Thomas Aquinas

International Bibliography

1977-1990

Richard Ingardia

BIBLIOGRAPHIES OF FAMOUS PHILOSOPHERS

The Philosophy Documentation Center publishes an ongoing series of "Bibliographies of Famous Philosophers." Published bibliographies include:

Alfred North Whitehead: A Primary-Secondary Bibliography
Edmund Husserl and His Critics: An International Bibliography (1894-1979)
Jean-Paul Sartre and His Critics: An International Bibliography (1938-1980), Second Edition
Martin Heidegger: Bibliography and Glossary
Hobbes Studies (1879-1979): A Bibliography
George Santayana: A Bibliographical Checklist (1880-1980)
Paul of Venice: A Bibliographical Guide
José Ortega y Gasset: A Bibliography of Secondary Sources
A Bibliography of Vico in English (1884-1984)
Henri Bergson: A Bibliography, Revised Edition
A Comprehensive Bibliography of the Published Works of Charles Sanders Peirce with a Bibliography of Secondary Studies
Bradley: A Research Bibliography
R. G. Collingwood: A Bibliographic Checklist
Thomas Aquinas: International Bibliography 1977-1990
Sartre: Bibliography 1980-1992

PHILOSPHICAL BIBLIOGRAPHIES

Philosophy Books, 1982-1986
Women Philosophers: A Bibliography of Books through 1990

Published by

The Philosophy Documentation Center
Bowling Green State University
Bowling Green, Ohio 43403-0189

ISBN 0-912632-92-5

TABLE OF CONTENTS

Introduction

Despite the heterogeneous character of contemporary Thomism, in this century alone it is abundantly clear that an extraordinary number of differing scholarly studies have appeared on Aquinas' thought in general and his philosophy in particular. It is extremely difficult to understand how the various versions of Thomism today are all able to be grouped under the same designation. For example, how can Transcendental Thomism and Existential Thomism share the same philosophical patrimony, if their methods, starting points, and conclusions are so radically opposed to each other? These differences are not merely minor matters of dispute but major areas of opposition rendering the use of the term "Thomistic" in each case apparently purely equivocal.

The two major bibliographies in English on Aquinas' thought list a total of 8,953 entries to 1978. These bibliographies do not claim to be comprehensive; indeed, many important philosophical works are omitted. The current bibliography from 1977 to 1990 contains more than 4,200 entries. If the scope were broadened to include strictly theological and other non-philosophical works, the number could have been easily doubled. Paradoxically, given this number of more than 13,000 citations to date, it is clear that Aquinas has received a considerable amount of scholarly attention today and may be the most discussed, yet the least influential, philosopher of the twentieth century.

The principal focus of this bibliography is limited to Aquinas' philosophy and those international studies about his philosophy from 1977-1990; therefore, many works of importance are intentionally omitted. Purely theological studies and other non-philosophically oriented discussions of Aquinas' views are not within the scope of this volume. In this regard, the perspective is quite selective. The guiding idea behind the construction of this study is to provide a complete international listing of titles for use by scholars interested in Thomistic philosophy and to provide these scholars with a useful research tool.

A complex problem arises, however, regarding works that contain philosophically valuable material discussed within an explicitly theological context. Are these works theological or philosophical? Or is the problem better stated not as a disjunction but as a conjunction? And if the answer is both, then how are we to understand the union? Should such titles be given in a work whose explicit interest is philosophical? The dichotomy, as well as the problem itself, is rooted in Aquinas' own development of his philosophy within his theological works. The answer is certainly not agreed upon by Thomistic scholars today, but whatever answer is adopted will have very important consequences for a bibliography on Thomas Aquinas' philosophy.

The historical fact that Aquinas' most original philosophical insights are contained within his theological treatises should not bar them from being listed here as philosophical works, as long as such "thought is based solely on what is both accessible, at least in principle, to unaided human cognition and, in fact, grasped by the natural power of human cognition in all the premises used in the philosophical reasoning."[1] Correspondingly, the same principles should hold for considering secondary studies on Aquinas' thought. Historically, Aquinas' most detailed philosophical discussions as the proof for God's existence, the real distinction between essence and existence, the nature of knowledge, truth, and reality, relations, method, nature, and division of the sciences, analogy, language, etc., are all contained within his theological writings. His Commentary on Lombard's *Sentences*, his unfinished Commentary on Boethius' *De Trinitate*, his *De ente et essentia*, and his *Summa Contra Gentiles* are just a few clear examples of this. Even Aquinas' Commentaries on Aristotle are not independent expositions produced without theological motives and Christian concerns.

For philosophers, however, it should not matter where a philosophical argument is given, nor the subjective motivation for advancing it by its author; the important thing, the only thing, is whether it keeps its essential rational character in the discussion of ultimates at all times and that it proceeds without the insertion of alien materials in its own internal development. When the reasoning is "even partly dependent upon revealed premises, the procedure has to be regarded as theological," and consequently cannot be considered Thomistic philosophy or any kind of philosophy in the traditional understanding of that term. Mediate knowledge does not suddenly cease to be knowledge because of the purposes of the thinker. Philosophy does not turn into theology by losing its essential character as a rational activity because of the external conditions within which it is performed. Significant philosophical material should not be omitted simply because it is part of a theological, scientific, or literary discussion. Precisely for this reason, works whose titles are clearly theological and whose focus is not principally philosophical, yet contain philosophically important discussions of Aquinas' arguments, are listed in this bibliography.

Aquinas discusses the same perennial philosophical problems we find in Plato and Aristotle, Kant and Hegel, Whitehead and Heidegger within his theology in a manner which has been and is philosophical in nature, but one in which the context of his faith essentially specifies his outlook and interest without altering internally or formally the rational component without which it could not be considered philosophical. This external condition of his philosophy does not make his philosophy theology, but sets a unique context for the properly philosophical arguments generated for extra-philosophical purposes. As this is true of Aquinas himself, it is equally as true for studies written about him. Secondary sources lacking genuine philosophical analysis are disregarded. It is clearly prejudicial, however, as well as completely arbitrary to dismiss a work as philosophically valuable simply because an author decides to philosophize within a religious, poetic, political, or scientific context.

The answer to the objection that *no* philosophy exists in Aquinas' writings, because it is all theological and done within a Christian context, then is clear. Aquinas' philosophy cannot be simply abstracted from his theological writings by an act of extraction, as a dentist would a tooth. This caricature of Thomistic philosophy as a self-enclosed existing entity in the fashion of a Platonic essence or form unaffected by time and history—an outlook that might be appealing to a logician for whom a tenseless world is a preference—is not found in the Thomistic corpus.

However, Aquinas never confused philosophical methodology with either religious faith or his understanding of his faith as its principles proceeded from revealed doctrine in actual practice. Failing to observe *these* distinctions have led to untold problems and another aberration. Those who deny the reality of Thomistic philosophy as a self-contradiction, contending that the adjective nullifies the noun as in Christian philosophy, often believe they are preserving the dignity and integrity of theology; they often believe they are countering the caricature of Thomism as a variety of Cartesianism. The reality, however, is they depreciate the genuine philosophical argumentation manifestly present in Thomas' thought in their praise of religious faith. Further they completely fail to understand that for Aquinas, his theology is completely unintelligible without the philosophical substructure without which it would collapse. One simply cannot have Aquinas' theology without his unique philosophy. In this limited sense, Aquinas' theology, not his faith, has been a handmaiden to his novel philosophy; Aquinas' theology requires philosophy for its very existence as a human science. It is not only impossible to separate Aquinas' philosophy from his theology, but perhaps even more so, it is impossible to separate his theology from his philosophy.

Consequently, the methodological principle governing the construction of this entire bibliography is not to fall victim to either aberration, especially the second. This bibliography cites those important works on Aquinas' philosophy wherever they appear in scholarly sources. In this way, the philosophical interests of the work will be genuinely preserved, a fidelity to philosophy's existential conditions recognized, and the anti-intellectual and fideistic tendencies avoided.

No matter how such difficult problems may be resolved, bibliographies by their nature can never be exhaustive. Important entries are always omitted in the best of compilations, either because of a lack of thoroughness on the compiler's part, ignorance, error in judgment, methodological errors used in the selection of entries, computer failure, or accidental deletions. Though extensive use of The *Philosopher's Index*, *Repertoire Bibliographique de la Philosophie*, *Rassegna di Letteratura Tomistica*, and *Tijdschrift voor Filosofie* were made in compiling this volume, in addition to numerous other sources, completeness, like perfection in life, is an ideal which is never actually achieved but is constantly sought after and desired. However, honesty demands the claim that this bibliography is the most extensive and nearly complete one within the stated time parameters available today. If omissions exist, the reader's critical comments and suggestions are *most* welcomed and appreciated, both to help bring this work to perfection in the future and to eliminate current errors. This is especially the case with respect to theological writings and studies judged lacking enough philosophical material to warrant inclusion into this bibliography. Also, probably some international titles that have been missed or judged incorrectly as lacking philosophical merit ought to be included.

The bibliography is divided into three unequal parts. In the first part, 143 primary source entries are given. The second part has 3,661 entries (761 books and 2,900 articles) of secondary sources, whereas the last part of miscellaneous entries consists of 427 entries. One unique feature of the bibliography is that it contains entries sorted according to different language groups for ease of research use and reference. The list should be of great value to Thomistic scholars in their own work. Further, the huge amount of international material on every facet of Aquinas' philosophy supports the contention that Thomistic philosophy has universal appeal among contemporary writers and that its immediate future at least is secure. Other advantages of the work are author abstracts of books and articles which are given when available; significant book reviews of secondary sources cited with the book entry itself for ease of reference; and dissertations, especially from American universities. The numerous indexes should be useful as well. The weakest part of the bibliography is the last part, specifically the list containing entries of unpublished papers. To make this complete would have accomplished very little from a research point of view, so the list was intentionally reduced in size—only a few American sources are mentioned.

I thank the Computer Center at St. John's University, Staten Island Campus, under Richard Lejune and his able staff, especially Timothy O'Connell, for its excellent technical support.

Like a Sherpa, who is the very skilled and knowledgeable tribesman responsible for obtaining the necessary supplies and equipment for a successful Himalayan climb, a bibliographer of philosophical literature provides a necessary tool for a successful philosophical journey. In providing this bibliography to Thomistic scholars and others, it is hoped that precious hours of time are saved by its use, a full global perspective achieved, and new and unexpected sources revealed. The objective of this bibliographer, analogous to the goal of the Sherpa, is to have supplied an indispensable tool for those interested in Thomistic philosophy and its future development, so that their climb to the summit is made easier, and as often happens with the Sherpa, to accompany them on their journey.

NOTES

1. Owens, Joseph, "Introduction," in *Towards a Christian Philosophy*, Washington, DC: The Catholic University of America Press, 1990, p. 24.

PRIMARY SOURCES

I. ENGLISH

A. BOOKS

1 Thomas Aquinas. *A Tour of the Summa*. Ed. Paul J. Glenn. Rockford, IL: Tan Books and Publishers, 1978. xi-466.

2 Thomas Aquinas. *Selected Writings of St. Thomas Aquinas, The Principles of Nature, On Being and Essence, On the Virtues in General, On Free Choice*. Trans. Robert P. Goodwin. 1965. Indianapolis, IN: The Liberal Arts Press, Inc., 1979. xxi-162.

3 Thomas Aquinas. *On Kingship, to the King of Cyprus*. Trans. Gerald B. Phelan. Rev. 1949. Westport, CT: Hyperion Press, 1979. xxxix-119. Introduction and notes by Ignatius T. Eschmann.

4 Thomas Aquinas. *Thomas Aquinas. Being and Essence: Trans. and Interpretation*. Trans. Joseph Bobik. 1965. Notre Dame, IN: University of Notre Dame Press, 1980. 286.

*The purpose of this book is to translate into as ordinary English as possible, and to present an intelligible interpretation of the doctrines put forth in Aquinas' treatise *On Being and Essence*. Following the treatise, the interpretation investigates a broad range of questions—linguistic, logical, and philosophical—in a most economical way, i. e.,, in terms of a reduction of the whole of human intellectual activity to its analytically first concepts, those of being and essence; uses of the words "being" and "essence," the essences of natural substance, the immateriality of the human soul and of the intelligences, the existence and the essence of God, and the foundations for distinguishing mind-derived ingredients of human knowledge from those which are object-derived. *

5 Thomas Aquinas. *Commentary on the Gospel of John, Part I*. Trans. James A. Weisheipl and F. R. Larcher. Albany, NY: Magi Books, 1980.

*Harrington, Wilfrid, *The Thomist* 47(1983): 151-155.*

6 Thomas Aquinas. *Treatise on Man*. Trans. James F. Anderson. 1962. Westport, CT: Greenwood Press, 1981. 178.

7 Thomas Aquinas. *Summa Theologiae: General Index*. Vol. 61. Ed. Thomas C. O'Brien. Blackfriars. London: Eyre & Spottiswoode, 1981. 383.

*Carlen, C., *The Thomist*, 48(1984): 475-457.*

8 Thomas Aquinas. *Summa Theologiae*. Trans. English Dominican Province. 1911. Westminster, MD: Christian Classics, 1981.

9 Thomas Aquinas. *Aquinas: Selected Political Writings*. Trans. A. R. D'Entrêves. Ed. S. G. Dawson. New York: Barnes and Noble, 1981. 136.

10 Thomas Aquinas. *St. Thomas Aquinas: Philosophical Texts*. Trans. Thomas Gilby. 1951. Durham, NC: The Labyrinth Press, 1982. xxii-405.

11 Thomas Aquinas. *St. Thomas Aquinas: Theological Texts*. Trans. Thomas Gilby. 1955. Durham, NC: The Labyrinth Press, 1982. 423.

12 Thomas Aquinas. *St. Thomas Aquinas, Quodlibetal Questions 1 and 2*. Trans. Sandra Edwards. Mediaeval Sources in Trans. 27. Toronto: Pontifical Institute of Mediaeval Studies, 1983. viii-128.

*Wippel, John F., *Journal of the History of Philosophy*, 23(1985): 585-586.*

13 Thomas Aquinas. *Disputed Questions on Evil*. Trans. John J. Oesterle. South Bend, IN: Notre Dame University Press, 1983.

14 Thomas Aquinas. *Questions on the Soul [Quaestiones de Anima]*. Trans. James H. Robb. Mediaeval Philosophical Texts in Trans. 27. Milwaukee, WI: Marquette University Press, 1984. iv-275.

*Bazán, Bernardo Carlos, *The Review of Metaphysics*, 38(1984-1985): 910-912.*
*Catania, Francis J., *The Modern Schoolman*, 64(1987): 301-303.*
*Lindblad, U., *Revue Théologique de Louvain*, 118(1986): 424-425.*

15 Thomas Aquinas. *Summa Theologica I*. Ed. Franklin Center, PA: Franklin Library Press, 1985.

16 Thomas Aquinas. *St. Thomas Aquinas. The Division and Methods of the Sciences. Questions V and VI of His Commentary on the De Trinitate of Boethius*. Trans. Armand Maurer. 4th rev. ed. 1953. Mediaeval Sources in Trans. 3. Toronto/Leiden: Pontifical Institute of Mediaeval Studies/E. J. Brill, 1986. xii-119.

17 Thomas Aquinas. *St. Thomas Aquinas: Faith, Reason and Theology. Questions I-IV of His Commentary on the De Trinitate of Boethius*. Trans. Armand Maurer. Mediaeval Sources in Trans. 32. Toronto: Pontifical Institute of Mediaeval Studies, 1987. xxxviii-127.

*Bonino, S. -T., *Revue Thomiste*, 90(1990): 355.*
*Van Steenberghen, F., *Revue Philosophique de Louvain*, 86(1988): 257-258.*

18 Thomas Aquinas. *Albert and Thomas: Selected Writings*. Trans. Simon Tugwell. Classics of Western Spirituality. New York: Paulist, 1988. xv-650.

*Berna, Francis, *Speculum*, 65(1990): 1067-1069.*
*Vansteenkiste, C., *Angelicum*, 67(1990): 257-259.*
*Woods, Richard, *The Thomist*, 54(1990): 541-545.*

19 Thomas Aquinas. *St. Thomas Aquinas, On Politics and Ethics*. Trans. Paul E. Sigmund. Ed. Paul E. Sigmund. New York/London: W. W. Norton Company, 1988. xxx-250.

*Weithman, P.J., *The Review of Metaphysics*, 42 (1988-1989): 639-340.*

20 Thomas Aquinas. *Saint Thomas Aquinas: On Law, Morality, and Politics*. Ed. William P. Baumgarth and Richard J. Regan. Indianapolis, IN: Hackett Publishing Company, 1988. xxviii-288.

*Lisska, Anthony J., *Teaching Philosophy*, 12(1989): 429-431.*

21 Thomas Aquinas. *An Aquinas Reader*. Ed. Mary Clark. New York: Fordham University Press, 1988.

*Teske, Roland J., *The Modern Schoolman*, 62(1984): 60-61.*

22 Thomas Aquinas. *An Aquinas Treasury: Religious Imagery. Selections Taken from the Writings of St. Thomas Aquinas*. Trans. Jules Brady. Ed. Jules Brady. Arlington, TX: Liberal Arts, 1988. 135.

23 Thomas Aquinas. *The Philosophy of Thomas Aquinas: Introductory Readings*. Ed. Christopher Martin. Croom Helm Philosophy. London: Routledge, 1988. 201.

*Anderson, Robert D., *The Thomist*, 56(1992): 149-151.
*García-Huidobro, Joaquin, *Anuario Filosofico*, 22(1989): 191-193.*

24 Thomas Aquinas. *Summa Theologiae: A Concise Translation*. Trans. Timothy McDermott. Ed. Timothy McDermott. Christian Classics. Westminster, MD: Eyre & Spottiswoode, 1989. xvii-651. See "Preface: What the *Summa* is About," xvii-lviii.

*Cessario, Romanus, *Theological Studies*, 52(1991): 147-149.
*Clarke, W. Norris, *International Philosophical Quarterly*, 30(1990): 265-266.*
*Davies, Brian, *New Blackfriars* 71(1990): 148-149.*
*Froelich, Gregory, *The Thomist* 54(1990): 727-730.*
*Murphy, Thomas, *The Heythrop Journal*, 32(1991): 440-441.*

25 Thomas Aquinas. *The Literal Exposition on Job: A Scriptural Commentary Concerning Providence*. Trans. Anthony Damico. Classics in Religious Studies 7. Atlanta, GA: Scholars Press, 1989. 496.

26 Thomas Aquinas. *On Faith: Summa Theologiae 2-2, Qq. 1-16 of St. Thomas Aquinas*. Trans. Mark D. Jordan. Readings in the *Summa Theologiae* 1. Notre Dame, IN: University of Notre Dame Press, 1990. x-208.

*Cessario, Romanus, *The Thomist*, 55(1991): 141-144.*

B. ARTICLES

27 Thomas Aquinas. "A New Disputed Question of St. Thomas Aquinas on the Immortality of the Soul." *Archives d'Histoire Doctrinale et Littéraire du Moyen Age* 45 (1979): 205-223. By Leonard A. Kennedy.

28 Thomas Aquinas. "Excerpts from the Commentary of Thomas Aquinas: Commentary on the Second Book of the Sentences of Master Peter Lombard Distinction 44." *Civil Authority in Medieval Philosophy: Lombard, Aquinas and Bonaventure*. Ed. Michael P. Molloy. New York: University Press of America, 1985. 143-173.

29 Thomas Aquinas. "*Peciae*, *Apopeciae*, and a Toronto Ms. of the Sententia Libri Ethicorum of Aquinas." *The Role of the Book in Medieval Culture*. Turnhout: Brepols, 1986. 71-82. By Leonard Boyle.

30 Thomas Aquinas. "The Nature of Truth." *Philosophy and Theology Disk Supplement* 4(1989): 93-108, 561-562. Trans. Karl Rahner and Andrew Tallon.

*This article is a translation of "A Verdade em S. Thomas de Aquino" by Karl Rahner, S. J. (*Revista Portuguesa de filosofia,* 7 [Tomo VII, fasc. 4, Oct. -Nov.] 1951: 353-370). The Portuguese article is itself a Trans. of a conference given by the authorat Innsbruck before an audience of nonscholastic philosophers; the Portuguese version is the work of Julio Fragata, S. J., with the assistance of the author. In answer to a request for a German original, the author replied that he knew of none. Perhaps what explains the style of this article and that of much of Rahner's work is its origin in spoken or dictated rather than written language.*

31 Thomas Aquinas. "Disputed Question on the Soul's Knowledge of Itself." Stillwater, OK: Oklahoma State University, Trans. Clearing House, 1990. 1-8. A-40-451. Trans. Richard T. Lambert.

32 Thomas Aquinas. "The Quodlibetal Questions (Selections: I, Q. 3, A. 4-5; II, Q. 10, A. 21-22; III, Q. 1, A. 1-2; IV, Q. 3, A. 4-5; VIII, Q. 1, A. 1; IX, Q. 1, A. 1; XII, Q. 3, A. (2)." Stillwater, OK: Oklahoma State University, Trans. Clearing House, 1990. 1-23. A-40-60i. Trans. by P. V. Spade.

33 Thomas Aquinas. "On the Mixture of the Elements, to Master Philip." Stillwater, OK: Oklahoma State University, Trans. Clearing House, 1990. 1-5. A-40-75s. Trans. by P. V. Spade.

II. FRENCH

A. BOOKS

34 Thomas d'Aquin. *Somme Théologique Vol. II: La Loi Nouvelle Questions 106-108.* Trans. J. Tonneau. Paris: Éditions du Cerf, 1981. 260.

*Anon., *Rassegna di Letteratura Tomistica*, 17(1981): 28-30.*

35 Thomas d'Aquin 1982. *Job: Un Homme Pour Notre Temps.* Trans. J. Kreit. Paris: Téqui, 1982. 656.

36 Thomas d'Aquin. *Questions Disputées sur La Vérité: Question XI: Le Maître (De Magistro).* Trans. Bernadette Jollés. Bibliothéque Des Textes Philosophiques. Paris: J. Vrin, 1983. 123.

*Composta, Dario, *Doctor Communis*, 37(1984): 263.*
*Imbach, R., *Revue de Théologie et de Philosophie*, 116(1984): 268-269.*
*Jolivet, J., *Revue Philosophique de la France et de l'étranger*, 110(1985): 249-250.*
*Reix, A., *Journal Philosophique*, 1(1985): 181-182.*

37 Thomas d'Aquin. *N. 1, 1983 [Trimestriel] Annevoie, N. de Montpellier.* Rue Des Jardins 47. B-5181. Belgrique: Étanger, 1983. 24.

38 Thomas d'Aquin. *Somme Théologique I: Introductions Générales et Premiére Partie.* Trans. Aimon-Marie Roguet. Ed. A. Raulin. Paris: Éditions du Cerf, 1984. 996. "Introduction à la Somme théologique" par Nicolas, Joseph; "Plan général de la Somme théologique. Vocabulaire de la Somme théologique" par Nicolas, Marie-Joseph. "Auteurs cités dans la Somme Théologique" par Neyrand, Édith. Prima pars: Introductions et notes par Geffré, Claude; Nicolas, Jean-Hervé; Maldamé, Jean-Michel; Dubarle, Andre-Marie; and Nicolas, Marie-Joseph.

39 Thomas d'Aquin. *Somme Theologique II: Premiére Section de la Deuxiéme Partie.* Trans. Aimon-Marie Roguet. Ed. Aimon-Marie Raulin. Paris: Éditions du Cerf, 1984. 827.

*Anon., *Rassegna di Letteratura Tomistica*, 20(1987): 41-50.*
*Delhaye, P., *Revue Philosophique de Louvain*, 16(1985): 359-361.*

40 Thomas d'Aquin. *Somme Théologique I-II.* Trans. Aimon-Marie Roguet. Paris: Éditions du Cerf, 1984. 966.

*Anon., *Rassegna di Letteratura Tomistica*, 20(1984): 41-50.*
*Labourdette, M. -M., *Revue Thomiste*, 85(1985): 302-305.*
*Ponton, L., *Laval Théologique et Philosophique*, 42(1986): 272-274.*
*Sieben, H. J., *Theologie und Philosophie*, 63(1988): 611-612.*

41 Thomas d'Aquin. *Opuscules Vol. I: Compendium Theologiae*. 1856. Paris: J. Vrin, 1984.

42 Thomas d'Aquin. *Opuscules Vol. II: Contra Erroes Graecorum. Contra Graecos, Armenos, et Saracenos. Ad Cantorem Antiochenum (De Rationibus Fidei)*. 1856 (Vivés). Paris: J. Vrin, 1984.

43 Thomas D'Aquin. *Opuscules Vol. III: De Differentia Divini Verbi et Humani; De Natura Verbi Intellectus; De Substantiis Separatis; De Unitate Intellectus Contra Averroystas*. 1857. Paris: J. Vrin, 1984.

44 Thomas d'Aquin. *Opuscules Vol. IV: De Perfectione Vitae Spiritualis. Contra Pestiferam Doctrinam Retrahentium Homines a Religionis Ingressu*. 1857. Paris: J. Vrin, 1984.

45 Thomas d'Aquin. *Opuscules Vol. V: Contra Impugnantes Dei Cultum et Religionem*. 1857. Paris: J. Vrin, 1984.

46 Thomas d'Aquin. *Opuscules Vol. VI: De Aeternitate Mundi. De Principio Individuationis. De Principiis Naturae. De Natura Materiae et Dimensionibus Interminatis*. 1857. Paris: J. Vrin, 1984.

47 Thomas d'Aquin. *L'être et L'essence*. Trans. Catherine Capelle. 8th ed. Bibliothéque Des Textes Philosophiques. Paris: J. Vrin, 1985. 94.

48 Thomas d'Aquin. *Bref Résumé de La Foi Chrétienne (Compendium Theologiae)*. Trans. Pére Kreit. Ed. Francis Ruello. Docteur Angélique 6. Paris: Nouvelles Editions Latines, 1985. xxxi-611.

*Petino, Cosimo, *Doctor Communis*, 40(1987): 312-313.*
*Saranyana, J. I., *Scripta Theologica*, 18(1986): 727.

49 Thomas d'Aquin. *Somme Théologique III: Second Volume de la Deuxiéme Partie*. Trans. Aimon-Marie Roguet. Ed. A. Raulin. Paris: Éditions du Cerf, 1985. 1158.

*Anon.,**Rassegna di Letteratura Tomistica*, 21(1985): 46-49.*
*De Grijs, F., *Bijdragen*, 47(1986): 421-435.*
*Kaczynski, E., *Angelicum*, 63(1986): 311-312.*

50 Thomas d'Aquin. *Les Collationes in Decem Preceptis de Saint Thomas D'Aquin. Revue des Sciences Philosophiques et Théologiques* 69(1985): 227-263. II. Trans. critique avec introduction et notes par Torrell, Jean-Pierre.

51 Thomas d'Aquin. *Somme Théologique III: Troisiéme Partie [Tertia Pars]*. Trans. Aimon-Marie Roguet. Paris: Éditions du Cerf, 1986. 767.

52 Thomas d'Aquin. *Somme Théologique IV*. Trans. Aimon-Marie Roguet. Ed. A. Raulin. Paris: Éditions du Cerf, 1986. 765.

*Anon., *Rassegna di Letteratura Tomistica*, 22(1986): 25-28.*
*Bonino, Serge-Thomas, *Revue de Théologie et de Philosophie*, 123(1991): 93-97.
*Steel, C., *Bulletin de Théologie Ancienne et Médiévale*, 14(1986): 144.*

B. ARTICLES

53 Thomas d'Aquin. "Fragments de Sermons de Gérard D'Abbeville: Etudes de Rosny et Thomas D'Aquin." *Archives d'Histoire Doctrinale et Littéraire du Moyen Age*, 51(1984): 257-268. Discussed by Louis F. Bataillon.

54 Thomas D'Aquin. "Les Collationes in Decem Preceptis de Saint Thomas D'Aquin." *Revue des Sciences Philosophiques et Théologiques* 69(1985): 5-40. Ed. Jean-Pierre Torrell.

55 Thomas d'Aquin. "Les Collationes in Decem Preceptis de Saint Thomas D'Aquin." *Revue des Sciences Philosophiques et Théologiques* 69(1985): 227-263. Ed. Jean-Pierre Torrell.

III. GERMAN

A. BOOKS

56 Thomas Von Aquin. *Fünf Fragen Über die Intellektuelle Erkenntnis (Questio 84-88 Des 1. Teils der Summa de Theologia).* Trans. Eugen Rolfes. Ed. Eugen Rolfes. Philosophische Bibliothek 191. Hamburg: Meiner, 1977. xiv-126.

57 Thomas von Aquin. *Die Deutsche Thomas-Ausgabe.* Kommentiert von Pesch, Otto Hermann. Trans. Philos. -Theol. Hochsch. Ed. Philos. -Theol. Hochsch. Heidelberg: Graz, Wien, Köln, Verlag Styria, 1977. 832.

58 Thomas von Aquin. *Thomas von Aquin: De Ente et Essentia: Das Seiende und das Wesen.* Trans. Leo Franz Beeretz. Ed. Leo Franz Beeretz. Universal-Bibliothek 1957. Stuttgart: Philipp Reclam Jun., 1979. 119.

59 Thomas von Aquin. *Die Deutsche Thomas Ausgabe. Summa Theologica.* Trans. O. Pesch. Das Gesetz 13. Heidelberg: Kerle, 1980. 832.

60 Thomas von Aquin. *Thomas von Aquin. Bd II: Philosophische Fragen.* Trans. Klaus Bernath. Wege der Forschung 538. Darmstadt: Wissenschaftliche Buchgesellschaft, Abt. Verl., 1981. viii-572.

*Anon., *Rassegna di Letteratura,* 17(1981): 461-462.*
*Albert, K., *Philosophischer Literaturanzeiger,* 37(1984): 197-199.
*De Vries, J., *Theologie und Philosophie,* 57(1982): 440-442.*
*Lindblad, Ulrika, *Freiburger Zeitschrift für Philosophie und Theologie,* 30(1983): 209-212.
*Pöltner, G., *Salzburger Jahrbuch für Philosophie,* 26-27(1981-1982): 277.*
*Walgrave, J. H., *Ephemerides Theologicae Lovanienses,* 59(1983): 386-387.*

61 Thomas von Aquin. *Summe Gegen die Heiden I.* Trans. Karl Albert and Paulus Engelhardt. Ed. Karl Albert and Paulus Engelhardt. Text Zur Forschung 15. Darmstadt, Wissenschaftliche Buchgesellschaft: Abt. Verlag, 1982. xx-513.

62 Thomas von Aquin. *Die Deutsche Thomas-Ausgabe, I: Dominikanern U Benediktinern Deutschlands U. österreichs:Summa Theologica: Bd I. Buch 1, Frage 1-119: Gottes Dasein und Wesen.* Aufl. Fotomenchan. Nachdr.: Graz, Wien, Köln, Verlag Styria, 1982. 551.

*Anon., *Rassegna di Letteratura Tomistica,* 18(1982): 38-40.*

63 Thomas von Aquin. *Die Deutsche Thomas-Ausgabe: Summa Theologica: Bd II.* Trans. Dominikanern u Benediktinern Deutschlands u. österreichs. 1960. Aufl. Fotomenchan. Nachdr.: Graz, Wien, Köln, Verlag Styria, 1982. 452.

*Anon., *Rassegna di Letteratura Tomistica,* 18(1982): 26-29.*

64 Thomas von Aquin. *Gottes Dasein und Wesen.* Die Deutsche Thomas-Ausgabe 1. Graz-Wien-Köln: Styria, 1982. 551.

*Anon., *Rassegna di Letteratura Tomistica,* 18(1985): 38-40.*

65 Thomas von Aquin. *Von der Wahrheit (De Veritate, Quaestio I)*. Trans. Albert Zimmermann. Philosophische Bibliothek 384. Hamburg: Felix Meiner Verlag, 1985. xlii-93.

*Albert, K., *Philosophischer Literaturanzeiger*, 39(1986): 313-314.*

*Imbach, R., *Freiburger Zeitschrift für Philosophie und Theologie* 34(1987): 264-267.*

*Van Steenberghen, Fernand, *Revue Philosophique de Louvain*, 84(1986): 264.*

66 Thomas von Aquin. *Summa Theologica Vol. 32*. Trans. Burkhard Neunheuser. Graz-Wien-Köln: Styria, 1985. 569.

*C. V., *Angelicum*, 64(1987): 148-150.*

67 Thomas von Aquin. *Die Gottesbeweise in der Summe Gegen die Heiden und der Summe der Theologie*. Trans. Horst Seidl. Philosophische Bibliothek 330. Hamburg: Meiner, 1986. xl-196.

*Leroy, M. V., *Revue Thomiste*, 83(1983): 120-121.*

*Wuppertal, Rainer B., *Philosophischer Literaturanzeiger*, 43(1990): 173-174.

68 Thomas von Aquin. *Von der Wahrheit: De Veritate, Quaestio I*. Trans. Albert Zimmermann. Philosophische Bibliothek 384. Hambourg: Meiner Verlag, 1986. xlii-98.

*Albert, K., *Philosophischer Literaturanzeiger*, 39(1986): 313-314.*

*Imachi, Ruedi, *Revue de Théologie et de Philosophie*, 119(1987): 242. *

*Saranyana, J. I., *Scripta Theologica*, 18(1986): 727.*

69 Thomas von Aquin. *De Ente et Essentia: Das Seiende und das Wesen*. Trans. Leo Franz Beeretz. Universal-Gibliothek 9957. Stuttgart: Philipp Reclam Jun., 1987. xx-513.

*Deronne, E., *Tijdschrift voor Filosofie*, 45(1983): 128-129.*

70 Thomas von Aquin. *Summa Contra Gentiles—Summe Gegen die Heiden II*. Trans. Karl Albert and Paulus Engelhardt. Ed. Karl Albert and Paulus Engelhardt. Darmstadt, Wissenschaftliche Buchgesellschaft: Abt. Verl., 1987. xx-533.

71 Thomas von Aquin. *Über die Einheit Des Geistes Gegen die Averroisten: De Unitate Intellectus Contra Averroistas. Über die Bewegung Des Herzens: De Motu Cordis*. Trans. Wolf-Ulrich Klünker. Stuttgart: Verlag Freies Geistesleben, 1987. 186.

*Cheneval, F., *Freiburger Zeitschrift für Philosophie und Theologie*, 36(1989): 199-204.*

72 Thomas von Aquin. *De Rationibus Fidei*. Ed. Ludwig Hagemann and Reinhold Glei. Corpus Islamo-Christianum: Series Latina 2.Altenberge: CIS-Verl., 1987. 167.

73 Thomas von Aquin. *Thomas von Aquin: Über die Einheit Des Geistes—De Unitate Intellectus*. Trans. W. -U. Klünker. Ed. Friedrich-Von-Hardenberg-Institut/Heidelberg 1987. Stuttgart: Verl. Freies Geistesleben, 1987. 186.

74 Thomas von Aquin. *Recht und Gerechtigkeit. Theol. Summe II-II, Fragen 57-79*. Trans. Josef F. Groner. Ed. Arthur F. Utz. Nacfolgefassung von 18. Bonn: IfG-Verl. -Ges., 1987. xxvi-544.

75 Thomas von Aquin. *Über Seiendes und Wesenheit—De Ente et Essentia*. Trans. Horst Seidl. Philosophische Bibliothek 415. Hamburg: Meiner, 1988. lxii-136.

*Schreier, Josep, *Philosophischer Literaturanzeiger*, 43(1990): 227-230.*

76 Thomas von Aquin. *Über Den Lehrer (De Magistro). Quaestiones Disputatae de Veritate, Quaestio XI. Summa Theologiae, Pars. I, Quaestio 117, Articulus 1.* Trans. Gabriel Jüssen, Gerhard Krieger, and Josef Hans Jakob Schneider. Ed. Gabriel Jüssen, Gerhard Krieger, and Josef Hans Jakob Schneider. Philosophische Bibliothek 412. Hamburg: Felix Meiner Verlag, 1988. lvi-189.

77 Thomas von Aquin. *Das Buch der Tugenden: Ein Compendium Des XIV: Jhts Über Moral und Recht Nach der Summa Theologiae II-II Des Thomas von Aquin und Eren Werken der Scholastik und Kanonistik.* Kl. Berg and M. Kasper, Eds. Texte und Textgeschichte 7-8. Tübingen: N. Niemeyer, 1984. 305.

78 Thomas von Aquin. *Über das Sein und das Wesen.* Trans. Rudolf Allers. Ed. Rudolf Allers. 1953. Darmstadt: Wissenschaftliche Buchgesellschaft, Abt. Verl., 1989. 166.

79 Thomas von Aquin. *Summe Gegen die Heiden.* Trans. Karl Allgaier. Ed. Karl Allgaier. Texte Zur Forschung 17. Darmstadt: Wiss. Buchges. Abt. Verl., 1990. xvi-363.

IV. ITALIAN

A. BOOKS

80 Tommaso d'Aquino. *Tommaso D' Aquino: Numbero Unico in Omaggio.* Trans. G. Giannini. Laterano: Pontifical Università del Laterano, 1978.

*Cartechini, Sisto, *Doctor Communis*, 32(1979): 387-389.*

81 Tommaso d'Aquino. *Diritto e Giustizia Nella Somme Teologica: II-II, Question 57-58.* Trans. Vittoria Cambilargiu. Sassari: Intituto di Filosofia, 1979. 124.

*Anon., *Rassegna di Letteratura Tomistica*, 18(1982): 414-416.*

82 Tommaso d'Aquino. *La Politica Dei Principi Cristiani (De Regmine Principum).* Siena: Cantagalli, 1981. 298.

83 Tommaso d'Aquino. *Fede e Opere: Testi Ascetici e Misitici.* Trans. E. M. Sonzini. Roma: Città Nuova, 1981. 286.

84 Tommaso d'Aquino. *La Conoscenza Di Dio Nella Somma Teologica.* Trans. Pietro Scapin. Classici Dello Spirito 4. Padova: Messaggero, 1982. 255.

85 Tommaso d'Aquino. *Opera Omnia. Tomus XXIII: Quaestiones Disputatae De Malo.* Ed. Fratrum Praedicatorum. Roma (Commissio Leonina): J. Vrin, 1982. 383.

86 Tommaso d'Aquino. *L'uomo e L'universo: Opuscoli Filosofici.* Trans. Antonio Tognolo. I Classici del Pensiero: Medioevo e Rinascimento 2. Milano: Rusconi, 1982. 415.

*Anon., *Rassegna di Letteratura Tomistica*, 18(1982): 41-42.*

87 Tommaso d'Aquino. *La Conoscenza Di Dio Nella Somma Teologica.* Trans. Marie-Dominique Chenu. Classici Dello Spirito. Padova: Ed. Messagero, 1982. 255.

88 Tommaso d'Aquino. *Scritti Politici.* Trans. L. Alberto Perotto. Studia Universitatis S. Thomae in Urbe 25. Milano: Massimo, 1985. 573.

*Anon., *Rassegna di Letteratura Tomistica*, 21(1985): 52-55.*

89 Tommaso d'Aquino. *La Somma Teologica.* Trans. Edizione Salani. Bologna: Edizioni Studio Domenicano, 1985.

90 Tommaso d'Aquino. *De Ente et Essentia: L'essenza Dell'esistente*. Trans. Pasquale Orlando. Napoli: Edizioni Dehoniane, 1986. 99.

*Sessa, D., *Sapienza*, 40(1987): 236-237.*

91 Tommaso d'Aquino. *Commento Al Libro Delle Cause*. Trans. Cristina D'Ancona Costa. I Classici del Pensiero: Medioevo e Rinascimento 2. Milano: Rusconi, 1986. 480.

*Anon., *Rassegna di letteratura Tomistica*, 22(1986): 31-34.*
*Wielockx, R., *Bulletin de Théologie Ancienne et Médiévale*, 14(1987): 369-372.*

92 Tommaso d'Aquino. *Pagine Di Filosofia [Antologia]*. Trans. Roberto Coggi. Philosophia 1. Bologna: Edizioni Studio Domenicano, 1988. 200.

*Pangallo, Mario, *Doctor Communis*, 42(1989): 95.*

B. ARTICLES

93 Tommaso d'Aquin. "Tratado: De Veritate: Questión IV (Divida en 8 Articulos)." Trans. Enrique Le-Beuffe Poblete. *Revista de Filosofia (Chile)*, 18(1980): 107-108.

94 Tommaso d'Aquino. "I Quattro Opposti." *Aquinas*, 24(1981): 50-103. Trans. A. Molinaro.

V. LATIN

A. BOOKS

95 Thomae de Aquino. *Compendium Theologiae: Responsio ad Magistrum Ioan de Vercellis de 108 Articulis*. Leonine. Vol. 42. 1979.

*Hissette, R., *Bulletin de Théologie Ancienne et Médiévale*, 13(1981): 128-129.*

96 Thomae de Aquino. *Opera omnia Vol. XLIII: Compendium Theologiae. De articulis fidei et ecclesiae sacramentis. Responis 108 articulis. Responsio de 43 articulis. Responis 36 articulis. Responsio de 43 articulis. Responsi 36 articulis. Responsio de 6 articulis. Epistola a Ducissam Brabantiae. De emptione et venditione ad tempus. Epistola ad Bernardum Abbatem Casinensem. Regno ad Regem Cypri. De secreto. Fratrum Praedicatorum*. Roma: Ed.i di San Tommaso. 1979. 529.

*Anon., *Rassegna di Letteratura Tomistica*, 15(1979): 24-32.*
*Wenin, C., *Revue Philosophique de Louvain*, 83(1985): 281-287.*

97 Thomae de Aquino. *Opera omnia: De articulis fidei*. H. F. Dondaine. Vol. 42. Rome: Ad Sanctae Sabinae. 1979.

98 Thomae de Aquino. *Opera omnia, ut sunt in Indice Tomistico additis scriptis ex aliis medii aevi auctoribus* Vols. I-VII. Ed. Roberto Busa. Stuttgart-Bad Cannstatt: Frommann Holzboorg. 1980. 723, 951, 667, 599, 525, 609, 837.

*Anon, *Rassegna di Letteratura Tomistica*, 16(1980): 38-39.*
*Burton, D. M., *Speculum*, 59(1984): 891-894.*
*Deronne, E., *Tijdschrift voor Filosofie*, 47(1985): 1223.*

99 Thomae de Aquino. *Summa Theologiae*. Blackfriars. Vol. 61. London: Blackfriars in conjunction with Eyre & Spottiswood. 1981.

100 Thomae de Aquino. *Opera Omnia*. Tomus XXIII: Quaestiones Disputatae De Malo. Roma/Paris: Fratrum Praedicaorum/J. Vrin. 1982. 384.
*Anon., *Rassegna di Letteratura Tomistica*, 18(1982): 31-38.*
*Bazán, Bernardo Carlos, *Dialogue*, 24(1985): 172-176.*
*Hissette, R., *Bulletin de Théologie Ancienne et Médiévale*, 80(1985): 340-341.*
*Holtz, L., *Revue des Études Latines*, 61(1983): 372-373.*
*Perini, G., *Divus Thomas*, 89-90(1986-1987): 582-588.*
*Zedler, B. H., *Speculum*, 59(1984): 704-706.*

101 Thomae de Aquino. *Opera Omnia II iussu Leonis XIII P. M. XLV. I: Sent. libri De Anima*. Fratrum Praedicatorum. Roma/Paris: J. Vrin. 1984. viii-294/313.
*Anon., *Rassegna di Letteratura Tomistica*, 20(1984): 29-41.*
*Elders, L. J., *Divus Thomas*, 88(1985): 212-214.*
*Escol, R., *Nouvelle Revue Theologie Ancienne et Médiévale*, 13(1985): 813-815.*
*Hissette, R., *Bulletin de Théologie Ancienne et Médiévale*, 80(1985): 813-815.*
*Jolivet, J., *Revue Philosophique de la France et de l'étranger*, 111(1986): 112-113.*
*Maer, A., *Rivista Rosminiana di Filosofia Cultura*, 44(1989): 178-188.*
*Solignac, A., *Aporia*, 49(1986): 485-486.*
*Wielockx, R., *Scriptorium*, 39(1985): 139-150.*
*Zedler, B. H., *Speculum*, 61(1986): 475-477.*

102 Thomae de Aquino. *Opera omnia. XLV. II: Sentencia Libri De Sensu et Sensato cuius secunduis tractatus est De memoria e reminiscencia*. Fratrum Praedicatorum. Roma/Paris: J. Vrin. 1985. xii-128/155.
*Anon., *Rassegna di Letteratura Tomistica*, 21(1985): 37-43.*
*Hissette, R., *Bulletin de Théologie Ancienne et Médiévale*, 14(1986): 144-146.*
*Jolivet, J., *Revue Philosophique de la France et de l'étranger*, 111(1986): 112-113.*
*Perini, G., *Divus Thomas*, 91(1988): 326-334.*
*Snyder, S. C., *Speculum*, 62(1987): 211-213.*
*Wielockx, R., *Scriptorium*, 39(1985): 150-157.*

103 Thomae de Aquino. *Codices manuscripti operum Thomae de Aquino III: Bibliothecae: Comissionis Leoninae*. H. V. Shooner. Paris: J. Vrin. xv-395.

104 Thomae de Aquino. *Opera omnia iussu Leonis XIII: Tomus I: Libri Peryemenias*. Fratrum Praedicatorum. Paris: J. Vrin. 1989. 110.

105 Thomae de Aquino. *Opera omnia iussu Leonis XIII: Tomus II: Expositio Libri Posteriorium*. Fratrum Praedicatorum. Paris: J. Vrin. 1989. 284.

VI. SPANISH

A. BOOKS

106 Tomás de Aquino. *El Regimen Politico*. Trans. Victorino P. Rodriquez. Madrid: Fuerza Nueva, 1978. 184.

107 Tomás de Aquino. *De Veritate*. Santiago, Chile: Ed. Universitaria, 1978. 172.

108 Tomás de Aquino. *Comentario Al Libro del Alma de Aristóteles*. Trans. Maria C. De Gandolfi Maggi Donadio. Buenos Aires: Fundación Arche, 1979. xv-503.

*Anon., *Rassegna di Letteratura Tomistica*, 18(1982): 414-416.*
*Perini, G., *Divus Thomas*, 88(1985): 215-216.*

109 Tomás de Aquino. *Compendio de Teologia.* Trans. José Ignacio Saranyana and Jaime Restrepo Escobar. Madrid: Ediciones Rialp, 1980. 396.

*Anon., *Rassegna di Letteratura Tomistica*, 16(1980): 40-42.*
*Bandera, A., *Ciencia Tomista*, 107(1980): 613-614.*
*Huerga, A., *Angelicum*, 58(1981): 241-242.*
*Perini, G., *Divus Thomas*, 83(1980): 316.*

110 Tomás de Aquino. *A Suma Teológica, I.* Trans. Alexandre Corrêa. Porto Alegre: Eda. Sulina, 1981. lxvi-456.

*Lorenzon, A., *Presença Filosófica*, 6(1980): 70-72.*
*Lorenzon, A., *Revista de Filosofia*, 17(1980): 144-145.*
*Lorenzon, A., *Ciências Humanas*, Rio de Janeiro, 4(1980): 64.*

111 Tomás de Aquino. *De los Principios de la Naturaleza*. Trans. Antonio José Miguez. 8th ed. Biblioteca de Iniciación Filosófica. Buenos Aires: Aguilar, 1981. 66.

112 Tomás de Aquino. *Sobre la Eternidad del Mundo*. Trans. Angel J Cappelletti. 2nd ed. Biblioteca de Iniciación Filosófica. Buenos Aires: Aguilar, 1981. 137.

113 Tomás de Aquino. *Ente y la Esencia*. Trans. Manuel Benot Fuentes. 9th ed. Buenos Aires: Aguilar, 1981. 80.

114 Tomás de Aquino. *Tratado de la Ley: Tratado de la Justicia. Opusculo Sobre el Gobierno de los Príncipes*. Trans. Ignacio Carlos González. 2nd ed. México City, México: Porrúa, 1981. 496.

*Anon., *Rassegna di Letteratura Tomistica*, 17(1981): 30-31.*

115 Tomás de Aquino. *Textos Económicos en Tomás de Aquino*. Trans. Joaquin Llanos Entrepueblos. Bogota: University Santo Tomás, 1982. 304.

116 Tomás De Aquino. *Comentario de la Etica a Nicómaco*. Trans. Maria Ana Mallea. Buenos Aires: Ciafic, 1983. xiii-607.

*La Croce, E., *Sapientia*, 41(1986): 151-153.*
*Lértora Mendoza, C. A., *Revista de Filosofia*, 18(1985): 178-180.*

117 Tomás De Aquino. *Comentario de la Etica a Nicómaco*. Ed. Ana Maria Mallea. Buenos Aires: Ciafic, 1983. 607.

*La Croce, E., *Sapientia*, 41(1986): 151-153.*
*Létora Mendoza, C. A., *Revista de Filosofia*, 18(1985): 178-180.*

118 Tomás de Aquino. *Traducción de la Lección II del Libro I de la Explicación de Santo Tomás a los Libros de Aristóteles "Sobre la Interpretación."* Trans. Oscar Rotella. *Sapientia*, 38(1983): 297-314.

119 Tomás de Aquino. *Comentario de la Politica de Aristoteles Libro IV*. Trans. Ana Maria Mallea. Buenos Aires: Boletin de la Biblioteca del Congreso de la Nacion, 1984. 12-123.

120 Tomás de Aquino. *Santo Tomás de Aquino. Exposición del De Trinitate de Boecio.* Trans. Alfonso Marqués Garcia and José Antonio Fernandez. Biblioteca Di Teologia 17. Pamplona: Ediciones Universidad de Navarra, 1986. 302.

*Anon., *Rassegna di Letteratura,* 22(1986): 29-31.*
*Leroy, Marie Vincent, *Revue Thomiste,* 90(1990): 689.*

121 Tomás de Aquino. *Filosofía del Ser: Introducción, Comentario, Texto, y Traduución del De Ente et Essentia.* Trans. Edualdo Forment. Barcelona: Promociones y Publicaciones Universitarias, 1988.215.

122 Tomás de Aquino. *Suma de Teologia I, Parte 1.* Trans. Provincias Dominicanas. Ed. Provincias Dominicanas. BAC Maior 31. Madrid: Editorial Católica, 1988. 992.

*Osuna, A., *La Ciencia Tomista,* 115(1988): 331-335.*

123 Tomás de Aquino. *La Monarquia.* Trans. Laureano Robles and Angel Chueca. Madrid: Techos, 1989. 92.

B. ARTICLES

124 Tomás de Aquino. "*Del Maestro* II." *Revista de Filosofia* 10. 6-7(1977): 121-144. Trans. Mauricio Beuchot.

125 Tomás de Aquino. "*Quaestiones Disputatae de Veritate*. Quaestio 21: De Bono." *Ethos* (Buenos Aires), 6-7(1978-1979): 245-309. Trans. Soaje, R. G. and Corbi, Gustavo.

126 Tomás de Aquino. "Cuestiones 4a, 5a. y 6a. De la *Summa Theologiae* (La Pars)." *Ethos* (Buenos Aires), 8(1980): 307-330. Trans. Gustavo Corbi.

127 Tomás De Aquino. "Tratado *De Veritate*: Question IV (Divida en 8 Articulos)." *Revista de Filosofia* (Chile), 18(1980): 107-108. Trans. Poblete Le-Beuffe.

128 Tomás De Aquino. "Traduction Du Proemium de Saint Thomas A Son Commentaire Du *De Sensu et Senato* D'Aristote." *Cahiers I. P. C. Faculté libre de Philosophie Comparée*, 24(1981): 69-79. Trans. Bernard d'Avezac de Castera and Florence Avezac de Castera.

129 Tomás De Aquino. "O Proêmio de St. Tomás de Aquino Ao *Commentário A Metafisica de Aristóteles.*" *Trans form açao,* 5(1982): 103-106. Trans. Francisco Benjamin de Souza Netto.

130 Tomás De Aquino. "Traducción de la Lección II del Libro I Explicación de Santo Tomás a los Libros de Aristóteles Sobre la Interpretación (Con Una Introducción, Notas y Un Léxico)." *Sapientia,* 38(1983): 297-314. Trans. by Oscar Sabino Rotella.

VII. MISCELLANEOUS

A. BOOKS

131 Sw. Tomasz z Akwinu. *Suma Teologiczna Tom 2: O Bogu Czesc II(13-26).* Trans. Pius Belch. London: Veritas, 1977. 379.

132 Sw. Tomasz z Akwinu. *Suma Teologiczna Tom 3: O Trójcy Przenajswietsaej.* Trans. Pius Belch. London: Veritas, 1978. 337.

133 Sw. Tomasz z Akwinu. *Opusculum De Ente et Essentia*. Trans. R. Gosselina. Warszawa: ATK, 1978. 394.

134 Sw. Tomasz z Akwinu. *Suma Teologiczna Tom. 5*. Trans. O. Pius Belch. London: Veritas, 1979. 325.

135 Thomas Aquinas. *Somme Théologique (2a, 2ae 34-56 De Odio, Etc.)*. Trans. Démétrius Cydonés. Corpus Philosophorum Graecorum Recentiorum II 17A. Athénes: Fondation de Recherche et d'éditíons de Philosophie Néohellénique, 1979. 281.

136 Thomas Aquinas. *Somme Théologique (II II, Q. 17-22)*. Trans. Démétrius Cydonés. Corpus Philosophorum Graecorum Recentiorum II. Athénes: Fondation de Recherche et d'éditíons de Philosophie Néohellénique, 1979. 94.

137 Tomás De Aquino. *O Ente e a Essência*. Trans. Odilào D. Moura. Rio de Janeiro: Presença, 1981. 180.

*Skarica Zuñiga, M., *Philosophica*, Valparaiso, 5(1982): 202.*

*Van Acker, L., *Revista Brasileira de Filosofia*, 32(1982): 330-333.*

138 Sw. Tomasz z Akwinu. *Suma Teologiczna. Malzenstwo*. Trans. F. W. Bednarski. London: Veritas, 1982. 398.

139 Sw. Tomasz z Akwinu. *Suma Teologiczna Tom 33: Zmartwychwstanie Cial*. Trans. Pius Belch. London: Veritas, 1983.

140 Sw. Tomasz Z Akwinu. *Suma Teologiczna*. Trans. O. W. F. Bednarski. London: Veritas, 1985. 296.

141 Thomas von Aquin. *Von der Wahrheit*. Trans. Albert Zimmermann. Hamburg: Meiner, 1985. xiii-96.

142 Sw. Tomasz z Akwinu. *Suma Teologiczna Tom. 34*. Trans. O. Pius Belch. London: Veritas, 1986. 326.

143 Thomas Aquinas. *Over Het Zijnde en Het Wezen: Ingeleid, Vertaald en Geannoteerd*. Trans. B. Delgaauw. Agora Editie. Kampen: Kok Agora, 1986. 152.

*Bos, E. P. *Algemeen Nederlands Tijdschrift voor Wijsbegeerte*, 79(1987): 236-237.*

144 Thomas Aquinas. *Over God Spreken. Een Tekst Van Thomas Van Aquino Uit de Summa Theologiae (I. Q. 13)*. Trans. H. W. M. Rikhof. Sleutelteksten in Godsdienst en Theologie 6.(1988) Delft: Meinema. 159.

145 Thomas Van Aquino. *Over Waarheid en Onwaarheid. Ingel., Vert. en Geann. Door*. Trans. R. A. Te Velde. Kampen: Kok Agora, 1988.

146 Thomas Aquinas. *Shingaku Taizen 14 Tomasu Akuinasu [Japanese Trans. of the Latin Text of Summa Theologiae* St. Thomae Aquinatis Secundae Secundum Queastiones 106-114]. Trans. Bernard Ryôsuke Inagaki. Tokyo: Sôbun-sha, 1989. 330.

B. ARTICLES

147 Thomas Aquinas. "Demetrius Kydones' Trans. of the *Summa Theologica*." *Jahrbuch der österreichischen Byzantinistik (Wien)*, 32(1982): 311-320. Trans. Demetracopoulos, Photios.

148 Sw. Tomasz z Akwinu. "O Wiecznosci Swiata (*De Aeternitate Mundi*)." *Przeglad Tomistyczny: Rocznik Poswiecony Historii Teologii*. Warszawa Instytut Tomistyczny Ojców Dominikanów, 1984. 163-170.

SECONDARY SOURCES

I. BOOKS

A. ENGLISH

149 Adler, Mortimer. *The Angels and Us*. New York: Macmillan Company, 1988. 205.

150 Aertsen, Johannes Adrianus. *Medieval Reflections on Truth: Adaequatio Rei et Intellectus*. Amsterdam: VU Boehandel, 1984. 32.

151 Aertsen, Johannes Adrianus. *Nature and Creature: Thomas Aquinas' Way of Thought*. Studien und Text Zur Geistesgeschichte Des Mittelaiters. Leiden: E. J. Brill, 1988. xiv-413.

*Bonino, S. -T., *Revue Thomiste*, 89(1989): 333-336.*

152 Allard, Jean-Louis, ed. *Jacques Maritain: Philosophe dans la Cité/ A Philosopher in the World*. Ottawa: University of Ottawa Press, 1985. 447.

*Allion, J. -M., *Revue Thomiste*, 86(1986): 345-346.*
*Bourke, Vernon J., *The New Schoolman*, 65(1988): 284-285.*
*Fortin, Pierre, *Canadian Philosophical Reviews*, 6(1986): 3-4.*

153 Allen, Diogenes. *Philosophy for Understanding Theology*. London: SCM Press, 1985. LX-287.

154 Allen, Prudence. *The Concept of Woman: The Aristotelian Revolution 750 B. C. -A. D. 1250*. Montréal: Eden Press, 1985. vii-578.

155 Alston, William P. *Divine Nature and Human Language*. Ithaca, NY: Cornell University Press, 1989.

156 Armour, Leslie. *The Faces of Reason*. Waterloo, Ontario: Wilfrid Laurier University Press, 1981.

157 Arraj, James. *God, Zen and the Intuition of Being*. Chiloquin, OR: Inner Growth Books, 1988. *The author describes the inner nature of Zen from the viewpoint of Thomistic metaphysics. The book includes an imagined conversation between Jacques Maritain, a twentieth century commentator of Thomistic metaphysics, and Toshihiko Izutsu, a foremost Zen philosopher. *

158 Autori vari. *The Ethics of St. Thomas Aquinas*. Studi Tomistici 25. Città del Vaticano: Libreria Editrice Vaticana, 1984.

159 Ayers, Robert H. *Language, Logic and Reason in the Church Fathers: A Study of Tertullian, Augustine, and Aquinas*. Altertiumswissenschaftliche Texte und Studien 6. Hildesheim, NY: Olms Press, 1979. Especially 82-120. vii-146.

*Jordan, M., *Rassengna di Letteratura Tomistica*, 15(1982): 211-214.*

160 Azar, Larry. *Man: Computer, Ape, or Angel?* Hanover, MA: The Christopher Publishing House, 1989. 432. Especially Chapter 31: "The nature, origin, and destiny of the human soul," 275-294.

161 Azar, Larry. *Twentieth Century in Crisis: Foundations of Totalitarianism*. Dubuque, IA: Kendall/Hunt Publishing Company, 1990. Especially Chapter VII: "The Natural Law," 263-296, 317.

*Ingardia, Richard, *The Thomist*, 55(1991): 168-172.*
*Seddon, F., *Studies in Soviet Thought*, 27(1984): 345-351.*
*Stack, G. J., *The Modern Schoolman*, 61(1983-1984): 131.*

162 Baseheart, Mary Catharine. *The Encounter of Husserl's Phenomenology and the Philosophy of St. Thomas in Selected Writings of Edith Stein*. Ann Arbor, MI: University Microfilms International, 1977. vi-203. Authorized facsimile of the dissertation of the University of Notre Dame, Ph. D., 1960.

163 Battaglia, Anthony. *Toward a Reformulation of Natural Law*. New York: The Seabury Press, 1981. ix-150.

*Moloney, R., *The Heythrop Journal*, 24(1983): 197-199.*

*Smith, Raymond, *The Thomist*, 43(1983): 461-462.*

164 Bignogiari, Dino, ed. *The Political Ideas of St. Thomas Aquinas*. 1953. New York: Hafner Press, 1981. Especially *Introduction*, vii-xxxvii.

165 Bogliolo, Don Luigi. *Philosophical Anthropology: A Complete Course of Scholastic Philosophy*. Trans. Noel Chin. Ed. Sebastian Kanotemprel. Vol. 2. Shillong, India: Sacred Hearth Theological College, 1984.

*Hasan, Noorul, *Doctor Communis*, 37(1984): 177.*

166 Bonansea, Bernardino M. *God and Atheism: A Philosophical Approach to the Problem of God*. Washington, DC: The Catholic University of America Press, 1979. xiv-378. Especially Chapter IV: "The Five Ways of St. Thomas," 71-221.

*Bérubé, C., *Collectanea Franciscana*, 51(1981): 425-426.*

*Cartechini, S., *Doctor Communis*, 35(1982): 78-85.*

*Davies, Brian, *Religious Studies*, 18(1982): 408-410.*

*Lacoste, Jean-Yves, *Revue Philosophique de Louvain*, 81(1983): 318-319.*

*Mangiagalli, M., *Rivista di Filosofia Neo-Scolastica*, 77(1985): 161-164.*

*Masterson, Patrick, *The Review of Metaphysics*, 34(1980): 128-129.*

*Pappin Joseph, *The Heythrop Journal*, 22(1981): 71-74.*

*Perego, A., *Divus Thomas* 83(1980): 293-295.*

*Sadowsky, James A., *International Philosophical Quarterly*, 21(1981): 463-465.*

*Tosetto, M. T., *Filosofia*, 32(1981): 259-260.*

*Walhout, D., *International Studies in Philosophy*, 13(1981): 82-83.*

*Wilder, A., *Angelicum*, 58(1981): 87-89.*

In this book Professor Bonansea considers the question of God's existence purely philosophical, rational grounds. In Part I he evaluates 19th and 20th century atheistic arguments. Part II is a survey of the main historical theistic arguments, such as the ideological, ontological, and Scotistic arguments, as well as the Five Ways of St. Thomas and Maurice Blondel's approach to God. Part III includes a discussion of St. Bonaventure's arguments against creation from eternity and the effects of modern science on traditional Judeo-Christian theories of creation.

167 Booth, Edward. *Aristotelian Aporetic Ontology in Islamic and Christian Thinkers*. Cambridge Studies in Medieval Life and Thought 20. Cambridge: Cambridge University Press, 1983. xxvi-314.

*Burrell, David B., *The New Scholasticism*, 60(1986): 243-245.*

*Murphy, Thomas, *The Heythrop Journal*, 27(1986): 471.*

168 Borresen, Kari Elisabeth. *Subordination and Equivalence: The Nature and Role of Woman in Augustine and Thomas Aquinas*. Trans. Charles H. Talbot. 1968. Washington, DC: University Press of America, 1981.

169 Boyle, Leonard E. *The Setting of the Summa Theologiae of Saint Thomas*. The Etienne Gilson Series 5. Toronto: Pontifical Institute of Mediaeval Studies, 1982. 30.

*Anon., *Rassegna di Letteratura Tomistica*, 18(1982): 45-46.*

170 Braine, David. *The Reality of Time and the Existence of God: The Project of Proving God's Existence*. Oxford: Clarendon Press, 1988. xvi-383.

*Burrell, David, *Faith and Philosophy*, 7(1990): 361-364.*
*Fisichella, Rino, *Gregorianum*, 72(1991): 146-147.*
*Quinn, Philip L., *The Review of Metaphysics*, 42(1988): 378-381.*

171 Brezik, Victor B., ed. *One Hundred Years of Thomism: Aeterni Patris* and Afterwards, A Symposium. Houston, TX: Center for Thomistic Studies, University of St. Thomas, 1981. 210.

*Murphy, Thomas, *The Heythrop Journal*, 24(1983): 95-97.*
*O'Brien, Thomas C., *The Thomist*, 48(1984): 473-475.*

172 Brezik, Victor B., ed. *Thomistic Papers I*. Notre Dame, IN: University of Notre Dame Press, 1984. 156.

*Haldane, John J., *Philosophical Books*, 27(1986): 79-82.*
*O'Brien, Thomas C., *The Thomist*, 48(1984): 473-475.*

This volume is a collection of previously unpublished essays relating the philosophy of Thomas Aquinas to contemporary issues. Henry B. Veatch writes about the relevance of natural law ethics, Vernon J. Bourke about the insanity plea, James A. Weisheipl about the concept of nature, Victor B. Brezik about evolution as the total explanation of human origin, Anton C. Pegis about intentionality in knowledge, and Joseph Owens about the notion of philosophy as ideology.

173 Brody, Baruch A., ed. *Suicide and Euthanasia*. Norwell: Kluwer, 1989. 39-75.

This volume analyzes the history of philosophical thought on suicide and euthanasia and discusses the implication of that history for the contemporary debate. The historical section contains an essay by John Cooper about Greek views, Barch Brody about Jewish casuistry, Darrel Amundsen about Christian values, Gary Ferngren about Renaissance and Reformation views, and Tom Beauchamp about views during the Enlightenment. Joseph Boyle and Tris Engelhardt debate the implications of the historical views for the contemporary discussion.

174 Brown, Barry F. *Accidental Being: A Study in the Metaphysics of St. Thomas Aquinas*. Washington, DC: University Press of America, 1985. xii-427.

*Anon., *Rassegna di Letteratura Tomistica*, 21(1985): 190-193.*
*Antoniotti, Louise-Marie, *Revue Thomiste*, 90(1990): 304-306.*
*Clarke, W. N., *Canadian Philosophical Reviews*, 7(1987): 391-393.*
*Ewbank, Michael B., *The Review of Metaphysics*, 44(1990): 406-409.*
*Pangallo, Mario, *Doctor Communis*, 42(1989): 95-96.*
*Stella, P. T., *Aquinas*, 29(1986): 196-197.*

This work investigates the ontological status of accidents in the metaphysics of St. Thomas Aquinas. Do accidents have their own being as existential acts? Strictly speaking, the answer is negative. Yet there is an accidental being, which belongs to and is exercised by the subject of an accident, i.e., by a substance. This multiple being is caused by its subject, is dependent upon it, and is really distinct from the single, substantial being of a substance.

175 Brown, Oscar James. *Natural Rectitude and Divine Law in Aquinas: An Approach to an Integral Interpretation of the Thomistic Doctrine of Law*. Studies and Texts 55. Toronto: Pontifical Institute of Medieval Studies, 1981. xiv-210.

*Anon., *Rassegna di Letteratura Tomistica*, 17(1981): 163-166.*
*Daly, P. H., *Revue d'Histoire Ecclésiastique*, 80(1985): 572-573.*
*Étienne, Jacques, *Revue Philosophique de Louvain*, 83(1985): 292-293.*
*Zedler, B. H., *Speculum*, 59(1984): 228-229.*

176 Browne, Joseph W. *Personal Dignity*. New York: Philosophical Library, 1983. 164. Especially Chapter 10: "Dignity: Natural and Supernatural," 151-164.

177 Burrell, David B. *Aquinas: God and Action*. London/Notre Dame, IN: Routledge & Kegan Paul/University of Notre Dame Press, 1979. xiii-194.

*Anon., *Rassegna di Letteratura*, 15(1979): 235-238.*
*Bourke, Vernon J., *The New Scholasticism*, 54(1980): 109-111.*
*Catan, John R., *Nous*, 18(1984): 125-132.*
*Desharnais, Richard P., *International Studies in Philosophy*, 12(1980): 95-96.*
*Elders, L. J., *Divus Thomas*, 83(1980): 92-94.*
*Innis, Robert E., *The Thomist*, 45(1981): 585-589.*
*Jordan, Mark D., *The Review of Metaphysics*, 33(1979-1980): 417-419.*
*Mascall, E. L., *Religious Studies*, 15(1979): 556-558.*
*M. D. J., *The Review of Metaphysics*, 33(1979): 417-419.*
*Murphy, Thomas, *The Heythrop Journal*, 21(1980): 348-349.*
*Peccorini, F. L., *Speculum*, 55(1980): 532-536.*
*Prozesky, Martin H., *Philosophical Papers*, 9(1980): 47-48.*
*Spitzer, Robert, *The Modern Schoolman*, 57(1980): 361-365.*
*Stump, Eleonore, *The Philosophical Review*, 90(1981): 162-164.*
*Walgrave, J. H., *Tijdschrift voor Filosofie*, 44(1982): 554-555.*

178 Burrell, David B. *Knowing the Unknowable God: Ibn Sina, Maimonides, Aquinas*. Notre Dame, IN: University of Notre Dame Press, 1986. 130.

*Broadie, A., *Religious Studies*, 24(1988): 541-542.*
*Catania, Francis J., *The Modern Schoolman*, 65(1988): 131-132.*
*De Grijs, F., *Bijdragen*, 49(1988): 87-89.*
*Doods, Michael, *New Blackfriars*, Jan.(1988): 45-46.*
*Hill, W. J., *The Thomist*, 51(1987): 699-709.*
*McCool, Gerald A., *International Philosophical Quarterly*, 27(1987): 110-111.*
*Owens, Joseph, *International Journal for Philosophy of Religion*, 23(1988): 119-121.*
*Rudavsky, T. M., *Religious Studies*, 24(1989): 468-470.*
*Rudavsky, T. M., *Journal of the History of Philosophy*, 27(1989): 468-470.*
*Sokolowski, Robert, *Faith and Philosophy*, 6(1989): 11-114.*

179 Burrell, David B., and Bernard McGinn. *God and Creation: An Ecumenical Symposium*. Notre Dame, IN: University of Notre Dame Press, 1990. xii-328.

180 Butterworth, Edward Joseph. *The Identity of Anselm's Proslogion Argument for the Existence of God with the Via Quarta* of Thomas Aquinas. Studies in the History of Philosophy 8. Lewiston: The Edwin Mellen Press, 1990.

181 Capestany, Edward J. *The Moral World.* Scranton, NJ: Ridge Row Press, 1988.

182 Caputo, John D. *Heidegger and Aquinas: An Essay on Overcoming Metaphysics.* New York: Fordham University Press, 1982. xii-308.

*Blanchette, Oliva, *International Studies in Philosophy*, 19(1987): 69-70.*
*Burch, Robert, *Canadian Philosophical Reviews*, 4(1984): 235-237.*
*Cronin, J., *Revue Philosophique de Louvain*, 82(1984): 285-288.*
*Dumoulin, B., *Les Études Philosophiques*, 2-3(1987): 347-349.*
*Marsh, J. L., *International Philosophical Quarterly*, 25(1985): 201-206.*
*O'Leary, Joseph Stephen, *The Thomist*, 49(1985): 477-481.*
*Pleydell-Pearce, A. G., *The Journal of the British Society for Phenomenology*, 18(1987): 79-82.*
*Wenin, Christian, *Revue Philosophique de Louvain*, 82(184): 285-290.*
*Wilkinson, Winston A., *The Modern Schoolman*, 63(1985): 71-73.*
*Zimmerman, Michael E., *The New Scholasticism*, 62(1988): 365-370.*

*This work contends that(1) past studies are hampered by uncritical allegiance to one of these thinkers and blindness to the merits of the other; (2) even granting a participationist reading of Aquinas, the notion of *esse* does not escape Heidegger's *Seinsvergessenheit*; (3) Heidegger's true concern is not with Being but *Ereignis*; hence no metaphysics of *esse* can address his critique; (4) there is a mystical element in Aquinas which "overcomes" metaphysics and is the real contact between the two thinkers.*

183 Carroll, William E., ed. *Nature and Motion in the Middle Ages.* Studies in Philosophy and the History of Philosophy 11. Washington, DC: The Catholic University of America Press, 1985. 287.

184 Carvin, Walter P. *Creation and Scientific Explanation.* Theology and Science at the Frontiers of Knowledge 10. Edinburgh: Scottish Academic Press, 1988. ix-106.

185 Cassell, Anthony K. *Dante's Fearful Art of Justice.* Toronto: University of Toronto Press, 1984. xiii-186.

186 Cassidy, T. G. *Experience and Theology: A Study of the Influence of Love on Knowledge in the Theology of St. Thomas.* Pontifical Studiorum University, 1984. 236.

187 Catan, John R., ed. *St. Thomas Aquinas on the Existence of God: Collected Papers of Joseph Owens, C. Ss. R.* Albany, NY: State University of New York Press, 1980. 291.

*O'Brien, Thomas C., *The Thomist*, 46(1982): 644-653.*

188 Catan, John R., ed. *Aristotle: The Collected Papers of Joseph Owens.* Albany, NY: State University of New York Press, 1981. 288.

*Ackrill, J. L., *Classical Review*, 97(1983): 64-66.*
*Brumbaugh, R. S., *Classical World*, 75(1981-1982): 377-378.*
*Grimaldi, W. M. A., *Philosophy and Rhetoric*, 16(1983): 275-277.*
*Husain, Martha, *International Studies in Philosophy*, 16(1984): 120-123.*
*Kachi, Y., *Archives Intérnationales d'Histoire des Sciences*, 34(1984): 269-271.*
*Konyndyk, K., *The Philosophical Review*, 92(1983): 297-302.*
*O'Brien, T. C., *The Thomist*, 46(1982): 644-653.*
*Spade, P. V., *Dialogue*, 21(1982): 772-773.*
*Turnbull, R. G., *Phoenix*, 36(1982): 366-370.*
*Van Rijen, J., *Archiv für Geschichte der Philosophie*, 66(1984): 216-217.*

189 Centore, Florestano. *Persons: A Comparative Account of the Six Possible Theories.* Contributions in Philosophy 13. Westport, CT: Greenwood Press, 1979.

*Englebretsen, George, *Dialogue*, 20(1981): 407-409.*

This book is an account of the various essentially different views which may be taken on the definition of the human person. These are related to their philosophy-of-being backgrounds, as well as to some of their main theoretical consequences in political and social philosophy. The paradigms are entitled Reductionistic Materialism, Nonreductionistic Materialism, Psychosomaticism Without Immortality, Psychosomaticism With Immortality, Vitalism, and Reductionistic Immaterialism.

190 Cessario, Romanus. *Christian Satisfaction in Aquinas: Towards a Personalist Understanding*. Lanham, MD: University Press of America, 1982. xxi-368.

*Anon., *Rassegna di Letteratura Tomistica*, 18(1985): 263-268.*
*Buckley, James, *The Thomist*, 51(1987): 524-526.*
*Perego, A., *Divus Thomas*, 87(1984): 110-111.*

191 Chandel, Bhuvaw, ed. *Nature of Violence*. Chandigarh: Panjab University Publication Bureau, 1980. vi-100.

192 Chesterton, Gilbert K. *St. Thomas Aquinas*. 1933. *G. K. Chesterton: Collected Works*. Eds. George Marlin, Richard Rabatlin, and John Swan. 2. San Francisco: Ignatius Press, 1986. 419-540.

193 Chin, Kyo-Hun. *Studies in Philosophical Anthropology I*. Seoul: Kyungmunsa, 1982. 209.

194 Christian, William A. *Doctrines of Religious Communities: A Philosophical Study*. New Haven, CT: Yale University Press, 1987.

Along with their primary doctrines about the settings of human activities and conduct in these settings, religious communities have norms to govern the development of their bodies of doctrines. They have criteria of authenticity, principles of internal consistency, rules for deriving and arguing for their doctrines, and other governing doctrines. These have consequences for their positions on alien claims and thus for the ways they face their social and intellectual environments.

195 Clarke, W. Norris. *The Philosophical Approach to God: A Neo-Thomist Perspective*. Ed. William E. Ray. Winston-Salem, NC: Wake Forest University Press, 1979. viii-115.

*Jordan, M. D., *Rassegna di Letteratura Tomistica*, 15(1982): 219-222.*
*Kondoleon, Theodore J., *The Thomist*, 46(1982): 156-161.*

196 Cobb, John B., and Franklin I. Gamwell, eds. *Existence and Actuality: Conversations with Charles Hartshorne*. Chicago: University of Chicago Press, 1984. xvii-196.

*Wood, Jr., F., *International Journal for Philosophy of Religion*, 18(1985): 166-168.*

This book is based on a conference on Hartshorne's thought held at the University of Chicago in 1981. Critics are Eugene Peters, Schubert Ogden, R. M. Martin, William Alston, John Smith, Paul Weiss, Manley Thompson, John Cobb, and George Wolf. Hartshorne's reply to each critic is included as well as an autobiography. The discussion ranges over issues of methodology, theism, and nature, and considers Hartshrone's relations to Quine, Aquinas, Anselm, and Peirce. The distinction between existence and actuality is affirmed by Hartshorne as one of his major philosophical contributions.

197 Colish, Marcia L. *The Mirror of Language: A Study in the Medieval Theory of Knowledge*. Ed. rev. ed. Lincoln, NB: University of Nebraska Press, 1983. xvii-339.

198 Copleston, Frederick Charles. *A History of Medieval Philosophy*. 1972. Notre Dame, IN: University of Notre Dame Press, 1990. 399.

199 Costanzo, Joseph F. *The Historical Credibility of Hans Kung*. North Quincy, MA: Christopher Press, 1979.

200 Craig, William Lane. *The Cosmological Argument from Plato to Leibniz*. Ed. John Hick. New York: Barnes & Noble, 1980. xi-305.

*Durant, Michael, *Religious Studies*, 17(1981): 289-291.*

*Weber, Stephen L., *Philosophical Books*, 23(1982): 452-453.*

This study explores the development of the cosmological argument in its various forms by means of a careful analysis of the arguments of thirteen of the proof's greatest proponents, including Plato, Aristotle, Ibn Sina, al-Ghazali, Ibn Rushd, Maimonides, Aquinas, Scotus, Spinoza, and Leibniz. A final chapter suggests a three-fold typology of cosmological arguments and delineates the most important critical issues raised by each.

201 Craig, William Lane. *The Problem of Divine Foreknowledge and Future Contingents from Aristotle to Suarez*. Leiden: E. J. Brill, 1988. Especially Chapter IV: "Thomas Aquinas," 99-126.

202 Creel, Richard E. *Divine Impassibility: An Essay in Philosophical Theology*. Cambridge: Cambridge University Press, 1986. xi-238.

*Bracken, J. A., *Theological Studies*, 46(1985): 707-708.*

*Davies, Brian, *The Heythrop Journal*, 30(1989): 239-240.*

*Feenstra, Ronald J., *Faith and Philosophy*, 5(1988): 456-458.*

*Ford, Lewis S., *International Journal for the Philosophy of Religion*, 24(1988): 194-198.*

*Keller, J. A., *Process Studies*, 15(1986): 290-296.*

*Oppenheimer, H., *The Journal of the Theological Studies*, 37(1986): 682-685.*

*Sia, Santiago, *Modern Theology*, 5(1989): 182-184.*

*Four respects in which God might be passible or impassible are discussed, with emphasis on Aquinas and Hartshorne: God's nature, will, knowledge, and feeling. The following related topics are discussed: divine eternality (vs. Stump, Kretzmann): evil (vs. Madden, Hare): creation *ex nihilo* (vs. Geach, Swinburne): a best possible world (vs. Adams, Reichenback). The conclusions reached are that God should be thought of as impassible in nature, will, and knowledge of abstract possibilities, but passible in knowledge of actuality and concrete possibilities.*

203 Crowe, Michael Bertram. *The Changing Profile of the Natural Law*. The Hague: Nijhoff, 1977. xii-321. Especially "Aquinas faces the natural law tradition," 136-165, and "Aquinas makes up his mind," 166-191.

*Anon, *Rassegna di Letteratura Tomistica*, 15(1982): 453-455.*

204 Crowley, Charles B. *Universal Mathematics in Aristotelian-Thomistic Philosophy: The Hermeneutics of Aristotelian Texts Relative to Universal Mathematics*. Washington, DC: University Press of America, 1980. xviii-221.

The purpose of this work is to examine critically certain texts of Aristotle(1026a25-28; 1064b5-15; 1077a9-12; 1077b12-22; 74a17-25; 85a36-85b1): which some of his modern Trans.s and commentators allege indicate that Aristotle held, at least implicitly, for a universal mathematical science prior to Arithmetic and Geometry, which, while being mathematical, treated quantity as quantity, its properties and axioms. The conclusion reached is that textually Aristotle did not implicitly hold for a universal mathematics prior to Arithmetic and Geometry, and that such a position is contrary to his philosophical principles.

205 Cunningham, Francis A. *Essence and Existence in Thomism: A Mental vs. the "Real Distinction?"* Lanham, MD: University Press of America, 1988. 552.

*Sweeney, Leo, *The Modern Schoolman*, 68(1991): 337-340.*

206 D'Arcy, Eric. *Conscience and Its Right to Freedom*. 1961. London: Sheed and Ward, 1979. x-277.

207 Dales, Richard C. *Medieval Discussions of the Eternity of the World*. Brill's Studies in Intellectual History 18. Leiden: E. J. Brill, 1990. v-303. Especially Chapter 7: "The development of the controversy," 109-128; Chapter 8: "The condemnations of 1270 and its aftermath, 129-155; Chapter 9: "The climax of the controversy," 156-177.

208 Davidson, Herbert Alan. *Proofs for Eternity, Creation and the Existence of God in Medieval, Islamic and Jewish Philosophy*. Oxford: Oxford University Press, 1987. xii-428. Especially Chapter 12: "Subsequent history of proofs from the concept of necessary existence, #1: Maimonides and Aquinas," 378-406.

*Redpath, Peter A., *The Thomist*, 53(1989): 528-531.*
*Taylor, Richard C., *Speculum*, 65(1990): 648-651.*

209 Davies, Brian. *An Introduction to the Philosophy of Religion*. Oxford: Oxford University Press, 1982. x-144.

*Stump, Eleonore, *The Thomist*, 49(1985): 128-131.*

210 Davies, Brian. *Language, Meaning, and God: Essays in Honour of Herbert McCabe, O. P.* London: Geoffrey Chapman, 1987.

*Clarke, W. Norris, *New Blackfriars*, 1988: 456-457.*

211 De Smet, Richard. *The Concept of Man in Thomism and Neo-Thomism*. Madras: University of Madras, 1982-1983. 32.

212 Dennehy, Raymond. *Reason and Dignity*. Washington, DC: University Press of America, 1981. viii-143.

213 Dodds, Michael J. *The Unchanging God of Love: A Study of the Teaching of St. Thomas Aquinas on Divine Immutability in View of Certain Contemporary Criticism of This Doctrine*. Studia Friburgensia, Nouvelle Série 66. Suisse: Éditions Universitaires Fribourg, 1986. xviii-492.

*Anon., *Rassegna di Letteratura Tomistica*, 22(1986): 195-198.*
*Rousseau, Mary F., *The Modern Schoolman*, 65(1988): 272-274.*
*Wielockx, R., *Louvain Studies*, 16(1991): 178-180.*
*Wilder, A., *Angelicum*, 65(1988): 134-137.*

214 Doering, Bernard E. *Jacques Maritain and the French Catholic Intellectuals*. Notre Dame, IN: University of Notre Dame Press, 1983. 268.

*Sutton, Michael, *The Heythrop Journal*, 27(1986): 99-101.*

215 Doig, James Conroy. *In Defense of Cognitive Realism: Cutting the Cartesian Knot*. Lanham, MD: University Press of America, 1987. 306.

216 Donagan, Alan. *Human Ends and Human Actions: An Exploration in St. Thomas' Treatment*. Milwaukee, WI: Marquette University Press, 1985. 43.

Aquinas distinguished two kinds of end, those pre-existing actions for their sake and those produced by actions for their sake. How this distinction affected his treatment of the Aristotelian doctrine that eudaemonia is the end of human actions is explored.

217 Donagan, Alan. *Choice: The Essential Element in Human Action*. New York: Routledge, 1987.

*Bishop, John, *Australasian Journal of Philosophy*, 67(1989): 375-376.*
*Hornsby, Jennifer, *Inquiry*, 32(1989): 95-106.*

218 Donceel, Joseph. *The Searching Mind: An Introduction to a Philosophy of God*. Notre Dame, IN: University of Notre Dame Press, 1979. viii-231.

*Honner, John, *The Heythrop Journal*, 22(1981): 308-309.*
*Ingardia, Richard, *The New Scholasticism*, 56(1982): 381-384.*
*Jordan, Mark D., *Rassengna di Letteratura Tomistica*, 15(1982): 219.*
*Kopaczynski, G., *Miscellanea Francescana*, 81(1981): 275-277.*
*Ogiermann, H., *Theologie und Philosophie*, 56(1981): 152-153.*
*Teske, Roland, *The Modern Schoolman*, 59(1982): 225-226.*

The book contains two parts:(1) Existence of God. Established by means of transcendental method: the affirmation of God is a condition of the possibility of human thought and action. Or again: If God is possible, he exists. The fact that we are aware of the finite as finite implies that we strive for the infinite. Such a striving implies the positive possibility of God. The human person is an embodied affirmation of God. (2) Nature of God. Studied briefly within the framework of (a) Thomistic philosophy. (b) process philosophy. Brief discussions of creation, problem of evil, panenthesim, atheism.

219 Eco, Umberto. *Art and Beauty in the Middle Ages*. Trans. Hugh Bredin. New Haven, CT: Yale University Press, 1986.

*Cheetham, Mark A., *Canadian Philosophical Reviews*, 7(1987): 229-230.*
*Collinson, Diané, *British Journal of Aesthetics*, 27(1987): 286-287.*
*Morris, Michael, *The Thomist*, 52(1988): 181-183.*
*Mothersill, Mary, *Journal of Aesthetics and Art Criticism*, 46(1987-1988): 311-312.*
*Wood, Robert E., *The Review of Metaphysics*, 43(1990): 859-863.*
*Zawilla, Ronald John, *The Modern Schoolman*, 68(1990): 84-86.*

220 Eco, Umberto. *The Aesthetics of Thomas Aquinas*. Trans. Hugh Bredin. 1970. Cambridge, MA: Harvard University Press, 1988. xii-287. Originally published in 1970 as *Il Problema estetico in Tommaso d'Aquin*.

*Barbiero, Daniel, *Critical Texts*, 6(1989): 103-109.*
*Culiani, Joan P., *The Journal of Religion*, 70(1990): 283-285.*
*Wood, Robert E., *The Review of Metaphysics*, 43(1990): 859-863.*

221 Edwards, Steven Anthony. *Interior Acts: Teleology, Justice, and Friendship in the Religious Ethics of Thomas Aquinas*. Lanham, MD: University Press of America, 1986. xi-171.

222 Elders, Léon J. *The Philosophical Theology of St. Thomas Aquinas*. Studien und Texte Zur Geistesgeschichte Des Mittelalters 26. Leiden: E. J. Brill, 1990. ix-332.

223 Elders, Léon J., and K. Hedwig, eds. *The Ethics of St. Thomas Aquinas*. Studi Tomistici 25. Città del Vaticano: Libreria Editrice Vaticana, 1984. 259.

*Composta, D., *Doctor Communis*, 38(1985): 181-187.*
*Lefévre, Ch., *Mélanges de Science Religieuse*, 41(1984): 177-180.*

224 Elders, Léon J., and K. Hedwig, eds. *Lex et Libertas: Freedom and Law According to St. Thomas Aquinas*. Studi Tomistici 30. Città del Vaticano, Pontificia Accademia di San Tommaso e di Religione Cattolica: Libreria Editrice Vaticana, 1987. 286.

*Composta, Dario, *Doctor Communis*, 41(1988): 96-97.*

225 Farthing, John Lee. *Thomas Aquinas and Gabriel Biel: Interpretations of St. Thomas Aquinas in German Nominalism on the Eve of the Reformation*. Duke Monographs in Medieval and Renaissance Studies 9. Durham, NC: Duke University Press, 1988. x-265.

*Bonino, S. -T., *Revue Thomiste*, 88(1988): 496-497.*
*Eire, Carlos M. N., *The Journal of Religion*, 70(1990): 91-92.*
*Lindberg, Carter, *Church History*, 58(1989): 379-380.*
*McInerny, Ralph, *Speculum*, 66(1991): 150-152.*
*Wawrykow, Joseph, *The Thomist*, 55(1991): 149-156.*

226 Figurski, Leszek Stanley. *Finality and Intelligence*. Washington, DC: University Press of America, 1978.

227 Fink, Hans. *Social Philosophy*. London: Methuen, 1981. 122.

228 Finnis, John M. *Natural Law and Natural Rights*. Oxford: Clarendon Press, 1980. xv-425.

*Anon., *Rassenga di Letteratura Tomistica*, 16(1980): 203-206.*
*Barry, Robert, *The Thomist*, 45(1981): 626-630.*
*Boyle, Jr.,, Joseph M., *The New Scholasticism*, 55(1981): 245-247.*
*Demmer, Klaus, *Gregorianum* 62(1981): 180-182.*
*Fitzgerald, P. J., *Canadian Philosophical Reviews*, 2(1982): 164-167.*
*Gómez-Lombo, A., *Revista Latinoamericana de Filosofia*, 8(1982): 282-284.*
*Greenawalt, Kent, *Political Theory*, 10(1982): 133-136.*
*Kalinowski, G., *Archives de Philosophie du Droit*, 26(81): 419-423.*
*Kalinowski, G., *Ethos*, 10-11(1982-1983): 344-370.*
*Langan, John, *International Philosophical Quarterly*, 21(1981): 217-218.*
*Massini, C. I., *Sapienza*, 41(1986): 76-77.*
*Paulson, S. L., *Philosophical Books*, 22(1981): 215-217.*
*Pollard, D. E. B., *Philosophical Studies*, 30(1984): 369-370.*
*Richards, David A. J., *Ethics*, 93(1982): 169-173.*
*Russman, Thomas, *The Review of Metaphysics*, 35(1982): 604-605.*
*Tuck, Richard, *Philosophical Quarterly*, 31(1981): 282-284.*
*Vitale, V., *Rivista Internazionale di Filosofia del Ditto*, 58(1981): 346-347.*
*Wilcox, W. H., *The Philosophical Review*, 92(1983): 599-604.*

229 Finnis, John M. *Fundamentals of Ethics*. Washington, DC: Georgetown University Press, 1983.

*Brown, Geoffrey, *The Philosophical Quarterly*, 35(1985): 210-211.*
*Donnelly, John, *Philosophical Books*, 25(1984): 227-229.*

*Fitzpatrick, F. J., *Philosophical Studies*, 31(1986-1987): 403-406.*
*Gordon, David, *International Philosophical Quarterly*, 24(1984): 329-330.*
*Hittinger, R., *The Modern Schoolman*, 63(1986): 295-298.*
*La Barge, J. A., *Theological Studies*, 45(1984): 753-754.*
*McCauley, H. C., *Irish Theological Quarterly*, 54(1988): 321-323.*
*McFetridge, I. G., *Mind*, 94(1985): 158-160.*
*Ricken, F., *Theologie und Philosophie*, 62(1987): 471-73.*
*Warnock, M., *The Journal of the Theological Studies*, 35(1984): 579-580.*
*Weiler, G., *Grazer Philosophische Studien*, 23(1985): 164-168.*

230 Flew, Anthony. *God: A Critical Enquiry*. 1964. La Salle, IL: Open Court Publishing Company, 1984. 450. Especially Chapters 3-5: *Natural Theology*, 52-117.

231 Freddoso, Alfred J., ed. *The Existence and Nature of God*. Notre Dame, IN: University of Notre Dame Press, 1983. 190.

*Burrell, David B., *International Journal for Philosophy of Religion*, 16(1984): 173-174.*
*Davies, Brian, *The Heythrop Journal*, 28(1987): 331-333.*
*Gill, Jerry H., *International Studies in Philosophy*, 19(1987): 74-75.*
*Mann, William E., *Faith and Philosophy*, 2(1985): 195-204.*
*Millar, Alan, *Religious Studies*, 20(1984): 173-174.*

This volume includes seven original essays that serve as critical reflections on classical discussions of God's existence and nature: N. Pike, "Over-Power and God's Responsibility for Sin"; R. Swinburne, "A Theodicy of Heaven and Hell"; P. Quinn, "Divine Conservation, Continuous Creation, and Human Action"; T. Flint and A. Freddoso, "Maximal Power"; J. Ross, "Creation II"; C. Dore, "Descartes' Meditation V: Argument for God's Existence"; and M. Jordan, "The Names of God and the Being of Names."

232 Geach, Peter. *The Virtues*. Cambridge: Cambridge University Press, 1977. xxxv-173.

233 Geraghty, Richard Patrick. *The Object of Moral Philosophy According to St. Thomas Aquinas*. Washington, DC: University Press of America, 1982. x-319.

234 Gerson, Lloyd P., ed. *Graceful Reason: Essays in Ancient and Medieval Philosophy Presented to Joseph Owens on the Occasion of His Seventy-fifth Birthday and the Fiftieth Anniversary of His Ordination*. Papers in Mediaeval Studies 4. Toronto: Pontifical Institute of Mediaeval Studies, 1983.

*Ashley, Benedict, *The Modern Schoolman*, 64(1987): 124-125.*
*Burrell, David, *The New Scholasticism*, 62(1988): 239-241.*
*Jordan, Mark D., *Speculum*, 60(1985): 1047-1048.*
*Kretzmann, Norman, *Dialogue*, 25(1986): 564-566.*
*Leroux, G., *Philosophiques*, 12(1985): 229-231.*
*Madigan, Arthur, *Ancient Philosophy*, 5(1985): 136-140.*

235 Gilson, Étienne Henry. *The Philosophy of St. Thomas Aquinas*. Trans. E. Bullough. New York: Avno Press, 1978.

236 Gilson, Étienne Henry. *Elements of Christian Philosophy*. 1960. Westport, CT: Greenwood, 1978. 358.

237 Gilson, Étienne Henry. *History of Christian Philosophy in the Middle Ages*. London: Sheed & Ward, 1978.

238 Gilson, Étienne Henry. *God and Philosophy*. 1941. New Haven, CT: Yale University Press, 1979. 147.

239 Gilson, Étienne Henry. *The Unity of Philosophical Experience*. 1937. Westminster: Christian Classics, 1982. xii-331.

240 Gilson, Étienne Henry. *The Christian Philosophy of St. Thomas Aquinas*. Trans. L. K. Shook. 1956. New York: Octagon Books, 1983. 502.

241 Gilson, Étienne Henry. *Thomist Réalism and the Critique of Knowledge*. Trans. Mark A. Wauck. 1939. San Francisco: Ignatius Press, 1986. 215. French original entitled, *Réalisme thomiste et critique de la connaissance*.

*Lee, Patrick, *The New Scholasticism*, 63(1989): 81-100.*

242 Gilson, Étienne Henry. *Linguistics and Philosophy: An Essay on the Philosophical Constants of Language*. Trans. John Lyon. Notre Dame, IN: University of Notre Dame Press, 1988. 256.

243 Gilson, Étienne Henry. *Letters of Étienne Gilson to Henri De Lubac*. Trans. Mary Emily Hamilton. San Francisco: Ignatius Press, 1988. 247. Trans. of *Lettres de M. Etienne Gilson addressées au P. Henri De Lubac.*

*Ols, D., *Angelicum*, 65(1988): 148-151.*
*Van Steenberghen, Fernand, *Revue Philosophique de Louvain*, 87(1989): 324-331.*

244 Gilson, Étienne Henry. *Methodical Realism*. Trans. Philip Trower. Front Royal, VA: Christendom Press, 1990. 190.

245 Gratsch, Edward J. *Aquinas' Summa: An Introduction and Interpretation*. Staten Island, NY: Alba House, 1985. xxxix-305.

246 Gutting, Gary. *Religious Belief and Religious Skepticism*. Notre Dame, IN: University of Notre Dame Press, 1982. Especially Part 1, Chapter 2: *Aquinas on religious language*, 50-78.

247 Haberman, Jacob. *Maimonides and Aquinas: A Contemporary Appraisal*. New York: Ktav Pub. House, 1979. xx-289.

*Anon., *Revue Théologique de Louvain*, 15(1979): 119-122.*
*Barbotin, E., *Revue d'Histoire et de Philosophie Religieuses*, 62(1982): 95-96.*
*Burrell, D. B., *The Journal of Religion*, 63(1983): 190-191.*
*Colonnello, P., *Sapienza*, 35(1982): 373-375.*
*Doyle, J. P., *The Modern Schoolman*, 59(1981-1982): 64-66.*
*Evans, G. R., *The Journal of the Philosophical Sciences*, 31: 640-641.*
*Feldman, S., *Philosophical Topics*, 12(1981): 283-288.*
*Heidrich, P., *Theologische Literaturzeitung*, 107(1982): 212-213.*
*Hill, W. J., *Theological Studies*, 41(1980): 208-210.*
*Jolivet, J., *Revue Philosophique de la France et de L'étranger*, 106(1981): 337-339.*
*Kraml, H., *Zeitschrift für Katholische Theologie*, 103(1981): 457-459.*
*Loth, H. -J., *Zeitschrift für Religions-und Geistesgeschichte*, 34(1982): 77-78.*
*Schneider, M., *Wissenschaft und Weisheit*, 46(1983): 76-79.*
*Stump, E., *Speculum*, 55(1980): 577-578.*
*Teske, Roland, *The Modern Schoolman*, 59(1981): 64-66.*
*Williams, Bruce A., *The Thomist*, 47(1983): 279-280.*

248 Hankey, Wayne J. *God in Himself: Aquinas' Doctrine of God as Expounded in Summa Theologiae*. Oxford: Oxford University Press, 1987. 196.

*Baertschi, Bernard, *Revue de Théologie et de Philosophie*, 121(1989): 107-108.*
*Bazán, B. Carlos, *Speculum*, 65(1990): 166-170.*
*Booth, Edward, *New Blackfriars*, Oct.(1988): 457-459.*
*Turco, Giovanni, *Sapienza*, 42(1989): 98-101.*

249 Haren, Michael. *Medieval Thought: The Western Intellectual Tradition from Antiquity to the Thirteenth Century*. New York: St. Martin Press, 1985. x-269.

*Colish, Marcia L., *History of European Ideas*, 8(1987): 108-109.*
*Decorte, J., *Tijdschrift voor Theologie*, 50(1988): 145-146.*
*McEvoy, J. *Bulletin de Théologie Ancienne et Médiévale*, 14(1986): 1-2.*
*Monti, Dominic V., *Church History*, 55(1986): 360-361.*

250 Harris, Errol. *The Problem of Evil*. Milwaukee, WI: Marquette University Press, 1977. 52.

251 Henle, John Robert. *Method in Metaphysics*. Milwaukee, WI: Marquette University Press, 1980.

252 Henle, John Robert. *Theory of Knowledge*. Chicago: Loyola University Press, 1983.

*Foster, David, *The Review of Metaphysics*, 40(1986): 126-128.*

253 Henninger, Mark Gerald. *Relations: Medieval Theories 1250-1325*. Oxford: Clarendon, 1989. 198. Especially #2, *Relation as being and ratio*: Thomas Aquinas, 13-29.

*Santogrossi, Ansgar, *The Review of Metaphysics*, 43(1990): 868-870.*

Is the existence of a relation, as color similarity, somehow reducible to that of the individuals related? If not, how does a relation exist extra-mentally? Or is a relation only our way of conceiving things? Through an analysis of the thought of Thomas Aquinas, Henry of Ghent, Richard Mediavilla, John Duns Scotus, Henry of Harclay, William of Ockham, and Peter Aueroli, I uncover a variety of medieval theories of relations, e.g., the strong realism of Duns Scotus, the modalism of Henry of Ghent, and the conceptualism of Peter Aureoli. I conclude that between 1250-1325 there was a significant change in the way a relation came to be conceived, less Aristotelian and more like some theories of the classical modern period.

254 Herr, William A. *Catholic Thinkers in the Clear: Giants of Catholic Thought from Augustine to Rahner*. Chicago: The Thomas More Press, 1985. 275. Especially Chapter 7: "Albert and Thomas," 87-99 and Chapter 8: "Thomas Aquinas," 100-112.

255 Hetzler, Florence M. *Introduction to the Philosophy of Nature*. American University Studies 5. New York: Peter Lang, 1990. 250.

*A study of Aquinas' commentary on the first book of the *Physics* of Aristotle, which summarizes the thought of the pre-Socratics and of Aristotle's approach to cosmology. A unit with all cross-reference in English, it clarifies the thought of the ancients and of the medieval Aquinas with regard to the philosophy of nature; it presents all of this as a basis for a subsequent philosophy of nature.*

256 Hittinger, Russell. *A Critique of the New Natural Law Theory*. Notre Dame, IN: University of Notre Dame Press, 1987. vi-232.

*Califano, Joseph J., *The Thomist*, 53(1989): 343-345.*
*Fortin, Ernest L., *The Review of Metaphysics*, 42(1989): 838-841.*

*Gordon, David, *International Philosophical Quarterly*, 29(1989): 103-106.*
*Grisez, Germain, *The New Scholasticism*, 62(1988): 438-465.*
*Veatch, Henry B., *The New Scholasticism*, 62(1988): 353-365.*

257 Honderich, Ted, ed. *Philosophy Through Its Past*. Harmondsworth: Penguin Books, 1984. 534.

258 Hopkin, Charles Edward. *The Share of Thomas Aquinas in the Growth of the Witchcraft Delusion*. 1980. New York: AMS, 1982. 188.

259 Hudson, Deal W., and Matthew J. Mancini, eds. *Understanding Maritain: Philosopher and Friend*. Macon, GA: Mercer University Press, 1987. xviii-334.

*Aeschliman, M. D., *The Thomist*, 53(1989): 727-731.*
*Copleston, Frederick C., *The Heythrop Journal*, 32(1991): 443-444.*
*Crosson, Frederick J., *Canadian Philosophical Reviews*, 9(1989): 270-272.*
*Hittinger, John P., *The Review of Metaphysics*, 42(1988): 390-393.*

260 Hughes, Christopher Mark. *On a Complex Theory of a Simple God: An Investigation in Aquinas' Philosophical Theology*. Cornell Studies in the Philosophy of Religion. Ithaca, NY: Cornell University Press, 1989. xi-281.

261 Inagaki, Bernard Ryôsuke. *The Philosophy of Habit*. Sobunsha, Tokyo, 1981.

262 Jaffa, Harry Victor. *Thomism and Aristotelianism: A Study of the Commentary by Thomas Aquinas on the Nicomachean Ethics*. 1952. Westport, CT: Greenwood, 1979. 230.

263 Jaki, Stanley L. *Cosmos and Creator*. Chicago: Gateway Editions, 1980.

*Demaret, J., *Revue des Questiones Scientifiques*, 153(1982): 536-537.*
*Soskice, O., *The Heythrop Journal*, 24(1983): 87-88.*

264 Janz, Denis R. *Luther and Late Medieval Thomism: A Study in Theological Anthropology*. Waterloo, Ontario: Wilfrid Laurier University Press, 1983. xiii-186.

*Olson, Jeannine, *Church History*, 56(1987): 395-396.*

265 Janz, Denis R. *Luther on Thomas Aquinas: The Angelic Doctor in the Thought of the Reformer*. Veröffentlichungen Des Instituts Für Europäische Geschichte Mainz, Abteilung Für Abendländische Religionsgeschichte 140. Stuttgart: Franz Steiner Verlag, 1989. 124.

*Tune, Anders S., *The Thomist*, 55(1991): 145-148.*

266 Johnson, Harold Joseph, ed. *The Medieval Tradition of Natural Law*. Studies in Medieval Culture 22. Kalamazoo, MI: Medieval Institute Publications, 1987. 211.

*Cvek, P. P., *Canadian Philosophical Reviews*, 8(1988): 22-24.*
*Henle, R. J., and Thro, Linus J., *The Modern Schoolman*, 67(1990): 238-242.*
*Hundersmarck, Lawrence F., *Vera Lex*, 9(1989): 21-22.*

267 Joós, Ernest. *Intentionality—Source of Intelligibility: The Genesis of Intentionality*. New York: Peter Lang, 1989.

The author has one objective: to show that intentionality belongs to the fabric of reality; hence it is also the source of intelligibility of this reality. As such, it has a reality; hence it is also the source of intelligibility of this reality. As such, it has an ontological status and a causality of its own which enables it to play its role as intermediary between the knowing subject and the object of thought. The work follows the changes in the nature of intentionality from the Greek antiquity through the Middle Ages up to Brentano, Husserl, Merleau-Ponty, and Heidegger.

268 Jordan, Mark D. *Ordering Wisdom: The Hierarchy of Philosophical Discourses in Aquinas*. Publications in Medieval Studies 24. Notre Dame, IN: University of Notre Dame Press, 1986. xviii-297.

*Aertsen, J., *Speculum*, 66(1991): 175-176.*
*Bourke, Vernon J., *The Modern Schoolman*, 68(1990): 91-93.*
*Kennedy, Leonard A., *The Review of Metaphysics*, 41(1987-1988): 142-143.*
*Moveno, Antonio, *The Thomist*, 52(1988): 745-749.*
*Stack, George J., *The Review of Metaphysics*, 44(1987): 142-143.*

269 Josol, Abdon Ma C. *Property and Natural Law in Rerum Novarum and the Summa Theologiae 2-2, Q. 66, AA. 1, 2, 7: An Expository and Comparative Study*. Roma: Pontificia Universitas, Academia Alfonsiana, 1985. xiii-239.

*Habiger, Matthew, *The Thomist*, 51(1987): 539-542.*

270 Kaminski, Stanislaw, Marian Kurdzialek, and Zofia Zdybicka, eds. *Theory of Being to Understand Reality*. Lublin: Towarzystwo Naukowe Katolickiego Uniwersytetu Lubelskiego, 1980. 322.

271 Kelley, Carl Franklin. *Meister Eckhart on Divine Knowledge*. New Haven, CT: Yale University Press, 1977. 285.

272 Kelly, William J., ed. *Theology and Discovery: Essays in Honor of Karl Rahner*. Milwaukee, WI: Marquette University Press, 1980.

273 Kennedy, Leonard A., ed. *Thomistic Papers III*. Houston, TX: University of St. Thomas, Center for Thomistic Studies, 1987. 140.

*Di Liscia, D. A., *Patristica et Mediaevalia*, 9(1988): 111-112.*

*In one paper Joseph Owens discusses the complex history of the essence existence distinction among Thomistic commentators. Benedict Ashley discusses the role of teleology in nature in constructing a postmodern view of science. Bernard Doering discusses Jacques Maritain's strong affinities with Saul Alinsky and Eduardo Frei. Edward Synan does some historical biography of Thomas Aquinas, and Gary Lessard reviews the critics of Maritain's *Integral Humanism*.*

274 Kennedy, Leonard A. *A Catalogue of Thomists, 1270-1900*. Notre Dame, IN: University of Notre Dame Press, 1987. 240.

*Carlen, Claudia, *The Thomist*, 53(1989): 166-169.*

This is a list, arranged by century and country, of more than 2,000 members of the School of Thomas Aquinas. Each entry give dates, works, and a reference for further information. The criteria for inclusion in the School, and the sources of information, are given in the introduction. The entries end at the year 1900 because twentieth century Thomists have been listed elsewhere.

275 Kennedy, Leonard A, ed. *Thomistic Papers IV*. Houston, TX: University of St. Thomas, Center for Thomistic Studies, 1988. 207.

*Kaczynski, E., *Angelicum*, 67(1990): 451-453.*
*Reichenbach, Bruce R., *The Thomist*, 54(1990): 371-376.*

276 Kennedy, Leonard A., and Jack C. Marler, eds. *Thomistic Papers II*. Houston, TX: University of St. Thomas, Center for Thomistic Studies, 1986. 160.

*Baldner, Steven, *Canadian Philosophical Reviews*, 6(1986): 492-493.*

277 Kenny, Anthony John Patrick, ed. *Aquinas: A Collection of Critical Essays*. Modern Studies in Philosophy. Notre Dame, IN: University of Notre Dame Press, 1977. 389.

*Villanueva, E., *Critica*, 13(1981): 109-113.*

278 Kenny, Anthony John Patrick. *The God of the Philosophers*. Oxford: Clarendon Press, 1979. vii-135.

*Burrell, David, *The New Scholasticism*, 57(1983): 410-415.*

*Butterworth, R., *The Heythrop Journal*, 21(1980): 425-426.*

*Collins, James, *The Modern Schoolman*, 59(1981): 66-69.*

*Donnelly, John, and Michael Wagner, *International Philosophical Quarterly*, 20(1980): 475-479.*

*Hasker, W., *The Philosophical Review*, 90(1981): 621-624.*

*Helm, Paul, *Philosophy*, 55(1980): 418-420.*

*Palmer, Humphrey, *Philosophical Books*, 22(1981): 50-52.*

*Reix, André, *Revue Philosophique de Louvain*, 81(1983): 317-318.*

*Ross, James F., *The Journal of Philosophy*, 79(1982): 410-417.*

*Sutherland, Stewart R., *Mind*, 90(1981): 312-314.*

*Swinburne, R., *Nous*, 16(1982): 477-479.*

*Teske, Roland, *The Modern Schoolman*, 59(1981): 66-68.*

*Tilley, T. W., *Theological Studies*, 41(1980): 594-595.*

*Wiles, M., *The Journal of the Theological Studies*, 31(1980): 687-689.*

*Young, Robert, *Philosophia*, Israel, 15(1985): 169-171.*

279 Kenny, Anthony John Patrick. *Aquinas*. Hill and Wang Book. Past Masters Series. Oxford: Oxford University Press, 1980. 86.

*Anon., *Rassegna di Letteratura Tomistica*, 16(1980): 11-12.*

*Kretzmann, Norman, *Faith and Philosophy*, 3(1986): 342-345.*

*Owens, Joseph, *Dialogue*, 23(1984): 352-353.*

*Villanueva, Enrique, *Critica*, 13(1981): 109-113.*

280 Kenny, Anthony John Patrick. *The Five Ways to St. Thomas Aquinas' Proofs of God's Existence*. 1969. Notre Dame, IN: University of Notre Dame Press, 1980. vii-131.

*Ogiermann, H., *Theologie und Philosophie*, 57(1982): 121-122.*

"To me it seems that if belief in the existence of God cannot be rationally justified, there can be no good reason for adopting any of the traditional monotheistic religions" (p. 4). Kenny therefore examines the Five Ways to help the reader discover within himself whether Aquinas' arguments constitute a rational proof of the existence of God. The respective bases of the Five Ways are motion, efficient causation, possibility and necessity, the gradation found in things, and the directedness of things (finality).

281 Kenny, Anthony John Patrick. *Faith and Reason*. New York: Columbia University Press, 1983.

*Meynell, Hugo, *The Thomist*, 48(1984): 303-305.*

*Meynell, Hugo, *The Heythrop Journal*, 28(1987): 97-98.*

*Swinburne, Richard, *The Journal of Philosophy*, 82(1985): 46-53.*

The book addresses the question whether belief in God and faith in a divine revelation is a rational state of mind. It investigates the nature of rationality, the intellectual virtue which stands between skepticism and credulity. It concludes that while theism may be defensible, faith, considered as an irrevocable commitment to the contents of an alleged revelation, is no virtue, but an irrational state of mind.

282 Kenny, Anthony John Patrick. *Reason and Religion: Essays in Philosophical Theology.* New York: Basil Blackwell, 1987. 182.

*Burrell, D., *The Journal of Religion*, 69(1989): 570-571.*
*Hiorth, F., *Philosophia*, 19(1989): 85-87.*
*McDonald, S., *The Philosophical Review*, 99(1990): 138-142.*
*Quinn, P. L., *The Thomist*, 53(1989): 709-713.*

283 Kenny, Anthony John Patrick. *The Metaphysics of Mind.* Oxford: Clarendon, 1989. Especially Chapter 8: *Imagination*, 113-122.

284 Klauder, Francis J. *The Wonder of the Real.* Rev. ed. North Quincy, MA: Christopher Press, 1979.

*The rev. ed. of *The Wonder of the Real* is an updated presentation of the Metaphysics of St. Thomas Aquinas, published on the 100th anniversary of Pope Leo XIII's encyclical in the restoration of Christian philosophy, and more recently urged by Pope John Paul II. The book is enhanced by more than 25 illustrative charts or diagrams which present at a glance some of the fundamental concepts of Scholastic Philosophy. Also, there are relevant comparisons of St. Augustine, St. Bonaventure, and St. Thomas with Kant, Newman, the Existentialists, Teihard de Chardin, Einstein, Rahner, and Karol Wojtyla (Pope John Paul II).*

285 Knasas, John F. X., ed. *Jacques Maritain: The Man and His Metaphysics.* Notre Dame, IN: University of Notre Dame Press, 1988. 279.

By the publication of this volume, the American Maritain Association initiates a project that will continue to offer to the world men and women animated by Maritain's legacy. The volume has three main parts. Articles by noted biographers of the Maritains comprise Part One. The occasion for Part Two is the 40th anniversary(1987) of Maritain's "Existence and the Existent." The subsections of Part Two come from the chapters of Maritain's book. Articles of the subsections either critically discuss points of the chapter or creatively utilize them to address other issues. Finally, the appendix contains inspiring addresses by the presidents of the American and Canadian Maritain societies.

286 Knasas, John F. X. *The Preface to Thomistic Metaphysics: A Contribution to the Neo-Thomist Debate on the Start of Metaphysics.* American University Series 5. New York: Peter Lang, 1990. 193.

287 Knowles, David. *The Evolution of Medieval Thought.* Eds. D. E. Luscombe and C. N. L. Brooke. 2nd ed. 1962. Harlow, Essex: Longman Group, 1988. 337. Especially Chapters 19-22: "*The Franciscan School at Paris; Albert the Great; St. Thomas Aquinas; Sieger of Brabant and the Faculty of Arts*," 201-251.

288 Konescsni, Johnemery. *A Philosophy for Living: A Sketch of Aquinate Philosophy.* 2nd ed. 1977. Lanham, MD: University Press of America, 1986. 178.

*An exercise in practical philosophy, this book translates Aquinas out of both Latin and scholastic English. It reviews the first and second parts of the *Summa Theologia* with reference only to philosophical content. It integrates some neo-Thomist writings from Maritain, Farrell, and Lonergan.*

289 Kopaczynski, Germain. *Linguistic Ramifications of the Essence-existence Debate.* Washington, DC: University Press of America, 1979. xii-199.

*Has linguistic philosophy anything of value to teach metaphysicians? The book answers in the affirmative. We use as a case in point the oft-discussed mediaeval question: Is there a real distinction between essence and existence in the writings of St.

Thomas Aquinas? Our analysis of the language of Aquinas and of his commentators leads us to a deeper awareness of the unique character of metaphysical language. Metaphysicians owe much to analytical philosophy for affording them invaluable insights into the workings of metaphysical language.*

290 Koren, Henry J. *An Introduction to the Philosophy of Animate Nature*. 1955. Needham Heights, MA: Ginn Press, 1990. 341.

291 Kovach, Francis J. *Scholastic Challenges to Some Mediaeval and Modern Ideas*. Stillwater, OK: Western Publications, 1987. 387.

292 Kovach, Francis J., and Robert W. Shahan, eds. *Albert the Great: Commemorative Essays*. Norman, OK: University of Oklahoma Press, 1980. 297. Especially Francis J. Kovach, "The Enduring Question of Action at a distance in St. Albert the Great," 161-235, and James Weisheipl, "Albertus Magnus and universal hylomorphism: Avicebron, a Note on thirteenth-century Augustinianism," 239-260.

293 Krapiec, Mieczyslaw Albert. *I-Man: An Outline of Philosophical Anthropology*. Trans. Marie Lescoe, Andrew Woznicki, and Theresa Sandok, et al. New Britain, CT: Mariel Publication, 1983. 502. Abridged version 1985, xxii-282.

*Knasas, John F. X., *The Thomist*, 50(1986): 474-478.*

294 Kretzmann, Norman, Anthony Kenny, and Jan Pinborg, eds. *The Cambridge History of Later Medieval Philosophy: From the Rediscovery of Aristotle to the Disintegration of Scholasticism 1100-1600*. 1982. New York: Cambridge University Press, 1988. xiv-1035.

*Beuchot, Mauricio, *Nôus*, 22(1988): 635-638.*
*Copleston, F. C., *Classical Review*, 98(1984): 223-224.*
*Courtney, W. I., *Speculum*, 60(1985): 165-167.*
*Delfgaauw, B., *Theological Studies*, 45(1983): 484-486.*
*Freddoso, A. J., *The Journal of Philosophy*, 81(1984): 150-156.*
*Ghisalberti, Alessandro, *Rivista Internazionale di Filosofia del Diritto*, 74(1982): 557-558.*
*Gombocz, W. L, *Philosophische Rundschau*, 34(1987): 239-247.*
*Gracia, J. J. E., *Journal of the History of Philosophy*, 22(1984): 233-236.*
*Hissette, Roland, *Bulletin de Théologie Ancienne et Médiévale*, 83(1985): 279-281.*
*Hissette, R., *Revue Philosophique de Louvain*, 83(1985): 279-281.*
*Hossefeld, P., *Zeitschrift für Religions-und Geistesgeschichte*, 35(1983): 371-373.*
*Lackner, G., *Siculorum Gymnasium*, 91(1984): 283-284.*
*Michel, A., *Revue des Études Latines*, 60(1982): 534-535.*
*Michel, J., *Revue d'Histoire Ecclésiastique*, 78(1983): 495-497.*
*Milton, J. R., *Philosophical Books*, 25(1984): 15-17.*
*Murphy, Thomas, *The Heythrop Journal*, 26(1985): 222-226.*
*Panaccio, C., *The Philosophical Review*, 93(1984): 155-157.*
*Reade, S., *Philosophical Quarterly*, 34(1984): 170.*
*Sirat, C., *Revue des Études Juives*, 143(1984): 173-175.*
*Stella, P. T., *Salesianum*, 46(1984): 601-602.*
*Synan, E. A., *Dialogue*, 22(1983): 741-743.*

This is a historical critical study of the philosophy of the great age of scholasticism, from Abelard to the rejection of Aristotelianism in the Renaissance, organized topically rather than chronologically. Its 46 chapters are arranged in parts dealing with medieval philosophical literature, the old logic, semantic theory, propositions and modalities, metaphysics and epistemology, natural philosophy, philosophy of mind and action, ethics, politics, and the defeat, neglect, and revival of scholasticism. The contributors are 41 scholars from 10 different countries. The volume includes biographies of medieval authors, a bibliography, and detailed indexes.

295 Kretzmann, Norman, and Eleonore Stump, eds. *The Cambridge Trans. of Medieval Philosophical Texts, Volume One: Logic and the Philosophy of Language*. Cambridge: Cambridge University Press, 1988.

*The first of a four-volume anthology intended as a companion to *The Cambridge History of Later Medieval Philosophy*, enabling nonspecialists to read the texts discussed in the *History*. Volume One is concerned with logic and philosophy of language and comprises 15 different important (hitherto untranslated) texts on questions of meaning and inference that formed the basis of medieval philosophy. As far as practicable, complete works or topically complete segments of larger works have been translated. Includes general introduction, introductory headnotes, and comprehensive index.*

296 Kreyche, Gerald F. *Thirteen Thinkers*: A Sampler of Great Philosophers. 1979. Lanham, MD: University Press of America, 1984. 172.

The purpose of this book is to provide an easy, non-technical introduction to a sampling of philosophers, ranging from Plato to Sartre.Philosophical ideas and problems are interwoven with biographical sketches of the thinkers in such a way that one can appreciate both the abstract and concrete character of the philosophical enterprise. Term paper projects are suggested, and review questions are given. Hence the book also serves as a basic study guide.

297 La Fleur, William R. *Dogen Studies*. Honolulu, HI: University of Hawaii Press, 1985. 165.

298 Lacroix, W. L. *Four Questions on Persons: A Philosophical Dialectic*. Washington, DC: University Press of America, 1982. viii-205.

299 Lamb, Matthew, ed. *Creativity and Method: Essays in Honor of Bernard Lonergan S. J.* Milwaukee, WI: Marquette University Press, 1981. x-584.

300 Landmann, Michael. *De Homine: Man in the Mirror of His Thought*. Ann Arbor, MI: Monograph, 1979.

*"Philosophical Anthropology" in German has nothing to do with "anthropology" in English (which, in German, is "ethnology"). The discipline is an attempt to understand the singularity of man and to find out his essential features. The book, a translation from German, deals with the history of this discipline from antiquity up to Nietzsche. The author also published the introduction *Philosophical Anthropology* (Westminster Press, Philadelphia, 1974) and *Fundamental Anthropologie* (Bonn, 1979, not yet in English).*

301 Langston, Douglas Charles. *God's Willing Knowledge: The Influence of Scotus' Analysis of Omniscience*. Philadelphia, PA: University of Pennsylvania Press, 1986. 145.

302 Lauer, Quentin. *The Nature of Philosophical Inquiry*. Milwaukee, WI: Marquette University Press, 1989. 131.

303 Lindbeck, George. *The Nature of Doctrine: Religion and Theology in a Postliberal Age*. Philadelphia, PA: Westminster Press, 1984.

304 Link-Salinger, Ruth et al., eds. *A Straight Path: Studies in Medieval Philosophy and Culture. Essays in Honor of Arthur Hyman*. Washington, DC: The Catholic University of America Press, 1988. xiv-310.

305 Little, Joyce A. *Toward a Thomist Methodology*. Toronto Studies in Theology 34. Lewiston, NY: The Edwin Mellen, 1988. 558.
This work is an inquiry into Thomist method. It proceeds on the basis of two fundamental assumptions with regard to theological method. First, theological method deals with the formal structural principles employed in systematic theology. Second, theology itself is not concerned solely with God or with man, but with the union of two. That union as given in Christ, the God-man, grounds the theological enterprise. Theological method is therefore a correlation of the revelation given in Christ with methodological principles drawn from one or another of the humanistic disciplines. This book deals explicitly with the correlation of the revelation and principles drawn from philosophy.

306 Lloyd, Genevieve. *The Man of Reason: Male and Female in Western Philosophy*. Minneapolis: University of Minneapolis Press, 1984. x-138.
*McLean, Jeanne P., *Ancient Philosophy*, 10(1990): 154-157.*
*Shute, Sara, *Journal of the History of Philosophy*, 25(1987): 464-465.*

307 Lohr, Charles H. *St. Thomas Aquinas: Scriptum Super Sententiis: An Index of Authorities Cited*. Amersham, Buckinghamshire: Avebury Company, 1980. vii-391.
*Deronne, E., *Tijdschrift voor Filosofie*, 47(1985): 123-124.*

308 Lonergan, Bernard. *Insight: A Study of Human Understanding*. San Francisco: Harper & Row, 1978.

309 Lonergan, Bernard. *Understanding and Being: The Halifax Lectures on Insight*. Ed. Frederick E. Crowe. Toronto: University of Toronto Press, 1990. xix-467.

310 Long, James, ed. *Philosophy and the God of Abraham: Essays in Memory of James A. Weisheipl, OP*. Toronto: Pontifical Institute of Mediaeval Studies, In press. 296.

311 Lyons, William. *Emotion*. Cambridge: Cambridge University Press, 1980. xiii-230.

312 MacIntyre, Alasdair. *After Virtue: A Study in Moral Theory*. 2nd rev. ed. 1981. Notre Dame, IN: University of Notre Dame Press, 1984. 320.
*Abelson, R., *Canadian Philosophical Reviews*, 2(1982): 175-179.*
*Blackburn, Simon, *Philosophical Investigations*, 5(1982): 146-153.*
*Brown, Grant, *Eidos*, 7(1988): 105-110.*
*Casey, J., *The Philosophical Quarterly*, 33(1983): 296-300.*
*Cauvel, Jane, *Teaching Philosophy*, 5(1982): 245-246.*
*Collins, Peter, *South African Journal of Philosophy*, 4(1985): 100-106.*
*Connolly, William E., *Political Theory*, 10(1982): 315-319.*
*Edel, Abraham, *Zygon*, 18(1983): 343-349.*
*Edel, Abraham and E. Flower, *Journal of the History of Philosophy*, 21(1983): 426-429.*
*Ellis, A., *Philosophy*, 57(1982): 551-553.*
*Evangeliou, C., *The Review of Metaphysics*, 37(1983-1984): 132-134.*
*Flower, E., *Journal of the History of Philosophy*, 21(983): 426-429.*
*Gowans, Christopher W., *International Philosophical Quarterly*, 22(1982): 215-218.*

*Haller, B., *Philosophisches Jahrbuch*, 92(1985): 431-446.*
*Hauerwas, Stanley and Paul Wadell, *The Thomist*, 46(1982): 313-322.*
*Hittinger, Russell, *The New Scholasticism*, 56(1982): 385-390.*
*Johnson, Mark, *Personalist Forum*, 2(1986): 156-159.*
*Kunneman, H., *Kennis en Methode*, 8(1984): 348-357.*
*Maidan, Michael, *Revista Latinoamericana de Filosofia*, 10(1984): 90-93.*
*Maidan, Michael, *History of European Ideas*, 6(1985): 209-212.
*McKenzie, G., *Australasian Journal of Philosophy*, 61(1983): 450-454.*
*Morrisey, W., *Interpretation*, 12(1984): 131-134.*
*Pinckaers, Servais-Th., *Revue Thomiste*, 86(1986): 137-142.*
*Phillips, D. Z., *Mind*, 93(1984): 111-124.*
*Prakash, M. S. and M. Weinstein, *Études*, 32(1982): 35-44.*
*Rasmussen, David M., *Philosophy and Social Criticism*, 9(1982): 383-394.*
*Rossi, Steven L., *The Journal of Value Inquiry*, 19(1985): 13-26.*
*Scherer, Donald, *International Journal of Applied Philosophy*, 2(1984): 97-107.*
*Scheffler, Samuel, *The Philosophical Review*, 92(1983): 443-447.*
*Spitz, J. -F., *Critique*, 41(1985): 1137-1158.*
*Steel, C., *Tijdschrift voor Filosofie*, 46(1984): 169-171.*
*Todd, Jennifer, *Philosophical Studies*, 29(1982-1983): 281-287.*
*Vegas, J. M., *Diálogo Filosófico*, 1(1985): 125-128.*
*Wallace, R. Jay, *History and Theory*, 28(1989): 326-348.*
*Wallach, J. R., *Telos*, 57(1983-1984): 233-240.*
*Walton, A. S., *Bulletin of the Hegel Society of Great Britain*, 6(1982): 41-43.*
*Weston, Anthony, *Free Inquiry*, 4(1984): 54-56.*

313 MacIntyre, Alasdair. *Whose Justice? Which Rationality?* Notre Dame, IN: University of Notre Dame Press, 1988. Especially *Aquinas on practical rationality and justice*, 164-208. xi-410.

*Appel, Fredrick, *Philosophy and the Social Sciences*, 20(1990): 135-138.*
*Barham, P., *HHS*, 2(1990): 253-258.*
*Barry, Brian, *Ethics*, 100(1989): 160-168.*
*Brodsky, Garry M., *Canadian Philosophical Reviews*, 9(1989): 276-279.*
*Fisher, Walter, *Philosophy and Rhetoric*, 23(1990): 242-247*.
*Harris, Roger, *Radical Philosophy*, 519(1989): 48-49.*
*Hartle, Ann, *The Journal of the History of Philosophy*, 28(1990): 470-473.*
*Iglesias, Teresa, *Philosophical Studies* (Ireland): 32(1989-90): 333-337.*
*Isaac, Jeffrey C., *Political Theory*, 17(1989): 663-672.*
*Kennedy, Terence, *Gregorianum*, 72(1991): 183-185.*
*Kerlin, Michael J., *The Thomist*, 53(1989): 512-515.*
*Larmore, Charles, *The Journal of Philosophy*, 86(1989): 437-442.*
*Lassman, P., *HHS*, 2(1989): 258-260.*
*Matson, Wallace I., *Philosophy*, 64(1989): 564-566.*
*Post, Stephen G., *Medical Humanities Review*, 3(1989): 48-50.*
*Schuller, Peter M., *Teaching Philosophy*, 11(1988): 373-375.*
*Snider, Eric W., *Metaphilosophy*, 20(1989): 387-390.*
*Stout, J., *The Journal of Religion*, 69(1989): 220-232.*
*Wallace, R. Jay, *History and Theory*, 28(1989): 326-348.*
*Wong, David, *Philosophical Books*, 31(1990): 7-14.*

314 MacIntyre, Alasdair. *First Principles, Final Ends, and Contemporary Philosophical Issues*. Milwaukee, WI: Marquette University Press, 1990. 69.

This is an investigation into the place of first principles within that conception of a perfected science, the achievement of which, so it is argued, is the final end of rational enquiry, as understood by Aristotle and by Aquinas. Their account of first principles is contrasted with that advanced by Cartesians and others for whom appeal to first principles has an epistemological function. The project of a genealogy of contemporary anti-Thomistic standpoints isproposed.

315 MacIntyre, Alasdair. *Three Rival Versions of Moral Enquiry: Encyclopedia, Genealogy, and Tradition*. Notre Dame, IN: University of Notre Dame Press, 1990. x-241. Especially Chapter III: "Too Many Thomisms," 58-81, and Chapter VI: "Aquinas and the rationality of tradition," 127-148. Gifford lectures delivered in the University of Edinburgh in 1988.

316 Madigan, Patrick. *Christian Revelation and the Completion of the Aristotelian Revolution*. Lanham, MD: University Press of America, 1988.

317 Malloy, Michael Patrick. *Civil Authority in Medieval Philosophy: Lombard, Aquinas and Bonaventure*. Lanham, MD: University Press of America, 1985. xv-223. Especially Chapter III: "*Excerpts from the Commentary of Thomas Aquinas*," 141-173, and Chapter IV: "*Aquinas' later writings*," 83-104.

318 Marenbon, John. *Later Medieval Philosophy (1150-1350): An Introduction*. London: Routledge & Kegan Paul, 1987. Especially Chapter 7: *Thomas Aquinas*, 116-130, xii-230.

*Follon, Jacques, *Revue Philosophie de Louvain*, 87(1989): 350-354.*
*Jordan, Mark D., *The Journal of Religion*, 69(1989): 247-248.*
*Leaman, O., *Philosophy*, 63(1988): 283-285.*
*MacDonald, S., *Archiv für Geschichte der Philosophie*, 71(1989): 84-89.*
*Macierowski, E. M., *The Thomist*, 54(1990): 187-189.*
*Maurer, Armand, *Journal of the History of Philosophy*, 28(1990): 288-289.*
*Moorhead, John, *The Heythrop Journal*, 32(1991): 117-118.*
*Perreiah, Alan, *Teaching Philosophy*, 12(1989): 83-84.*
*Tweedale, Martin M., *Canadian Philosophical Reviews*, 8(1988): 351-354.*

This book aims to combine an historical approach to medieval works with philosophical analysis. Part One provides the reader with basic information for understanding medieval thinkers' arguments. Part Two examines in detail the problem of intellectual knowledge in the works of Aristotle, Avicenna, Averroes, William of Auvergne, Thomas Aquinas, Martin and Boethius of Dacia, Radulphus Brito, Henry of Ghent, Duns Scotus, and William of Ockham.

319 Maritain, Jacques. *Existence and the Existent*. Trans. Lewis Galantiere and Gerald B. Phelan. 1948. Lanham, MD: University Press of America, 1987. 156.

320 Maurer, Armand Augustine. *St. Thomas and Historicity*. Milwaukee, WI: Marquette University Press, 1979. 57.

321 Maurer, Armand Augustine. *Medieval Philosophy*. 2nd with additions, and a bibliographic supplement corrections. The Etienne Gilson Séries 4. Toronto: Pontifical Institute of Mediaeval Studies, 1982. xii-455.

*Ewbank, Michael B., *The New Scholasticism*, 61(1987): 490-491.*

322 Maurer, Armand Augustine. *About Beauty: A Thomistic Interpretation*. Houston, TX: Center for Thomistic Studies, 1983. 135.

*Eaton, Marcia Muelder, *Idealistic Studies*, 16(1986): 173.*
*Kovach, Francis J., *The Review of Metaphysics*, 38(1985): 662-664.*
*Leroy, M. -V., *Revue Thomiste*, 86(1986): 343-344.*
*McCullough, E. J., *Dialogue*, 26(1987): 199-201.*
*Murphy, Thomas, *The Heythrop Journal*, 27(1986): 472-473.*
*Wilder, A., *Angelicum*, 62(1985): 126-127.*

This book brings together statements of St. Thomas bearing on the following themes: beauty and existence, the perception of beauty, beauty and the birth of the universe, beauty and the human person, beauty and art, and beauty and God. The Thomistic conception of beauty is confronted with certain modern views of the subject. The conclusion is reached that beauty, no less than the transcendentals truth and goodness, is ultimately grounded on the actuality of existence.

323 Maurer, Armand Augustine. *Being and Knowing: Studies in Thomas Aquinas and Later Medieval Philosophers*. Papers in Mediaeval Studies 10. Toronto: Pontifical Institute of Mediaeval Studies, 1990. 496.

324 McCool, Gerald A. *Nineteenth-Century Scholasticism: The Search for a Unitary Method*. New York: Fordham University Press, 1980. Originally published as *Catholic Theology in the Nineteenth Century* 1977. 301.

*Lauder, Robert, *The Thomist*, 55(1991): 301-319.*

325 McCool, Gerald A., ed. *The Universe as Journey: Conversations with W. Norris Clarke, S. J.* New York: Fordham University Press, 1988.

*Madigan, Patrick, *Revue Philosophique de Louvain*, 87(1989): 354-357.*

326 McCool, Gerald A. *From Unity to Pluralism: The Internal Evolution of Thomism*. New York: Fordham University Press, 1989. 248.

*Hudson, Deal W., *International Philosophical Quarterly*, 30(1990): 367-369.*
*Lauder, Robert, *The Thomist*, 55(1991): 301-319.*
*McDermott, John M., *Gregorianum*, 72(1991): 150-151.*

327 McGrath, Margaret, comp. *Etienne Gilson: A Bibliography*. Etienne Gilson 3. Toronto: Pontifical Institute of Mediaeval Studies, 1982. xxviii-124.

*Dougherty, Jude P., *The Review of Metaphysics*, 8(1984): 132-133.*

328 McInerny, Ralph. *Rhyme and Reason: St. Thomas and Modes of Discourse*. Milwaukee, WI: Marquette University Press, 1981. viii-70.

329 McInerny, Ralph. *Ethica Thomistica: The Moral Philosophy of Thomas Aquinas*. Washington, DC: The Catholic University Press of America, 1982. x-129.

*Anon., *Rassegna di Letteratura Tomistica*, 18(1982): 196-197.*
*Anon., *Rassegna di Letteratura Tomistica*, 7(1984): 168-170.*
*Bertoncini, L., *Divus Thomas*, 88(1985): 431-435.*
*Bodéus, Richard, *Revue Philosophique de Louvain*, 82(184): 284-285.*
*Bourke, Vernon J., *The Modern Schoolman*, 62(1984): 64.*
*Composta, Dario, *Doctor Communis*, 37(1984): 92-93.*
*Hittinger, R., *The Review of Metaphysics*, 36(1982-1983): 939-941.*
*MacIntyre, A., *Teaching Philosophy*, 7(1984): 168-170.*
*Micallef, Paul J., *Laval Théologique et Philosophique*, 39(1983): 107-108.*

330 McInerny, Ralph. *St. Thomas Aquinas*. 1977. Twayne's World Authors. Notre Dame, IN: University of Notre Dame Press, 1982. 197.

*Anon., *Rassegna di Letteratura Tomistica*, 13(1977): 12-14.*
*Bobik, Joseph, *The Thomist*, 44(1980): 455-457.*
*Bourke, V. J., *Speculum*, 53(1978): 828-829.*
*King, Peter, *International Philosophical Quarterly*, 23(1983): 227-229.*
*Murphy, Thomas, *The Heythrop Journal*, 26(1985): 222-226.*

331 McInerny, Ralph. *Being and Predication: Thomistic Interpretations*. Studies in Philosophy and the History of Philosophy 16. Washington, DC: The Catholic University of America Press, 1986. xii-323.

*Murphy, Thomas, *The Heythrop Journal*, 30(1989): 240-241.*
*Pangallo, Mario, *Doctor Communis*, 40(1987): 313-314.*

332 McInerny, Ralph. *Art and Prudence: Studies in the Thought of Jacques Maritain*. Jacques Maritain Center 1. Notre Dame, IN: University of Notre Dame Press, 1988. 224.

333 McInerny, Ralph. *A First Glance at St. Thomas Aquinas: A Handbook for Peeping Thomists*. Notre Dame, IN: University of Notre Dame Press, 1990. 192.

334 McInerny, Ralph. *Boethius and Aquinas*. Washington, DC: The Catholic University of America Press, 1990. xiv-268. Especially Part Two: *De Trinitate*, #3, *Thomas comments on Boethius,* 97-120, and Part Three: *De hebdomadibus*, #7, *The Exposition of St. Thomas*, 199-231.

335 Merriell, Donald Juenval. *To the Image of the Trinity: A Study in the Development of Aquinas' teaching*. Studies and Texts 96. Toronto: Pontifical Institute of Mediaeval Studies, 1990. x-266. Especially #5, "Thomas' doctrine of the image in the *Summa theologiae*," 153-235.

336 Midgley, E. Brian F. *The Ideology of Max Weber: A Thomist Critique*. Totowa, NJ: Barnes & Noble, 1983. xv-166.

This critique of Weber' ideology includes a review of the assessments of Weber made by Voegelin, Strauss, Gouldner, Aron, Mommsen, Rex, and others. Weber's misconceptions concerning natural law and political philosophy are examined, and his atheism is considered in relation to the Christianities both Catholic and Protestant. Finally, this critique of Weber is developed in the context of the author's Thomistic critique of liberalism and of the more revolutionary atheisms of Marx and Nietzsche.

337 Miethe, Terry L., and Vernon J. Bourke, comps. *Thomistic Bibliography 1940-1978.* Westport, CT/London: Greenwood Press, 1980. xxii-318.

*Anon., *Rassegna di Letteratura*, 16(1980): 460-461.*
*Wenin, Christian, *Revue Philosophique de Louvain*, 80(1982): 303-308.*

A reference work listing 4,097 entries from the field of Thomistic studies. This bibliography includes items in 15 languages of scholarship. The materials are classified in five main categories: Life of Aquinas, his writings, philosophical teachings (in 10 subdivisions): theological doctrines, relations: historical and doctrinal. No analyses or critiques of the entries are included. The Introduction surveys the present situation in Thomistic studies. A chronological list of Aquinas' works and extensive indexes (of names and periodicals cited) are provided.

338 Mihalich, Joseph C. *Existentialism and Thomism*. 1960. Ann Arbor, MI: University Microfilms International, 1984. 91.

339 Mitchell, Timothy. *Hedonism and Eudemonism in Aquinas—not the Same as Happiness*. Chicago: Franciscan Herald, 1983. 71.

340 Montross, Constance M. *Virtue or Vice: Sor Juana's Use of Thomistic Thought*. Washington, DC: University of Press of America, 1981.

341 Morreall, John S. *Analogy and Talk About God: A Critique of the Thomistic Approach*. Washington, DC: University Press of America, 1978. 137.

342 Morris, Thomas V., ed. *Divine and Human Action: Essays in the Metaphysics of Theism*. Ithaca, NY: Cornell University Press, 1988.

This is a book of newly commissioned essays by some of the leading American philosophers who write on religious topics. Its focus is on providing pioneering work in theistic metaphysics centering on the relation between God and the world.

343 Moskop, John Charles. *Divine Omniscience and Human Freedom: Thomas Aquinas and Charles Hartshorne*. Macon, GA: Mercer University Press, 1984. xviii-105.

344 Mothersill, Mary. *Beauty Restored*. New York: Oxford University Press, 1984. vii-438.

*Budd, Malcolm, *The Philosophical Quarterly*, 36(1986): 89-92.*
*Carter, Curtis, *The Modern Schoolman*, 64(1986): 53-57.*
*Charlton, W., *British Journal of Aesthetics*, 26(1986): 71-72.*
*Cohen, Ted, *The Journal of Philosophy*, 87(1990): 702-708.*
*Falk, Barry, *Philosophical Books*, 27(1986): 2-13.*
*Scott, James H., *Philosophical Topics*, 13(1985): 179-183.*

345 Mtega, Norbert W. *Analogy and Theological Language in the Summa Contra Gentiles*: A Textual Survey of the Concept of Analogy and Its Theological Application by St. Thomas Aquinas. European University Studies: Theology, 241. Frankfurt: Lang, 1984. 207.

*Anon., *Rassegna di Letteratura Tomistica*, 20(1987): 51-55.*

346 Mullady, Brian Thomas. *The Meaning of the Term 'moral' in St. Thomas Aquinas*. Studi Tomistici 27. Città del Vaticano, Pontificia Accademia di S. Tommaso: Libreria Editrice Vaticana, 1986. Especially Chapter Two: *The meaning of moral in St. Thomas: The role of the will*, 43-84. 262.

*Composta, Dario, *Doctor Communis*, 40(1987): 210-212.*

347 Munk, Arthur W. *Saint Thomas Aquinas*. Meerut: Sadhna Prakashan, 1980. Especially "St. Thomas: The man and the philosopher," 61-97.

348 Murphy, Edward F. *St. Thomas' Political Doctrine and Democracy*. Cleveland, OH: Zubal, 1983. xiv-297.

349 Murray, Alexander. *Reason and Society in the Middle Ages*. Oxford: Clarendon Press, 1978.

350 O'Connor, Bernadette. *Martin Heidegger, Saint Thomas Aquinas, and the Forgottenness of Being*. Ann Arbor, MI: University Microfilms International, 1982. xiv-495.

351 O'Hear, Anthony. *Experience, Explanation and Faith*. London: Routledge & Kegan Paul, 1984. Especially #3: "*Religion, truth and morality*," 56-88.

352 O'Keefe, Martin D. *Known from the Things That Are: Fundamental Theory of Moral Life*. Houston, TX: Center for Thomistic Studies, University of St. Thomas, 1987. ix-339.

*Naus, John, *The Modern Schoolman*, 67(1990): 314-315.*

353 Oesterle, John A. *Ethics: The Introduction to Moral Science*. 1957. Needham Heights, MA: Ginn Press, 1990. 269.

354 Owens, Joseph. *The Doctrine of Being in the Aristotelian Metaphysics: A Study in the Greek Background of Mediaeval Thought*. 3rd rev. ed. Toronto: The Pontifical Institute of Mediaeval Studies, 1978. xxxvi-540.

*Mansion, Suzanne, *Revue Philosophique de Louvain*, 78(1980): 138-140.*

355 Owens, Joseph. *St. Thomas Aquinas on the Existence of God: Collected Papers of Joseph Owens, C. Ss. R.* Ed. John R. Catan. Albany, NY: State University of New York Press, 1980. xii-291.

*Konyndyk, K., *The Philosophical Review*, 92(1983): 297-302.*
*O'Brien, Thomas C., *The Thomist*, 46(1982): 644-653.*
*Spade, Paul V., *Dialogue*, 21(1982): 772-773.*
*Stump, E., *International Studies in Philosophy*, 14(1982): 114-115.*
*Zimmermann, A., *Archiv für Geschichte der Philosophie*, 65(1983): 315-320.*

356 Owens, Joseph. *Aquinas on Being and Thing*. Niagara University, NY: Niagara University Press, 1981. 35.

*Ewbank, Michael B., *The New Scholasticism*, 59(1985): 238-243.*
*Roccaro, G., *Giornale di Metafisica*, 4(1982): 606-610.*

357 Owens, Joseph. *Human Destiny: Some Problems for Catholic Philosophy*. Washington, DC: The Catholic University of America Press, 1985. Especially Chapter 2: "Human destiny in Aquinas," 31-49. viii-117.

*Bodéüs, R., *Revue Philosophique de Louvain*, 87(1989): 101-102.*
*Centore, F. F., *Dialogue*, 26(1987): 216-219.*
*Desharnais, Richard P., *International Studies in Philosophy*, 20(1988): 135-136.*
*Henle, Robert J., *The Modern Schoolman*, 65(1988): 142-145.*
*Penna, James V., *Canadian Philosophical Reviews*, 6(1986): 240-242.*

In answer to Kant's third question "What may I hope for?" this study examines typical conceptions of human destiny in Aristotle, Aquinas, and modern ideologies in confrontation with liberal democracies. It faces important questions that arise for Catholic philosophy from these various conceptions, especially in regard to freedom, human rights, and tolerance. In those problems it shows how the Aristotelian notion of focal meaning can smooth out satisfactorily the basic difficulties in philosophy of religion today.

358 Owens, Joseph. *Towards a Christian Philosophy*. Studies in Philosophy and the History of Philosophy 21. Washington, DC: The Catholic University of America Press, 1990. 332.

359 Owens, Joseph. *An Elementary Christian Metaphysics*. 1963. Houston, TX: The Center for Thomistic Studies, 1990. 384.

*Dewan, L., *Dialogue* 26(1987): 572-574.*
*Ewbank, Michael B., *The New Scholasticism*, 62(1988): 474-479.*

360 Owens, Joseph. *An Interpretation of Existence.* 1968. Houston, TX: The Center for Thomistic Studies, 1990. 153.
*Dewan, L., *Dialogue*, 26(1987): 572-574.*
*Ewbank, Michael B., *The New Scholasticism*, 62(1988): 474-479.*
*Harper, Albert W. J., *Irish Philosophical Journal*, 5(1988): 121-126.*
*Harper, Albert W. J., *Indian Philosophical Quarterly*, 16(1989): 237-244.*
*Wilhelmsen, Frederick D., *Faith and Philosophy*, 4(1987): 348-350.*

361 Owens, Joseph. *Aristotelian Epistemology.* Notre Dame, IN: University of Notre Dame Press, In press.

362 Parel, Anthony, ed. *Calgary Aquinas Studies.* Toronto: Pontifical Institute of Mediaeval Studies, 1978. 174.

363 Pieper, Josef. *Guide to Thomas Aquinas.* Trans. Richard Winston and Clara Winston. 1962. New York: Octagon Books, 1982. 181.
The author "presents the thirteenth-century philosopher who reconciled the pragmatic 9dangerous' Aristotle with the Church. Though himself a true pragmatist, Aquinas performed the near miracle of proving that realistic knowledge need not preclude belief in the supramundane realities of religion...." Topics include "the voluntary poverty movement, the beginnings of the Dominican order, the Inquisition, the fomenting universities, St. Thomas as a Socratic teacher, the vital literature in medieval Latin...."

364 Pieper, Josef. *Living the Truth: The Truth of All Thing and Reality and the Good.* San Francisco: Ignatius Press, 1989. 190.

365 Pieper, Josef. *"The Truth of All Things" and "Reality and the Good"* 1966/1963. San Francisco: Ignatius Press, 1989. Trans. of *Wahreit der Dinge* and *Die Wirklichkeit und das Gute.*

366 Plantinga, Alvin, and Nicholas Wolterstorff, eds. *Faith and Rationality: Reason and Belief in God.* Notre Dame, IN: University of Notre Dame Press, 1983. 321.
*Levine, M. P., *Philosophia*, 16(1986): 447-460.*
*Swinburne, R., *The Journal of Philosophy*, 82(1985): 46-53.*
*Tomberlin, J. E., *Nous*, 20(1986): 401-413.*
*Westphal, M., *International Journal for Philosophy of Religion*, 16(1984): 183-184.*
*Wykstra, S., *Faith and Philosophy*, 3(1986): 206-213.*
This book contains four long essays in the epistemology of religious belief: "Reason and Belief in God" by Alvin Plantinga, "Christian Experience and Christian Belief" by William P. Alston, "Can Belief in God be Rational If It Has No Foundations?" by Nicholas Wolterstorff, and "Jerusalem and Athens Revisited" by George Mavorodes. It also contains an essay on the theology of W. Panneburg, "Faith, Reason and the Resurrection" by David Holwerda, an essay by George Marsden entitled "The Collapse of American Evangelical Academia," and two fables by George Mavrodes. Perhaps the unifying theme of the book is consideration and rejection of the evidentialist objection to theistic belief, the claim that theistic belief is rational or appropriate only if there is adequate evidences for it of the general sort provided by sound theistic arguments.

367 Porreco, Rocco, ed. *The Georgetown Symposium on Ethics.* Lanham, MD: University Press of America, 1984.

368 Porter, Mildred Jean. *The Recovery of Virtue: The Relevance of Aquinas for Christian Ethics.* Louisville, KY: John Knox Press, 1990. 208.
*Anon., *Rassegna di Letteratura Tomistica*, 16(1980): 208-210.*
*Cessario, Romanus, *The Thomist*, 55(1991): 141-144.*

369 Potts, Timothy C. *Conscience in Medieval Philosophy*. Cambridge: Cambridge University Press, 1980. xii-152.

*Bourke, V. J., *Speculum*, 56(1981): 935-936.*
*Clarke, P. A., *Mind*, 92(1983): 128-129.*
*Follon, Jacques, *Revue Philosophique de Louvain*, 79(1981): 268-271.*
*Fortin, Ernest, *The Review of Metaphysics*, 35(1981): 160-161.*
*Murphy, Thomas, *The Heythrop Journal*, 22(1981): 295-327.*

*Trans.s of treatises on conscience by Philip the Chancellor, Bonaventure and Aquinas and of their sources, with critical essay on the texts: distinction between *synderesis* and *conscientia*, concluding that it is necessary although historically introduced for the wrong reason; also a priori nature of dictates of conscience, their logical structure (Aquinas' conditional analysis) and method of justification. Bonaventure's moral intuitionism is criticized. Appendix with plan for course in medieval philosophy based on the texts is given.*

370 Powell, Ralph. *Freely Chosen Reality*. Washington, DC: University Press of America, 1983.

*Sanguineti, G., *Divus Thomas*, 88(1985): 174-175.*

371 Principe, Walter H. *Thomas Aquinas' Spirituality*. The Etienne Gilson Series 7. Toronto: Pontifical Institute of Mediaeval Studies, 1984. 30.

372 Quinn, John M. *The Doctrine of Time in St. Thomas Aquinas: Some Aspects and Applications*. Washington, DC: Catholic University Press of America, 1986.

373 Redpath, Peter. *A Simplified Introduction to the Wisdom of St. Thomas*. Washington, DC: University Press of America, 1980. 170.

*Kennedy, Leonard A., *The New Scholasticism*, 51(1982): 110.*
*Veatch, P., *International Philosophical Quarterly*, 22(1982): 218-219.*

374 Redpath, Peter. *The Moral Wisdom of St. Thomas: An Introduction*. Washington, DC: University Press of America, 1983. x-206.

A general introduction to the moral teaching of St. Thomas Aquinas written for a non-specialized, secular audience. This work approaches the moral teaching of St. Thomas in a way markedly different from standard Thomistic approaches. It consciously avoids attempting to dissect a moral philosophy distinct from the theology of Aquinas; it disagrees with the view that Aquinas' moral teaching is a natural law doctrine; and it attempts to be readable.

375 Regan, Richard J. *The Moral Dimensions of Politics*. New York: Oxford University Press, 1986. x-206.

*Gueguen, John A., *The Modern Schoolman*, 68(1991): 175-176.*

376 Reilly, James P. *St. Thomas on Law*. Etienne Gilson 12. Toronto: Pontifical Institute of Mediaeval Publication, 1990. 17.

377 Ricoeur, Paul. *The Reality of the Historical Past*. Milwaukee, WI: Marquette University Press, 1984. 51.

378 Roberts, Lawrence D., ed. *Approaches to Nature in the Middle Ages*. Medieval & Renaissance Texts & Studies 16. Binghamton, NY: Center for Medieval & Early Renaissance Studies, 1982. 220.

379 Ross, James F. *Portraying Analogy*. New York: Cambridge University Press, 1981. xi-244.

*Burrell, D., *The New Scholasticism*, 59(1985): 347-357.*
*Frank, W. A., *The Review of Metaphysics*, 38(1984-1985): 401-404.*
*Raposa, Michael L., *The New Scholasticism*, 59(1985): 233-237.*
*Stern, J., *The Journal of Philosophy*, 84(1987): 392-437.*
*Wierenga, E., *Philosophy and Phenomenological Research*, 46(1986): 692-696.*

How do wrong meanings fit to contrasting verbal surroundings (drop/eyes; drop/courses)? This is a systematic account of the "classical" analogy phenomena: mere equivocation (charge/account; charge/gun) proportionality (collect/books; collect/debts): denomination (play/piano; play/Chopin): metaphor, paronymy (healthy/healthful) and of figurative discourse. Two universals, linguistic force and inertia, explain the fit: words are dominated by other words to fit, notch-wise, resisting various kinds of unacceptability by dropping affinities and opposition to other words. Craftbound discourse, in religion, law, and science, exhibits those structures, too. Resulting infinite polysemy and evolving expressive capacity, explained here, have massive consequences for analysis, philosophy of language, and philosophy of mind.

380 Rudavsky, Tamar, ed. *Divine Omniscience and Omnipotence in Medieval Philosophy: Islamic, Jewish, and Christian Perspectives*. Dordrecht: D. Reidel Publishing Company, 1985.

*Decorte, J., *Tijdschrift voor Filosofie*, 50(1988): 148-149.*
*Mulligan, R. W., *The Modern Schoolman*, 64(1987), 207-209.*
*Redpath, P. A., *The Thomist*, 51(1987): 716-718.*

381 Russell, Frederick H. *The Just War in the Middle Ages*. Cambridge: Cambridge University Press, 1977. xi-322.

*Fay, Thomas, *The New Scholasticism*, 54(1980): 253-255.*

382 Russman, Thomas A., ed. *Thomistic Papers V*. Houston, TX: Center for Thomistic Studies, University of Saint Thomas, 1990. 96.

383 Schall, James V. *The Politics of Heaven and Hell: Christian Themes from Classical, Medieval, and Modern Political Philosophy*. Washington, DC: University Press of America, 1984. 360.

384 Schall, James V. *Reason, Revelation, and the Foundations of Political Philosophy*. Baton Rouge, LA: Louisiana University Press, 1987.

*Rehg, William R., *The Modern Schoolman*, 67(1990): 161-163.*

The relation of revelation and reason in political philosophy has not been thoroughly investigated. Aristotle had said that if man were the highest being, politics would be the highest science. The problem of modernity in political philosophy is precisely what to do when metaphysics and revelation are no longer allowed a place in political philosophy. To understand the consequences of this position, it is necessary to study classical, medieval, and modern political philosophy, to find its unity and the relation of the systems to one another. This book presents a coherent and critical study of the unity of political philosophy from the tradition of reason and revelation.

385 Schall, James V., John Schrems, and Charles N. R. McCoy, eds. *On the Intelligibility of Political Philosophy: Essays of Charles N. R. McCoy*. Washington, DC: The Catholic University of America Press, 1989.

386 Schmitz, Kenneth L. *The Gift—Creation*. Milwaukee, WI: Marquette University Press, 1982. 142.

387 Schmitz, Kenneth L. *What Has Clio to Do with Athena? Etienne Gilson, Historian and Philosopher*. The Etienne Gilson Series 10. Toronto: Pontifical Institute of Mediaeval Studies, 1987. 24.

388 Scordis, Peter. *The Three Ways, A Philosophy of Theism*. Newbury, CT: Philosophy Publications, 1986. 83.

389 Sheehan, Thomas. *Karl Rahner: The Philosophical Foundations*. Athens, OH: Ohio University Press, 1987. 320.

390 Shook, Laurence K. *Etienne Gilson*. The Etienne Gilson Series 6. Toronto: Pontifical Institute of Mediaeval Studies, 1984. x-412.

*Donneaud, Henry, *Revue Thomiste*, 90(1990): 343-345.*

*Elders, L., *Divus Thomas*, 87(1984): 273-274.*

*Fitzgerald, Desmond, *Journal of the History of Philosophy*, 24(1986): 571-573.*

*Van Steenberghen, Fernand, *Revue Philosophique de Louvain*, 84(1986): 521-525.*

391 Sigmund, Paul. *Thomism in Contemporary Politics: Europe and Latin America*. Milwaukee, WI: Marquette University Press, 1990.

392 Simpson, Peter. *Goodness and Nature*. Dordrecht: Martinus Nijhoff, 1987.

393 Smart, Ninian. *The Philosophy of Religion*. 1970. New York: Oxford University Press, 1979. Especially Chapter Five: "*On Religion and Nature*," 139-166.

394 Smith, Gerard, and Lottie H. Kendzierski. *The Philosophy of Being, Metaphysics I*. Milwaukee, WI: Marquette University Press, 1983.

395 Smith, Samuel. *Ideas of the Great Educators*. New York: Barnes & Noble, 1979.

396 Smith, Wolfgang. *Cosmos and Transcendence: Breaking Through the Barrier of Scientific Belief*. La Salle: Open Court, 1988.

*The author presents an insider's critique of the scientific world-view based upon the sharp but oft-overlooked distinction between scientific truth and scientistic faith. He shows, first, how contemporary cosmologies continue to be vitiated through the Cartesian postulate of bifurcation; next, he argues that the theory of evolution is little more than a scientistic myth; and in two separate chapters he argues the same for the theories of Freud and Jung. Most importantly, however, he brings to light—ina scientific context—some of the long-forgotten insights belonging rightfully to the *cosmologia perennis*, especially in its Platonic and Christian forms.*

397 Sokolowski, Robert. *The God of Faith and Reason*. Notre Dame, IN: University of Notre Dame Press, 1982. xiv-172.

*Kondoleon, Theodore J., *The Thomist*, 48(1984): 667-671.*

398 Sokolowski, Robert. *Moral Action: A Phenomenological Study*. Bloomington, IN: Indiana University Press, 1985. ix-224.

399 Sorabji, Richard. *Time, Creation and the Continuum: Theories in Antiquity and the Middle Ages*. Ithaca, NY: Cornell University Press, 1983. xviii-473.

400 Soupios, Michael A. *European Political Theory: Plato to Machiavelli.* Lanham, MD: University Press of America, 1986.

401 Spangler, Mary Michael. *Principles of Education: A Study of Aristotelian Thomism Contrasted with Other Philosophies.* Washington, DC: University Press of America, 1983. viii-297.

402 Srzednicki, Jan T. J., and Wladyslaw Tatarkiewicz, eds. *A History of Six Ideas.* The Hague: Nijhoff Press, 1980.

403 Steiner, Rudolf. *The Redemption of Thinking: A Study in the Philosophy of Thomas Aquinas.* 3 lectures given in Dornach, Switzerland. Trans. A. P. Shepherd and Mildred Robertson Nicoll. Ed. A. P. Shepherd and Mildred Robertson Nicoll. 1956. Spring Valley, NY: Anthroposophic, 1983. 191.

404 Surin, Kenneth, ed. *The Turnings of Darkness and Light: Essays in Philosophical and Systematic Theology.* Cambridge: Cambridge University Press, 1989.

This collection of essays, written between 1975 and 1987, covers the doctrine of analogy, the Trinity, "theological realism," the problems of evil and suffering, the doctrine of God, tragedy and Christian life, the doctrine of the atonement, Christology, the theology of religions, ecclesiology, discipleship, and the so-called theistic "proofs." The earlier essays reflect the author's training as a philosopher in the Anglo-American "analytic" tradition. Later essays have a more explicitly theological focus. More importance is attached to issues in hermeneutics and literary and social theory in the later essays. This collection therefore tends to address a wider list of topics than is usual in works of philosophical theology.

405 Sweeney, Leo, with William J. Carroll and John Furlong. *Authentic Metaphysics in an Age of Unreality.* 1965. New York: Peter Lang, 1988. xi-419.

*Zedler, Beatrice, *The Modern Schoolman*, 68(1991): 333-337.*

406 Swinburne, Richard. *The Existence of God.* Oxford: Clarendon Press, 1979. Especially #7: "The Cosmological argument," 116-132, and #8: "Teleological arguments," 133-151.

407 Tanner, Kathryn. *God and Creation in Christian Theology: Tyranny or Empowerment?* Oxford: Basil Blackwell, 1988. Especially #3: "God and the efficacy of Creatures," 81-119.

408 Thro, J. Linus, ed. *History of Philosophy in the Making: A Symposium of Essays to Honor Professor James D. Collins on His 65th Birthday.* Washington, DC: University Press of America, 1982. ix-330.

*Teske, Roland J., *The Modern Schoolman*, 62(1984): 60-61.*

409 Torre, Michael D., ed. *Freedom in the Modern World: Jacques Maritain, Yves R. Simon, Mortimer J. Adler.* American Maritain Association. Notre Dame, IN: University of Notre Dame Press, 1989. 289.

410 Tracey, David, ed. *Celebrating the Medieval Heritage: A Colloquy on the Thought of Aquinas and Bonaventure. The Journal of Religion*, Supplement 58. Chicago: University of Chicago Press, 1978. 239.

411 Trigg, Roger. *Ideas of Human Nature: An Historical Introduction.* Oxford: Blackwell, 1988.

This book forms an introduction to views about human nature held by some of the most influential thinkers in the Western philosophical tradition. Chapters are devoted to each of 10 thinkers from Plato to Wittgenstein, and including Aristotle, Aquinas, Hobbes, Hume, Darwin, Marx, Nietzsche, and Freud. Each is put in his historical context, and his relevance to modern philosophical debates is shown. The aim is demonstrate how assumptions made about human nature form the basis of how we live and of how society is organized. The book is intended to be both a historical introduction and a stimulus to further philosophical thought.

412 Trusted, Jennifer. *Free Will and Responsibility*. Oxford: Oxford University Press, 1984. x-195.

413 Tugwell, Simon. *Human Immortality and the Redemption of Death*. London: Longmann and Todd, 1990. 196.

414 Ugorji, Lucius Jwejuru. *The Principle of Double Effect: A Critical Appraisal of Its Traditional Understanding and Its Modern Reinterpretation*. Bern: Peter Lang, 1985. 150.

415 Van Steenberghen, Fernand. *Thomas Aquinas and Radical Aristotelianism*. Trans. Dominic J. O'Meara, John F. Wippel, and Stephen F. Brown. Washington, DC: The Catholic University of America Press, 1980. x-114.

*Bonino, S. -T., *Revue Thomiste*, 87(1987): 513-515.*
*Brown, S. F., *Speculum*, 56(1981): 224.*
*Kennedy, Leonard A., *The New Scholasticism*, 56(1982), 110-111.*
*Mahoney, E. P., *Journal of the History of Philosophy*, 20(1982): 429-432.*
*Rothschild, J. -P., *Revue de l'Histoire des Religione*, 202(1985): 446-448.*

Three lectures at the Catholic University of America. Purpose: To show how Thomas combated important errors of Radical Aristotelianism.(1) Eternity of the world in the past: This cannot be demonstrated (although reason no more can prove that the world began to exist). (2) Averroes' monopschism: Thomas rigorously proves that every man has a personal intelligence. (3) Rationalism, provoked by invasion of pagan philosophy in the 13rd century: Thomas clearly develops the laws which command relationship between reason and faith. [in connection with this:] nobody defended the double-truth theory in the Middle Ages.

416 Veatch, Henry B. *Swimming Against the Current in Contemporary Philosophy: Occasional Essays and Papers*. Studies in Philosophy and the History of Philosophy 20. Washington, DC: Catholic University of America Press, 1990. 337. Especially "Introduction: On Trying to be an Aristotelian or a Thomist in Today's World," 1-20.

A collection of papers written to return the attention of contemporary philosophers to the implications of the teaching of Aristotle and Aquinas in order to revive the realism in philosophy. Particular attention is paid to ethics, the philosophy of nature, and the philosophy of human nature.

417 Vos, Arvin. *Aquinas, Calvin, and Contemporary Protestant Thought: A Critique of Protestant Views on the Thought of Thomas Aquinas*. Christian College Consortium. Grands Rapids, MI: Christian University Press & William B. Eerdmans Publication Company, 1985. xvii-178.

*Brito, E., *Revue Théologique de Louvain*, 18(1987): 391-392.*
*De Boer, J., *The Review of Metaphysics*, 40(1986-1987): 406-408.*
*O'Brien, Thomas C., *The Thomist*, 52(1988): 148-152.*
*Sell, Alan P., *Philosophical Studies*, 37(1988-1990): 377-379.*
*Teselle, Eugene, *Church History*, 55(1986): 517-518.*

418 Wallace, William A. *The Elements of Philosophy: A Compendium for Philosophers and Theologians*. New York: Alba House, 1977. 338.

419 Wallace, William A. *From a Realist Point of View: Essays on the Philosophy of Science*. 2nd ed. 1979. Washington, DC: University Press of America, 1983. xi-340.

*Blackwell, Richard J., *The Review of Metaphysics*, 33(1980): 650-651.*

*Koterski, Joseph W., *The New Scholasticism*, 55(1981): 256-258.*

This is a collection of 16 essays, all by the author; many have been published previously, but two were written specially for this volume and two more considerably enlarged. Its focus is not on problems of formal logic, but rather on those of realist epistemology. Successive sections deal with the definition of philosophy of science; with problems of methodology; with the ontology of gravitational and elementary particle theories; with the modeling of man and the human science; and with problems of ultimate explanation.

420 Watts, C. D. F. *The Mathematical God: A Brief Study of the First Way of the Demonstration of God's Existence as Presented in the Theologiae of Saint Thomas Aquinas*. Oxford: Blackwell, 1984. 16.

421 Wauck, Mark A. *Thomist Realism and the Critique of Knowledge*. Trans. Mark A. Wauck. By Étienne Gilson. A Trans. of *Réalisme thomiste et critique: De la connaissance*. San Francisco: Ignatius Press, 1986.

*Lee, Patrick, *The New Scholasticism*, 63(1989): 81-100.*

422 Weisheipl, James A. *Thomas D'Aquino and Albert His Teacher*. The Etienne Gilson Series 2. Toronto: Pontifical Institute of Mediaeval Studies, 1980. 22.

423 Weisheipl, James A. *Friar Thomas D'Aquino: His Life, Thought, and Works: With Corrigenda and Addenda*. 1974. Washington, DC: The Catholic University of America Press, 1983. Contains *A brief catalogue of authentic works*, 355-405. A German translation by G. Kirstein is entitled *Thomas von Aquin: Sein Leben und Seine Theologie*, Graz, 1980. 587.

*Alvira, T., *Anuario Filosófico*, 12(1979): 198-201.*

*Anon., *Rassegna di Letteratura Tomistica*, 19(1983): 15-16.*

*Flood, D., *Speculum*, 52(1977): 449-451.*

*Inciarte, F., *Philosophisches Jahrbuch*, 85(1978): 398-419.*

*Krajski, S., *Journal Philosophique*, 9(1986): 276-279.*

*Leroy, M. -V., *Revue Thomiste*, 78(1978): 665-669.*

*Yarnold, E. J., *The Journal of the Theological Studies* 28(1977): 214-215.*

This intellectual and biographical history of St. Thomas Aquinas tries (1) to place his remarkable philosophical and theological thought in the context of his life and writings considered chronologically and (2) to place the life and times of Aquinas (c 1125-1274) in the wider context of intellectual history of the medieval university and academic teaching. There is also a brief catalogue of Thomas' writings with dates, place of composition, purpose, etc.

424 Weisheipl, James A. *Nature and Motion in the Middle Ages*. Ed. William E. Carroll. Studies in Philosophy and the History of Philosophy 11. Washington, DC: The Catholic University of America Press, 1985. Selected Bibliography of the works of James A. Weisheipl, 283-285. 292.

*Baldner, Steven, *The New Scholasticism*, 62(1988): 479-483.*

*Kelley, Francis E., *The Thomist*, 51(1987): 81-383.*

425 White, Reginald E. O. *Christian Ethics*. Atlanta, GA: John Knox Press, 1981. 442.

426 Wicksteed, Philip Henry. *The Reactions Between Dogma and Philosophy Illustrated from the Works of St. Thomas Aquinas*. 1920. New York: AMS, 1980. xxxvi-669.

427 Wilhelmsen, Frederick D. *Christianity and Political Philosophy*. Athens, GA: University of Georgia Press, 1978.

*Carpino, Joseph L., *Interpretation*, 8(1980): 204-222.*
*Dannhauser, Werner J., *International Studies in Philosophy*, 14(1982): 108-109.*
*Gueguen, John A., *The Modern Schoolman*, 57(1979): 94-95.*
*Lemos, Ramon M., *International Journal for Philosophy of Religion*, 13(1982): 50-51.*

**Christianity and Political Philosophy* addresses itself principally to the ways in which Christian philosophers came to terms with the problem of political power. Arguing that classical political philosophy had no adequate solution to problems centering around power, virtue, and the forces of irrationality, the author details solutions proffered by St. Augustine, Sir John Fortesque, Donoso Cortez, and the Natural Law Tradition as summed up by St. Thomas Aquinas. The book concludes with a plea for the restoration and development of a Christian political philosophy.*

428 Wippel, John F. *The Metaphysical Thought of Godfrey of Fontaines: A Study in Late Thirteenth-century Philosophy*. Washington, DC: The Catholic University of America, 1981. 413.

*Brown, Jerome V., *The New Scholasticism*, 57(1983): 123-125.*
*Kretzmann, Norman, *International Studies in Philosophy*, 18(1986): 113-115.*
*Macken, R., *Franziskanische Studien*, 69(1987): 116-117.*
*Martinez-G., L., *Pensamiento*, 41(1985): 75-77.*
*McEvoy, J., *Philosophical Studies*, 31(1986-1987): 425-426.*
*Sacchi, Mario Enrique, *Sapientia*, 42(1987): 73-75.*
*Thro, Linus J., *The Modern Schoolman*, 61(1983): 68-69.*
*Wagner, Claus, *Freiburger Zeitschrift für Philosophie und Theologie*, 31(1984): 214-220.*
*Weisheipl, James A., *The Review of Metaphysics*, 35(19): 639-641.*
*Wells, N. J., *The Journal of the History of Philosophy*, 21(1983): 280-281.*

429 Wippel, John F. *Metaphysical Themes in Thomas Aquinas*. Studies in Philosophy and the History of Philosophy 10. Washington, DC: The Catholic University of America Press, 1984. xi-293.

*Anon., *Rassegna di Letteratura Tomistica*, 20(1984): 162-164.*
*Bianchi, L., *Rivista di Storia della Filosofia*, 43(19): 220-221.*
*Burrell, David B., *The New Scholasticism*, 62(1988): 228-229.*
*Desharnais, Richard, *International Studies in Philosophy*, 20(1988): 154-155.*
*Kelley, Francis E., *The Thomist*, 50(1986): 703-705.*
*Kretzmann, Norman, *Faith and Philosophy*, 3(1986): 336-341.*
*Leroy, Marie-Vincent, *Revue Thomiste*, 84(1984): 667-671.*
*McEvoy, J., *Philosophical Studies*, 31(1986-1987): 423-424.*
*Van Steenberghen, Fernand, *Revue Philosophique de Louvain*, 83(1985): 287-289.*
*Weisheipl, James A., *The Review of Metaphysics*, 38(1985): 699-700.*
*Wilder, A., *Angelicum*, 63(1986): 150-152.*

430 Wippel, John F., ed. *Studies in Medieval Philosophy*. Studies in Philosophy and the History of Philosophy 17. Washington, DC: The Catholic University of America Press, 1987. viii-302.

*Buijs, Joseph A., *Canadian Philosophical Reviews*, 8(1988): 372-374.*

*Van Steenberghen, F., *Bulletin de Théologie Ancienne et Médiévale*, 14(1989): 618-619.*

431 Wissink, J. B. M., ed. *The Eternity of the World in the Thought of Thomas Aquinas and His Contemporaries*. Studien und Texte Zur Geistesgeschichte Des Mittelalters 27. Leiden: E. J. Brill, 1990. viii-100.

432 Wojtyla, Karol (Pope John Paul II). *The Acting Person*. Trans. Andrzej Potocki. Ed. A. T. Tymieniecka. Hingham, MA: D. Reidel, 1979. xxiii-367.

*Abbà, G., *Salesianum*, 42(1980): 102-103.*

*Blakeley, T. J., *Studies in Soviet Thought*, 20(1979): 373-376.*

*Chisholm, R. M., *Religious Studies*, 17(1981): 408-409.*

*Elders, L. J., *Divus Thomas*, 83(1980): 49-57.*

*Hartshorne, Charles, *Philosophy and Phenomenological Research*, 40(1979-1980): 443-444.*

*Kerr, F., *The Journal of the British Society for Phenomenology*, 10(1979): 138.*

*Köchler, H., *Philosophischer Literaturanzeiger*, 33(1980): 52-56.*

*Long, Eugene T., *The Review of Metaphysics*, 33(1979-1980): 453-454.*

*Marabotto de Grau, M. I., *Antropos*, 4-5(1980-1981): 127-132.*

*McNicholl, Ambrose, *Philosophical Studies*, 37(1980): 237-241.*

*Muscari, P. G., *The Modern Schoolman*, 65(1987-1988): 221-223.*

*Pappin, Joseph, *The Thomist*, 45(1981): 472-480.*

*Pegueroles, J., *Espiritu*, 28(1979): 185-187.*

*Sánches, J. R. P., *Revista de Philosophie*, Mexico, 117(14): 546-550.*

*Skousgaard, S., *International Journal for Philosophy of Religion*, 13(1982): 43-44.*

*Stohrer, Walter J., *The Modern Schoolman*, 57(1980): 265-267.*

*Vacek, E., *Theological Studies*, 41(1980): 228-229.*

*Valori, P., *Gregorianum*, 60(1979): 763-766.*

The book stresses that Man must ceaselessly unravel his mysteries and strive for a new and more mature expression of his nature. The author sees this expression as an emphasis on the significance of the individual living in community and on the person in the process of performing an action. The author states in his preface that he has tried to face the major issues concerning life, nature, and the existence of Man directly as they present themselves to Man in his struggles to survive while maintaining the dignity of a human being, but who is torn apart between his all too limited condition and his highest aspirations to set himself free. The author hopes that his book "contributes to this disentangling of the conflicting issues facing Man, which are crucial for man's own clarification of his existence and direction of his conduct." The author's analysis of the human being is a dynamic counter to the materialistic and positivistic tendencies in various schools of modern philosophy. Ever since Descartes, the knowledge of Man and his world has been identified through cognition. This book is a reversal of the post-Cartesian attitude toward Man in that it characterizes him as the person in action.

433 Woznicki, Andrew Nicholas. *A Christian Humanism: Karol Wojtyla's Existential Personalism*. New Britain, CT: Mariel Press, 1980.

*Kuczynski, Janusz, *Dialectical Humanism*, 14(1987): 270-274.*

434 Woznicki, Andrew Nicholas. *The Dignity of Man as a Person*. San Francisco: Christ Publications, 1988. xvi-174.

*McDermott, John M., *Gregorianum*, 72(1991): 149-150.*

435 Woznicki, Andrew Nicholas. *Being and Order: The Metaphysics of Thomas Aquinas in Historical Perspective*. Catholic Thought from Lublin. New York: Peter Lang, 1990. xiv-309.

*Lauder, Robert E., *The Thomist*, 56(1992): 151-154.*

436 Wright, Thomas. *The Passions of the Mind in General*. New York: Garland Press, 1986.

437 Yearley, Lee H. *Mencius and Aquinas: Theories of Virtue and Conceptions of Courage*. SUNY Series Toward a Comparative Philosophy of Religion. Albany, NY: State University of New York, 1990. 280.

438 Zagar, Janko. *Acting on Principle: A Thomistic Perspective in Making Moral Decisions*. Lanham, MD: University Press of America, 1984. xxiv-227.

The purpose of this work is to present Aquinas' fundamental moral principles, not as a historical interest for a medieval thinker, but as a contemporary vehicle in making moral decisions. Within the philosophical and theological unity of moral experience, the book analyzes the great moral themes of motivation, responsibility, conscience, and moral formation, with particular explanation of the meaning of objective morality as both highly personal yet socially sound and workable.

439 Zedler, Beatrice Hope. *How Philosophy Begins: The Aquinas Lecture 1983*. Milwaukee, WI: Marquette University, 1983. 52.

Plato and Aristotle said that philosophy begins in wonder. The lecture first considers what it means to say this. It then looks at incidents in the lives of philosophers from Augustine to Kierkegaard, but especially Thomas Aquinas, to see more concretely how philosophy begins. It concludes by examining the philosophical basis for the connection between life and philosophy and finds such a basis in Thomas Aquinas' view of the hylemorphic nature of the human person.

440 Zeitz, James V. *Spirituality and Analogia Entis* According to Erich Przywara, S. J. Washington, DC: University Press of America, 1988. xii-346.

B. FRENCH

441 Armogathe, Jean R. *Theologia Cartesiana: L' Explication Physique de L'Eucharistie Chez Descartes et Dom Desgabets*. Archives Internationales D'Histoire Des Idées 84. La Haye: Nijhoff, 1977. xi-146.

442 Bastit, Michel. *Naissance de la Loi Moderne: La Pensée de la Loi de Saint Thomas A Suarez*. Paris: Presses Universitaires de France, 1990. 389.

443 Belmans, Théo G. *Le Sens Objectif de L'Agir Humanin: Pour Relire la Morale Conjugale de Saint Thomas*. Studi Tomistici 8. Città del Vaticano. Pontificia Accademia di S. Tommaso: Libreria Editrice Vaticana, 1980. 457.

*Anon., *Rassegna di Letteratura Tomistica*, 16(1983): 196-198.*
*G. S. R., *Ethos*, 10-11(1982-1983): 391-393.*

444 Blanco, A., and Georges Cottier, eds. *La Doctrine de la Révelation Divine de Saint Thomas D'Aquin*. Studi Tomistici 37. Roma: Ed. Vaticana, 1990. 278.

445 Bruun, Emilie, and Alain De Libera. *Maître Eckhart: Métaphysique der Verbe et Théologie Négative*. Bibliothéque Des Archives de Philosophie 42. Paris: Beauchesne, 1984. 252.

446 Caldera, Rafael-Tomas. *Le Jugement par Inclination Chez Saint Thomas D'Aquin*. Paris: Librairie Philosophique J. Vrin, 1980. v-140.

*Owens, J., *The Review of Metaphysics*, 35(1981-1982): 369-370.*
*Paván-S., C., *Revista Venezolana de Filosofia*, 22(1986): 163-167.*
*Wéber, E., *Les Études Philosophiques*, 2(1986): 272-273.*

447 Capelle, Catherine. *Thomas D'Aquin Feministe? Avant-propos de Jean-Marie Aubert*. Bibliothéque Thomiste 43. Paris: J. Vrin, 1982. iv-180.

*Derksen, L. D., *Stoicheia*, 1(1986): 63-68.*
*Escol, R., *Nouvelle Revue Théologique*, 105(1983): 442.*
*Mathon, G., *Bulletin de Théolgie Ancienne et Médiévale*, 13(1984): 673-675.*
*Nicholas, S., *Revue Thomiste*, 88(1988): 171-172.*

448 Casin, Renée. *Saint Thomas D'Aquin Ou L'Intelligence de la Foi: Quatre Points Chauds*. 2nd ed. Montsurs: Résiac, 1986. 137.

449 Caspar, Ph. *La Saisie Du Zygote Humain par L'esprit: Destin de L'ontogénése Aristotélicienne*. Horizon 17. Paris: Lethielleux, 1987. 512.

*Pangallo, Mario, *Doctor Communis*, 42(1989): 102-103.*

450 Cattin, Yves. *Le Preuve de Dieu*. Paris: Vrin, 1989.

*Follon, Jacques, *Revue Philosophie de Louvain*, 87(1989): 354-357.*

451 Chalmel, P. *Biologie Actuelle et Philosophie Thomiste: Essai de Philosophie*. Paris: Téqui, 1984. 326.

452 Champlin, T. S. *Reflexive Paradoxes*. London: Routledge & Kegan Paul, 1988. viii-235. [Should be in English Books]

*Borst, Clive, *Philosophical Books*, 31(1990): 28-29.*
*Grattan-Guinness, I., *History and Philosophy of Logic* 11(1990): 247-248.*
*Noonan, Harold W., *Philosophy*, 64(1989): 568-569.*

453 Chatelet, François. *Le Philosophie: De Platon A Saint Thomas I*. Rev.. Marabout Université 311. Verviers: Marabout, 1979. 306.

454 Châtillon, Jean. *D'Isidore de Séville A Saint Thomas D'Aquin: Etudes D'histoire et de Théologie*. London: Variourum Reprints, 1985. 336.

455 Chenu, Marie-Dominique. *Saint Thomas D'Aquin et la Théologie*. Maîtres Spirituels. Paris: Le Seuil, 1977. 192.

456 Chesterton, Gilbert K. *Saint Thomas Du Créateur (Saint Thomas Aquinas)*. Trans. Antoine Barrois. Paris: D. Martin Morin, 1977. 148.

*Lechartier, J. -J., *Bulletin du Cercle Thomiste*, 82(1978): 47-50.*

457 Chevallier, Jean-Jacques. *Histoire de la Pensée Politique Vol. I: De la Cité-Etat A L'apogée de L'Etat-nation*. Paris: Payot, 1979. 370.

458 Clément, André. *La Sagesse de Thomas D'Aquin*. Collection Docteur Angélique 1. Paris: Nouvelles Éditions Latines, 1983. 366.

*Anon., *Rassegna di Litteatura Tomistica*, 19(1983): 122-125.*
*De Castera, B., *Thomas Aquinas*, 4(1983): 23-29.*
*De Finance, J., *Gregorianum*, 64(1983): 749-750.*
*Leroy, M. -V., *Revue Thomiste*, 83(1983): 673-675.*
*Widow, J. A., *Philosophica*, Valparaiso, 6(1983): 243-244.*

459 Congar, Yves. *Thomas D'Aquin: Sa Vision de Théologie et de L'église*. Collected Studies 190. Londres: Variorum Reprints, 1984. 334.

*Burr, David, *Church History*, 54(1985): 100-101.*

460 Corbin, Michel. *L'inouï de Dieu*. Paris: Desclée de Brouwer, 1980.364.

461 Cromp, Germaine. *Les Sources de L'abstraction de L'intellect Agent, dans la Somme de Théologie de Thomas D'Aquin I*. Montréal: L'Universite de Montréal, 1980. 202.

462 Cromp, Germaine. *Le Phantasme dans L'abstraction de L'intellect Agent: Dans la Somme de Theologie de Thomas D'Aquin II*. Montréal: L'Universite de Montréal, 1980. 276. Deuxiéme partie d'une thése de doctorat en Philosophie, 1980, Montreál, L'Universite de Montréal, Institut d'études Médiévales.

463 Cromp, Germaine. *L'espéce Intelligible dans L'abstraction de L'intellect Agent: Dans la Somme de Théologie de Thomas D'Aquin III*. Montréal: L'Universite de Montréal, 1980. 252. Troisieme partie d'une thése de doctorat en Philosophie, 1980, Montreál, L'Universite de Montréal, Institut d'études Médiévales.

464 Cromp, Germaine. *L'intellect Agent et Son Rôle D'abstraction: Les Sources de L'abstraction de L'intellect Agent dans la Somme de Theologie de Thomas D'Aquin IV*. Montréal: L'Universite de Montréal, 1980. 228. Quatriéme partie d'une thése de doctorat en Philosophie, 1980, Montreál, L'Universite de Montréal, Institut d'études Médiévales.

465 De Boylesve, Pierre Faucon. *Etre et Savoir, Etude Du Fondement de L'intelligibilité dans la Pensée Mediévale*. Bibliotéque Thomiste 45. vii-383. Paris: Vrin, 1985.

*Imbach, Ruedi, *Revue de Théologie et de Philosophie*, 119(1987): 243-244.*

466 De Finance, Joseph. *L'ouverture et la Norme: Questions sur L'agir Humain. Teologia e Filosofia 13*. Città del Vaticano: Libreria Editrice Vaticana, 1989. xii-200.

467 De Rijk, Lambert Marie. *La Philosophie Au Moyen Age*. Trans. P. Swiggers. 1977. Leiden: E. J. Brill, 1985. xii-244.

*De Genaro, J., *Patristica et Mediaevalia*, 8(1987): 118-119.*
*Imbach, R., *Freiburger Zeitschrift für Philosophie und Theologie*, 34(1987): 243-256.*
*Reix, A., *Revue Thomiste* 88(1988): 150-152.*

468 De Weiss, Roger. *Amor Sui Sens et Fonctions de L'amour de Soi dans L'ontologie de Thomas D'Aquin*. Genéve: Imprimerie du Belvédére, 1977. 135.

469 Delégue, Y. *Les Machines Du Sens: Fragments D'une Sémiologie Médiévale, Textes de Hugues de Saint-Victor, Thomas D'Aquin et Nicolas de Lyre Traduits et Présentés*. Paris: Vrin, 1987. 122.

470 Delhaye, Philippe. *Enseignement et Morale Au XIIe Siécle*. Vestigia 1. Paris: Ed.s du Cerf, 1988. viii-136.

471 Dubarle, A. -M. *Le Péché Originel: Perspectives Théologiques*. Paris: Le Cerf, 1983. 180.

472 Dubarle, Dominique. *Le Modernisme*. Paris: Beauchesne, 1980. 272.

473 Dubarle, Dominique. *Dieu avec L'être: De Parménide A Saint Thomas*. Philosophie 2. Paris: Beauchesne, 1986. 372.

474 Duroux, Benoît. *La Pschologie de la Foi Chez St. Thomas D'Aquin*. Paris: Téqui, 1977. 235.

475 Elders, Léon J., ed. *Quinque Sunt Viae: Actes Du Symposium sur les Cinq Voies de la Somme Théologique*. 1979. Studi Tomistici 9. Città del Vaticano, Pontificia Accademia di S. Tommaso: Libreria Editrice Vaticana, 1980. 150.

476 Elders, Léon J., ed. *La Philosophie de la Nature de Saint Thomas D'Aquin. Studi Tomistici 18.* Cittá del Vaticano, Pontificia Accademia di San Tommaso: Libreria Editrice Vaticana, 1982. 178.

*Van Steenberghen, F., *Revue Philosophique de Louvain*, 83(1985): 289-292.*

477 Elders, Léon J. *Autour de Saint Thomas D'Aquin: Recueil D'études sur Sa Pensée Philosophique et Théologique I: Les Commentaires sur les Oeuvres D'Aristote. La Métaphysique de L'être*. Paris: FAC-éditions et Bruges, Tabor, 1987. x-247.

*De Jong, E., *The Review of Metaphysics*, 42(1988-1989): 137-140.*

*Pangallo, Mario, *Doctor Communis*, 41(1988): 95-96.*

*Van Steenberghen, F., *Revue Philosophique de Louvain*, 86(1988): 255-257.*

478 Elders, Léon J. *Autour de Saint Thomas D'Aquin: Recueil D'études sur Sa Pensée Philosophique et Théologique II: L'agir Moral Approches Théologiques*. Paris: FAC-éditions et Bruges, Tabor, 1987. 229.

479 Floucat, Yves. *Métaphysique et Religion, Vers une Sagesse Chrétienne Intégrale*. Téqui: Paris, 1989. 208.

*Contat, Alain, *Doctor Communis*, 43(1990): 90-92.*

480 Gaboriau, Florent. *Edith Stein Philosophie*. Paris: FAC, 1989. 164.

*Labato, Abelardo, *Angelicum*, 67(1990): 438-440.*

481 Gilson, Étienne Henry. *L'esprit de la Philosophie Médiévale*. 4th rev. ed. 1944. Etudes de Philosophie Médiévale 33. Paris: Vrin, 1978. viii-446. Gifford lectures, Université d' Aberdeen.

482 Gilson, Étienne Henry. *L'Athéisme Difficile*. Problémes et Controverses. Paris: J. Vrin, 1979. Trans. A. Contess under the title, *L'Atesimo Difficile*, Milano: Pensiero, 1983. 96.

*Deschepper, Jean-Pierre, *Revue Philosophique de Louvain*, 83(1985): 125-126.*

*Livi, Antonio, *Rivista di Filosofia Neo-Scholastica*, 75(1983): 343-347.*

483 Gilson, Étienne Henry. *Index Scolastico-Cartésien*. 2nd rev. 1913. Etudes de Philosophie Médiévale 62. Paris: J. Vrin, 1980. 410.

*Barcala, A., *Revista Espanola de Teologia*, 38(1978): 194-195.*

484 Gilson, Étienne Henry. *Pourquoi Saint Thomas a Critiqué Saint Augustin: Avicenne et le Point Départ de Duns Scot*. 1926-1927. Paris: J. Vrin, 1981. 189.

485 Gilson, Étienne Henry. *Christianisme et Philosophie*. 1949. Paris: Vrin, 1981. 168.

486 Gilson, Étienne Henry. *Autour de Saint Thomas. Reprint 1931-1973*. Paris: Vrin, 1983. 126.

*Pasqua, H., *Revue Philosophique de Louvain*, 86(1988): 258-259.*

487 Gilson, Étienne Henry. *Constantes Philosophiques de L'être*. Paris: Vrin, 1983. 256.

*Pasqua, Hervé, *Revue Philosophique de Louvain*, 83(1985): 123-125.*

488 Gilson, Étienne Henry. *Etudes Médiévales*. Paris: Vrin-reprisé, 1983. 225.

*Pasqua, Hervé, *Revue Philosophique de Louvain*, 86(1988): 258-259.*

489 Gisel, P., and Ph. Secrétan, eds. *Analogie et Dialectique: Essais de Théologie Fondamentale*. Genéve: Labor et Fides, 1982.

490 Gorce, Matthieu-Mazime. *L'essor de la Pensée Au Moyen Age: Albert le Grand, Thomas D'Aquin*. 1933. Paris: Champion, 1978. xviii-422.

491 Hadot, P. *Dieu et L'être*. Paris: Centre d'etudes des réligions du livre, 1978.

492 Hissette, Roland. *Enquête sur les 219 Articles Condamnés A Paris le 7 Mars 1277*. Philosophes Médiévaux 22. Paris: Vander-Oyez, 1977. 340.

493 Jacquement, Maurice. *La Priére Chrétienne en Saint Augustin et Saint Thomas D'Aquin*. Paris: Téqui, 1989. 72.

494 Jugnet, Louis. *Pour Connaître la Pensée de Saint Thomas D'Aquin*. 2nd ed. Bordeaux: Éditions Ulysse, 1979. iii-240.

495 Kalinowski, Georges. *L'impossibile Métaphysique, en Annexe Trois Lettres Inédites de Etienne Gilson*. Bibliothéque Des Archives de Philosophie 33. Paris: Beauchesne, 1981. 251.

*Bogliolo, Luigi, *Doctor Communis*, 37(1984): 284-286.*
*Pasqua, Hervé, *Revue Philosophique de Louvain*, 83(1985): 117-122.*

496 Kreit, J. *Thomas D'Aquin, Job, Un Homme Pour Notre Temps*. Paris: Téqui, 1980. 656.

497 Lafleur, Claude. *Quatre Introductions A la Philosophie Au XIII Siécle*. Montreal: University of Montreal Press, 1988.

*Bataillon, Louis-Jacques, *Laval Théologique et Philosophique*, 45(1989): 470-472.*

498 Lafont, Ghisiain. *Dieu, le Temps et L'être*. Cogitatio Fidei 139. Paris: Le Cerf, 1986. 373.

499 Largeault, Jean. *Principes D'une Philosophie Réaliste*. Paris: Klincksieck, 1985. 271.

500 Le Goff, J. *L'Imaginaire Médiéval: Essais*. Paris: Gallimard, 1985. 352.

501 Lelyveld, M. *Les Logia de la Vie dans L'Evangile Selon Thomas: A la Recherche D'une Tradition et D'une Rédaction*. Leiden: E. J. Brill, 1987. 166.

502 Lindblad, Ulrika Margareta. *L'intelligibilité de L'être Selon Saint Thomas D'Aquin et Selon Martin Heidegger*. Publications Universitaires Européennes 20. Berne, Frankfurt a. m.: Peter Lang, 1987. iv-337.

503 Lohr, Charles H. *Commentateurs D'Aristote Au Moyen Age Latin*. Etudes et Documents de Philosophie Antique et Médiévale 2. Fribourg: Ed.s Universitaires Fribourg, 1988. 255.

504 Lotz, Johannés Baptist. *Martin Heidegger et Thomas D'Aquin: Homme-temps-être*. Trans. Philibert Secretan. Paris: Presses Universitaires de France, 1988. x-232.

505 Lubac, Henri de. *La Postérité Spirituelle de Joachim de Fiore I*. Paris: Lethielleux, 1979. 416.

506 Maitre Eckhart. *Sermons II*. Trans. Jeanne Ancelet-Hustache. Paris: Le Seuil, 1979. 200/216.

507 Maritain, Jacques. *Les Degrés Du Savoir. Jacques et Raïssa Maritain: Oeuvres Complétes*. 4. Paris, 1983.

508 Mucchielli, Roger. *Histoire de la Philosophie et Des Sciences Humanines*. 2nd rev. ed. Paris: Bordas, 1979. 304.

509 Nicolas, Marie-Joseph. *L'idée de Nature dans la Pensée de St. Thomas D'Aquin*. Paris: Téqui, 1979. 62.

510 Patfoort, Albert. *Saint Thomas D'Aquin: Les Cléfs D'une Théologie*. Paris: Pac Éditions, 1983. 130.

*Anon., *Rassegna di Letteratura Tomistica*, 19(1983): 204-208.*
*East, S. -P., *Laval Théologique et Philosophique*, 41(1985): 122-123.*
*Leroy, M. -V., *Revue Thomiste*, 84(1984): 298-303.*

511 Philippe, Marie-Dominique. *De L'etre A Dieu: De la Philosophie Premiére A la Sagesse*. Paris: Tégui, 1977. 525.

512 Piclin, Michel. *Philosophie et Théologie Chez Saint Thomas D'Aquin*. Paris: Klincksieck, 1983. 170.

*Leroy, M. -V., *Revue Thomiste*, 84(1984): 303-304.*

513 Pinckaers, Servais. *Les Sources de la Morale Chrétienne. Sa Méthode, Son Contenu, Son Histoire*. Freiburg: Universitätsverlag, 1985. 523.

*Furger, F., *Theologische Revue*, 82(1986): 418.*
*Poutet, Y., *Divus Thomas*, 88(1985): 159-160.*

514 Pinckaers, Servais. *La Priére Chrétienne*. Fribourg (Suisse): Editions universitaires, 1989. 318.

515 Przywara, E. *Analogia Entis*. Trans. P. Secretan. Théologiques. Paris: University de France, 1990. 190.

516 Rassam, Joseph. *Le Silence comme Introduction A la Métaphysique*. Série A 44. Toulouse: Toulouse Publications de l'Université, 1980. 148.

517 Regnault, François. *Dieu Est Inconscient: Etudes Lacaniennes Aútour de Saint Thomas D'Aquin*. Paris: Navarin, Seuil, 1985. 160.

518 Risset, Jacqueline. *Dante Écrivain Ou L'intelletto D'amore*. Paris: Le Seuil, 1982. 258.

519 Roulier, Fernand. *Jean Pic de la Mirandole(1463-1494): Humaniste, Philosophe et Théologien*. Genéve: Slatkine, 1989. 671.

*Valin, Pierre, *Recherches de Science Religieuse*, 78(1990): 309-310.*

520 Rousseau, Félicien. *La Croissance Solidaire Des Droits de L'homme: Un Retour Aux Sources de L'éthique*. Philosophie 29. Montréal: Parigi Tournai, 1982. 315.

*Composta, Dario, *Doctor Communis*, 37(1984): 182-184.*

521 Rousseau, Félicien. *Courage Ou Resistance et Violence*. Montréal: Bellarmin, 1985. 311.

522 Ruello, Francis. *La Christologie de Thomas D'Aquin*. Théologie Historique 76. Paris: Beauchesne, 1987. 397.

523 Shooner, H. V., ed. *Codices Manuscripti Operum Thomae de Aquino*. Montréal: Les Presses del' Université de Montréal, 1985. xiii-396.

524 Swiezawski, Stefan. *Redécouvrir Thomas D'Aquin*. Trans. Marie Stakowska and Éric Ibarra. Paris: Nouvelle Cité, 1989. 220.

525 Thivierge, Guy-Réal. *Le Commentaire Des Noms Divins de Denys L'Aréopagite: L'occassion D'une Recontre Entre Platonisme et Aristotélisme Chez Thomas D'Aquin*. Roma: Pontifical Studiorum University a Thomas Aq. in Urbe, 1986. 107.

526 Trigeaud, J. M. *La Possession Des Biens Immobiliers*. Paris: Economica, 1981. 632.

527 Van Steenberghen, Fernand. *Le Probléme de L'existence de Dieu dans les Écrits de S. Thomas D'Aquin*. Philosophes Médiévaux 23. Louvain-la-Neuve: Éditions de l'Institut Supérieur de Philosophie, 1980. 375.

*Anon., *Rassegna di Letteratura Tomistica*, 16(1980): 227-239.*
*Bascour, H., *Bulletin de Théologie Ancienne et Médiévale*, 13(1981): 130-131.*
*Bérubé, C., *Collectanea Franciscana*, 51(1981): 178-182.*
*Bogliolo, L., *Doctor Communis*, 35(1982): 185-204.*
*Bonansea, B. M., *International Philosophical Quarterly*, 21(1981): 461-463.*
*Elders, L., *Divus Thomas*, 86(1983): 171-187.*
*Hissette, R., *Revue Théologique de Louvain*, 14(1983): 376-377.*
*Igartua, J. M., *Pensamiento*, 38(1982): 231-232.*
*Lefévre, C., *Mélanges de Science Religieuse*, 39(1982): 31-33.*
*Leroy, M. -V., *Revue Thomiste*, 83(1983): 121-125.*
*Macken, R., *Franziskanische Studien*, 63(1981): 349-435.*
*McEvoy, J., *Philosophical Studies*, 31(1986-1987): 420-421.*
*Reix, A., *Revue Philosophique de la France et de l'étranger*, 108(1983): 460-462.*
*Rovighi Vanni, *Rivista di Filosofia Neo-Scolastica*, 74(1982): 380-383.*
*Sanabria, J. R., *Revista de Filosofia*, 16(1983): 139-143.*

528 Van Steenberghen, Fernand. *Le Thomisme (Que Sais-je? 587)*. Paris: Presses Universitaires de France, 1983. 127.

*Anon., *Rassegna di Letteratura Tomistica*, 19(1983): 125-129.*
*Bazán, Bernardo Carlo, *Dialogue*, 23(1984): 729-732.*
*Bérubé, C., *Collectanea Franciscana*, 53(1983): 422.*
*Étienne, Jacques, *Revue Théologique de Louvain*, 15(1984): 109-110.*
*Jolivet, J., *Revue Philosophique de la France et de l'étranger*, 108(1983): 458-459.*
*Leroy, M. -V., *Revue Thomiste*, 83(1983): 668-671.*
*McEvoy, J., *Philosophical Studies*, 30(1984): 314-315.*

*Miele, M., *Sapienza*, 36(1983): 356-357.*
*Musco, A., *Giornale di Metafisica*, 5(1983): 570-572.*
*Musco, A., *Schede Medievali*, 5(1983): 525-526.*
*Ruello, F., *Recherches de Science Religieuse*, 72(1984): 124-125.*
*Struyker Boudier, C. E. M., *Tijdschrift voor Filosofie*, 46(1984): 660-661.*
*Wenin, Christian, *Revue Philosophique de Louvain*, 82(1984): 282-283.*
*Wielockx, R., *Ephemerides Theologicae Lovanienses* 65(1989): 192.*

529 Van Steenberghen, Fernand. *Etudes Philosophiques (Collection Essais)*. 2nd rev. ed. 1985. Longueuil, Québec: Éditions du Préambule, 1988. 321.

*Bazán, B. C., *Dialogue*, 25(1986): 579-584.*
*Bogliolo, L., *Doctor Communis*, 40(1987): 103-105.*
*De Montpellier, G., *Revue Théologique de Louvain*, 17(1986): 463.*
*Deschepper, J. P., *Revue Philosophique de Louvain*, 86(1988): 603-604.*
*Druart, T. -A., *The Review of Metaphysics*, 43(1989-1990): 183-184.*
*McEvoy, J., *Philosophical Studies*, 31(1986-1987): 421-422.*
*Reix, A., *Revue Philosophique de la France et de l'étranger*, 112(1987): 231.*
*Sanabria, J. R., *Revista de Filosofia*, 20(1987): 475-480.*
*Wenin, C., *Revue Philosophique de Louvain*, 84(1986):146-147.*

530 Van Steenberghen, Fernand. *Philosophie Fondamentale*. Longueuil, Québec: Préambule, 1989. 512.

*McEvoy, J., *Revue Philosophique de Louvain*, 87(1989): 626-628.*

531 Verbeke, Gérard. *D'Aristote A Thomas D'Aquin: Antécédents de la Pensée Moderne*. Ancient and Medieval Philosophy: De Wulf-Mansion Centre 1. Leuven: University Press, 1990. xvii-644.

532 Vernier, Jean-Marie. *Les Anges Chez Saint Thomas D'Aquin: Fondements Historiques et Principes Philosophiques*. Angelologia 3. Paris: Nouvelles Éditions Latines, 1986. 146.

*Dalledonne, Andrea, *Doctor Communis*, 50(1987): 110-111.*

533 Veysset, Philippe. *Situation de la Politique dans la Pensée de S. Thomas D'Aquin*. Paris: Ed.s du Cédre, 1981. 152.

534 Vignaux, Paul. *Philosophie Au Moyen Age*. Albeuve (Suisse): Éditions Catella, 1987. 280.

*Bonino, S. -T., *Revue Thomiste*, 88(1988): 487-488.*
*Suarez-Nani, T., *Rivista di Storia della Filosofia*, 44(1989): 87-97.*
*Wenin, C., *Revue Philosophique de Louvain*, 86(1988): 241-242.*

535 Villey, Michel. *Philosophie Du Droit I-IV*. Paris: Précis Dalloz, 1979.

*Bozzi, Rodolfo, *Gregorianum*, 64(1983): 379-381.*
*Dagory, J., *Archives de Philosophie du Droit*, 30(1985): 396-399.*
*Gardies, Jean-Louis, *Revue Philosophique de la France et de l'Etranger*, 2(1979): 271-272.*
*Quan-Yan-Chui, René, *Revue Thomiste*, 83(1983): 343-345.*

536 Villey, Michel. *Le Droit et les Droits de L'homme*. Paris: Presses Universitaires de France, 1983. 171.

*Liggieri, Maria Carmela, *Rivista Internazionale di Filosofia del Diritto*, 65(1988): 386-387.*
*Massini, C. I., *Filosofar Cristiano* (Córdoba, Argentina): 8-9(1984-1985): 287-289.*

537 Villey, Michel. *Questiones de Saint Thomas sur le Droit et la Politique Ou le Bon Usage Des Dialogues*. Paris: Presses Universitaires de France, 1987. 184.

*Gervais, R., *Laval Théologique et Philosophique*, 43(1987): 405-407.*
*Jolivet, J., *Revue Philosophique de la France et de l'étranger*, 114(1989): 392-393.*
*Parain-Vial, J., *Les Études Philosophiques*, 1(1989): 120-121.*
*Reix, A., *Journal Philosophique*, 15(1987): 263-266.*

538 Wéber, Édouard-Henri. *Le Christ Selon Saint Thomas D'Aquin*. Paris: Desclée, 1988. 336.

539 Wohlman, Avital. *Thomas D'Aquin et Maïmonide: Un Dialogue Exemplaire*. Paris: Cerf, 1988. 417.

*Bonino, S. -T., *Revue Thomiste*, 89(1989): 330-332.*
*Horowitz, M., *Nouvelle Revue Théologique*, 111(1989): 981.*
*Imbach, Ruedi, *Revue de Théologie et de Philosophie*, 122(1990): 131-132.*

C. GERMAN

540 Aertsen, Johannes Adrianus. *Natura en Creatura: De Denkweg Van Thomas Van Aquino I, II*. Amsterdam: Vrije Universiteit Boekhandel-Uitgeverij, 1982. In German Trans. xiv-539.

*Anon., *Rassegna di Letteratura Tomistica*, 18(1985): 110-115.*
*Delfgaauw, B., *Algemeen Nederlands Tijdschrift voor Wijsbegeerte*, 74(1982): 276-277.*
*Marlet, M., *Philosophia Reformata*, 50(1985): 85-89.*

541 Anzenbacher, Arno. *Analogie und Systemgeschichte*. Uberlieferung und Aufgabe 16. Wien/München: R. Oldenbourg Verl., 1978. 179.

542 Arroyabe, Estanislao. *Das Reflektierende Subjekt: Zur Erkenntnistheorie Des Thomas von Aquin. Athenäums Monografien Philosophie 253*. Frankfurt: Athenäum, 1988. xii-122.

543 Baader, Franz Xaver von. *Sämtliche Werke: Systemat. Geodnete, Durch Reiche Erl. von D. Hand D. Verf. Bedeutend Verm. Vollst. Elementarbegriffe Über die Zeit, Vorlesungen Über Philosophie der Sozietät. Erläuterungen Zu Stellen Aus Thomas von Aquin*. Ed. Franz Hoffmann, Schlüter and Lutterbeck. Aalen: Scientia-Verl., 1987. 488.

544 Bathen, Norbert. *Thomistische Ontologie und Sprachanalyse*. Symposion 85. Freiburg: Karl Alber, 1988. 236.

*Truyen, F., *Tijdschrift Voor Filosofie*, 3(1990): 541-542.*

545 Beckmann, J. P. et al., eds. *Philosophie Im Mittelalter: Festschrift in Honor of Wolfgang Kluxen*. Hamburg: Felix Meiner Verlag, 1987. 413.

*Van Steenberghen, F., *Revue Philosophique de Louvain-La Neuve*, 87(1989): 348-349.*

546 Belmans, Théo G. *Der Objektive Sinn Menschlichen Handelns: Zur Ehemoral Des Hl. Thomas*. Trans. Theo G. Belmans. Ed. D. Franz. Vallendar-Schönstatt: Patris-Verlag, 1984. 514.

547 Berg, Klaus, and M. Kasper, eds. *Das Buch der Tugenden: Ein Compendium Des XIV: Jhts Über Moral und Recht Nach der Theologiae II-II Des Thomas von Aquin und Eren Werken der Scholastik und Kanonistik*. Texte und Textgeschichte 7-8. Tübingen: N. Niemeyer, 1984. 305.

548 Bernath, Klaus, ed. *Thomas von Aquin. Bd I: Chronologie und Werkanalyse*. Wege der Forschung 188. Darmstadt, Wissenschaftliche Buchgesellschaft: Abt. Verl., 1978. x-491.

*Bonansea, B. M., *The Review of Metaphysics*, 36(1982-1983): 160-161.*
*Lindblad, Ulrika, *Freiburger Zeitschrift für Philosophie und Theologie*, 30(1983): 209-212.*
*Pöltner, G., *Salzburger Jahrbuch für Philosophie*, 23-24(1978-1979): 329-330.*
*Volpi, F., *Veritas*, 12(1983): 286-288.*

549 Bien, Günther, ed. *Die Frage Nach dem Glück*. Problemata 74. Stuttgart: Bad Cannstatt, 1978.

550 Brugger, Walter. *Summe einer Philosophischen Gotteslehre*. München: Johannes Berchmans Verlag, 1979. 583.

*Mondin, B., *Divinitas*, 25(1981): 101-102.*

551 Bubner, R., ed. *Geschichte der Philosophie in Text und Darstellung II*. Stuttgart: Reclam, 1980-1984. 542. Especially Chapter 9: "Thomas von Aquin: Über die Art unseres Erkennens, Probleme der Ethik."

552 Bujo, Bénézet. *Moralautonomie und Normenfindung bei Thomas von Aquin: Unter Einbeziehung der Neutestamentlichen Kommentare*. Veröffentlichungen Des Grabmann-Institutes Zur Erforschung der Mittelalterlichen Theologie und Philosophie, N. F. 29. Paderborn, Wien, Zürich: Ferdinand Schöningh, 1979. 382.

*Mathon, G., *Bulletin de Théologie Ancienne et Médiévale*, 13(1984): 675-676.*
*Pinckaers, S., *Freiburger Zeitschrift für Philosophie und Theologie*, 474-481.*

553 Bujo, Bénézet. *Die Begründung Des Sittlichen: Zur Frage Des Eudämonismus bei Thomas von Aquin*. Münchener Universitätschriften, Veröffentlichungen Des Grabmann-Institutes Zur Erforschung der Mittelalterlichen Theologie und Philosophie 33. Paderborn: F. Schöningh, 1984. 199. Katholisch-Theologische Fakultät.

554 Chenu, Marie-Dominique. *Thomas von Aquin in Selbstzeugnissen U. Bilddokumenten Aus D. Fraz*. Trans. Otto M. Pesch. Rowohlts Monographien 45. Hamburg: Rowohlt, 1981. 181.

555 Chenu, Marie-Dominique. *Das Werk Des Hl. Thomas von Aquin*. Trans. Otto H. Pesch. Graz-Wien-Köln: Styria, 1982. 452.

556 Cubells, S. C. *Die Anthropologie Des Suarez: Beiträge Zur Spanischen Anthropologie Des XVI. und XVII. Jahrhunderts*. Freiburg: Alber, 1982. 207.

557 Darms, Gion. *Symbolik: Die Rolle Des Symbolhaften Nach Thomas von Aquin*. Schwyz: Albertus Magnus-Verlag, 1987. 44.

558 De Vries, Josef. *Grundbegriffe der Scholastik*. Darmstadt: Wissenschaft, 1980. 120.

559 De Wohl, Louis. *Licht Über Aquino. Thomas von Aquin*. Freiburg: Walter-Verlag, 1978. 367.

560 Dierkes, Hans, ed. *Philosophische Anthropologie Arbeitstexte Für Den Unterricht.* Ditzingen: Reclam, 1989. 168.

561 Domanyi, Thomas. *Der Römerbriefkommentar Des Thomas von Aquin: Ein Beitrag Zur Untersuchung Seiner Auslegungsmethoden.* Basler und Berner Studien Zur Historischen und Systematischen Theologie 39. Bern: P. Lang, 1979. 285.

562 Elders, Léon J. *Die Metaphysik Des Thomas von Aquin in Historischer Perspeketive, I: Das Ens Commune.* Trans. Klaus Hedwig. Studien Zur Philosophie 16. Salzburg, München: Verlag Anton Pustet, 1985. 256.

*Contat, A., *Doctor Communis*, 39(1986): 184-201.*
*Hissette, R., *Archiv für Geschichte der Philosophie*, 69(1987): 113-114.*
*Owens, Joseph, *The Thomist*, 50(1986): 463-465.*

563 Elders, Léon J. *Die Metaphysik Des Thomas von Aquin in Historischer Perspeketive II.* Salzburger Studien Zur Philosophie 17. Salzburg-München: Universitätsverlag Anton Pustet, 1987. 331.

*Owens, Joseph, *The Thomist*, 53(1989): 337-339.*
*Schmitz, R. M., *Doctor Communis*, 41(1988): 294-296.*

564 Elders, Léon J. *De Filosofische Godsleer Van St. Thomas Van Aquino.* Brugge: Tabor, 1987. In German Trans.. 505.

565 Fiasch, K. *Das Philosophische Denken Im Mittelalter: Von Augustin Zu Machiavelli.* Stuttgart: Reclam, 1986. 220.

566 Fleischmann-Kessler, Eva. *Funktion und Bedeutung der Himmelskoerper in der Theologica Des Thomas von Aquin.* Zürich: ADAG Administration und Druck AG, 1983. 198.

*Anon., *Rassegna di Letteratura Tomistica*, 20(1987): 421-422.*

567 Grabmann, Martin. *Gesammelte Akademieabhandlungen.* Veröffentlichungen Des Grabmann-Institutes, Neue Folge 25. 2. Paderborn: Ferdinand Schöningh, 1979. xxxii-2220.

*Van Steenberghen, Fernand, *Revue Philosophique de Louvain*, 78(1980): 294-296.*

568 Grabmann, Martin. *Die Geschichte der Scholastischen Method, Bd II: Die Scholastische Method Im 12. und Beginnenden 13. Jahrhundert.* 1911. Berlin: Akademie-Verl., 1988. xiii-586. A French Trans. by Mercurio Candela and Paola Buscaglione Candela: *Storia del metodo scolastico condotta su fonti edite e inedite.* Vol. I: Il metodo scolastico dai suoi primi inizi nella letteratura patristica fino al principio del secolo XII. Vol. II: Il metodo scolastico nel XII e all'inizio del XIII secolo (Il pensiero filosofico, 15, 1-2): Firenze: La Nuova Italia Editrice, 1980, pp. 408 and 692.

569 Günzler, C. et al. *Perfectio Omnium Perfectionum: Studien Zur Seinskonzeption bei Thomas von Aquin und Hegel.* Libreria Editrice Vaticana: Città del Vaticano, 1984. 208.

570 Häring, H., and K. -J. Kuschel, eds. *Gegenentwürfe: 24 Lebensläufe Für eine Andere Theologie.* München: Piper, 1988. 378.

571 Hartmann, Otto Julius. *Angst, ein Krankheitssymptom Unserer Zeit. Gedächtnis und Erinnerung: Garanten Unserer Pérsonalität. Das Mysterium Des Seins bei Thomas von Aquino: D. Mensch Zwischen Theologie und Physik. Antworten auf aktuelle Lebensfragen, von Julius Hartmann* 7(1979) Freiburg: Verlag die Kommenden. 61.

572 Höhler, Gertrude. *Das Glück: Analyse einer Sehnsucht*. Düsseldorf: Verlag Herder, 1981.

573 Honnefelder, Ludger. *Ens Inquantum Ens: Der Begriff Des Seienden Als Solchen Als Gegenstand der Metaphysikcnach der Lehre Des Johannes Duns Scotus*. Beiträge Zur Geschichte der Philosophie und Theologie Des Mittelalters. Neue Folge 16. Münster: Aschendorff, 1979. xii-468.

*Hartmann, N., *Wissenschaft und Weisheit*, 43(1980): 72-76.*
*Manzano, I., *Antonianum*, 55(1980): 533-535.*

574 Jauss, Hans R. *Alterität und Modernität in der Mittelalterlichen Literatur: Gesammelte Aufsätze 1956-1976*. München: Verlag Herder, 1977.

*Aertsen, J. A., *Vivarium*, 24(1986): 143-157.*
*Albert, K., *Philosophischer Literaturanzeiger*, 37(1984): 203-204.*
*Hissette, R., *Bulletin de Théologie Ancienne et Médiévale*, 13(1985): 849-850.*
*Lobato, A., *Angelicum* 61(1984): 196-197.*
*Owens, Joseph, *The Review of Metaphysics*, 38(1984) 129-130.*
*Pattin, A., *Tijdschrift voor Filosofie*, 45(1983): 307-308.*
*Wielockx, Robert, *Revue Philosophique de Louvain*, 82(1984): 280-283.*

575 Kim, Jung-Hi. *Caritas bei Thomas von Aquin Im Blick auf Den Konfuzianischen Zentralbegriff Jen*. Regensburger Studien Zur Theologie 25. Frankfurt: Peter D. Lang, 1981. viii-360.

576 Kleber, Hermann. *Glück Als Lebensziel: Untersuchungen Zur Philosophie Des Glücks bei Thomas von Aquin*. Beiträge Zur Geschichte der Philosophie und Theologie Des Mittelalters, Neue Folge 31. Münster: Aschendorff, 1988. 328.

577 Klünker, Wolf-Ulrich, ed. *Thomas von Aquin: Über die Einheit Des Geistes*. Stuttgart: Freies Geistesleben, 1987.

*Cheneval, Francis, *Freiburger Zeitschrift für Philosophie und Theologie*, 36(1989): 199-204.*

578 Klünker, Wolf-Ulrich. *Menschliche Seele und Kosmischer Geist. Siger von Brabant in der Ausinandersetzung mit Thomas von Aquin*. Beiträge Zur Bewusstseinsgeschichte 3. Stuttgart: Verl. Freies Geistesleben, 1988. 140.

579 Kluxen, Wolfgang. *Philosophische Ethik bei Thomas von Aquin*. Walberberger Studien der Albertus-Magnus. Akademie Philosophische Reihe 2. Hamburg: Felix Meiner Verlag, 1980. xlv-264.

*Abbà, G., *Salesianum*, 43(1981): 926-927.*
*Elders, L. J., *The Review of Metaphysics*, 36(1982-1983): 456-457.*
*Elders, L. J., *Rassegna di Letteratura Tomistica*, 16(1980): 191-193.*
*Korff, W., *Philosophical Journal*, 89(1982): 411-423.*
*Solignac, A., *Aporia*, 45(1982): 684-685.*

580 Korff, Wilhelm. *Norm und Sittlichkeit: Untersuchungen Zur Logik der Normativen Vernuft. 2. Grundlagenanalyse Des Normproblems. Der Gründungszusammenhang Des Normativen Nach Thomas von Aquin*. Freiburg-München: Alber, 1985. 216.

581 Koslowski, Peter, ed. *Gnosis und Mystik in der Geschichte der Philosophie*. Zürick: Artemis Verlag, 1988. 408.

*Stephenson, Günther, *Philosophischer Literaturanzeiger*, 43(1990): 41-46.*

582 Kreiml, J. *Zwei Auffassungen Des Ethischen bei Heidegger: Ein Vergleich von Sein und Zeit*. Philosophie und Theologie 2. Regenburg: Roderer, 1987. 179.

583 Kühn, Wilfried. *Das Prinzipienproblem in der Philosophie Des Thomas von Aquin*. Bochumer Studien Zur Philosophie 1. Amsterdam: Verlag B. R. Grüner, 1982. xxxviii-531.

584 Lakebrink, Bernhard. *Perfectio Omnium Perfectionum: Studien Zur Seinskonzeption bei Thomas von Aquin und Hegel*. Ed. C. Günzler et al. Studi Tomistici 24. Città del Vaticano: Pontificia Accademia di S. Tommaso e di Religione Cattolica, 1984. 206.

*Anon., *Rassegna di Letteratura Tomistica*, 20(1987): 164-166.*

585 Lantz, Göran. *Eigentumsrecht, ein Recht oder ein Unrecht? Eine Kritische Beurteilung der Ethischen Argumente Für das Privateigentum bei Aristoteles, Thomas von Aquino, Grotius, Locke, Hegel, Marx und in Den Modernen Katholischen Sozialenzykliken*. Uppsala Studies in Social Ethics 4. Uppsala, Stockholom: Almqvistoch Wiksell Internat. [in Komm.], 1977. 154.

586 Lutz-Bachmann, Matthias, ed. *Ontologie und Theologie: Beiträge Zum Problem der Metaphysik bei Aristoteles und Thomas von Aquin. Europäische Hochschulschriften, Reihe 23, Theologie, 331*. Frankfurt/New York: Bern/Lang, 1988. 109.

587 Meier, B. *Die Lehre Des Thomas von Aquino de Passionibus Animae in Quellenanalytischer Darstellung*. Vol. 11. Librairie des Arts et métiers. xv-160.

588 Merks, Karl-Wihelm. *Theologische Grundlegung der Sittlichen Autonomie: Strukturmomente Eines Autonomen Normbegründungsverständnisses Im Lex-Traktat der Theologiea Des Thomas von Aquin*. Düsseldorf: Patmos, 1978. 364.

589 Michel, Elsabeth. *Nullus Potest Amare Aliquid Incognitum: Ein Beitrag Zur Frage Des Intellektualismus bei Thomas von Aquin*. Studi Friburgensia: Neue Folge 57. Freiburg: Universitätsverlag, 1979. iv-190.

590 Michelitsch, Antonius. *Kommentatoren Zur Summa Theologiae Des Hl. Thomas von Aquin*. 1924. Hildesheim: Georg Olms, 1981. xii-203.

591 Mostert, Wilhelm. *Menschwerdung: Eine Historische und Dogmatische Untersuchung Über das Motiv der Inkarnation Des Gottessohnes bei Thomas von Aquin*. Tübingen: Möhr, 1978. vi-189.

592 Müller, Klaus. *Thomas von Aquins Theorie und Praxis der Analogie: Der Streit Um das Rechte Vorurteil und die Analyse einer Aufschlussreichen Diskrepanz in der Theologiae*. Regensburger Studien Zur Theologie 29. Bern: Lang, 1983. 368.

*Anon., *Rassegna di Letteratura Tomistica*, 19(1983): 178-181.*
*Vansteenkiste, C., *Angelicum*, 62(1985): 121-126.*

593 Müller, Max. *Sein und Geist. Systemat. Unters. Über Grundproblem U. Aufbau Mittelaltere*. Ontologie 2. Freiburg: Alber, 1981. viii-245.

594 Mundhenk, Johannes. *Die Seele Im System Des Thomas von Aquin: Ein Beitrag Zur Klärung und Beurteilung der Grundbegriffe der Thomistischen Psychologie*. 1934. Hamburg: Felix Meiner Verlag, 1980. xi-284.

*Anon., *Rassengna di Letteratura Tomistica*, 16(1983): 152-155.*
*Albert, K., *Philosophischer Literaturanzeiger*, 37(1984): 201-202.*
*Senner, W., *Bulletin de Théologie Ancienne et Médiévale* 13(1982): 304-305.*

595 Naab, E. *Zur Begründung der Analogia Entis bei Erich Przywara*. Eichst. Beitr. 21. Regensburg: Pustet, 1987. 140.

596 Nwigwe, Boniface Enyeribe. *Die Lehre von der Göttlichen Vorsehung und Menschlichen Freiheit bei Thomas von Aquin und Ihre Zeitlogisch Kritik Durch A. N. Prior and P. T. Geach*. Münster: Verlag Peter Lawg, 1985. 259.

597 Oeing-Hahnhoff, Ludger. *Ens et Unum Convertuntur: Stellung und Gehalt Des Grundsatzes in der Philosophie Des Hl. Thomas von Aquin*. Nogent Le Roi: Librairie des Arts et Métiers Ed.s. xv-194.

598 Oemüller, W., R. Doelle-Oemüller, and C. -F. Geyer, eds. *Philosophische Arbeitsbücher 6: Diskurs, Metaphysik*. Paderborn: Schöningh, 1983.

599 Papadis, Dimitrios. *Die Rezeption der Nikomachischen Ethik Des Aristoteles bei Thomas von Aquin: Eine Vergleichende Untersuchung*. Frankfurt: R. G. Fischer, 1980. v-184.

600 Pesch, Otto Hermann. *Kommentar Zu Summa Theologiae II/qq. 90-105*. Beiträge Zur Geschichte der Philosophie und Theologie Des Mittelalters 20. Heidelberg: Graz, 1977.

601 Pesch, Otto Hermann. *Thomas von Aquin. Grenze und Grösse Mittelalterlicher Theologie: Eine Einf.* Mainz: Matthias-Grünewald-Verl., 1988. 452.

*McCool, Gerald, *Theological Studies*, 50(1989): 796-798.*

*Torrell, Jean-Pierre, *Freiburger Zeitschrift für Philosophie und Theologie*, 36(1989): 493-498.*

602 Pieper, Josef. *Scholastik: Gestalten und Probleme der Mittelalterlichen Philosophie 1*. Philosophie 4303. München: Deutscher Taschenbuch-Verlag, 1978. 156.

*Anon., *Rassegna di Letteratura Tomistica*, 14(1978): 109-112.*

603 Pieper, Josef. *Scholastik: Gestalten und Probleme der Mittelalterlichen Philosophie 2*. München: Kösel, 1978. 253.

604 Pieper, Josef. *Thomas von Aquin. Leben und Werk 3*. München: Kösel-Verlag, 1984. 245.

605 Pöltner, Günther, ed. *Schönheit: Eine Untersuchung Zum Ursprung Des Denkens bei Thomas von Aquin 1978*. Especially "Die Repräsentation Als Grundlage Analogen Sprechens von Gott Im Denken Des Thomas von Aquin." *Salzburger Jahrbuch für Philosophie* 21-22(1976-1977): 23-43. Wien, Freiburg: Herder, 1978. 214.

*Anon., *Rassegna di Letteratura Tomistica*, 14(1978): 180-185.*

*Czapiewski, W., *Salzburger Jahrbuch für Philosophie*, 23-24(1978-1979): 330-334.*

*Hissette, R., *Bulletin de Théologie Ancienne et Médiévale*, 13(1981): 131-132.*

*Marmiroli, E., *Theologie und Philosophie*, 57(1982): 439-440.*

*Scherer, Georg, *Zeitschrift für Philosophische Forschung*, 34(1980): 686-689.*

*Wucherer-Huldenfeld, A. K., *Philosophisches Jahrbuch*, 87: 421-423.*

606 Rhonheimer, Martin. *Natur Als Grundlage der Moral: D. Personale Struktur Des Naturgesetzes bei Thomas von Aquin: Eine Auseinandersetzung mit Autonomer und Teleologischer Ethik*. Innsbruck: Tyrolia-Verlag, 1987. 443.

607 Rohls, Jan. *Wilhelm von Auvergne und der Mittelalterliche Aristotelismus: Gottesbegriff und Aristotelische Philosophie Zwischen Augustin und Thomas von Aquin*. Münchener Monographien Zur Historischen und Systematischen Theologie 5. München: Kaiser, 1980. 226.

608 Rolfes, Eugen, trans. *Thomas von Aquin: Fünf Fragen Über die Intellektuelle Erkenntnis, Summa Theologiae I, 84-88*. Hamburg: Meiner, 1977. xiv-126.

609 Sapaemann, R., ed. *Ethik-Lesebuch: Von Platon Bis Heute*. München: Piper, 1987. 450.

610 Sarnowsky, Jürgen. *Die Aristotelisch-Scholastische Theorie der Bewegung: Studien Zum Kommentar Alberts von Sachsen Zur Physik Des Aristoteles*. Beiträge Zur Geschichte der Philosophie und Theologie Des Mittelalters 32. Münster: Aschendorffsche Verlagsbuchhandlung Gmbh & Co., 1989. 501.

611 Schachten, Winfried H. J. *Ordo Salutis: Das Gesetz Als Weise der Heilsvermittlung: Zur Kritik Des Hl. Thomas von Aquin an Joachim von Fiore*. Beiträge Zur Geschichte der Philosophie und Theologie Des Mittelalters 20. Münster: Aschendorff, 1980. viii-234.

612 Schaeffler, Richard. *Fähigkeit Zum Glück*. Theologische Meditationen 46. Zürich, 1977.

613 Schenk, R. *Die Gnade Vollendeter Endlichhkeit: Zur Transzendentaltheologischen Auslegung der Thomanischen Anthropologie*. Freiburger Theologische Studien 135. Freiburg: Herder, 1989. 638.

614 Schmidl, Wolfgang. *Homo Discens: Studien Zur Pädagogischen Anthropologie bei Thomas von Aquin*. österreichische Akademie der Wissenschaften: Philosophisch-Historische Klasse, Sitzungsberichte, 487. Wien: Verlag der österreichischen Akademie der Wissenschaften, 1987. 210.

*Aertsen, Jan A., *Speculum*, 65(1990): 231-232.*
*Fuchs, M., *Theologie und Philosophie*, 66(1991): 261-266.*
*McClement, C., *Revue Philosophique de Louvain*, 88(1990): 441-443.*

615 Schmitz, Rudolph B. *Sein-Wahrheit-Wort: Thomas von Aquin und Die. Lehre von der Wahrheit der Dinge*. Philosophie 1. Münster: Lit Verlag, 1984. 656.

*Elders, L., *Divus Thomas*, 89-90(1988): 479-480.*

616 Schneider, G. *Glück—was ist Das? Traum und Wirklichkeit*. München: Piper, 1978.

617 Schockenhoff, Eberhard. *Bonum Hominis: Die Anthropologischen und Theologischen Grundlagen der Tugendethik Des Thomas von Aquin*. Tübinger Theologische Studien 28. Mainz: Matthias-Grünewald-Verlag, 1987. 613.

*Lippens, Elisabeth, *Tijdschrift voor Filosofie*, 2(1990): 540-541.*
*Pinckaers, Servais, *Revue Thomiste*, 89(1989): 118-125.*
*Schuster, J., *Theologie und Philosophie*, 66(1991): 266-269.*

618 Schönberger, Rolf. *Nomina Divina: Zur Theologie Semantik bei Thomas von Aquin*. Philosophie 72. Frankfurt: Lang, 1981.

619 Schönberger, Rolf. *Die Transformation Des Klassischen Seinsbegriffs Im Mittelalter*. Berlin: Walter de Gruyter, 1986.

620 Schulze, Werner. *Zahl, Proportion, Analogie: Ein Untersuchung Zur Metaphysik und Wissenschaftshaltung Des Nikolaus von Kues VII*. Eds. E. Meuthen and Joseph Stallmach. Münster: Aschendorff, 1978. xiv-157.

621 Schütz, Ludwig. *Thomas-Lexikon*. Stuttgart-Bad Cannstatt: Frommann-Holzboog, 1983. x-889.

622 Siewerth, Gustav. *Gesammelte Werke Bd II: Der Thomismus Als Identitätssystem*. Eds. von Wolfgang Behler and Alma von Stockhausen. Düsseldorf: Patmos-Verlag, 1979. 372.

623 Siewerth, Gustav. *Gesammelte Werke: Bd IV: Das Schicksal der Metaphysik von Thomas Zu Heidegger*. Ed. von Wolfgang Behler and Alma von Stockhausen. Düsseldorf: Patmos-Verlag, 1987.

624 Speck, Josef, ed. *Grundprobleme der Grossen Philosophen*. UTB Für Wissenschaft: Uni-Taschenbücher 146. Göttingen: Vandenhoeck und Ruprecht, 1983. 261.

625 Stachowiak, H., ed. *Pragmatisches Denken von Den Ursprüngen Bis Zum 18 Jahrhundert*. Trans. C. Baldus. Hamburg: Meiner, 1986. 1-578.

626 Steiner, Rudolf. *Die Philosophie Des Thomas von Aquino*. Taschenbuchausg. Dornach/ Schweiz: Rudolf-Steiner-Verlag, 1984. 125.

627 Stroick, Clemens, ed. *Ein Anonymer Kommentar Zum Opusculum De Ente et Essentia Des Thomas von Aquino*. Studia Friburgensia Neue Folge 65. Fribourg, Switzerland: Universitätsverlag, 1985. 254.

*Hissette, Roland, *Revue Philosophique de Louvain*, 83(1985): 304-305.*
*Wielockx, R., *Scriptorium*, 40(1986): 164.*

628 Teuwsen, Rudolf. *Familienähnlichkeit und Analogie: Zur Semantik Genereller Termini bei Wittgenstein und Thomas von Aquin*. Symposion 84. Freiburg: Karl Alber, 1988. 234.

*Bharati, Agehananda, *Philosophischer Literaturanzeiger*, 43(1990): 138-142.*

629 Van Groenewoud, A. J. H. *Kunst en Schoonheid Volgens de Beginselen Van de Thomistische Filosofie*. Amsterdam: Goor, 1986.

630 Van Steenberghen, Fernand. *Die Philosophie Im XIII. Jahrhundert*. Trans. Raynald Wagner. München: F. Schöningh, 1977. 579.

631 Virt, Gübter. *Epikie: Verantwortlicher Umgang mit Normen: Eine Historisch-systematische Untersuchung Zu Aristoteles, Thomas von Aquin und Franz Suarez*. Tübinger Theologische Studien 21. Mainz: Matthias-Grünewald-Verlag, 1983. 299.

632 Wagner, M. *Die Philosophischen Implikate der Quarta Via: Eine Untersuchung Zum Vierten Gottesbeweis bei Thomas von Aquin (S. Th., I, 2, 3 (c)*. Studium Zur Problemgeschichte der Antiken und Mittelalterlichen Philosophie 12. Leiden: E. J. Brill, 1989. xviii-146.

633 Waibl, Elmar. *Ökonomie und Ethik: Die Kapitalismusdebatte in der Philosophie der Neuzeit*. Stuttgart: Fromann, 1984. 390.

634 Weber, Ludwig. *Theologie Als Meditation Unter Verwendung Des Heideggerschen Denkens: Mit einem Exkurs Über das Sein bei Thomas und bei Heidegger*. Reihe Philosophie 4. Pfaffenweiler: Centaurus-Verlagsgesllschaft, 1985. vii-136.

635 Weisheipl, James. *Thomas von Aquin: Sein Leben und Seine Theologie*. Trans. Gregor Kirstein. Graz-Wien-Köln: Styria, 1980. 391.

636 Welp, Dorothée. *Willensfreiheit bei Thomas von Aquin: Versuch einer Interpretation.* Studia Friburgensia 58. Freiburg (Schweiz): Universitätsverlag, 1979. 247.

*Anon. , *Rassenga di Letteratura Tomistica*, 15(1979): 159-160.*
*Caroti, S., *Memorie Domenicane*, 11(1980): 654-655.*
*Fetz, R. L., *Studia Philosophica* 39(1980): 229-231.*
*Igartua, J. M., *Pensamiento*, 37(1981): 370-372.*

637 Welte, Bernard. *Uber das Böse: Eine Thomistische Untersuchung*. Ed. Bernhard Casper. Freiburg: Herder, 1986. 54.

638 Wieland, Georg. *Ethica—Scientia Practica: Die Anfänge der Philosophischen Ethik Im 13 Jahrhundert.* Beiträge Zur Geschichte der Philosophie und Theologie Des Mittelalters 21. Münster: Aschendorff, 1981.

639 Wipfler, Heinz. *Grundfragen der Trinitätsspekulation: Die Analogiefrage in der Trinitätstheologie.* Regensburg: Habbel, 1977. 222.

640 Wulf, Berthold. *Thomas von Aquin: Doctor Angelicus.* Stuttgart: Verlag Freies Geistesleben, 1982. 101. Korrigierter Nachdr. d. Ausg: *Doctor Angelicus*, Ahrweiler, 1964.

641 Zimmermann, Albert, ed. *Studien Zur Mittelalterlichen Geistesgeschichte und Ihren Quellen.* Miscellanea Mediaevalia 15. Berlin: Walter de Gruyter, 1982. viii-318.

642 Zimmermann, Albert, and Clemens Kopp, eds. *Thomas von Aquin: Werk und Wirkung Im Licht Neuerer Forschungen.* Miscellanea Mediaevalia 19. Berlin: Walter de Gruyter, 1988. xi-507.

*Jolivet, J., *Revue Philosophique de la France et del'étranger*, 114(1989): 390-391.*
*Schenk, Richard, *The Thomist*, 54(1990): 376-379.*
*Wielockx, R., *Bulletin de Théologie Ancienne et Médiévale*, 14(1989): 730-745.*

D. ITALIAN

643 Abbà, Giuseppe. *Lex et Virtus: Studi Sull'evoluzione Della Dottrina Morale Di San Tommaso D'Aquino.* Biblioteca Di Scienze Religiose 56. Roma: Libreria Ateneo Salesiano, 1983. 293.

*Anon., *Rassegna di Letteratura Tomistica*, 19(1983): 247-256.*
*Elders, L., *Revue Théologique de Louvain*, 16(1985): 242-243.*
*Étienne, Jacques, *Ephemerides Theologicae Lovanienses*, 60(1984): 426-427.*
*Flecha, J. R., *Salmanticensis*, 23(1985): 128-130.*
*Lazcano, R., *Revista Agustiniana*, 26(1985): 500-501.*
*Mathon, G., *Bulletin de Théolgoie Ancienne et Médiéval*, 13(1985): 853-855.*
*Rivera, E., *Naturaleza y Gracia*, 31(1984): 214-215.*
*Silva, C. Ferreira, *Salesianum* 46(1984): 151-152.*
*Toubeau, A., *Nouvelle Revue Théologique* 106(1984): 598-599.*

644 Allegro, Calogero. *Il Metodo e Il Pensiero Di San Tommaso D'Aquino.* Roma: Città Nuova, 1978. 231.

*Anon., *Rassegna di Letteratura Tomistica*, 14(1978): 50-53.*

645 Ambrosetti, Giovanni. *Diritto Naturale Cristaino. Profili Di Metodo, Di Storia e Di Teoria.* 2nd ed. Milano: Giuffré, 1985. 340.

*Pizzorni, R. M., *Divus Thomas*, 88(1985): 175-177.*

646 Bagnulo, Roberto. *Il Concetto Di Diritto Naturale in San Tommaso D'Aquino*. Milano: Ed. Giuffré, 1983. xiii-232.

*Composta, D., *Doctor Communis*, 37(1984): 184-185.*
*Mangiagalli, M., *Rivista di Filosofia*, 76(1984): 651-655.*

647 Balthasar, Hans Urs von. *Gloria: Una Estetica Teologica*. Trans. M. Fiorillo. Milano: Jaca Book, 1978. 334.

648 Battaglia, Felice. *Thomasio Filosofo e Giurista*. Unknown: Clueb, 1982.

*Cesareo, Rosa, *Filosofia*, 34(1983): 190-192.*
*Faralli, C., *Rivista Internazionale di Filosofia del Diritto*, 60(1983): 488-492.*

649 Bednarski, Felice Adalberto. *L'educazione Dell'affettività Alla Luce Della Psicologia Di S. Tommaso D'Aquino*. Milano: Massimo, 1986. 207.

*Di Marco, Nazareno, *Aquinas*, 29(1986): 395-398.*

650 Bergomo, Petrus A. *Concordantiae Textuum Discordantium Divi Thomae Aquinatis*. Trans. Innocentius Colosio. Firenze: Libreria Editrice Fiorentina, 1982. vi-555.

*Rábanos, J. M. Soto, *Revista Espanola de Teologia*, 43(1983): 536-537.*

651 Bernardi, Brenno. *Studio Sul Significato Di Esse, Forma, Essentia Nel Primo Libro Dello Scriptum in Libros Sententiarum Di San Tommaso D'Aquino*. Philosophie 148. Berne/New York: Peter Lang, 1984. 344.

*Alarcón, E., *Anuario Filosófico*, 21(1988): 187-188.*

652 Berti, E., and Giuseppe Casetta, eds. *Origini e Sviluppi Dell'analogia: Da Parmenide a S. Tommaso*. Settimane Filosofiche Di Vallombrosa 1. Roma: Edizioni Vallombrosa, 1987. 178.

653 Bianchi, Luca. *L'errore Di Aristotle: La Polemica Contro L'eternità del Mondo Nel XIII Secolo*. Pubblicazioni D. Facoltà Di Lettere e Filosofia D. Università Di Milano 104. Florence: La Nuova Italia, 1984. xviii-210.

654 Bianchi, Luca. *Il Vescovoei Filosofi: La Condanna Parigina del 1277 e L'evoluzione Dell'Aristotelismo Scolastico*. Quodlibet 6. Bergamo: Pierluigi Lubrina, 1990.

655 Bianchi, Luca, and Eugenio Randi. *Le Verità Dissonanti: Aristotele Alla Fine del Medioevo*. Biblioteca Di Cultura Moderna 991. Roma: Laterza, 1990.

656 Biffi, Inos. *La Teologia e Un Teologo: San Tommaso D'Aquino*. Casale Monferrato: Marietti, 1984. 121.

657 Blandino, Giovanni. *Discussioni Sul Neo-tomisimo: Per Il Progresso Della Filosofia Cristiana*. Vatican City: Pontifical U. Lateranense, 1990.

658 Bogliolo, Don Luigi. *Come si Fa Filosofia*. Genova: Quadrivium, 1980. 124.

*Cartechini, Sisto, *Doctor Communis*, 35(1982): 379-387.*

659 Bogliolo, Don Luigi. *Essere e Conoscere*. Studi Tomistici 21. Città del Vaticano, Pontificia Accademia di S. Tommaso: Libreria Editrice Vaticana, 1983. 350.

*Antoniotti, L. -M., *Revue Thomiste*, 90(1990): 295-298.*
*Cardoletti, P., *La Civiltà Cattolica*, 135(1984): 95-96.*
*Radice, G., *Aquinas*, 26(1983): 283-288.*
*Rolandetti, Vittorio, *Doctor Communis*, 37(1984): 87-88.*
*Van Steenberghen, F., *Revue Philosophique de Louvain*, 83(1985): 115-116.*

660 Bogliolo, Luigi. *Metafisica e Teologia Razionale*. S. Urbaniana 7. Roma: Urbaniana University Press, 1983. 342.

661 Bondolfi, Alberto. *Pena e Pena Di Morte*. Temi Etici Nella Storia 2. Bologna: Ed. Dehoniane, 1985. 303.

662 Borgiae, Francesco. *Praecipiae Divi Thomae Aquinatis Materiae in Litaniarum Rationem Redactae*. Ed. B. De Margerie. Studi Tomistici 22. Città del Vaticano, Pontifica Accademia di San Tommaso: Libreria Editrice Vaticana, 1983. 93.

663 Borresen, Kari Elisabeth. *Natura e Ruolo Della Donna in Agostino e Tommaso D'Aquino*. Teologia Attraverso. Assisi: Citadella, 1979. 327.

664 Briguglia, Alfio, Giuseppe Savagnone, and Francesco Viola. *La Vita Nella Verità Secondo San Tommaso D'Aquino*. Palermo: Centro di Formazione Cristiana, 1979. xii-187.

*Cavadi, A., *Sapienza*, 33(1980): 240-242.*

665 Brocchieri, Mt. Fumagalli Beonio, and M. Parodi. *Storia Della Filosofia Medievale: Da Boezio a Wyclif*. Roma: Editori Laterza & Figli Bari, 1989. xix-500.

666 Buscaroli, Silvano. *Appunti Per Una Storia Dell'ascesi: Duns Scoto, Bonaventura, Valla, Tommaso, Nietzsche, Schopenhauer, Heidegger, Gentile, Carabellese*. Argomenti 1. Bologna: G. Barghigiani, 1979. 149.

667 Buttiglione, Rocco. *Il Pensiero Di Karol Wojtyla*. Milano: Jaca Book, 1982.

*Tripoli, G., *Rivista Internazionale di Filosofia del Diritto*, 60(1983): 493-494.*

668 Buttiglione, Rocco. *Metafisica Della Cognoscenza e Politica in S. Tommaso D'Aquino*. Bologna: Centro Studi Europa Orientale, 1985.

669 Cambilargiu, Vittoria. *Attualità Di San Tommaso D'Aquino—esistenza e Fede*. Università Di Sassari, Memorie del Seminario Di Storia Della Filosofia Della Facoltà Di Magistero 9. Sassari, Istituto di Filosofia: Ed. Ballizzi, 1978. 35.

*Anon., *Rassengna di Letteratura Tomistica*, 14(1978): 113-114.*

670 Campodonico, Angelo. *Alla Scoperta Dell'essere: Saggio Sul Pensiero Di Tommaso D'Aquino*. Filosofia 16. Milano: Ed.iale Jaca Book, 1986. 208.

*Anon., *Rassegna di Letteratura Tomistica*, 22(1986): 142-145.*

*Contat, Alain, *Doctor Communis*, 40(1987): 301-304.*

*Paggi, C., *Aquinas*, 31(1988): 424-425.*

*The book is concerned with Aquinas' metaphysics of creation, particularly with immediacy of God's immanence permanently pervades the universe because He is being, *esse*, i.e., the cause of created things, and Spirit. The difference that exists in creatures between *esse* and *essentia* and the hierarchical participation of immediate immanence is the basis of entities value, action, and complimentarity. The last chapter is concerned with Aquinas' metaphysical experience.*

671 Caparello, Adriana. *Esegesi Aristotelico-tomista e Terminologia Greca*. Studi Tomistici 7. Roma, Pontificia Accademia di San Tommaso e di Religione Cattolica: Coletti Editore, 1979. 244.

*Anon., *Rassegna di Letteratura Tomistica*, 15(1982): 45-48.*

672 Caparello, Adriana. *La Perspectiva in Sigieri Di Brabante*. Vatican: Lib. Ed. Vaticana, 1987.

673 Carlo, Lupi. *Il Problema Della Creazione in San Tommaso*. Genova: Studio ed. di Cultura, 1979. 75.

*Petino, Cosimo, *Doctor Communis*, 36(1983): 93-94.*

674 Cecchelli, Marco, ed. *San Bonaventura e San Tommaso D'Aquino*. Cento: Il Centro studi G. Baruffaldi, 1978. 263. Atti del Convengno di studi promosso dalla Collegiata di S. Biagio nel VII centenario della morte(1274-1979).

675 Cenacchi, Giuseppe. *Il Lavoro Nel Pensiero Di Tommaso D'Aquino*. Studi Tomistici 5. Roma: Coletti Ed.e—Pontificia Accademia di San Tommaso e di Religione Cattolica, 1977. 196.

*Anon., *Rassegna di Letteratura Tomistica*, 13(1977): 215-218.*
*Miele, M., *Sapienza*, 30(1970): 363-364.*
*Ozaeta, J. M., *Ciudad de Dios*, 190(1977): 640.*
*Van Steenberghen, Fernand, *Revue Philosophique de Louvain*, 76(1978): 256-257.*
*Verecke, L., *Revue d'Histoire Ecclésiastique*, 73(1978): 698-700.*

676 Cenacchi, Giuseppe. *Antropologia Filosofica*. Saggi Filosofici 3. Cité du Vatican: Pontificia Accademia di S. Tommaso-Libreria Editrice Vaticana, 1981. 319.

*Mezzogori, Ivo, *Sapienza*, 35(1982): 367-368.*

677 Centi, Tito S. *Nel Segno del Sole: San Tommaso D'Aquino*. Roma: S. Sisto Vecchio, 1982. 164.

*Malatesta, Michele, *Sapienza*, 37(1984): 467-469.*
*Petino, Cosimo, *Doctor Communis*, 34(1984): 289.*

678 Chenu, Marie-Dominique. *San Tommaso D'Aquino e la Teologia*. Trans. Corrado Camandone. Ritorno Alle Fonti 8. Torino: P. Gribaudi, 1977. 136.

679 Chenu, Marie-Dominique. *La Teologia Come Scienza Nel XIII Secolo*. Trans. M. Spranzi and M. Vigevani. Ed. G. Colombo. Milano: Jaca Books, 1985. 180.

680 Colafrancesco, G. Battista. *L'Aquinate: Saggio Critico Sul Luogo Di Nascita*. Aquino: Ed La Voce di Aquino, 1983. 121.

*Anon., *Rassegna di Letteratura Tomistica*, 19(1983): 13-15.*

681 Colombo, Anna, trans. *Tommaso D'Aquino*. By Anthony Kenny. Milano: Dall'Oglio, 1981. 122.

682 Composta, Dário. *La Nuova Morale e I Suoi Problem: Critica Sistematica Alla Luce del Pensiero Tomistico*. Studi Tomistici 38. Roma: Pontificia Accademia di S. Tommaso, 1990. 194.

683 Corvino, Francesco, ed. *Linguistica Medieval: Anselmo D'Aosta, Abelardo, Tommaso D'Aquino, Pietro Ispano, Gentile Da Cingoli, Occam*. Bari: Ed. Adriatica, 1983. 315.

*Lunetta, L., *Studi Medievali*, 26(1985): 1027-1029.*
*Müller, P., *Rivista di Filosofia Neo-Scolastica*, 77(1985): 673-675.*

684 Costantino, Salvatore. *Filosofia Politica e Società in Jacques Maritain*. Valentia: Mapograf, 1986.

685 Cristaldi, Giuseppe. *Cristianesimo e Filosfia*. Milano: Ed. Vita e Pensiero, 1980. 282.

686 Dalledonne, Andrea. *Problematica Metafisica del Tomismo Essenziale*. Roma: Ed. Elia, 1980. 237.

687 Dalledonne, Andrea. *Implicazioni del Tomismo Originario*. Genova: Quadrivium, 1981. 141.

688 Dalledonne, Andrea. *Tomisimo Contro Sovversione*. Milano: Marzorati, 1987.

*Turco, Giovanni, *Sapienza*, 42(1989): 468-470.*

689 De Angelis, R. Padellaro. *L'influenza del Pensiero Neoplatonico Sulla Metafisica Di San Tommaso D'Aquino*. Rome: Abete, 1981. 277.

690 Di Mari, Carmelo. *San Tommaso D'Aquino Oggi*. Siracusa: Centro Studi San Tommaso d'Aquino, 1982. 135.

691 Di Mari, Carmelo. *Il Problema Critico e la Metafisica Secondo San Tommaso D'Aquino*. Siracusa: Edizioni Centro Studi San Tommaso d'Aquino, 1985. 143.

*Wilder, A., *Angelicum*, 64(1987): 182.*

692 Di Mari, Carmelo, and Giuseppe Di Mari. *Criticismo Kantiano e Filosofia Tomista*. Roma: Ciranna, 1980. 127.

693 Eco, Umberto. *Il Problema Estetico in Tommaso D'Aquino*. 2nd augmented ed. 1970. Milano: Bompiani, 1982. 272. Translated as *The Aesthetics of Thomas Aquinas*, 1988.

694 Fabriziani, Anna. *Blondel, Interprete Di Tommaso: Tra Rinascita del Tomismo e Condanna del Pensiero Modernista*. Pubblicazioni Dell'Istituto Di Storia Della Filosofia e del Centro Per Ricérche Di Filosofia Medioeval: Nuova Serie 32. Padova: Antenore, 1984. xiv-213.

695 Fabro, Cornelio. *Riflessioni Sulla Libertà*. Rimini: Maggioli Editore, 1983. xi-349.

696 Fabro, Cornelio. *Introduzione a San Tommaso: La Metafisica Tomista e Il Pensiero Moderno*. Faretra 9. Milano: Ares, 1983. Especially pp. 324-354, "Futuro del Tomismo." 390.

*Anon., *Rassegna di Letteratura Tomistica*, 19(1983): 116-122.*
*Cardoletti, P., *La Civiltà Cattolica*, 135(1984): 436-438.*
*Cardona, C., *Anuario Filosófico*, 18(1985): 208-211.*
*Composta, Dario, *Doctor Communis*, 37(1984): 283-284.*
*D'Eredità, P. L., *Schede Medievali*, 8(1985): 166-167.*
*Derisi, Octavio N., *Sapientia*, 41(1986): 145-147.*
*Fontana, S., *Studia Patavina*, 31(1984): 437-438.*
*Fontana, S., *Bollettino Filosofico*, 18(1984): 35-36.*
*Giannini, G., *Filosofia Oggi*, 8(1985): 132-134.*
*Leroy, M. -V., *Revue Thomiste*, 83(1983): 671-673.*

697 Galati, Vincenzo. *La Guerra Praticamente Impossibile: Una Lettura Di Tommaso D'Aquino (Con Appendice Sul Pacifismo Di Voltaire)*. Collana Di Studi Sul Problema Della Pace 1. Palermo: Edizioni Augustinus, 1984. 124.

698 Galeazzi, Umberto. *L'etica Filosofica in Tommaso D'Aquino. Dalla Summa Theologiae Alla Contra Gentiles: Per Una Riscoperta Dei Fondamenti Della Morale*. Roma: Città Nuova Editrice, 1989. 293.

699 Garfagnini, Gian Carlo. *Aristotelismo e Scolastica*. Filosofia 19. Turin: Loescher Ed.e, 1979. 303.

700 Gennaro Fallica, Concettina, ed. *Tractatus Beati Thomae de Aquino De Natura Universalis*. Testi e Studio Critico. Siracusa: Ed. Centro Studi *San Tommaso d'Aquino*, 1983. 116.

*Anon., *Rassegna di Letteatura Tomistica*, 19(1983): 35-38.*
*Pizzorni, R. M., *Angelicum*, 61(1984): 534.*
*Stella, P. T., *Aquinas*, 27(1984): 237-238.*

701 Gennaro Fallica, Concettina, and Giuseppe Di Mari. *Problemi Fondamentali del Tomismo*. Siracusa: Centro Studi di Tommaso d'Aquino, 1982. 152.

*Anon., *Rassegna di Letteratura Tomistica*, 189(1982): 270-274.*

702 Gherardini, Brunero. *La Conoscenza Sapienziale Di Dio in San Tommaso*. Roma: Città del Vaticano, 1980.

703 Giacon, Carlo. *Itinerario Tomistico*. Rome: La Goliardica: Editrice Universitaria di Roma, 1983. 244.

704 Giannini, Giorgio. *Tesi Di Ontologia Tomista*. Filosofia 9. Roma, Pontificia Università Lateranense: Città Nuova, 1980. 136.

*Anon., *Rassegna di Letteratura Tomistica*, 16(1980): 174-176.*
*Stefani, M., *Filosofia Oggi*, 6(1983): 113-115.*

705 Gigante, Mario. *Genesi e Struttura Dell'atto Libero in S. Tommaso (I Principii, 19)*. Napoli: Giannini Ed.e, 1980. xii-132.

*Anon., *Rassegna di Letteratura Tomistica*, 16(1980): 155-157.*
*Petino, Cosimo, *Doctor Communis*, 34(1981): 351-352.*

706 Gigante, Mario. *San Tommaso e la Storia Della Salvezza: La Polemica Con Gioacchino Da Fiore*. La Ripresa 3. Salerno: Istituto Superiore di Scienze Religiose, 1986. 382.

707 Gilson, Étienne Henry. *L'essere e L'essenza*. Scienza Umane e Filosofia. Milano: Ed. Massimo, 1988.

708 González, Angel Luis. *Filosofia Di Dio*. Filosofia e Realta. Florence: Le Monnier, 1988. viii-284.

709 Grabmann, Martin. *Storia del Metodo Scolastico*. Strumenti: Ristampe Anastatiche 59. 1-2. Florence: La Nuova Italia, 1980. xxiv-410/vi-694. Translated from the German.

710 Grabmann, Martin. *San Tommaso D'Aquino: Introduzione Alla Sua Personalità e Al Suo Pensiero*. 5th ed. Classici del Tomismo 2. Città del Vaticano: Libreria Editrice Vaticana, 1986. 136.

*Composta, Dario, *Doctor Communis*, 42(1989): 306-307.*
*Lluch-Baixauli, M., *Scripta Theologica*, 18(1986): 725-726.*
*Orlando, Pasquale, *Doctor Communis*, 40(1987): 108-109.*
*Turco, G., *Sapienza*, 41(1988): 344-346.*

711 Grabmann, Martin. *Introduzione Alla Summa Theologiae Di S. Tommaso D'Aquino*. 2nd ed. Classici del Tomismo 4. Città del Vaticano, Pontificia Accademia di S. Tommaso: Editrice Vaticana, 1989. 118.

*Pangallo, Mario, *Doctor Communis*, 43(1990): 79-82.*
*Turco, G., *Sapienza*, 41(1988): 344-346.*

712 Grabmann, Martin. *San Tommaso D'Aquino*. Città del Vaticano: Vaticana, n. d.

*Turco, Giovanni, *Sapienza*, 41(1988): 344-346.*

713 Gratsch, Edward J. *Manuale Introduttivo Alla Summa Teologica Di Tommaso D'Aquino*. Trans. Monache Benedettine di Marionasco. Piemme: La Spezia Casale Monferrato, 1988. 342.

714 Hugolini de Urbe Veteri, Oesa. *Commentarius in Quatro Libros Sententiarum I-II*. Ed. Willigis Eckermann. Cassiciacum. Suppl. 8. Würzburg: Augustinus Verlag, 1980. lxi-407.

*Anon., *Rassegna di Letteratura Tomistica*, 20(1984): 324-326.*
*Decorte, J., *Bulletin de Théologie Ancienne et Médiévale*, 14(1986): 171-173.*
*Decorte, J., *Scriptorium*, 39(1985): 146-147.*
*Kafel, S., *Collectanea Franciscana*, 55(1985): 370-371.*

715 Klein, Alessandro. *Meister Eckhart: La Dottrina Mistica Della Giústificazione. Biblioteca di Filosofia. Ricerche* 4. Milano: Mursia. 1977. 189.

716 Knowles, David. *L'evoluzione del Pensiero Medievale*. Trans. Bernardino Loschi. 1962. Bologna: Mulino, 1984. viii-478.

*Anon., *Rassegna di Letteratura Tomistica*, 20(1987): 131-134.*

717 La Spisa, Mauro. *San Tommaso e Il Pensiero Post-moderno*. Studia Pontificiae Universitatis San Thomae Aquinatis, 19. Milano: Massimo, 1983. 480.

*Anon., *Rassegna di Letteratura Tomistica*, 19(1983): 416-418.*
*Bogliolo, Luigi, *Doctor Communis*, 37(1984): 287.*
*Iammarrone, L., *Miscellanea Francescana*, 84(1984): 331-332.*

718 Lacordaire, P. Henri Dominique. *San Tommaso Il Dottore Dei Dottori*. Perennità del Tomismo: Testimonianze e Document 2. Roma, Città del Vaticano: Libreria Editrice Vaticano, 1989. 76.

719 Lonergan, Bernard. *Conoscenza e Interiorità: Il Verbum Nel Pensiero Di San Tommaso*. Trans. Natalino Spaccapelo. Nuovi Saggi Teologici 21. Bologna: Edizioni Dehoniane, 1984. 262.

*Sala, Giovanni B., *Rivista di Filosofia Neo-Scolastica*, 77(1985): 174-178.*
*Wilder, A., *Angelicum*, 63(1986): 145-148.*
*Zürich, A., *Divus Thomas*, 88(1985): 444.*

720 Lupi, Carlo. *Il Problema Della Creazione in San. Tommaso*. Filosofia Oggi 11. Genova: Studio Editoriale di Cultura, 1979. 75.

*Beuchot, M., *Revista de Filosofia*, 16(1983): 144-145.*
*Petino, Cosimo, *Doctor Communis*, 36(1983): 93-94.*

721 Malusa, Luciano. *Neotomismo e Intransigentismo Cattolico: II Contributo Di Giovanni Maria Cornoldi Per la Rinascita del Tomismo. Ricerche Di Filosofia e Di Storia Della Filosofia 3*. Milano: Istituto Propaganda Libraria, 1986. xxxii-510.

*Giannini, G., *Doctor Communis*, 40(1987): 198-201.*
*Manno, A. G., *Sapienza*, 39(1986): 473-475.*
*Nicola Curcio, Vicenza, *Philosophischer Literaturanzeiger*, 42(1989): 75-76.*
*Quintino, R., *Rivista di Filosofia Neo-Scolastica*, 78(1986): 690-691.*

722 Marengo, Gilfredo. *Trinità e Creazione: Indagine Sulla Teologia Di Tommaso D'Aquino*. Roma: Città Nuova Editrice, 1990. 197.

723 Maritain, Jacques. *I Diritti Dell'uomo e la Legge Naturale*. Milano: Vita e Pensiero, 1977. 114.

724 Maritain, Jacques. *Nove Lezioni Sulle Prime Nozioni Della Filosofia Morale*. Milan: Vita e Pensiero, 1979. 263.

*Composta, Dario, *Doctor Communis*, 36(1983): 96-97.*

725 Maritain, Jacques. *Da Bergson a Tommaso D'Aquino: Saggi Di Metafisica e Di Morale*. 1944. Milano: Vita e Pensiero, 1980. 271.

*Anon., *Rassegna di Letteratura Tomistica*, 16(1980): 403-406.*
*Amato, S., *Rivista Internazionale di Filosofia del Diritto*, 58(1981): 358-359.*
*Visconti, G., *Divus Thomas*, 87(1984): 236-246.*

726 Maritain, Jacques. *Sette Lezioni Sull'essere e Sui Primi Principi Della Ragione Speculativa*. Scienze Umane e Filosofia 10. Milano: Ed. Massimo, 1981. 284.

*Visconti, G., *Divus Thomas*, 87(1984): 246-252.*

727 Maritain, Jacques. *Nove Lezioni Sulla Legge Naturale*. Trans. Francesco Viola. Milano: Jaca Book, 1985. 202.

*Composta, Dario, *Doctor Communis*, 39(1986): 221-222.*
*Tripodi, A. M., *Filosofia Oggi*, 10(1987): 476.*

728 Maritain, Jacques. *Riflessioni Sull'intelligenza e la Sua Vita Propria*. 1924. Scienze Umane e Filosofia 23. Milano: Massimo, 1987. 279.

*Capone, Domenico, *Studia Moralia*, 26(1988): 319-321.*

729 Mazzarella, Pasquale. *Controversie Medievali: Unità e Pluralità Delle Forme*. Napoli: Giannini, 1978. 395.

*Ghisalberti, Alessandro, *Rivista de Filosofia* 71(1979): 611-614.*

730 Melchiorre, Virgilio. *Il Corpo*. 2nd ed. 1984. Brescia: La Scuola, 1988. 248.

731 Melina, Livio. *La Conoscenza Morale: Linee Di Riflessione Sul Commento Di San Tommaso All'Etica Nicomachea*. Roma: Città Nuova, 1987. 253.

732 Mondin, Battista. *L'ermeneutica Metafisica Di San Tommaso Nel Commento Alle Sentenze*. Quaderni Di Presenza Culturale 2. Caltanisetta: Edizioni del Seminario, 1977. 75.

*Maglione, G., *Asprenas*, 24(1977): 447-449.*
*Petino, Cosimo, *Divinitas*, 22(1978): 132-133.*

733 Mondin, Battista. *Antropologia Filosofica*. Roma: Pontificia University Urbaniana, 1983.

*Cavadi, Augusto, *Sapienza*, 36(1983): 487-489.*

734 Mondin, Battista. *I Valori Fondamentali*. Roma: Dino Editore, 1985. 210.

*Cennacchi, Giuseppe, *Doctor Communis*, 50(1987): 305-307.*

735 Mondin, Battista. *Il Sistema Filosofico Di Tommaso D'Aquino: Per Una Lettura Attuale Della Filosofia Tomista*. Problemi del Nostro Tempo 62. Milano: Massimo, 1985. 270.

*Anon., *Rassegna di Letteratura Tomistica*, 21(1985): 133-136.*
*De Finance, J., *Gregorianum*, 671(1986): 183-184.*

*Fontana, S., *Studia Patavina*, 32(1985): 389-390.*
*Manzanedo, M. F., *Angelicum*, 63(1986): 148-150.*
*Rigobello, A., *Per la Filosofia*, Milano, 2(1985): 81-82.*
*Roccaro, G., *Schede Medievali*, 11(1986): 398-402.*

736 Mondin, Battista. *Storia Della Filosofia Medievale*. Pontifica Universitas Urbaniana Subsidia Urbaniana 12. Roma: Pontificia Università Urbaniana, 1985. Especially pp. 296-379. 425.

*Anon., *Rassegna di Letteratura Tomistica*, 21(1985): 126-129.*
*Derisi, Octavio N., *Sapientia*, 41(1986): 78-80.*
*Derisi, Octavio N., *Doctor Communis*, 39(1986): 96-97.*
*Pizzorni, R., *Angelicum*, 63(1986): 138-140.*

737 Mondin, Battista. *Scienze Umane e Teologia*. Subsidia Urbaniana 203. Roma: Pontificia Università Urbaniana, 1988. 510.

*Lobato, Abelardo, *Doctor Communis*, 42(1989): 302-304.*

738 Musco, Alessandro. *Pensiero Medievale e Medioevo Per Differenza*. Palermo: Manfredi, 1979.

*Catechini, P. Sisto, *Doctor Communis*, 33(1980): 97-100.*

739 Musco, Alessandro, ed. *Il Concetto Di Sapientia in San Bonaventura e San Tommaso*. Biblioteca Dell'Enchiridion 1. Parma: Officina di Studi Medievale, 1983. x-95.

*Vela, Luis, *Pensamiento*, 43: 222-223.*

740 Nicolas, Marie-Jean. *Evoluzione e Cristianesimo: Da Teilhard de Chardin a San Tommaso D'Aquino*. Milano: Massimo, 1978.

741 Orosz, Ladislao Mariano. *De Sacrificio Ad Mentem S. Thomae Aquinatis*. Milano: Massimo, 1985. 191.

742 Ottonello, Pier Paolo. *L'attualità Di Rosmini*. Filosofia Oggi 5. Genova: Studio Editoriali di Cultura, 1978. 122.

*Cartechini, Sisto, *Doctor Communis*, 33(1980): 111-113.*
*Composta, Dario, *Doctor Communis*, 37(1984): 192-194.*
*Lacoste, Jean-Yves, *Revue Philosophique de Louvain*, 79(1981): 413-414.*

743 Padellaro De Angelis, Rosa. *L'influenza del Pensiero Neoplatonico Sulla Metafisica Di San Tommaso D'Aquino*. Collana Di Filosofia Antica 6. Roma: Abete, 1981. 277.

*Anon., *Rassegna di Letteratura Tomistica*, 18(1985): 422-424.*

744 Pangallo, Mario. *L'essere Come Atto Nel Tomismo Essenziale Di Cornelio Fabro*. Studi Tomistici 22. Roma: Libreria Editrice Vaticana, 1987. 168.

*Antoniotti, L. -M., *Revue Thomiste*, 90(1990): 291-295.*
*Livi, Antonio, *La Ciencia Tomista*, 41(1988): 303-305.*
*Livi, Antonio, *Doctor Communis*, 51(1988): 303-305.*
*Lobato, A., *Angelicum*, 65(1988): 629-631.*

745 Parente, Pietro. *Terapia Tomistica: Per la Problematica Modern de Leone XIII a Paolo VI*. Bibl. University Crist. 36. Roma: Ed. Logos, 1979. 176.

*Anon., *Rassegna di Letteratura Tomistica*, 15(1979): 405-407.*
*Composta, D., *Doctor Communis*, 33(1980): 91-96.*

746 Pera, Ceslao. *Le Fonti de Pensiero Di San Tommaso D'Aquino Nella Somma Teologica*. Turin: Marietti, 1979. 123.

*Spiazzi, R., *Divinitas*, 25(1981): 99-100.*

747 Percivale, Franco. *Rosmini, San Tommaso e L'Aeterni Patris*. Biblioteca Della Rivista Rosminiana 2. Stresa: Libraria Editoriale Sodalitas, 1983. 47.

*Tripodi, A. M., *Filosofia Oggi*, 8(1985): 357-358.*

748 Perotto, Lorenzo Alberto. *Stato e Giustizia Distributiva: La Dimensione Morale-politica Della Giustizia Distributiva Nel De Justitia Di San Tommaso*. Milano: Massimo, 1984. 644.

749 Petrus a Bergomo. *Concordantiae Textuum Discordantium Divi Thomae Aquinatis*. Ed. Innocentius Colosio. Firenze: Libreria Editrice Fiorentina, 1982. vi-479-555.

*Anon., *Rassegna di Letteratura Tomistica*, 18(1985): 334-335.*
*Wenin, C., *Revue Philosophique de Louvain*, 82(1984): 294-296.*

750 Piolanti, Antonio. *La Conoscenza Sapienziale Di Dio in San Tommaso Summa Theologiae II-II, Q. 45*. Lectura Aquinatis 1. Città del Vaticano: Libreria Editrice Vaticana, 1980. 47.

751 Piolanti, Antonio, ed. *Atti Dell' VIII Congresso Tomistico Internazionale I: Enciclica Aeterni Patris Nell' Arco Di Un Secolo*. Città del Vaticano: Pontificia Accademia di San Tommaso, 1981.

*O'Brien, Thomas C., *The Thomist*, 48(1984): 473-475.*

752 Piolanti, Antonio. *Il Tomismo Come Filosofia Cristiana Nel Pensiero de Leone XIII*. Studi Tomistici 20. Città del Vaticano: Pontificia Accademia di San Tommaso, 1983.

753 Pizzorni, Reginaldo. *Il Diritto Naturale Dalle Origini a San Tommaso D'Aquino: Saggio Storico-critico*. 2nd ed. Diritto 3. Roma, Pontificia Università Lateranense: Città Nuova, 1978. 522.

*Composta, Dario, *Salesianum*, 40(1978): 676-677.*
*Composta, Dario, *Divus Thomas*, 88(1985): 177-179.*
*Composta, Dario, *Doctor Communis*, 39(1986): 96-97.*
*Ferrari, V., *Angelicum*, 55(1978): 643-645.*
*Ferrari, V., *Sapienza*, 31(1978): 363-364.*

754 Pizzorni, Reginaldo. *Filosofia del Diritto*. 2nd ed. Roma: Pontificia Università Lateranense Roma, 1982. 461.

*Composta, Dario, *Doctor Communis*, 36(1983): 99-100.*
*Composta, Dario, *Divus Thomas*, 87(1984): 110-111.*
*Ferrari, V., *Angelicum*, 60(1983): 156-158.*
*Ferrari, V., *Aquinas*, 25(1982): 372-373.*
*Ferrari, V., *Sapienza*, 26(1983): 113-114.*

755 Pizzorni, Reginaldo. *Il Diritto Naturale Dalle Origini a San Tommaso D'Aquino: Saggio Storico-critico*. 2nd ed. Roma, Pontificia Università Lateranense: Città Nuova Editrice, 1985. 632.

*Bucci, Onorato, *Apollinaris*, 58(1985): 775-784.*
*Composta, D., *Divus Thomas*, 88(1985): 177-179.*
*Composta, D., *Doctor Communis*, 39(1986): 98-100.*

756 Pizzorni, Reginaldo. *Il Fondamento Etico Religioso del Diritto Secondo San Tommaso D'Aquino*. 2nd ed. Studia Universitatis S. Thomae in Urbe 30. Milano: Massimo, 1989. 288.

*Ferrari, Valentino, *Doctor Communis*, 42(1989): 202-203.*

757 Poppi, Antonino. *La Verità*. Brescia: Editrice la Scuola, 1984. 286.

*Bogliolo, Luigi, *Doctor Communis*, 39(1986): 219-220.*

758 Poppi, Antonino. *Classicità del Pensiero Medievale: Anselmo, Bonaventura, Tommaso, Duns Scoto Alla Prova Dell'élenchos*. Scienze Filosofiche 39. Milano: Vita e Pensiero, 1988. viii-191.

*Bonino, S. -T., *Revue Thomiste*, 89(1989): 340-342.*
*Elders, Léon, *Doctor Communis*, 42(1989): 94-95.*
*Jori, A., *Bollettino Filosofico*, 22(1988): 102-103.*
*Mauro, L., *Verifiche*, 18(1989): 219-220.*
*Nicola Curcio, Vicenza, *Philosophischer Literaturanzeiger*, 43(1990): 173-174. *
*Pizzorni, R., *Angelicum*, 67(1990): 147.*

759 Possenti, Vittorio. *Giorgio La Pira e Il Pensiero Di San Tommaso*. Studia Universitatis San Thomae in Urbe 20. Milano: Massimo Ed., 1983. 150.

*Composta, Dario, *Doctor Communis*, 37(1984): 288-289.*

760 Possenti, Vittorio. *Una Filosofia Per la Transizione: Metafisica, Persona e Politica in Jacques Maritain*. Milano: Massimo, 1984. 286.

*Composta, Dario, *Doctor Communis*, 38(1985): 203-205.*

761 Pulvirenti, Rosalia Azzaro. *La Rinascita del Tomismo in Sicilia Nel Sec. XIX*. Città del Vaticano: Libreria Editrice Vaticana, 1986. 151.

762 Righi, Giulio. *Studio Sulla Analogia in San Tommaso*. Pubblicazioni Dell'Istituto Di Filosofia, Facoltà Di Magistero Dell'Università Di Genova 28. Milano: Marzorati, 1981. 164.

*Anon., *Rassegna di Letteratura Tomistica*, 17(1981): 139-142.*

763 Riva, F. *L'analogia Metaforica: Una Questione Logico-metaforica Nel Tomismo*. Scienze Filosofiche 46. Milano: Vita e Pensiero, 1989. xii-204.

764 Romani, Aegidii. *Opera Omnia, III, I: Apologia*. Ed. Robert Wielockx. Firenze: Leo S. Olschki, 1985. xvi-292.

765 Romano, Carla. *Figure e Momenti del Pensiero Medievale: Gioacchino Da Fiore, Pier Giovanni Olivi, San Tommaso D'Aquino*. Salerno: Palladio Ed., 1985. 132.

766 Rosset, Vincent. *L'Index Thomisticus: Mode D'emploi*. Ed. J. P. Torrelli. Fribourg: Université de Fribourg (Suisse): 1989. 44.

*Bonino, Serge Thomas, *Revue Thomiste*, 90(1990): 333.*

767 Sainati, Vittorio. *Il Problema Della Teologia Nell'età Di San Tommaso*. Biblioteca Di Cultura Contemporanea 133. Messina-Firenze: G. D'Anna, 1977. 190.

*Tacchella, E., *Filosofia Oggi*, 1(1978): 297-299.*

768 Sánchez Sorondo, Marcelo. *Aristotele e San Tommaso: Un Confronto Nelle Nozioni Di Assoluto e Di Materia Prima*. Filosofia 2. Roma: Pontificia Universita Lateranense and Città Nuova, 1981. 100.

*Composta, Dario, *Doctor Communis*, 36(1983): 94-95.*
*Derisi, Octavio N., *Sapientia*, 37(1982): 238-239.*

769 Sanchez Sorondo, Marcelo. *Aristotele e San Tommaso*. Roma: Cità Nuova, 1981. 100.

*Anon., *Rassegna di Letteratura Tomistica*, 17(1981): 47-50.*
*Composta, Dario, *Doctor Communis*, 36(1983): 94-95.*
*Derisi, O. N., *Sapientia*, 37(1982): 238-239.*

770 Sanguineti, Juan José. *La Filosofia del Cosmo in Tommaso D'Aquino*. Ragione e Fede 5. Milan: Edizioni Ares, 1986. 264.

*Jordan, Mark D., *The Thomist*, 45(1981): 333-337.*
*Volta, S., *Journal Philosophique*, 15(1987): 260-261.*

771 Savagnone, Giuseppe. *Il Convito Della Sapienza: Il Concetto Di Sapientia Secondo San Tommaso D'Aquino*. Quaderni Di Presenza Culturale 20. Caltanissetta: Edizioni del Seminario, 1985. 110.

772 Scola, Angelo. *La Fondazione Teologica Della Legge Naturale Nello Scriptum Super Sententiis Di San Tommaso D'Aquino*. Studia Friburgensia: Neue Folge 60. Freiburg (Schweiz): Universitätsverlag, 1982. 298.

*Anon., *Rassegna di Letteratura Tomistica*, 18(1985): 251-255.*

773 Selvaggi, Filippo. *Filosofia del Mondo: Cosmologia Filosofica*. Roma: University Gregoriana Ed., 1985. 591.

774 Sertillanges, A. D. *S. Tommaso D'Aquino*. Trans. A. Piolanti. 4th ed. Classici del Tomismo 3. Rome: Ed du Vatican Pontificia accademia di San Tommaso, 1988. 122.

775 Simi Varanelli, Emma. *Tommaso e Giotto: I Fondamenti Dell'estetica Tomistica e la Renovatio Umanistica Delle Arti*. Roma: Tip. Rondoni, 1989. 115.

776 Spiazzi, Raimondo. *Tesi Politiche Di San Tommaso D'Aquino*. Palermo: Thule, 1980. 61.

*Anon., *Rassegna di Letteratura Tomistica*, 16(1980): 218-219.*

777 Staffa, Dino. *Il Tomismo E Vivo*. Perennità del Tomismo 1. Citta del Vaticano: Vaticana, 1989.

778 Stagnitta, Antonino. *L'autocoscienza: Per Una Rilettura Antropologica Di Tommaso D'Aquino*. Napoli: E. D. I. Editrice, 1979. 175.

*Corvez, M., *Revue Thomiste*, 82(1982): 165-166.*
*Sessa, D., *Sapienza*, 35(1982): 486-487.*

779 Stagnitta, Antonino. *L'antropologia in Tommaso D'Aquino: Saggio Di Ricerca Comparata Sulle Passioni e Abitudini Dell'uomo*. Napoli: E. D. I. Editrice, 1979. 142.

*Corvez, M., *Revue Thomiste*, 82(1982): 163-165.*
*Sessa, D., *Sapienza*, 35(1982): 486-487.*

780 Stella, P. T. *Videmus Ad Sensum a Superioribua Nubium Imbres Effluere (Principium: Rigans Montes). La Prolusione Di Tommaso D'Aquino e Il Suo Contesto*. Inculturazione e Formazione Salesiana. Rome: Editrice S. D. B., 1984. 448.

781 Szaszkiewicz, Jerzy. *Filosofia Dell'uomo*. Roma: University Gregoriana, 1981.

*Blandino, G., *Aquinas*, 25(1982): 191-202.*

782 Talamo, Salvatore. *Il Rinnovamento del Pensiero Tomistico*. Città del Vaticano: Libreria Editrice Vaticana, 1986. 134.

*Orlando, Pasquale, *Doctor Communis*, 40(1987): 107-108.*
*Turco, Giovanni, *Sapienza*, 41(1988): 319-321.*

783 Tognolo, Antonio. *Due Saggi Sull'accezione Metafisica del Concetto Di Separatio in Tommaso D'Aquino*. Padova: Ed. Gregoriana, 1983. 39.

784 Tozzi, Roberto. *Cogito Ergo Sum*. Milano: Mursia, 1987. 388.

785 Vanni Rovighi, Sofia. *Studi Di Filosofia Medioevale II: Secoli XIII e XIV*. Scienze Filosofiche 20. Milano: Vita e Pensiero, 1978. 311.

*Mathon, G., *Bulletin de Théologie Ancienne et Médiévale*, 13(1982): 198.*
*Pavan, C., *Episteme NS*, Caracas, 2(1982): 271-280.*

786 Vanni Rovighi, Sofia. *Uomo e Natura: Appunti Per Una Antropologia Filosofica*. Milano: Vita e Pensiero, 1980. 237.

787 Vanni Rovighi, Sofia. *Introduzione a Tommaso D'Aquino*. 3rd ed. I Filosofi 16. Bari: Latenza, 1986. 214.

*D'Agostino, F., *Rivista Internazionale di Filosofia del Diritto, 59*(1982): 329-331.*
*Quintino, R., *Bulletin de Théologie Ancienne et Médiévale*, 14(1989): 729-730.*
*Turco, Giovanni, *Sapienza*, 41(1988): 316-318.*

788 Vanni Rovighi, Sofia. *La Filosofia e Il Problema Di Dio*. Milano: Vita e Pensiero, 1986. 170.

789 Viola, Francesco. *Concezioni Dell'Autorita e Teorie del Diritto*. Nomoi 6. L'Aquila: L. U. Japadre, 1982. 200.

*Rivero, Manuel, *Revue Thomiste*, 88(1988): 172.*

790 Weisheipl, James A. *Tommaso D'Aquino: Vita, Pensiero, Opere*. Trans. Inos Biffi and Costante Marabelli. Biblioteca Di Cultura Medievale 213. Milano: Jaca Book, 1987. xiv-426.

*Tomadini, Raffaella, *Revue Philosophique de Louvain*, 88(1990): 439-440.*

791 Wojtyla, Karol. *I Fondamenti Dell'ordine Etico*. Città del Vaticano: Libreria Editrice Vaticana, 1980.

792 Zoffoli, Enrico. *Mistero Della Sofferenza Di Dio? Il Pensiera Di San Tommaso*. Studi Tomistici 34. Cittá del Vaticano: Libreria Editrice Vaticana, 1988. 82.

*Stramare, Tarcisio, *Doctor Communis*, 51(1988): 302-303.*

793 Zubiri, Xavier. *Natura Storia Dio*. Palermo: Augustinus, 1985. 349.

E. SPANISH

794 Alvira, Tomás. *Naturaleza y Libertad: Estudio de los Conceptos Tomistas de Voluntas Ut Natura y Voluntas Ut Ratio*. Publicaciones de la Facultad de Filosofica 44. Pamplona: Ediciones Universidad de Navarra, 1985. 210.

795 Alvira, Tomás, Luis Clavell, and Tomás Melendo. *Metafísica*. Pamplona: Ed. Universidad de Navarra (EUNSa): 1986. 252.

796 Ansaldo, Aurelio. *El Primer Principio del Obrar Moral y Las Normas Especificas en el Pensamiento de G. Grisez y J. Finnis*. Roma: Pontificia Università Lateranense, 1990. xii-255.
*May, William E., *The Thomist*, 55(1991): 332-337.*

797 Beuchot, Mauricio. *El Problema de los Universales*. Fac. de Filos. y Letras, Opúsculos: Investigaciones. México City, México: U. N. A. M., 1981. 520.

798 Beuchot, Mauricio. *Aspectos Históricos de la Semiótica y la Filosofia del Lenguaje*. Cuadernos del Seminario de Poética 11. México City, México: Instituto de Investigacione Filógicas UNAM, 1987. 196.

799 Byrne, D., ed. *San Tomás de Aquino, Suma de Teologia*. Ed. Regentes de Estudios de las Provincias Dominicanas en Espana. Biblioteca de Autores Cristianos 31. Madrid: La Ed.ial Católica, 1988. xxxviii-992.
*Osuna, A., *La Ciencia Tomista*, 115(1988): 331-335.*

800 Cappelletti, Angel J. *La Teoria Aristotélica de la Visión*. Caracas: Sociedad Venezolana de Ciencias Humanas, 1977. 97.

801 Cayetano, Tomás. *Del Ente y de la Esencia*. Buenos Aires: Universidad Central de Venezuela, 1977. 319.

802 Chesterton, Gilbert K. *Santo Tomás de Aquino*. Trans. M. Mercader, Buenos Aires: Carolos Lohlé, 1986. 180.

803 Clavell, Luis. *El Nombre Proprio de Dios Según Santo Tomás de Aquino*. Colección Filosófica 34. Pampelune: Ediciones Universidad de Navarra, 1980. 201.
*Anon., *Rassengna di Letteratura Tomistica*, 16(1980): 249-250.*
*Zurich, A., *Divus Thomas*, 84(1981): 361.*

804 Copleston, Frederick. *Historia de la Filosofia Tomo 2*. Trans. J. C. Garcia Borrón. 3rd ed. Barcelona: Ariel, 1978. 584.

805 Corti, Maria. *La Felicità Menale: Nuove Prospettive Per Cavalcanti e Dante*. Einaudi Paperbacks 147. Torino: Einaudi, 1983. x-172.

806 Costa, E. Colom. *Dios y el Obrar Humano*. Pamplona: EUNSA, 1977. 201.
*Lopéz, Clemente Garciá, *Revista Espanola de Teologia*, 38(1977): 202.*

807 Cúnsulo, Rafael R. *El Libre Albedrio: Santo Tomás y Cornelio Fabro*. Roma: Pontificia Studiorum Universitas a San Tommaso d'Aquino in Urbe, 1989. 206.

808 Darós, William R. *Razón e Inteligencia*. Filosofia Oggi 24. Genova: Studio Ed.iale di Cultura, 1984. 129.

809 Derisi, Octavio Nicolás. *La Doctrina de la Inteligencia de Aristóteles a Santo Tomás*. Buenos Aires: Club de Lectores, 1980.

810 Derisi, Octavio Nicolás. *Santo Tomás de Aquino y la Filosofià Actual*. Buenos Aires: Club de Lectores (Dist. Tres Américas): 1981.

811 Derisi, Octavio Nicolás. *Esencia y Vida de la Persona Humana*. Buenos Aires: Ed. Universitaria, 1979. 211.

812 Derisi, Octavio Nicolás. *La Palabra*. Buenos Aires: Emecé Editores, 1978. 296.
*Reix, André, *Revue Philosophique de Louvain*, 79(1981): 122-123.*

813 Derisi, Octavio Nicolás. *Los Fundamentos Metafisicos del Orden Moral*. 4th ed. Buenos Aires: Universidad Católica (EDUCa): 1980. 504.

814 Derisi, Octavio Nicolás. *Estudios de Metafísica y Gnoseología I-II*. Buenos Aires: EDUCA, 1985.

*Di Pietro, Alfredo, *Sapientia* 41(1986): 148-151.*

815 Echauri, Raúl. *El Pensamiento de Etienne Gilson*. Pampelune: Ediciones Universidad de Navarra S. A., 1980. 243.

*Derisi, Octavio Nicolás, *Sapientia*, 36(1981): 316-317.*
*Sanabria, José Rubén, *Revista de Filosofia* 14(1981): 522-523.*

816 Esquirol I Calaf, Josep M. *Raó I Fonament: Estudi Sobre la Doctrina Cartesiana de Las Verdades Eternes*. Barcelona: Promociones y Publicaciones Universitarias (PPU): 1988. 144.

817 Esteban Perruca, Joaquin. *Tomás de Aquino*. 3rd ed. Madrid: Palabra, 1984. 400.

818 Fabro, Cornelio. *Percepción y Pensamiento*. Pampelune: Ediciones Universidad de Navarra S. A., 1978. 645.

819 Fabro, Cornelio. *Introducción Al Problemá del Hombre*. Col. C. Fundamentales. Madrid: Rialp, 1983. 328.

*Arregui, J. V., *Anales de Filosofia*, 17(1984): 184-186.*

820 Farrell, Walter. *Guia de la Suma Teológica. I*. Madrid: Palabra, 1982. 236.

821 Fernández, Clemente. *Los Filósofos Médievales I-II*. Madrid: Católica, 1979. 772.

*Cruz, J., *Anuario Filosófico*, 14(1981): 220-222.*
*De Andrés Hernansanz, T., *Pensamiento*, 37(1981): 204-206.*

822 Forment, Edualdo. *Filosfia del Ser*. Barcelona: Edicions de la Universitat de Barcelona, 1988. 215.

823 Forment, Edualdo. *Ser y Persona*. 2nd ed. Barcelona: Ed. Universidad de Barcelona, 1983. 528.

824 Forment, Edualdo. *El Problema de Dios en la Metafísica*. Biblioteca Universitaria de Filosofia 12. Barcelona: Promociones Publicaciones Universitarias (PPU): 1986. 402.

825 Garcia, Cándido. *Teoria de la Memoria en Santo Tomás*. Zamora: Ed. Monte Casino, 1978. 61.

826 Garcia del Castillo, Julián. *La Imagen es Mensaje*. Caracas: Ed. Tripode, 1987. 208.

827 Garcia Lopez, Jesús. *Tomás de Aquino: Razón y Fe*. Madrid: Cincel, 1985. 232.

828 García Marqués, Alfonso. *Necesidad y Substancia: Averroes y Su Proyección en Tomás de Aquino*. Filosófica 59. Pamplona: Ediciones Universidad de Navarra, 1989. 300.

829 Giannini, Humberto. *Breve Historia de la Filosofia*. Santiage de Chile: Editorial Universitaria, 1985. 365.

830 Gilson, Etienne. *Elementos de Filosofia Cristiana*. Trans. A. Garcia-Arias. 2nd ed. Madrid: Rialp, 1977. 368.

831 Gilson, Etienne. *El Espiritu de la Filosofia Medieval*. Trans. A. Garcia-Arias. Madrid: Rialp, 1981. 448.

832 Gilson, Etienne. *Lo Spirito Della Filosofia Medioevale*. 3rd ed. Brescia: Morcelliana, 1983. 560.

833 Gilson, Etienne. *El Ser y los Filósofos*. Trans. A. Garcia-Arias. 2nd ed. Pamplona: EUNSA, 1985. 348.

834 González, Angel Luis. *Ser y Participación: Estudio Sobre la Cuarta Via de Tomás de Aquino*. Colección Filosófica 31. Pamplona: Eunsa, 1985. 262.

*Pasqua, H., *Revue Philosophique de Louvain*, 86(1988): 259-263.*

835 Grenet, Paul B. *Veinticuatro Tesis Tomistas de la Evolución a la Existencia*. Buenos Aires: Club de Lectores (Dist. Tres Américas), 1981.

836 Gugzmán del Rey, Francisco. *Santo Tomás: Sintesis y Comentario*. Picos 17. Almeria: Autor-Ed., 1984. 20.

837 Haag, Herbert. *El Problema del Mal*. Bacelona: Herder, 1981. 340.

838 Hernández Pacheco Sanz, Javier. *Acto y Substancia: Estudio a Través de Santo Tomás de Aquino*. Col. S. Filosofia y Letras 71. Sevilla: Universidad de Sevilla, 1984. 330.

*Anon., *Rassegna di Letteratura Tomistica*, 20(1987): 169-174.*

839 Lain Entralgo, Pedro. *Sobre la Amistad*. Madrid: Ed. Espasa-Calpe, 1985. 334.

840 Larga, P. *San Agustin y el Hombre de Hoy*. Madrid: Rialp, 1988. 333.

841 López, Jesús Garcia. *Los Derechos Humanos en Santo Tomás de Aquino*. Baranain, Pamplona: Universidad de Navarra, 1979. 248.

*Fernández Rodriguez, J. L., *Anuario Filosófico*, 13(1980): 207-210.*
*Vitale, V., *Rivista Internazionale di Filosofia del Diritto*, 54(1981): 667-668.*

842 Malavassi-V., Guillermo. *El Ente y la Esencia de Santo Tomás de Aquino*. San José: Univerisidad de Costa Rica, 1981. 85.

843 Manzanedo, Marcos F. *La Imaginación y la Memoria Según Santo Tomás*. Studia Universitatis S. Thomae in Urbe 9. Roma: Herder, 1978. 395.

*Anon., *Rassegna di Letteratura Tomistica*, 14(1978): 157-162.*
*Soria, F., *Estudios Filosóficos*, 29(1980): 390-391.*

844 Manzanedo, Marcos F. *Las Pasiones O Emociones Según Santo Tomás*. Filosofia 8. Madrid: Inst. Pontificios Filos. y Teo., 1984. 80.

845 Maritain, Jacques. *El Doctor Angélico*. Buenos Aires: Club de Lectores, 1979. 214.

846 Méndez, Julio Raúl. *El Amor Fundamento de la Participación Metafisica: Hermenéutica de la Summa Contra Gentiles*. Buenos Aires: Editorial Sudamericana, 1990. 530.

847 Olgiati, Francisco. *El Concepto de Juridicidad en Santo Tomás de Aquino*. Trans. T. Diorki. Barañain: Ed. Universidad de Navarra, 1977. 368.

*Villey, M., *Archives de Philosophie du Droit*, 26(1981): 442-443.*

848 Pérez Ruiz, Francisco. *Metafísica del Mal*. Madrid: UPGM, 1982. xv-268.

*Perego, A., *Divus Thomas*, 87(1984): 407.*

849 Pieper, Josef. *Filosofia Medieval y Mundo Moderno*. Trans. 2nd ed. Madrid: Rialp, 1979. 405.

*Derisi, Octavio N., *Sapientia*, 37(1982): 312-313.*

850 Pieper, Josef. *Las Virtudes Fundamentales*. Trans. 2nd ed. Madrid: Rialp, 1980. 574.

851 Platts, Mark, ed. *La Ética a Través de Su Historia*. Mexico City, México: Instituto de Investigaciones Filosóficas Unam, 1988. 141. Especially Beuchot, M., "Etica y justica en Tomás de Aquino."

852 Ponferrada, Gustavo Eloy. *Introducción Al Tomismo*. 2nd ed. 1970. Temas de Eudeba Filosofía 2. Buenos Aires: Club de Lectores, 1978. xii-223.

*Anon., *Rassegna di Letteratura Tomistica*, 14(1978): 116-117.*
*Clavell, L., *Anuario Filosófico*, 13(1980): 228-231.*

853 Ramos, Alice. *Signum: De la Semiótica Universal a la Metafísica del Signo*. Colección Filosófica 51. Pamplona: EUNSA, 1987. 434. Especially Chapter II, Section 4: "Noción tomista del signo," 221-253 and Chapter III, Sections 1-3: "Metafísica del signo," 281-417.

854 Rassam, Joseph. *Introducción a la Filosofia de Santo Tomás de Aquino*. Trans. Julían Urbistondo. Madrid: Rialp, 1980. 344.

*Derisi, Octavio N., *Anales de Filosofia*, 16(1983): 224-226.*
*Fuentes, M., *Mikael*, 24(1980): 156-157.*
*Magraner, Rulián J., *Sapientia*, 38(1983): 316-317.*

855 Ruspoli Morenés, Enrique. *Lectura Transcendental del Problema del Conocimiento en Tomás de Aquino*. Madrid: Autor-Ed., 1984. 100.

856 Sacchi, Mario Enrique. *Aristóteles, Santo Tomás de Aquino y el Orden Militar*. Col. Ensayos Doctrinarios 5. Buenos Aires: Cruz y Fierro Ed., 1982. 158.

*Perini, G., *Divus Thomas*, 86(1983): 366-367.*

857 Sánchez del Bosque, Manuel. *Una Raiz de la Modernidad: Doctrina Tomista Sobre la Vida*. Biblioteca Salmanticensis Studios 78. Salamanca: Editorial Universitas, 1985. 164.

858 Sanchez Sorondo, Marcelo. *La Gracia Como Participación de la Naturaleza Divina Según Santo Tomás de Aquino*. Estudios 28. Buenos-Aires: Salamanca Universidades Pontificias, 1979. 358.

*Composta, Dario, *Doctor Communis*, 35(1982): 104-107.*

859 Sanguineti, Juan José. *La Filosofia del Progreso en Kant y Tomás de Aquino. Anuario Filosófico* 18(1985): 341-352.

860 Sanguineti, Juan José. *La Filosfía de la Ciencia Según Santo Tomás*. Colección Filosófica 25. Barañaom, Pamplona: Ediciones Universidad de Navarra, 1977. 372.

*Anon., *Rassegna di Letteratura Tomistica*, 13(1977): 131-135.*
*Jordan, Mark D., *The Thomist*, 45(1981): 333-337.*
*Rebaglia, A., *Filosofia*, 35(1984): 151-156.*
*Roldán, A., *Pensamiento*, 34(1978): 334-336.*

861 Saranyana, José Ignacio. *Joaquín de Fiore y Tomás de Aquino: Historia Doctrinal de Una Polémica*. Pamplona: Ediciones Universidad de Navarra, 1979. 174.

*Ghisalberti, Alessandro, *Rivista di Filosofia Neo-Scolastica*, 72(1980): 563-565.*
*Huerga, A., *Revista Espanola de Teologica*, 154-161(1979-1980): 457-458.*
*Manselli, R., *Revue d'Histoire Ecclésiastique*, 78(1983): 863-867.*

862 Saranyana, José Ignacio. *História de la Filosofiá Medieval*. Pampelune: Ediciones Universidad de Navarra, Especially pp. 212-231. 1985. 306.

*Elders, L. J., *Forum Katholisch Theologie*, 1(1985): 316-317.*
*Musco, A., *Schede Medievali*, 8(1985): 207.*
*Van Steenberghen, Fernand, *Revue Philosophique de Louvain*, 84(1986): 258-259.*

*The Spanish Jewish philosopher Ibn-Gabirol, better known as Avicebrón(1020-1058), wrote a treatise entitled *Fons vitae*, which was discovered by Munk(1857) and edited by Baeumker(1895). It is of enormous importance for the history of mediaeval philosophy because it was the principle inspirer of "universal hylomorphism," systematized in the 13rd century by Saint Bonaventure and Duns Scotus. Saint Thomas took Avicebrón as his opposite number in his discussion of the perfect or positive immateriality of the angels and of the human soul. Discussing with Ibn-Gabirol, the Angelic Doctor was able to crystallize his great discovery of the *actus essendi*, declaring that not all potency is necessarily prime matter. He also showed that his way of philosophizing was incompatible with the metaphysics of Bonaventure and of Duns Scotus.*

863 Van Steenberghen, Fernand. *História Da Filosofia: Periodo Cristaò*. Trans. J. M. Pontes Da Cruz, Lisboa: Gradiva, n. d. 213.

*Wenin, C., *Revue Philosophique de Louvain*, 84(1986): 259.*

864 Zabalza Iriarte, Joaquin. *Lectura Sobre el Derecho: Tomás de Aquino y Latinoamérica*. Bogotá: Universidad de Santo Tomás, 1978. 232.

F. MISCELLANEOUS

865 Bjelke, Johan Fredrik. *Den Europeiske Filosofi: Fra Thomas Aquinas Til Henri Bergson*. Oslo: Universitetsfori, 1981. 207.

866 Bor, J., and S. Teppema, eds. *25 Eeuwen Filosofie*. Meppel: Boom, 1982. 303.

867 Bychowski, B. E. *Die Erosion der Ewigen Philosophie: Kritik Des Neothomismus*. Ed. Max Kühn. Berlin: Verlag, 1977. 155.

868 Chudy, Wojciech. *Refleksja a Poznanie Bytu: Refleksja in Actu Exercito I Jejfunkcja W Poznaniu Metafizykalnym*. Lublin: Katolicki Uniwersytet Lubelski, 1984. 127. Especially "La notion et le rôle de la réflexion dans la philosophie de Thomas d'Aquin."

869 De Rijk, L. M. *Middeleeuwse Wijsbegeerte*. Philosophie Médiévale. Assen/Amsterdam: Van Gorcum, 1977. xii-290.

*Anon., *Rassegna di Letteratura Tomistica*, 13(1980): 122-125.*

870 De Wijsgerige, Thomas. *Terugblik Op Het Neothomisme*. Trans. M. I. Delfgaauw. Annalen Van Het Thijmgenootschap Jg. 72. Baarn: Amboboeken, 1984. 168.

871 Delfgaauw, B. *Thomas Van Aquino: Een Kritische Benadering Van Zijn Filosofie*. Wijsgerige Monografieë. Bussum: Wereldvenster, 1980. 210.

Anon., Rassegna di Letteratura Tomistica, 16(1983): 121-125.
*Lippens, E., *Tijdschrift voor Filosofie*, 48(1986): 634-636.*
*Van Velthoven, Th., *Algemeen Nederlands Tijdschrift voor Wijsbegeerte*, 73(1981): 200-201.*

872 Delfgaauw, B. *Thomas Van Aquino: De Wereld Van Een Middeleeuws Denker*. 1980. Rééd (Antwerpen): De Nederlandsche Boekhandel, 1985. 210.

*Lippens, E., *Tijdschrift voor Filosofie*, 48(1986): 634-936.*

873 Delfgaauw, B. et al., eds. *De Wijsgerige Thomas: Terugblik Op Het Neothomisme*. Annals of the Thijmosciety 72. Baarn: Ambo, 1984. 164.

874 Dominicus De Flandria. *Quaestiones in Thomae de Aquino Commentaria Super Libros Posteriorum*. Frankfurt: Minerva, 1982. 160.

875 Elders, Léon J. *De Metafysica Van St. Thomas Van Aquino in Historisch Perspectief, I: Het Gemeenschappelijk Zijnde*. Vol. Studia Rodensia 3. Brugge. Uitg. Tabor: Vught. Uitg. J. Richt., 1982. Translated into German, *Die Metaphysik des Thomas von Aquin in historischer Perspektive*, Salzburg, 1984. 327.

*Anon., *Rassegna di Letteratura Tomistica*, 18(1982): 164-169.*

*Dudley, John, *Revue Philosophique de Louvain*, 82(1984): 283-284.*

*Hedwig, K., *Revue Thomiste*, 83(1983): 128-129.*

*Ravensloot, V. Ch., *Algemeen Nederlands Tijschrift voor Wijsbegeerte*, 75(1983): 376-377.*

*Steel, C., *Tijdschrift voor Filosofie*, 45(1983): 467-474.*

876 Elders, Léon J. *De Metafysica Van St. Thomas Van Aquino in Historisch Perspectief: II: Filosofische Godsleer*. Studia Rodensia 4. Brugge: Uitgeverij Tabor, 1987. 504.

*Hedwig, K., *Revue Thomiste*, 88(1988): 508-510.*

877 Elders, Léon J. *De Natuurfilosofie Van Saint-Thomas Van Aquino. Algemene Natuurfilosofie: Kosmologie. Filosofie Van de Organische Natuur: Wijsgerige Mensleer*. Brugge: Uitgeverij Tabor, 1989. 436.

878 Frankowska-Terlecka, Malgorzata. *L'unité Du Savoir Aux XII et XIII Siécles*. Trans. Hanna Sitkowska. Ossolineum: Polish Academy of Sciences, 1980.

879 Gogacz, Mieczyslaw, ed. *Metafizyczne Ujecia Jednosci: Platon, Tomasz Z Akwinu, Giovanni Pico Della Mirandola, Aristoteles*. Opera Philosophorum Medii Aevi. Textus et Studia 6. Warszawa: Akademia teologii Katoliskie, 1985. 219.

880 Gogacz, Mieczyslaw. *L'homme et Ses Relations*. Warszawa: Akademia Teologii Katolickiej, 1985. 200.

881 Gogacz, Mieczyslaw. *Subsystencja I Osoba Wedlug Sw Tomasza Z Akwinu*. Opera Philosophorum Medii Aevi: Textus et Studia 8. Warszawa: Akademia Teologii Katolickiej, 1987. 214.

882 Gogacz, Mieczyslaw. *Elemenmtarz Metafizyki*. Warsaw: Akademia Teologii Katolickiej, 1987.

883 Goossens, Charles. *Het Recht Van de Moraal: De Stuctuur Van Moraalrechtvaardiging en Van Moraalkritiet: Aquinas en Nietzsche*. Amsterdam: Rodopi, 1980. x-106.

884 Hallebeek, Jan. *Quia Natura Nichi Privatum: Aspecten Van de Eigendomsvraag in Het Werk Van Thomas Van Aquino (1225-1274)*. Uitagaven Van Het Gerard Noodt Instituut 9. Nijmegen: Gerard Noodt Instituut, 1986. 174.

885 Kaminski, Stanislaw, Marian Kurdzialek, and Zofia Zdybicka, eds. *Saint-Thomas D'Aquin Pour le Septiéme Centenaire de Sa Mort: Essai D'actualisation de Sa Philosophie*. Lublin: Towarzystwo Naukowe Katolickiego Uniwersytetu Lubelskiego, 1978. 351.

886 Karawa, N. *Nauka O Bogu Jako Ipsum Esse Subsistens Wedlug Tomasza Z Akwinu*. Lublin: Université Catholique, 1985. xliii-403.

887 Kattackal, Jacob. *Aquinas-Sankara-Ramanuja-Madhva. Darsanankalum.* Kottayam: St. Thomas Ap. Seminary, 1979. xiv-347.

888 Krajski, S. *Zawartosé Tresciowa Traktau De Ente et Essentia Tomasza Akwinu*. Warszawa: Akademia Teologii Katolickiej, 1985. 511.

889 Krapiec, Mieczyslaw A., ed. *Tomasz a Akwinu, De Ente et Essentia*. Lublin, 1980.

890 Krapiec, Mieczyslaw A. *Metafizyka*. Lublin: Redakcja Wydawnictw Kul, 1985.

891 Lindborg, Rolf. *Om Gud Och Världen: Thomas Ab Aquinos Lära Om Skapelsen*. Lund: Bodafors Doxa, 1983. 178.

892 Menezes, Djacir. *A Juridicidade Em Tomás de Aquino e Em Karl Marx*. Brasilia: Ed. Catedra, 1982. 121.

893 Prokopowicz, M. *Porzadek Natury Wedlug Sw. Tomasza Z Akwinu*. Warszawa: Akademia Teologii Katolickiej, 1985. 321.

894 Schavemaker, C., and H. Willemsen, eds. *Over Het Weten Van de Mens*. Alphen aan den Rijn: Samson, 1986. 198.

895 Swiezawski, Stefan. *Swiety Tomasz Na Nowo Odczytany: Wyklady W. Laskach*. Kraków: Wyd. Znak, 1983. 219.

896 Swiezawski, Stefan, and Jan Czerkawskiego. *Dziejow Mysli Swietego Tomasza Z Akwinu*. Lublin: Towarzystwo Naukowe Polskiego Uniwersytetu, 1978.

897 Swiezawski, Stefan, and Jan Czerkawskiego. *Studia Z Dziejów Mysli Swietego Tomasza Z Akwinu*. Lublin: Towarzystwo Naukowe Katolickiego Uniwersytetu Lubelskiego, 1978. 401.

898 Van Acker, L. *O Tomismo e O Pensamento Contemporâneo*. Biblioteca Di Pensamento Brasileiro. Sao Paulo: Editora Convivio c Editora da Univcrsidaddc Sao Paulo, 1983. 238.

*Rodrigues, A. M. Moog, *Presença Filosófica*, 9(1983): 164-165.*

899 Van Den Eijnden, J. G. J. *Thomas Van Aquino in de Theologie: Een Draaiboek Voor Receptienonderzoek*. Werkgroep Tomas Van Aquino 1. Amsterdam: Robert Scottstvaat, 1985. vii-245.

900 Van Steenberghen, Fernand. 1990. *O Tomismo*. Trans. J. M. da Pontes Cruz. Trajectos 14. Lisboa: Gradiva, 1990. 180.

901 Veres, Tomo. *Iskonski Mislilac*. Zagreb: Dominikanska Naklada, 1978. 201.

902 Weisheipl, James A. *Tomasz Z Akwinu. Zycie, Mysl I Dzielo*. Trans. Cz Wesolowski. Poznan: W. drodze, 1985. 519.

903 Wójcik, J. *Rola Pracy W Ksztaltowanii Rodziny Jako Wspólnoty Osób W Filozofii Tomasza Z Akwinu*. Warszawa: Akademia Teologii Katolickiej, 1985. 121.

904 Yamada, Akira. *Studies in Res* in Thomas Aquinas. Tokyo, 1986. v-979.

*Miyauchi, H., *Studies in Medieval Thought*, 29(1987): 142-145.*

II. ARTICLES

A. ENGLISH

905 Aertsen, Johannes Adrianus. "The Convertibility of Being and Good in St. Thomas Aquinas." *The New Scholasticism* 59(1985): 449-470.

906 Aertsen, Johannes Adrianus. "The Circulation-motive and Man in the Thought of Thomas Aquinas." *L'homme et Son Univers Au Moyen Age I: Actes Du Septiéme Congrés International de Philosophie Médiéval.* Ed. Christian Wenin. Philosophes Médiévaux 26. Louvain-la-Neuve: Éditions de l'Institut Supérieur de Philosophie, 1986. 432-439.

907 Aertsen, Johannes Adrianus. "Natural Law in the Light of the Doctrine of Transcendentals." *Lex et Libertas. Freedom and Law According to St. Thomas Aquinas.* Eds. L. J. Elders and K. Hedwig. Studi Tomistici 30. Città del Vaticano: Pontificia Accademia di San Tommaso e di Religione Cattolica, 1987. 99-112.

908 Aertsen, Johannes Adrianus. "Method and Metaphysics: The *Via Resolutionis* in Thomas Aquinas." *The New Scholasticism* 63(1989): 405-418.

909 Algozin, Keith. "Whence the Infinite God." *Proceedings of the Catholic Philosophical Association* 55(1981): 73-84.
There are two main options in metaphysics, spiritualism and materialism. The issue is whether being, which we always understand on the model of our human experience is best understood as a self, as power serving an ideal, as God. This paper, after setting forth the alternatives, especially the argument of Thomist spiritualism for an infinite God, rejects spiritualism in favor of materialism. The self, human or divine is a mythical entity; this truth can bring detachment from the world, in the image of the infinite God.

910 Allen, Prudence. "Two Medieval Views on Women's Identity: Hildegard of Bingen and Thomas Aquinas." *Studies in Religion* 16(1987): 21-36.

911 Alonso, Luz García. "The Perspectives of the Distinction Between *Agere* and *Facere*." *Diotima* 12(1984): 97-103.

912 Alston, William P. "Hartshorne and Aquinas: A *Via Media*." *Existence and Actuality: Conversations with Charles Hartshorne.* Eds. John Cobb, Jr., and Franklin I. Gamwell. Chicago: University of Chicago Press, 1984. 78-98. Response by Charles Hartshorne, pp. 98-102.
*Aquinas' "classical" theology and Hartshorne's process theology are contrasted on 10 points on which Hartshorne has criticized Aquinas. Hartshorne suggests that each view must be accepted or rejected as a whole, but I suggest a more discriminating position. I divide the issues into two groups, on one of which I side with Hartshorne and on the other with Aquinas. I argue that Hartshorne's criticisms are cogent for the first but not for the second group, and that my *via media* is coherent.*

913 Alston, William P. "Functionalism and Theology." *American Philosophical Quarterly* 22(1985): 221-230.

914 Altmann, Alexander. "Maimonides and Thomas Aquinas: Natural or Divine Prophecy?" *Association for Jewish Studies* 3(1978): 1-19. Reprinted in A. Altmann, *Essays in Jewish Intellectual History*, Hanover, NH: Brandeis University, 77-96.

915 Anderson, Robert. "Laying Bare Speculative Grammar: Some Remarks." *The New Scholasticism* 61(1987): 13-24.

916 Anscombe, G. E. M. "Truth: Anselm or Thomas." *New Blackfriars* 66(1985): 82-98.

917 Ardagh, David W. "Aquinas on Happiness: A Defence." *The New Scholasticism* 53(1979): 428-459.

It is argued via a review of the relevant works of Aquinas that criticisms of his account of happiness as the ultimate end of human life offered by three contemporary philosophers (D. J. O'Connor, A. J. Kenny, and J. Rawls) largely miss the mark. This is done by distinguishing the elements of Aquinas' mature treatment from similar but less plausible theses ascribed to him by these three authors. By respecting a distinction Aquinas draws between the natural wish for happiness "in the common notion" and the specific ingredients of a truly happy life, one can show Aquinas' account to be sophisticated, plausible, and worthy of renewed study.

918 Ardley, Gavin. "The Eternity of the World." *Philosophical Studies* 29(1982-1983): 55-67.

919 Arges, Michael. "New Evidence Concerning the Date of Thomas Aquinas' *Lectura on Matthew*." *Mediaeval Studies* 49(1987): 517-523.

920 Ashley, Benedict M. "Aquinas and the Theology of the Body: What Can Thomism Contribute to Post-modern Theology?" *Thomistic Papers III*. Ed. Leonard A. Kennedy. Houston, TX: University of St. Thomas, Center for Thomistic Studies, 1987. 55-89.

921 Ashley, Benedict M. "The River Forest School and the Philosophy of Nature Today." *Philosophy and the God of Abraham: Essays in Memory of James A. Weisheipl, OP*. Ed. James Long. Toronto: Pontifical Institute of Mediaeval Studies, In press. 1-15.

922 Aumann, Jordan. "Beauty and the Esthetics Response." *Angelicum* 54(1977): 489-519.

923 Aumann, Jordan. "Thomistic Evaluation of Love and Charity." *Angelicum* 55(1978): 534-556.

924 Bäck, Allan. "Aquinas on the Incarnation." *The New Scholasticism* 56(1982): 127-145.

In this paper the author deals with Aquinas' solution to the problem, whether the doctrine of the Incarnation is consistent. He first shows why there is a problem of consistency with this doctrine, given orthodox Christian beliefs. He then claims that Aquinas has two solutions, and that both fail. The first solution, as Scotus also observes, does not resolve the apparent inconsistency, and the other depends on making humanity accidental to Christ, and hence on abandoning the orthodox position.

925 Balas, David L. "A Thomist View on Divine Infinity." *Proceedings of the American Catholic Philosophical Association* 55(1981): 91-98.

926 Baldner, Steven Earl. "St. Thomas and Charles Hartshorne on Change and Process." *Philosophy and the God of Abraham: Essays in Memory of James A. Weisheipl, OP*. Ed. James Long. Toronto: Pontifical Institute of Mediaeval Studies, In press. 17-29.

927 Barad, Judith A. "Aquinas on Faith and the Consent/assent Distinction." *Journal of the History of Ideas* 24(1986): 311-321.

928 Barad, Judith A. "Aquinas' Inconsistency on the Nature and the Treatment of Animals." *Between Species* 4(1988): 102-111.

According to St. Thomas Aquinas, the only reason to restrict human conduct with regard to the use and treatment of nonhuman animals is grounded upon obligations to other human beings. He thought that cruelty to animals could lead to cruelty to humans. In holding this view of how animals should be treated, Aquinas reduces animals to mere instruments or things. Yet his ontological placement of animals above inanimate objects and vegetative life does not accord withhis ethical view that animals are mere instruments on the order of inanimate objects. Moreover, because human beings should be treated in a manner consonant with their ontological status (as Aquinas insists): then animals should be accorded opposite treatment on the same basis. Aquinas' failure to recommend that animals be treated this way, a failure which has had a far-reaching influence, points to a blatant inconsistency in his view. The purpose of this paper is to investigate Aquinas' diverse teachings on the issue and hence expose his inconsistency and the implications of this inconsistency.

929 Barad, Judith A. "Aquinas' Assent/consent Distinction and the Problem of *Akrasia*." *The New Scholasticism* 62(1988): 98-111.

*The purpose of this paper is to provide a fresh account of the problem of *akrasia* (moral weakness) by analyzing St. Thomas Aquinas' doctrine between assent and consent. Aquinas' explicit development of a faculty of will allows him to recognize that the problem of moral weakness is not merely a matter of abstract knowledge. The moral agent may assent to a universal principle as expressive of the way he should act, and yet his will may incline him to act otherwise. It is my contention in this analysis that Aquinas' discussion of consent presents the function of end as regulating the individual's moral choices and thus provides a new perspective to the perennial problem of *akrasia*.*

930 Barad, Judith A. "Aquinas on the Role of Emotion in Moral Judgment and Activity." *The Thomist* 55(In press): 397-413.

931 Barden, Garrett. "Defending Self-defence." *Irish Philosophical Journal* 1(1984): 25-35.

*A study of Aquinas' *Sum Theo.* IIaIIae, 64. 7. One may intend to defend oneself; this may involve killing; one may not intend to kill. It is argued that the non-intention to kill is based on the irregularity of the association between self-defense and killing rather than on the simple desire of the actor to defend himself.*

932 Barral, Mary Rose. "The Philosophy of St. Thomas from a Phenomenological Viewpoint." *Tommaso Nel Suo Settimo Centenario VI: Atti del Congresso Internazionale: L'essere*. Napoli: Edizioni Domenicane Italiane, 1977. 480-486.

933 Barral, Mary Rose. "Thomas Aquinas and Merleau-Ponty." *Philosophy Today* 26(1982): 204-216.

The purpose of the work is to compare Aquinas and Merleau-Ponty and see whether the thought of Thomas is relevant today. It is, as presenting a different insight into being. They agree in their purposes, but seek reality differently. Thomas looks for ultimate cause, eternal truths, and claims the soul of man is an independent, spiritual entity; Merleau-Ponty looks to phenomena to find essences, sees truth as elusive, and claims the soul is developmental. Both affirm the unity of man, however.

934 Barrois, G. Antoine. "Two Metaphysics of the Divine Being: Thomism and Palamism." *Diotima* 7(1979): 21-25.

The metaphysics of Thomism, whether defined as an essentialism, or as a metaphysics of the existent, does not allow for a direct contact with the divine Being, prisoner of its own transcendence, whereas the communications of man with the Divine calls for intermediaries, the way of causality, analogical knowledge, and the Western theological notion of grace. Palamism, by its real distinction, in God, of Essence and Energy, makes the communication between man and the divinity immediately possible through a vital participation in the energies of the divine Being, while safeguarding the absolute transcendence of the Superessence.

935 Basti, Gianfranco. "A Cybernetical, Operational Re-proposal of the Aristotelian-Thomistic Theory of Intentionality." *Energeia: Etudes Aristotéliciennes Offertes A Mgr. Antonio Jannone*. Ed. Evanghélos A. Moutsopoulos. Recherches 1. Centre International d'études platoniciennes et aristotéliciennes. Paris: J. Vrin, 1986. 322-349.

936 Baumer, Michael R. "The Role of "Inevitability at Time T" in Aquinas' Solution to the Problem of Future Contingents." *The New Scholasticism* 53(1979): 147-167.

*Aquinas' discussion of future contingents is designed to solve the problem raised by Augustine in *De Libero Arbitro* and *De Civitate Dei*—namely, is God's foreknowledge consistent with creatures' freedom of choice? The fundamental distinction upon which Aquinas bases his solution is that between a contingent event as potential and that event as actual. In one sense of "contingent," an event may be contingent as potential and yet necessary as actual. Because God knows it as actual, He knows it as "having happened" or "determined to one," and there is no inconsistency between His certainty and any indetermination in the event. The necessity is the same as absolute necessity, but this could not be what Aquinas means. If we consider eternity to be a moment, we can admit that everything is inevitable as of eternity. But this does not entail the absence of freedom or contingency in created things, because eternity is not "already" with respect to them.*

937 Baumer, Michael R. "Whitehead and Aquinas on the Eternity of God." *The Modern Schoolman* 62(1984): 27-42.

938 Baumgarth, William P., and Richard J. Regan, eds. "Introduction." *Saint Thomas Aquinas: On Law, Morality, and Politics*. By Thomas Aquinas. Indianapolis, IN: Hackett Publishing Company, 1988. xi-xxviii.

939 Bazán, Bernardo Carlos. "*Intellectum Speculativum*: Averroes, Thomas Aquinas, and Siger of Brabant on the Intelligible Object." *Journal of the History of Philosophy* 19(1981): 425-446.

*The notion *intellectum speculativum* and of its double support (imagination and intellect) applies, in Averroes' noetic, to the *object* of knowledge. In Siger's noetic it applies to the *subject* of knowledge in act. In Thomas' noetic it becomes the *species intelligibilis*, which is no longer the object known. Both transformations evince all the difficulties of Averroes' thesis of the unicity of the separated intellect and explain the undermining of the Averroistic convictions of the Brabatine Master.*

940 Beards, Andrew. "Kenny and Lonergan on Aquinas." *Method* 4(1986): 115-123.

Anthony Kenny proposes a theory of mind based on Wittgenstenian correction of Aquinas. Kenny is influenced by Lonergan's work on Aquinas, but is not in complete agreement with it. In this article, I argue that Kenny's presentation of both Aquinas and Lonergan is oversimplified and misleading. Kenny's account of mind is also too dependent on Aristotelian physics. I also propose a Lonerganian, rather than a Wittgenstenian answer to questions Kenny raises.

941 Beer, Samuel H. "The Role of the Wise and the Holy: Hierarchy in the Thomistic System." *Political Theory* 14(1986): 391-422.

942 Belch, S. "Aquinas' *Summa Theologica* in the Polish Trans.." *Atti Dell'VIII Congresso Tomistico Internazionale VIII: San Tommaso Nella Storia del Pensiero*. Studi Tomistici 17. Cittá del Vaticano: Pontificia Accademia di San Tommaso e di Religione Cattolica, 1982. 169-172.

943 Bigger, Charles P. "St. Thomas on Essence and Participation." *The New Scholasticism* 62(1988): 319-348.

*The paper contends that Plato attempted to express the phenomenological possibility of unconcealment in *Timaeus*, where soul is the condition for the appearing of beings and their being known; but when this phenomenological open was made immanent in the soul and the gap defined in terms of expressivist, conceptual thought and its phantasm, then the gap became unbridgeable. Conceptualism as represented by Aristotle, Kant, and Aquinas has in its theory of judgments a variety of ways of trying to bridge the gap. It attempts to respect in its passive view of sense the real thing and, by making its intelligibility a function of mind, to avoid positing the reality of the object of knowledge as such. On its face, the most likely candidate as the architect of this spanning is St. Thomas.*

944 Billy, Denis J. "Grace and Natural Law in the *Super Epistola and Romanos Lectura*: A Study in Thomas' Commentary on *Romans* 2: 14-16." *Studia Moralia* 26(1988): 15-37.

945 Billy, Denis J. "Aquinas on the Content of Synderesis." *Studia Moralia* 29 (In press): 61-83.

946 Black, A. "Society and the Individual from the Middle Ages to Rousseau: Philosophy, Jurisprudence and Constitutional Theory." *History of Political Thought* 1(1980): 145-166.

This article aims to demonstrate the diversity of views held in the Middle Ages about the individual and society, and the continuity with the early-modern period.

947 Black, Deborah L. "The Influence of the *De Divinis Nominibus* on the Epistemology of St. Thomas Aquinas." *Proceedings of the Patristic, Medieval and Renaissance Conference* 10(1985): 41-52.

948 Black II, C. Cl. "St. Thomas' Commentary on the Johannine Proloque: Some Reflections on Its Character and Implications." *The Catholic Biblical Quarterly* 48(1986): 681-698.

949 Blandino, Giovanni. "Remarks Concerning the Doctrine of Act and Potency." *Aquinas* 32(1989): 337-352.

950 Blandino, Giovanni. "Remarks on General Neo-Thomistic Metaphysics: The Contribution of Christian Revelation to Philosophy." *Aquinas* 32(1989): 57-71.

The author accepts all the theses of Neo-Thomistic metaphysics, except the thesis of the act and potency. He underlines that the principal ideas of Thomistic metaphysics are due not to Aristotle, but to the indication of Judeo-Christian revelation.

951 Blumberg, Harry. "The Problem of Immortality in Avicenna, Maimonides, and St. Thomas Aquinas." *Essays in Medieval, Jewish and Islamic Philosophy*. Ed. Arthur Hyman. New York: KTAV Publishing House, 1977. 95-115.

952 Blumberg, Harry. "The Problem of Immortality in Avicenna, Maimonides and St. Thomas Aquinas." 1965. *Eschatology in Maimonidean Thought*. Ed. Jacob Dienstag. New York: KTAV Publishing House, 1983. 76-96.

953 Blythe, James Morgan. "The Mixed Constitution and the Distinction Between Regal and Political Power in the Work of Thomas Aquinas." *Journal of the History of Ideas* 47(1986): 547-565.

954 Blythe, James Morgan. "Family, Government and the Medieval Aristotelian." *History of Political Thought* 10(1989): 1-16.

955 Boadt, Lawrence. "St. Thomas Aquinas and the Biblical Wisdom Tradition." *The Thomist* 49(1985): 575-611.

956 Bobik, Joseph. "Immortality." *Philosophical Studies (Ireland)* 25(1977): 69-85.

If man's soul is immortal, then(1) it will survive death, (2) with consciousness, (3) forever. The purpose of this article is to note certain important things which have, and certain others, which have not (but need to): been done with respect to making out a case for the soul's immortality, in the sense of "immortality" just indicated. This purpose is achieved by presenting, and critically reflecting on, certain contributions of Plato, Aristotle, Aquinas, Descartes, the Wurzburg psychologists, parapsychology, eschatology. Though it is quite clear what must be shown—namely, that there is some conscious activity of man which proceeds, during life, completely independently of the body and all its functions—in order to conclude that immortality is a fact; it is not so clear that it has been shown, or that it can be.

957 Bobik, Joseph. "The Sixth Way of St. Thomas Aquinas." *The Thomist* 42(1978): 373-399.

*The purpose of this paper is to call attention to an unnoticed argument for God's existence by St. Thomas Aquinas. This argument is an *a posteriori* argument, but one which is closer to Jacques Maritain's Sixth Way in its point of departure than it is to any of the Five Ways. The point of departure is an introspective one, though not (as it is for Maritain) an intuition that the thinking I has always existed; rather, it is any man's introspective experience of universal forms in human knowledge. This paper presents the argument, reformulates its premises for reasons of economy and clarity, and considers the evidence which Aquinas gives, or would give, for their truth.*

958 Bobik, Joseph. "Aquinas on *Communicatio*, the Foundation of Friendship and *Caritas*." *The Modern Schoolman* 64(1986): 1-18.

*The purpose of this article is to make clear the meaning of *communicatio* in Aquinas' views on friendship and its forms, especially friendship with God (charity). It has three meanings (not the five suggested by the combined efforts of earlier writers), namely (1) a social relational context which is the foundation out of which friendship can arise; (2) the activities of friendship; and (3) the activity of offering a gift which provides a foundation (where there was none) out of which friendship can arise.*

959 Bobik, Joseph. "Aquinas on Friendship with God." *The New Scholasticism* 60(1986): 257-271.

960 Bobik, Joseph. "Aquinas' Fourth Way and the Approximating Relation: I." *The Thomist* 51(1987): 17-36.

This paper tries, by a review of and reflection on five suggestions (those of Harvanek, Maritain, Brady, Annice, and Van Steenberghen) to clarify the meaning, and the role of the approximating relation in Aquinas' Fourth Way. The approximating relation is, in fact, the relation of exemplary causality, and its role is to establish the existence of God as what is Most a Being. And so, causality does function in proving God's existence. This done, the Fourth Way then uses another sort of causality, agent causality, to argue further that God (the Most a Being) is the source of the being, goodness, truth, and the like, in all else.

961 Bobik, Joseph. "Aquinas' Fourth Way and the Approximating Relation: II." *The Thomist* 51(1987): 37-50.

962 Boh, Ivan. "Metalanguage and the Concept of *Ens Secundae Intentionis*." *Thomas von Aquin. Werk und Wirkung Im Licht Neuerer Forschungen*. Ed. Albert Zimmermann. Misçellanea Mediaevalia 19. Berlin: Walter de Gruyter, 1988. 53-70.

963 Bonansea, Bernardino M. "The Human Mind and the Knowledge of God." *Franciscan Studies* 40(1980): 5-17.

In this paper an attempt has been made to present the positions of Thomas Aquinas and John Duns Scotus on the human mind's ability to know God. After a careful analysis and interpretation of Aquinas' seemingly contradictory statements on the subject, Scotus' position is proposed within the context of his notion of being as the proper object of the human intellect and the doctrine of univocity. The paper concludes with the author's reflections on the controversial issue.

964 Bonansea, Bernardino M. "Scotus and Aquinas on the Human Mind's Ability to Know God." *Homo et Mundus: Acta Quinti Congressus Scotistici Internationalis*. Ed. Camille Bérubé. Studia Scholastico-scotistica 8. Romae: Societas Internationalis Scotistica, 1984. 229-238.

965 Bonnette, Dennis. "A Variation on the First Way of St. Thomas Aquinas." *Reason & Faith* 8(1982): 34-56.

966 Booth, Edward. "A Confrontation Between the Neo-Platonisms of St. Thomas Aquinas and Hegel." *Angelicum* 63(1986): 56-89.

967 Booth, Edward. "The Three *Pecia* Systems of St. Thomas Aquinas' Commentary in *I Sententiarum*." *La Production Du Livre Universitaire Au Moyen Âge: Exemplar et Pecia*. Ed. Louis J. Bataillon, Bertrand G. Guyot, and Richard H. Rouse. Actes Du Symposium Tenu Au Collegio San Bonaventura de Grottaferrata en Mai 1983. Paris: Éditions du Centre National de la Recherche Scientifique, 1988. 225-251.

968 Borgosz, Józef, and Maria Paczynska, Trans. "Controversies and Discussions About the Post-Council Aspect of Catholic Philosophy." *Dialectical Humanism* 14(1988): 233-248.

969 Botterill, Steven. "Doctrine, Doubt and Certainty: *Paradiso* XXXII." *Italian Studies* 42(1987): 20-36.

970 Bourke, Vernon J. "Right Reason as the Basis for Moral Action." *Tommaso Nel Suo Settimo Centenario 5: Atti del Congresso Internazionale: L'agire Morale*. Napoli: Edizioni Domenicane Italiane, 1977. 122-127.

971 Bourke, Vernon J. "The Ethical Justification of Legal Punishment." *American Journal of Jurisprudence* 22(1977): 1-18.

972 Bourke, Vernon J. "*Aeterni Patris*, Gilson and Christian Philosophy." *Proceedings of the American Catholic Philosophical Association* 53(1979): 5-15.

973 Bourke, Vernon J. "The New Center and the Intellectualism of St. Thomas." *One Hundred Years of Thomism: Aeterni Patris and Afterwards*. Ed. Victor B. Brezik. Houston, TX: Center for Thomistic Studies: University of St. Thomas, 1981. 165-172.

974 Bourke, Vernon J. "Justice as Equitable Reciprocity: Aquinas Updated." *American Journal of Jurisprudence* 27(1982): 17-31.

975 Bourke, Vernon J. "The Background of Aquinas' Synderesis Principle." *Graceful Reason: Essays in Ancient and Medieval Philosophy Presented to Joseph Owens on the Occasion of His Seventy-fifth Birthday and the Fiftieth Anniversary of His Ordination.* Ed. Lloyd P. Gerson. Papers in Mediaeval Studies 4. Toronto: Pontifical Institute of Mediaeval Studies, 1983. 345-360.

976 Bourke, Vernon J. "The Synderesis Rule and Right Reason." *The Monist* 66(1983): 71-82.

Many regard the rule "good should be done, evil avoided" as originating in Thomas Aquinas' famous article on natural law, where he says that it is knowable through the habit of synderesis. As governing all uses of right reasoning, it provides a bridge between speculative knowledge and obligatory decisions concerning human actions. Such decisions, in Aquinas' view, are never morally neutral but always of ethical significance. Formal in character, the rule does not specify what acts are good or evil. So one cannot deduce from it the more specific precepts of natural law: they are knowable by reasoning from actual life experiences.

977 Bourke, Vernon J. "Voluntariness and the Insanity Plea." *Thomistic Papers I.* Ed. Victor B. Brezik. Houston, TX: Center for Thomistic Studies: University of St. Thomas, 1984. 45-64.

978 Bourke, Vernon J. "Aquinas." *Ethics in the History of Western Philosophy.* Ed. Robert J. Cavalier. New York: St. Martin's Press, 1989. 98-124.

*Thomas Aquinas changed Western ethics from Christian Platonism to a more naturalistic moral theory in which Aristotle's ethics played a role. Besides the *Summa of Theology* and Book II, *Summa contra Gentiles*, seven other writings indicate how Aquinas used analyzes of human virtue, natural law precepts, and right reason to develop this new ethics. His handling of some special problems (homicide in self-defence, usury, gambling, just war) illustrates how Thomistic ethics works. It influenced later ethics: the Spanish Commentators, Cambridge Platonists and Caroline Casuists, and recent moralities of human virtue.*

979 Boyle, Joseph M. "*Praeter Intentionem* in Aquinas." *The Thomist* 42(1978): 649-665.

*In this paper I consider Aquinas' views on whether and how one can distinguish between what an agent intends in acting and what he foresees but does not intend. First, I consider his views on what is within the intention: both ends and means are within the intention. Second, I consider his views on what can be outside the intention: I discuss *S. T.* II-II 64, 7—on killing in self-defense—at some length. I argue for the following conclusion: the consequences or properties of intended ends and chosen means need not—on Aquinas' view—fall within the intention. They can be *praeter intentionem* if they are not essentially connected with what is within the intention.*

980 Boyle, Joseph M. "Aquinas, Kant, and Donagan on Moral Principles." *The New Scholasticism* 58(1984): 391-408.

981 Boyle, Joseph M. "Natural Law, Ownership and the World's Natural Resources." *The Journal of Value Inquiry* 23(1989): 191-207.

982 Boyle, Leonard E. "A Remembrance of Pope Leo XIII: The Encyclical *Aeterni Patris.*" *One Hundred Years of Thomism: Aeterni Patris and Afterwards.* Ed. Victor B. Brezik. Houston, TX: Center for Thomistic Studies: University of St. Thomas, 1981. 7-22.

983 Boyle, Leonard E. "Thomas Aquinas and the Duchess of Brabant." *Proceedings of the Patristic, Mediaeval, and Renaissance Studies* 8(1983): 25-35.

984 Boyle, Leonard E. "*Alia Lectura Fratris Thomae.*" *Mediaeval Studies* 45(1983): 418-429.

985 Boyle, Leonard E. "*Peciae, Apopeciae,* and a Toronto Ms. of the *Sententia Libri Ethicorum* of Aquinas." *The Role of the Book in Medieval Culture I.* Turnhout: Brepols, 1986. 71-82.

986 Bracken, Jerry. "Thomas Aquinas and Anselm's Satisfaction Theory." *Angelicum* 62(1985): 501-530.

987 Bradley, Denis J. M. "Rahner's *Spirit in the World*: Aquinas or Hegel?" *The Thomist* 41(1977): 167-199.

Despite Rahner's reliance on Thomistic terminology, his central problem is Kantian: to provide, against Kant, a transcendental justification for traditional (dogmatic) metaphysics. But Rahner's transcendental deduction raises Hegelian issues which are not sufficiently explored and which threaten Rahner's intended argument.

988 Bradley, Denis J. M. "Aristotelian Science and the Science of Thomistic Theology." *The Heythrop Journal* 22(1981): 162-171.

989 Bradley, Denis J. M. "Thomistic Theology and the Hegelian Critique of Religious Imagination." *The New Scholasticism* 59(1985): 60-78.

990 Brezik, Victor B. "The Descent of Man According to Thomas Aquinas." *Thomistic Papers I.* Ed. Victor B. Brezik. Houston, TX: Center for Thomistic Studies: University of St. Thomas, 1984. 83-108.

991 Brito, Emilio. "The Happiness of God: Hegel and Thomas Aquinas." *American Catholic Philosophical Quarterly* (formerly *The New Scholasticism*) 64(1990): 491-508.

992 Broadie, Alexander. "Maimonides and Aquinas on the Names of God." *Religious Studies* 23(1987): 157-170.

*Maimonides and Aquinas present what appear to be radically different answers to the question of the correct way to interpret terms used to signify divine attributes. It is argued in this paper that Maimonides' *via negativa* and Aquinas' *via analogica* are not different in substance, only in formation. Consideration of their accounts of God's knowledge confirms this.*

993 Bronaugh, Richard N. "Thomas Aquinas on Promises." *The Medieval Tradition of Natural Law.* Ed. Harold J. Johnson. Studies in Medieval Culutre 22. Kalamazoo, MI: Medieval Institute Publications, 1987. 5-12.

994 Bronson, Larry L. "My Heard is Harden'd: Marlowe's Dr. Faustus and the Thomistic Concepts of *Desperatio* and *Acedia.*" *Aquinas* 25(1982): 465-478.

995 Brown, Montague. "Permanent Creation in Saint Thomas Aquinas." *New Blackfriars* 67(1986): 362-371.

996 Brown, Montague. "Aquinas and the Real Distinction: A Re-evaluation." *New Blackfriars* 67(1988): 170-177.

997 Brown, Oscar James. "Aquinas' Doctrine of Slavery in Relation to Thomistic Teaching on Natural Law." *Proceedings of the American Catholic Philosophical Association* 53(1979): 173-181.

*The problem of the relation of slavery and natural law in Thomistic teaching cannot be probed apart from the indispensable Aristotelian background. In the most general terms the paper ties together the teaching of the two as follows: That while in one way Aquinas' doctrine is even more pro-slavery than is Aristotle's (if, that is to say, we consider slavery on the levels either of secular natural law or secondary natural law *ex peccato*): in another way Aquinas' doctrine of slavery is a quite considerably mitigated, not to say minimalist, one—if we consider the matter from what the paper presents as the predominant perspective of St. Thomas, that of the theological or specifically Christian doctrine of natural law and justice.*

998 Brown, Oscar James. "Individuation and Actual Existence in Scotistic Metaphysics: A Thomistic Assessment." *The New Scholasticism* 53(1979): 347-361.

*The issue of individuation vis-à-vis existence as it appears in Scotus is introduced in its historical context against the background of the treatment of the same problem by his immediate predecessors. Then the structure of Scotus' arguments on the issue (in 2 *Sent.* (Ox.) 3. 3 and 2 *Sent.* (Paris) 12:7) is closely examined along with his solution of the problem, and both are submitted to critical analysis and evaluation. Finally, the issue is addressed from the perspective of comparative metaphysics—Scotus' solution as seen from the Thomistic perspective of the primacy of existence. The study concludes that, although for Aquinas the role of existence in individuation is quite crucial, for Scotus actual existence is, as it were, an "epiphenomenal" aspect of anything: Existence contributes nothing and essence explains everything; that is to say, an essence is individuated exclusively in its own order.*

999 Brown, Oscar James. "St. Thomas, the Philosophers and Felicity: Some Reflections on *Summa Contra Gentiles* III, 63, 10." *Laval Théologique et Philosophique* 37(1981): 69-82.

*At the very end of the first part of Book III of the *Summa contra Gentiles* 63. 10, and as the culmination of his consideration of human happiness, Aquinas informs us that "the philosophers...were not able to get full knowledge of this ultimate happiness." Why not? The answer to that question inevitably entails the examination of three incidental issues, to wit:(1) Whether the pagan philosophers could have known the beatific vision at all; (2) Whether to know the felicity of this life is to know something that is in no sense ultimate; (3) Whether the knowledge of immortality was the one step that was absolutely necessary to a proper realization of ultimate beatitude. The first issue is answered in the affirmative; the other two in the negative.*

1000 Brown, Robert F. "A Reply to Kelly on Aquinas' Third Way." *International Journal for Philosophy of Religion* 12(1982): 225-228.

Kelly's defense involves the stipulation that a "possible-not-to-exist" is that which at one time did not exist. Yet Aquinas himself doesn't use such a restrictive sense of contingency elsewhere in his philosophy. Thus Kelly unwittingly shows that the first part of the "third way" has only hypothetical force and is not a conclusive demonstration.

1001 Bruening, William H. "Aquinas and Wittgenstein on God-talk." *Sophia* (Australia) 16(1977): 1-7.

*This essay compares Aquinas' discussion of analogy with Wittgenstein's discussion of God in his Lectures on *Religious Belief.* Aquinas' doctrine of analogy is discussed in terms of his doctrine of showing and saying. The thesis is that Aquinas and Wittgenstein take very similar views about talking about God, and that Wittgenstein sees the issue of God-talk more clearly than does Aquinas.*

1002 Buersmeyer, Keith A. "Predication and Participation." *The New Scholasticism* 55(1981): 35-51.

*The main concern of this article is to clarify Thomas Aquinas' theory of predication, showing its coherence and possible relevance for current discussions on this topic. A number of scattered texts from the *In Peri Hermeneias, In Posteriorum Analyticorum*, and *De Hebdomadibus* and other works of Aquinas are examined in the attempt to discover a unified theory. Points touched upon include Aquinas' treatment of proper names, universals, the copula, analogy, and the possibility of predicating terms of God. Two recent articles by F. Wilhelmsen are used as a framework for this discussion of predication. In these articles, Wilhelmsen re-opened the debate between judgment and participation as the key to Aquinas' thought, siding with the former. I have attempted to show the danger of this opposition, arguing that judgment and participation have a mutual dependence for Aquinas.*

1003 Buersmeyer, Keith A. "The Verb and Existence." *The New Scholasticism* 60(1986): 145-162.

1004 Buersmeyer, Keith A. "Aquinas on the *Modi Significandi*." *The Modern Schoolman* 64(1987): 73-95.

1005 Buijs, Joseph A. "The Negative Theology of Maimonides and Aquinas." *The Review of Metaphysics* 41(1988): 723-738.

*Isaac Franck recently defended what he called a *radical* negative theology. He took both Maimonides and Aquinas to be at the root of such a theology. However, his understanding of negative theology, I argue, conflates two distinct theses: an epistemic one concerning the unknowability of God with a semantic one concerning the intelligibility of language about God. On the basis of this distinction I argue for a fundamental philosophical difference in the respective negative theologies of Maimonides, Aquinas, and Franck.*

1006 Bukowski, Thomas P. "John Pecham, Thomas Aquinas, et al. on the Eternity of the World." *Recherches De Théologie Ancienne et Médiévale* 46(1979): 216-221.

1007 Bukowski, Thomas P. "Siger of Brabant Vs. Thomas Aquinas on Theology." *The New Scholasticism* 61(1987): 25-32.

1008 Bukowski, Thomas P. "A Note on Thomas' *In Physics. Libro* 8um." *Recherches de Théologie Ancienne et Médiévale* 61(1989): 224-227.

1009 Burns, J. H. "St. German, Gerson, Aquinas, and Ulpian." *History of Political Thought* 4(1983): 443-450.

1010 Burns, Robert M. "The Divine Simplicity in St. Thomas." *Religious Studies* 25(1989): 271-293.

Aquinas' arguments for divine simplicity are essentially attempts to specify the nature of the source of cosmic intelligibility. They fail because no account is taken of the possibility of complexity as opposed to compositeness in the first principle, even though Aquinas eventually resorts to it in his defense of the doctrine of the Trinity. Moreover, he fails to reconcile divine simplicity with omniscience and free will. His preoccupation with divine simplicity is traced to the influence of Arabic Neoplatonized Aristotelianism mediated especially through Avicenna and Maimonides. More satisfactory approaches are found in Plotinus, Marius Victorinus, Al-Ghazali, and Schelling.

1011 Burns, Robert M. "The Agent Intellect in Rahner and Aquinas." *The Heythrop Journal* 29(1988): 423-449.

*Karl Rahner's "historical investigation," in his *Spirit in the World*, of Aquinas' cognitional theory is found to be flawed because it largely ignores its context in the thirteenth-century debate on the agent intellect, reading into Aquinas' conceptions derived ultimately from German idealism. Rahner ignores Thomas' downgrading of the agent intellect and corresponding upgrading of the possible intellect compared with the Averroist account, confuses the agent intellect with the will and the will with natural desire, and distorts Thomas' account of the emanation of the powers of the soul in several respects.*

1012 Burrell, David B. "The Performative Character of the "Proofs" for the Existence of God." *Listening* 13(1978): 20-26.

*This essay explores the purpose or the point of so-called "proofs" for God's existence and offers a typology of two kinds of *justification* in an effort to ascertain what a successful "proof" would be expected to accomplish.*

1013 Burrell, David B. "Religious Belief and Rationality." *Rationality and Religious Belief*. Ed. C. F. Delaney. Notre Dame, IN: University of Notre Dame Press, 1979. 84-115.

*"Rationality and religious belief" offers ways of understanding how *justification* may be construed in such a way as to allow the very practice and perspectives of a life of faith to be brought to bear on one's assessment of the activity. Although this proposal is inevitably circular, the article shows how it cannot be called viciously so and offers a way of discriminating between "prospective" and "retrospective" justification. It attempts to show that the latter is in fact a more natural paradigm than the former for assessing humanly significant activities and accounting for our participation in them responsibly.*

1014 Burrell, David B. "Aquinas and Maimonides: A Conversation About Proper Speech." *Immanuel* 16(1983): 70-86.

1015 Burrell, David B. "Reply to Burrell's Misconstruals of Scotus: An Exercise in Reading." *The New Scholasticism* 57(1983): 81-82.

How does Scotus really differ from Aquinas? A great deal, I have contended, and significantly. Douglas Langston disagrees: they offer but minor variations on medieval epistemological themes. What is at issue, however, is the critical character of that enterprise, especially as Aquinas engaged in it. Some reminders to that effect are assembled here.

1016 Burrell, David B. "Maimonides, Aquinas and Gersonides on Providence and Evil." *Religious Studies* 20(1984): 335-351.

This essay shows how interfaith and intercultural was the treatment of issues in medieval times, as two Jewish and one Christian thinkers' commentaries on Job are compared to determine the parameters for the "problem of evil" and to set the stage for an analysis of Aquinas' treatment. One reading of Aquinas (Peter Geach) is considered, and a constructive alternative is offered which keeps God's knowledge rigorously in the practical mode.

1017 Burrell, David B. "Creation, Will and Knowledge in Aquinas and Scotus." *Pragmatisches I*. Ed. H. Stuchowiak. Hamburg: FelixMeiner, 1986.

1018 Burrell, David B. "Distinguishing God from the World." *Language, Meaning, and God: Essays in Honour of Herbert McCabe*. Ed. Brian Davies. London: Chapman, 1987. 75-91.

1019 Burrell, David B. "Aquinas' Debt to Maimonides." *A Straight Path: Studies in Medieval Philosophy and Culture. Essays in Honor of Arthur Hyman*. Eds. Jeremiah Hackett et al. Washington, DC: The Catholic University of America, 1988. 37-48.

Aquinas lived in an interfaith, intercultural intellectual situation, and the greatest proof was his debt to Moses Maimonides: for the state of argumentation regarding the "eternity" of the world, for the pattern of reasoning regarding God's existence, and even for the question of "divine names," although Aquinas' more sophisticated semantics led him to a more nuanced solution. All this argues for a re-visioning of the medieval philosophical world, as one in which Jewish, Christian, and Islamic philosophers were treating common subjects in a shared idiom.

1020 Burrell, David B. "Ghazali and Aquinas on the Names of God." *Literature and Theology* 3(1989): 173-180.

1021 Burt, Robert K. "Facts, Fables, and Moral Rules: An Analysis of the Abortion Debate." *The New Scholasticism* 62(1988): 400-411.

Most moral arguments are combinations of facts, principles, and exemplary cases which serve as the basis for an argument from analogy. The debate about abortion is an example of this. There are facts about the humanity and rights of the fetus, facts about the place of the individual in the universe, and then the facts of the particular situation under consideration. There are also principles such as justice and "Do not harm," and more specifically, "One has absolute control over what is to be done to one's body," or "it is always forbidden to directly will to kill an innocent person." This paper argues that the prohibition of killing the innocent is not absolute in the Judaic-Christiantradition (as shown by the thought of Augustine and Aquinas).

1022 Busa, Roberto. "How Quantitative Information on Words, Forms and Lemmas is Presented in the *Index Thomisticus*." *Biblioteca dell'Archivum Romanicum, Serie II: Linguistica* 37(1980): 887-892.

1023 Busa, Roberto. "On Law and Freedom—Hermeneutical Methods for Interpreting St. Thomas from the *Index Thomisticus*." *Lex et Libertas: Freedom and Law According to St. Thomas Aquinas*. Eds. L. J. Elders and K. Hedwig. Studi Tomistici 30. Città del Vaticano, Pontificia Accademia di San Tommaso e di Religione Cattolica: Libreria Editrice Vaticana, 1987. 25-40.

1024 Butterworth, Edward Joseph. "On the Rationale for Proving the Existence of God." *Existence of God: Essays from the Basic Issues Forum*. Eds. R. Jacobson and Robert Lloyd Mitchell. Lewiston, NY: Mellen Press, 1988. 97-114.

1025 Byrne, Patrick H. "The Thomist Sources of Lonergan's Dynamic World-View." *The Thomist* 46(1982): 108-145.

1026 Calhoun, David H. "Can Human Beings Be Friends of God?" *The Modern Schoolman* 66(1989): 209-219.

Thomas Aquinas begins his analysis of charity by asserting that charity is equivalent to friendship, and that God and human beings, who are bound by charity, share a relationship of friendship. Although Thomas recognizes that there are problems with the identification of friendship and charity, he omits the most important difficulty arising from his reliance on Aristotle's account of friendship: the vast inequality between the human and the divine. However, while true friendship between God and human beings appears impossible, I argue that Thomas' initial insight about the relation between human beings and God can be saved by modification.

1027 Callangan Aquino, Ranhilio. "St. Thomas and Existentialists: Links in Epistemology." *Philippiniana Sacra* (Manila) 14(1979): 303-348.

1028 Camara, Helder. "What Would Saint Thomas Aquinas, the Aristotle Commentator, Do If Faced with Karl Marx?" *Celebrating the Medieval Heritage: A Colloquy on the Thought of Aquinas and Bonaventure*. Ed. David Tracy. *The Journal of Religion* 58. Chicago: University of Chicago Press, 1978. 174-182. See also "What would St. Thomas Aquinas do if faced with Karl Marx" in *New Catholic World*, June, 1977, 108-113.

1029 Caputo, John D. "The Problem of Being in Heidegger and Aquinas." *The Thomist* 41(1977): 62-91.

*This article is based on Heidegger's discussion of the scholastic doctrine of essence and existence in the recently published *Grundproblem der Phaenomenologie*; the author confronts the scholastic and, particularly, the Thomistic theory of being with Heidegger's *Seinsdenken*. He takes up the common (and conflicting) claim made by Heidegger and the followers of Saint Thomas that each has alone achieved an insight into being as being, being itself, and that the history of metaphysics represents an oblivion in which the unique, irreducible quality of being has been covered. The different methodologies of Heidegger and Aquinas are found to lie at the root of the difference between their interestingly comparable understanding of being.*

1030 Caputo, John D. "Heidegger's 'Dif-ference' and the Distinction Between *Esse* and *Ens* in St. Thomas." *International Philosophical Quarterly* 20(1980): 161-182.

*After a discussion of the distinction between *esse* and *ens* in the metaphysics of St. Thomas, a discussion which argues that there is not and can be no oblivion of Being in a philosophy of *esse*, it is shown that Heidegger's critique of metaphysics is deeper than such a defense of Thomism admits, and that it has to do with the very difference (*Austrag*) which opens up all such metaphysical distinctions, a dif-ference unthought by Thomas.*

1031 Caputo, John D. "Heidegger and Aquinas: The Thought of Being and the Metaphysics of *Esse*." *Philosophy Today* 26(1982): 194-203.

*This article sketches the argument of a forthcoming book of the same title to the effect that the ground must be shifted on which the confrontation of Heidegger and Aquinas has usually been carried out. The author argues that, contrary to the protest of the Thomists, the metaphysics of *esse* is not an exception to the "forgetfulness" of Being, but on the contrary part and parcel of it. The genuine response, from a Thomistic standpoint, to the Heideggerian critique lies elsewhere in what the author calls the "mystical element" in Saint Thomas' thought, a dimension in which metaphysical or ontotheological reason gives way to an aletheological experience of the mystery of the divine Being.*

1032 Cardman, Francine. "The Medieval Question of Women and Orders." *The Thomist* 42(1978): 582-599.

How the question of women's ordination arose in medieval theology, what reasons were advanced for not ordaining women, and what authority Sentences commentators gave their arguments are questions addressed here. Structural and theological development of treatment of the sacrament of orders in Alexander of Hales, Albert, Thomas, Bonaventure, and Duns Scotus is investigated, then located in the context of concurrent systematization of canon law. Conclusions are that medieval discussions of women and orders varied greatly in theological rationale and estimate of authority, that established liturgical practice and interaction of canon law and theology produced a position of limited historical and theological merit.

1033 Carlin, Jr., David R. "Assimilating Kohlberg to Aquinas." *The Thomist* 45(1981): 124-131.

*Lawrence Kohlberg's three levels of moral thinking (pre-conventional, conventional, and post-conventional) roughly correspond to Aquinas' three levels of human inclination (existential, animal, and rational) and to the moral imperatives based on these inclinations. Implicit in Aquinas is an ontologically grounded scheme of moral development which the act of assimilating Kohlberg requires us to render explicit. Mention is made of benefits both parties will gain by such a merger. The whole argument rests upon a liberal interpretation of the Thomistic text under consideration (*Summa Theologica*, I-II, 94, art. (2).*

1034 Carney, Frederick. "On McCormick and Teleological Morality." *Journal of Religious Ethics* 6(1978): 81-107.

This essay, after setting forth four different types of teleology employed in various moralities (a teleology of persons, of nature, of human institutions, and of moral obligation) and identifying the teleology advocated by McCormick as an instance of the fourth type, critically examines an assumption by McCormick that an acknowledgement of teleology of any of the first three types is equivalent to, or leads to the affirmation of, a teleology of the fourth type. Then it explores the relation of McCormick's teleology of moral obligation to utilitarianism and to the classic Catholic morality of Thomas Aquinas, finding an identity with the former and a discontinuity with the latter. Finally, this essay suggests some considerations against adopting the teleological morality advocated by McCormick.

1035 Carr-Wiggen, Robert. "God's Omnipotence and Immutability." *The Thomist* 48(1984): 44-51.

1036 Casey, Gerard N. "A Problem of Unity in St. Thomas' Account of Human Action." *The New Scholasticism* 61(1987): 146-161.

1037 Casey, Gerard N. "An Explication of the *De Hebdomadibus* of Boethius in the Light of St. Thomas' Commentary." *The Thomist* 51(1987): 419-434.

1038 Casey, Gerard N. "Angelic Interiority." *Irish Philosophical Journal* 6(1989): 82-118.

*In this article I examine St. Thomas' application of some basic metaphysical and epistemological principles to purely intellectual beings (angels). I consider an apparent inconsistency in St. Thomas' angelology having to do with an angel's transparency to self but not other angels, and I attempt to show both that is not an inconsistency and why it is not an inconsistency. The dissolution of the inconsistency depends crucially upon the distinction of *esse naturale*, *esse intentionale*, and *esse intelligibile* from one another, and upon a clear grasp of the role of the will as a principle of interiority in all created intellectual beings.*

1039 Celano, Anthony John. "The Concept of Worldly Beatitude in the Writings of Thomas Aquinas." *Journal of the History of Philosophy* 25(1987): 215-226.

*The article concerns Thomas Aquinas' understanding of the meaning of Aristotle's statement in the *Nichomachean Ethics* that living men can be called blessed, but only "blessed as me"(1101a18-20). Thomas views this assertion as Aristotle's admission that a human life is inherently imperfect, especially when compared to the perfect life of eternal contemplation that divine beings enjoy. Thomas does not, however, introduce here theological ideas into his understanding of beatitude but poses the question in terms of how human goods affect human happiness. His resolution may go further than Aristotle's answer, but it does not do an injustice to the spirit of Aristotle's moral philosophy.*

1040 Centore, Florestano. "Lovejoy and Aquinas on God's 'Need' to Create." *Angelicum* 59(1982): 23-36.

1041 Centore, Florestano. "Logic, Aquinas, and *Ultrum Deus Sit*." *Angelicum* 63(1986): 213-226.

1042 Centore, Florestano. "Thomism and the Female Body as Seen in the *Summa Theologiae*." *Angelicum* 67(1990): 37-56.

1043 Charlesworth, Max. "St. Thomas Aquinas and the Decline of the Kantian- Kierkegaardian Philosophy of Religion." *Tommaso Nel Suo Settimo Centenario VI: Atti del Congresso Internazionale: L'essere*. Napoli: Edizioni Domenicane Italiane, 1977. 50-60.

1044 Charlesworth, Max. "Augustine and Aquinas: Church and State." *Political Thinkers*. Ed. David Muschamp. Basingstoke: Macmillan Education Ltd., 1986. 39-50.

1045 Chenu, Marie-Dominique. "Body and Body Politic in the Creation Spirituality of Thomas Aquinas." *Listening* 13(1978): 214-232.

1046 Christianson, Joseph M. "The Necessity and Some Characteristics of the Habit of First Indemonstrable (Speculative) Principles." *The New Scholasticism* 62(1988): 249-296.

*This article examines Aquinas' doctrine regarding habits in general and the habit of first (speculative) principles in particular. It shows that, according to St. Thomas, only certain powers (the intellect and will) of finite rational beings can be the proper subjects of habits as such. Why this author posits that habits are necessary is investigated and determined. The remainder of the article presents Aquinas' thought on the following points with respect to the habit of first principles, specifically our knowledge of the existence of this *habitus*; why this habit is necessary; whether this habit is a virtue, in the strict sense; the function of the *habitus principiorum* in man's attainment of truth. The paper is not meant to be exhaustive but to explicate certain noteworthy details in St. Thomas' teaching on habits, and especially the habit of first principles.*

1047 Chydenius, J. "Humanism in Medieval Concepts of Man and Society." *Commentationes Humanarum Litterarum* 77(1985): 1-53.

1048 Clark, Mary T. "Towards a Thomistic Philosophy of Death." *Tommaso D'Aquino Nel Suo Settimo Centenario: Atti del Congresso Internazionale VII: L'Uomo*. Napoli: Edizioni Domenicane Italiane, 1978. 450-456.

1049 Clark, Mary T. "What Maritain Meant by Abstractive Intuition." *Jacques Maritain. Philosophe dans la Cité/ A Philosopher in the World*. Ed. Jean-Louis Allard. Philosophica 28. Ottawa: University of Ottawa Press, 1985. 85-91.

1050 Clark, Mary T. "Willing Freely According to Thomas Aquinas." *A Straight Path: Studies in Medieval Philosophy and Culture. Essays in Honor of Arthur Hyman*. Eds. Jeremiah Hackett et al. Washington, DC: The Catholic University of America Press, 1988. 49-56.

1051 Clarke, W. Norris. "The Role of Essence Within St. Thomas' Essence-existence Doctrine: Positive or Negative Principle? A Dispute Within Thomism." *Tommaso Nel Suo Settimo Centenario VI: Atti del Congresso Internazionale: L'essere*. Napoli: Edizioni Domenicane Italiane, 1977. 109-115.

1052 Clarke, W. Norris. "Fifty Years of Metaphysical Reflection: The Universe as Journey." *The Universe as Journey: Conversations with W. Norris Clarke*. Ed. Gerard A. McCool. New York: Fordham University Press, 1979. 49-92.

1053 Clarke, W. Norris. "Action as the Self-Revelation of Being: A Central Theme in the Thought of St. Thomas." *History of Philosophy in the Making: Essays in Honor of James Collins*. Ed. L. J. Thro. Washington, DC: The Catholic University of America Press, 1982. 63-80.

1054 Clarke, W. Norris. "The Metaphysics of Religious Art: Reflections on a Text of St. Thomas Aquinas." *Graceful Reason: Essays in Ancient and Medieval Philosophy Presented to Joseph Owens on the Occasion of His Seventy-fifth Birthday and the Fiftieth Anniversary of His Ordination*. Ed. Lloyd P. Gerson. Papers in Mediaeval Studies 4. Toronto: Pontifical Institute of Mediaeval Studies, 1983. 301-314.

1055 Clarke, W. Norris. "Thomism and Contemporary Philosophical Pluralism." *The Modern Schoolman* 67(1990): 123-139.

1056 Cleary, John J. "On the Terminology of Abstraction in Aristotle." *Phronesis* 30(1985): 13-45.

1057 Cohen, Sheldon M. "St. Thomas Aquinas on the Immaterial Reception of Sensible Forms." *The Philosophical Review* 91(1982): 193-209.

The received interpretation holds that Aquinas holds that in perception there are two events—a physical event taking place in the sense organ, and a non-physical event, a spiritual reception of form, taking place in the soul. On this interpretation, the latter event culminates in a mental image. The author argues on textual and doctrinal ground that Aquinas holds that no non-physical event is involved in perception. His "spiritual reception of sensible form" is a type of physical event, and it issues in a physical likeness, not a mental image.

1058 Collins, James. "Przywara's *Analogia Entis*." *Thought* 65(1990): 359-375.

1059 Connell, Desmond. "St. Thomas on Reflection and Judgment." *Irish Theological Quarterly* 45(1978): 234-247.

1060 Connell, Richard J. "Preliminaries to the Five Ways." *Thomistic Paper IV*. Ed. Leonard A. Kennedy. Notre Dame, IN: University of Notre Dame Press, 1988. 129-167.

This paper argues that for three reasons the Five Ways are widely misunderstood. First, the arguments are not complete but are only sketches. Second, they are ordered among themselves, the first to the second and second to the third, which alone of the first three fully proves that God exists; both the first and second ways argue from formalities too narrow to draw that conclusion perfectly. The fifth way argues to God's intelligence, not to his existence. Third, the arguments, especially the first and second ways, presuppose certain empirical propositions (indicated in the paper) to be rightly understood.

1061 Connery, John R. "The Teleology of Proportionate Reason." *Theological Studies* 44(1983): 489-496.

1062 Cooke, Vincent M. "Human Beings." *International Philosophical Quarterly* 26(1986): 269-275.

1063 Cooper, John W. "Natural Law and Economic Humanism." *Jacques Maritain: The Man and His Metaphysics*. Ed. John F. X. Knasas. Mishawaka, IN: The American Maritain Association, 1988. 147-157.

1064 Corrigan, Kevin. "A Philosophical Precursor to the Theory of Essence and Existence in St. Thomas Aquinas." *The Thomist* 48(1984): 219-240.

1065 Cortest, Luis. "Was St. Thomas Aquinas a Platonist?" *The Thomist* 52(1988): 209-219.

1066 Cos, Joseph. "Evidences of St. Thomas' Dictating Activity in the Naples Manuscript of His *Scriptum in Metaphysicam* (Naples, BN VIII F. 16)." *Scriptorium* 38(1984): 231-253.

1067 Courtenay, William J. "The King and the Leaden Coin: The Economic Background of 9Sine Qua Non' Causality." 1972. *Covenant and Causality in Medieval Thought: Studies in Philosophy, Theology and Economic Practice*. London: Variorum Reprints, 1984. 185-209.

1068 Craig, William Lane. "The Cosmological Argument and the Possibility of Infinite Temporal Regression." *Archiv für Geschichte der Philosophie* 59(1977): 261-279.

1069 Craig, William Lane. "Dilley's Misunderstandings of the Cosmological Argument." *The New Scholasticism* 53(1979): 388-392.

Contemporary philosophers of religion often betray an unfortunate ignorance of the history of philosophy and its principal figures. A case in point is Frank Dilley's attempted clarification of Thomas Aquinas' cosmological argument by interpreting it to conclude to a final cause. Dilley's assertion is easily refuted by numerous references in Aquinas that all of his first three ways terminate in an efficient cause. This single fact vitiates the remainder of Dilley's argument, because problems such as the question of infinite causal regression cannot then be dismissed as he suggests. Dilley's misinterpretation of Aquinas seems to be because of(1) ignorance of the arguments of Aquinas himself and (2) the desire to press Aquinas' proofs into the service of process theology, a Procrustean bed into which they do not fit.

1070 Craig, William Lane. "Was Thomas Aquinas a B-theorist of Time?" *The New Scholasticism* 59(1985): 475-483.

1071 Craig, William Lane. "Aquinas on God's Knowledge of Future Contingents." *The Thomist* 54(1990): 33-79.

*A thorough examination of the primary texts of the primary texts, dealing with God's timeless *scientia visionis* and analyzing the implications for Thomas' theory of time, the doctrine of God's knowing all things through His essence, and the doctrine of God's knowledge asthe cause of things.*

1072 Cranz, Edward F. "The Publishing History of the Aristotle Commentaries of Thomas Aquinas." *Traditio* 34(1978): 157-192.

1073 Creel, Richard E. "Happiness and Resurrection: A Reply to Morreall." *Religious Studies* 17(1981): 387-394.

*John Morreall argues in "*Perfect Happiness and the Resurrection of the Body*" (*Religious Studies* 16, 29-35) that the Christian doctrine of the resurrection is otiose because, according to orthodox theology, the perfect bliss that we enjoy in life after death is entirely because of our vision of the essence of God, a vision for which the body is not needed. I critique two of Morreall's implicit assumptions about happiness and defend the meaningfulness of the resurrection.*

1074 Crosby, John. "The Idea of Value and the Reform of the Traditional Metaphysics of *Bonum*." *Aletheia* 1(1977): 231-336.

*I deal with the Thomistic teaching that good (*bonum*) is not something which a being has in itself but rather only in relation to something else, namely to the appetite of some being. I bring to evidence that good in all its kinds is "more" than being (*ens*) considered as desirable (*appetibile*); good is a distinct character or moment of a being.

I also show that the great value phenomenologist, von Hildebrand, brought to light an objective kind of good (value) which has a metaphysical impact which would be unintelligible if it existed only as the desirability of being. I conclude by showing that the unity of being and value, far from being compromised by this idea of value, is established more adequately than in the Thomistic teaching.*

1075 Crosson, Frederick J. "Proof and Presence." *Experience, Reason and God.* Ed. E. Long. 1980. 55-67.

1076 Crosson, Frederick J. "*Fides and Credere*: W. C. Smith on Aquinas." *The Journal of Religion* 65(1988): 399-412.

1077 Crowe, Frederick. "Thomas Aquinas and the Will: A Note on Interpretation." *Method* 22(1990): 13-26.

1078 Crowe, Michael Bertram. "The Pursuit of the Natural Law." *Irish Theological Quarterly* 44(1977): 3-29.

1079 Crowe, Michael Bertram. "Natural Law Terminology in the Late 12th and Early 13rd Centuries." *Tijdschrift voor Filosofie* 39(1977): 409-420.

*The terminology in which Thomas Aquinas and his numerous successors discuss the natural law is the result of a lengthy development. The analysis of connected notions (synderesis, conscience) and of competing definitions (Ulpian's, Gratian's) contributed powerfully to this development. The terms and definitions are studied in important canonists, civil lawyer and theologians of the period—William of Auxerre, Philip the Chancellor, Alexander of Hales, Bonaventure, Albert the Great and others, leading up to Aquinas. The article summarizes part of the argument of my book, *The Changing Profile of the Natural Law* (Nijhoff, The Hague, 1977).*

1080 Crowe, Michael Bertram. "St. Thomas' Natural Law and Some Contemporary Approaches." *Tommaso D'Aquino Nel Suo Settimo Centenario VIII: Atti del Congresso Internazionale: L'Uomo.* Napoli: Edizioni Domenicane Italiane, 1978. 271-281.

1081 Crowe, Michael Bertram. "Aquinas and Natural Law: Terminology and Definitions in Late 12th and Early 13th Centuries." *Sprache und Erkenntnis Im Mittelalter: Akten Des VI. Internationalen Kongresses Für Mittelalterliche Philosophie der Sociéte Internationale Pour L'étude de la Philosophie Médiévale 1981.* Eds. Jan P. Beckmann et al. Miscellanea Medievalia 13. Berlin: Walter de Gruyter, 1981. 614-621.

1082 Crowe, Michael Bertram. "Thomism and Today's Crisis in Moral Values." *One Hundred Years of Thomism: Aeterni Patris* and Afterwards. Ed. Victor B. Brezik. Houston, TX: Center for Thomistic Studies: University of St. Thomas, 1981. 74-89.

1083 Damich, Edward J. "The Essence of Law According to Thomas Aquinas." *American Journal of Jurisprudence* 30(1985): 79-96.

1084 Dammann, R. M. J. "Metaphors and Other Things." *Proceedings of the Aristotelian Society* 78(1977-1978): 125-140.

1085 Daniel, William. "Double Effect and Resisting Evil." *Australasian Catholic Record* 56(1979): 377-387.

1086 Davenport, Manuel M. "Saint Thomas and Arming the *Contras*." *Southwestern Philosophy Review* 4(1988): 49-60.

Do recent efforts by citizens of the United States to overthrow the government of Nicaragua violate the just war theory criterion of legitimate authority? St. Thomas describes a legitimate authority as one who has a right established prior to a conflict to select and depose rulers and argues that God has willed that nonlegitimate persons shall never initiate or engage in wars. In these terms, the legitimate authority in the United States is Congress, and even if Casey, North, and others were acting under presidential orders, they were morally wrong. A secular, rule-utilitarian version of just war theory leads to the same conclusion.

1087 Davies, Brian. "Heads in the Clouds: Thomas Aquinas and Professor John Hick on Faith." *New Blackfriars* 60(1979): 242-257.

1088 Davies, Brian. "Natural Law in the Age of Reason: The Emergence of Relativistic Utilitarianism." *Fides* 13(1981): 62-72.

1089 Davies, Brian. "Kenny on God." *Philosophy* 57(1982): 105-117.

1090 Davies, Brian. "Classical Theism and the Doctrine of Divine Simplicity." *Language, Meaning, and God: Essays in Honour of Herbert McCabe*. Ed. Brian Davies. 1987. 51-74.

1091 Davies, Brian. "Is *Sacra Doctrina* Theology?" *New Blackfriars* 71(1990): 141-147.

1092 Day, Timothy Joseph. "Aquinas on Infinite Regresses." *International Journal for Philosophy of Religion* 22(1987): 151-164.

I discuss Aquinas' views about infinite regresses, in particular why he allows some and rejects others. I use two of the Five Ways arguments to illustrate how Aquinas uses infinite regress arguments. I also look at an infinite regress argument that Aquinas rejects. I draw a distinction to separate acceptable from unacceptable regresses as Aquinas does. Finally, I suggest some reasons to explain why Aquinas rejects the regresses he does reject.

1093 De Kirchner, Beatriz Bossi. "Aquinas as Interpreter of Aristotle on the End of Human Life." *The Review of Metaphysics* 40(1986-1987): 41-54.

1094 De Mello Gomide, Fernando. "Hypothesis and Theory in Physics and St. Thomas Aquinas' Epistemology." *Atti Dell'VIII Congresso Tomistico Internazionale VII: L'uomo e Il Mondo Nella Luce Dell'Aquinate*. Studi Tomistici 16. Cittá del Vaticano: Pontificia Accademia di San Tommaso e di Religione Cattolica, 1982. 286-296.

1095 De Rijk, L. M. "Did Parmenides Reject the Sensible World?" *Graceful Reason: Essays in Ancient and Medieval Philosophy Presented to Joseph Owens on the Occasion of His Seventy-fifth Birthday and the Fiftieth Anniversary of His Ordination*. Ed. Lloyd P. Gerson. Papers in Mediaeval Studies 4. Toronto: Pontifical Institute of Mediaeval Studies, 1983. 29-53.

1096 De Vogel, Cornelia J. "*Deus Creator Omnium*: Plato and Aristotle in Aquinas' Doctrine of God." *Graceful Reason: Essays in Ancient and Medieval Philosophy Presented to Joseph Owens on the Occasion of His Seventy-fifth Birthday and the Fiftieth Anniversary of His Ordination*. Ed. Lloyd P. Gerson. Papers in Mediaeval Studies 4. Toronto: Pontifical Institute of Mediaeval Studies, 1983. 203-207.

1097 Dedek, John F. "Intrinsically Evil Acts: An Historical Study of the Mind of St. Thomas." *The Thomist* 43(1979): 385-413.

*The purpose of this article is to show that St. Thomas never held that any acts are intrinsically evil, that is to say, so deformed in themselves that they can never be licit for any purpose or under any circumstances. Thomas never used the expression "intrinsically evil act"; rather he said that some actions like theft, adultery, and murder are *secundum se* evil. A study of this expression, not only in the writings of Thomas but also in the published and unpublished writings of his immediate predecessors, shows that this expression is a tautology: it denotes an act done *ex libidine*, i.e., lawlessly out of sinful desire. For instance, adultery is *secundum se* evil in the sense of *coire cum no sua ex libidine*, but not in the sense of *coire cum non sua*.*

1098 Dedek, John F. "Moral Absolutes in the Predecessors of St. Thomas." *Theological Studies* 38(1979): 654-680.

1099 Dedek, John F. "Intrinsically Evil Acts: The Emergence of a Doctrine." *Recherches de Théologie Ancienne et Médiévale* 50(1983): 191-226.

1100 Degnan, Jr., Daniel A. "Two Models of Positive Law in Aquinas: A Study of the Relationship of Positive Law and Natural Law." *The Thomist* 46(1982): 1-32.

1101 Dennehy, Raymond. "The Ontological Basis of Human Rights." *The Thomist* 42(1978): 434-463.

1102 Dennehy, Raymond. "Reply to Mr Schedler on Human Rights." *The New Scholasticism* 55(1981): 488-494.

Schedler's critique of the Thomist theory of rights—the conclusion of which is that Thomists "... are unable to make out a basis for rights for humans which are incapable of rational choice"—rests upon a failure to understand the metaphysical basis of the theory. For example, he confuses essential and accidental qualities of man and equivocates on the term "human essence," thereby erroneously attributing to Thomism the extreme realism of the Platonic solution to the problem of universals.

1103 Dennehy, Raymond. "Understanding Maritain: His Epistemological Doctrine of Judgment and His Metaphysical Doctrine of the Subject." *Notes et Documents de L'Institut International Jacques Maritain*. Rome: L' Institut Interanational J. Maritain, 1984. 123-143.

1104 Dennehy, Raymond. "Maritain's Intellectual Existentialism: An Introduction to His Metaphysics and Epistemology." *Understanding Maritain: Philosopher and Friend*. Eds. Deal W. Hudson and Matthew J. Mancini. Macon, GA: Mercer University Press, 1987. 201-233.

1105 Devenish, Philip E. "Omnipotence, Creation, Perfection: Kenny and Aquinas on the Power and Action of God." *Modern Theology* 1(1985): 105-117.

1106 Dewan, Lawrence. "St. Thomas, Capreolus, and Entitative Composition." *Divus Thomas* 80(1977): 355-375.

1107 Dewan, Lawrence. "Being *Per Se*, Being *Per Accidens* and St. Thomas' Metaphysics." *Science et Esprit* 30(1978): 169-184.

1108 Dewan, Lawrence. "St. Thomas and the Causality of God's Goodness." *Laval Théologique et Philosophique* 34(1978): 291-304.

1109 Dewan, Lawrence. "St. Thomas and the Possibles." *The New Scholasticism* 53(1979): 76-85.

Zedler claims that for Saint Thomas the possibles as possible is the result of God freely willing, indeed that God gives possibility to things by creating them. I show the meaning of "absolute possible" for Saint Thomas; the priority of such possibles to any creation, some things being possible and never created; the priority of the possibility of possibles to the divine will; the need to see the possibles as pertaining to the divine being and God's natural knowledge of his being (prior even to his conception of himself as agent); that this conception pertains to the very intelligibility of God's freedom in creating.

1110 Dewan, Lawrence. "St. Thomas, Ideas, and Immediate Knowledge." *Dialogue* 18(1979): 392-404.

Saint Thomas Aquinas teaches that ideas are essentially known objects, pertaining, not to the primary theory of knowledge, but to the theory of reflexive knowledge, i.e., knowledge of oneself knowing things. In the primary theory of knowledge he teaches that the knowing has as principle a likeness of the known, present in the knower. This is not an idea, is not something known. It is rather a programming of the knower, by the thing to be known, prior to any act of knowing. The knowing which results from this principle is entirely thing-oriented, and thus is "immediate knowledge."

1111 Dewan, Lawrence. "St. Thomas and the Divine Names." *Science et Esprit* 32(1980): 19-33.

1112 Dewan, Lawrence. "St. Thomas and the Ground of Metaphysics." *Proceedings of the American Catholic Philosophical Association* 54(1980): 144-154.

*St. Thomas Aquinas held that at the origin of wisdom in man, and of all intellectual knowledge, is the natural apprehension of *ens*: "a being." In opposition to Cornelio Fabro, I stress that this apprehension is abstractive (pointing out the nobility of abstraction). I show that it is an apprehension of pure form. I explore how this apprehension of *ens* is the principle for our intellectual knowledge of the actual existence (*esse*) of things.*

1113 Dewan, Lawrence. "St. Thomas, Metaphysics, and Formal Causality." *Laval Théologique et Philosophique* 36(1980): 285-316.

*This study of Aquinas' *Commentary on Aristotle's Metaphysics* first establishes his view that, for Aristotle, metaphysics as science about being demonstrates its conclusions primarily through the formal cause. (1) It aims to examine the influence of this view upon Thomas' commentary on books seven and eight. This necessitates (2) an examination of the conception Thomas proposes of the general drift of these books, as a movement from mere logical to truly philosophical consideration. The two books are seen (3) to take the form of an exhibition of substantial form, as distinct from mere "quiddity" (a more merely "logical" item).*

1114 Dewan, Lawrence. "The Distinctiveness of St. Thomas' Third Way." *Dialogue (Canada)* 19(1980): 201-218.

*The third of the Five Ways to prove the existence of God (*Summa Theologia* 1, 2, (3) has so distinctive an argumentative procedure that one finds even sympathetic commentators attempting to replace it with so-called "other versions" of it (e.g., *Contra Gentiles 1, 15, 5*). I aim to show that the procedure is entirely intended, on St. Thomas' part, and is in accordance with the focus on substance, which special focus I claim is the whole raison d'être of the way. In the course of the presentation, I attempt to reply to some recent criticism of the argument.*

1115 Dewan, Lawrence. "The Real Distinction Between Intellect and Will." *Angelicum* 57(1980): 556-593.

1116 Dewan, Lawrence. "*Obiectum*: Notes on the Invention of a Word." *Archives d'Histoire Doctrinale et Littéraire du Moyen Age* 48(1981): 37-96.

1117 Dewan, Lawrence. "Jacques Maritain, St. Thomas and the Philosophy of Religion." *Revue de l'Universíte d'Ottawa* 51(1981): 644-653.

1118 Dewan, Lawrence. "St. Thomas Aquinas Against Metaphysical Materialism." *Atti Del'VIII Congresso Tomistico Internazionale V: Problemi Metafisici.* Studi Tomistici 14. Città del Vaticano, Pontificia Accademia di San Tommaso e di Religione Cattolica: Libreria Editrice Cattolica, 1982. 412-434.

1119 Dewan, Lawrence. "St. Thomas, Joseph Owens, and Existence." *The New Scholasticism* 56(1982): 399-441.

*Father Owens says that existence, as grasped in the judgment, is grasped as a flux. I(1) present his view in some detail, together with an alternative conception, namely that existence is grasped in judgment as an absolute actuality, an immobility, beyond movement, beyond rest, beyond operation. (2) I criticize Father Owens' interpretation of texts of Saint Thomas on time and existence, at the same time arguing that it is rather my view which is to be found in Saint Thomas' texts on time and existence. (3) I examine Saint Thomas' doctrine of divine conservation of creatures, because I find there further confirmation that it is my view of existence which Saint Thomas actually held. This is because there Saint Thomas stresses not only the distinction between existence and change, but also the *per se* relationship between form and existence: and Father Owens admits that form relates primarily to immobility.*

1120 Dewan, Lawrence. "Saint Thomas, Joseph Owens, and the Real Distinction Between Being and Essence." *The Modern Schoolman* 61(1984): 145-156.

1121 Dewan, Lawrence. "St. Albert, Creation, and the Philosophers." *Laval Théologique et Philosophique* 40(1984): 295-308.

1122 Dewan, Lawrence. "St. Thomas and the Integration of Knowledge Into Being." *International Philosophical Quarterly* 24(1984): 383-393.

The paper aims to show the role of the distinction between substance and accident in Saint Thomas' view of the relation between the knower and the act of knowing. It presents first the nature of the distinction between the act of being and the act of knowing. It secondly presents the productive causal relation between the knower and its knowing power. It concludes with a view of the immaterial nature of the knowing substance.

1123 Dewan, Lawrence. "Saint Thomas and the Principle of Causality." *Jacques Maritain: Philosophie dans la Cité/ A Philosopher in the World.* Ed. Jean-Louis Allard. Philosophica 28. Ottawa: University of Ottawa Press, 1985. 53-71.

Il y a déjà eu quelques débats relatifs à l'existence du principe de causalité et au rôle qu'un tel principe pourrait jouer dans une métaphysique thomiste. Dans la même veine. L'auteur présente d'abord la conception qu'avait saint Thomas du rôle et de la responsabilité de la métaphysique en ce qui concerne la discussion et la discussion et lad défense des premiers principes dela connaissance démonstrative; et il note aussi l'espéce de proposition qui, selon lui, consitue un tel principe. De là, il examine le principe un effet dépend de sa cause, parce que saint Thomas lui-même se servait de ce principe de facon non négligeable et qu'il a pris la peine de nous en laisser une réflexion bréve mais pénetrante, où il en expose les multiples sens et les degrés d'intelligibilité. Enfin il s'interroge à savoir si ce principe pourrait contribuer à résoudre la controverse sur la causalité au sein de la philosophie moderne, controverse suscitée surtout par Hume. Et la résponse est affirmative. A cet effet, il introduit certaines considérations de saint Thomas à propos des divers modes d'être de l'objet de l'intelligence humaine.

1124 Dewan, Lawrence. "Death in the Setting of Divine Wisdom." *Angelicum* 65(1988): 117-129.

1125 Dewan, Lawrence. "St Thomas, St. Bonaventure, and the Need to Prove the Existence of God." *Philosophy and Culture III*. Ed. Venant Cauchy. 1988. 841-844.

Aquinas opposed the view that God's existence is known by virtue of itself to the human mind. Gilson held that in this Aquinas was criticizing Bonaventure. A. C. Pegis argues that Bonaventure was not an appropriate target for such criticism. I argue that Aquinas and Gilson were right.

1126 Dewan, Lawrence. "Saint Thomas, Alvin Plantinga, and the Divine Simplicity." *The Modern Schoolman* 66(1989): 141-153.

Plantinga challenges divine simplicity as incompatible with divine personhood and agency. He rejects Aquinas' doctrine, including the analogical nature of being, as a way of maintaining both simplicity and personhood. I say Plantinga's presentation of analogy is inadequate. I also say that Plantinga fails to enter into authentic dialogue with Aquinas and trace this to Plantinga's position on our knowledge of God's existence. I use Aquinas' criticism of Anselm to suggest a reason for Plantinga's weakness.

1127 Dewan, Lawrence. "St. Thomas, Metaphysical Procedure, and the Formal Cause." *The New Scholasticism* 63(1989): 173-182.

1128 Dewan, Lawrence. "St. Thomas, Our Natural Lights." *Angelicum* 67(1990): 285-307.

1129 Dewan, Lawrence. "Aristotelian Features of the Order of Presentation in St. Thomas Aquinas' *Summa Theologiae*, Prima Pars, Qq. 3-11." *Philosophy and the God of Abraham: Essays in Memory of James A. Weisheipl, OP*. Ed. James Long. Toronto: Pontifical Institute of Mediaeval Studies, In press. 41-53.

1130 Di Noia, J. A. "Philosophical Theology in the Perspective of Religious Diversity." *Theological Studies* 49(1988): 401-416.

1131 Dobbs-Weinstein, Idit. "Medieval Biblical Commentary and Philosophical Inquiry as Exemplified in the Thought of Moses Maimonides and St. Thomas Aquinas." *Moses Maimonides and His Time*. Ed. Eric L. Ormsby. Studies in Philosophy and the History of Philosophy 19. Washington, DC: The Catholic University of America Press, 1989. 101-120.

The paper examines Maimonides' and Aquinas' biblical exegetical practice as an instance of philosophical prudence through an inquiry into their respective approaches to interpretation in general, to that of the Book of Job in particular. In contrast to the predominant scholarship on the questions of providence and theodicy which address the tension among divine knowledge, human freedom, and evil, this study focuses upon the possibility, nature, and scope of human knowledge of providence. The conclusion reached is that for both thinkers Job's transgression consists of an intellectual hubris of a kind that precludes a true understanding of providence and of evil.

1132 Dodds, Michael J. "St. Thomas Aquinas and the Motion of the Motionless God." *New Blackfriars* 68(1987): 232-242.

1133 Dombrowski, Daniel A. "Rorty and Mirror Images in St. Thomas." *Method* 4(1986): 108-114.

I show that an analysis of St. Thomas' use of mirror metaphors has surprising ramifications not only for our understanding of Richard Rorty, but also for the way we should view some largely neglected texts of St. Thomas.

1134 Dombrowski, Daniel A. "Noncombatant Immunity and St. Thomas: Carrying the Debate Further." *New Blackfriars* 67(1986): 216-221.

1135 Dombrowski, Daniel A. "Barad, Aquinas, and 'From-to' Perspective." *Between Species* 5(1989): 20-24.

Relying on Judith Barad's treatment of Aquinas' inconsistent attitude toward animals, I suggest that we refocus our "from-to perspectives" to consider in detail the period from Aquinas to Descartes, in particular, and from premodern to modern philosophy, in general, so as to better understand the roots of modern speciesism.

1136 Donagan, Alan. "Teleology and Consistency in Theories of Morality as Natural Law." *The Georgetown Symposium on Ethics*. Ed. R. Porreco. Washington, DC: Georgetown University Press, 1984. 91-107.

1137 Donagan, Alan. "Thomas Aquinas on Human Action." 1982. *The Cambridge History of Later Medieval Philosophy: From the Rediscovery of Aristotle to the Disintegration of Scholasticism*. Eds. Norman Kretzmann, Anthony Kenny, and Jan Pinborg. Cambridge: Cambridge University Press, 1988. 642-654.

1138 Donceel, Joseph. "God in Transcendental Thomism." *Logos* 1(1980): 50-63.

*Transcendental Thomism (TT) reaches God not as the cause of the universe, but as the "whereunto" of the basic thrust of our intellect and will. Uses a refurbished from of Leibniz' argument: "If God is possible, he exists. But God is possible. Therefore..." It tries to show that this possibility is implied in an undeniable *fact*, the dynamism of our intellect. Kant's objections are briefly considered. Regarding God's essence TT favors a mild form of panentheism, which holds that the relations between God and creatures are reciprocal. However, creation is not constitutive of God's essence, but a free result of His infinite Love.*

1139 Donnelly, Dorothy F. "Aquinas and Some Subsequent Thinkers on the Renewal of Utopian Speculation." *The Thomist* 46(1982): 539-572.

*This study explores utopian thinking in which Aquinas' departure from the Augustinian notion of the state as a consequence of, and remedy for, sin and his reaffirmation of the integrity of the *polis* are seen as a bridge between Plato's *Republic* and More's *Utopia*. This seminal thought, furthered but altered in Dante and Marsilius, makes clear that what is at issue in the discussion is an understanding of the relationship between reason and faith.*

1140 Dougherty, Jude P. "Toward a Thomistic Philosophy of Religion." *Proceedings of the American Catholic Philosophical Association* 57(1983): 105-115.

The thesis defended here is that Aquinas has a theory of religion at least as rich as that of Hume and Kant. Although not the author of a specific philosophical treatise on the structure and value of religion, he nevertheless has much to say on many topics which are normally discussed in the philosophy of religion. He can tell us what religion is and does, the nature of belief, and the function of a religious community. He understand the role of symbol and the importance of rites.

1141 Dougherty, Jude P. "Keeping the Common Good in Mind." *The Ethics of St. Thomas Aquinas*. Eds. L. Elders and K. Hedwig. Studi Tomistici 25. Città del Vaticano: Libreria Editrice Vaticana, 1984. 188-201.

1142 Dougherty, Jude P. "The Thomistic Element in the Social Philosophy of John Paul II." *Proceedings of the American Catholic Philosophical Association* 60(1984): 156-165.

1143 Dougherty, Jude P. "Aquinas on Punishment." *Lex et Libertas: Freedom and Law According to St. Thomas Aquinas*. Eds. L. J. Elders and K. Hedwig. Studi Tomistici 30. Città del Vaticano: Pontificia Accademia di San Tommaso e di Religione Cattolica, 1987. 160-170.

1144 Du Lac, Henri. "A First Incredulous Reaction to Faith and Rationality." *Thomistic Papers IV*. Ed. Leonard A. Kennedy. Notre Dame, IN: University of Notre Dame Press, 1988. 65-72.

1145 Dubois, M. "Mystical and Realistic Elements in the Exegesis and Hermeneutics of Thomas Aquinas." *Creative Biblical Exegesis*. Eds. B. Uffenheimer and H. G. Reventlow. 1988. 39-54.

1146 Dulles, Avery. "The Spiritual Community of Man: The Church According to Saint Thomas." *Calgary Aquinas Studies*. Ed. Anthony Parel. Toronto: Pontifical Institute of Mediaeval Studies, 1978. 125-153.

1147 Dulles, Avery. "Vatican II and Scholasticism." *New Oxford Review* 57(1990): 5-11.

1148 Duncan, Roger. "Analogy and the Ontological Argument." *The New Scholasticism* 54(1980): 25-33.

*St. Thomas rejects the ontological argument but does not deny that the concept of God entails his essence. Instead, he relies on the distinction between a proposition's being necessary and its being known *a priori*, the Achilles heel of contemporary modal arguments. Why can we not know God's possibility *a priori*? The doctrine of analogy claims that God-language is too obscure to authorize such deductions. The rejection of irreducibly analogous language leads to rationalism, which accepts the ontological argument, or to fideism/agnosticism, which reject it. Modern philosophers were in tacit agreement in ignoring the distinction between *a priority* and necessity and on the irrelevance of analogy. Hence they oscillated between acceptance of the ontological argument and the total rejection of significant God-talk. Recent trends are favorable to a reconsideration of both points and to an appreciation of their adumbration in the writing of Aquinas.*

1149 Dunphy, William. "Maimonides and Aquinas on Creation: A Critique of Their Historians." *Graceful Reason: Essays in Ancient and Medieval Philosophy Presented to Joseph Owens on the Occasion of His Seventy-fifth Birthday and the Fiftieth Anniversary of His Ordination*. Ed. Lloyd P. Gerson. Papers in Mediaeval Studies 4. Toronto: Pontifical Institute of Mediaeval Studies, 1983. 361-379.

1150 Dunphy, William. "Maimonides' Not-so-secret Position on Creation." *Moses Maimonides and His Time*. Ed. Eric L. Ormsby. Studies in Philosophy and the History of Philosophy 19. Washington, DC: The Catholic University of America Press, 1989. 151-172.

1151 Durbin, Paul T. "Aquinas, Art as an Intellectual Virtue, and Technology." *The New Scholasticism* 55(1981): 265-280.

*Can Aristotelian/Thomistic causal categories be applied to contemporary philosophical discussions of technology as well as, say, the categories of Martin Heidegger? The paper addresses this question in two parts:(1) Can the traditional definition of *techne, ars*, in its broadest sense, be extended to modern technology? And if so, (2) Does this provide an adequate definition? The paper addresses the issue as raised by Carl Mitcham and concludes that no adequate Aristotelian/Thomistic causal definition of technology has yet been proposed, and that such attempts as have been made have somewhat paradoxical consequences.*

1152 Edwards, Sandra. "Some Medieval Views on Identity." *The New Scholasticism* 51(1977): 62-74.

The purpose of this article is to examine and reconstruct two contrasting medieval views of identity and nonidentity. First, the relativist positions of Aquinas and Scotus are examined, and an attempt is made to reconstruct them to accommodate relativization to Leibniz's Law via different levels of discernibility and indiscernibility. Next, the absolutist position of Ockham is examined along with his reasons for rejecting relativization. An attempt is made to show how he could handle the problems of his predecessors through the doctrine of supposition of terms rather than relativization. Ockham's view is briefly compared with some twentieth century absolutist positions.

1153 Edwards, Sandra. "Aquinas on Unity and Identity." *Proceedings of the Patristic and Mediaeval and Renaissance Conference* 3(1978): 41-50.

1154 Edwards, Sandra. "Saint Thomas Aquinas on 'The Same Man.'" *The Southwestern Journal of Philosophy* 10(1979): 89-97.

The purpose of this article is to present Saint Thomas Aquinas' account of what it is to be the same man at different times. Because a man is essentially both a material body and a substantial form or soul, identity of a man must consist of both identity of body and identity of soul. The first part of the article deals with Aquinas' account of individuation and material identity. The second part deals with identity of souls through time. The third part puts together the findings of the first parts into a set of sufficient conditions for being the same man and evaluates this set.

1155 Edwards, Sandra, trans. "Introduction." *St. Thomas Aquinas, Quodlibetal Questions 1 and 2*. By Thomas Aquinas. Mediaeval Sources in Trans. 27. Toronto: Pontifical Institute of Mediaeval Studies, 1983. 1-25.

1156 Edwards, Sandra. "Aquinas on Individuals and Their Essences." *Philosophical Topics* 13(1985): 155-164.

Occasionally philosophers like Henry Veatch have argued that Aquinas did not believe in individual essences, i.e., essences unique to the individuals which have them as opposed to the essences of kinds of things. I argue that there is much evidence to support the claim that Aquinas did accept individual essences; a close look at individuation and identity through time indicates that the individual essences of material objects consist largely in the way the individual's matter is composed.

1157 Edwards, Sandra. "The Realism of Aquinas." *The New Scholasticism* 59(1985): 79-101.

1158 Elders, Léon J. "The Criteria of the Moral According to Aristotle and Their Criticism by St. Thomas." *Doctor Communis* 31(1978): 362-375.

1159 Elders, Léon J. "St. Thomas Aquinas and the Problems of Speaking About God." *Doctor Communis* 35(1982): 305-316.

1160 Elders, Léon J. "Saint Thomas Aquinas' *Commentary on the Physics* of Aristotle." *La Philosophie de la Nature de Saint Thomas D'Aquin*. Ed. Léon Elders. Studi Tomistici 18. Cittá del Vaticano: Pontificia Accademia di San Tommaso, Libreria Editrice Vaticana, 1982. 107-133.

1161 Elders, Léon J. "St. Thomas Aquinas' *Commentary on the Metaphysics* of Aristotle." *Divus Thomas* 86(1983): 307-326.

1162 Elders, Léon J. "St. Thomas Aquinas' *Commentary on the Nicomachean Ethics.*" *The Ethics of St. Thomas Aquinas.* Eds. L. Elders and K. Hedwig. Studi Tomistici 25. Città del Vaticano: Libreria Editrice Vaticana, 1984. 9-49.

1163 Elders, Léon J. "The Spirit of Mediaeval Philosophy." *Doctor Communis* 38(1985): 243-254.

1164 Elders, Léon J. "St. Thomas Aquinas' Doctrine of Conscience." *Lex et Libertas: Freedom and Law According to St. Thomas Aquinas.* Eds. L. J. Elders and K. Hedwig. Studi Tomistici 30. Città del Vaticano: Pontificia Accademia di San Tommaso e di Religione Cattolica, 1987. 125-134.

1165 Elders, Léon J. "Values According to St. Thomas Aquinas." *Doctor Communis* 41(1988): 18-33.

1166 Eschmann, Ignatius T. "Introduction." *On Kingship, to the King of Cyprus.* Trans. Gerald B. Phelan. Rev. By Thomas Aquinas. 1949. Toronto: Pontifical Institute of Mediaeval Studies, 1982. i-xviii. Under the title *On the governance of rulers.*

1167 Eschmann, Ignatius T. "A Catalogue of St. Thomas' Works: Bibliographical Notes." 1956. *The Christian Philosophy of St. Thomas Aquinas.* Ed. L. K. Shook. New York: Octagon Books, 1983. 381-437.

1168 Eslick, Leonard J. "From the World to God: The Cosmological Argument." *The Modern Schoolman* 60(1983): 145-169.

The cosmological argument is critically examined in the historical contexts of Plato, Aristotle, and Thomas Aquinas. Its validity is seen to hinge upon establishment of an essentially subordinated causal series. Such a causal series seems to negate freedom and contingency in the effects. Further, it seems difficult to maintain such a series in the light of relativity physics and quantum mechanics. The article suggest that such problems can only be resolved by a different model of causality, such as that of Whitehead and Charles Hartshorne.

1169 Etzwiler, James P. "Man as Embodied Spirit." *The New Scholasticism* 54(1980): 358-377.

*It is misleading to maintain that Thomas Aquinas held the theory of man as "rational animal." Although it is customarily assumed that he simply took over Aristotle's view on this point, Aquinas actually developed a position quite different; in fact, he inverted Aristotle's theory. Aquinas held that, whereas in other entities the form and matter exist by the *esse* of the composite, the human composite exists by the *esse* of the soul. To do justice to Aquinas' view, it is suggested that we adopt a new model for his theory of man, that of "embodied soul" or "incarnate spirit."*

1170 Evans, G. R. "Newman and Aquinas on Assent." *The Journal of the Theological Studies* 30(1979): 202-211.

1171 Ewbank, Michael Berton. "Remarks on Being in St. Thomas Aquinas' *Expositio de Divinis Nominibus.*" *Archives d'Histoire Doctrinale et Littéraire du Moyen Age* 56(1989): 123-149.

1172 Ewbank, Michael Berton. "Diverse Orderings of Dionysius's *Triplex Via* by St. Thomas Aquinas." *Mediaeval Studies* 52(1990): 82-109.

1173 Fabro, Cornelio. "The Overcoming of the Neoplatonic Triad of Being, Life, and Intellect by Saint Thomas Aquinas." *Neoplatonism and Christian Thought.* Ed. Dominic J. O'Meara. Studies in Neoplatonism 3. Albany, NY: State University of New York Press, 1982. 97-108, 250-255.

1174 Farley, Margaret A. "Fragments for an Ethic of Commitment in Thomas Aquinas." *Celebrating the Medieval Heritage: A Colloquy on the Thought of Aquinas and Bonaventure*. Ed. David Tracy. *The Journal of Religion* 58. Chicago: University of Chicago Press, 1978. 135-155.

1175 Farthing, John Lee. "The Problem of Divine Exemplarity in St. Thomas." *The Thomist* 49(1985): 183-222.

1176 Fay, Thomas A. "Bonaventure and Aquinas on God's Existence: Points of Convergence." *The Thomist* 41(1977): 585-595.

This paper takes under consideration a question which is of pivotal importance in the thought of the two great 13th century masters, Bonaventure and Thomas, with the purpose of discovering the relationship between the two; that is, is there a basic opposition between the two, because of differing epistemological starting points, which is so fundamental as to preclude any meaningful encounter between them, or are there perhaps unsuspected areas of substantive agreement. This paper takes as its methodological starting point the thought of Bonaventure, and after a brief exposition of his position concerning the problem of our knowledge of God's existence, attempts to effect an encounter between his thought and that of Thomas Aquinas which might prove mutually fruitful for the followers of each of these great Doctors.

1177 Fay, Thomas A. "The Problem of God-language in Thomas Aquinas: What Can and Cannot Be Said." *Rivista di Filosofia Neo-Scolastica* 69(1977): 385-391.

*Concerning man's ability to know God and express such knowledge in meaningful language, Aquinas defends both Divine Transcendence and man's ability to know God. In defending Divine Transcendence he is careful to point out what cannot be known and said about God. He is equally insistent, however, through his theories of causality and analogy on what can be said about God, and thus he is able to avoid on the one hand the Scylla of rationalism, which compromises the Divine Transcendence, and on the other Charybdis of agnosticism, which robs man of his noblest activity: the *contemplatio Dei*.*

1178 Fay, Thomas A. "Maritain on Rights and Natural Law." *The Thomist* 55 (In press): 439-448.

1179 Feldman, Seymour. "A Scholastic Misinterpretation of Maimonides' Doctrine of Divine Attributes." 1968. *Maimonides: A Collection of Critical Essays*. Ed. J. Buijs. 1988. 267-283.

1180 Ferraro, Joseph. "The Marxian Basis of the Thomist Arguments for the Existence of God." *Aquinas* 24(1981): 104-131.

1181 Ferré, Frederick. "In Praise of Anthropomorphism." *International Journal for Philosophy of Religion* 16(1984): 203-212.

Anthropomorphic language about the ultimate is rejected in strands of Judaism, Islam, and Christianity. Revulsion from describing God with words drawn from the vulgar human domain is valuationally understandable. As logical doctrine, however, negative theology, from Avicenna and Maimonides through Kant and Kierkegaard, proves theoretically and religiously self-defeating. Religious prohibitions against anthropomorphic speech should themselves not be taken literally. Clues to appropriate use of anthropomorphism are found in Midgley's treatment of talk about animals.

1182 Field, Richard W. "St. Thomas Aquinas on Properties and the Powers of the Soul." *Laval théologique et philosophique* 40(1984): 203-215.

For Aquinas the vegetative powers of the soul (viz. nutrition, growth, and reproduction) are properties of living organisms: that is, they are characteristics of living organisms which, while not being essential characteristics, can nevertheless be predicated necessarily and convertibility of living organism. Furthermore, they are active powers in the sense that they are capacities to perform certain actions which can have effects. But such an interpretation of Aquinas leads to the conceptual difficulty of allowing for the possibility of non-active living organisms (i.e., organisms which do nothing). This difficulty can be avoided if we consider at least one of the vegetative powers as being a capacity which is of necessity always exercised.

1183 Finnis, John M., and Germain Grisez. "The Basic Principles of Natural Law: A Reply to Ralph McInerny." *American Journal of Jurisprudence* 26(1983): 21-31.

1184 Finnis, John M. "Human Goods and Practical Reasoning." *Proceedings of the American Catholic Philosophical Association* 58(1984): 23-36.

1185 Finnis, John M. "Practical Reasoning, Human Goods, and the End of Man." *New Blackfriars* 66(1985): 438-451.

1186 Finnis, John M. "Natural Inclinations and Natural Rights: Deriving Ought from Is according to Aquinas." *Lex et Libertas: Freedom and Law According to St. Thomas Aquinas*. Eds. L. J. Elders and K. Hedwig. Studi Tomistici 30. Città del Vaticano: Pontificia Accademia di San Tommaso e di Religione Cattolica, 1987. 43-55.

1187 Finnis, John M. "Object and Intention in Aquinas." *The Thomist* 55 (In press): 1-27.

1188 Fitzgerald, John. "Aquinas on Goodness." *The Downside Review* 105(1987): 23-31.

1189 Fitzgerald, L. P. "St. Thomas Aquinas and the Two Powers: Is the De Regno Authentic?" *Angelicum* 56(1979): 515-556.

1190 Fitzgerald, L. P. "St. Thomas Aquinas and the Two Powers." *Angelicum* 56(1979): 515-556.

1191 Fitzpatrick, F. J. "Aristotle, Aquinas and Ryle: Thought Processes and Judgment." *Philosophical Studies* 31(1986-1987): 197-227.

1192 Flippen, Douglas. "A Problem Concerning Relation in Sensation." *Tommaso D'Aquino Nel Suo Settimo Centenario IX: Atti del Congresso Internazionale: Il Cosmo e la Scienza*. Napoli: Edizioni Domenicane Italiane, 1978. 307-314.

1193 Flippen, Douglas. "Immanence and Transcendence in Human Knowledge: The Illumination of a Problem in St. Thomas." *The New Scholasticism* 53(1979): 324-346.

In a philosophical account of how immanent cognitive acts apprehend objects transcending the knower, that immanent element which directs the cognitive act to its object seems to be an object, in some way, in its own right. There are texts from St. Thomas on this topic which read as though they were penned by an idealist. This problem of distinguishing, and yet uniting, knower and object known has been treated of in different ways by non-Thomists such as Husserl and the American school of critical realism. And yet there is a solution to this specific difficulty in the writings of St. Thomas himself. The solution depends on a correct understanding of the rather controversial distinction between essence and existence.

1194 Flippen, Douglas. "On Two Meanings of Good and the Foundation of Ethics in Aristotle and St. Thomas." *Proceedings of the American Catholic Philosophical Association* 58(1984): 56-64.

There are two definitions of good in Aristotle and St. Thomas:(1) the naturally desirable, (2) the smooth functioning of a thing. Hume takes the first definition and makes ethics non-cognitive. Grisez avoids Hume by grounding ethics on practical reason. Aristotle and Thomas agree with Hume against Grisez on practical reason, and with Grisez against Hume on the intellectual basis of ethics. To understand them we must understand the systematic ambiguity of "ought" and "good."

1195 Flippen, Douglas. "Intentionality and the Concept in Jacques Maritain." *Jacques Maritain. Philosophie dans la Cité/ A Philosopher in the World.* Ed. Jean-Louis Allard. Philosophica 28. Ottawa: University of Ottawa Press, 1985. 93-102.

1196 Flippen, Douglas. "Natural Law and Natural Inclinations." *The New Scholasticism* 60(1986): 284-316.

1197 Flynn, J. G. "St. Thomas and Averroes on the Knowledge of God." *Abr-Nahrain* (Leiden) 18(1978-1979): 19-32.

1198 Fogelin, Robert J. "A Reading of Aquinas' Five Ways." *American Philosophical Quarterly* 27(1990): 305-313.

1199 Ford, Lewis S. "Whitehead's Transformation of Pure Act." *The Thomist* 41(1977): 381-399.

1200 Ford, Lewis S. "Thomas Aquinas and Contemporary Philosophical Options." *Listening* 14(1979): 237-248.

Although there are many philosophical excellencies to commend Thomism, it can no longer serve as an instrument for achieving that goal which Thomas intended: the reconciliation of the Christian faith with science. Were Thomas alive today, there are several reasons to think his philosophy would more closely resemble Whitehead's. Both philosophies are metaphysically oriented, hospitable to Christian concern, and espouse a realistic epistemology. More particularly, both are creationist philosophies. Thomas has a monistic, transcendent version, whereby an uncreated God creates a world incapable of creation. Whitehead has a pluralistic, immanent version, whereby each actuality creates itself out of others, and God is its chief exemplification. If this shift is accepted, evolutionary development can be seen as the most natural way in which God could persuade the world to create itself.

1201 Fortin, Ernest L. "Augustine, Thomas Aquinas, and the Problem of Natural Law." *Mediaevalia* 4(1978): 178-208.

1202 Fortin, Ernest L. "St. Thomas Aquinas." 2nd ed. *History of Political Philosophy*. Eds. Leo Strauss and Joseph Cropsey. Chicago: University of Chicago Press, 1981. 223-250.

1203 Fortin, Ernest L. "Thomas Aquinas and the Reform of Christian Education." *Interpretation* 17(1989): 3-17.

1204 Foster, David Ruel. "Aquinas on the Immateriality of the Intellect." *The Thomist* 55(1990): 415-438.

1205 Foster, Kenelm. "St. Thomas and Dante." *The Two Dantes and Other Studies: Collected Essays of Kenelm Foster*. London: Darton, Longman & Todd, 1977. 56-65.

1206 Fox, Marvin. "Maimonides and Aquinas on Natural Law." *Interpreting Maimonides: Studies in Methodology, Metaphysics, and Moral Philosophy*. Eds. William Scott Green and Calvin Goldscheider. Chicago Studies in the History of Judaism. Chicago: The University of Chicago Press, 1990. 124-151.

1207 Franck, Isaac. "Maimonides and Aquinas on Man's Knowledge of God: A Twentieth Century Perspective." *Maimonides: A Collection of Critical Essays*. Ed. Joseph A. Buijs. Notre Dame, IN: University of Notre Dame Press, 1988. 284-305.

1208 Franck, Isaac. "Maimonides and Aquinas on Man's Knowledge of God: A Twentieth Century Perspective." *A Philosopher's Harvest: The Philosophical Papers of Isaac Franck*. Ed. William Gerber. Washington, DC: Georgetown University Press, 1988. 3-24. Also in *Review of Metaphysics*, 38(1984-1985): 591-615.

1209 Freddoso, Alfred J. "Human Nature, Potency, and the Incarnation." *Faith and Philosophy* 3(1986): 27-53.

According to the Christian doctrine of the Incarnation, the son of God is truly but only contingently a human being. But is it also the case that Christ's individual human nature is only contingently united to a divine person? The affirmative answer to this question, explicitly espoused by Duns Scotus and William Ockham, turns out to be philosophically untenable, while the negative answer, which is arguably implicit in St. Thomas Aquinas' explication of the Incarnation, has some surprising and significant metaphysical consequences.

1210 Froelich, Gregory Lawrence. "The Equivocal Status of *Bonum Commune*." *The New Scholasticism* 63(1989): 38-57.

*Much has been said about the elusive character of the common good and how it admits of various senses, some legitimate, some counterfeit. Although this is done often in connection with the works of St. Thomas Aquinas, little attention has been paid to the different uses that Thomas himself makes of the expression *bonum commune*. This article investigates three senses found in Thomas' writings, all of which carry a fair amount of importance in the science of politics, and then argues that one of these is what St. Thomas usually has in mind in discussion about the common good.*

1211 Fry-Revere, Sigrid. "Ontic Evil: How St. Thomas Understood It, and How Some Contemporary Authors Have Deviated from His Meaning." *Kinesis* 17(1987): 56-86.

1212 Fu, Pei-Jung. "Some Reflections on the Principles of Individuation and Unification in Neo-Thomism." *The Philosophical Review* 92(1983): 163-180.

1213 Fuller, Timothy. "Compatibilities on the Idea of Law in Thomas Aquinas and Thomas Hobbes." *Hobbes Studies* 3(1990): 112-134.

The central theme is that Aquinas and Hobbes have similar views of the relation between natural and civil law, and of the general purpose of civil law. Contrary to the opinion of many, Hobbes's discussion has many traditional elements of natural law theory, and Aquinas anticipates some "modern" conclusions about law. The distinction of classical and modern natural law ideas are not so sharp as is often thought. Some collateral issues about the nature of political authority are also considered.

1214 Gabriel, Pedro. "Dialogue Between St. Thomas and the Panentheist." *Philippiniana Sacra* (Manila) 14(1979): 472-495.

1215 Gabriel, Pedro. "Aquinas and Kant on the Existence of God." *Philippiniana Sacra* (Manila) 12(1979): 75-101.

1216 Gelinas, Elmer. "The Natural Law According to Thomas Aquinas." *American Journal of Jurisprudence*(1982): 13-36.

1217 Gendreau, Bernard A. "The Integral Humanism of Jacques Maritain and the Personalism of John Paul II." *Jacques Maritain. Philosophe dans la Cité/ A Philosopher in the World*. Ed. Jean-Louis Allard. Philosophica 28. Ottawa: University of Ottawa Press, 1985. 43-52.

1218 Genovesi, Vincent J. "Just War Doctrine: A Warrant for Resistance." *The Thomist* 45(1981): 503-540.

The article reaches two conclusions:(1) that the just-war criteria are meant for consideration not only by public authorities but also by private citizens who must determine the legitimacy of their own participation in a proposed war; (2) that the just-war doctrine itself offers warrant for an individual's resistance to a particular war in the light of even plausible argumentation against the war's justice.

1219 George, Robert P. "Moral Particularism, Thomism, and Traditions." *The Review of Metaphysics* 42(1989): 593-605.

1220 Germino, Dante. "Saint Thomas Aquinas and the Idea of the Open Society." *Calgary Aquinas Studies*. Ed. Anthony Parel. Toronto: Pontifical Institute of Mediaeval Studies, 1978. 105-124.

1221 Gerson, Lloyd P. "Joseph Owens, CSSR: A Bibliography." *Graceful Reason: Essays in Ancient and Medieval Philosophy Presented to Joseph Owens on the Occasion of His Seventy-fifth Birthday and the Fiftieth Anniversary of His Ordination*. Ed. Lloyd P. Gerson. Papers in Mediaeval Studies 4. Toronto: Pontifical Institute of Mediaeval Studies,1983. 419-433.

1222 Gerson, Lloyd P. "Plato, Aquinas, and the Universal Good." *The New Scholasticism* 58(1984): 131-144.

1223 Gewirth, Alan. "Natural Law, Human Action, and Morality." *The Georgetown Symposium on Ethics*. Ed. R. Porreco. Washington, DC: Georgetown University Press, 1984. 67-90.

1224 Girodat, Clair Raymond. "The Thomistic Theory of Personal Growth and Development." *Angelicum* 58(1981): 137-150.

1225 Glowienka, E. "Aquinas with the Linguists on 'Matter.'" *Proceedings of the American Catholic Philosophical Association* 57(1983): 180-188.

This paper combines insights of Thomas Aquinas with contemporary linguists on the concept of "matter," showing it is only a construct, whereas what we primordially know about experienced things, before perceiving or conceiving anything, is their "exist—ing" (be—ing). It is concluded (a) "Death" is merely cessation of some functions of a being, constructed as "life"; (b) "Persons" do not die but merely cease operating in so—called "material" ways; (c) "Immortality" is a continuance of nonmaterial functions.

1226 Godfrey-Smith, William. "Beginning and Ceasing to Exist." *Philosophical Studies* 32(1977): 393-402.

*The Frege-Russell claim that the notion of existence is exhausted by construing it as a second-level predicate of concepts is inadequate for a satisfactory account of an object beginning and ceasing to exist. To express the facts of beginning and ceasing to exist, a (first-level) predicative sense of existence is required in addition to that expressed by the existential quantifier (Section I). However, although existence in the temporal sense is construed as a property, it is not a property which can be acquired or lost. This raises problems for a satisfactory account of beginning to exist (Section II); the resolution of which entails, *inter alia*, accepting the ineliminability of tense.*

1227 Goerner, E. A. "Thomistic Natural Right: The Bad Man's View of Thomistic Natural Law." *Political Theory* 7(1979): 101-122.

Contrary to common opinion, natural law is not the foundation of Saint Thomas Aquinas' teaching about natural ethics and politics. Natural law is merely an external corrective for a defect: lack of natural virtue. Consequently, the doctrine about natural law is radically subordinate theoretically to the doctrine about virtue which, in turn, is not defined by adherence to general rules or law. Seen in this way, the natural law teaching of Thomas loses the strangely impractical and impolitic rigidity of the legalistic ethics with which it is so often clothed and which leaves so many textual and theoretical difficulties.

1228 Goerner, E. A. "Thomistic Natural Right: The Good Man's View of Thomistic Natural Law." *Political Theory* 11(1983): 393-418.

*Aquinas conventionally viewed as a natural law thinker, in fact, radically subordinates law to justice as equity (*epieikeia*) understood as the intention of a just legislator, an intention that cannot be formulated in any universally applicable propositions because that intention, the highest standard of justice, is ultimately determined by a form of prudence (*gnome* or *eugnomosyne*) that, like divine providence, is also beyond adequate expression in law-like rules.*

1229 Goerner, E. A. "Response to Hall's Goerner on Thomistic Natural Law." *Political Theory* 18(1990): 650-655.

1230 Goodwin, Robert. "Aquinas' Justice: An Interpretation." *The New Scholasticism* 63(1989): 275-285.

1231 Gottfried, Paul E. "The Western Case Against Usury." *Thought* 60(1985): 89-98.

1232 Gracia, Jorge J. E. "Numerical Continuity in Material Substance: The Principle of Identity in Thomistic Metaphysics." *The Southwestern Journal of Philosophy* 10(1979): 73-92.

*This paper investigates the problem of numerical continuity in Thomistic metaphysics and attempts to point out the principle of identity in material substances. It has three parts: The first clarifies the issue and presents the possible alternatives; the second rejects various solutions which have been proposed by interpreters of Thomas Aquinas, such as matter, form, accidents, and substance; and the third part argues that within Thomistic metaphysics it is only existence (*esse*) that may be considered as an acceptable candidate for this ontological role.*

1233 Gracia, Jorge J. E. "What the Individual Adds to the Common Nature According to Suarez." *The New Scholasticism* 53(1979): 221-233.

*In *Metaphysical Disputation* V, Section 2, Suarez criticizes the views of Thomas, Ockham, and Scotus on what the individual adds to the common nature. Then he proceeds to state his own view as follows:(1) the individual adds something real to the common nature, (2) nonetheless, what the individual adds is not really or modally distinct from the common nature, (3) rather, it is conceptually distinct from it, because (4) a conceptual distinction does not require that what is added be conceptual. In this paper I shall examine briefly the nature of the problem at stake, Suarez's view, and submit (a) that Suarez's position is fully consistent, (b) although different from those of Thomas, Scotus, and Ockham, with which it has been compared often and (c) that the apparent inconsistency is due to an ambiguity in the use of the term "addition."*

1234 Graeser, Andreas. "Aristotle and Aquinas on Being as Being True." *Métaphysique: Histoire de la Philosophie*. Neuchâtel: Eds. de la Baconniére, 1981. 85-97.

1235 Gram, Moltke S., and Richard M. Martin. "The Perils of Plenitude: Hintikka Contra Lovejoy." *Journal of the History of Ideas* 41(1980): 497-511.

1236 Gray, Christopher Berry. "Specification of Norm in the Jurisprudence of Aquinas, Austin and Kelsen." *Aquinas* 23(1980): 79-92.

1237 Grisez, Germain. "A Critique of Russell Hittinger's Book, *A Critique of the New Natural Law Theory*." *The New Scholasticism* 62(1988): 438-465.

1238 Guagliardo, Vincent Anthony. "Aquinas and Heidegger: The Question of Philosophical Theology." *The Thomist* 53(1989): 407-442.

*Reason cannot be deconstructed from Aquinas' thought, as Caputo argues, because of the place reason occupies in Aquinas' understanding of the human as finite, temporal, this—worldly conditioned. Aquinas' conception of reason relates positively, not just negatively, to Heidegger's philosophy, where reason as discursive and indirect is the index of finitude presupposing the relation of *Dasein* to Being. In Aquinas, transcendental being bespeaks a finite clearing which makes revealment of being (world) possible and in which reason ineluctably presupposes the prior negativing of being's concealment. Theology as a thinking and questioning elaboration of faith (Heidegger) involves reason in this sense.*

1239 Gueguen, John A. "Teaching Aquinas in the Secular University, The Synthesis of Classical Wisdom." *Atti Dell'VIII Congresso Tomistico Internazionale VIII: San Tommaso Nella Storia del Pensiero*. Studi Tomistici 17. Cittá del Vaticano: Pontificia Accademia di San Tommaso e di Religione Cattolica, 1982. 405-416.

1240 Gueguen, John A. "Beyond the Natural Law-legal Positivism Debate: A Reinterpretation of Aquinas." *Proceedings of the IX World Congress, International Association for Philosophy of Law and Social Philosophy II*. 1982. 465-487.

1241 Haldane, John J. "Aquinas on Sense-perception." *The Philosophical Review* 2(1983): 233-239.

In giving an account of sense-perception, Aquinas invokes the idea of the intentional reception of the sensible form of the object perceived and contrasts this with the natural mode of reception, as when something acquires a physical property by being acted upon. The question arises: is the intentional mode immaterial? Two opposing interpretations are considered, and it is shown that both find support in Thomist texts.

1242 Haldane, John J. "Chesterton's Philosophy of Education." *Philosophy* 65(1990): 65-80.

This is a study of the educational philosophy of Chesterton. It considers his credentials as a philosopher, noting that several distinguished thinkers, including Aurel Kolnai, Ernst Bloch, Etienne Gilson, and John Anderson, cite his work with respect, and it explores something of the character of his views about the role of philosophy and the nature of education, showing them to be closely related to the epistemology, metaphysics, and value theory of Aquinas.

1243 Hall, Douglas C. "Immediacy and Mediation in Aquinas: In *I Sent.* , Q. 1, A. 5." *The Thomist* 53(1989): 31-55.

1244 Hall, Pamela. "Goerner on Thomistic Natural Law." *Political Theory* 18(1990): 638-649.

This essay criticizes the interpretation of Thomistic natural law given by E. A. Goerner. It is argued that Goerner, discussing the two standards of right action in Aquinas' ethics (natural law and prudence): improperly relegates natural law to the minimal role of government of so-called "bad men." But this view fails to recognize the way in which natural law and prudence are interdependent for Thomas: the core sense of natural law is that of directedness to our connatural goods, and as such the natural law must guide prudence. Thus the natural law is not transcended even by the virtuous.

1245 Hallman, Joseph M. "The Necessity of the World in Thomas Aquinas and Alfred North Whitehead." *The Modern Schoolman* 60(1983): 264-272.

Thomas Aquinas and Alfred North Whitehead are not absolutely opposed in their understanding of the necessity of the world. Although Whitehead held that some sort of world is necessary for God's prehension, any given set of existent is contingent. Thomas held that creatures exist by a necessity of supposition which is relative and extrinsic, but a necessity nonetheless. His theory of necessity allows for thinking of creatures as relatively and extrinsically necessary for God's well being.

1246 Hallman, Joseph M. "Aquinas and the Trinity of A. N. Whitehead." *The Journal of Religion* 70(1990): 36-47.

1247 Hankey, Wayne J. "The Place of the Psychological Image of the Trinity in the Arguments of Augustine's *De Trinitate*, Anselm's *Monologion*, and Aquinas' *Summa Theologiae*." *Dionysius* 3(1979): 99-110.

*Thomas Aquinas' *Summa Theologiae* and Anselm's *Monologion* treat the Trinity in the inverse order of Augustine's *De Trinitate*. Augustine moves from the three persons known in scripture toward understanding the Trinity through its psychological image in man. Aquinas and Anselm begin from the unity and arrive at the Trinity through the psychological image. The crucial and significant point is that the difference between Thomas and Augustine is reducible to a difference between the Proculan and Plotinian Neoplatonisms. Anselm's place relative to these two Neoplatonism is not decided.*

1248 Hankey, Wayne J. "Aquinas' First Principle: Being or Unity?" *Dionysius* 4(1980): 133-172.

1249 Hankey, Wayne J. "The *De Trinitate* of St. Boethius and the Structure of the *Summa Theologiae* of St. Thomas Aquinas." *Atti Congresso Internazionale Di Studi Boeziani*. Ed. Luca Obertello. Roma: Editrice Herder, 1981. 367-375.

1250 Hankey, Wayne J. "The Structure of Aristotle's Logic and the Knowledge of God in the *Pars Prima* of the *Summa Theologiae* of Thomas Aquinas." *Sprache und Erkenntnis Im Mittelalter*. Eds. Jan P. Beckmann et al., Miscellanea Mediaevalia 13/2. Berlin: Walter de Gruyter, 1981. 961-968.

1251 Hankey, Wayne J. "Pope Leo's Purposes and St. Thomas' Platonism." *Atti Dell'VIII Congresso Tomistico Internazionale VIII: San Tommaso Nella Storia del Pensiero*. Studi Tomistici 17. Cittá del Vaticano: Pontificia Accademia di San Tommaso e di Religione Cattolica, 1982. 39-52.

1252 Hankey, Wayne J. "Theology as System and as Science: Proclus and Thomas Aquinas." *Dionysius* 6(1982): 83-93.

*The article shows how theology as science (deriving from Aristotle) and theology as system (deriving from Proclus) complement each other and also conflict with one another in the theological *summa* of Thomas Aquinas. The piece concludes that for better or worse his *summae* are onto-theo-logy and that a more honest confrontation with Heidegger is required.*

1253 Hankey, Wayne J. "The Place of the Proof for God's Existence in the *Summa Theologiae* of Thomas Aquinas." *The Thomist* 46(1983): 370-393.

*Given the sacred doctrine originates from God's self-revelation, how and why does Aquinas' *Summa Theologiae* begin with a proof for God's existence? The paper shows that the philosophical theological framework enabling both the beginning from

God's simplicity and the placing of a proof starting with sensibly perceived nature in the second question is derived from Proclus mediated through the Pseudo-Dionysius. It is in this context that Aristotle became theologically acceptable.*

1254 Hankey, Wayne J. "Making Theology Practical: Thomas Aquinas and the Nineteenth Century Religious Revival." *Dionysius* 9(1985): 85-127.

1255 Hanley, Katherine Rose. "Freedom and Fault." *The New Scholasticism* 51(1977): 494-512.

Adopting the questioning perspectives from contemporary European phenomenology, this study articulates a textually based retrieve of Saint Thomas Aquinas' reflective analysis of the subjective nature of moral fault. Saint Thomas' description and interpretation of the elements of consciousness preceding sin, the process of deliberation, and the actual election of moral fault identify those elements of one's cognitive, affective, and volitional life that constitute moral fault and highlight the distinctive and determinative role of human freedom in its creation. Conscious conflicts and contrariety, a strange mixture of willing-unwilling, knowing-unknowing, emerge as the distinguishing and essential characteristics of that peculiar human act we call sin.

1256 Hanley, Terry. "St. Thomas' Use of Al-Ghazali's *Maqasid Al-Falasifa*." *Mediaeval Studies* 44(1982): 243-270.

This study investigates all 30 of the passages where Thomas of Aquinas refers explicitly to al-Ghazali. The results suggest, against the opinion of certain scholars (e.g., D. Salman, R. E. Abu Shanab), that, with the possible exception of one minor point (the possibility of there being an actual infinity of human souls), al-Ghazali's influence on Thomas was altogether negligible or even non-existent.

1257 Hannon, Patrick. "Aquinas, Morality and Law." *Irish Theological Quarterly* (Ireland) 56(1990): 278-286.

1258 Harak, G. Simon. "The Passions, the Virtues, and Agency: Modern Research and Thomistic Reflection." *Logos* 8(1987): 31-44.

1259 Harper, A. W. J. "St. Thomas and Free Will." *Indian Philosophical Quarterly* 7(1979): 93-99.

1260 Harris, Errol. "Natural Law and Naturalism." *International Philosophical Quarterly* 23(1983): 115-124.

Natural Law theorists are frequently accused of the naturalistic fallacy. John Finnis admits the fallacy, but denies that it is committed by Aquinas. Both are wrong in their rigid separation of fact from value, of which the criterion is here shown to be the same. If proper conceptions of "reason," "nature," and "human nature" are adopted values can legitimately be derived from facts, so that Natural Law and "naturalism" are reconcilable without fallacy. Thus Aquinas and Suarez (attacked by the critics) are both justified.

1261 Harris, James F. "An Empirical Understanding of Eternality." *International Journal for Philosophy of Religion* 22(1987): 165-183.

1262 Harvey, Warren Z. "Maimonides and Aquinas on Interpreting the Bible." *American Academy for Jewish Research: Proceedings* 55(1988): 59-77.

1263 Hasker, William. "Simplicity and Freedom: A Response to Stump and Kretzmann." *Faith and Philosophy* 3(1986): 192-201.

*In "*Absolute Simplicity*," Stump and Kretzmann claim to show how all of God's acts are conditionally necessitated while preserving divine free choice as well as creaturely contingency and freedom; they also claim to show how the cosmological argument can be rehabilitated in the face of the objection by William Rowe. I show that they either fail to preserve divine freedom or fail to show that God's acts are conditionally necessitated; in any case, their view is inconsistent with human free will, and their answer to Rowe's objection fails.*

1264 Hassing, R. F. "Thomas Aquinas on *Physics* VII. 1 and the Aristotelian Science of the Physical *Continuum.*" *Nature and Scientific Method.* Ed. Daniel O. Dahlstrom. Studies in Philosophy and the History of Philosophy 22. Washington, DC: The Catholic University ofAmerica Press. 109-140.

1265 Hauerwas, Stanley. "Aristotle and Thomas Aquinas on the Ethics of Character." 1975. *Character and the Christian Life: A Study in Theological Ethics.* San Antonio, TX: Trinity University Press, 1985. 35-82.

1266 Hayden, Mary R. "The Paradox of Aquinas' Altruism: From Self-love to Love of Others." *Proceedings of the American Catholic Philosophical Association* 63(1990): 72-83.

1267 Henle, John Robert. "A Catholic View of Human Rights: A Thomistic Reflection." *The Philosophy of Human Rights.* Westport, CT: Greenwood Press, 1980. 87-94.

1268 Henle, John Robert. "Transcendental Thomism: A Critical Assessment." *One Hundred Years of Thomism: Aeterni Patris* and Afterwards. Ed. Victor B. Brezik. Houston, TX: Center for Thomistic Studies: University of St. Thomas, 1981. 90-116.

1269 Henle, John Robert. "St. Thomas Aquinas and American Law." *Thomistic Papers II.* Eds. Leonard A. Kennedy and Jack C. Marler. Houston, TX: University of St. Thomas, Center for Thomistic Studies, 1986. 59-83.

1270 Henle, John Robert. "Sanction and the Law According to St. Thomas Aquinas." *Vera Lex* 10(1990): 5-6, 18.

1271 Hennesey, James. "Leo XIII's Thomistic Revival: A Political and Philosophical Event." *Celebrating the Medieval Heritage: A Colloquy on the Thought of Aquinas and Bonaventure.* Ed. David Tracy. *The Journal of Religion* 58. Chicago: University of Chicago Press, 1978. 185-197.

1272 Henninger, Mark Gerald. "Thomas Aquinas and the Ontological Status of Relations." *Journal of the History of Ideas* 25(1987): 491-515.

*The article examines Thomas Aquinas' doctrine on the ontological status of categorical relations such as equality, similarity, and various causal relations. It shows that he takes a middle way between two extremes. According to Duns Scotus' strong realism, statements of the form *aRb* ("*a* is really related to *b*") are true if and only if *a* and *b* with their foundations really exist, and there is a real relation *R*, an extra-mental thing with its own accidental reality really distinct from that of its foundation in *a*. If there is no such extra-mental thing, there is no real relation. According to Peter Aureoli's conceptualism, statements of the form *aRb* are true if and only if *a* and *b* with their foundations really exist, and there exists in some mind a concept or judgment joining *a* and *b*. If there is no such concept, there is no real relation. This article shows that for Thomas, real relations are extra-mentally real but do not have their own accidental reality really distinct from their foundations. It then briefly examines Thomas' views on the relations of God and creatures.*

1273 Herrera, Robert A. "Saint Thomas and Maimonides on the Tetragrammaton: The *Exodus* of Philosophy." *The Modern Schoolman* 59(1982): 179-193.

An attempt to ascertain the relationship between the "God of Religion" and the "God of philosophy" using St. Thomas' and Maimonides' speculations of the unique status of the Tetragrammaton as a point of departure. Maimonides' thought is viewed as ensconced within his theory of negative attributes, that of St. Thomas within the context of the analogy of being. The religious God is seen to appear only on the distant horizon, together with the realization that God transcends human thought.

1274 Herrera, Robert A. "An Episode in Medieval Aristotelianism: Maimonides and St. Thomas on the Active Intellect." *The Thomist* 47(1983): 317-338.

*A comparative study using Aristotle's theory of *Poietikon* (Activity) as an index to measure the degree of penetration of Aristotelian rationalism and naturalism in Christian and Jewish medieval thought, taking into consideration its variations and historical vicissitudes.*

1275 Hess, Charles R. "Aquinas' Organic Synthesis of Plato and Aristotle." *Angelicum* 58(1981): 339-350.

1276 Hibbs, Thomas Stewart. "Principles and Prudence: The Aristotelianism of Thomas' Account of Moral Knowledge." *The New Scholasticism* 61(1987): 271-284.

1277 Hibbs, Thomas Stewart. "Against a Cartesian Reading of *Intellectus* in Aquinas." *The Modern Schoolman* 66(1988): 55-69.

1278 Hibbs, Thomas Stewart. "Divine Irony and the Natural Law: Speculation and Edification in Aquinas." *International Philosophical Quarterly* 30(1990): 419-429.

Readers of Aquinas often suppose that his doctrine of natural law provides an autonomous and a complete moral theory. Yet Aquinas sees the natural law as but part of a more nearly comprehensive moral pedagogy. He highlights the dialectical and instrumental status of law. The law fosters self-knowledge and intensifies the sense of the need for divine assistance. The engagement of the natural by the supernatural operates through dialectic and irony, through strategies that demand and allow for the reappropriation and perfection of the self.

1279 Hibbs, Thomas Stewart. "A Rhetoric of Motives: Thomas on Obligation as Rational Persuasion." *The Thomist* 54(1990): 293-309.

1280 Hibbs, Thomas Stewart. "The Hierarchy of Moral Discourse in Aquinas." *American Catholic Philosophical Quarterly* (formerly *The New Scholasticism*) 64(1990): 199-214.

1281 Hill, John. "Philosophy and the Priesthood." *Metaphilosophy* 10(1979): 215-226.

1282 Hill, William J. "In What Sense is God Infinite? A Thomistic View." *The Thomist* 42(1978): 14-27.

1283 Hill, William J. "Two Gods of Love: Aquinas and Whitehead." *Listening* 10(1979): 249-264.

*Philosophers studying Thomism and Process Thought agree that human agency is the analogue for conceiving deity as interacting with world, and that such agency is, in the final analysis, that of love. The two metaphysical systems differ in that, for the Thomist, God is Pure Act and ultimate reality, whereas for the Whiteheadian the category of the ultimate belongs to Creativity, itself not actual. God is thus differently identified as love: for followers of Whitehead divine love is akin to Greek *eros*, a love wherein God ever seeks further self-fulfillment; for followers of Aquinas, it is the altruistic love which the New Testament names *agape*, the love of purely actual God for his creatures.*

1284 Hill, William J. "Seeking Foundations for Faith: Symbolism of Person or Metaphysics of Being?" *The Thomist* 45(1981): 219-242.

1285 Hill, William J. "Rescuing Theism: A Bridge Between Aquinas and Heidegger." *The Heythrop Journal* 27(1986): 377-393.

*This study attempts to counter Heidegger's overthrow of metaphysics as grounding classical theism, not by equating Aquinas' identification of God as *Esse Subsistens* with Heidegger's *Sein* as is frequently done, but by suggesting that the objective and causal character of *esse* as *actus essendi* provides a perspective wherein Being can attain a personal character in the act of positing itself in an approximation to Heidegger's *Ereignis* (event) and *Anwesen* (presencing).*

1286 Hill, William J. "On Knowing the Unknowable God: A Review Discussion." *The Thomist* 51(1987): 699-709.

1287 Hittinger, Russell. "When It is More Excellent to Love Than to Know: The Other Side of Thomistic Realism." *Proceedings of the American Catholic Philosophical Association* 57(1983): 171-179.

*In *De Veritate* and the *Summa* Aquinas tries to settle the issue of whether the intellect or the will is the superior power. If they are compared "absolutely" (simply as powers): the intellect is superior; if they are compared "relatively" (in relation to things): the will is superior because it is capable of a more perfect union with entities which exceed the nobility of the human soul. Thomists have usually stressed the "absolute" mode of comparison, but the "relative" mode is central to Aquinas' understanding of the theological virtues.*

1288 Hoenen, J. F. M. "Can God Be Proved to Act Freely? Ockham's Criticism of an Argument in Thomas." *Ockham and Ockhamists*. Eds. E. P. Bos and H. A. Krop. Artistarium, Supplementa 4. Nijmegen: Ingenium Publishers, 1987. 15-23.

1289 Hoffman, Paul. "The Unity of Des Cartes's Man." *The Philosophical Review* 95(1986): 339-370.

1290 Hoffman, Paul. "St. Thomas Aquinas on the Halfway State of Sensible Being." *The Philosophical Review* 99(1990): 73-92.

1291 Hoffmaster, Barry C. "Natural Law and Legal Obligation." *The Medieval Tradition of Natural Law*. Ed. Harold J. Johnson. Studies in Medieval Culture 22. Kalamazoo, MI: Medieval Institute Publications, 1987. 67-74.

1292 Hoye, William J. "The Unknowability of the Universe in the Thought of Thomas Aquinas." *Doctor Communis* 38(1985): 46-61.

1293 Hoye, William J. "The Thought of Being as the Necessary Reason for Supernatural Faith in the Theology of Thomas Aquinas." *Doctor Communis* 41(1988): 173-183.

1294 Hudson, Deal W. "The Ecstasy Which is Creation." *Understanding Maritain: Philosopher and Friend*. Eds. Deal Hudson and Matthew J. Mancini. Macon, GA: Mercer University Press, 1988. 235-256.

1295 Hudson, Deal W. "Maritain and Happiness in Modern Thomism." *From Twilight to Darwin: The Cultural Vision of Jacques Maritain*. Notre Dame, IN: University of Notre Dame Press, 1990. 263-276.

1296 Hughes, Gerard T. "Aquinas and the Limits of Agnosticism." *The Philosophical Assessment of Theology: Essays in Honour of Frederick C. Copleston*. Washington, DC: Georgetown University Press, 1987. 35-63.

1297 Hughson, Thomas. "Dulles and Aquinas on Revelation." *The Thomist* 52(1988): 445-471.

*H.-G. Gadamer's hermeneutic brings Avery Dulle's *Models of Revelation* into exploratory dialogue with Thomas Aquinas' theology of revelation (*Summa Theologiae* 2a2ae, 173, 2). The principle of "symbolic mediation" (Dulles) and the principle that prophecy consists essentially in divinely enlightened judgment mutually provoke one another. The former needs to integrate interpretation with symbol, and the latter can be read as an act of interpreting symbols. In general, the article proceeds from an affinity with Dulles' proposal but offers a reorientation to its further development.*

1298 Hurd, Robert L. "Heidegger and Aquinas: A Rahnerian Bridge." *Philosophy Today* 28(1984): 105-137.

1299 Hurd, Robert L. "Being is Being-present-to-self: Rahner's Key to Aquinas' Metaphysics." *The Thomist* 52(1988): 63-78.

1300 Inagaki, Bernard Ryôsuke. "The Contemporary Significance of Thomistic Ethics. " *Tommaso Nel Suo Settimo Centenario V: Atti del Congresso Internazionale: L'agire Morale*. Napoli: Edizioni Domenicane Italiane, 1977. 527-531.

1301 Inagaki, Bernard Ryôsuke. "The Degrees of Knowledge and *Habitus* According to Thomas Aquinas." *Sprache und Erkenntnis Im Mittelalter*. Eds. Jan P. Beckmann et al. Berlin: Walter de Gruyter, 1981. 270-282.

1302 Inagaki, Bernard Ryôsuke. "Virtue and Justification— A Consideration on Thomas Aquinas' Treatise of Virtue." *Actes Du Septiéme Congrés International de Philosophie Médiéval II: L'homme et Son Univers Au Moyen Age*. Ed. Christian Wenin. Philosophes Médiévaux 26-27. Louvain-la-Neuve: Éditions de l'Institut Supérieur de Philosophie, 1986. 791-798.

1303 Inagaki, Bernard Ryôsuke. "*Habitus* and *Natura* in Aquinas." *Studies in Medieval Philosophy*. Ed. John F. Wippel. Studies in Philosophy and the History of Philosophy, 17. Washington, DC: The Catholic University of America Press, 1987. 159-175.

1304 Innis, Robert E. "Aquinas' God and the Linguistic Turn: A Review Discussion of David B. Burrell, *Aquinas: God and Action*." *The Thomist* 45(1981): 585-598.

1305 Irwin, T. H. "The Scope of Deliberation: A Conflict in Aquinas." *The Review of Metaphysics* 44(1990): 21-42.

1306 Jaki, Stanley L. "Maritain and Science." 1984. *Understanding Maritain: Philosopher and Friend*. Eds. Deal W. Hudson and Matthew J. Mancini. Macon, GA: Mercer University Press, 1987. 183-200.

1307 Jaki, Stanley L. "Thomas and the Universe." *The Thomist* 53(1989): 545-572.

1308 Janssens, Louis. "Ontic Evil and Moral Evil." 1972. Ed. *Readings in Moral Theology I*. Eds. Charles Curran and Richard McCormick. New York: Paulist Press, 1979. 40-93.

1309 Janssens, Louis. "Saint Thomas Aquinas and the Question of Proportionality." *Louvain Studies* 9(1982): 26-46.

1310 Janz, Denis R. "Thomas Aquinas, Martin Luther, and the Origins of the Protestant Reformation." *Philosophy and the God of Abraham: Essays in Memory of James A. Weisheipl, OP*. Ed. James Long. Toronto: Pontifical Institute of Mediaeval Studies, In press. 71-83.

1311 Jaroszynski, Piotr. "On the Nature of Beauty." *Angelicum* 65(1988): 77-98.

1312 John Paul II (Wojtyla, Karol). "Perennial Philosophy of St. Thomas for the Youth of Our Times." *Angelicum* 57(1980): 133-146.

1313 John Paul II (Wojtyla, Karol). "Perennial Philosophy of St. Thomas for the Youth of Our Times." *The Jacques & Raissa Maritain*. Ed. Donald A. Gallagher and Ralph J. Masiello. Niagara, NY: Maritain Institute: Niagara University Press, 1981. 209-227.

1314 John Paul II (Wojtyla, Karol). "Method and Doctrine of St. Thomas in Dialogue with Modern Culture." *The Jacques & Raissa Maritain*. Eds. Donald A. Gallagher and Ralph J. Masiello. Niagara, NY: Maritain Institute: Niagara University Press, 1981. 262-280.

1315 Johnson, Harold Joseph. "*Via Negationis* and *Via Analogiae*: Theological Agnosticism in Maimonides and Aquinas." *Actas del V Congreso Internacional de Filosofia Medieval II*. Madrid: Nacional, 1979. 843-855.

1316 Johnson, Harold Joseph. "*Contra Anselum* but *Contra Gentiles*: Aquinas' Rejection of the Ontological Argument." *Schede Medievali* 8(1985): 18-27.

1317 Johnson, Harold Joseph. "Ethical Relativism and Self-determination: Political Theory in Aquinas and Some Others." *Actes Du Septiéme Congrés International de Philosophie Médiéval II: L'homme et Son Univers Au Moyen Age*. Philosophes Médiévaux 26-27. 1986. 835-844.

1318 Johnson, Harold Joseph. "Just Price, Aquinas, and the Labor Theory of Value." *The Medieval Tradition of Natural Law*. Ed. Harold J. Johnson. Studies in Medieval Culutre 22. Kalamazoo, MI: Medieval Institute Publications, 1987. 75-86.

1319 Johnson, John F. "The Structure of *Ens Commune* as the Subject of Thomistic Metaphysics." *Kinesis* 12(1982): 19-35.

1320 Johnson, John F. "Biblical Authority and Scholastic Theology." *Inerrancy and the Church*. Ed. J. Hannah. 1982. 67-97.

1321 Johnson, Mark F. "St. Thomas' *De Trinitate*, Q. 5, A. 2, Ad 3: A Reply to John Knasas." *The New Scholasticism* 63(1989): 58-65.

*In a recent article which appeared in the periodical *Angelicum*, John Knasas of the University of St. Thomas in Houston dealt with the question of the starting point for Thomistic metaphysics ("Immateriality and Metaphysics," *Angelicum* 65, 1988, 44-76). In defense of his own thesis, Knasas interprets St. Thomas' *In Boethii de Trinitate*, q. 5, a2,ad3 in a way which, while in accord with his own conviction that, for St. Thomas, natural philosophy does not attain to the immaterial, seems to me to be diametrically opposed to the straightforward meaning of the text. Examining the text in some detail, I criticize the reading of Knasas and show that St. Thomas' response in this *ad tertium* can be understood only if we see him conceding that natural philosophy does, in fact, attain to the immaterial. This leaves open, I think, the important discussion about the relationship of natural philosophy to metaphysics.*

1322 Johnson, Mark F. "Did St. Thomas Attribute a Doctrine of Creation to Aristotle?" *The New Scholasticism* 63(1989): 129-155.

This historical sketch seeks to show that Thomas Aquinas did attribute to Aristotle a doctrine of the total dependence in being of all things upon God: a doctrine of creation. Examining several key texts of Aquinas, it shows that he held this view for the entirety of his career.

1323 Johnson, Mark F. "Immateriality and the Domain of Thomistic Natural Philosophy." *The Modern Schoolman* 67(1990): 285-304. Reply by John Knasas, "Materiality and Aquinas' Natural Philosophy: A Reply to Johnson," *The Modern Schoolman*, 68(1991): 245-257.

1324 Johnson, Mark F. "*Alia Lectura Fratris Thome*: A List of the New Texts of St. Thomas Aquinas Found in Lincoln College, Oxford, MS. Lat. 95." *Recherches de Théologie Ancienne et Médiévale* 57(1990): 34-61.

1325 Johnson, Mark F. "The Sapiential Character of the First Article of the *Summa Theologiae*." *Philosophy and the God of Abraham: Essays in Memory of James A. Weisheipl, OP*. Ed. James Long. Toronto: Pontifical Institute of Mediaeval Studies, In press. 85-98.

1326 Johnstone, Brian V. "The Meaning of Proportionate Reason in Contemporary Moral Theology." *The Thomist* 49(1985): 223-247.

This article seeks to clarify the notion of proportionate reason as used by contemporary proponents of the method of moral analysis commonly called "proportionalism." Contemporary theories seek to determine the moral quality of acts by an assessment of the presence or absence of proportion. There are at least three distinct meanings and functions of proportions and Five Ways of calculating proportion. The notion is insufficiently clear to provide an instrument for moral analysis.

1327 Johnstone, Brian V. "The Structures of Practical Reason: Traditional Theories and Contemporary Questions." *The Thomist* 50(1986): 417-446.

1328 Jones, David C. "The Supreme Good." *Prebyterion* 11(1985): 124-141.

1329 Jones, John D. "The Ontological Difference for St. Thomas and Pseudo-Dionysius." *Dionysius* 4(1980): 119-132.

The article offers an analysis of the quite different ways in which Pseudo-Dionysius and St. Thomas understand the relation of being and beings. I argue that despite the priority of being over essence for Aquinas, he ultimately understands being to be a being. Pseudo-Dionysius, in contrast, denies being to be a being, even an infinite being. That is, Pseudo-Dionysius offers the more thoroughgoing "existentialist" metaphysics. In consequence, I show that Gerald Phelan's "existentialist" interpretation of St. Thomas remains fundamentally "essentialistic." I also discuss what I believe to be serious distortions of Neoplatonic thought.

1330 Jones, L. Gregory. "The Theological Transformation of Aristotelian Friendship in the Thought of St. Thomas Aquinas." *The New Scholasticism* 61(1987): 373-399.

1331 Jordan, Mark D. "Disputed Question in Seifert's "Essence and Existence." *Aletheia* 1(1977): 461-466.

1332 Jordan, Mark D. "The Order of Lights: Aquinas on Immateriality as Hierarchy." *Proceedings of the American Catholic Philosophical Association* 52(1978): 113-120.

*Aquinas suggests in his *De substantis separatis* that immaterial substances must be understood as primarily hierarchical. He sees hierarchy as an order of participation beings brought together on a shared esse-ground. Ps.-Dionysus sees hierarchy as having the same features. But Aquinas denies Ps.-Dionysus' insistence on mediation in order to bring into prominence the immediacy of the esse-ground. This leads him to consider pure being as a kind of "spatiality" within which hierarchy stands.*

1333 Jordan, Mark D. "Aquinas Manuscripts in the Admont Collection: Corrections." *Bulletin de Philosophie Médiévale* 22(1980): 86.

1334 Jordan, Mark D. "Modes of Discourse in Aquinas' Metaphysics." *The New Scholasticism* 54(1980): 401-446.

*There is in Aquinas a vivid awareness of the importance for metaphysics of discriminating among modes of discourse. This awareness plays partly an exegetical and partly a compositional role; in both, it grasps as central the hierarchy of the modes which structure metaphysical language. A picture of Aquinas' understanding of that hierarchy can be had in four sets of remarks:(1) the doctrine of cosignification in terms; (2) the use of the disputed question as a format for parsing contradictory texts; (3) the model for the plural sense of Scripture; and (4) the ordering of the "sciences." A careful reading of these four will secure the fact and the sense of the hierarchy of discursive modes. To see that hierarchy is to begin re-thinking certain hinges in Aquinas' work, including the question of his authorship, his handling of the philosophical tradition, his stand on the philosophy/theology dilemmas, and his teaching on *esse*.*

1335 Jordan, Mark D. "The Grammar of *Esse*: Re-reading Thomas on the Transcendentals." *The Thomist* 44(1980): 1-26.

*Working from *De Veritate*, q. 1, a. 1, the paper investigates Thomas' description of the transcendentals in themselves and as expressions of *esse*. It traces the five transcendentals back to three (*unum*, *bonum*, *verum*) and shows that these are derived from the ways in which any *ens* is intrinsically ordinable. The transcendentals can be 9translated' as completeness, finality, and manifestness. This triplet corresponds to the aesthetic notes of *integritas*, *consonantia*, and *claritas*. These, in turn, are related to the pure perfections—*existere, vivere, intelligere*. In them, one sees how far Thomas has expanded the Aristotelian notion of act and how deeply he interprets *esse* as grounding a particular hierarchy.*

1336 Jordan, Mark D. "The Modes of Thomistic Discourse: Questions for Corbin's *Le Chemin de la Théologie Chez Thomas D'Aquin*." *The Thomist* 45(1981): 80-98.

1337 Jordan, Mark D. "The Controversy of the *Correctoria* and the Limits of Metaphysics." *Speculum* 51(1982): 292-314.

1338 Jordan, Mark D. "The Names of God and the Being of Names." *The Existence and Nature of God*. Ed. Alfred J. Freddoso. Notre Dame, IN: University of Notre Dame Press, 1983. 161-190.

1339 Jordan, Mark D. "The Intelligibility of the World and the Divine Ideas in Aquinas." *The Review of Metaphysics* 38(1984): 17-32.

1340 Jordan, Mark D. "The Terms of the Debate Over Christian Philosophy." *Communio* 12(1985): 293-311.

1341 Jordan, Mark D. "Aquinas' Construction of a Moral Account of the Passions." *Freiburger Zeitschrift für Philosophie und Theologie* 33(1986): 71-97.

1342 Jordan, Mark D. "The Protreptic Structure of the *Summa Contra Gentiles*." *The Thomist* 50(1986): 173-209.

1343 Jordan, Mark D. "Theological Exegesis and Aquinas' Treatise *Against The Greeks*." *Church History* 66(1987): 445-456.

1344 Jordan, Mark D. "Medicine and Natural Philosophy in Aquinas." *Thomas von Aquin: Werk und Wirkung Im Licht Neuerer Forschungen*. Ed. Albert Zimmermann. Miscellanea Mediaevalia 19. Berlin/New York: Walter de Gruyter, 1988. 233-246.

1345 Jordan, Mark D. "The Evidence of the Transcendentals and the Place of Beauty in Thomas Aquinas." *International Philosophical Quarterly* 29(1989): 393-407.

1346 Jordan, Mark D. "Thomas Aquinas' Disclaimers in the Aristotelian Commentaries." *Philosophy and the God of Abraham: Essays in Memory of James A. Weisheipl, OP*. Ed. James Long. Toronto: Pontifical Institute of Mediaeval Studies, In press. 99-112.

1347 Kainz, Howard P. "Angelology, Metaphysics and Intersubjectivity: A Reply to G. N. Casey." *Irish Philosophical Journal* 6(1989): 119-132.

1348 Kato, M. "Thomas Aquinas on *Ratio Individiui*." *Studies in Medieval Thought* 27(1985): 133-141.

1349 Kayser, John R., and Ronald J. Lattieri. "Aquinas' *Regimen Bene Commixtum* and the Medieval Critique of Classical Republicanism." *The Thomist* 46(1982): 195-220.

1350 Kearney, R. J. "Analogy and Inference." *The New Scholasticism* 51(1977): 131-141.

1351 Keller, James A. "Reflections on a Methodology for Christian Philosophers." *Faith and Philosophy* 5(1988): 144-158.

1352 Kelley, Francis E. "The Egidean Influence in Robert Orford's Doctrine on Form." *The Thomist* 47(1983): 77-99.

1353 Kelley, Francis E. "Robert Orford's Attack on Giles of Rome." *The Thomist* 51(1987): 70-96.

*The paper reviews the historical context of Robert Orford's work directed against Giles of Rome, *Reprobationes dictorum a fratre Egido in primum Sententiarum*. Orford, a first generation Oxford Thomist, finds fault with Giles over such trivial matters that one might wonder why he wrote the book at all. In the paper, I suggest that Orford's attack on Giles was politically, rather than doctrinally, inspired.*

1354 Kelly, Charles J. "Some Fallacies in the First Movement of Aquinas' Third Way." *International Journal for Philosophy of Religion* 12(1981): 39-54.

1355 Kelly, Charles J. "The Third Way and the Possible Eternity of the World." *The New Scholasticism* 56(1982): 273-291.

Critics have contended that Thomas Aquinas' opening to the possible eternity of the world invalidates and is otherwise inconsistent with his Third Way purporting to demonstrate the existence of God, contradicts his view that an actually infinite multitude cannot exist, and undermines his ascription of a timeless eternity to God. The paper centers on the presentation and evaluation of three arguments alleging the first incoherency. The thesis is that the methodology employed by Aquinas is a demonstrative argument, his recognition of the eternity of the world as only a supposition and not as an assumption of inquiry, and his essentially predicative concept of time serving to preclude a quantifier shift fallacy and to obviate a recognition of a time when nothing existed as even a possible state of affairs combine to deflect the force of the objections as cogent internal criticisms.

1356 Kelly, Charles J. "The Third Way and the Temporally Infinite: A Rejoinder." *International Journal for Philosophy of Religion* 15(1984): 81-84.

The article replies to two objections made against Kelly's previous attempt to dissolve some fallacies ascribed to Aquinas' third way. The first objection is that the proposed definition of a contingent being as that which once did not exist is unduly restrictive in its exclusion of temporally everlasting contingent beings. The second is that Aquinas is obligated to show that an infinite past time inhabited only by contingent beings would have been a time when no beings existed.

1357 Kelly, Charles J. "The Third Way and the Temporally Infinite: A Rejoinder." *International Journal for Philosophy of Religion* 15(1984): 81-84.

1358 Kelly, Charles J. "Circularity and Contradiction in Aquinas' Rejection of Actually Infinite Multitudes." *The Modern Schoolman* 61(1984): 73-100.

*Aquinas' rejection of an infinity of caused causes as precluding a first cause has been assessed as a *petitio principii*, while his affirmation of the possibility of a temporally infinite universe has been regarded as contradictory to his assertion of the impossibility of an actually infinite multitude. The paper develops these difficulties, proposes and assesses ways of overcoming the *petitio*, and analyzes the charge of contradiction in the light of the argumentative strategies of the Aristotelian *Organon*.*

1359 Kelly, Charles J. "Aquinas' Third Way from the Standpoint of the Aristotelian Syllogistic." *Monist* 69(1986): 189-206.

*Critics have diagnosed Aquinas' claim in his *Third Way* that "everything at some time does not exist" entails "at some time nothing existed" not only as a quantifier reversal fallacy but also as an illicit inference in its deduction that the dismal moment must have been some time in the past. But, by construing Aquinas as using "time" adverbially and by viewing the entailment as an enthymeme with "whatever at some time does not (yet) exist at that time did not exist" as the suppressed necessarily true premise, we can assess his argument as sound. Interpretation of the principle *ex nihilo nihil fit* as "if that which at some time does not (yet) exist presently exists, then some thing at that time existed" confirms this assessment and provides the key to validating the further inference to the claim that nothing now exists.*

1360 Kelly, Charles J. "The Logic of Eternal Knowledge from the Standpoint of the Aristotelian Syllogistic." *The Modern Schoolman* 66(1988): 29-54.

1361 Kelly, Eugene. "Aquinas and the Deconstruction of History." *Vera Lex* 10(1990): 6-8.

1362 Kelly, Matthew J. "Agency in Aquinas." *Laval Théologique et Philosophique* 33(1977): 33-37.

Although St. Thomas holds the axioms "Nothing divisible can move itself" and "Every self-mover is composed of two parts, a part that only moves and a part that is moved only," I show that he can consistently think of living bodies as self-movers, i.e., as agents. I show that he thinks that everybody is an agent, i.e., performs at least one action, and I claim that he thinks the same of every substance. He does not think that these views are incompatible with his claim that there is a being that causesall agents to perform their actions.

1363 Kelly, Matthew J. "Action in Aquinas." *The New Scholasticism* 52(1978): 261-267.

*I use certain texts of St. Thomas to show that he does not think that the division of action usually referred to by Scholastics with phrases like *actio immanens* and *actio transitiva* is exclusive. I show furthermore that it is his view that *actio* refers primarily to a perfection which remains in an agent and that such a perfection is neither essentially productive nor essentially non-productive. The agents in his universe are not linked together by necessary connections in virtue of their actions, for their actions are neither essentially productive nor essentially non-productive.*

1364 Kelly, Matthew J. "Power in Aquinas." *The Thomist* 43(1979): 474-479.

I show, by using examples of Aquinas' use of "power," that the sufficient condition for the exercise of the power of persons differs from the sufficient condition for the exercise of the power of things because "power" in "power of persons" refers to capacities for action while "power" in "power of things" refers to actions. In the former case, "exercise" picks out the action the power is a capacity for, while in the latter case "exercise" picks out the effect the action of a thing (its power) happens to have.

1365 Kelly, Matthew J. "St. Thomas and Transeunt Causality." *The New Scholasticism* 54(1980): 34-45.

I cite some texts which show that many post-medieval philosophers, Descartes, Kant, Locke, Leibniz, and Malebranche, have thought that transeunt causality involves the transmission or transference of a property from cause to effect. I show that St. Thomas did not so conceive of transeunt causality and try to show how he did conceive of it in terms of his theories of agency, action, and power. I then list his view of the necessary and sufficient conditions of an episode of transeunt causality.

1366 Kelly, Matthew J., and George Schedler. "St. Thomas and the Judicial Killing of the Innocent." *Journal of Thought* 14(1982): 17-22.

We use certain texts of Saint Thomas to show that he thinks a judge is justified in knowingly condemning an innocent person to death and that an executioner, knowing this, is justified in carrying out the judge's sentence. These texts show, contrary to Joseph Pieper, that for Saint Thomas justice is not a matter of what is actually done to persons but a matter of what the system (the order of justice) demands. They show that he was not an absolutist when it comes to justice but a proceduralist, for these texts justify the killing of the innocent for the sake of the system.

1367 Kelly, Matthew J. "A Note: Aquinas and the Moral Agent." *The Thomist* 46(1982): 307-312.

Aquinas should have taught that the person who does right thinking it wrong acts as involuntarily as the person who does wrong thinking it right. I conclude that the moral agent for him is the person who knows the moral quality of his action and performs it freely. For Aquinas, it is not sufficient to be a moral agent that a person think about the moral quality of his action and perform it freely.

1368 Kelly, Matthew J. "St. Thomas and the Nature of Moral Precepts." *The New Scholasticism* 61(1987): 427-439.

Because Aquinas holds that it is of the essence of precepts to "prescribe what is useful or necessary for an end," I argue that "Good is to be done and pursued and evil avoided" expresses for St. Thomas the first principle of morality. "Good" refers, therefore, as "evil" does, to actions and not to the human end in terms of which actions are morally right or wrong nor to some chosen end in terms of which actions are right or wrong in a merely practical sense.

1369 Kelsey, David H. "Aquinas and Barth on the Human Body." *The Thomist* 50(1986): 643-689.

1370 Kennedy, Leonard A., ed. "The Soul's Knowledge of Itself: An Unpublished Work Attributed to St. Thomas Aquinas." *Vivarium* 15(1977): 31-45.

1371 Kennedy, Leonard A., ed. "A New Disputed Question of St. Thomas Aquinas on the Immortality of the Soul." *Archives d'Histoire Doctrinale et Littéraire du Moyen Age* 45(1978): 205-223.

1372 Kennedy, Leonard A. "Thomism and Divine Absolute Power." *Thomistic Papers V*. Ed. Thomas A. Russman. Houston, TX: Center for Thomistic Studies, University of Saint Thomas, 1990. 49-62.

1373 Kenny, Anthony John Patrick. "Intentionality: Aquinas and Wittgenstein." *The Legacy of Wittgenstein*. Ed. Anthony Kenny. 1984. 61-76.

1374 Kenny, Anthony John Patrick. "Philosophy of Mind in the Thirteenth Century." *Actes Du Septiéme Congrés International de Philosophie Médiéval II: L'homme et Son Univers Au Moyen Age*. Philosophes Médiévaux 26-27. Louvain-la-Neuve: Éditions de l'Institut Supérieur de Philosophie, 1986. 42-55.

1375 Kenny, Anthony John Patrick. "The Definition of Omnipotence." 1979. *The Concept of God*. Ed. T. Morris. 1987. 125-33. Previously published in author's *The God of the Philosophers*, Oxford: Oxford University Press, 1979, 91-98.

1376 Kenny, Anthony John Patrick. "Aquinas on Knowledge of Self." *Language, Meaning, and God: Essays in Honour of Herbert McCabe*. Ed. Brain Davies. 1987. 104-119.

1377 Kenny, Anthony John Patrick. "The Self." Milwaukee, WI: Marquette University Press, 1988. 34.

1378 Kent, Bonnie Dorrick. "Transitory Vice: Thomas Aquinas on Incontinence." *Journal of the History of Ideas* 27(1989): 199-223.

*Most modern interpreters agree on two points concerning Aristotle's analysis of incontinence (*akrasia*):(1) the agent does not choose the act he performs, and (2) he does not believe his act to be good. According to Aquinas, however, the incontinent does judge his act to be good and docs choose to perform it, though he does not act *from* choice. Using both Aquinas' theological works and his commentary on the *Nichomachean Ethics*, this study shows how his analysis of incontinence follows partly from his conception of the will and partly from his reading of Aristotle.*

1379 Kevane, Eugene. "Augustine's Illumination and Aquinas' *Intellectus Agens*: A Comparative Study." *L'anima nell'antropologia di San Tommaso D'Aquino IX: Atti del Congresso Societá Internazionale San Tommaso D'Aquino*. Ed. Abelardo Lobato. Milano: Editrice Massimo, 1987. 81-93.

1380 Kianka, Frances. "Demetrius Cydones and Thomas Aquinas, Appendix: Demetrius Cydones on Thomas Aquinas. Letter 333 to Maximus Chrysoberges (*Corr.* II, 266-268)." *Byzantion* 52(1982): 264-286.

1381 Killoran, John B. "Aquinas and Vitoria: Two Perspectives on Slavery." *The Medieval Tradition of Natural Law*. Ed. Harold J. Johnson. Studies in Medieval Culutre 22. Kalamazoo, MI: Medieval Institute Publications, 1987. 87-101.

1382 Killoran, John B. "Divine Reason and Virtue in St. Thomas' Natural Law Theory." *Vera Lex* 10(1990): 17-18.

1383 King-Farlow, John. "Historical Insights on Miracles: Babbage, Hume, Aquinas." *International Journal for Philosophy of Religion* 13(1982): 209-218.

*Charles Babbage, outstanding 19th century figure on theory of computing, urges on proto-Goodmanian and neo-Maimonidean grounds that Hume is quite wrong about the probability of miracles occurring. Aquinas' classification of miracles indicates that no single probable judgment is always right. Babbage's work on computing still circulates, but his *Ninth Bridgewater Treatise (On Miracles)* has long deserved republication.*

1384 King-Farlow, John. "Simples, Third Men and Logical Constructions." *Philosophical Inquiry* 7(1985): 13-20.

1385 Kirchner, Bossi Beatriz. "Aquinas as an Interpreter of Aristotle on the End of Human Life." *The Review of Metaphysics* 40(1986): 41-54.

1386 Klein, Sherwin. "Plato's Parmenides and St. Thomas' Analysis of God as One and Trinity." *The Thomist* 55 (In press): 229-244.

1387 Klima, Gyula. "*Libellus Pro Sapiente*—a Criticism of Allan Back's Argument Against St. Thomas Aquinas' Doctrine of the Incarnation." *The New Scholasticism* 58(1984): 207-219.

1388 Kluge, E. H. W. "St. Thomas, Abortion and Euthanasia: Another Look." *Philosophy Research Archives* 7(1981): No. 1472.

St. Thomas is usually thought to have rejected abortion and euthanasia as murder (viz. the statement of The Sacred Congregation for the Doctrine of the Faith "On Procured Abortion"). By going back to Aquinas' own words I show that this is a mistaken view: that he explicitly states abortion prior to a certain point of fetal development to be non-murderous and that his position, when consistently developed, allows for euthanasia under analogous circumstances. These claims are argued by presenting an analytical exposé of Aquinas' metaphysics of man and of human ontogenesis. The implications of this for current bioethical concerns are sketched briefly.

1389 Kluxen, Wolfgang. "Thomas Aquinas: On What Makes an Action Good." *Contemporary German Philosophy* 4(1984): 163-177.

1390 Knasas, John F. X. "Necessity in the *Tertia Via*." *The New Scholasticism* 52(1978): 373-394.

*A look at the *tertia via* reveals that Aquinas is perfectly aware of the difference between real and propositional necessity and of the further distinctions within the last category. These senses of necessity he creatively weaves into an argument for the Christian God that he philosophically understands as subsistent existence. Aquinas is able to neutralize the volatile chemistry contemporary debate has uncovered in the various senses of necessity. Logically necessary being is not logically absurd, if what that proposition is designating is subsistent existence. As a result no need exists for placing factual, or real, necessity and logical necessity into water-tight compartments. Both can be present in one and the same argument and be of one and the same thing. Finally, because no genuine conceptual grasp of existence is available in this life, "God exists" can be *per se notum* in itself yet approached through demonstration. Logical necessity does not preclude demonstration. The *tertia via*, then, offers an understanding of necessity that can creatively further present debate on necessary being.*

1391 Knasas, John F. X. "Aquinas and Finite Gods." *Proceedings of the American Catholic Philosophical Association* 53(1979): 88-97.

1392 Knasas, John F. X. "Making Sense of the *Tertia Via*." *The New Scholasticism* 54(1980): 476-511.

*Aquinas looks at generable and corruptible things and says in Latin what Aristotle says in Greek, *possibile esse et non esse*. But the phrase can be a front for two different metaphysical worlds. Where Aristotle sees things possessing a shaky relationship between their matter and form, Aquinas also perceives a relation of openness between the thing's nature and its existence. This perception is in back of the phrase when Aquinas employs it in theistic reasoning. True, Aquinas can use the phrase in the Aristotelian way. Yet when the context is proving the God of his belief, Aquinas shifts the sense of the phrase to the absolutely possible. The absolutely possible is the possible of the *tertia via*. The absolutely possible is respectful of the language of the first part of the *via* and allows it to make sense.*

1393 Knasas, John F. X. "Super-God: Divine Infinity and Human Self-Determination." *Proceedings of the American Catholic Philosophical Association* 55(1981): 197-209.

1394 Knasas, John F. X. "Aquinas: Prayer to an Immutable God." *The New Scholasticism* 57(1983): 196-221.

My paper effects a critical comparison between the classical theist, Thomas Aquinas, and the process theist, Lewis Ford, on the issue of prayer. For both prayer is an act of love to God by the rational creature. For Ford prayer is loving insofar as the creature contributes to the divine perfection. Prayer is our expression of feeling that is assumed by God to "flesh out his intellectual aridity." For Aquinas prayer takes a loving form in adoration which is a submission, or giving, of our wills to God. Yet Aquinas' view of prayer is more exalted and so can be more bold. Our free prayers of adoration are understood to be infallible effects of God's infinite causality, which has as an apt secondary cause our prayers of petition. In short, for Aquinas prayer is the means by which we can obtain graces, infallibly bringing us to freely love God no matter how difficult our circumstances. Aquinas' reduction of God's immutability to God's being infinite act makes his position intelligible. Ford's process understanding of God does not include infallible effects that are our free acts. Hence, his view of prayer pales in comparison to Aquinas'.

1395 Knasas, John F. X. "*Esse* as the Target of Judgment in Rahner and Aquinas." *Proceedings of the American Catholic Philosophical Association* 59(1985): 114-131.

*My paper critically investigates Rahner's *Spirit in the World*. My conclusion is that the work contains a massive misconstrual of the *esse* grasped in judgment. This is no esoteric point of Thomistic exegesis. A correct appreciation of the *esse* targeted in judgment shows that no necessity for making the transcendental turn exists. Such a turn, at least in Rahner's case, ineluctably leads to a curtailment of metaphysics. Kant is not beaten at his own game.*

1396 Knasas, John F. X. "Thomistic Existentialism and the Silence of the *Quinque Viae*." *The Modern Schoolman* 63(1986): 157-171.

1397 Knasas, John F. X. "*Ad Mentem Thomae*: Does Natural Philosophy Prove God?" *Proceedings of the American Catholic Philosophical Association* 61(1987): 209-220. *My paper investigates a long-simmering controversy: is the *prima via* of Aquinas' famous Five Ways to God an argument of Aristotelian natural philosophy or Thomistic metaphysics? Distinguishing two versions of the physical interpretation, my paper shows that neither has textual support. Points include(1) matter/form principles lead only to a first body; (2) Aquinas relegates philosophical knowledge of God to metaphysics; (3) texts contrary to(1) and (2) are not withstanding; (4) even separate substances, i.e., angels, are beyond the proof of physical principles and they also are relegated to metaphysics; (5) texts apparently contrary to (4) are not withstanding. By this process, my paper fosters the metaphysical solution of the *prima via*.*

1398 Knasas, John F. X. "*Esse* as the Target of Judgment in Rahner and Aquinas." *The Thomist* 51(1987): 222-245.

*Rahner's *Spirit in the World* contains a massive misconstrual of the *esse* grasped in judgment. For Rahner, judgment grasps a universal and non-proper *esse* in reference to which a thing is called a being. For Aquinas, judgment grasps *esse* as radically diverse and most profound, and deeply set in the thing. This disagreement is no esoteric point of Thomistic exegesis. A correct appreciation of the *esse* targeted in judgment shows no necessity for making a transcendental turn exist.*

1399 Knasas, John F. X. "Aquinas, Analogy, and the Divine Infinity." *Doctor Communis* 40(1987): 64-84.

1400 Knasas, John F. X. "Immateriality and Metaphysics." *Angelicum* 65(1988): 44-76.

1401 Knasas, John F. X. "The Liberationist Critique of Maritain's New Christendom." *The Thomist* 52(1988): 247-267.

The article assesses two understandings of radical Christian temporal involvement—Maritain's New Christendom and Gutierrez's Liberationism. Because both positions claim Thomistic inspiration, my assessment proceeds by comparison with Aquinas. In sum, the Lubacian basis for Gutierrez's liberationist turn is not necessary. The human nature able to be called to the supernatural need not be radically and constitutively oriented to the vision of God. Aquinas, however, supports the distinction of planes in Maritain's New Christendom. The correlative Thomistic points are perfect and imperfect happiness.

1402 Knasas, John F. X. "How Thomistic is the Intuition of Being?" *Jacques Maritain: The Man and His Metaphysics*. Ed. John F. X. Knasas. Notre Dame, IN: University of Notre Dame Press, 1988. 83-91.

*The ambiguity of the intuition of being is noted. It can refer to the judgmental grasp of the act of existing (esse) of a sensible thing. It can also refer to the grasp of "ens" understood as a transphysical commonality. As such a commonality, *ens* is seen as able to be realized both in bodies and possibly immaterial instances. Different as these two senses are, an intimate connection exists between them. To have the first is to have the second. One cannot grasp *esse* and fail to see that its actualizing capacity extends to possible immaterial things. After noting the standard neo-Thomist critique, a partial defense of Maritain's doctrine is given. Crucial here is the realization that Thomistic remarks on the transphysicality of *ens* as the subject of metaphysics (*In De Trin.* V, 4c and *In Meta.* , proem) are not intended to refer to the subject of metaphysics at its start.*

1403 Knasas, John F. X. "Does Gilson Theologize Thomistic Metaphysics?" *Thomistic Papers V*. Ed. Thomas A. Russman. Houston, TX: Center for Thomistic Studies, University of Saint Thomas, 1990. 3-24.

1404 Knasas, John F. X. "Does Natural Philosophy Prove the Immaterial?: An Answer to Mark Johnson." *American Catholic Philosophical Quarterly* 64(1990): 265-269.

1405 Knasas, John F. X. "Gilson Vs Maritain: The Start of Thomistic Metaphysics." *Doctor Communis* 43(1990): 250-265.

1406 Knasas, John F. X. "Transcendental Thomism and the Thomistic Texts." *The Thomist* 54(1990): 81-95. Response to J. Donceel, "A Thomistic misapprehension?" *Thought*, 32(1957): 189-198.

*Some time ago Father Joseph Donceel published an unchallenged article alleging that American Thomism was too *a posteriori* in its appreciation of Aquinas' metaphysical stance. Donceel counters by spotlighting various Thomistic texts that speak of an *a priori* contribution of the intellect to human knowledge. The texts cited by Donceel are all found in Maréchal's *Cahier V*. There Maréchal mentions many other besides. By employing the Maréchalian collection, I seek to determine if Aquinas is an a priorist. The texts include *De Ver.* 1, 4, ad 5m; *De Ver*. XXII, 2 ad1m; *S. T.* I, 88, 3c; *De Ver*. X, 6c; *In IV Meta.* lect. 6; *S. T.* I, 84, 6c; *C. G.* I, 43.*

1407 Knauer, Peter. "The Hermeneutic Function of the Principle of Double Effect." *Readings in Moral Theology: Moral Norms and Catholic Tradition*. Eds. Charles E. Curran and Richard McCormick. New York: Paulist Press, 1979. 1-39.

1408 Knuuttila, Simo. "Being *Qua* Being in Thomas Aquinas and John Duns Scotus." *The Logic of Being: Historical Studies*. Eds. Simo Knuuttila and Jaakko Hintikka. Synthese Historical Library 28. Dordrecht: Reidel, 1986. 201-222.

1409 Kondoleon, Theodore J. "Substance and Accidents, Potency and Act." *The New Scholasticism* 51(1977): 234-239.

1410 Kondoleon, Theodore J. "The Third Way: Encore." *The Thomist* 44(1980): 325-356.

1411 Kondoleon, Theodore J. "The Free Will Defense: New and Old." *The Thomist* 47(1983): 1-42.

1412 Konyndyk, Kenneth. "Faith and Evidentialism." *Rationality, Religious Belief, and Moral Commitment: New Essays in the Philosophy Religion*. Eds. Robert Audi and William J. Wainwright. Ithaca, NY: Cornell University Press, 1986. 82-108.

1413 Kopaczynski, Germain. "Some Franciscans on St. Thomas' Essence-existence Doctrine." *Franciscan Studies* 38(1978): 283-298.

*Did St. Thomas hold a real distinction between essence and existence? The article tries to answer the question by taking a rather roundabout approach, namely, by seeing what the Franciscans—those traditional adversaries of Aquinas' metaphysics—have to say on the matter. Texts of Scotus, Ockham, and Mastrius lead us to conclude, according to the Franciscans who opposed it, St. Thomas Aquinas did indeed hold a doctrine of a real distinction between essence and *esse*.*

1414 Kopaczynski, Germain. "The Essence-Existence Question in a Linguistic Key." *Miscellanea Francescana* 80(1980): 67-79.

1415 Kopaczynski, Germain. "A Real Distinction in St. Thomas Aquinas? 20th Century Opponents and the Linguistic Turn." *Philosophy Research Archives* 11(1985): 127-140.

The objective of this study is to analyze the writing of three neo-scholastic writers of the twentieth century—Marcel Chossat, Pedro Descoqus, and Francis Cunningham—who happen to dispute the prevailing view of Thomists that St. Thomas Aquinas does indeed hold a doctrine of the real distinction of essence and existence in created being. The approach utilized will be basically historical: we start with the year 1910, the year in which Marcel Chossat rekindled the ever-smoldering embers of the essence-existence controversy with his claim that Aquinas never held such a doctrine. To justify another treatment of what has been called "the endlessly rehashed question," we try to show that the arguments put forth by the three thinkers in question all are based on considerable and weighty linguistic grounds which others in the debate have tended to dismiss. We conclude by saying that any discussion of the real distinction controversy must take a "linguistic turn" if it is to have any hope of being fruitful.

1416 Kottman, Karl A. "16th and 17th Century Iberian Controversy Over St. Thomas' Theory of *Jus Gentium* and Natural Law: The Interpretation of Antonio Vieira, S. J." *Tommaso D'Aquino Nel Suo Settimo Centenario VIII: Atti del Congresso Internazionale.* Napoli: Edizioni Domenicane Italiane, 1978. 295-305.

1417 Kovach, Francis J. "The Transcendality of Beauty Revisited." *The New Scholasticism* 52(1978): 404-412.

1418 Kovach, Francis J. "Saint Thomas Aquinas: Limitation of Potency by Act, a Textual and Doctrinal Analysis." *Atti Del'VIII Congresso Tomistico Internazionale V: Problemi Metafisici.* Studi Tomistici 14. 1982. 387-411.

1419 Kovach, Francis J. "Action at a Distance in St. Thomas Aquinas." *Thomistic Papers II.* Eds. Leonard A. Kennedy and Jack C. Marler. Houston, TX: University of St. Thomas, Center for Thomistic Studies, 1986. 85-132.

This paper aims at identifying the various sources and models of Aquinas' causal continguism, according to which neither corporeal agents nor God can act directly at a distance. Among the findings are (1) Thomas' physical contiguism is originally Aristotelian; the implicit models of his metaphysical contiguism are patristic; and the explicit source of the same, Albert; (2) Thomas' two proofs of physical contiguism are Aristotelian and Neoplatonic, respectively; and (3) Aquinas' belief in and contiguist accounts of various apparent actions at a distance, like magnetism, fascination, magic acts, and celestial influences, are partly Aristotelian-Alexandrian and partly influenced by ancient Greek and Roman poetic and scientific ideas.

1420 Kovach, Francis J. "Human Purposiveness in Saint Thomas Aquinas." *Religion and Human Purpose: A Cross Disciplinary Approach.* Eds. W. Horosz and T. Clements. Vol. 1. Studies in Philosophy and Religion 6. Dordrecht: Martinus Nijhoff, 1987. 143-164.

Aquinas treats human purposiveness in a philosophical and a theological theory of man's ultimate end. Philosophically, this end has three components. One is the intellectual contemplation of God, rendering human life an ever-exciting voyage of the mind toward God, filled with the sweetness of its concomitant intellectual joy. The second is aesthetic: glimpses, as if through a veil, of God's enigmatic, since incomprehensible, beauty in which every creature proportionately participates. The third is ethical; virtuous life. Because, however, our acts of the intellect and will, like human nature, are limited and imperfect, the philosophically recognized end is only relatively ultimate. Its absolutely ultimate counterpart is a matter of theology: beatific vision.

1421 Kovach, Francis J. "A Novel Argument from Contingency for the Existence of God." *Scholastic Challenges to Some Mediaeval and Modern Ideas.* Ed. Francis J. Kovach. Stillwater, OK: Western Publications, 1987. 3-21.

1422 Kovach, Francis J. "The Infinity of the Divine Essence and Power in the Works of St. Albert the Great." *Scholastic Challenges to Some Mediaeval and Modern Ideas.* Ed. Francis J. Kovach. Stillwater, OK: Western Publications, 1987. 23-41.

1423 Kovach, Francis J. "St. Thomas Aquinas: Limitation of Potency by Act, A Textual and Doctrinal Analysis." *Scholastic Challenges to Some Mediaeval and Modern Ideas*. Ed. Francis J. Kovach. Stillwater, OK: Western Publications, 1987. 45-66.

1424 Kovach, Francis J. "Divine Art in Saint Thomas Aquinas." *Scholastic Challenges to Some Mediaeval and Modern Ideas*. Ed. Francis J. Kovach. Stillwater, OK: Western Publications, 1987. 69-79.

1425 Kovach, Francis J. "The Transcendentality of Beauty in Thomas Aquinas." *Scholastic Challenges to Some Mediaeval and Modern Ideas*. Ed. Francis J. Kovach. Stillwater, OK: Western Publications, 1987. 83-90.

1426 Kovach, Francis J. "Angelic Locution in Albert the Great." *Scholastic Challenges to Some Mediaeval and Modern Ideas*. Ed. Francis J. Kovach. Stillwater, OK: Western Publications, 1987. 111-126.

1427 Kovach, Francis J. "Bonaventure's and Aquinas' Theories of the Infinite and Their Roles in Later Mediaeval Thought." *Scholastic Challenges to Some Mediaeval and Modern Ideas*. Ed. Francis J. Kovach. Stillwater, OK: Western Publications, 1987. 129-145.

1428 Kovach, Francis J. "Aquinas' Theory of Action at a Distance—A Critical Analysis." *Scholastic Challenges to Some Mediaeval and Modern Ideas*. Ed. Francis J. Kovach. Stillwater, OK: Western Publications, 1987. 149-177.

1429 Kovach, Francis J. "The Temporality of the World and the Concept of the Infinite in Thomas Aquinas." *Scholastic Challenges to Some Mediaeval and Modern Ideas*. Ed. Francis J. Kovach. Stillwater, OK: Western Publications, 1987. 181-195.

1430 Kovach, Francis J. "The Empirical Foundations of Thomas Aquinas' Philosophy of Beauty." *Scholastic Challenges to Some Mediaeval and Modern Ideas*. Ed. Francis J. Kovach. Stillwater, OK: Western Publications, 1987. 201-210.

1431 Kovach, Francis J. "The Influence of Pseudo-Dionysius's *De Divinis Nominibus* on Thomas Aquinas' Philosophy of Beauty." *Scholastic Challenges to Some Mediaeval and Modern Ideas*. Ed. Francis J. Kovach. Stillwater, OK: Western Publications, 1987. 213-240.

1432 Kovach, Francis J. "The Role of Nature in the Aesthetics of Thomas Aquinas." *Scholastic Challenges to Some Mediaeval and Modern Ideas*. Ed. Francis J. Kovach. Stillwater, OK: Western Publications, 1987. 2432-49.

1433 Kovach, Francis J. "Aesthetic Disinterestedness in Thomas Aquinas." *Scholastic Challenges to Some Mediaeval and Modern Ideas*. Ed. Francis J. Kovach. Stillwater, OK: Western Publications, 1987. 253-258.

1434 Kovach, Francis J. "Is Maritain's Philosophy of Beauty Truly Thomistic?" *Scholastic Challenges to Some Mediaeval and Modern Ideas*. Ed. Francis J. Kovach. Stillwater, OK: Western Publications, 1987. 297-330.

1435 Kovach, Francis J. "Lie and Protective Statement: Their Nature and Morality." *Scholastic Challenges to Some Mediaeval and Modern Ideas*. Ed. Francis J. Kovach. Stillwater, OK: Western Publications, 1987. 333-372.

1436 Krapiec, Mieczyslaw Albert. "The Theory of Analogy of Being." *Theory of Being to Understand Reality*. Ed. Stanislaw Kaminski et al. Lublin: Towarzystwo Naukowe Katolickiego Uniwersytetu Lubelskiego, 1980. 31-106.

1437 Krapiec, Mieczyslaw A. "The Human Soul: The Approach of St. Thomas and Some Contemporary Thinkers." *L'anima Nell'antropologia Di San Tommaso D'Aquino IX: Atti del Congresso Societá Internazionale San Tommaso D'Aquino*. Ed. Abelardo Lobato. Milano: Editrice Massimo, 1987. 469-482.

1438 Kretzmann, Norman. "Goodness, Knowledge, and Indeterminacy in the Philosophy of Thomas Aquinas." *The Journal of Philosophy* 80(1983): 631-649.

Four apparent inconsistencies in Aquinas' philosophy are examined in the form of these questions:(1) Is God free to choose whether to create? (2) Is God free to choose what to create? (3) Are the beginninglessness and immutability of God's knowledge of all particulars compatible with the fact that some of them are contingent? (4) Is the purely active character of God's knowledge of all particulars compatible with the fact that some of them are contingent?

1439 Kretzmann, Norman. "*Lex Iniusta Non Est Lex*: Laws on Trial in Aquinas' Court of Conscience." *American Journal of Jurisprudence* 33(1988): 99-122.

1440 Kretzmann, Norman. "Christian Faith." *Philosophy and the Christian Faith*. Ed. Thomas V. Morris. University of Notre Dame Studies in the Philosophy of Religion 5. Notre Dame, IN: University of Notre Dame Press, 1988. 172-195.

1441 Kretzmann, Norman. "Warring Against the Law of My Mind: Aquinas on *Romans* 7." *Philosophy and the Christian Faith*. Ed. Thomas V. Morris. University of Notre Dame Studies in the Philosophy of Religion 5. Notre Dame, IN: University of Notre Dame Press, 1988. 172-195.

*Discussions of *akrasia* or weakness of will rely on Romans 7 for a paradigm of that state. Gareth Matthews interprets the passage in terms of *akrasia* compounded by two orders of hypocrisy. Drawing on Aquinas' discussions of incontinence and his commentary on Romans, the article rejects both those interpretations in favor of Aquinas' dual man-of-sin and man-of-grace interpretation, which recognizes the condition Paul portrays as one that is a feature of the moral life quite generally.*

1442 Kretzmann, Norman, and Eleonore Stump. "Being and Goodness." *Divine and Human Action*. Ed. Thomas V. Morris. Ithaca, NY: Cornell University Press, 1988. 281-312.

Aquinas' naturalism supplies for his virtue-centered morality the sort of metaethical foundation that recent virtue-centered morality has been criticized for lacking, and it complements Aquinas' Aristotelian emphasis on rationality as a moral standard by supplying a method for determining degrees of rationality. It also effects a connection between morality and theology that offers an alternative to divine-common morality, construing morality not merely as a dictate of God's will but as an expression of his nature. Finally, it illuminates an often overlooked side of the problem of evil, raising the question whether recent defenses against the argument from evil are compatible with the doctrine of God's goodness.

1443 Kries, Douglas Lee. "Thomas Aquinas and the Politics of Moses." *The Review of Politics* 52(1988): 84-104.

1444 Kuntz, Paul Grimley. "The Analogy of Degrees of Being: A Critique of Cajetan's *Analogy of Names*." *The New Scholasticism* 56(1982): 51-79.

*What Cajetan neglected in *De Nominum Analogia* was the fact that St. Thomas introduced analogy in the *Summa Theologia* in commenting on *De Divinis Nominibus*. Dionysius asked the question: how should man use names of creatures in talking about the Creator? St. Thomas accepted the solution that *good*, *wise*, etc., are attributes that "exist in Him in a more excellent way." St. Thomas then accepts hierarchy coming from Neo-Platonism and uses Biblical metaphor. Cajetan's treatise, which deserves great esteem as the first treatise on analogy, is nevertheless in error in drawing Thomistic analogy solely from Aristotle. Just as recent scholarship has called our attention to participation, so now we need to go a further step. *Analogia entis* does solve the logical problem of finding a mean between univocity and ambiguity, but this is not sufficient to solve the metaphysical problem of connecting the levels of hierarchy. To this end we must formulate *analogia graduum entis*, even if Cajetan did reject *analogia inequalitatis* as "pseudo-analogy."*

1445 Kuntz, Paul Grimley. "*De Analogia Graduum Entis* on Cardinal Cajetan's Neglect of Thomistic Hierarchy." *The New Scholasticism* 52(1986): 72-79. 1986.

1446 Kuntz, Paul Grimley. "A Formal Preface and an Informal Conclusion to the Great Chain of Being: The Universality and Necessity of Hierarchical Thought." *Jacob's Ladder and the Tree of Life*. Eds. M. Kuntz and Paul Kuntz. 1987. 3-14.

1447 Kuykendall, George. "Thomas' Proofs as *Fides Quarens Intellectum*: Towards a Trinitarian *Analogia*." *Scottish Journal of Theology (London)* 31(1978): 113-132.

1448 La Croix, Richard R. "Aquinas on God's Omnipresence and Timelessness." *Philosophy and Phenomenological Research* 42(1982): 391-399.

Aquinas holds the view that God is both omnipresent and timeless. But if God is omnipresent, then it would appear that he must have been in the United Nations Building yesterday as well as the day before yesterday. And if God was in the United Nations Building both yesterday and the day before, then it would appear that he is in time and that temporal predications do actually apply to him. So, it would appear that God is not a timeless being if he is omnipresent. The author shows that this argument holds against Aquinas' way of understanding the doctrines of divine omnipresence and divine timelessness and, hence, that two doctrines crucial to the theology of Aquinas are logically incompatible.

1449 La Plante, Harry. "Person and Thomism." *The Modern Schoolman* 63(1986): 193-215.

1450 Lacugna, Catherine Mowry. "The Relational God: Aquinas and Beyond." *Theological Studies* 46(1986): 647-663.

1451 Lacugna, Catherine Mowry. "Philosophers and Theologians on the Trinity." *Modern Theology* 2(1986): 168-181.

1452 Lambert, Richard Thomas. "Habitual Knowledge of the Soul in Thomas Aquinas." *The Modern Schoolman* 60(1982): 1-19.

*Aquinas' *De Veritate* referred to "habitual knowledge" of the soul, although almost no mention of it reappears in later works. This knowledge is not a specific act of disposition but the soul's immediate readiness, from its identity with itself, to know its own existence whenever it performs a conscious act. While this capability clearly differs from ordinary habitual knowledge, the retention of concepts, it is, like that retention, midway between actual and potential knowledge.*

1453 Lambert, Richard Thomas. "A Textual Study of Aquinas' Comparison of the Intellect to Prime Matter." *The New Scholasticism* 56(1982): 80-99.

Aquinas notes similarities between the possible intellect and prime matter, especially in their potentiality to all forms; while matter holds the last place among all things, the intellect is last among "intelligences" or "intelligibles." These terms need clarifications. "Intelligences" (intellectual knowers) are differentiated from "intelligibles" (things knowable by an intellect) in that immateriality is a sufficient condition of the latter but only a necessary condition of the former; intellectual likenesses, for instance, are intelligible but not intelligent. Further, intelligences are real existent, but intelligibles need not be in the order of existence. Intelligibles are ranked according to their degrees of inherent actuality, the criterion for which is the number of species one must receive to know something. Ranked in accordance with these principles, the entire order of intelligibles ranges from God through angelic essences, likenesses, and powers, to the agent intellect, concepts, and possible intellect in the human soul.

1454 Lambert, Richard Thomas. "Nonintentional Experience of Oneself in Thomas Aquinas." *The New Scholasticism* 59(1985): 253-275.

1455 Lang, Helen S. "Aristotelian Physics: Teleological Procedure in Aristotle, Thomas and Buridan." *The Review of Metaphysics* 42(1989): 569-591.

1456 Langan, John Patrick. "Beatitude and Moral Law in St. Thomas." *Journal of Religious Ethics* 5(1977): 183-195.

The author interprets the ethical theory of Saint Thomas Aquinas as a kind of deontological intuitionism. Although the concept of the supreme good or beatitude does not serve as the criterion of right action, it is shown that it does play an important role as a guiding and unifying thread in the life of the human agent.

1457 Langan, John Patrick. "Morality, Egoism and Punishment in Thomas Aquinas." *The Heythrop Journal* 22(1981): 378-393.

1458 Langston, Douglas Charles. "Burrell's Misconstruals of Scotus." *The New Scholasticism* 57(1983): 71-80.

In two publications, David Burrell has argued that Scotus has an "incredible position" on religious language. Burrell claims this because he thinks that Scotus subscribes to a theory of concept formations that commits him to what Sellars calls "the myth of the given" as well as the claim that intuition is a source of knowledge. In this paper, I show that Scotus does not subscribe to the dangerous theory of concept formation; on the contrary, he holds a theory very similar to Aquinas'. Moreover, I show that Scotus' doctrine of intuitive cognition is not the doctrine of intuition Burrell thinks it is. Having shown Burrell's misconstruals of Scotus, I caution that one must suspect Burrell's evaluation of Scotus' position on religious language and Burrell's comparisons between the theories of Scotus and Aquinas.

1459 Lash, Nicholas. "Ideology, Metaphor and Analogy." *Philosophical Frontiers of Christian Theology*. Eds. B. Hebblethwaite and S. Sutherland. Cambridge: Cambridge University Press, 1982. 68-94.

1460 Lash, Nicholas. "Considering the Trinity." *Modern Theology* 2(1986): 183-196.

1461 Lauder, Robert. "On Being or not Being a Thomist." *The Thomist* 55 (In press): 301-319.

1462 Leclerc, Ivor. "God and the Issue of Being." *Religious Studies* 20(1984): 63-78.

1463 Lee, William Patrick. "St. Thomas and Avicenna on the Agent Intellect." *The Thomist* 45(1981): 41-61.

Taking cues from Aristotle, Avicenna (an llth century Muslim thinker) concludes that the agent intellect is a separate substance, a thesaurus of forms, and that man understands when intelligible forms emanate from this agent intelligences into his own passive intellect. For Avicenna, all intelligibility is from above (just as in his cosmology, all real causal efficacy is from above). Concerned as always, with dignity of terrestrial creatures, Aquinas subjects Avicenna's notion of agent intellect to a significant critique—significant not only for the questions at issue, but also for Aquinas' whole metaphysics and for his relation to Aristotle.

1464 Lee, William Patrick. "St. Thomas and the Permanence of the Ten Commandments." *Theological Studies* 42(1981): 422-443.

1465 Lee, William Patrick. "Aquinas and Scotus on Liberty and Natural Law." *Proceedings of the American Catholic Philosophical Association* 56(1982): 70-78.

1466 Lee, William Patrick. "Language About God and the Theory of Analogy." *The New Scholasticism* 58(1984): 40-66.

1467 Lee, William Patrick. "The Relation Between Intellect and Will in Free Choice According to Aquinas and Scotus." *The Thomist* 49(1985): 321-342.

1468 Lee, William Patrick. "Aquinas on Knowledge of Truth and Existence." *The New Scholasticism* 60(1986): 46-71.

1469 Lee, William Patrick. "Existential Propositions in the Thought of St. Thomas Aquinas." *The Thomist* 52(1988): 605-626.

1470 Lee, William Patrick. "Etienne Gilson: *Thomist Réalism and the Critique of Knowledge*." *The New Scholasticism* 53(1989): 81-100.

1471 Lee, William Patrick. "Reply to Mark Wauck." *American Catholic Philosophical Quarterly* 64(1990): 411-413.

1472 Leftow, Brian. "The Roots of Eternity." *Religious Studies* 24(1988): 189-212.

1473 Leftow, Brian. "Aquinas on Time and Eternity." *American Catholic Philosophical Quarterly* 64(1990): 387-399.

1474 Lescoe, Francis J. "Existential Personalism." *Proceedings of the American Catholic Philosophical Association* 60(1986): 2-10.

1475 Lewis, Delmas. "Eternity, Time and Tenselessness." *Faith and Philosophy* 5(1988): 72-86.

*In this paper I argue that the classic concept of eternity, as it is presented in Boethius, Anselm, and Aquinas, must be understood to involve not only the claim that all temporal things are epistemically present to God, but also the claim that all temporal things are *existentially* present to God insofar as they coexist timelessly in the eternal present. I further argue that the concept of eternity requires a tenseless view of time. If this is correct, then the existence of an eternal God logically depends on the truth of the tenseless account of time. I conclude by suggesting that the Christian theologian ought to reject a tenseless ontology.*

1476 Lewis, John Underwood. "The Power of Law: Mill, Devlin, and Aquinas on the Relation Between Law and Morality." *Proceedings of the American Catholic Philosophical Association* 53(1979): 141-149.

1477 Lewis, John Underwood. "Saint Thomas Aquinas' *S. T.* I-II. 94. 2 and 4: Two Renaissance Interpretations and Their Significance to Contemporary Value Theory." *The Medieval Tradition of Natural Law*. Ed. Harold J. Johnson. Studies in Medieval Culutre 22. Kalamazoo, MI: Medieval Institute Publications, 1987. 119-127.

1478 Lewry, Osmund. "Two Continuators of Aquinas: Robertus de Vulgarbia and Thomas Sutton on the *Perihermeneias* of Aristotle." *Mediaeval Studies* 43(1981): 58-130.

1479 Lindbeck, George. "Responses to Marshall's Aquinas as Postliberal Theologian." *The Thomist* 53(1989): 403-406.

1480 Lindsay, Ronald A. "Thomas Aquinas' Complete Guide to Heaven and Hell." *Free Inquiry* 10(1990): 38-39.

*This article summarizes in a humorous fashion the orthodox Christian philosopher's conception of the afterlife. All quotes are from the Supplement to Part Three of the *Summa Theologica*. Problems with this conception are discussed; in particular, the Christian philosopher's understanding of the afterlife diverges sharply from the understanding of the ordinary lay person. The article suggest that the ordinary lay person may not find the prospect of immortality attractive as it is described by the philosopher.*

1481 Lints, Richard. "Attempts to Bridge the Gap in the *Tertia Via*." *The Southwestern Journal of Philosophy* 24(1986): 531-539.

1482 Lobo-Gomez, Alfonso. "Natural Law and Naturalism." *Proceedings of the American Catholic Philosophical Association* 59(1985): 232-249.

1483 Lohr, Charles H. "The Medieval Interpretation of Aristotle." *The Cambridge History of Later Medieval Philosophy: From the Rediscovery of Aristotle to the Disintegration of Scholasticism. 1100-1600.* Eds. Norman Kretzmann et al. Cambridge: Cambridge University Press, 1982. 80-98.

1484 Lonergan, Bernard. "Aquinas Today: Tradition and Innovation." *Celebrating the Medieval Heritage: A Colloquy on the Thought of Aquinas and Bonaventure*. Ed. David Tracy. *The Journal of Religion*, Supplement 58. Chicago: University of Chicago Press, 1978. 1-17.

1485 Longeway, John. "Nicholas of Cusa and Man's Knowledge of God." *Philosophy Research Archives* 13(1987-1988): 289-313.

*I argue that Nicholas of Cusa agrees with Thomas Aquinas on the metaphysics of analogy in God, but differs on epistemology, taking a Platonic position against Aquinas' Aristotelianism. As a result Cusa has to rethink Thomas' solution to the problem of discourse about God. In *De docta ignorantia* he uses the mathematics of the infinite as a clue to the relations between a thing and its measure and this allows him, he thinks, to adapt Aquinas' approach to the problem of his own epistemology. The resulting approach, I maintain, is coherent and reasonable if the metaphysical behind it are.*

1486 Losoncy, Thomas A. "The Platonic Ideas: Some Permanent Contributions to Medieval Philosophies of Man." *Diotima* 7(1979): 105-110.

This article endeavors to identify the Platonic notion of the immaterial as such and to show that the basic insight remains a key element in Medieval philosophies of man where it is employed, expanded and more fully developed. Initially, the feature of the immaterial found in the Platonic dialogues are presented. Then various views of man through the Middle Ages are surveyed to show how the notion of the immaterial is attributed to man's knowing, employed in man's efforts to know of immaterial beings, and finally used to assign man a precise metaphysical niche in the universe of beings.

1487 Lukac de Stier, María Lillana. "Theoretical and Practical Knowledge in Hobbes and Thomas Aquinas." *The New Scholasticism* 61(1987): 1-12.

1488 Luscombe, David E. "Natural Morality and Natural Law." *The Cambridge History of Later Medieval Philosophy: From the Rediscovery of Aristotle to the Disintegration of Scholasticism. 1100-1600.* Eds. Norman Kretzmann et al. Cambridge: Cambridge University Press, 1982. 705-719.

1489 Luscombe, David E. "Thomas Aquinas and Conceptions of Hierarchy in the Thirteenth Century." *Thomas von Aquin: Werk und Wirkung Im Licht Neuerer Forschungen.* Ed. Albert Zimmermann. Berlin/New York: Walter de Gruyter, 1988. 261-277.

1490 MacBeath, Murray. "Omniscience and Eternity." *The Aristotelian Society Supplement* 63(1989): 55-73.

Problem: Can a timeless God know what time it is (now)? Simple answer: At any time God, even if timeless, can answer the question "What time is it now?" simply in virtue of knowing at what time it is asked, and it follows from this that at any time he knows what time it is. Objection: There is a nonpropositional kind of knowledge, knowing what-it-is-like-to, and knowing what it is like to experience some event as past is not possible for a timeless God. Conclusion: The simple answer to the problem is inadequate, and so is the traditional propositional definition of omniscience.

1491 MacDonald, Scott. "The *Esse/Essentia* Argument in Aquinas' *De Ente et Essentia.*" *Journal of the History of Philosophy* 22(1984): 157-172.

*The purpose of the article is to offer a detailed exegetical analysis of the argument in Chapter Four of *De ente et essentia*, in which Aquinas argues for a distinction between *esse* and essence and to develop an interpretation of it on the basis of the analysis. I argue that the reconstructed argument shows that Aquinas argues for a real distinction and that he established it earlier in the argument than some commentators have thought. I criticize a rival interpretation of the argument defended recently by Joseph Owens.*

1492 MacKenzie, Charles S. "Augustine's Trinitarian Ideal and Aquinas' Universal Christendom." *Building a Christian World View II.* Eds. W. Hoffecker and G. Smith. 1988. 189-220.

1493 Mackey, Louis. "Entreatments of God: Reflections on Aquinas' Five Ways." *Franciscan Studies* 37(1977): 103-119.

*Aquinas' Five Ways are not cosmological arguments that begin with the actual world and conclude to God as its first cause, but ontological arguments that demonstrate the necessary existence of God as the cause of any possible world exhibiting the features of motion, efficient causality, contingency, hierarchy, and teleology. Not *a posteriori* but *a priori*, they elicit God's being from a few principles *per se nota*. Experiences occasions and interprets the proofs; it does not provide them with premises. Augustinian in form, the proofs rely on faith to provide an interpretation of the world as sign/effect which legitimatize the conclusion to God as signified/cause.*

1494 Maguire, Daniel C. "*Ratio Practica* and the Intellectualistic Fallacy." *Journal of Religious Ethics* 10(1982): 22-39.

*The epistemology of ethics in both philosophical and theological quarters is broadly guilty of what can be called the intellectualistic fallacy. This fallacy ignores the animating affective mold of moral knowing and so wreaks reductionism on ethical epistemology and method. Specifically, the neglect of the affective as a dimension of moral cognition leads to a failure to see the relationship of all moral awareness to mysticism, contemplation, faith, and religious experience. It also leads to the adoption of false paradigms for moral knowing drawn from science, mathematics, or linguistics. This essay studies *ratio practica* in Thomas Aquinas and the derivative theory of affective knowledge in John of St. Thomas. Then the author proceeds to develop his own theory on the place of affectivity in the overall epistemology of ethics.*

1495 Mahoney, Edward P. "Metaphysical Foundations of the Hierarchy of Being According to Some Late Medieval and Renaissance Philosophers." *Philosophies of Existence*. Ed. Parviz Morewedge. New York: Fordham University Press, 1982. 165-257.

1496 Mahoney, Edward P. "Sense, Intellect, and Imagination in Albert, Thomas, and Siger." *The Cambridge History of Later Medieval Philosophy: From the Rediscovery of Aristotle to the Disintegration of Scholasticism. 1100-1600*. Eds. Norman Kretzmann et al. Cambridge: Cambridge University Press, 1982. 602-622.

1497 Mahoney, Edward P. "Lovejoy and the Hierarchy of Being." *Journal of the History of Ideas* 48(1987): 211-230.

1498 Mahoney, Marianne. "Prudence as the Consequence of the Contemporary Thomistic Philosophy of Freedom." *Freedom in the Modern World: Jacques Maritain, Yves R. Simon, Mortimer J. Adler*. Ed. Michael D. Torre. Notre Dame, IN: University of Notre Dame Press, 1989. 117-129.

1499 Makin, Stephen. "Aquinas, Natural Tendencies and Natural Kinds." *The New Scholasticism* 63(1989): 253-274.

1500 Maloney, Christopher J. "*Esse* in the Metaphysics of Thomas Aquinas." *The New Scholasticism* 55(1981): 159-177.

*Thomas Aquinas developed a theory of individual substance based largely upon Aristotelian notions of matter, form, and essence. Aquinas augmented and altered Aristotle's system, introducing *esse* and distinguishing designated and undesignated matter. Aquinas also differed with Aristotle regarding the essence of a material substance, and this led Aquinas to introduce *esse* into his general theory of individual substances. My purpose is to reconstruct Thomas' theory, proposing an analysis of the structure of material and spiritual substances and their essences, noting selected inconsistencies, and revealing theses to which he is committed.*

1501 Marshall, Bruce D. "Aquinas as a Postliberal Theologian." *The Thomist* 53(1989): 353-402.

*The purpose of this essay is to discuss the relation between Thomas Aquinas' account of religious and theological truth and a "postliberal" one such as that sketched in George Lindbeck's *The Nature of Doctrine*. Most reviewers assume that Lindbeck's approach is on this point incompatible with the mainstream of the tradition, and Colman O'Neill, writing in *The Thomist* symposium on Lindbeck's book, thinks it contradicts Aquinas in particular. This paper presents the case to the contrary. After outlining O'Neill's problem, it argues that he misreads Lindbeck and, at greater length, that Aquinas' views on truth are, as Lindbeck affirms, compatible with postliberal emphases.*

1502 Marshall, David J., trans. "Socrates Est/There is No Such Thing as Pegasus. Thomas Aquinas and W. Van Orman Quine on the Logic of Singular Existence Statements." *Contemporary German Philosophy* 3(1983): 159-178.

1503 Martin, Richard M. "Some Thomistic Properties of Primordiality." *Notre Dame Journal of Formal Logic* 18(1977): 567-582.

1504 Mascall, E. L. "Does God Change? Mutability and Incarnation: A Review Discussion." *The Thomist* 50(1986): 447-457.

1505 Masiello, Ralph J. "A Note on Substance and *Quod Quid Erat Esse* According to St. Thomas." *Doctor Communis* 40(1987): 285-288.

1506 Masterson, Patrick. "Aquinas' Notion of God Today." *Irish Theological Quarterly* 44(1977): 79-89.

1507 Matsumoto, Masao. "Equality of Human Rights and the Principle of Individuation." *Reason, Action, Experience: Essays in Honor of R. Klibansky*. Ed. H. Kohlenberger. Hamburg: Meiner, 1979. 153-165.

1508 Maurer, Armand Augustine. "St. Thomas and Changing Truths." *Tommaso Nel Suo Settimo Centenario: Atti del Congresso Internazionale Vol. VI: L'essere*. Napoli: Edizioni Domenicane Italiane, 1977.

1509 Maurer, Armand Augustine. "Time and the Person." *Proceedings of the American Catholic Philosophical Association* 53(1979): 182-193.

1510 Maurer, Armand Augustine, trans. "Introduction." *St. Thomas Aquinas: The Division and Methods of the Sciences. Questions V and VI of His Commentary on the De Trinitate of Boethius*. By Thomas Aquinas. 4th rev. ed. 1953. Mediaeval Sources in Trans. 3. Toronto/Leiden: Pontifical Institute of Mediaeval Studies/E. J. Brill, 1986. vii-xli.

1511 Maurer, Armand Augustine. "Reflections on Metaphysics and Experience." *Proceedings of the American Catholic Philosophical Association* 61(1987): 26-34.

*This paper aims to show that it is not necessary to opt for the empiricism of Locke and Hume without metaphysics or the transcendentalism of Kant without experience. There is no metaphysics without experience, and experience naturally leads to the insights of metaphysics. There are necessary *a posteriori* propositions. Moreover, the progress of metaphysics is bound up with advances in the sciences, art, and religion.*

1512 Maurer, Armand Augustine. "Introduction." *Thomas Aquinas: The Division and Methods of the Sciences*. 4th rev. ed. 1953. Toronto: Pontifical Institute of Mediaeval Studies, 1987. vii-xli.

1513 Maurer, Armand Augustine, trans. "Introduction." *St. Thomas Aquinas: Faith, Reason and Theology. Questions I-IV of His Commentary on the De Trinitate of Boethius*. By Thomas Aquinas. Mediaeval Sources in Trans. 32. Toronto: Pontifical Institute of Mediaeval Studies, 1987. vii-xxxviii.

1514 Maurer, Armand Augustine. "Siger of Brabant and Theology." *Mediaeval Studies* 50(1988): 257-278.

1515 Maurer, Armand Augustine. "Maimonides and Aquinas on the Study of Metaphysics." *A Straight Path: Studies in Medieval Philosophy and Culture. Essays in Honor of Arthur Hyman*. Ed. Jeremiah Hackett et al. Washington, DC: The Catholic University of America Press, 1988. 206-215.

The essay compares the views of Maimonides and Aquinas on the place of metaphysics in education. They agree that a long preparation in the liberal arts and sciences is needed before undertaking metaphysics. It should not be taught to the young. They also agree that there are divine gifts superior to all rational speculation, such as prophecy and mysticism. But their conceptions of these gifts and their relation to the natural sciences and metaphysics were widely different. They did not see eye to eye on the nature of metaphysics itself or its relation to scriptural theology or prophecy.

1516 Maurer, Armand Augustine. "The *De Quiditatibus Entium* of Dietrich of Freiberg and Its Criticism of Thomistic Metaphysics [Rev. and Corrected]." 1956. *Being and Knowing: Studies in Thomas Aquinas and Later Medieval Philosophers*. Papers in Mediaeval Studies 10. Toronto: Pontifical Institute of Mediaeval Studies, 1990. 177-199.

1517 Maurer, Armand Augustine. "St. Thomas and Historicity [Rev. and Corrected]." 1979. *Being and Knowing: Studies in Thomas Aquinas and Later Medieval Philosophers*. Papers in Mediaeval Studies 10. Toronto: Pontifical Institute of Mediaeval Studies, 1990. 95-116.

1518 Maurer, Armand Augustine. "St. Thomas and the Analogy of Genus [Rev. and Corrected]." 1955. *Being and Knowing: Studies in Thomas Aquinas and Later Medieval Philosophers*. Papers in Mediaeval Studies 10. Toronto: Pontifical Institute of Mediaeval Studies, 1990. 19-31.

1519 Maurer, Armand Augustine. "The Unity of a Science: St. Thomas and the Nominalists." 1974. *Being and Knowing: Studies in Thomas Aquinas and Later Medieval Philosophers*. Papers in Mediaeval Studies 10. Toronto: Pontifical Institute of Mediaeval Studies, 1990. Revised and corrected. 71-93.

1520 Maurer, Armand Augustine. "A Neglected Thomistic Text on the Foundation of Mathematics [Rev. and Corrected]." 1959. *Being and Knowing: Studies in Thomas Aquinas and Later Medieval Philosophers*. Papers in Mediaeval Studies 10. Toronto: Pontifical Institute of Mediaeval Studies, 1990. 33-58.

1521 Maurer, Armand Augustine. "St. Thomas on Eternal Truths [Rev. and Corrected]." 1970. *Being and Knowing: Studies in Thomas Aquinas and Later Medieval Philosophers*. Papers in Mediaeval Studies 10. Toronto: Pontifical Institute of Mediaeval Studies, 1990. 43-58.

1522 Maurer, Armand Augustine. "St. Thomas on the Sacred Name Tetragrammaton [Rev. and Corrected]." 1972. *Being and Knowing: Studies in Thomas Aquinas and Later Medieval Philosophers*. Papers in Mediaeval Studies 10. Toronto: Pontifical Institute of Mediaeval Studies, 1990. 59-69.

1523 Maurer, Armand Augustine. "Form and Essence in the Philosophy of St. Thomas." 1951. *Being and Knowing: Studies in Thomas Aquinas and Later Medieval Philosophers*. Papers in Mediaeval Studies 10. Toronto: Pontifical Institute of Mediaeval Studies, 1990. 3-18.

1524 Maurer, Armand Augustine. "Gilson's Use of History in Philosophy." *Thomistic Papers V*. Ed. Thomas A. Russman. Houston, TX: Center for Thomistic Studies, University of Saint Thomas, 1990. 25-48.

1525 Maurer, Armand Augustine. "Reflections on Thomas Aquinas' Notion of Presence." *Philosophy and the God of Abraham: Essays in Memory of James A. Weisheipl, OP*. Ed. James Long. Papers in Mediaeval Studies 12. Toronto: Pontifical Institute of Mediaeval Studies, In press. 113-127.

1526 May, William E. "The Meaning and Nature of the Natural Law in Thomas Aquinas." *American Journal of Jurisprudence* 22(1977): 168-189.

1527 May, William E. "Aquinas and Janssens: On the Moral Meaning of Human Acts." *The Thomist* 48(1984): 566-606.

This essay challenges Janssens' interpretation of Thomistic texts on the moral meaning of human acts. Janssens claims that for Aquinas the agent's intention is so decisive that one can will evil for the sake of a higher good. This claim is not, it is argued, supported by a close study of Aquinas, who taught that an act morally wicked by reason of its object and known to be such cannot be made good by any end.

1528 Maydole, Robert E. "A Modal Model for Proving the Existence of God." *American Philosophical Quarterly* 17(1980): 135-142.

1529 McArthur, Robert P. "Timelessness and Theological Fatalism." *Logique et Analyse* 20(1977): 475-490.

This paper is a reconstruction of and an attack on the view developed by Saint Thomas Aquinas to explain how it is that God knows the future without the future being determined. The paper opens with a formal version of the argument derived from Aristotle showing that if the future is knowable, then it must be determined. Saint Thomas' position, which I call "The Timelessness Solution," agrees with Aristotle that if the future were knowable then it would be determined, but claims that God's omniscience does not count as future knowledge because He knows all events timelessly. Thus Aquinas holds both that future knowledge would be determining (if there were any) and that God is omniscient and yet future events are not determined. I argue that this position is not tenable; either the timelessness solution must be abandoned or Aristotle's original position must be radically altered. Either side of this dilemma is unappealing to someone of Aquinas' bent, so the question posed by theological fatalism remains open.

1530 McBride, Joseph. "Christianity, Ethics and Alienation in Contemporary Atheistic Humanism: F. Nietzsche and St. Thomas Aquinas." *Philosophy and Totality*. Ed. J. McEvoy. Belfast: The Queen's University of Belfast, 1977. 111-131.

1531 McCabe, Herbert. "Aquinas on Good Sense." *New Blackfriars* 67(1986): 25-30.

1532 McCarthy, John F. "The Perennial Value of Thomism." *Atti Dell'VIII Congresso Tomistico Internazionale VIII: San Tommaso Nella Storia del Pensiero*. Studi Tomistici 17. Cittá del Vaticano: Pontificia Accademia di S. Tommaso e di Religione Cattolica, 1982. 382-386.

1533 McCauley, Joseph. "The Teaching -learning Relationship: A Thomist Perspective on the Standard Thesis." *Philosophy and Totality* Ed. J. McEvoy. Belfast: The Queen's University of Belfast, 1977. 63-89.

1534 McCool, Gerald A. "Twentieth Century Scholasticism." *Celebrating the Medieval Heritage: A Colloquy on the Thought of Aquinas and Bonaventure*. Ed. David Tracy. *The Journal of Religion* 58. Chicago: University of Chicago Press, 1978. 198-221.

1535 McCool, Gerald A. "Maritain's Defense of Democracy." *Thought* 54(1979): 132-142.

1536 McCool, Gerald A. "Karl Rahner and the Christian Philosophy of St. Thomas Aquinas." *Theology and Discovery*. Ed. W. Kelly. 1980. 63-93.

1537 McCool, Gerald A. "An Alert and Independent Thomist: William Norris Clarke, S. J." *International Philosophical Quarterly* 26(1986): 3-22.

1538 McCool, Gerald A. "History, Insight and Judgment in Thomism." *International Philosophical Quarterly* 27(1987): 299-313.

1539 McCool, Gerald A. "Neo-Thomism and the Tradition of St. Thomas." *Thought* 62(1987): 113-146.

1540 McCool, Gerald A. "The Tradition of Saint Thomas in North America: At 50 Years." *The Modern Schoolman* 65(1988): 185-206.

1541 McCool, Gerald A. "Why St. Thomas Stays Alive?" *International Philosophical Quarterly* 30(1990): 275-287.

1542 McDermott, John Michel. "Maritain on Two Infinities: God and Matter." *International Philosophical Quarterly* 28(1986): 257-269.

Maritain presupposes matter's unintelligibility insofar as concepts, which grasp being, abstract from it. Yet poetic, moral, and mystical knowledge are based on nonconceptual intuition of the existential singular, attained at the soul's essence, where existential and essential orders coincide. Correspondingly rational proofs for God's existence arrive only at the pure form of Aristotle's Prime Mover without the prephilosophical intuition into the essence-existence distinction, which occurs at the soul's essence. The singular's nonconceptual intelligibility is thus grounded in God's pure infinity. Maritain maintains a "sacramental vision": finite intelligibilities pointing to God's infinite mystery.

1543 McEvoy, James. "*Philia* and *Amicita*: The Philosophy of Friendship from Plato to Aquinas." *Sewanee Mediaeval Colloquium Occasional Papers* 2(1985): 1-23.

1544 McEvoy, James. "The Divine as the Measure of Being in Platonic and Scholastic Philosophy." *Studies in Medieval Philosophy*. Ed. John F. Wippel. Studies in Philosophy and the History of Philosophy 17. Washington, DC: The Catholic University of America Press, 1987. 85-116.

1545 McGovern, Mark. "Prime Matter in Aquinas." *Proceedings of the American Catholic Philosophical Association* 61(1987): 221-234.

*In this article the author attempts to show that by paying attention to a seldom noticed distinction in Aquinas between prime matter as an essence and prime matter as it exists in things, much confusion can be avoided concerning Aquinas' concept of prime matter. As a result the author hopes to make the concept a more acceptable concept in the philosophical world today. The author's procedure is to "investigate the texts of Aquinas in the order of time in which he wrote them." He begins with the *Commentary on the Sentences* and concludes with the *Summa*.*

1546 McGrath, Alister E. "The Influence of Aristotelian Physics Upon St. Thomas Aquinas' Discussion of the *Processus Iustificationis*." *Recherches de Théologie Ancienne et Médiévale* 51(1984): 223-229.

1547 McGrew, Timothy. "The Missing Link: Aquinas and Kant Revisited." *Dialogue* 30(1987): 11-16.

Aquinas and Kant both approach the problem of religious knowledge by separating the sensible and suprasensible worlds. Aquinas unifies these by extending scientific knowledge into the suprasensible realm; Kant, loyal to Newtonian physics, could not include teleology among the categories, and therefore he had to reject Aquinas' synthesis. Kant's use of teleological reflective judgment in his third Critique is a product of both his fidelity to Newton and his commitment to the realm of the transcendent.

1548 McInerny, Ralph. "On Behalf of Natural Theology." *Proceedings of the American Catholic Philosophical Association* 54(1980): 63-73.

1549 McInerny, Ralph. "The Principles of Natural Law." *American Journal of Jurisprudence* 25(1980): 1-15.

1550 McInerny, Ralph. "Reflections on Christian Philosophy." *One Hundred Years of Thomism: Aeterni Patris* and Afterwards. Ed. Victor B. Brezik. Houston, TX: Center for Thomistic Studies: University of St. Thomas, 1981. 63-73.

1551 McInerny, Ralph. "The Principles of Natural Law." *American Journal of Jurisprudence* 25(1981): 1-15.

1552 McInerny, Ralph. "The Nature of Book Delta of the Metaphysics According to the Commentary of St. Thomas Aquinas." *Graceful Reason: Essays in Ancient and Medieval Philosophy Presented to Joseph Owens on the Occasion of His Seventy-fifth Birthday and the Fiftieth Anniversary of His Ordination*. Ed. Lloyd P. Gerson. Papers in Mediaeval Studies 4. Toronto:Pontifical Institute of Mediaeval Studies, 1983. 331-343.

1553 McInerny, Ralph. "Fideism in the Philosophical Fragments." *Knowledge and Action*. Ed. G. Stengren. 1984. 74-85.

1554 McInerny, Ralph. "*Esse Ut Actus Intensivus*." 1964. *Being and Predication: Thomistic Interpretations*. Studies in Philosophy and the History of Philosophy 16. Washington, DC: The Catholic University of America Press, 1986. 229-235.

1555 McInerny, Ralph. "A Note on Thomistic Existentialism." 1955. *Being and Predication: Thomistic Interpretations*. Studies in Philosophy and the History of Philosophy 16. Washington, DC: The Catholic University of America Press, 1986. 165-172.

1556 McInerny, Ralph. "Albert and Thomas on Theology." 1981. *Being and Predication: Thomistic Interpretations*. Studies in Philosophy and the History of Philosophy 16. Washington, DC: The Catholic University of America Press, 1986. 131-142.

1557 McInerny, Ralph. "Albertus Magnus on Universals." 1980. *Being and Predication: Thomistic Interpretations*. Studies in Philosophy and the History of Philosophy 16. Washington, DC: The Catholic University of America Press, 1986. 115-129.

1558 McInerny, Ralph. "Analogy and Foundationalism in Thomas Aquinas." *Rationality, Religious Belief, and Moral Commitment: New Essays in the Philosophy of Religion*. Eds. Robert Audi and William J. Wainwright. Ithaca, NY: Cornell University Press, 1986. 271-288.

1559 McInerny, Ralph. "Apropos of Art and Connaturality." 1958. *Being and Predication: Thomistic Interpretations*. Studies in Philosophy and the History of Philosophy 16. Washington, DC: The Catholic University of America Press, 1986. 287-302.

1560 McInerny, Ralph. "Aquinas on Divine Omnipotence." *L'homme et Son Univers Au Moyen Age: Actes Du Septiéme Congrés International de Philosophie Médiéval II*. Ed. Christian Wenin. Philosophes Médiévaux 26-27. Louvain-la-Neuve: Éditions de l'Institut Supérieur de Philosophie, 1986. 440-444.

1561 McInerny, Ralph. "Being and Predication." 1959. *Being and Predication: Thomistic Interpretations*. Studies in Philosophy and the History of Philosophy 16. Washington, DC: The Catholic University of America Press, 1986. 173-228.

1562 McInerny, Ralph. "Boethius and St. Thomas Aquinas." 1974. *Being and Predication: Thomistic Interpretations*. Studies in Philosophy and the History of Philosophy 16. Washington, DC: The Catholic University of America Press, 1986. 89-114.

1563 McInerny, Ralph. "Can God Be Named by Us?" 1978. *Being and Predication: Thomistic Interpretations*. Studies in Philosophy and the History of Philosophy 16. Washington, DC: The Catholic University of America Press, 1986. 259-278.

1564 McInerny, Ralph. "On Behalf of Natural Theology." 1980. *Being and Predication: Thomistic Interpretations*. Studies in Philosophy and the History of Philosophy 16. Washington, DC: The Catholic University of America Press, 1986. 247-258.

1565 McInerny, Ralph. "Ontology and Theology in the Metaphysics of Aristotle." 1968. *Being and Predication: Thomistic Interpretations*. Studies in Philosophy and the History of Philosophy 16. Washington, DC: The CatholicUniversity of America Press, 1986. 59-66.

1566 McInerny, Ralph. "Philosophizing on Faith." 1972. *Being and Predication: Thomistic Interpretations*. Studies in Philosophy and the History of Philosophy 16. Washington, DC: The Catholic University of America Press, 1986. 237-246.

1567 McInerny, Ralph. "Scotus and Univocity." 1968. *Being and Predication: Thomistic Interpretations*. Studies in Philosophy and the History of Philosophy 16. Washington, DC: The Catholic University of America Press, 1986. 159-164.

1568 McInerny, Ralph. "St. Bonaventure and St. Thomas." 1974. *Being and Predication: Thomistic Interpretations*. Studies in Philosophy and the History of Philosophy 16. Washington, DC: The Catholic University of America Press, 1986. 143-158.

1569 McInerny, Ralph. "St. Thomas Aquinas: An Overview." 1982. *Being and Predication: Thomistic Interpretations*. Studies in Philosophy and the History of Philosophy 16. Washington, DC: The Catholic University of America Press, 1986. 1-24.

1570 McInerny, Ralph. "The Analogy of Names is a Logical Doctrine." 1974. *Being and Predication: Thomistic Interpretations*. Studies in Philosophy and the History of Philosophy 16. Washington, DC: The Catholic University of America Press, 1986. 279-286.

1571 McInerny, Ralph. "The Prime Mover and the Order of Learning." 1956. *Being and Predication: Thomistic Interpretations*. Studies in Philosophy and the History of Philosophy 16. Washington, DC: The Catholic University of America Press, 1986. 49-57.

1572 McInerny, Ralph. "Thomas on Book Delta of the Metaphysics." 1983. *Being and Predication: Thomistic Interpretations*. Studies in Philosophy and the History of Philosophy 16. Washington, DC: The Catholic University of America Press, 1986. 67-78.

1573 McInerny, Ralph. "Ultimate End in Aristotle." 1982. *Being and Predication: Thomistic Interpretations*. Studies in Philosophy and the History of Philosophy 16. Washington, DC: The Catholic University of America Press, 1986. 79-88.

1574 McInerny, Ralph. "Action Theory in St. Thomas Aquinas [Ultimate Ends and Natural Law]." *Thomas von Aquin: Werk und Wirkung Im Licht Neuerer Forschungen*. Ed. Albert Zimmermann. Berlin: Walter de Gruyter, 1988. 13-22.

1575 McInerny, Ralph. "The Right Deed for the Wrong Reason: Comments on Belmans." *Doctor Communis* 43(1990): 234-249.

1576 McKeon, Richard. "Philosophy and Theology, History and Science in the Thought of Bonaventura and Thomas Aquinas." *Celebrating the Medieval Heritage: A Colloquy on the Thought of Aquinas and Bonaventure*. Ed. David Tracy. *The Journal of Religion* 58. Chicago: University of Chicago Press, 1978. 24-51.

1577 McLaughlin, Robert J. "Men, Animals and Personhood." *Proceedings of the American Catholic Philosophical Association* 59(1985): 166-181.

On which side of the person-thing divide do animals belong? In the face of current talk of "animal rights," this paper aims at identifying various arguments developed by St. Thomas Aquinas in support of man's privileged moral status, at displaying the key presuppositions of these arguments, and at understanding why recent literature on the subject largely ignores the Thomistic contribution.

1578 McMahon, Kevin A. "Economics, Wisdom and the Teaching Role of the Bishops in the Theology of Thomas Aquinas." *The Thomist* 53(1989): 91-106.

*Thomas Aquinas refers in the *Summa theologiae* to uniquely authoritative moral teachers he call the "wise men." Their function is to teach the moral principles that are not self-evident to all. It is argued that this quality of wisdom cannot be identified with the virtue of prudence or with the acquired virtue of wisdom, which is not concerned with action at all, but only with the infused wisdom that is a gift of the Holy Spirit. It is, indeed, a special form of this gift, received by those who succeed sacramentally to Christ as teacher and sanctifier—the bishops.*

1579 McMullin, Ernan. "The Motive for Metaphor." *Proceedings of the American Catholic Philosophical Association* 55(1981): 27-39.

1580 McMullin, Ernan. "Introduction: Evolution and Creation." *Evolution and Creation*. Ed. Ernan McMullin. University of Notre Dame Studies in the Philosophy of Religion 4. Notre Dame, IN: University of Notre Dame Press, 1985. 1-56.

1581 McNicholl, Ambrose. "On Judging Existence." *The Thomist* 43(1979): 507-580.

The judgment does not require two concepts, nor is it the mental union of such. It is adequately explained as a simple and an original act by which the intellect attributes a form, signified by a concept, to that being to which it originally belongs and which is denoted by the subject of the judgment. Such attribution does not seem to be needed for all types of judgment, in particular for purely existential ones; the normal type of attributive judgments does not require more than this. All judgments imply, directly or indirectly, a reference to what has been known, in the first place, as individual and actually existing. What is specific in judging is reference to the act of existing.

1582 McNicholl, Ambrose. "A Chant in Praise of What is." *Angelicum* 57(1980): 172-196.

1583 Mensch, James R. "Existence and Essence in Thomas and Husserl." *The Horizons of Continental Philosophy: Essays on Husserl, Heidegger, and Merleau-Ponty*. Eds. Hugh J. Silverman et al. Martinus Nijhoff Philosophy Library 30. Dordrecht: Kluwer Academic Publishers, 1988. 62-92.

1584 Merchen, Paul. "Transformations of the Ethics of Aristotle in the Moral Philosophy of Thomas Aquinas." *Tommaso Nel Suo Settimo Centenario V: Atti del Congresso Internazionale: L'agire Morale*. Napoli: Edizioni Domenicane Italiane, 1977. 151-162.

1585 Merleau-Ponty, J. "Ideas of Beginning and Endings in Cosmology." *The Study of Time*. Ed. Lawrence Nathaniel. New York: Springer, 1978. 333-350.

As far as the philosophy of time is concerned, more specifically of cosmic time, the ancient Greek philosophers still provide a basic reference. Out of the small number of possible solutions, they clearly formulated three: those of Democritus, Plato, and Aristotle. Among the three, one, at best, that of Plato, if carefully qualified, implied a beginning of the world. By contrast, such a beginning was categorically asserted in the Book of Genesis. It was taken by the Christians as an untouchable dogma. They were at pains to build a philosophy grounded on the Greek tradition and the Judaic dogma.

1586 Meynell, Hugo. "Wilfred Sellars: A Thomist Estimate." *The Thomist* 50(1986): 223-237.

1587 Miceli, Vincent P. "St. Thomas, Human Liberty and Academic Freedom." *Atti Dell'VIII Congresso Tomistico InternazionaleVI Morale e Diritto Nella Prospettiva Tomistica*. Studi Tomistici 15. Cittá del Vaticano: Pontificia Accademia di San Tommaso e di Religione Cattolica, 1982. 329-340.

1588 Midgley, E. Brian F. "Thomism and the Promethean Ideology of Hobbes." *Atti Dell'VIII Congresso Tomistico Internazionale VIII: San Tommaso Nella Storia del Pensiero*. Studi Tomistici 17. Cittá del Vaticano: Pontificia Accademia di San Tommaso e di Religione Cattolica, 1982. 181-190.

1589 Miethe, Terry L. "The Cosmological Argument." *The New Scholasticism* 52(1978): 285-305.

Within the past two decades or so there has been a gradual renewal of interest in metaphysics in general and in the theistic arguments in particular. "The era is past when all metaphysical statements or arguments can simply be dismissed as silly or senseless, since they do not meet a preestablished criterion of verifiability." This article is the most comprehensive bibliography ever done on the cosmological Argument for God's existence, with more than 330 items listed. The article is divided into the following categories: Introduction, General Works on the cosmological Argument, The Argument from 428 B. C. to 430 A. D., from 1135 to 1349 A. D., from 1548-1753 A. D., in Hume and Kant, the relationship of the cosmological to Ontological Argument, the Principle of Sufficient Reason, the Principle of Causality, and Works of General Importance to the Argument.

1590 Miethe, Terry L. "Natural Law, the Synderesis Rule, and St. Augustine." *Augustinian Studies* 11(1980): 91-97.

1591 Milhaven, John Giles. "Thomas Aquinas on Sexual Pleasure." *Journal of Religious Ethics* 5(1977): 157-181.

A key to understanding the sexual ethics of Thomas Aquinas is his position that spouses sin whenever their purpose in having intercourse is the pleasure of it. The pleasure itself, Thomas declares, is not sinful, but necessary, natural, and good. Nevertheless, it cannot be rational man's intended end. Other sense pleasures can be, inasmuch as they are pleasures of knowing something, e.g., a beautiful color. Sexual pleasure is a pleasure of knowing, too, but the kind of knowing is so minimal and negligible that it is not worthy of being an end intended by rational man. In modern critical dialogue one can ask: Is Thomas' ethical thinking radically handicapped by a model of knowledge that is valid, but unrealistically exclusive?

1592 Miller, Barry. "Exists and Other Predicates." *The New Scholasticism* 53(1979): 475-479.

1593 Miller, Clyde L. "Maimonides and Aquinas on Naming God." *The Journal of Jewish Studies* (London) 28(1977): 65-71.

1594 Mondin, Battista. "Faith and Reason in Roman Catholic Thought from Clement of Alexandria to Vatican II." *Dialogoue Alliance* 1(1987): 18-26.

1595 Montaldi, Daniel F. "Toward a Human Rights Based Account." *Social Theory and Practice* 11(1985): 123-161.

I argue that just wars are possible only if respect for rights is morally prior to their enjoyment. Wars kill the innocent as well as the guilty. Defending the rights of some cannot justify infringing the rights of others if the enjoyment of rights is the only moral concern. I argue that the importance of stopping the conscious violation of rights is a different and higher concern.

1596 Montaldi, Daniel F. "A Defense of St. Thomas and the Principle of Double Effect." *Journal of Religious Ethics* 14(1986): 296-332.

1597 Moonan, Lawrence. "Aquinas' Quodlibet XII, Question 14." *New Blackfriars* 69(1988): 325-329.

1598 Moreno, Antonio. "The Subject, Abstraction, and Methodology of Aquinas' Metaphysics." *Angelicum* 61(1984): 580-601.

1599 Morreall, John S. "Divine Simplicity and Divine Properties." *The Journal of Critical Analysis* (NJ) 7(1978): 67-70.

1600 Morreall, John S. "Aquinas' Fourth Way." *Sophia* 18(1979): 20-28.

Aquinas argues that the various degrees of perfections like goodness we find in things point to something which is the maximum of each of those perfections—God—who causes those perfections in creatures. I criticize his argument as based on a misunderstanding of the comparison of adjectives (and the properties they name) and on an incoherent notion of causality. A further problem is that there is no single scale of "good things" and so no logical place for the best thing. I conclude with a caution that Aquinas' thinking in the fourth Way tends to compromise the transcendence of God.

1601 Mueller, Franz. "Person and Society According to St. Thomas Aquinas." *Aquinas Papers* (St. Paul, MN) 17 (N. d.): no pagination.

1602 Mullady, Brian Thomas. "The Crucible of Human Unity." *L'anima Nell'antropologia Di San Tommaso D'Aquino IX: Atti del Congresso Societá Internazionale San Tommaso D'Aquino*. Ed. Abelardo Lobato. Milano: Editrice Massimo, 1987. 579-596.

1603 Nelson, Daniel Mark. "Karl Rahner's Existential Ethics: A Critique Based on St. Thomas' Understanding of Prudence." *The Thomist* 51(1987): 461-479.

1604 Nijenhuis, John. "To Be or to Exist: That is the Question." *The Thomist* 50(1986): 353-394.

1605 Noonan, J. T. "Agency, Bribery and Redemption in Thomas Aquinas." *Recherches de Théologie Ancienne et Médiévale* 49(1982): 159-173.

1606 Normore, Calvin G. "Compatibilism and Contingency in Aquinas." *The Journal of Philosophy* 80(1983): 650-652.

1607 Novak, Joseph A. "Aquinas and the Incorruptibility of the Soul." *History of Philosophy Quarterly* 4(1987): 405-421.

*The thesis argued is that a key argument for the incorruptibility of the soul, given at *SCG* II, 79, contains an equivocation on the term "immaterial" which vitiates the argument. Three construals are presented of the argument, and each is seen to involve problems related to this term. The failure of the argument is philosophically interesting for it points to a split of the intentional and entitative, which becomes important for subsequent epistemology and metaphysics.*

1608 Novak, Michael. "We Mediterraneans: Nature or History?" *Celebrating the Medieval Heritage: A Colloquy on the Thought of Aquinas and Bonaventure*. Ed. David Tracy. *The Journal of Religion* Supplement 58. Chicago: University of Chicago Press, 1978. 160-173.

1609 O'Brien, Thomas C. "*Sacra Doctrina* Revisited: The Context of Medieval Education." *The Thomist* 41(1977): 475-509.

*This is an exegesis of Aquinas on *Sacra doctrina* (theology) in Saint Thomas Aquinas, *Summa Theologiae*, Volume 1. The exegesis takes Question One as embodying the scholastic "method of disputation" and centers on two phrases in art. 1: *doctrina praeter philosophicas disciplinas* as raising the problem; *doctrina secundum revelationem divinam* as key to the resolution. The force of *praeter* (over and above) *philosophicus disciplinas* in the medieval setting, especially from Hugh of St. Victor's *Didascalicon* is that theology has no place or epistemological standing because the given "philosophical disciplines" exhaustively make up the whole corpus of human learning. The force of *secundum* (following on and according to) *revaltionem divinam* is that theology has existence and receives its epistemological distinctiveness and epistemological status as consequent on and conformed to the new intelligibility given to reality by divine revelation.*

1610 O'Hara, M. L. "Truth in Spirit and Letter: Gregory the Great, Thomas Aquinas and Maimonides on the *Book of Job*." *From Cloister to Classroom: Monastic and Scholastic Approaches to Truth 1986*. Ed. E. R. Elder. Cistercian Studies 90. Kalamazoo, MI: Cistercian Publications, 1986. 47-79.

1611 O'Meara, Dominic J. "Eriugena and Aquinas on the Beatific Vision." *Eriugena Redivivus*. Ed. von Werner Beierwaltes. Heidelberg: Abhandlungen der Heidelberger Akademie der Wissenschafter: Philosophisch-Historische Klasse, Jg Abh. 1, 1987. 214-236.

1612 O'Meara, Thomas F. "Albert the Great and Martin Luther on Justification." *The Thomist* 44(1980): 539-559.

A look at Albert the Great's theology of how human, fallen freedom meets God's saving will; the examination is done from the perspective of Luther's critique of elements of Pelagianism in medieval thought. The ecclesiastical controversies over Semi-pelagianism were unknown to many medieval thinkers prior to Thomas Aquinas. Albert, Aquinas' teacher, struggles to give all active primacy and power to God, but his language at times has a suggestion of semi-pelagianism which is absent in Thomas Aquinas.

1613 O'Meara, Thomas F. "Thomas Aquinas and German Intellectuals: Neoscholasticism and Modernity in the Late 19th Century." *Gregorianum* 68(1987): 719-736.

1614 O'Meara, Thomas F. "Grace as a Theological Structure in the *Summa Theologiae* of Thomas Aquinas." *Recherches de Théologie Ancienne et Médiévale* 55(1988): 130-153.

1615 O'Reilly, Paul. "What is Intelligible Matter?" *The Thomist* 53(1989): 74-90.

1616 Oesterle, John A. "St. Thomas, Moral Evil, and the Devil." *Tommaso Nel Suo Settimo Centenario V: Atti del Congresso Internazionale: L'agire Morale*. Napoli: Edizioni Domenicane Italiane, 1977. 510-515.

1617 Olshewsky, Thomas M. "Thomas' Conception of Causation." *Nature and System* 2(1980): 101-122.

1618 Omoregbe, J. I. "The Moral Philosophy of St. Thomas Aquinas: A Critical Look." *Nigerian Journal of Philosophy* 2(1982): 20-28.

1619 Owens, Joseph. "Darkness of Ignorance in the Most Refined Notion of God." *Bonaventure and Aquinas: Enduring Philosophers*. Ed. Robert Shahan and Francis Kovach. Norman, OK: University of Oklahoma Press, 1978. 69-86.

1620 Owens, Joseph. "Being in Early Western Tradition." *The Question of Being: East-West Philosophers*. Ed. Merryn Sprung. University Park, PA: Pennsylvania State Press, 1978. 17-30.

1621 Owens, Joseph. "Value and Person in Aquinas." *Atti del Congresso Internazionale: Tommaso D'Aquino Nel Suo Settimo Centenario*. Naples: Kraus, reprint, 1978. 56-62.

1622 Owens, Joseph. "Being *Per Se*, Being *Per Accidens* and St. Thomas' Metaphysics." *Science et Esprit* 30(1979): 169-184.

1623 Owens, Joseph. "Existence as Predicated." *The New Scholasticism* 53(1979): 480-485.

1624 Owens, Joseph. "The Notion of Actuality in Aquinas." *Proceedings of the Patristic Mediaeval and Renaissance Studies Conference* 4(1979): 13-23.

1625 Owens, Joseph. "The Relation of God to World in the Metaphysics." *Etudes sur la Métaphysique D'Aristote*. Paris: Vrin, 1979. 207-228.

1626 Owens, Joseph. "*Quandoque* and *Aliquando* in Aquinas' *Tertia Via*." *The New Scholasticism* 54(1980): 447-475.

*The time factor in the *tertia via* of Aquinas has been much discussed of late. In the text, the word "now" (*nunc*) can scarcely mean anything else than present time. It grounds a strong presumption that the two immediately preceding adverbs, *quandoque* and *aliquando*, are also to be taken in an ordinary temporal sense. So taken, the argument has come under attack. This article defends the argument by suggesting that *quandoque* refers to real past time while *aliquando* refers to imaginary time, in a setting in which both temporal adverbs denote the metaphysical condition of preceding non-existence required by generated things.*

1627 Owens, Joseph. "Actuality in the *Prima Via* of St. Thomas." 1967. *St. Thomas Aquinas on the Existence of God: Collected Papers of Joseph Owens, C. Ss. R.* Ed. John R. Catan. Albany, NY: State University of New York Press, 1980. 192-207. Originally published in *Mediaeval Studies*, 29(1967): 26-64.

1628 Owens, Joseph. "Aquinas and the Five Ways." 1974. *St. Thomas Aquinas on the Existence of God: Collected Papers of Joseph Owens, C. Ss. R.* Ed. John R. Catan. Albany, NY: State University of New York Press, 1980. 132-41. Originally published in *The Monist*, 58(1974): 16-35.

1629 Owens, Joseph. "Aquinas as Aristotelian Commentator." 1974. *St. Thomas Aquinas on the Existence of God: Collected Papers of Joseph Owens, C. Ss. R.* Ed. John R. Catan. Albany, NY: State University of New York Press, 1980. 1-19. Originally published in *St. Thomas Aquinas 1274-1974: Commemorative Studies*, ed. Armand Maurer, C. S. B., Toronto: Pontifical Institute of Mediaeval Studies, 1(1974): 213-238.

1630 Owens, Joseph. "Aquinas on Infinite Regress." 1962. *St. Thomas Aquinas on the Existence of God: Collected Papers of Joseph Owens, C. Ss. R.* Ed. John R. Catan. Albany, NY: State University of New York Press, 1980. 228-30. Originally published in *Mind*, N. S. 71(1962): 244-246.

1631 Owens, Joseph. "Aquinas on Knowing Existence." 1976. *St. Thomas Aquinas on the Existence of God: Collected Papers of Joseph Owens, C. Ss. R.* Ed. John R. Catan. Albany, NY: State University of New York Press, 1980. 20-33. Originally published in *The Review of Metaphysics*, 29(1976): 670-690.

1632 Owens, Joseph. "Diversity and Community of Being in St. Thomas Aquinas." 1960. *St. Thomas Aquinas on the Existence of God: Collected Papers of Joseph Owens, C. Ss. R.* Ed. John R. Catan. Albany, NY: State University of New York Press, 1980. 97-131. Originally published in *Mediaeval Studies*, 22(1960): 257-302.

1633 Owens, Joseph. "Existence and the Subject of Metaphysics." *Science et Esprit* 32(1980): 255-260.

1634 Owens, Joseph. "Immobility and Existence for Aquinas." 1968. *St. Thomas Aquinas on the Existence of God: Collected Papers of Joseph Owens, C. Ss. R.* Ed. John R. Catan. Albany, NY: State University of New York Press, 1980. 208-27. Originally published in *Mediaeval Studies*, 30(1968): 22-46.

1635 Owens, Joseph. "Judgment and Truth in Aquinas." 1970. *St. Thomas Aquinas on the Existence of God: Collected Papers of Joseph Owens, C. Ss. R.* Ed. John R. Catan. Albany, NY: State University of New York Press, 1980. 34-51. Originally published in *Mediaeval Studies*, 32(1970): 138-158.

1636 Owens, Joseph. "Philosophy—an *Est* and *Quid Est*." *Proceedings of the American Catholic Philosophical Association* 54(1980): 37-48.

1637 Owens, Joseph. "The Accidental and Essential Character of Being in the Doctrine of St. Thomas Aquinas." 1958. *St. Thomas Aquinas on the Existence of God: Collected Papers of Joseph Owens, C. Ss. R.* Ed. John R. Catan. Albany, NY: State University of New York Press, 1980. 52-96. Originally published in *Mediaeval Studies*, 20(1958): 1-40.

1638 Owens, Joseph. "The Conclusion of the *Prima Via*." 1952-1953. *St. Thomas Aquinas on the Existence of God: Collected Papers of Joseph Owens, C. Ss. R.* Ed. John R. Catan. Albany, NY: State University of New York Press, 1980. 142-68. Originally published in *The Modern Schoolman*, 30(1952/53): 33-53; 109-121; 203-215.

1639 Owens, Joseph. "The Starting Point of the *Prima Via*." 1967. *St. Thomas Aquinas on the Existence of God: Collected Papers of Joseph Owens, C. Ss. R.* Ed. John R. Catan. Albany, NY: State University of New York Press, 1980. 169-191. Originally published in *Franciscan Studies*, 5(1967): 249-294.

1640 Owens, Joseph. "*Diversificata in Diversis*: Aquinas in *I Sent.* , Prol., 1, 2." *La Scolastique: Certitude et Recherche. En Hommage a Louis-Marie Régis*. Ed. Ernest Joós. Montréal: Les Éditions Bellarmin, 1980. 113-129.

1641 Owens, Joseph. "Actuality in Aristotle and Aquinas." *Proceedings of the World Congress on Aristotle II*. Athens: Publication of the Ministry of Culture and Sciences, 1981. 192-196.

1642 Owens, Joseph. "Aristotle—Cognition a Way of Being." *Aristotle: The Collected Papers of Joseph Owens*. Ed. Merryn Sprung. Albany, NY: State University of New York Press, 1981. 74-81.

1643 Owens, Joseph. "Stages and Distinction in (*De Ente*): A Rejoinder." *The Thomist* 45(1981): 99-123.

1644 Owens, Joseph. "The Future of Thomistic Metaphysics." *One Hundred Years of Thomism: Aeterni Patris and Afterwards*. Ed. Victor B. Brezik. Houston, TX: Center for Thomistic Studies: University of St. Thomas, 1981. 142-161.

1645 Owens, Joseph. "Barry Miller Vs Owens." *The New Scholasticism* 56(1982): 371-380.

1646 Owens, Joseph. "Material Substance— Temporal or Eviternal?" *The New Scholasticism* 56(1982): 442-461.

1647 Owens, Joseph. "Natures and Conceptualization." *The New Scholasticism* 56(1982): 376-380.

1648 Owens, Joseph. "The Relevance of Thomistic Metaphysics for Christian Life." *Actas del Tercer Congreso Nacional de Filosofia II*. Buenos Aires: Universidad, 1982. 413-418.

1649 Owens, Joseph. "Being and Nature in Aquinas." *The Modern Schoolman* 61(1984): 157-168.

There is persistent philosophical tension between being as the most impoverished of human notions, and being as the infinitely rich nature of God. For Aquinas, the natures of things are known through conceptualization. Their being is known originally through judgment, and not as a nature but as an actuality outside the nature. Quidditatively assessed, being thereby appears devoid of content. Demonstrated as a nature in God, being shows content, really different from any finite nature it actualizes.

1650 Owens, Joseph. "Ideology and Aquinas." *Thomistic Papers I*. Ed. Victor B. Brezik. Houston, TX: Center for Thomistic Studies: University of St. Thomas, 1984. 135-152.

1651 Owens, Joseph. "A Note on Aquinas, *In Boethius De Trin.*, 2, 2 Ad Lm." *The New Scholasticism* 59(1985): 102-108.

1652 Owens, Joseph. "Aquinas and Philosophical Pluralism." *Thomistic Papers II*. Eds. Leonard A. Kennedy and Jack C. Marler. Houston, TX: University of St. Thomas, Center for Thomistic Studies, 1986. 133-158.

*Interpretations of Aquinas differ radically. This is but an instance of what occurs in all genuine philosophical thinking. Each philosopher or commentator, built differently, thinks in accord with the individual mentality in which he or she has been trained. Aristotle (*Metaph.* 2. 3. 994b32) pointed this out even for theoretical discourse. The result is that philosophy is genuinely pluralistic. Yet it is not relativistic, because each philosophy can have its absolute grounds for judging truth.*

1653 Owens, Joseph. "Aquinas' Distinction at *De Ente et Essentia* 4. 119-123." *Mediaeval Studies* 48(1986): 264-287.

*In the *De Ente et Essentia*, Aquinas shows that being is not contained in natures such as man or phoenix. He straightway extends this conclusion to all beings, with only one exception. Two recent writers have contended that a real distinction between being and finite nature is thereby established. The present article examines that contention and finds it insufficient to explain the profoundly metaphysical tenet that a finite thing is really distinct from its own being.*

1654 Owens, Joseph. "Further Thoughts on Knowledge of Being and Truth." *The New Scholasticism* 60(1986): 454-470. A response to Lee, Patrick, *Aquinas on Knowledge of Truth and Existence*, *New Scholasticism*, 60(1986): 46-71.

1655 Owens, Joseph. "Metaphysics—The Fulfillment of Natural Desire." *The Modern Schoolman* 65(1986): 1-13.

1656 Owens, Joseph. "Aquinas on Being and Thing." *Thomistic Papers III*. Ed. Leonard A. Kennedy. Houston, TX: University of St. Thomas, Center for Thomistic Studies, 1987. 3-34.

Early in the present century Marcel Chossat, followed by others, maintained that the first appearance of real distinction between essence and existence is to be found in Giles of Rome, some years after the death of Thomas Aquinas. Examination of the texts of Aquinas, however, shows that real distinction between thing and being in creatures is the very warp and woof of Aquinas' metaphysical thinking, and on occasion is expressly qualified by the designation "real."

1657 Owens, Joseph. "Aquinas on the Inseparability of Soul from Existence." *The New Scholasticism* 61(1987): 249-270.

1658 Owens, Joseph. "The Neoplatonic Leaven in Western Culture." *Philosophy and Culture V*. Ed. V. Cauchy. Montreal: Ed Montorency, 1988. 181-185.

1659 Owens, Joseph. "The Self in Aristotle." *The Review of Metaphysics* 41(1988): 707-722.

1660 Owens, Joseph. "Thomas Aquinas: Dimensive Quantity as Individuating Principle." *Mediaeval Studies* 50(1988): 279-310.

1661 Owens, Joseph. "Introduction." *Towards a Christian Philosophy*. Studies in Philosophy and the History of Philosophy 21. Washington, DC: The Catholic University of America Press, 1990. 1-59.

1662 Owens, Joseph. "Epilogue." *Toward a Christian Philosophy*. Washington, DC: The Catholic University of America Press, 1990. 307-326.

1663 Owens, Joseph. "Cause of Necessity in Aquinas' *Tertia Via*." *Towards a Christian Philosophy*. Studies in Philosophy and the History of Philosophy 21. Washington, DC: The Catholic University of America Press, 1990. 225-249.

1664 Owens, Joseph. "Darkness of Ignorance in the Most Refined Notion of God." *Towards a Christian Philosophy*. Studies in Philosophy and the History of Philosophy 21. Washington, DC: The Catholic University of America Press, 1990. 207-224.

1665 Owens, Joseph. "Aquinas on the Inseparability of Soul from Existence." *Towards a Christian Philosophy*. Studies in Philosophy and the History of Philosophy 21. Washington, DC: The Catholic University of America Press, 1990. 291-306.

1666 Owens, Joseph. "Aquinas on the Intimacy and Contingency of Existence." *American Catholic Philosophical Quarterly* 64(1990): 261-264.

1667 Owens, Joseph. "Christian Conscience Vs Aristotelian Right Reason." *Toward a Christian Philosophy*. Washington, DC: The Catholic University of America Press, 1990. 150-173.

1668 Owens, Joseph. "Faith, Ideas, Illumination, and Experience." 1982. *The Cambridge History of Later Medieval Philosophy: From the Rediscovery of Aristotle to the Disintegration of Scholasticism*. Eds. Norman Kretzmann, Anthony Kenny and Jan Pinborg. Cambridge: Cambridge University Press, 1990. 440-459.

1669 Owens, Joseph. "God in Philosophy Today." *Toward a Christian Philosophy*. Washington, DC: The Catholic University of America Press, 1990. 177-188.

1670 Owens, Joseph. "Is Nature Something Complete?" *Towards a Christian Philosophy*. Studies in Philosophy and the History of Philosophy 21. Washington, DC: The Catholic University of America Press, 1990. 76-96.

1671 Owens, Joseph. "Soul as Agent in Aquinas." *Towards a Christian Philosophy*. Studies in Philosophy and the History of Philosophy 21. Washington, DC: The Catholic University of America Press, 1990. 266-290.

1672 Owens, Joseph. "The Christian Philosophy of *Aeterni Patris*." *Towards a Christian Philosophy*. Studies in Philosophy and the History of Philosophy 21. Washington, DC: The Catholic University of America Press, 1990. 63-75.

1673 Owens, Joseph. "The Distinguishing Feature in Catholic Philosophy." *Towards a Christian Philosophy*. Studies in Philosophy and the History of Philosophy 21. Washington, DC: The Catholic University of America Press, 1990. 119-136.

1674 Owens, Joseph. "The Notion of Catholic Philosophy." *Towards a Christian Philosophy*. Studies in Philosophy and the History of Philosophy 21. Washington, DC: The Catholic University of America Press, 1990. 97-118.

1675 Owens, Joseph. "This Truth Sublime." *Towards a Christian Philosophy*. Washington, DC: The Catholic University of America Press, 1990. 189-206.

1676 Owens, Joseph. "Human Reason and the Moral Order in Aquinas." *Studia Moralia* 28(1990): 155-173.

1677 Owens, Joseph. "St. Thomas Aquinas on Individuation." *Individuation in Scholasticism: The Late Middle Ages and the Counter-Reformation*. Ed. Jorge J. E. Gracia. München: Philosophia Verlag, In press. no pagination.

1678 Pangle, Thomas L. "A Note on the Theoretical Foundation of the Just War Doctrine." *The Thomist* 43(1979): 464-473.

This note addresses the theoretical grounding, not the substance, of the Just War Doctrine in Thomas Aquinas and his successors. Building on an analysis of how Thomas corrects Aristotle's doctrine of the natural basis for morality, the author raises the question whether the Just War Doctrine is, for Thomas, based on natural (as opposed to Divine) Law—i.e., has a grounding independent of Christian revelation. It is shown that although Thomas claims to ground the Just War Doctrine on Natural Law, he in fact fails to do so. The difficulties with which Vitoria and Suarez wrestle only highlight this failure. Thomas' doctrine is thus found to be rhetorical rather thanphilosophical.

1679 Parel, Anthony. "Bibliography." *Calgary Aquinas Studies*. Ed. Anthony Parel. Toronto: Pontifical Institute of Mediaeval Studies,. 1978. 155-161.

1680 Parel, Anthony. "The Thomistic Theory of Property, Regime, and the Good Life." *Calgary Aquinas Studies*. Ed. Anthony Parel. Toronto: Pontifical Institute of Mediaeval Studies, 1978. 77-104.

1681 Parel, Anthony. "Aquinas' Theory of Property." *Theories of Property*. Eds. A. Parel and Thomas Flanagan. Waterloo, Ontario: University of Waterloo Press, 1979. 89-111.

1682 Park, Katharine, and Eckhard Kessler. "The Concept of Psychology." *The Cambridge History of Renaissance Philosophy*. Eds. Quentin Skinner, Charles B. Schmitt, and Eckhard Kessler. New York: Cambridge University Press, 1988. 455-463.

1683 Patt, Walter. "Aquinas' Real Distinction and Some Interpretations." *The New Scholasticism* 62(1988): 1-29.

*This article reviews the debate between J. Owens and J. Wippel as to where in Chapter 4 of *De ente et essentia* Thomas Aquinas arrives at the real distinction between essence and existence. Contrary to both authors, it is argued that the *intellectus essentiae* argument establishes a real distinction between that which is conceptual (essence) and that which is nonconceptual (existence). Aquinas' proofs of God's uniqueness and of the first cause do not concentrate on that distinction itself but introduce a distinction between two types of beings.*

1684 Paul, Harry W. "Thomism and Science: Wonderful Harmony Under the Shield and Authority of the Angelic Doctor." *The Edge of Contingency: French Catholic Reaction to Scientific Change from Darwin to Duheim*. Ed. Harry W. Paul. Gainesville, FL: University Presses of Florida, 1979. 179-194.

1685 Paulhus, Normand. "Uses and Misuses of the Term Social Justice in the Roman Catholic Tradition." *Journal of Religious Ethics* 15(1987): 261-282.

A considerable amount of confusion surrounds the use of the term "social justice" in contemporary ethical dialogue, as can be seen in the Roman Catholic bishops' pastoral letter on the economy. By examining its first appearances in Catholic writings influenced by the neo-Thomistic revival, this paper discerns numerous confusions arising from misunderstandings of Aquinas' vision because of the pervasive influence of modern political philosophies. To avoid such confusions, commutative and distributive justice ought to remain our main tools in ethical analyzes of the economy, while social justice, with its focus on the common good, social solidarity, and the primacy of duties, ought to be reserved for issues that relate directly to the common good.

1686 Payer, Pierre J. "Prudence and the Principles of Natural Law: A Medieval Development." *Speculum* 54(1979): 55-70.

1687 Pearson, Paul. "Creation Through Instruments in Thomas' *Sentence* Commentary." *Philosophy and the God of Abraham: Essays in Memory of James A. Weisheipl, OP*. Ed. James Long. Toronto: Pontifical Institute of Mediaeval Studies, In press. 147-160.

1688 Pegis, Anton Charles. "Saint Thomas and the Meaning of Human Existence." *Calgary Aquinas Studies*. Ed. Anthony Parel. Toronto: Pontifical Institute of Mediaeval Studies, 1978. 49-64.

1689 Pegis, Anton Charles. "St. Thomas Aquinas and Husserl on Intentionality." *Thomistic Papers I*. Ed. Victor B. Brezik. Houston, TX: Center for Thomistic Studies: University of St. Thomas, 1984. 109-134.

1690 Pegis, Anton Charles. "Cosmogony and Knowledge: I. St. Thomas and Plato." *Thought* 65(1990): 359-375.

1691 Pelikan, Jaroslav. "*Imago Dei*: An Explication of *Summa Theologiae*, Part 1, Question 93." *Calgary Aquinas Studies*. Ed. Anthony Parel. Toronto: Pontifical Institute of Mediaeval Studies, 1978. 27-48.

1692 Penelhum, Terence. "The Analysis of Faith in St. Thomas Aquinas." *Religious Studies* 13(1977): 133-154.

1693 Peters, Calvin B., and Jon A. Hendricks. "Synderesis and Phenomenology: Intermediate Concepts of Value and Law in Social Science." *Philosophy of the Social Sciences* 7(1977): 229-238.

It has been argued that Thomistic natural law theory has no place in modern social science accounts of the origin and nature of law. However, it can be shown that an accurate understanding of natural law and the Thomist concept of synderesis yields striking similarity to the phenomenological sociology of law of Guvitch, Scheler, and Znaniecki. Synderesis, the capacity to recognize and apply natural law in various existential settings, is paralleled by phenomenology's casting of man as possessing an ideal intuition which relates moral ideal to empirical law through the medium of justice. In both formulas man occupies intermediate position between the ideal realm of values and the empirical world of law.

1694 Petrik, James. "Freedom as Self-determination in the *Summa Theologiae*." *The Southwestern Journal of Philosophy* 27(1989): 87-100.

This paper is a critical exposition and analysis of Thomas Aquinas' theory of free action. Using the modern distinction between liberty of indifference and liberty of spontaneity, it is argued that Thomas rejected the former and embraced the latter. In addition, reasons are sketched for maintaining that liberty of spontaneity is a better account of human freedom than liberty of indifference.

1695 Philibert, P. J. "Addressing the Crisis in Moral Theory: Clues from Aquinas and Gilligan." *Theology Digest* 34(1987): 103-113.

1696 Pike, Nelson. "If There is No Necessary Being, Nothing Exists." *Nous* 11(1977): 417-420.

1697 Pike, Nelson. "Over-power and God's Responsibility for Sin." *The Existence and Nature of God*. Ed. Alfred J. Freddoso. Notre Dame, IN: University of Notre Dame Press, 1983. 11-36.

1698 Plantinga, Alvin. "Reason and Belief in God." *Faith and Rationality: Reason and Belief in God*. Eds. Alvin Plantinga and Nicholas Wolterstorff. Notre Dame, IN: University of Notre Dame Press, 1983. 16-93.

1699 Plantinga, Alvin. "On Ockham's Way Out." *Faith and Philosophy* 3(1986) 235-269.

1700 Platthy, Jeno. "Aristotle's Concept of Time in Medieval Philosophies." *Faith and Philosophy* 3(1981) 212-219.

1701 Porter, Mildred Jean. "Desire for God: Ground of the Moral Life in Aquinas." *Theological Studies* 47(1986): 48-68.

1702 Porter, Mildred Jean. "*De Ordine Caritatis*: Charity, Friendship, and Justice in Thomas Aquinas' *Summa Theologiae*." *The Thomist* 53(1989): 197-213.

1703 Porter, Mildred Jean. "Moral Rules and Moral Actions: A Comparison of Aquinas and Modern Moral Theology." *Journal of Religious Ethics* 17(1989): 123-149.

This essay compares Aquinas' understanding of the precepts of justice with the various accounts of moral rules developed in the debate over proportionalism among contemporary moral theologians. It is argued that both sides in this debate oversimplify Aquinas' account of moral rules so drastically as to misread him. Moreover, it is argued that because Aquinas' account reflects a sense of the communal context for moral discernment, it is superior to both traditionalism and proportionalism.

1704 Postow, B. C. "Thomas on Sexism." *Ethics* 90(1980): 251-256.

Several claims made by Thomas give the appearance of supporting the view that sexist epithets are not extremely abusive. By untangling Thomas' notion of a phenomenon readily lending itself to a morally unobjectionable description, I show that his remarks give no support to the view that sexist epithets are less abusive than racist epithets. I also argue that Thomas is unduly pessimistic about the prospects of inducing men to give up sexism and that he provides only modest illumination on the differences between sexism and racism.

1705 Potts, Timothy. "Conscience." *The Cambridge History of Later Medieval Philosophy: From the Rediscovery of Aristotle to the Disintegration of Scholasticism. 1100-1600.* Eds. Norman Kretzmann et al. Cambridge: Cambridge University Press, 1982. 687-704.

1706 Powell, Ralph. "Degenerate Secondness in Peirce's Belief in God." *Proceedings of the Catholic Philosophical Association* 62(1988): 116-123.

1707 Presa, W. K. "St. Thomas on Religious Belief." *Sophia (Australia)* 19(1980): 22-26.

1708 Principe, Walter H. "Affectivity and the Heart in Thomas Aquinas' Spirituality." *Spiritualities of the Heart: Approaches to Personal Wholeness in Christian Tradition.* Ed. Annice Callahan. New York: Paulist, 1990. 45-63.

1709 Principe, Walter H. "'The Truth of Human Nature' According to Thomas Aquinas: Theology and Science in Interaction." *Philosophy and the God of Abraham: Essays in Memory of James A. Weisheipl, OP.* Ed. James Long. Toronto: Pontifical Instituteof Mediaeval Studies, In press. 161-177.

1710 Prufer, Thomas. "Heidegger, Early and Late, and Aquinas." *Edmund Husserl and the Phenomenological Tradition: Essays in Phenomenology.* Ed. Robert Sokolowski. Studies in Philosophy and the History of Philosophy 18. Washington, DC: The Catholic University of America Press, 1988. 197-215.

1711 Quinn, John M. "The Third Way to God: A New Approach." *The Thomist* 42(1978): 50-68.

One formidable difficulty in the Third Way arises from the claim, "If only physical possibles exist, then at one time nothing exists." Endless generation and corruption make appeal to an infinite time untenable. The crux seems solved when we recognize that Aquinas' claim supposes equivocal causation, in particular the operation of a universal physical cause (a necessary being of nature) that causes and conserves species. Suppress this primary cosmic agent, and all species vanish: absolutely nothing in nature remains. Whether or not regarded as scientifically admissible today, a universal physical cause supplies an indispensable key to understanding the Third Way.

1712 Quinn, John M. "A Few Reflections on The Third Way: Encore." *The Thomist* 46(1982): 75-91.

*This article is a rejoinder to T. Kondoleon's "*The Third Way: Encore*" that criticized my earlier article on Aquinas' Third Way to God. Kondoleon overlooks Aquinas' contrary-to-fact strategy, misconstrues equivocal causation, inflates primary matter into a necessary being, and attempts a reconstruction on dubious grounds. Thus the Third Way terminates not in subsistent existence but in a being necessary of itself. The mature Aquinas did not simultaneously reach the existence and nature of God.*

1713 Quinn, Patrick. "The Relationship Between Human Transcendence and Death in the Philosophy of St. Thomas Aquinas." *Milltown Studies* 25(1990): 63-75.

1714 Radcliffe, Elizabeth S. "Kenny's Aquinas on Dispositions for Human Acts." *The New Scholasticism* 58(1984): 424-446.

1715 Rahner, Karl. "Thomas Aquinas on the Incomprehensibility of God." *Celebrating the Medieval Heritage: A Colloquy on the Thought of Aquinas and Bonaventure.* Ed. David Tracy. Chicago: University of Chicago Press, 1978. 107-125.

1716 Rasmussen, Douglas B. "Rorty, Wittgenstein, and the Nature of Intentionality." *Proceedings of the American Catholic Philosophical Association* 57(1983): 152-162.

Richard Rorty claims that intentionality is not a criterion of the mental, but as Wittgenstein suggests, the functional. The reluctance we feel to identify the mental with the material is not because of any special feature of the mental, but rather it is because of the fact that we do not know how to relate what we observe to what it means. The intentional features of a brain state are like those of a mark or sound: they are a function of their relation to a larger context. Once we grasp how they function in relation to a larger whole, then brainstates, as well as marks on a page, will manifest intentional properties. This Wittgensteinian view of intentionality can, however, be challenged, and this work will take up this challenge.

1717 Ratzinger, Joseph. "Faith, Philosophy and Theology." *Pope John Paul II.* Ed. College of St. Thomas. Lecture Series. St. John Vianney Seminary, 1985. 10-14.

1718 Redpath, Peter. "Romance of Wisdom: The Friendship Between Jacques Maritain and Saint Thomas Aquinas." *Understanding Maritain: Philosopher and Friend.* Eds. Deal W. Hudson and Matthew J. Mancini. Macon, GA: Mercer University Press, 1987. 91-113.

The purpose of this article is to determine what in particular attracted Maritain to Aquinas, how faithfully Maritain interprets Aquinas, and what, if anything, is distinctive about Maritain's interpretation of St. Thomas. The article concludes that Maritain's attraction to Aquinas was primarily theological, rather than, as often thought and as Maritain would himself have maintained, philosophical. This conclusion is based upon a radical reinterpretation of Christian philosophy, scholasticism, and the development of modern philosophy.

1719 Redpath, Peter. "Classifying the Moral Teaching of St. Thomas." *The Medieval Tradition of Natural Law.* Ed. Harold J. Johnson. Studies in Medieval Culture 22. Kalamazoo, MI: Medieval Institute Publications, 1987. 137-148.

1720 Reese, William L. "Dipolarity and Monopolarity in the Idea of God." *Dialogos* 18(1983): 51-58.

*Reviewing the argument of *Philosophers Speak of God* (Hartshorne and Reese, 1953, 1976) I argue that dipolarity successfully resolves the problems generated by the monopolar conception of God, but that the panentheistic version of dipolarity resolves some problems only, while posing others. Whitehead turns out to be a dipolarist but not a panentheist; and Hartshorne's panethesim is not Whiteheadian. In turning from classical theism one must search for nonpanentheistic forms of dipolarity.*

1721 Regan, Richard J. "Aquinas on Political Obedience and Disobedience." *Thought* 56(1981): 77-88.

The article analyzes Aquinas' views on society, government, and political obedience, especially from the perspective of contemporary Western democracies. According to Aquinas, the aim of a rightly ordered society is to promote common material, intellectual, and moral well-being. Rulers should be subject to law, and the burdens and rewards of government should be shared by all citizens proportionately. Although Aquinas' political theory is historically limited, he recognized the essential linkage of virtue to regime. Contemporary Western democracies need to do likewise.

1722 Reichmann, James B. "Aquinas, God and Historical Process." *Tommaso D'Aquino Nel Suo Settimo Centenario IX: Atti del Congresso Internazionale: Il Cosmo e la Scienza.* Napoli: Edizioni Domenicane Italiane, 1978. 427-436.

1723 Reichmann, James B. "The *Cogito* in St. Thomas: Truth in Aquinas and Descartes." *International Philosophical Quarterly* 26(1986): 341-352.

*The article contrasts Descartes' and Aquinas' theories on truth, tracing their basic difference to a divergent view concerning the act of judgment. Descartes' *Cogito* is held to be internally inconsistent precisely because it strives to unite an aprioristic *intellectus* with a reasoning process. Such an attempt is made, it is claimed, because, artificially separating understanding and judgment, Descartes misreads the hidden presuppositions of the act of reasoning as a way to fuller understanding. This occurs because Descartes, unlike Aquinas, seeks to ground human knowing upon a theory of pure essences.*

1724 Reichmann, James B. "Language and the Interpretation of Being in Gadamer and Aquinas." *Proceedings of the American Catholic Philosophical Association* 62(1988): 225-234.

The article contrasts Gadamer's hermeneutical ontology with the epistemological theory of Aquinas. It presents a sketch of Gadamer's theory of interpretation and of language relating these to his hermeneutical notion of truth. It focuses on the developmental aspect of Gadamer's interpretation theory and on the unique role language plays as the horizon of hermeneutical ontology. Aquinas' position on truth and language is next outlined, and the sense in which he views the knowing process as authentically hermeneutical is considered. The two hermeneutical positions are found to differ significantly. The article concludes by suggesting that the line of demarcation between the two lies in Gadamer's neglect of the distinction between material and formal cause.

1725 Reilly, James P. "The Leonine Enterprise: An Exercise in Historical Discovery." *Proceedings of the Patristic, Medieval and Renaissance Conference* 7(1982): 1-12.

1726 Reilly, James P. "The *Alia Littera* in Thomas Aquinas' *Sententia Libri Metaphysicae*." *Mediaeval Studies* 50(1988): 559-583.

1727 Reilly, James P. "The Numbering Systems of the *Pecia* Manuscripts of Aquinas' *Commentary on the Metaphysics*." *La Production Du Livre Universitaire Au Moyen Äge: Exemplar et Pecia.* Eds. Louis J. Bataillon, Bertrand G. Guyot, and Richard H. Rouse. Actes Du Symposium Tenu Au Collegio San Bonaventura de Grottaferrata en Mai 1983. Paris: Éditions du Centre National de la Recherche Scientifique, 1988. 209-223.

1728 Reimers, Adrian J. "St. Thomas' Intentions at *De Veritate* 1, 1." *Doctor Communis* 42(1989): 175-183.

1729 Reitan, Eric A. "Aquinas and Weisheipl: Aristotle's *Physics* and the Existence of God." *Philosophy and the God of Abraham: Essays in Memory of James A. Weisheipl, OP.* Ed. James Long. Toronto: Pontifical Institute of Mediaeval Studies, In press. 179-190.

1730 Renna, Thomas. "Augustinian Kingship and Thomas Aquinas." *Proceedings of the Patristic, Mediaeval and Renaissance Conference* 5(1980): 151-158.

1731 Rentto, Juha-Pekka. "What Can a Discursive Theory of Morality Learn from Aquinas." *Vera Lex* 10(1990): 1-4.

1732 Reynolds, Lyndon P. "Bonaventure on Gender and Godlikeness." *The Downside Review* 106(1988): 171-194.

1733 Ricoeur, Paul. "Response to Rahner." *Celebrating the Medieval Heritage: A Colloquy on the Thought of Aquinas and Bonaventure*. Ed. David Tracy. *The Journal of Religion* 58. Chicago: University of Chicago Press, 1978. 126-131. Response to Rahner, Karl, *Thomas Aquinas on the incomprehensibility of God.*

1734 Riedl, John O. "Thomas Aquinas' *Commentary on the Fourth Proposition of the Book of Causes* Appraised as a Measure of His Mature Understanding of the Platonist Philosophy." *Proceedings of the Patristic, Mediaeval and Renaissance* 6(1981): 145-160.

1735 Rikhof, H. "Whose Mistake? Some Critical Remarks About a Reading of *ST* I, Q. 13, A. 5." *Werkgroep Thomas Van Aquino*. Amsterdam: Jaarboek, 1985. 23-38.

1736 Ritacco de Gayoso, Graciela L. "Intelligible Light and Love: A Note on Dionysius and Saint Thomas." *The New Scholasticism* 63(1989): 156-172.

1737 Robb, James. "St. Thomas and the Infinity of Human Beings." *Proceedings of the American Catholic Philosophical Association* 55(1981): 118-125.

1738 Robb, James. "Introduction." *Questions on the Soul*. By Thomas Aquinas. Trans. James H. Robb. Mediaeval Philosophical Texts in Trans. 27. Milwaukee, WI: Marquette University Press, 1984. 1-12.

1739 Robb, James. "The Unity of Adequate Knowing in St. Thomas Aquinas." *The Monist* 69(1986): 447-457.

1740 Roberts, Lawrence D. "A Comparison of Duns Scotus and Thomas Aquinas on Human Freedom of Choice." *Homo et Mundus: Acta Quinti Congressus Scotistici Internationalis*. Ed. Camille Bérubé. Studia Scholastico- scotistica 8. Romae: Societas Internationalis Scotistica, 1984. 265-272.

1741 Rocca, Gregory Philip. "The Distinction Between *Res Significata* and *Modus Significata* in Aquinas' Theological Epistemology." *The Thomist* 55 (In press): 173-197.

1742 Rojas, José. "St. Thomas on the Direct/indirect Distinction." *Ephemerides Theologicae Louvanienses* 64(1988): 371-392.

1743 Romano, Joseph J. "Between Being and Nothingness: The Relevancy of Thomistic Habit." *The Thomist* 44(1980): 427-440.

*Aquinas' notion of human habits is considered and compared with some contemporary views. Specifically, a comparison is made with Gilbert Ryle's chapter on "Dispositions" in the *Concept of Mind*. The ontological status of habits is considered in reference to the objection that "habits" may imply occult entities. A comparison is then made with Sartre's notion of spontaneous freedom that would seem to rule out any continuity of human action. The Thomistic sense of habits allows a spontaneity that implies "reliability" on self and others in facing new situations. In comparing these views, the article concludes that Aquinas' theory of habits is relevant in both a theoretical and practical sense.*

1744 Ross, George M. "Angels." *Philosophy* 60(1985): 495-511.

How should we interpret alien beliefs, such as Plato's myths, or Aquinas' belief in angels? Davidson's principle of charity (also found in Hobbes, and taken up by Bennett) is patronizing, because it assumes the superiority of modern, Western concepts. If we translate everything into our own terms, we falsify history, and we lose the capacity to learn from the past. The origin of the image of angels dancing on points of needles is also discussed.

1745 Ross, James F. "Creation II." *The Existence and Nature of God*. Ed. A. Freddoso. 1983. 115-141.

1746 Ross, James F. "Aquinas on Belief and Knowledge." *Essays Honoring Allen B. Wolter*. Eds. William A. Frank and Girard J. Etzkorn. St. Bonaventure, NY: St. Bonaventure University Press, 1985. 245-269.

1747 Ross, James F. "Aquinas on Annihilation." *Studies in Medieval Philosophy*. Ed. John F. Wippel. Studies in Philosophy and the History of Philosophy, 17. Washington, DC: The Catholic University of America Press, 1987. 177-199.

1748 Ross, James F. "The Crash of Modal Metaphysics." *The Review of Metaphysics* 43(1989): 251-279.

1749 Ross, James F. "Aquinas' Exemplarism; Aquinas' Voluntarism." *American Catholic Philosophical Quarterly* 64(1990): 171-198.

1750 Rousseau, Edward L. "St. Anselm and St. Thomas: A Reconsideration." *The New Scholasticism* 54(1980): 1-24.

This article is not an historical assessment of Anselm's argument and Thomas' refutation, but a metaphysical essay showing a line of thought where their deepest intentions converge. Their definitions of truth, different as they are, both imply an obscure presence in the mind of that than which there can be no greater. Our intellectual activity mirrors a transcendent subject, the effective exemplar of truth and source of moral obligation. We transcend and judge the objects of our thinking by sharing the infinite horizon of divine light. The horizon is supplied by God. He could not supply it unless real. But for Thomas what is immediately judged in this horizon is the material thing. Hence the historical Aquinas, who began demonstrating God's existence with the objects known and not with the subject's activity, rejects Anselm's argument and has no temptation to construct a similar proof.

1751 Rousseau, Mary F. "Avicenna and Aquinas on Incorruptibility." *The New Scholasticism* 51(1977): 524-536.

*A comparison shows that Saint Thomas *Summa Theologiae* I, 75, 6 is modeled, with careful selectivity, on Avicenna's *De Anima* V, IV. Aquinas parallels the Persian's division of the question, his rejection of indirect corruptibility on the grounds of the soul's substantiality, his rejection of direct corruptibility on the grounds of the soul's simplicity, and his establishment of that simplicity by analysis of abstract intellection. He replaces the "flying man" argument for substantiality with one based on our ability to understand all material natures. Thus, while rejecting Avicenna's spiritualist view of man, his separation of the agent intellect, and his derivation of the content of our knowledge from higher substances, Aquinas adopts the form and most of the content of his proof for the incorruptibility of the soul.*

1752 Rousseau, Mary F. "The Natural Meaning of Death in *Summa Theologiae*." *Proceedings of the American Catholic Philosophical Association* 52(1978): 87-95.

This article is an effort to understand what death is and why we die, without appeal to any religious beliefs. Death is a diminution, because of the loss of phantasms, of knowledge, freedom, and virtue. Yet it is natural in a universe of generation and corruption, in which the tendency of matter to corrupt is not overcome even when actuated by an incorruptible form. The study confirms Aquinas' hylomorphic anthropology, instances his development of the concept of nature, and intensifies his positive evaluation of bodily life.

1753 Rousseau, Mary F. "Elements of a Thomistic Philosophy of Death." *The Thomist* 43(1979): 581-602.

A test of the consistency between Aquinas' hylomorphic theory of man and his philosophy of death through an analysis of his theory of the cognition of the separated soul. Consistency is shown to be complete: the optimism with which the soul's embodied existence is made its natural, fully human mode is confirmed by a pessimism in which the humanity of the separated soul is diminished in several important respects. Thanks to the absence of phantasms, knowledge is vague, general, and restricted to the past rather than perfected in existential contact with material singulars. Such diminished cognition implies diminished freedom and love as well as diminished exercise of the moral and intellectual virtues. Thus the ways in which "a separated soul is not a complete being" are spelled out in terms of operations.

1754 Rousseau, Mary F. "Process Thought and Traditional Theism." *The Modern Schoolman* 63(1986): 45-64.

1755 Roy, Louis. "Wainwright, Maritain, and Aquinas on Transcendent Experiences." *The Thomist* 54(1990): 655-672.

1756 Rudavsky, Tamar. "The Doctrine of Individuation in Duns Scotus." *Franziskanische Studien* 62(1980): 62-83.

1757 Russman, Thomas A. "Reformed Epistemology." *Thomistic Papers IV*. Ed. Leonard A. Kennedy. Houston, TX: Center for Thomistic Studies, University of Saint Thomas, 1988. 185-207.

1758 Ryan, Eugene E. "Bartolomeo Cavalcanti as a Critic of Thomas Aquinas." *Vivarium* 20(1982): 84-95.

*An analysis of the central treatises of the work by Bartolomeo Cavalanti, *Trattati sopra gli ottimi Reggimenti delle Repubbliche antiche e moderne*, indicates that these form an independent work. Though the work is ostensibly concerned with commenting on Aristotle's *Politics*, it turns out to be less interested in clarifying Aristotle's positions than with showing the mistakes in Aquinas' understanding of those positions. Cavalcanti displayed a high level of scholarly acumen as he went about his task.*

1759 Ryden, Edmund. "Aquinas on the Metaphorical Expression of Theological Truth." *Philosophisches Jahrbuch* 27(1986): 409-419.

This article seeks to apply the fruits of contemporary linguistic and aesthetic theories of metaphor to the theological language of Aquinas. In dialogue with Kant and Hegel, metaphorical assertions are shown to be uniquely adapted for conveying the truths of revelation. Although Aquinas gives no explicit theory of metaphor, reasons for this are suggested. Yet the theory here proposed is shown to be compatible with his analysis of theological discourse.

1760 Saint-Laurent, George. "Avicenna, Maimonides, Aquinas, and the Existence of God." *Festschrift in Honor of Morton C. Fierman*. Ed. Joseph Kalir. Fullerton, CA: California State University, 1982. 165-191.

1761 Sasaki, T. "The Origin of Thomas Aquinas' Theory on Law." *Studies in Medieval Thought* 27(1985): 124-132.

1762 Scalise, Charles J. "The *Sensu Literalis*: A Hermeneutical Key to Biblical Exegesis." *Scottish Journal of Theology* 42(1989): 45-65.

1763 Schall, James V. "Human Destiny and World Population: The Individual as Horizon and Frontier." *The Thomist* 41(1977): 92-104.

Current population and ecological theories about the meaning of human numbers and the ultimate destiny of the earth are surprisingly couched in terms and concepts originally forged by Aquinas in quite a different context, namely, those of the ultimate number of people—a finite number for Aquinas—and their condition in the Parousia. This means that the philosophical background of current movements represent another instance of attempts to secularize original Christian concepts and place them in terms of a philosophy confined to the ongoing process of the planet Earth. The metaphysical reason for this consists in replacing the value of the person's destiny with that of the species, its ongoing process, the destiny Aristotle gave to animals.

1764 Schall, James V. "The Reality of Society in St. Thomas." *Divus Thomas* 83(1980): 13-23.

1765 Schall, James V. "Revelation, Reason and Politics." *Gregorianum* 62(1981): 349-365.

Professor Leo Strauss made an original contribution to the understanding of political things. In particular, he was open to the question of the relation of reason and revelation, how this question arose from classical thought, how it varied in the three revealed religious traditions of Christianity, Islam, and his own Judaism. Christian, and particularly Catholic, thinkers have been slow to grasp the importance of Professor Strauss' contributions. However, there are a number of studies by Catholics which are of some considerable value. Strauss himself was familiar with Aquinas, and it seems evident that his understanding of Aquinas plays a key role in understanding how Strauss is to be understood. Essentially, Strauss was open to the possibility of revelation and did not allow philosophy to close the question. On the other hand, he wanted to preserve a legitimate place for reason, as was the case in the Thomist tradition. In this sense, Professor Strauss is a key thinker in the philosophical understanding of religion, on how faith can contribute to reason and politics.

1766 Schedler, George. "A Catholic Non-Thomist View of Human Rights." *The New Scholasticism* 54(1980): 153-167.

*In this paper, I demonstrate the incoherence of the arguments advanced by secular Anglo-American philosophers which purport to establish the basis for human rights. I then provide a rationale for the Catholic view, as reflected in the concrete stand taken in *Pacem in Terris*. A logical reconstruction of the Church's position shows that she has avoided the difficulties secular theorists have been unable to resolve. Finally, I show that the Thomist account of human nature does not provide the ontological basis for the same rights the Church has sought to protect. Both Thomists and secular theorists, it turns out, are unable to make out a basis for rights for humans who are incapable of rational choice.*

1767 Schedler, George. "Anselm and Aquinas on the Fall of Satan: A Case Study of Retributive Punishment." *Proceedings of the American Catholic Philosophical Association* 56(1982): 61-69.

On the one hand, the punishment of Satan seems to be a paradigm case of (the Kantian version of) retributive punishment, insofar as Satan was punished for a fully voluntary and knowledgeable act of will. But, on the other hand, it appears that because Satan achieved precisely what he willed (to be cut off from his final end): he was not punished in a retributive sense at all. This paper considers this and other puzzles created by the deontontological and natural law explanations of Satan's punishment.

1768 Schedler, George. "Retributive Punishment and the Fall of Satan." *American Journal of Jurisprudence* 30(1985): 137-154.

1769 Schindler, David L. "Whitehead's Challenge to Thomism on the Problem of God: The Metaphysical Issues." *International Philosophical Quarterly* 19(1979): 285-299.

1770 Schmidt, Robert W. "The Unifying Sense: Which?" *The New Scholasticism* 57(1983): 1-21.

1771 Schmitz, Kenneth L. "A Moment of Truth: Present Actuality." *The Review of Metaphysics* 33(1980): 673-688.

1772 Schmitz, Kenneth L. "Analysis by Principles and Analysis by Elements." *Graceful Reason: Essays in Ancient and Medieval Philosophy Presented to Joseph Owens on the Occasion of His Seventy-fifth Birthday and the Fiftieth Anniversary of His Ordination*. Ed. Lloyd P. Gerson. Papers in Mediaeval Studies 4. Toronto: Pontifical Institute of Mediaeval Studies, 1983. 315-330.

1773 Schmitz, Kenneth L. "Entitative and Systemic Aspects of Evil." *Dialectical Humanism* 5(1986): 149-161.

1774 Schmitz, Kenneth L. "Purity of Soul and Immortality." *The Monist* 69(1986): 396-415.

1775 Scholz, Franz. "Problems on Norms Raised by Ethical Borderline Situations: Beginnings of a Solution in Thomas Aquinas and Bonaventure." *Moral Norms and Catholic Tradition*. Ed. C. E. Curran. New York: Paulist Press, 1979. 158-183.

1776 Schoonenberg, Piet. "God as Relating and (Be) Coming: A Meta-thomistic Consideration." *Listening* 14(1979): 265-278.

1777 Schultz, Janice Lee. "Is-Ought: Prescribing and a Present Controversy." *The Thomist* 49(1985): 1-23.

Germain Grisez and John Finnis do not neglect nature as a basis for moral value, as some critics imply they do. However, owing to their interpretation of "ought"-judgments as prescriptive rather than descriptive, these authors incorrectly separate the realms of "is" and "ought." I offer an analysis of moral "ought"—judgments as inherently descriptive, recognizing prescriptive uses in which the descriptive component remains the ground of the directive.

1778 Schultz, Janice Lee. "The Ontological Status of Value Revisited." *The Modern Schoolman* 63(1986): 133-137.

1779 Schultz, Janice Lee. "Ought-judgments: A Descriptivist Analysis from a Thomistic Perspective." *The New Scholasticism* 61(1987): 400-426.

1780 Schultz, Janice Lee. "St. Thomas Aquinas on Necessary Moral Principles." *The New Scholasticism* 62(1988): 150-178.
*This paper shows how, according to St. Thomas Aquinas, basic descriptive moral principles can be both substantive and necessarily true. Aquinas' position on reference (the function of the subject term) is similar to that of the contemporary logician, Saul Kripe, who argues for necessary informative propositions. Such propositions in Aquinas (which are analyzed in detail in the paper) include definitions—e. g., "human beings, or men, are rational animals"—and property statements. The latter encompass those concerned with natural inclinations.From this foundation the necessity of fundamental moral principles is explained. Still, moral principles can be refined as we discover more about human nature; if true, such statements will be necessarily true. The paper ends with an explanation of how basic moral principles canbe considered to be not simply *per se*, but also *per se nota*.*

1781 Schultz, Janice Lee. "Thomistic Metaethics and a Present Controversy." *The Thomist* 52(1988): 40-62.

1782 Schultz, Janice Lee. "Appetite, Goodness, and Choice." *The New Scholasticism* 63(1989): 286-294.

1783 Scully, Edgar. "Aquinas' State: A Tyrannical Household Writ Large?" *Science et Esprit* 33(1981): 379-393.

1784 Scully, Edgar. "The Place of the State in Society According to Thomas Aquinas." *The Thomist* 45(1981): 407-429.

Aquinas' varied renditions of the Aristotelian formula, "man is by nature a political animal," bespeak fundamental principles of his social and political philosophy. For him, both society and the State as a civically governed society have a positive value arising from and serving the nature of man. But he does not favor the notion of a State or political society so exalted and all-encompassing that it would deny any autonomy to component communities and individual citizens. State-government remains essentially a part of the society it governs and is subject to that society not only as its origin and end on the natural plane but also as ordered in its individual members to a supernatural end.

1785 Scully, Edgar. "Aquinas and Hierocracy or Church Supremacy." *Sacris Erudiri* 36(1984): 233-248.

1786 Scully, Edgar. "The Political Limitations of Natural Law in Aquinas." *The Medieval Tradition of Natural Law*. Ed. Harold J. Johnson. Studies in Medieval Culture 22. Kalamazoo, MI: Medieval Institute Publications, 1987. 149-159.

1787 Sedgwick, Peter. "The Compulsion to Be Good: Aquinas on the Formation of Human Character." *Theology* 74(1988): 194-200.

1788 Seebohm, Thomas M. "Isidore of Seville Versus Aristotle in the Questions on Human Law and Right in the *Summa Theologiae* of Thomas Aquinas." *Graduate Faculty of Philosophy Journal* 11(1986): 83-105.

1789 Seidel, George J. "Hermeneutics and Prayer." *Proceedings of the American Catholic Philosophical Association* 62(1988): 189-201.
*The article bumps Thomas Aquinas' treatment of prayer, as the *interpres nostri desiderii apud Deum*, up against contemporary hermeneutics. The article is divided into four parts. Part I includes a discussion of St. Thomas' disquisition on prayer. Part

II is a little *jeu d'esprit* on Hermes which arrives at what the author believes to be the concern of hermeneutics, namely the inspired author/text relationship. Part III contrasts the emphasis upon the author ("romantic") and upon the text ("structuralist"), pointing out the good and bad points of each. And Part IV argues that the meaning of the author/text relationship, to which hermeneutics would ideally relate, is the Muse, drawing also upon Aquinas' understanding of prayer as inspired by the Spirit.*

1790 Seidl, Horst. "The Concept of Person in St. Thomas Aquinas: A Contribution to Recent Discussions." *The Thomist* 51(1987): 435-460.

Concerning the classical definition of person in Boethius and St. Thomas Aquinas, that person is "an individual substance of rational nature," the reader is confronted with a recent existentialist interpretation (Degl'Innocenti et al.) according to which the essential feature of person would consist in the act of existence of the individual, not in the rational nature. But this nature is misunderstood as a universal possibility whereas it is in truth the formal act principle in every man.

1791 Seifert, Josef. "Answer to Disputed Questions Concerning Essence and Existence." *Aletheia* 1(1977): 467-480.

1792 Seifert, Josef. "Essence and Existence I." *Aletheia* 1(1977): 17-157.

1793 Seifert, Josef. "Essence and Existence II." *Aletheia* 1(1977): 371-459.

1794 Seifert, Josef. "*Esse*, Essence, and Infinity: A Dialogue with Existentialist Thomism." *The New Scholasticism* 58(1984): 84-98.

1795 Seniff, Dennis F. "Introduction to Natural Law in Didactic, Scientific and Legal Treatises in Medieval Iberia." *The Medieval Tradition of Natural Law*. Kalamazoo, MI: Medieval Institute Publications, Western Michigan University, 1987. 161-178.

1796 Serene, Eileen F. "Medieval Theology Minus Aquinas: Jaroslav Pelikan's *The Growth of Medieval Theology (600-1300)*." *Religious Studies* 16(1980): 487-492.

1797 Serequeberhan, Tsenay. "Aquinas and Kant: A Comparative Study." *Dialogue (PST)* 26(1984): 40-48.

Aquinas and Kant stand on radically different terrains in the history of philosophy. Nonetheless, implicitly and indirectly the concepts of Kant's epistemology exhibit a fundamental similitude to Aquinas' reflections on the question of human knowledge. The thesis of this paper is that certain concepts from Aquinas are secularized, transformed, and carried over into Kant's epistemic position. The argument is not that Kant consciously takes over certain positions from Aquinas, but rather that the radically different positions of Kant and Aquinas share certain fundamental conceptions which are not obvious.

1798 Shea, John Michael. "St. Thomas Aquinas on the Principle *Ananké Stênai*." *The New Scholasticism* 55(1981): 139-158.

*The subject of this essay is the Aristotelian-Thomistic principle *ananké stênai*: it is impossible to go to infinity in efficient causes. This principle serves as a premise in St. Thomas Aquinas' First and Second Ways. It enables him to posit a first cause, which, he says, everyone calls God.*

1799 Shea, Joseph. "Two Conceptions of the Structure of Happiness." *Dialogue* (Canada) 26(1987): 453-464.

*Aristotle's conception of *eudaimonia* is both determinate and capable of incorporating different activities. Aristotle views happiness as the desirable novel emergent which orders other desired activities into a unified whole that is more than a mere preference ordering. Aquinas misinterpreted Aristotle's views and saddled the tradition with a view of the *summum bonum* as a single activity, to which all other activities are means. Traditional criticisms of an ethics positing a summum bonum are inapplicable to Aristotle's account of happiness.*

1800 Sheehan, Thomas. "Heidegger's Topic: Excess, Recess, Access." *Tijdschrift voor Filosofie* 41(1979): 615-635.

*The article discusses(1) the ambivalence of the word *Sein*; (2) the theme of metaphysics: beingness; (3) the categorical intuition in *Logical Investigations*: the immediate presentation of beingness; and (4) the unity of Heidegger's thought: man has access to entities as meaningfully present (*aletheia*) on the basis of his excess (transcendence) to the privatize recess (*lethe*) that characterizes the disclosure process.*

1801 Sheehan, Thomas. "A Way Out of Metaphysics." *Research in Phenomenology* 15(1985): 229-234.

1802 Shewmon, D. Alan. "The Metaphysics of Brain Death, Persistent Vegetative State and Dementia." *The Thomist* 49(1985): 24-80.

*Three neurologic conditions are analyzed in terms of modern medicine and Aristotelian-Thomistic philosophy. The minimum part of the body necessary for human life is shown to be the organ of *sensus communis*, which corresponds to what modern neuroanatomy knows as the "tertiary association areas" of the cerebral cortex. Therefore, brain death, persistent vegetative state, and severe dementia are valid manifestations of personal death. Theoretical and practical consequences are discussed.*

1803 Shook, Laurence K. "Maritain and Gilson: Early Relations." *Thomistic Papers II*. Eds. Leonard A. Kennedy and Jack C. Marler. Houston: University of Houston, Center for Thomistic Studies, 1986. 7-27.

*During early 1923, Etienne Gilson wrote Jacques Maritain, asking him for a frank opinion about his recently published second ed. of *Le Thomisme*. The answer Gilson received (Maritain to Gilson, March 11, 1923) transformed Gilson from an historian of philosophy into an authentic metaphysician and philosopher.*

1804 Sigmund, Paul E. "Thomistic Natural Law and Social Theory." *Calgary Aquinas Studies*. Ed. Anthony Parel. Toronto: Pontifical Institute of Mediaeval Studies, 1978. 65-76.

1805 Sigmund, Paul E. "Maritain on Politics." *Understanding Maritain*. Eds. Deal Hudson and Matthew Mancini. Macon, GA: Mercer University Press, 1987. 153-170.

The article traces the evolution of Maritain's political thought from the mid-twenties until his death in 1973. It argues(1) that his writings marked an important development of Thomist and Catholic political thought on modern democratic politics that helped to overcome the longstanding alienation between the Catholic church in Latin countries and democratic pluralism; (2) that he reformulated Thomist theories of natural law and the good society in ways that made them applicable to modern political conditions; and (3) that his thinking provided an important theoretical source for the ideologies of major Christian Democratic parties and movements in Europe and Latin America.

1806 Simpson, Peter. "St. Thomas on the Naturalistic Fallacy." *The Thomist* 51(1987): 51-69.

The article first states the key ideas behind ethical non-naturalism, namely the supervenience and action-guiding force of value terms. Aquinas' position is developed in response to these, using his distinction between transcendental and category terms to account for supervenience, and his theory of mind, or his analysis of the interplay between thought and will, to account for action-guiding force. These accounts enable Aquinas to be a logically coherent ethical naturalist.

1807 Simpson, Peter. "Practical Knowing: Finnis and Aquinas." *The Modern Schoolman* 67(1990): 111-122.

I argue that Finnis' account of practical knowing is false. It falls foul of dilemmas about the meaning of good, reasons for action, and truth. It is also not an accurate interpretation of Aquinas. Aquinas' own theory, when correctly stated, escapes all three dilemmas and makes for more sense. Finnis, however, may be right about the priority of good to nature in the order of knowing, if not about practical knowing as such.

1808 Skinner, Quentin. "Political Philosophy." *The Cambridge History of Renaissance Philosophy*. Eds. Quentin Skinner, Charles B. Schmitt, and Eckhard Kessler. New York: Cambridge University Press, 1988. 388-452.

1809 Smith, Marc. "Is There a Thomistic Alternative to Lonergan's Cognitional Structure?" *The Thomist* 43(1979): 626-636.

*Bernard Lonergan's insistent claim that the cognitional structure elaborated in *Insight* cannot be revised entails for him the question *quid sit* preceding the question *an sit*. St. Thomas Aquinas, who explicitly maintains the reverse ordering, might thus be thought to provide an alternative pattern of conscious operations. However, the study concludes that the two are not opposed; for, according to St. Thomas, prior to the intellectual act of knowing *an sit*, there is a grasp of what the question is about, and this is precisely what knowing *quid sit* achieves, in Lonergan's view: a grasp of the unity-identity-whole in data.*

1810 Smith, Philip A. "The Beginning of Personhood: A Thomistic Perspective." *Laval Théologique et Philosophique* 39(1983): 195-214.

**Le commencement de la personne: une perspective thomiste* explore le statut de la vie du foetus immédiatement aprés la fécondation. On le fait à l'inteérieur d'un cadre comprenant à la fois la dimension empirique et la dimension philosophique. L'examen des données biologiques et leur analyse philosophique suggérent que, dans les Étapes initiales de son existence, le foetus ne devrait pas être considéré comme une personne, vu que son individualité n'est pas encore arrêtée de maniére définitive. Toutefois, lcs changements observables à la suite de l'apparition de l'organisateur primaire durant la seconde ou la troisiéme semaine de gestation sont tellement dramatiques qu'un philosophie thomiste peut raisonnablement présumer la présence de la forme substantielle humaine (l'âme intellective) qui, tant spécifiquement que numériquement, constitute le foetus comme personne.*

1811 Smith, Philip A. "Brain Death: A Thomistic Appraisal." *Angelicum* 67(1990): 3-35.

1812 Smith, Philip A. "Transient Natures at the Edges of Human Life: A Thomistic Exploration." *The Thomist* 54(1990): 191-227.

1813 Snyder, David C. "Faith and Reason in Locke's *Essay Concerning Human Understanding*." *Journal of the History of Ideas* 47(1986): 197-213.

1814 Sommers, Mary C. "*Manifestatio*: The Historical Presencing of Being in Aquinas' *Expositio Super Job*." *Proceedings of the American Catholic Philosophical Association* 62(1988): 147-156.

*In his philosophical confrontation between Martin Heidegger and Thomas Aquinas, John Caputo argues that Aquinas is implicated in what Heidegger calls the "oblivion of Being." Aquinas' lack of historical consciousness leaves him trapped in a tradition of understanding Being, unable to know it as a tradition. Without trying to acquit St. Thomas of the charge of *Seinsvergessenheit*, I will argue that there is in Aquinas a teaching concerning the historical presencing of Being. This teaching is found in the *Expositio super Job*. It centers on the notion of the *manifestatio* of divine providence in the particular event.*

1815 Sprokel, Nico S. I. "The *Index Thomisticus*." *Gregorianum* 59(1978): 739-750.

1816 Stacer, John R. "Integrating Thomistic and Whiteheadian Perspectives on the Philosophy of God." *International Philosophical Quarterly* 21(1981): 355-378.

A framework to synthesize analogous philosophical knowledge about God includes five areas: divine identity and total capability, divine reflecting, creative relating, and curative relating. Divine identity situates most of Aquinas' attributes of God and Whitehead's affirmation that God as primordial is the one non-derivative actuality.

1817 Staley, Kevin Michael. "Natural Law and the Community of Being." *Proceedings of the Patristic, Mediaeval, and Renaissance Studies* 9(1984): 77-87.

1818 Staley, Kevin Michael. "Happiness: The Natural End of Man?" *The Thomist* 53(1989): 215-234.

1819 Staley, Kevin Michael. "Thomas Aquinas and Contemporary Ethics of Virtue." *The Modern Schoolman* 66(1989): 285-300.

1820 Steel, Carlos. "The Devil's Faith: Some Considerations on the Nature of Faith in Augustine and Aquinas." *Louvain Studies* 13(1988): 291-304.

1821 Steger, E. Ecker. "*Verbum Cordis*: Mediation Between I and Thou." *Divus Thomas* á81(1978): 40-53.

1822 Stegman, Thomas D. "Saint Thomas Aquinas and the Problem of *Akrasia*." *The Modern Schoolman* 66(1989): 117-128.

*Aquinas' account of *akrasia* marked an advance over those of Plato and Aristotle because of the former's emphasis on the role of the will—and in particular, to the act of consent. His distinction between assent and consent allowed him to give a more plausible explanation of what really happens when a person acts against his knowledge. Aquinas recognized that there is ignorance involved in an incontinent act, but this ignorance is the result of a voluntary focusing of one's attention on the object of concupiscence (cf. consent): which also involves voluntary inattention to a moral precept previously assented to.*

1823 Stengren, George L. "Connatural Knowledge in Aquinas and Kierkegaardian Subjectivity." *Kierkegaardiana X*. Kobenhavn: C. A. Reitzels Boghandel, 1977. 182-189.

1824 Stevens, Clifford. "A Prologue to *De Ente et Essentia*." *Angelicum* 57(1980): 389-400.

1825 Strasser, Michael W. "Anselm and Aquinas: Center and Epicenters." *From Cloister to Classroom: Monastic and Scholastic Approaches to Truth*. Ed. Rozanne E. Elder. The Spirituality of Western Christendom 3. Kalamazoo, MI: Cistercian Publications Inc., 1986. 130-153.

1826 Strozewski, Wladyslaw. "Remarks on the Nature and Origin of Good and Evil." *Dialectical Humanism* 5(1978): 173-179.

1827 Stubbens, Neil A. "Naming God: Moses Maimonides and Thomas Aquinas." *The Thomist* 54(1990): 229-267.

Moses Maimonides(1135-1204) and Thomas Aquinas (c. 1225-1274): two of the greatest theologians of the Jewish and Christian faith, had much in common. Like other Christian writers, Aquinas made several criticisms of Maimonides' views on divine predication. In this article I will discuss these criticisms and evaluate them by means of a detailed exposition of Maimonides' position. I will then offer an account of Aquinas' justification of analogical predication and make some suggestions as to the role of causality in naming God.

1828 Stump, Eleonore. "Petitionary Prayer." *American Philosophical Quarterly* 16(1979): 81-91.

On the face of it, belief in the efficacy of petitionary prayer appears inconsistent with belief in an omniscient, omnipotent, perfectly good God. The strongest sort of argument for this inconsistency is based on the assumption that an omniscient, omnipotent God will bring about all and only those good states of affairs which it is logically possible for him to bring about, so that petitionary prayers for good states of affairs are prayers for something God would bring about in any case, and those for bad states of affairs are prayers for something God will never bring about, and hence petitionary prayer is pointless. I consider and reject some traditional and contemporary attempt to explain the inconsistency and then suggest my own solution, which depends on taking seriously the theistic belief that God is a person.

1829 Stump, Eleonore. "Dante's Hell, Aquinas' Moral Theory, and the Love of God." *Canadian Journal of Philosophy* 16(1986): 181-198.

That certain human beings suffer in hell is a basic Christian doctrine, but it seems hard to reconcile it with the fundamental Christian claims that God is good and loving. On the basis of Aquinas' views of the nature of God's goodness and love, however, together with Dante's particular understanding of hell as a place where human beings are treated in accordance with the acquired nature they have chosen for themselves, it is possible to construct a philosophically interesting defense of the claim that God is both good and loving and yet consigns some persons to hell.

1830 Stump, Eleonore. "Atonement According to Aquinas." *Philosophy and the Christian Faith*. Ed. Thomas V. Morris. University of Notre Dame Studies in the Philosophy of Religion 5. Notre Dame, IN: University of Notre Dame Press, 1988. 61-91.

The doctrine of the atonement is the central doctrine of Christianity, but it has not received much attention in contemporary philosophy of religion, in part because it tends to be known only in an unreflective version full of philosophical and theological problems. I present an alternative version of the doctrine, taken from Aquinas, argue that it is a cogent and consistent account, and show that it does not suffer from the problems of the unreflective version.

1831 Stump, Eleonore. "Faith and Goodness." *Philosophy* 25(1989): 167-191.

Current work in philosophy of religion on the subject of faith has tended to consider such issues as whether beliefs held on faith are rational or whether belief in God may be properly basic. Such work has been useful in drawing our attention to certain issues in the epistemology of religion, but it has also left unanswered some longstanding perplexities about faith. I look at Aquinas' account of the nature of faith to show a side of faith neglected in contemporary accounts. For these purposes, the most important thing about Aquinas' account is that it assigns the will a role in faith. This added element in Aquinas' account provides a resolution for some common puzzles about the notion of faith.

1832 Stump, Eleonore, and Norman Kretzmann. "Absolute Simplicity." *Faith and Philosophy* 2(1985). 353-382.

1833 Stump, Eleonore, and Norman Kretzmann. "Simplicity Made Plainer: A Reply to Ross's 'Absolute Simplicity.'" *Faith and Philosophy* 4(1987): 198-201.

The authors try to show that many differences between Ross and themselves are only apparent, masking considerable agreement. Among the real disagreements, at least one is over the interpretation of Aquinas' account of divine simplicity, but the most central disagreement consists in the authors' claim that their concern was not with a distinction between the way God is and the way he might have been (as Ross suggests) but with the difference between the way God is necessarily and the way he is contingently. Finally, the authors argue that the concept of simplicity is indeed required for the solution of the problems discussed at the end of their original article.

1834 Sullivan, Thomas D. "Concepts." *The New Scholasticism* 56(1982): 146-168.

The Classical Theory of Thinking, as H. H. Price describes it, holds that thinking is distinguished from other forms of cognition not only by being a special sort of activity, but also by bearing on special sorts of objects, "universal concepts" or "abstract ideas." Recently, philosophers have tended to reject this position. For them, thinking is the exercise of certain dispositions, such as the use of general words, and not, in Thomas Heath's phrase, "the discovery, acquisition and storage of mental or transcendental furniture." The author suggests that this theory—the "Disposition Theory"—is inadequate to the cognitive facts and that it wins adherents mainly because it is thought that the Classical Theory cannot be formulated without reliance upon intra-or extra-mentally existing abstract entities. This assumption, he argues, is mistaken.

1835 Suttor, Timothy L. "Thomas of Aquino and Ibn Al-Arabi." *Hamdard Islamicus* (Karachi) 6(1983): 87-101.

1836 Swanston, H. F. G. "Reading, Writing, and Aquinas." *New Blackfriars* 70(1989): 4-14.

1837 Sweeney, Leo. "Can St. Thomas Speak to the Modern World?" *One Hundred Years of Thomism: Aeterni Patris and Afterwards*. Ed. Victor B. Brezik. Houston, TX: Center for Thomistic Studies: University of St. Thomas, 1981. 119-141.

This essay answers two questions: What constitutes the "modern mind"? Has Aquinas anything significant to say to "moderns"? The "modern mind" entails two eras: 1925 to 1960, wherein Luther, Descartes, and Rousseau were influential. In the second era(1960 seq.) Einstein, Darwin, and Freud were influential, and Sartre and other radical existentialists reacted against them. Aquinas offers moderns an authentic existentialism, which is theistic and which grounds helpful theories of natural law, creation, and unselfish love.

1838 Sweeney, Leo. "The Christian Existentialism of Jacques Maritain." *Jacques Maritain. Philosophe dans la Cité/ A Philosopher in the World*. Ed. Jean-Louis Allard. Philosophica 28. Ottawa: University of Ottawa Press, 1985. 31-41.

1839 Synan, Edward A. "Aquinas and His Age." *Calgary Aquinas Studies*. Ed. Anthony Parel. Toronto: Pontifical Institute of Mediaeval Studies, 1978. 1-25.

1840 Synan, Edward A. "Thomas Aquinas: Propositions and Parables." The Etienne Gilson Series. Toronto: Pontifical Institute of Mediaeval Studies, 1979. 1-20.

1841 Synan, Edward A. "Saint Thomas Aquinas: His Good Life and Hard Times." *Thomistic Papers III*. Ed. Leonard A. Kennedy. Houston, TX: University of St. Thomas, Center for Thomistic Studies, 1987. 35-53.

This is the text of a "Saint Thomas Day" lecture in which it is argued that aspects of the two worlds of Aquinas, one private and familial, the other his public world of feudalism and the Dominican vocation of preaching and teaching, made the life of Aquinas a hard one despite his holiness. A spontaneous attraction to a life of contemplative prayer was sacrificed for the "mixed vocation" of preacher and teacher for the sake of others.

1842 Synan, Edward A. "St. Thomas Aquinas and the Profession of Arms." *Mediaeval Studies* 50(1988): 404-437.

1843 Synan, Edward A. "Aquinas and the Children of Abraham." *Philosophy and the God of Abraham: Essays in Memory of James A. Weisheipl, OP*. Ed. James Long. Toronto: Pontifical Institute of Mediaeval Studies, In press. 203-216.

1844 Tallon, Andrew. "Connaturality in Aquinas and Rahner: A Contribution to the Heart Tradition." *Philosophy Today* 28(1984): 138-147.

The heart tradition stretches from Egyptian and Hebrew origins, through the medieval philosopher-theologians and their notion of affective connaturality, into the twentieth century ideas of affective (presentational—or presence—rather than representational) intentionality. First by a negative approach (heart is not-mind, mind is not nature, etc.), and then by the idea of connaturality in Aquinas and Rahner, I try briefly to say something helpful about the modern meaning of the basic word "heart."

1845 Tavuzzi, Michael M. "Aquinas on the Preliminary Grasp of Being." *The Thomist* 51(1987): 555-574.

1846 Tavuzzi, Michael M. "Aquinas on the Operation of *Additio*." *The New Scholasticism* 62(1988): 297-318.

*It is argued that an adequate understanding of Aquinas' scientific methodology, as it is operative in the three theoretical sciences of physics, mathematics, and metaphysics, requires the recognition that in the process of *compositio* effected by each of these sciences is exercised a special type of mental operation that Aquinas calls *additio*. This operation is to be seen as being parallel to, and as important for each of these three sciences as, the operation of *distinctio* of which the three specific types of total abstraction, formal abstraction and metaphysical separation are effected within their processes of *resolutio*. Each type of *additio*—correspondingly designated as "total addition," "formal addition," and "metaphysical addition"—is considered separately and its significance for the science in which it is especially operative is assessed.*

1847 Tavuzzi, Michael M. "Aquinas on Resolution in Metaphysics." *The Thomist* 55 (In press): 199-227.

1848 Taylor, Richard C. "St. Thomas and the *Liber de Causis* on the Hylomorphic Composition of Separate Substances." *Mediaeval Studies* 41(1979): 506-513.

*This article deals with the question of the hylomorphic composition of separated substances in the thought of Thomas Aquinas and in the Pseudo-Aristotelian *Liber de Causis* (Dc). It examines and evaluates the interpretation by Aquinas of Chapter 8 (Latin Chapter 9) of the DC where Aquinas found the word *yliatim*. The Latin text of the DC and the Commentary of Aquinas are studied in the light of the Arabic text of the DC. The conclusions are that Aquinas was mistaken in his analysis, but that he correctly saw that the author of the DC held that there is no hylomorphic composition of separate substances.*

1849 Tekippe, Terry Joseph. "Lonergan's Analysis of Error: An Experiment." *Gregorianum* 7(1990): 353-374.

1850 Tester, S. J. "Saint Thomas Aquinas." *Fides Quarens Intellectum: Mediaeval Philosophy from Augustine to Ockham*. Ed. S. J. Tester. United Kingdom: Bristol Classical Press, 1989. 117-132.

1851 Thelakat, Paul. "Process and Privation: Aquinas and Whitehead on Evil." *International Philosophical Quarterly* 26(1986): 287-296.

1852 Theron, Stephen. "*Esse*." *The New Scholasticism* 53(1979): 206-220.
*This paper is a critique of Kenny's critique of "Aquinas' theory of God as subsistent being" in *The Five Ways*. First, I compare his and Geach's views on Aquinas and *esse*, and discuss a remark about *quidditas*. Then, I find fault with several of his interpretations of Aquinas' texts in a way which brings out, I think, the latter's real sense. I argue that Kenny confuses the two senses of "Deus est" Aquinas had distinguished and that he misrepresents *esse* as essentially dependent upon form. After this analysis I advance texts, with comment, supporting my argument. Finally, I close with some general remarks on *esse*, arguing that Platonic parallels are only superficially similar.*

1853 Theron, Stephen. "St. Thomas Aquinas and *Epieicheia*." *Lex et Libertas: Freedom and Law According to St. Thomas Aquinas*. Ed. L. J. Elders and K. Hedwig. Studi Tomistici 30. Città del Vaticano: Pontificia Accademia di San Tommaso e di Religione Cattolica, 1987. 171-181.

1854 Theron, Stephen. "The Divine Attributes in Aquinas." *The Thomist* 51(1987): 37-50.

1855 Theron, Stephen. "Intentionality, Immateriality and Understanding in Aquinas." *The Heythrop Journal* 30(1989): 151-159.

1856 Theron, Stephen. "Subject and Predicate Logic." *The Modern Schoolman* 66(1989): 119-129.

1857 Thomas, J. L. H. "The Identity of Being and Essence in God." *The Heythrop Journal* 27(1986): 394-408.

1858 Tierney, Brian. "Hierarchy, Consent, and the Western Tradition." *Political Theory* 15(1987): 646-652.

1859 Tirosh-Rothschild, Hava. "Maimonides and Aquinas: The Interplay of Two Masters in Medieval Jewish Philosophy." *Conservative Judaism* 39(1986): 54-66.

1860 Tomasic, Michael Thomas. "Natural Moral Law and Predestination in St. Thomas Aquinas: An Incurable Contradiction?" *The Medieval Tradition of Natural Law*. Ed. Harold J. Johnson. Studies in Medieval Culture 22. Kalamazoo, MI: Medieval Institute Publications, 1987. 179-189.

1861 Tracy, Thomas F. "The Soul as Boatman of the Body: Presocratics to Descartes." *Diotima* 7(1979): 195-199.
In formulating his position on the body-soul problem, Descartes seems curiously concerned with the analogy that soul is to body as pilot is to ship. It has been suggested that the analogy "reaches back into the distant past." It does in fact go back to the Presocratics; to trace its occurrence is to follow the history of the body-soul problem through the centuries, from Anaximander, Parmenides, Heraclitus, Regimen I, Diogenes of Apollonia, through Plato, Aristotle, Menander, to Plutarch, Clement of Alexandria, Plotinus, the Byzantine commentators, Aquinas, and the Jesuit commentators on Aristotle. Descartes adopts the analogy but with unsatisfactory results.

1862 Tracy, Thomas F. "The Moral Perfections of God." *The Thomist* 47(1983): 473-500.

1863 Trapani, John G., Jr., "Are Persons Intrinsically Valuable?" *Journal of the West Virginia Philosophical Society* 17(1979): 4-6.

*After acknowledging that values are of different kinds, this paper includes the argument(1) that there is an *intrinsic unity* proper to natural substance (from Aristotle's distinction between existence and subsistence); (2) that there is an *intrinsic metaphysical value* proper to all natural substances (from Aquinas' notion of the participation of natural substance in *esse*); and (3) that the unique mode of subsistence proper to persons provides evidence of a participation not only in *esse* but also in spirit. The article concludes that it is precisely this *intrinsic spiritual value* which grounds man's *intrinsic moral value*.*

1864 Treloar, John L. "Pomponazzi's Critique of Aquinas' Arguments for the Immortality of the Soul." *The Thomist* 54(1990): 453-470.

1865 Tummers, Paul M. J. E. "Geometry and Theology in the XIIIth Century." *Vivarium* 18(1980): 112-142.

*Descriptions of the contents of five tracts (ff 1-15) of Ms. Admont 442: (a) Definitions from Book I of Euclid; (b) Book I and II of Euclid (Adelard); (c) proofs of Prop. 132 of Euclid; (d) tract on the incommensurability of side and diameter. Text and study of the fourth tract, on the horn—angle (*angulus contingentie*): the properties of which are used for the theological question of whether the sum goodness of human soul can be eliminated by an infinite number of sins, and for the analogical question concerning the intercessions of the church. Of the main 13th century authors, only William Auxerre mentions this example.*

1866 Twetten, David B. "Why Motion Requires a Cause: The Foundation for a Prime Mover in Aristotle and Aquinas." *Philosophy and the God of Abraham: Essays in Memory of James A. Weisheipl, OP*. Ed. James Long. Toronto: Pontifical Institute of Mediaeval Studies, In press. 235-254.

1867 Udo, Kinkichi. "Being, Truth and Cognition in St. Thomas Aquinas." *Actes Du Septiéme Congrés International de Philosophie Médiéval: L'homme et Son Univers Au Moyen Age II*. Ed. Christian Wenin. Philosophes Médiévaux 26-27. Louvain-la-Neuve: Éditions de l'Institut Supérieur de Philosophie, 1986. 530-564.

1868 Urban, Linwood. "Understanding St. Thomas' Fourth Way." *History of Philosophical Quarterly* 1(1984): 281-296.

1869 Van Melsen, A. G. "Some Key Concepts of the Thomistic Philosophy of Nature Reconsidered." *La Philosophie de la Nature de Saint Thomas D'Aquin*. Ed. Léon Elders. Studi Tomistici 18. Cittá del Vaticano: Pontificia Accademia di San Tommaso, Libreria Editrice Vaticana, 1982. 66-81.

1870 Van Uytven, Raymond. "The Date of Thomas Aquinas' *Epistola Da Ducissam Brabantiae*." *Pascua Mediaevalia*. Mediaevalia Lovaniensia 1. Leuven: Universitaire Pers Leuven, 1983. 631-643.

1871 Vander Walt, Johannes. "The Encounter of Arabic and Christian Civilizations in Medieval Philosophy with Particular Reference to the Conflict Between Faith and Reason: A Comparison Between the Viewpoints of Averroes and Thomas Aquinas." *Actas del V Congreso Internacional de Filosofia Medieval II*. Madrid: Nacional, 1979. 1331-1338.

1872 Vander Weel, Richard L. "A Note on Some Puzzling Phrases in Aquinas." *The New Scholasticism* 63(1989): 510-513.

1873 Veatch, Henry B. "Are There Non-moral Goods?" *The New Scholasticism* 52(1978): 471-499.

1874 Veatch, Henry B. "Philosophy, Thou Art in a Parlous State!" *Thomistic Papers I.* Ed. Victor B. Brezik. Houston, TX: Center for Thomistic Studies: University of St. Thomas, 1984. 9-44.

1875 Veatch, Henry B. "Preliminary Statement of Apology, Analysis, and Critique." *Thomistic Papers IV*. Ed. Leonard A. Kennedy. Center for Thomistic Studies, Houston, TX: University of St. Thomas, 1988. 5-63.

1876 Vedder, A. "St. Thomas Aquinas, Ockham and Buridan on the Possibility of a Normative Theory of Ethics." *Ockham and Ockhamists*. Eds. E. P. Bos and H. A. Krop. Artistarium, Supplementa IV. Nijmegen: Ingenium, 1987. 119-124.

1877 Vermeulen, B. P. "Some Remarks Concerning the Influence of Thomas Aquinas on Hugo Grotius' *Natural Law Thinking*." *Werkgroep Thomas Van Aquino*. Amsterdam: Jaarboek, 1985. 92-100.

1878 Viviano, Benedict T. "The Kingdom of God in Albert the Great and Thomas Aquinas." *The Thomist* 44(1980): 502-522.

The concept of the kingdom of God is important today as providing a biblical basis for social and political involvement of Christian believers and for meeting the Marxist challenge of hope for the future. It is shocking that the great theologians of the Middle Ages neglect or downplay this concept, except for Joachim of Flora. Four reasons for St. Thomas' neglect are given:(1) Rejection of exaggerated Joachimism; (2) High Christology and present pneumatology; (3) Close association with status quo represented by Pope and Emperor; and (4) Lack of awareness of Jewish apocalyptic. Then it is shown that Albert the Great treats the concept at length but gives it a Platonic interpretation which confuses psychology and political science and also lacks the apocalyptic dimension.

1879 Wainwright, William J. "Monotheism." *Rationality, Religious Belief, and Moral Commitment: New Essays in the Philosophy of Religion*. Eds. Robert Audi and William J. Wainwright. Ithaca, NY: Cornell University Press, 1986. 289-314.

1880 Walgrave, J. H. "Understanding of God According to Thomas Aquinas." *Louvain Studies* 7(1978-1979): 85-90.

1881 Walgrave, J. H. "*Tertia Via*." *Quinque Sunt Viae*. Ed. Léon Elders. Studi Tomistici 9. Città del Vaticano, Pontificia Accademia di San Tommaso: Libreria Editrice Vaticana, 1980. 65-74.

1882 Walgrave, J. H. "The Personal Aspects of St. Thomas Ethics." *The Ethics of St. Thomas Aquinas*. Eds. L. Elders and K. Hedwig. Studi Tomistici 25. Città del Vaticano: Libreria Editrice Vaticana, 1984. 202-215.

1883 Walgrave, J. H. "Reason and Will in Natural Law." *Lex et Libertas: Freedom and Law According to St. Thomas Aquinas*. Eds. L. J. Elders and K. Hedwig. Studi Tomistici 30. Città del Vaticano: Pontificia Accademia di San Tommaso e di Religione Cattolica, 1987. 67-81.

1884 Wallace, William A. "Causality, Analogy, and the Growth of Scientific Knowledge." *Tommaso D'Aquino Nel Suo Settimo Centenario IX*. Naples: Edizioni Domenicane Italiane, 1977. 26-40.

1885 Wallace, William A. "St. Thomas' Conception of Natural Philosophy and Its Method." *La Philosophie de la Nature de Saint Thomas D'Aquin*. Ed. Léon Elders. Studi Tomistici 18. Cittá del Vaticano: Pontificia Accademia di San Tommaso, Libreria Editrice Vaticana, 1982. 7-27.

1886 Wallace, William A. "St. Thomas' Conception of Natural Philosophy and Its Method." *La Philosophie de la Nature de Saint Thomas D'Aquin*. Ed. Leon Elders. Studi Tomistici 18. Rome: Editrice Vaticana, 1982. 7-27.

1887 Wallace, William A. "Aquinas, Galileo and Aristotle." *Proceedings of the American Catholic Philosophical Association* 57(1983): 17-24.

1888 Wallace, William A. "The Intelligibility of Nature: A Neo-Aristotelian View." *The Review of Metaphysics* 38(1984): 33-56.

1889 Wallace, William A. "Thomas Aquinas on Dialectics and Rhetoric." *A Straight Path: Studies in Medieval Philosophy and Culture. Essays in Honor of Arthur Hyman*. Eds. Jeremiah Hackett et al. Washington, DC: The Catholic University of America Press, 1988. 244-254.

1890 Wallace, William A. "Aquinas and Newton on the Causality of Nature and of God: The Medieval and Modern Problematic." *Philosophy and the God of Abraham: Essays in Memory of James A. Weisheipl, OP*. Ed. James Long. Toronto: Pontifical Institute of Mediaeval Studies, In press. 255-279.

1891 Wallis, R. T. "Divine Omniscience in Plotinus, Proclus, and Aquinas." *Neoplatonism and Early Christian Thought: Essays in Honour of A. H. Armstrong*. Eds. H. J. Blumenthal and R. A. Markus. London: Variorum Publications, 1981. 223-235.

1892 Walter, Edward F. "The Modernity of St. Thomas' Political Philosophy." *Vera Lex* 10(1990): 12-13.

1893 Walter, Edward F., and Bruce Bubacz. "The Common Good in Thomas Aquinas' Politics." *The Medieval Tradition of Natural Law*. Ed. Harold J. Johnson. Studies in Medieval Culture 22. Kalamazoo, MI: Medieval Institute Publications, 1987. 201-211.

1894 Wanjohi, Gerald J. "St. Thomas Aquinas' Philosophy of Education." *Euntes Docete (Roma)* 38(1985): 179-194.

1895 Watobe, Kikuo. "The Intellectual Cognition of Man According to St. Thomas Aquinas (Nipponice)." *Studies in Medieval Thought* 27(1985): 77-100.

1896 Wauck, Mark A. "A Response to Patrick Lee." *American Catholic Philosophical Quarterly* 64(1990): 401-409.

1897 Webster, Richard T. "Thomism and Empiricism." *Atti del Congresso Societá Internazionale Tommaso D'Aquino Nel Suo Settimo Centenario VI: L'essere*. Napoli: Edizioni Domenicane, 1977. 425-430.

1898 Weidemann, Hermann. "The Logic of Being in Thomas Aquinas." *The Logic of Being: Historical Studies*. Eds. Simo Knuuttila and Jaakko Hintikka. Synthese Historical Library 28. Dordrecht: Reidel, 1986. 181-200.

*The author examines how the ontological distinction between the *actual* being of something which falls under one of the 10 categories and the being *true* of something which is the case, which Aquinas borrows from Aristotle, is related in his writings to the familiar distinction between the "is" of existence, the "is" of predication, and the "is" of identity. It is shown that in drawing these distinctions Aquinas does not commit himself to the view that the verb "be" is genuinely ambiguous.*

1899 Weiher, Charles F. "Knowing and Symbolic Functioning." *The New Scholasticism* 62(1988): 412-437.

Notwithstanding the danger of mixing disparate philosophical perspectives and idioms, this author attempts to discuss a theory of knowledge which recognizes the role of symbolic functioning as it is discussed in the works of Ernst Cassirer and Michael Polanyi and as it appears to fit within the general framework of St. Thomas' cognitional doctrine. Pierre Rousselot sketches this latter system in broader outline and scope than is common and shows thereby the role of substitutes for pure assimilative knowing and the understanding of the essences of things and situations. To extend our grasp of meaning (a pivotal notion) as it is available in the span of cultural activity—science, art, myth, religion, etc. —we use inventive forms of construction of concepts, comparable to Cassirer's symbolic functioning, and proceed in ways describable in terms of Polany's "tacit" knowing. The locus of this activity is the interior senses, the cogitative sense in particular.

1900 Weiler, Anton Gerard. "Christianity and the Rest: The Medieval Theory of a Holy and Just War." *Concilium* 200(1988): 109-119.

1901 Weinandy, Thomas. "Aquinas and the Incarnational Act: Become as a Mixed Relation." *Doctor Communis* 22(1979): 15-31.

1902 Weingartner, Paul. "Aquinas' Theory of Conscience from a Logical Point of View." *Conscience: An Interdisciplinary View*. Eds. Paul Weingartner and Gerhard Zecha. Dordrecht: Reidel, 1987. 201-261.

The proceedings and discussions of an interdisciplinary colloquium on ethics, this book contains original contributions from developmental and social psychology, from social philosophy, the history of philosophy, moral theology, jurisprudence, and psychiatry. The purpose of the project was to analyze the notions of consciences as used in different disciplines and to find a common denominator. As a result, the life-serving function of conscience in its various forms is depicted, especially in relation to many current problems.

1903 Weinreb, Lloyd L. "Natural Law and Justice." Cambridge, MA: Harvard University Press, 1987. Especially Chapter 2: "The Law of Nature," 43-66.

1904 Weisheipl, James A. "The Nature, Scope and Classification of the Sciences." *Science in the Middle Ages*. Ed. David C. Lindberg. Chicago: University of Chicago Press, 1978. 461-82. Appears in *Studia Medie*, 18(1977): 85-101.

1905 Weisheipl, James A. "The Validity and Value of Natural Philosophy." *Atti del Congresso Internazionale IX: Tommaso D'Aquino Nel Suo Settimo Centenario*. 1978. 263-266.

1906 Weisheipl, James A. "The Axiom, *Opus Naturae Est Opus Intelligentiae* and Its Origins in Albert Magnus." *Albert Magnus Doctor Universalis: 1280/1980*. Eds. Gerbert Meyer and Albert Zimmermann. Mainz: Matthias-Grunewald, 1980. 441-463.

1907 Weisheipl, James A. "Albert's Disclaimers in the Aristotelian Paraphrases." *Proceedings of the Patristic, Medieval, and Renassiance Conference* 5(1980): 1-27.

1908 Weisheipl, James A. "Aristotle's Concept of Nature: Avicenna and Aquinas." *Approaches to Nature in the Middle Ages*. Ed. Lawrence D. Roberts. Medieval & Renaissance Texts & Studies 16. Binghamton, NY: Center for Medieval & Early Renaissance Studies, 1982. 137-60. Comment by William A. Wallace, 161-169.

1909 Weisheipl, James A. "A Brief Catalogue of Authentic Works." 1974. *Friar Thomas D'Aquino: His Life, Thought & Works: With Corrigenda and Addenda*. Washington, DC: The Catholic University of America, 1983. 355-405.

1910 Weisheipl, James A. "The Date and Context of Aquinas' *De Aeternitate Mundi*." *Graceful Reason: Essays in Ancient and Medieval Philosophy Presented to Joseph Owens on the Occasion of His Seventy-fifth Birthday and the Fiftieth Anniversary of His Ordination*. Ed. Lloyd P. Gerson. Papers in Mediaeval Studies 4. Toronto: Pontifical Institute of Mediaeval Studies, 1983. 239-271.

1911 Weisheipl, James A. "Mystic on Campus: Friar Thomas?" *An Introduction to the Medieval Mystics of Europe*. Ed. P. E. Szarmach. Albany, NY: State University of New York Press, 1984. 135-160.

1912 Weisheipl, James A. "Science in the Thirteenth Century." *The History of the University of Oxford I*. Ed. J. I. Catto. Oxford: Oxford University Press, 1984. 435-469.

1913 Weisheipl, James A. "The Concept of Nature: Avicenna and Aquinas." *Thomistic Papers I*. Ed. Victor B. Brezik. Houston, TX: Center for Thomistic Studies: University of St. Thomas, 1984. 65-82.

1914 Weisheipl, James A. "Athens and Jerusalem: The Spirituality of St. Thomas Aquinas." *The Canadian Catholic Review* 3(1985): 23-28.

1915 Weisheipl, James A. "Classification of the Sciences in Medieval Thought." 1965. *Nature and Motion in the Middle Ages*. Ed. William E. Carroll. Studies in Philosophy and the History of Philosophy, 11. Washington, DC: The Catholic University of America Press, 1985. 203-237.

1916 Weisheipl, James A. "Medieval Natural Philosophy and Modern Science." 1965. *Nature and Motion in the Middle Ages*. Ed. William E. Carroll. Studies in Philosophy and the History of Philosophy, 11. Washington, DC: The Catholic University of America Press, 1985. 261-276.

1917 Weisheipl, James A. "Motion in a Void: Aquinas and Averroes." 1974. *Nature and Motion in the Middle Ages*. Ed. William E. Carroll. Studies in Philosophy and the History of Philosophy, 11. Washington, DC: The Catholic University of America Press, 1985. 121-142.

1918 Weisheipl, James A. "Philosophy and the God of Abraham." *Pope John Paul II, Lecture Series*. College of St. Thomas Centennial. St. John Viannery Seminary, 1985. 16-22.

1919 Weisheipl, James A. "The Commentary of St. Thomas on the *De Caelo* of Aristotle." 1974. *Nature and Motion in the Middle Ages*. Ed. William E. Carroll. Studies in Philosophy and the History of Philosophy, 11. Washington, DC: The Catholic University of America Press, 1985. 177-201.

1920 Weisheipl, James A. "The Concept of Nature." 1955. *Nature and Motion in the Middle Ages*. Ed. William E. Carroll. Studies in Philosophy and the History of Philosophy 11. Washington, DC: The Catholic University of America Press, 1985. 1-23.

1921 Weisheipl, James A. "The Principle *Omne Quod Movetur Ab Alio Movetur* in Medieval Physics." 1965. *Nature and Motion in the Middle Ages*. Ed. William E. Carroll. Studies in Philosophy and the History of Philosophy, 11. Washington, DC: The Catholic University of America Press, 1985. 75-97.

1922 Weitz, Morris. "Aquinas." *Theories of Concepts*. Ed. Morris Weitz. New York: Routledge, 1988. 43-59.

1923 Wennemann, J. "Saint Thomas' Doctrine of Extrinsic Denomination as Mediate Correspondence in Naming God *Ex Tempore*." *The Modern Schoolman* 65(1988): 119-129.

1924 Westberg, Daniel. "Reason, Will and Legalism." *New Blackfriars* 68(1987): 431-436.

1925 Westra, Laura. "The Soul's Noetic Ascent to the One in Plotinus and to God in Aquinas." *The New Scholasticism* 58(1984): 99-126.

1926 Westra, Laura. "Truth and Existence in Thomas Aquinas [*De Veritate* I. 1]." *Doctor Communis* 37(1984): 135-144.

1927 Westra, Laura. "Knowing Un-truth and the Truth of Non-being in Thomas Aquinas and Jacques Maritain." *Jacques Maritain: Philosophe dans la Cité/ A Philosopher in the World*. Ed. Jean-Louis Allard. Philosophica 28. Ottawa: University of Ottawa Press, 1985. 113-125.

*En premier lieu, l'auteur explique la relation qui existe entre le "connaître" et la vérité et la non-vérité chez saint Thomas. Il montre ensuite comment la doctrine de ce dernier, lorsqu'elle est bien comprise, place les composantes privatize et négative du jugement là même où Maritain le fait en suivant sa propre maniére d'aborder les questions connexes de la connaissance de la novérité et du non-être. De fait, dans son *De veritate*, saint Thomas arrive à la même conclusion en partant de la nature de la nature de la vérté comme telle, que Maritain lui-même, dans les Approches sans entraves. A partir de son point de vue sur la nature blessée. Les deux doctrines, semble-t-il, convergent dans une certaine mesure et s'éclairent mutuellement.*

1928 White, Victor. "Aristotle, Aquinas and Man." 1952. *God and the Unconscious*. Dallas, TX: Spring Publications Inc., 1982. 81-106.

1929 Whitney, Barry. "Divine Immutability in Process: Philosophy and Contemporary Thomism." *Horizons* 7(1980): 49-68.

1930 Wieland, Georg. "The Reception and Interpretation of Aristotle's Ethics." *The Cambridge History of Later Medieval Philosophy: From the Rediscovery of Aristotle to the Disintegration of Scholasticism. 1100-1600*. Eds. Norman Kretzmann et al. Cambridge: Cambridge University Press, 1982. 657-672.

1931 Wierenga, Edward. "Anselm on Omnipresence." *The New Scholasticism* 62(1988): 30-41.

*Divine omnipresence is traditionally understood in terms of God's knowledge and power. Anselm, I claim, understands omnipresence solely in terms of God's knowledge. I defend this interpretation of Anselm's view by supplementing his explicit discussion of the topic in the *Monologion* with several ideas introduced in the *Prosologion*. According to Anselm, an incorporeal being is present at a place if it has "inner sense" there, and in the case of God this amounts to having "immediate knowledge" of what is happening there.*

1932 Wilder, Alfred. "St. Albert and St. Thomas on Aristotle's *De Interpretatione*: A Comparative Study." *Angelicum* 57(1980): 496-532.

1933 Wilder, Alfred. "Are Essences Good? A Comparative Study." *La Teologia Morale Nella Storia e Nella Problematica Attuale*. Ed. Louis Bertrand Gillon. Studia Universitatis S. Thomae in Urbe 13. Milano: Massimo, 1982. 337-361.

1934 Wilder, Alfred. "St. Thomas and the Real Distinction of the Potencies of the Soul from Its Substance." *L'anima Nell'antropologia Di San Tommaso D'Aquino IX: Atti del Congresso Societá Internazionale San Tommaso D'Aquino*. Ed. Abelardo Lobato. Milano: Editrice Massimo, 1987. 431-454.

1935 Wilder, Alfred. "St. Thomas: Master Teacher in the Thought of Maritain." *Angelicum* 64(1987): 85-100.

1936 Wilhelmsen, Frederick D. "The I and Aquinas." *Proceedings of the American Catholic Philosophical Association* 51(1977): 47-55.

The absence of any articulated theory of the ego in Aquinas heightens the dominating role commanded by a presumed substantive ego in the rationalist tradition, German idealism, and phenomenology. Arguing that the supposed primacy of the ego is actually posterior and not prior because the ego is itself intended as an object by Descartes, the author also rejects Sartre's pre-conscious ego because the latter is known, as well, only in an "after-the-fact" situation. The ego in Aquinas is not substantive but is a reflective moment in spirit (in cognitive act) and is, hence, totally functional with reference to the object known. "Self" emerges as "self" possession of intellectual activity in judgment. A substantive ego, hence, is superfluous within Aquinas' theory of cognition.

1937 Wilhelmsen, Frederick D. "The Concept of Existence and the Structure of Judgment: A Thomistic Paradox." *The Thomist* 41(1977): 317-349.

1938 Wilhelmsen, Frederick D. "Creation as a Relation in Saint Thomas Aquinas." *The Modern Schoolman* 56(1979): 107-133.

The author argues that for Aquinas creation is an inhering accident following on the creature. Given, however, that the intelligibility of this relation is rooted neither in the essence nor in the existence of the creature, that intelligibility is prior to the creature and is identically the Creator.

1939 Wilhelmsen, Frederick D. "Foreword." *Thomist Realism and the Critique of Knowledge*. By Etienne Gilson. Trans. Mark A. Wauck. San Francisco: Ignatius Press, 1983. 7-25.

1940 Wilhelmsen, Frederick D. "A Note: The Absolute Consideration of Nature in *Quaestiones Quodlibetales*, VIII." *The New Scholasticism* 57(1983): 352-361.

1941 Wilhelmsen, Frederick D. "Response to Joseph Owens' 'Aquinas and Philosophical Pluralism'." *Thomistic Papers II*. Eds. Leonard A. Kennedy and Jack C. Marler. Houston, TX: University of St. Thomas, Center for Thomistic Studies, 1986. 159-163.

1942 Wilson, Gordon A. "Thomas Aquinas and Henry of Ghent on the Succession of Substantial Forms and the Origin of Human Life." *Proceedings of the American Catholic Philosophical Association* 63(1990): 117-131.

1943 Winiewicz, David Casimer. "A Note on *Alteritas* and Numerical Diversity in St. Thomas Aquinas." *Dialogue* 16(1977): 693-707.

*The author examines the doctrine of otherness (*alteritas*) as presented in the fourth question of Thomas Aquinas' *Exposition Super Librum De Trinitate* and, in particular, the interpretation given to the Boethian view that the principle of plurality is otherness. It is argued that the nature (*ratio*) of diversity follows upon plurality insofar as there remains with it the power (*virtus*) of its cause, namely, the radical opposition between being (*ens*) and non-being (*non ens*). The ultimate source of diversity is an entity's *esse proprium* whereby it is undivided in itself and divided from all others. Within this framework otherness is most properly considered as a concept which exerts formal causality in the mind designating two things as other; however, otherness being (the *esse* of an *ens*). Following this, the overall problem of individuation and Boethius' claim that the accident of place is responsible for numerical diversity are considered. The paper closes with a comment on Aquinas' relation to the "historical Boethius."*

1944 Wippel, John F. "The Condemnations of 1270 and 1277 at Paris." *The Journal of Medieval and Renaissance Studies* 7(1977): 169-201.

1945 Wippel, John F. "Metaphysics and *Separatio* According to Thomas Aquinas." *The Review of Metaphysics* 31(1978): 431-470.

1946 Wippel, John F. "Aquinas' Route to the Real Distinction: A Note on *De Ente et Essentia*." *The Thomist* 43(1979): 279-295.

1947 Wippel, John F. "Did Thomas Aquinas Defend the Possibility of an Eternally Created World? (The *De Aeternitate Mundi* Revisited)." *Journal of the History of Ideas* 19(1981): 21-38.

1948 Wippel, John F. "The Reality of Nonexisting Possibles According to Thomas Aquinas, Henry of Ghent, and Godfrey of Fontaines." *The Review of Metaphysics* 34(1981): 729-758.

1949 Wippel, John F. "The Quodilbetal Question as a Distinctive Literary Genre." *Les Genres Littéraires dans les Sources Thélogiques et Philosophiques Médiévales. Definition, Critique, et Exploitation.* 1982. 67-84.

1950 Wippel, John F. "Quidditative Knowledge of God According to Thomas Aquinas." *Graceful Reason: Essays in Ancient and Medieval Philosophy Presented to Joseph Owens on the Occasion of His Seventy-fifth Birthday and the Fiftieth Anniversary of His Ordination.* Ed. Lloyd P. Gerson. Papers in Mediaeval Studies 4. Toronto: Pontifical Institute of Mediaeval Studies, 1983. 273-299.

1951 Wippel, John F. "First Philosophy According to Thomas Aquinas." 1974. *Metaphysical Themes in Thomas Aquinas.* Studies in Philosophy and the History of Philosophy 10. Washington, DC: The Catholic University of America Press, 1984. 55-67.

1952 Wippel, John F. "Aquinas and Avicenna on the Relationship Between First Philosophy and the Other Theoretical Sciences (In *De Trin.*, Q. 5, A. 1, Ad 9)." 1973. *Metaphysical Themes in Thomas Aquinas.* Studies in Philosophy and the History of Philosophy 10. Washington, DC: The Catholic University of America Press, 1984. 37-53.

1953 Wippel, John F. "Divine Knowledge, Divine Power, and Human Freedom in Thomas Aquinas and Henry of Ghent." 1982. *Metaphysical Themes in Thomas Aquinas.* Studies in Philosophy and the History of Philosophy 10. Washington, DC: The Catholic University of America Press, 1984. 243-270.

1954 Wippel, John F. "Essence and Existence in the *De Ente*, Ch. 4." 1979. *Metaphysical Themes in Thomas Aquinas.* Studies in Philosophy and the History of Philosophy 10. Washington, DC: The Catholic University of America Press, 1984. 107-120.

1955 Wippel, John F. "Essence and Existence in Other Writings." *Metaphysical Themes in Thomas Aquinas*. Studies in Philosophy and the History of Philosophy 10. Washington, DC: The Catholic University of America Press, 1984. 133-161.

1956 Wippel, John F. "Metaphysics and *Separatio* in Thomas Aquinas." 1978. *Metaphysical Themes in Thomas Aquinas*. Studies in Philosophy and the History of Philosophy 10. Washington, DC: The Catholic University of America Press, 1984. 69-104.

1957 Wippel, John F. "Quidditative Knowledge of God." 1983. *Metaphysical Themes in Thomas Aquinas*. Studies in Philosophy and the History of Philosophy 10. Washington, DC: The Catholic University of America Press, 1984. 215-241.

1958 Wippel, John F. "The Possibility of a Christian Philosophy: A Thomistic Perspective." *Faith and Philosophy* 1(1984): 272-290.

1959 Wippel, John F. "Thomas Aquinas and the Problem of Christian Philosophy." 1965. *Metaphysical Themes in Thomas Aquinas*. Studies in Philosophy and the History of Philosophy 10. Washington, DC: The Catholic University of America Press, 1984. 1-33.

1960 Wippel, John F. "Thomas Aquinas on the Possibility of Eternal Creation." 1981. *Metaphysical Themes in Thomas Aquinas*. Studies in Philosophy and the History of Philosophy 10. Washington, DC: The Catholic University of America Press, 1984. 191-214.

1961 Wippel, John F. "Thomas Aquinas, Henry of Ghent, and Godfrey of Fontaines on the Reality of Nonexisting Possible." 1981. *Metaphysical Themes in Thomas Aquinas*. Studies in Philosophy and the History of Philosophy 10. Washington, DC: The Catholic University of America Press, 1984. 163-189.

1962 Wippel, John F. "Divine Knowledge, Divine Power and Human Freedom in Thomas Aquinas and Henry of Ghent." *Divine Omniscience and Omnipotence in Medieval Philosophy: Islamic, Jewish and Christian Perspectives*. Ed. Tamar Rudavsky. Synthese Historical Library 25. Dordrecht: D. Reidel Publishing Company, 1985. 213-241.

1963 Wippel, John F. "Thomas Aquinas on the Distinction and Derivation of the Many from the One: A Dialectic Between Being and Nonbeing." *The Review of Metaphysics* 38(1985): 563-590.

1964 Wippel, John F. "Quodlibetal Questions Chiefly in Theology Faculties." *Les Questions Disputées et les Questions Quodlibétiques dans les Facultés de Théologie de Droit et de Médecine*. Eds. Bernado C. Bazan et al. Turnhout: Brepols, 1985. 151-222.

1965 Wippel, John F. "Substance in Aquinas' Metaphysics." *Proceedings of the American Catholic Philosophical Association* 61(1987): 2-16.

1966 Wippel, John F. "Thomas Aquinas and Participation." *Studies in Medieval Philosophy*. Ed. John F. Wippel. Studies in Philosophy and the History of Philosophy 17. Washington, DC: The Catholic University of America Press, 1987. 117-158.

1967 Wippel, John F. "Thomas Aquinas on Substance as a Cause of Proper Accidents." *Philosophie Im Mittelalter: Entwicklungslinien und Paradigmen*. Eds. Jan P. Beckmann et al. Hamburg: Felix Meiner Verlag, 1987. 201-212.

1968 Wippel, John F. "Thomas Aquinas' Derivation of the Aristotelian Categories (Predicaments)." *Journal of the History of Philosophy* 25(1987): 13-34.

1969 Wippel, John F. "Thomas Aquinas and the Axiom 'What is Received is Received According to the Mode of the Receiver.'" 1971. *A Straight Path: Essays in Honor of Arthur Hyman*. Ed. R. Link-Salinger. Washington, DC: The Catholic University of America Press, 1988. 279-289.

1970 Wippel, John F. "Truth in Thomas Aquinas, Part I." *The Review of Metaphysics* 43(1989): 295-326.

1971 Wippel, John F. "Essence and Existence." 1982. *The Cambridge History of Later Medieval Philosophy: From the Rediscovery of Aristotle to the Disintegration of Scholasticism*. Eds. Norman Kretzmann, Anthony Kenny, and Jan Pinborg. Cambridge: Cambridge University Press, 1990. 385-410.

1972 Wippel, John F. "The Latin Avicenna as a Source of Thomas Aquinas' Metaphysics." *Freiburger Zeitschrift für Philosophie und Theologie* 37(1990): 51-90.

1973 Wippel, John F. "Truth in Thomas Aquinas, Part II." *The Review of Metaphysics* 43(1990): 543-567.

1974 Wolterstorff, Nicholas. "The Migration of the Theistic Arguments: From Natural Theology to Evidentialist Apologetics." *Rationality, Religious Belief, and Moral Commitment: New Essays in the Philosophy Religion*. Eds. Robert Audi and William J. Wainwright. Ithaca, NY: Cornell University Press, 1986. 38-81.

1975 Wood, Robert C. "Aquinas." *A Path Into Metaphysics Phenomenological, Hermeneutical, and Dialogical Studies*. Ed. Robert E. Wood. New York: State University of New York Press, 1990. 177-203.

1976 Woods, Martin T. "The Reduction of Essence in Aquinas and Husserl." *The Thomist* 53(1989): 443-460.

1977 Wörner, Markus H. "Eternity." *Irish Philosophical Journal* 6(1989): 3-26.
Contemporary interpretations of "eternity" in terms of sempiternity, omnitemporality, or atemporality are flawed if they do not primarily refer to "possession of life" (Boethius) or "having one's being" (Aquinas) as systematic starting points.

1978 Woznicki, Andrew Nicholas. "Dialogistic Thomism and Dialectical Materialism." *The New Scholasticism* 52(1978): 214-242.

1979 Woznicki, Andrew Nicholas. "Lublinism—A New Version of Thomism." *Proceedings of the American Catholic Philosophical Association* 60(1986): 23-37.

1980 Woznicki, Andrew Nicholas. "Rev. Thomism: Existential Personalism Viewed from Phenomenological Perspectives." *Existential Personalism*. Ed. Daniel O. Dahlstrom. 1986. 38-49.

1981 Woznicki, Andrew Nicholas. "Natural Sciences and Natural Philosophy of St. Thomas Aquinas." *Dialectical Humanism* 14(1987): 219-231.

*To resolve the conflicts which exist between sciences and philosophy, one must take into consideration the historical perspective of a given time. In this article the author examines the question of the codependency existing between natural philosophy and sciences in Thomas Aquinas in a two-fold way, i.e., his attitude towards both the natural sciences and the philosophy of natural sciences. In this regard the author argues that, although St. Thomas did not always *de facto* distinguish between natural philosophy and sciences, nevertheless this distinction can be *de jure* justified in Aquinas' doctrine.*

1982 Woznicki, Andrew Nicholas. "The Order of Being and Truth in St. Thomas and Heidegger." *Proceedings of the American Catholic Philosophical Association* 62(1988): 157-164.

*In order of being and truth, there is, according to St. Thomas, a mutual reference based on their transcendental characteristics of reality. In his analysis of the mutual reference between being and truth, Aquinas gives the priority of being over truth, if it is considered in the ontological order, but then he attributes the priority of truth over being if it is considered in the cognitive order. This article presents the existential and ontological foundation of being and truth as exemplified in the metaphysics of *esse* by Aquinas and the ontological phenomenology of Dasein by Heidegger.*

1983 Wyschogrod, M. "A Jewish Reading of St. Thomas Aquinas on the Old Law." *Understanding Scripture*. Eds. C. Thoma and M. Wyschogrod. 1987. 125-138.

1984 Yaffe, M. "Providence in Medieval Aristotelianism: Moses Maimonides and Thomas Aquinas on the *Book of Job*." *Hebrew Studies* 20-21(1979-1980): 62-74.

1985 Yearley, Lee H. "A Comparison Between Classical Chinese Thought and Thomistic Christian Thought." *Journal of the American Academy of Religion* 51(1983): 427-458.

1986 Zagzebski, Linda. "Divine Foreknowledge and Human Free Will." *Religious Studies* 21(1985): 279-298.

1987 Zedler, Beatrice Hope. "Why Are the Possibles Possible?" *The New Scholasticism* 55(1981): 113-130.

*This is a reply to an article by Lawrence Dewan in "St. Thomas and the Possibles" (*New Scholasticism*, Winter 1979). Fr. Dewan questions some statements about St. Thomas in my article, "Another Look at Avicenna" (*New Scholasticism*, 1976). In "Why are the Possibles Possible?" the context of those statements is pointed out: that is, the contrast of the positions of Avicenna and St. Thomas. That a thing be-able-to-be also requires a Being Who can freely will to create it. The inclusion of existential as well as essential possibility in the very meaning of the possible distinguishes the view of St. Thomas from that of Avicenna.*

1988 Zellner, Harold. "The Third Way: The Opening Move." *Philosophy Research Archives* 6(1980): 43-64.

B. FRENCH

1989 Aduszkiewicz, Adam. "Le Beau et L'amour dans la Pensée Philosophique de Saint Thomas D'Aquin." *SPC* 21(1985): 9-22.

1990 Anawati, Georges C. "Théologie Musulmane et Théologie de S. Thomas: Quelques Thémes Comparés." *Année Charniére—Mutations et Continuités*. Ed. Colloques internationaux du Centre national de la recherche scientifique. Paris: Éditions du Centre national de la rechereche scientifique, 1977. 105-115.

1991 Anawati, Georges C. "Saint Thomas D'Aquin et les Penseurs Arabes: Les Loquentes in Lege Maurorum et Leur Philosophie de la Nature." *La Philosophie de la Nature de Saint Thomas D'Aquin*. Ed. Léon Elders. Studi Tomistici 18. Cittá del Vaticano, Pontificia Accademia di San Tommaso: Libreria Editrice Vaticana, 1982. 155-171.

1992 Andujar, Eduardo. "La Loi et le Droit Naturel Chez Saint Thomas: Une Bibliographie." *De Philosophia* 3(1982): 10-32.

1993 Antoniotti, Louise-Marie. "Le Prémotion Divine: Saint Thomas D'Aquin et L'auteur Du *Liber de Causis*." *Atti Dell'VIII Congresso Tomistico Internazionale VIII: San Tommaso Nella Storia del Pensiero*. Studi Tomistici 17. Cittá del Vaticano: Pontificia Accademia di San Tommaso e di Religione Cattolica, 1982. 60-70.

1994 Antoniotti, Louise-Marie. "L'étant, L'essence et L'être." *Revue Thomiste* 90(1990): 289-306.

1995 Armogathe, Jean R. "Les Sources Scolastiques Du Temps Cartésien: Eléments D'un Débat." *Revue Internationale de Philosophie* 37(1983): 326-336.

1996 Aubert, Jean-Marie. "La Morale Chrétienne Selon Saint Thomas." *Saint Thomas Aquinas in hodierna formatione sacerdotali: Seminarium* 29(1977): 780-811.

1997 Aubert, Jean-Marie. "La Fonction Éthique de la Représentation Selon Saint Thomas D'Aquin." *Actes Du XVIII Congrés Des Sociétés de Philosophie de Langue Française*. Strasbourg: Université des Sciences Humaines de Strasbourg, 1982. 90-95.

1998 Aubert, Jean-Marie. "Le Monde Physique en Tant Que Totalité et la Causalité Universelle Selon Saint Thomas D'Aquin." *La Philosophie de la Nature de Saint Thomas D'Aquin: Actes Du Symposium sur la Pensée de Saint Thomas*. Ed. Léon Elders. Studi Tomistici 18. Cittá del Vaticano: Pontificia Accademia di San Tommaso, Libreria Editrice Vaticana, 1982. 82-106.

1999 Aubert, Jean-Marie. "Nature de la Relation Entre Lex Nova et Lex Naturalis Chez Saint Thomas D'Aquin." *Atti Dell'VIII Congresso Tomistico Internazionale VI: Morale e Diritto Nella Prospettiva Tomistica*. Studi Tomistici 15. Cittá del Vaticano: Pontificia Accademia di San Tommaso e di Religione Cattolica, 1982. 34-38.

2000 Aubert, Jean-Marie. "Sociéte et Libertés Individuelles dans la Doctrine de Saint Thomas D'Aquin sur le Bien Commun." *Le Supplément* 155(1985): 7-13.

2001 Aubert, Jean-Marie. "L'analogie Entre la Lex Nova et la Loi Naturelle." *Lex et Libertas: Freedom and Law According to St. Thomas Aquinas*. Ed. L. J. Elders and K. Hedwig. Studi Tomistici 30. Città del Vaticano: Pontificia Accademia di San Tommaso e di Religione Cattolica, 1987. 248-253.

2002 Aubert, Jean-Marie. "Subtil et Subtilite Chez Saint Thomas D'Aquin." *Revue du Moyen Age Latin* 44(1989): 6-13.

2003 Baertschi, Bernard. "*Sensus Est Quodammodo Ipsa Sensibilia*: Le Réalisme Aristotélicien et le Probéme Des Erreurs Des Sens." *Revue de Théologie et de Philosophie* 118(1986): 237-253.

The author tries to elucidate a problem that comes from Aristotle's conception of sense knowledge when confronted with his description of sense illusions. For this philosopher, sensation consists in the reception of the object's form. But in illusions, this is not the case: the experienced form is not identical with the object's form. It is possible, however, to explain this difficulty away by distinguishing three types of forms in the process of sensation (object, medium, and sense). Texts of Aristotle and Aquinas are afforded to sustain this point of view.

2004 Balmés, Marc. "A Propos D'une Lecture Nouvelle de Saint Thomas." *Revue de Théologie et de Philosophie* 11(1979): 173-184.

2005 Barré, Michel. "Pour une Philosophie de la Religion Selon L'esprit de Saint Thomas et de Jacques Maritain." *Atti Dell'VIII Congresso Tomistico Internazionale VIII: San Tommaso Nella Storia del Pensiero*. Studi Tomistici 17. Cittá del Vaticano: Pontificia Accademia di San Tommaso e di Religione Cattolica, 1982. 272-284.

2006 Barreto de Macedo, José Silvio. "L'amour et Sa Fonction Cognitive dans la Philosophie Thomiste." *Tommaso D'Aquino Nel Suo Settimo Centenario: Atti del Congresso Internazionale VII: L'Uomo*. Napoli: Edizioni Domenicane Italiane, 1978. 368-374.

2007 Barrois, G. Antoine. "Saint Thomas Du Créateur." *Itinéraires* 214(1977): 117-124.

2008 Bastait's, Marc M. "*Similitudo Sensibilis* Chez Aristotle, Avicenne et Saint Thomas." *L'homme et Son Univers Au Moyen Age: Actes Du Septiéme Congrés International de Philosophie Médiéval II*. Ed. Christian Wenin. Philosophes Médiévaux 26-27. Louvain-la-Neuve: Éditions de l'Institut Supérieur de Philosophie, 1986. 554-559.

2009 Bataillon, Louis-Jacques. "Status Quaestionis sur les Instruments et Techniques de Travail de Saint Thomas et Saint Bonaventure." *Année Charniére—Mutations et Continuités: Colloques Internationaux Du Centre National de la Recherche Scientifique*. Paris: Éditions du Centre national de la rechereche scientifique, 1977. 647-657.

2010 Bataillon, Louis-Jacques. "La Commission Léoine A Grottaferrata(1973-1977)." *Archivum Franciscanum Historicum* 70(1977): 569-571.

2011 Bataillon, Louis-Jacques. "Problémes Posés par L'ed. Critique Des Textes Latins Médiévaux." *Revue Philosophique de Louvain* 75(1977): 234-250.

New technical procedures, and particularly the use of informatics, have and will continue to furnish valuable aid to the Ed.s of mediaeval texts. The works of the latter will have to take more and more into account, in regard to works later than the start of the 13rd century, the possible use of the "pecia" process; for works transmitted in this way a piece-by-piece study is necessary as a rule: each piece is liable to have been damaged and restored; several sets of pieces may have been in use differently in each individual case. For a considerable number of texts, honest but not fully critical ed.s would be sufficient.

2012 Bataillon, Louis-Jacques. "Bulletin D'histoire Des Doctrines Médiévales III: Le Haut Moyen Age." *Revue des Sciences Philosophiques et Théologiques* 61(1977): 605-623.

2013 Bataillon, Louis-Jacques. "Bulletin D'histoire Des Doctrines Médiévales: Le Treiziéme Siécle." *Revue des Sciences Philosophiques et Théologiques* 63(1979): 83-108.

2014 Bataillon, Louis-Jacques. "Bulletin D'histoire Des Doctrines Médiévales. Le Treiziéme Siécle (Suite)." *Revue des Sciences Philosophiques et Théologiques* 64(1980): 101-131.

2015 Bataillon, Louis-Jacques. "L'édition Léonine Des Oeuvres de Saint Thomas et les Études Médiévales." *Atti Dell'VIII Congresso Tomistico Internazionale I*. Ed. L'enciclica *Aeterni Patris* nell'arco di un secolo. Studi Tomistici 10. Cittá del Vaticano: Pontificia Accademia di San Tommaso e di Religione Cattolica, 1981. 452-464.

2016 Bataillon, Louis-Jacques. "Bulletin D'historie Des Doctrines Mediévales: La Fin Du Moyen Age." *Revue des Sciences Philosophiques et Théologiques* 65(1981): 455-481.

2017 Bataillon, Louis-Jacques. "Bulletin D'historie Des Doctrines Mediévales: Le Treiziemé Siécle." *Revue des Sciences Philosophiques et Théologiques* 65(1981): 101-122.

2018 Bataillon, Louis-Jacques, ed. "Fragments de Sermons de Gérard D'Abbeville: Eudes de Rosny et Thomas D'Aquin." *Archives d'Histoire Doctrinale et Littéraire du Moyen Age* 51(1984): 257-268.

2019 Bataillon, Louis-Jacques. "Les Sermons Attribués A Saint Thomas: Questions D'authenticité." *Thomas von Aquin: Werk und Wirkung Im Licht Neuerer Forschungen*. Ed. Albert Zimmermann. Miscellanea Mediaevalia 19. Berlin/New York: Walter de Gruyter, 1988. 323-341.

2020 Bataillon, Louis-Jacques. "Bulletin D'histoire Des Doctrines Médiévales. Le Treiziéme Siécle: Thomas D'Aquin." *Revue des Sciences Philosophiques et Théologiques* 73(1989): 585-604.

2021 Bazán, Bernardo Carlos. "Précisions sur la Doctrine de L'intelligence Selon Thomas D'Aquin." *Sprache und Erkenntnis Im Mittelalter II*. Eds. Jan P. Beckmann et al. Miscellanea Mediaevalia 13/2. Berlin: Walter de Gruyter, 1981. 1066-1073.

2022 Bazán, Bernardo Carlos. "La Corporalité Selon Saint Thomas." *Revue Philosophique de Louvain* 81(1983): 369-409.

2023 Bazán, Bernardo Carlos. "Le Commentaire de Saint Thomas D'Aquin sur le Traité de L'âme: Un Événement— L'édition de la Commission Léonine." *Revue des Sciences Philosophiques et Théologiques* 69(1985): 521-547.

2024 Bednarski, Feliks Wojciech. "Les Fondements de L'éducation Sociale Selon St. Thomas D'Aquin." *Roczniki Filozoficzne: Etyka*. Lublin: Towarzystwo Naukowe Katolickiego Uniwersytetu Lubelskiego, 1978. 109-123.

2025 Bednarski, Feliks Wojciech. "La Psychologie de L'agressivité A la Lumiére de la Psychosynthése de Saint Thomas D'Aquin." *Angelicum* 58(1981): 384-419.

2026 Bedouelle, J. -J., and M. -M. Labourdette. "Bulletin D'historire de L'église." *Revue Thomiste* 79(1979): 315-340.

2027 Belmans, Théo G. "La Spécification de L'agir Humain par Son Objet Chez Saint Thomas D'Aquin, I." *Divinitas* (Roma) 22(1978): 336-356.

2028 Belmans, Théo G. "La Spécification de L'agir Humain par Son Objet Chez Saint Thomas D'Aquin, II." *Divinitas* (Roma) 23(1979): 7-61.

2029 Belmans, Théo G. "Autour Du Probléme de la Défense Légitime de Saint Thomas." *Atti Dell'VIII Congresso Tomistico Internazionale: Morale e Diritto Nella Prospettiva Tomistica*. Studi Tomistici 15. Cittá del Vaticano: Pontificia Accademia di San Tommaso e di Religione Cattolica, 1982. 162-170.

2030 Belmans, Théo G. "Saint Thomas et la Notion de Moindre Mal Moral." *Revue Thomiste* 83(1983): 40-58.

Is it allowed to choose the minor of two sins in a conflict situation? Some authors seem to be convinced that Thomas Aquinas would not oppose himself to an affirmative answer to this question, and logically, that contraceptive devices could be justified to save a marriage that otherwise would probably break down. That this does by no means correspond to Thomas' thinking is demonstrated in the paper.

2031 Belmans, Théo G. "Le Volontarisme de Saint Thomas D'Aquin." *Revue Thomiste* 85(1985): 181-196.

2032 Belmans, Théo G. "L'immutabilité de la Loi Natureele Selon Saint Thomas D'Aquin." *Revue Thomiste* 87(1987): 23-44.

*Modern moralists want us to believe that norms of "natural law" underlie a continual change because of the socio-cultural evolution of humanity throughout history. This is by no means what Thomas Aquinas teaches us. As our very nature (*natura speciel*) does not change at all, he says, natural law will never lose its binding force on men. But as a result of sin, every human being (*natura individui*) finds itself exposed to the danger of deprivation of its will.*

2033 Belmans, Théo G. "Au Croisement Des Chemins en Morale Fondamentale." *Revue Thomiste* 89(1989): 264-278.

*As for me, the widespread neo-Thomistic theory of a double judgment of conscience should be struck out of our manuals of fundamental morals. Indeed, the term of "prudence" used by Thomas reveals itself as equivalent of "right reason"; moreover, speaking of *judicium electionis*, he does not mean any judgment at all in the cognitive sense of the word; what is really meant is the decision of the will itself, whose congenital defectibility explains the possibility of sinful choices. The very significant synonyms of "error" or even *ignorantia electionis* might enable us to establish the genuine thought of the Doctor Communis.*

2034 Bernath, Klaus. "Bibliographie." *Thomas von Aquin Bd I: Chronologie und Werkanalyse*. Ed. Klaus Bernath. Wege der Forschung 188. Darmstadt: Wissenschaftliche Buchgesellschaft, 1978. 471-482.

2035 Bodéüs, Richard. "L'influence de L'histoire Des Doctrines Grecques sur L'anthropologie Thomiste." *Actes Du Septiéme Congrés International de Philosophie Médiéval: L'homme et Son Univers Au Moyen Age I*. Ed. Christian Wenin. Philosophes Médiévaux 26-27. Louvain-la-Neuve: Éditions de l'Institut Supérieur de Philosophie, 1986. 252-289.

2036 Bonamy-Manteau, H. M. "La Liberté de L'homme Selon Thomas D'Aquin (La Datation de la *Q. Disp. De Malo*)." *Archives d'Histoire Doctrinale et Littéraire du M. â Paris* 46(1979): 7-34.

2037 Borella, Jean. "La Doctrine Thomiste de la Valeur." *Pensée Catholique* 188(1980): 76-80.

2038 Borella, Jean. "Situation de la Politique dans la Pensée de Saint Thomas D'Aquin." *Pensée Catholique* 200(1982): 30-41.

2039 Borresen, Kari Elisabeth. "L'Anthropologie Théologique D'Augustin et de Thomas D'Aquin." *Recherches de Science Religieuse* 69(1983) 393-406.

2040 Bossier, F. "Une Traduction Fragmentaire Du Commentaire Au *De Caelo* de Simplicius et Son Influence sur *Le Commentaire In Metaphysicam* de Thomas D'Aquin. *Recherches de Science Religieuse* 69(1981): 168-172.

2041 Bougerol, Jacques-Guy. "Saint Thomas D'Aquin et Saint Bonaventure Fréres Amis." *Année Charniére—Mutations et Continuités: Colloques Internationaux Du Centre National de la Recherche Scientifique*. Paris: Éditions du Centre national de la rechereche scientifique, 1977. 741-747.

2042 Boyer, Charles. "Le Sens D'un Texte de Saint Thomas: *De Veritate*, Q. 1, A. 9." *Doctor Communis* 31(1978): 3-19.

2043 Breton, Stanislas. "L'unité de L'intellect: Réflexions sur le Sens et la Portée D'une Controverse." *Revue des Sciences Philosophiques et Théologiques* 62(1978): 225-233.

*Reading of the *De unitate intellectus contra Averroistas* of Saint Thomas Aquinas. The article sums up, first, the position of Averroes, commentator on Aristotle, concerning the intellect: immaterial, it cannot be individualized, it is common to all and is thus one and unique. Then it details the objections, philosophers, summoned up by Saint Thomas to counter these positions which contradict the Catholic doctrine of personal immortality.*

2044 Briot, Emilio. "Infinité et Omniprésence Divines: Thomas D'Aquin et Hegel." *Giornale di Metafisica* 11(1989): 163-190.

2045 Brito, Emilio. "Connaissance et Inconnaissance de Dieu Selon Thomas D'Aquin et Hegel." *Ephemerides Theologicae Lovanienses* 63(1987): 327-353.

2046 Brito, Emilio. "Dieu en Mouvement? Thomas D'Aquin et Hegel." *Revue des Sciences Philosophiques et Théologiques* 62(1988): 111-136.

2047 Brito, Emilio. "Dieu Est-il Simple? Thomas D'Aquin et Hegel." *Nouvelle Revue Théologique* 110(1988): 514-536.

2048 Brito, Emilio. "La Puissance Divine: Thomas D'Aquin et Hegel." *Rivista di Filosofia Neo-Scolastica* 80(1988): 549-579.

2049 Brito, Emilio. "Nommer Dieu: Thomas D'Aquin et Hegel." *Revue Théologique de Louvain* 19(1988): 160-190.

2050 Brito, Emilio. "Infinité et Omniprésence Divines: Thomas D'Aquin et Hegel." *Giornale di Metafisica* 11(1989): 163-190.

2051 Brito, Emilio. "La Volonté en Dieu: Thomas D'Aquin et Hegel." *Revue Philosophique de Louvain* 87(1989): 391-426.

The present study compares the Thomist doctrine of the will in God with the Hegelian theory of the will of the Idea and of the freedom of the Spirit. Hegel's Idea, which unlike Thomas' God, lacks any truly ecstatic volitional tendency, articulates only the assimilating moment of the self-knowledge of the absolute Spirit. But Thomas does not sufficiently show the link between divine freedom, which Hegel is wrong to deny, and the necessary rationality of divine freedom, which Hegel perceived in depth. Hence an attempt has been made, finally, to decipher the absoluteness of freedom in conciliating the Thomist projection of possibles with the Hegelian introjection of necessity.

2052 Browne, M. -D. "L'authenticité Du Commentaire de Saint Thomas sur *La Politique* D'Aristote." 1920. *Thomas von Aquin*. Ed. Klaus Bernath. Darmstadt: Wissenschaftliche Buchgesellschaft, 1978. 24-33.

2053 Bruges, J. -L. "La Loi Morale et la Formation Du Jugement Moral Chez S. Thomas D'Aquin." *Universalité et Permanence Des Lois Morales (Etudes D'Ethique Chrétienne)*. Eds. S. Pinckaers and C. J. Pinto de Oliveira. Studien Zur Theologischen Ethik 16. Fribourg (Suisse): Éditions Universitaires, 1986. 136-148.

2054 Brugger, Walter. "*Index Thomisticus*." *Theologie und Philosophie* 52(1977): 435-444.

2055 Brunet, Louis. "Le Sujet de la Logique Selon Saint Thomas D'Aquin." *Angelicum* 58(1981): 55-72.

2056 Busa, Roberto. "Ordo dans les Oeuvres de St. Thomas D'Aquin." *Ordo*. Ed. Marta Fattori and Massimo Bianchi. Roma: Edizioni dell'Ateneo & Bizzarri, 1979. 59-184.

2057 Busa, Roberto. "L'originalité Linguistique de Saint Thomas D'Aquin." *Archivum Latinitatis Medii Aevi* 44-45(1983-1985): 65-90.

2058 Busa, Roberto. "L'ontologie Générative Chez Saint Thomas D'Aquin." *Actes Du Septiéme Congrés International de Philosophie Médiéval: L'homme et Son Univers Au Moyen Age II*. Ed. Christian Wenin. Philosophes Médiévaux 26-27. Louvain-la-Neuve: Éditions de l'Institut Supérieur de Philosophie, 1986. 496-504.

2059 Bush, William. "Raïssa Maritain et Jacques." *Understanding Maritain*. Ed. Deal W. Hudson. Macon, GA: Mercer University, 1987. 57-70.

2060 Cabral, Roque. "Réflexions sur la Prudence: Aristotle, Saint Thomas, Aujourd'hui." *Tommaso Nel Suo Settimo Centenario V: Atti del Congresso Internazionale: L'agire Morale*. Napoli: Edizioni Domenicane Italiane, 1977. 403-408.

2061 Cardonnel, Sylvain. "Principe de la Connaissance Chez Saint Thomas D'Aquin D'aprés le Commentaire D'étienne Gilson." *Journal Philosophique* 1(1985): 164-169.

2062 Cattin, Yves. "De L'homme Humain: La Question de L'homme dans la Pensée de Thomas D'Aquin." *Revue de Théologique et de Philosophie* 121(1989): 1-25.

La foi chrétienne affirme que l'homme accéde à la plénitude de son humanité dans l'acte gratuit du salut réalisé en Christ. Thomas d'Aquin pense qu'il y a une certaine précédence de l'humanité de l'homme par rapport au salut. L'homme accéde à son humanité dans l'acte par lequel il s'ouvre à un monde en se posant comme sujet. Dés lors, le mot "humain" dont on qualifie l'homme n'est pas univoque mais analogue. Une telle anthropologie, que l'auteur de cette Étude rappelle à partir des textes fondamentaux de Thomas d'Aquin, apparaît comme la condition de possibilité de l'ontologie et elle permet le dialogue de la foi avec l'incroyance.

2063 Cauchy, Venant. "A Propos Du De Interpretatione: Aristotle et Thomas D'Aquin." *Proceedings of the World Congress on Aristotle* 2(1981): 276-280.

2064 Charette, Léon. "Droit Naturel et Droit Positif Chez Saint Thomas D'Aquin." *Philosophiques* 8(1981): 113-130.

2065 Charette, Léon. "Quelques Considérations sur la Méthode de la Philosophie Morale Selon Saint Thomas D'Aquin." *Revue de l'Universíte d'Ottawa* 53(1983): 135-146.

2066 Charette, Léon. "La Phénoménologie et la Théorie de L'abstraction Selon Jacques Maritain." *Jacques Maritain: Philosophe dans la Cité/ A Philosopher in the World*. Ed. Jean-Louis Allard. Philosophica 28. Ottawa: University of Ottawa Press, 1985. 103-112. Proceedings of the International Congress of Ottawa on Jacques Maritain.

2067 Chenu, Marie-Dominique. "Der Plan der *Summa*." 1939. *Thomas von Aquin: Chronologie und Werkanalyse*. Ed. Klaus Bernath. Wege der Forschung 188. Darmstadt: Wissenschaftliche Buchgesellschaft, 1978. 173-195.

2068 Chenu, Marie-Dominique. "L'interpréte de Saint Thomas D'Aquin." *Etienne Gilson et Nous: La Philosophie et Son Histoire*. Eds. M. -Th. D'Alvery and P. Aubenque. Bibliothéque D'histoire de la Philosophie. Paris: J. Vrin, 1980. 43-48.

2069 Chenu, Marie-Dominique. "Un Ecole de Theologie: Le Saulchoir." *Une Ecole de Theologie*. Ed. G. Alberigo. 1985. 91-176.

2070 Clément, Marcel. "Est-ce la Méme Chose D'être Thomiste Ou D'être Disciple de Saint Thomas." *Atti Dell'VIII Congresso Tomistico Internazionale VIII: San Tommaso Nella Storia del Pensiero*. Studi Tomistici 17. Cittá del Vaticano: Pontificia Accademia di San Tommaso e di Religione Cattolica, 1982. 396-404.

2071 Comparot, Andrée. "Montaigne, Lecteur de Thomas D'Aquin." *Cahiers de Philosophie Politique et Juridique* 6(1984): 75-99.

2072 Congar, Yves. "Orientations de Bonaventure et Surtout de Thomas D'Aquin dans Leur Vision de L'église et Celle de L'état." *Année Charniére—Mutations et Continuités: Colloques Internationaux Du Centre National de la Recherche Scientifique*. Paris: Éditions du Centre national de la rechereche scientifique, 1977. 691-708.

2073 Congar, Yves. "Le Saint Esprit dans le Théologie Thomiste de L'agir Moral." *Atti del Congresso Internazionale. Tommaso D'Aquino Nel Suo Settimo Centenario V: L'agire Morale*. Napoli: Edizioni Donemicane, 1977. 9-19.

2074 Contat, Alain. "Réalisme de L'être et Structure de la Métaphysique." *Doctor Communis* 39(1986): 107-12. Reprinted L. J. Elders, *Die Metaphysik des Thomas von Aquin, I: Das ens commune*, 184-201.

2075 Corbin, Michel. "Le Pain de la Vie, la Lecture de Jean VI par Saint Thomas D'Aquin." *Recherches de science Religieuse* 65(1977): 107-138.

2076 Corbin, Michel. "La Parole Devenue Chair: Lecture de la Premiére Question de La Tertia Pars de la *Somme Théologique*." *Revue des Sciences Philosophiques et Théologiques* 62(1978): 5-40.

*The author studies the successive and conjunct modifications of the arguments of conveyance and the structures of the treatise on the Incarnation throughout Saint Thomas' itinerary. It is proposed to contest the habit of reducing the place of Christ in the *Summa Theologia* to a simple redemptive causality. An attentive reading of the first question of the *Tertia Pars* of the *Summa Theologica* establishes that the habitual opposition between Incarnation and Redemption is found to be surpassed in the discovery of the Pascal Mystery of Jesus as the manifestation and reality of the always greater God. The Christology is then quite other than a mere appendix: the *consummatio totius theologici negotii*, keystone and principle of all theology.*

2077 Corbin, Michel. "L'homme Passe L'homme: Essai sur L'éthique Théologique Chez Saint Thomas D'Aquin." *Ethique, Religion et Foi: Travaux de L'U. E. R. de Théologie et de Sciences Religieuses*. Ed. J. Doré. Le Point Théologique 43. Paris: Beauchesne, 1985. 155-193.

2078 Corvez, M. "La Quatriéme Voie Vers L'existence de Dieu Selon Saint Thomas." *Quinque Sunt Viae*. Ed. Léon Elders. Studi Tomistici 9. Città del Vaticano, Pontificia Accademia di San Tommaso: Libreria Editrice Vaticana, 1980. 75-83.

2079 Corvez, M. "La Quartriéme Voie Vers L'existence de Dieu Selon Saint Thomas." *Nouvelle Revue Théologique* 103(1981): 375-384.

2080 Costantini, Elio. "Persona e Teoria Della Conoscenza in S. Tommaso e Rosmini." *Tommaso D'Aquino Nel Suo Settimo Centenario: Atti del Congresso Internazionale*. Napoli: Edizioni Domenicane Italiane, 1978.

2081 Cottier, Georges. "Philosopher Sous le Ciel de la Foi." *Nova et Vetera (Genéve)* 53(1978): 260-278.

2082 Cottier, Georges. "L'individu comme Personne Responsable." *Studia Philosophica*, Switzerland 13(1987): 331-346.

2083 Cottier, Georges. "*Intellectus et Ratio*." *Revue Thomiste* 88(1988): 215-228.

2084 Courtine, Jean-François. "Philosophie et Théologie. Remarque sur la Situation Aristotélicienne de la Détermination Thomiste de la Theologia (*S. Th.* Ia, Qu. 1, A. 1 et 5)." *Revue Philosophique de Louvain* 84(1986): 315-344.

2085 Courtois, Gérard. "La Loi Chez Spinoza et Saint Thomas D'Aquin." *Archives de Philosophie du Droit* 25(1980): 159-189.

2086 Daujat, Jean. "Corruption et Salut de L'intelligence." *Thomas Aquinas* (Annevoie, Belgique) 2(1983): 1-6.

2087 De Contenson, Pierre Marie. "L'édition Critique Des Oeuvres de Saint Thomas D'Aquin: Principes, Méthodes, Problémes et Perspectives." *Hilfswissenschaften und Quellenkunde*. Eds. Ludwig Hödl and Dieter Wuttke. Boppard: H. B. Verlag, 1978. 55-74.

2088 De Finance, Joseph. "L'échelle Des Consciences Chez Bergson et Chez Saint Thomas." *Scritti in Onore Di N. Petuzzellis*. 93-103.

2089 De Finance, Joseph. "La Métaphysique de Saint Thomas dans le Contexte Sprituel de Notre Temps." *Saint Thomas Aquinas in hodierna formatione sacerdotali: Seminarium* 29(1977): 699-723.

2090 De Finance, Joseph. "La Foi Bienfaitrice de la Raison: Réflexions sur la Doctrine Thomiste de la Volonté." *Cahiers I. P. C. Faculté libre de philosophie comparée* 23(1980): 25-47.

2091 De Finance, Joseph. "La Foi Bienfaitrice de la Raison: Réfexions sur la Doctrine de la Volonté Saint Thomas." *Cahiers I. P. C. Faculté libre de philosophie comparée* 23(1980): 25-46.

2092 De Finance, Joseph. "La Foi Bienfaitrice de la Raison: Réflexions sur la Doctrine Thomiste de la Volonté." *Atti Dell'VIII Congresso Tomistico Internazionale I: L'enciclica Aeterni Patris Nell'arco Di Un Secolo*. Studi Tomistici 10. Cittá del Vaticano: Pontificia Accademia di San Tommaso e di Religione Cattolica, 1981. 380-393.

2093 De Finance, Joseph. "Les Degrés de L'être Chez Saint Thomas D'Aquin." *Analecta Husserliana*. Ed. Angela Bello. Dordrecht: Reidel, 1981. 51-57.

The degrees of being can be considered either as classes of beings or as ontological levels in the same being. As classes, they are ordered, in the material world, upward according to their distance from matter, in the spiritual world, downward, according to their distance from the principle which they participate of. In the same being, degrees are not really distinct. Does Aquinas admit a true analogy between the degrees of being?

2094 De Finance, Joseph. "Vision Du Monde et Métaphysique: Une Philosophie Qui Se Veut Thomiste Peut-elle Accueillir L'évolution?" *Gregorianum* 63(1982): 419-451.

*Un thomisme cohérent peut-il intégrer l'evolution comme il avait jadis intégré la génération spontanée? L'auteur distingue "metaphysique," science rationnelle de l'être, et "vision du monde," intégrant des Éléments, non encore rationalisés. L'évolution contredit la vision thomiste du monde amputée de la doctrine des corps célestes, admise par saint Thomas, mais elle peut s'intéger dans la métaphysique thomiste de l'*esse*, qui Échappe au fixisme de la métaphysique de le forme.*

2095 De Finance, Joseph. "L'*esse* dans la Philosophie Chrétienne d' Etienne Gilson." *Doctor Communis* 38(1985): 269-278.

2096 De Grijs, Ferdinand. "La *Summa Theologiae* Traduite en Français." *Bijdragen* 47(1986): 421-435.

2097 De Groglie, Guy. "La Doctrine de Saint Thomas sur le Fondement Communautaire de la Chasteté." *Tommaso Nel Suo Settimo Centenario V: Atti del Congresso Internazionale: L'agire Morale*. Napoli: Edizioni Domenicane Italiane, 1977. 297-307.

2098 De Koninck, Thomas. "Réflexions sur L'intelligence." *Jacques Maritain: The Man and His Metaphysics*. Ed. John F. X. Knasas. Mishawaka, IN: The American Maritain Association, 1988. 55-67.

2099 De La Soujeole, Benoît-Dominique. "Société et Communion Chez Saint Thomas D'Aquin." *Revue Thomiste* 90(1990): 587-622.

2100 De Ligny, Jean-Bernard. "Saint Thomas Sépare-t-il L'appréhension Du Jugement?" *Bulletin du Cercle Thomiste* 102(1984): 1-22.

2101 De Ligny, Jean-Bernard. "Saint Thomas Sépare-t-il L'appréhension Du Jugement?" *Bulletin du Cercle Thomiste* 103(1984): 1-31.

2102 De Ligny, Jean-Bernard. "Saint Thomas Sépare-t-il L'appréhension Du Jugement?" *Bulletin du Cercle Thomiste* 104-105(1984): 1-29.

2103 De Margerie, Bertrand. "L'objet, L'ordre et les Cheminements de la Révélation: Commentaire D'un Chapitre de la *Somme Contre les Gentils* (III. 154) A la Lumiére Des Autres Oeuvres de Saint Thomas D'Aquin." *Divus Thomas* 87(1984): 3-47.

2104 De Margerie, Bertrand. "La Relation Religieuse avec Dieu, Totalisation de Toutes les Relations Humaines Selon Saint Thomas D'Aquin (*In Boetium de Trinitate*, Lect 1, Quaest. 1, A. (2)." *Journal Philosophique* 1(1985): 90-100.

2105 De Margerie, Bertrand. "L'animal Irrationnel, Symbole de la Condition Historique de la Personne Humaine Chez Saint Thomas D'Aquin." *Journal Philosophique* 9(1986): 268-275.

2106 De Margerie, Bertrand. "Rôle Des Images et de L'imagination Reproductrice et Créatrice dans L'exposition de la Pensée Philosophique et Théologique de Saint Thomas D'Aquin. Artiste de la Pensée." *Journal Philosophique* 7(1986): 116-133.

2107 De Margerie, Bertrand. "De L'intuition Sensible de Mon Être Corporel par la Déduction Des Etres Immatériels-mon Ame et Dieu-vers L'intuition Spirituelle de Dieu en Mon Ame et de Mon Ame en Dieu: Que Dirait Aujourd'hui Saint Thomas A Un Jeune Agnostique?" *Journal Philosophique* 12(1987): 35-47.

2108 De Margerie, Bertrand. "L'âme Humaine Selon Thomas le Théologie." *L'anima Nell'antropologia Di San Tommaso D'Aquino IX: Atti del Congresso Societá Internazionale San Tommaso D'Aquino*. Ed. Abelardo Lobato. Milano: Editrice Massimo, 1987. 181-200.

2109 De Margerie, Bertrand. "La Connaissance Rationnelle de Dieu dans la Pensée de Saint Thomas D'Aquin." *Divus Thomas* 91(1988): 23-71.

2110 De Medeiros, François. "Les Cultures Africaines Face A la Pensée de Saint Thomas." *Année Charniére—Mutations et Continuités: Colloques Internationaux Du Centre National de la Recherche Scientifique*. Paris: Éditions du Centre national de la rechereche scientifique, 1977. 769-777.

2111 De Monleon, Jacques. "La Présence de Dieu dans les Etres." *Cahiers de l'Ecole Saint Jean* 106(1985): 47-52.

2112 De Monleon, Jacques. "Les Anges." *Cahiers de l'Ecole Saint Jean* 106(1985): 53-58.

2113 De Muralt, André. "La Doctrine Médiévale Des Distinctions et L'intelligibilité de la Philosophie Moderne I." *Revue de Théologie et de Philosophie* 30(1980): 113-131.

Cette Étude montre que la philosophie moderne de Descartes á Kant est régie par les structures de pensée issues du scotisme médieval interprété par Occam. Aprés une analyse des distinctions réele, de raison et formelle, défendues par l'aristotélisme et le scotisme, elle montre leur application dans la théorie du connaître et de l'agir chez Descartes, Spinoza, Leibniz ainsi que l'apparition de la pensée dialectique, bien avant la synthése hégélienne.

2114 De Muralt, André. "La Doctrine Médiévale Des Distinctions et L'intelligibilité de la Philosophie Moderne II." *Revue de Théologie et de Philosophie* 30(1980): 217-240.

2115 De Muralt, André. "Actuation de L'intellect par la Forme Intelligibile et Représentation de L'objet A L'intellect. Le Débat Entre les Critiques Thomasienne et Scotiste Du Concept." *Cahiers de l'Ecole Saint Jean* 107(1985): 18-27.

2116 De Muralt, André. "La Métaphysique Thomiste de la Causalité Divine: Pour Comprendre la Doctrine Occamienne de la Toute-puissance Divine." *Die Philosophie Im 14. und 15. Jahrhundert*. Ed. Olaf Pluta. Bochumer Studien Zur Philosophie 10. Amsterdam: Verlag B. R. Grüner, 1988. 303-320.

2117 De Sousa Alves, V. "La Catégorie de Quantité en S. Thomas D'Aquin." *Tommaso D'Aquino Nel Suo Settimo Centenario IX: Atti del Congresso Internazionale: Il Cosmo e la Scienza*. Napoli: Edizioni Domenicane Italiane, 1978. 298-306.

2118 De Vogel, Cornelia J. "L'éthique D'Aristote Offre-t-elle une Base Appropriée A une Éthique Chrétienne?" *Tommaso nel suo settimo centenario V: Atti del Congresso internazionale: L'agire morale*. Napoli: Edizioni Domenicane Italiane: 135-143. 1977.

2119 Delfgaauw, B. "La Date Du *De Ente et Essentia* de Saint Thomas D'Aquin." *Studia in Honorem Willem Noomen*. Amsterdam: Groningen, 1984. 47-51.

2120 Delhaye, Philippe. "Pourquoi une Morale Révélée?" *Tommaso Nel Suo Settimo Centenario V: Atti del Congresso Internazionale: L'agire Morale*. Napoli: Edizioni Domenicane Italiane, 1977. 128-134.

2121 Delhaye, Philippe. "Les Morales de L'esprit et de la Nature dans les Commentaires Bibliques de Saint Thomas." *The Ethics of St. Thomas Aquinas*. Ed. L. Elders and K. Hedwig. Studi Tomistici 25. Città del Vaticano: Libreria Editrice Vaticana, 1984. 226-253.

2122 Delhaye, Philippe. "Les Quatre Forces de la Vie Morale D'aprés Saint Paul et Saint Thomas I." *Esprit et Vie* 94(1984): 57-60.

2123 Delhaye, Philippe. "Les Quatre Forces de la Vie Morale D'aprés Saint Paul et Saint Thomas II." *Esprit et Vie* 94(1984): 113-127.

2124 Delhaye, Philippe. "La Loi Nouvelle comme Dynamisme de L'Esprit-Saint." *Lex et Libertas: Freedom and Law According to St. Thomas Aquinas*. Eds. L. J. Elders and K. Hedwig. Studi Tomistici 30. Città del Vaticano: Pontificia Accademia di San Tommaso e di Religione Cattolica, 1987. 265-280.

2125 Delhaye, Philippe. "Quelques Aspects de la Doctrine Thomiste et Néo-thomiste Du Travail." *Le Travail Au Moyen Age: Une Approache Interdisciplinaire*. Eds. Jacqueline Hamesse and Colette Muraille-Samaran. Institut D'études Médiévales: Textes, Études, Congrés 10. Louvain-la-Neuve: Université Catholique de Louvain, 1990. 157-175.

2126 Dondaine, Antoine. "Exemplars de la *Summa Contra Gentiles*." *Miscellanea Codicologica F. Masai*. Eds. P. Cockshaw, M. -C. Garand, and P. Jodobne. Les Publications de Scriptorium 8. Gand: E. Story-Scientia, 1979. lvii-608.

*Silagi, G., *Daem*, 37(1981): 321-323.*

2127 Dondaine, H. F. "*Alia Lectura Fratris Thome*? (*Super I Sent.*)." *Mediaeval Studies* 42(1980): 308-336.

2128 Dorval-Guay, Georgette. "Document—Sur le Sens Du Terme Placet dans la Définition Thomiste Du Beau." *Laval Théologique et Philosophique* 41(1985): 443-447.

2129 Drapeau, Jean. "Selon Saint Thomas D'Aquin, L'homme Est-il Maitre de la Nature?" *Ecologie et Environnement*, 5(1986): 135-139.

2130 Dubarle, Dominique. "Causalité et Finalité Chez Saint Thomas et Au Niveau Des Sciences Modernes de la Nature." *Tommaso D'Aquino Nel Suo Settimo Centenario IX: Atti del Congresso Internazionale: Il Cosmo e la Scienza*. Napoli: Edizioni Domenicane Italiane, 1978. 9-25.

2131 Dubois, Marcel-Jacques. "L'analogie et la Signification Face A L'ordinateur." *Revue Thomiste* 77(1977): 593-599.

2132 Dubois, Marcel-Jacques, and Avital Wohlman. "L'usage de la Notion Aristotélicienne de Forme dans L'explication de la Causalité Chez Maïmonide et Chez Thomas D'Aquin." *Aquinas* 30(1987): 3-26.

2133 Dufeil, Michel-Marie. "Regard D'amour." *Amour, Mariage et Transgression Au Moyen Age*. 535-559.

2134 Dufeil, Michel-Marie. "Regards D'historien sur la Métaphysique Du Devenir D'un Théologien." *Tommaso Nel Suo Settimo Centenario VI: Atti del Congresso Internazionale: L'essere*. Napoli: Edizioni Domenicane Italiane, 1977. 699-705.

2135 Dufeil, Michel-Marie. "Trois Sens de L'histoire Affrontés Vers 1250-1260." *Année Charniére—Mutations et Continuités: Colloques Internationaux Du Centre National de la Recherche Scientifique*. Paris: Éditions du Centre national de la recherche scientifique, 1977. 815-848.

2136 Dufeil, Michel-Marie. "Ierarchia: Un Concept dans la Polémique Universitaire Parisienne Du XIII Siécle." *Soziale Ordnungen Im Selbstverständnis Des Mittelalters I*. Ed. Albert Zimmermann. Miscellanea Mediaevalia 12. Berlin: Walter de Gruyter, 1979. 56-83.

2137 Dufeil, Michel-Marie. "Deux Méthodes de Composition Guillaume de Saint-Amour et Thomas D'Aquin." *Culture et Travail Intellectuel dans L'Occident Médiéval*. Eds. Geneviéve Hasenohr and Jean Longére. Colloques D'humanisme Médiéval. Paris: Centre National Recherche Scientifique, 1981. 177-186.

2138 Dufeil, Michel-Marie. "Oriens Apud Thomam." *Sénéfiance* 11(1982): 165-176.

2139 Dufeil, Michel-Marie. "Simple Note sur L'eau Chez Thomas." *Sénéfiance* 15(1985): 149-155.

2140 Dufeil, Michel-Marie. "Thomas D'Aquin et la Découverte de L'historicité." *Journal Philosophique* 8(1986): 38-150.

2141 Dumas, J. -L. "L'égalité Des Droits et le Principe D'individuation Chez Saint Thomas." *Bulletin du Cercle Thomiste* 88-89(1980): 52-55.

2142 Dumas, Marie-Noëlle. "La Définition de la Prudence Chez Thomas D'Aquin et Ses Relations avec la Définition D'Aristote I." *Bulletin du Cercle Thomiste* 82(1978): 19-30.

2143 Dumas, Marie-Noëlle. "La Définition de la Prudence Chez Thomas D'Aquin et Ses Relations avec la Définition D'Aristote II." *Bulletin du Cercle Thomiste* 83(1978): 3-14.

2144 Dumoulin de Castro, Françoise. "Le Langage de la Contemplation dans le *Somme Théologique*." *Vie Spirituelle* 60(1978): 422-444.

2145 El Khodeiry, Zeynab. "St. Thomas D'Aquin Entre Avicenne et Averroés." *Thomas von Aquin. Werk und Wirkung Im Licht Neuerer Forschungen*. Ed. Albert Zimmermann. Berlin: Walter de Gruyter, 1988. 156-160.

2146 Elders, Léon J. "La Morale de Saint Thomas: Une Éthique Philosophique?" *Doctor Communis* 30(1977): 192-205.

2147 Elders, Léon J. "Structure et Fonction de L'argument *Sed Contra* dans la *Somme Théologique* de Saint Thomas." *Divus Thomas* 80(1977): 245-260.

2148 Elders, Léon J. "La Phénoménologie de Sartre A la Lumiére de la Philosophie de Saint Thomas." *Incontri Culturali* 11(1978): 509-519.

2149 Elders, Léon J. "Les Sciences Historiques dans la Formation Sacerdotale et le Probléme de L'historicité de Notre Connaissance." *Incontri Culturali* 11(1978): 384-409.

2150 Elders, Léon J. "Morale Chrétienne et Nature." *Espirit et Vie* 7(1978): 187-192.

2151 Elders, Léon J. "L'ordre Des Attributs Divins dans la *Somme Théologique*." *Divus Thomas* 82(1979): 225-232.

2152 Elders, Léon J. "Les Rapports Entre la Doctrine de la Prophétie Selon Saint Thomas et Le Guide Des Égarés de Maïmonide." *Actas del V Congreso Internacional de Filosofia Medieval I*. Madrid: Nacional, 1979. 677-697.

2153 Elders, Léon J. "La Connaissance de L'être et L'entrée en Métaphysique." Trad. Néerlandaise. *Articuli*, 1980, 24-45.

2154 Elders, Léon J. "Les Cinq Voies et Leur Place dans la Philosophie de Saint Thomas." *Quinque Sunt Viae*. Ed. Léon Elders. Studi Tomistici 9. Città del Vaticano, Pontificia Accademia di San Tommaso: Libreria Editrice Vaticana, 1980. 133-146.

2155 Elders, Léon J. "Justification de Cinq Voies." 1961. *Thomas von Aquin*. 1981. 136-162.

2156 Elders, Léon J. "Le Commentaire de Saint Thomas D'Aquin sur le *De Caelo* d'Aristote." *Proceedings of the World Congress on Aristotle II*. Athens: Publication of the Ministry of Culture and Sciences, 1981. 173-187.

2157 Elders, Léon J. "La Connaissance de L'être et L'entrée en Métaphysique." *Atti Dell'VIII Congresso Tomistico Internazionale I: L' Enciclica Aeterni Patris Nell'arco Di Un Secolo*. Studi Tomistici 10. Cittá del Vaticano: Pontificia Accademia di San Tommaso e di Religione Cattolica, 1981. 273-290.

2158 Elders, Léon J. "Saint Thomas Aquinas' *Commentary on the Physics* of Aristotle." *Actes Du Symposium sur la Pensée de Saint Thomas: La Philosophie de la Nature de Saint Thomas D'Aquin*. Ed. Léon Elder. Studia Tomistici 18. Città del Vaticano: Libr. Ed. Vaticana, 1982. 107-133.

2159 Elders, Léon J. "La Doctrine de la Conscience de Saint Thomas D'Aquin." *Revue Thomiste* 83(1983): 533-557.

2160 Elders, Léon J. "Le Probléme de L'existence de Dieu dans les Écrits de S. Thomas D'Aquin: A Propos Du Livre de F. Van Steenberghen." *Divus Thomas* 86(1983): 171-187.

2161 Elders, Léon J. "Le Commentaire de Saint Thomas D'Aquin sur le *De Anima* D'Aristote." *Atti del Congresso Società Internazionale San Tommaso D'Aquino IX: L'anima Nell'antropologia Di San Tommaso D'Aquino*. 1987. 33-51. Also in *Autour de saint Thomas d'Aquin, I*. 55-76.

2162 Elders, Léon J. "Les Citations de Saint Augustin dans la *Somme Théologique* de Saint Thomas D'Aquin." *Doctor Communis* 40(1987): 115-167.

2163 Elders, Léon J. "Bibliographie Académique de L. J. Elders." *Autour de Saint Thomas D'Aquin: Recueil D'études sur Sa Pensée Philosophique et Théologique II: L'agir Moral Approches Théologiques*. Ed. Léon J. Elders. Paris: FAC-éditions et Bruges, Tabor, 1987. 215-219.

2164 Elders, Léon J. "Articles." *Lexikon der Philosophischen Werke*. Eds. F. Volpi et al. Stuttgart, 1988. Entries on 16 works of St. Thomas Aquinas.

2165 Elders, Léon J. "Matthias Joseph Scheeben et Saint Thomas D'Aquin." *Divinitas* 32(1988): 491-504.

2166 Elders, Léon J. "*Philosophia Perennis*." *Doctor Communis* 51(1988): 207-223.

2167 Elders, Léon J. "Saint Thomas D'Aquin Aujourd'hui." *Divus Thomas* 91(1988): 3-22.

2168 Elders, Léon J. "Saint Thomas D'Aquin et Aristote." *Revue Thomiste* 88(1988): 357-376.

2169 Elders, Léon J. "Normes Ethiques et Faits Pre-moraux." *Doctor Communis* 42(1989): 166-174.

2170 Elders, Léon J. "Saint Thomas D'Aquin et la Métaphysique Du *Liber de Causis*." *Revue Thomiste* 89(1989): 427-442.

2171 Étienne, Jacques. "Loi et Grâce: Le Concept de Loi Nouvelle dans la *Somme Théologique* de Saint Thomas D'Aquin." *Revue de Théologique de Louvain* 16(1985): 5-22.

2172 Evain, François. "La Sagesse de St. Thomas comme Méthode en Philosophie Selon L'Encyclique *Aeterni Patris*." *Atti Del'VIII Congresso Tomistico Internazionale II: L'enciclica Aeterni Patris 1981*. Studi Tomistici 11. Città del Vaticano, Pontificia Accademia di San Tommaso e di Religione Cattolica: Libreria Editrice Cattolica, 1981. 90-97.

2173 Fabro, Cornelio. "Le Liber de *Bona Fortuna* et L'éthique a Eudéme D'Aristote et la Dialectique la Divine Providence Chez Saint Thomas." *Revue Thomiste* 88(1988): 556-572.

2174 Floucat, Yves. "Libres Réflexions Philosophiques sur L'expérience Mystique de L'intimité Divine." *Revue Thomiste* 80(1980): 13-56.

2175 Floucat, Yves. "Approche Métaphysique Du Mal." *Cahiers Jacques Maritain 12*. 1985. 33-50.

2176 Floucat, Yves. "Sagesse Du Beau: En Relisant Jacques Maritain." *Revue Thomiste* 88(1988): 377-392.

2177 Fontan, Pierre. "Histoire et Philosophie: Critique et Tradition Chez Saint Thomas." *Revue Thomiste* 77(1977): 533-577.

Chez Saint Thomas, nul parti pris de rupture ou de départ à zéro. Mais, s'il remonte à des sources particuliéres, c'est au nom de l'universel et de l'humain. Elles représentent moins un cadre de pensée qu'un donné à explorer d'un regard critique, matiére à Élaboration orginale à proportion del'impersonnalité du vrai. Lui-même parle du scribe qui tire de son trésor de l'ancien et du nouveau, et rien n'est plus neuf que ce qui ne périme pas. Il vérifie pour sa part la remarque de Saint-Beure: "La tradition ne se continue jamais par des disciples mais par de noureaux maîtres."

2178 Gaboriau, Florent. "Edith Stein Philosophie." *Revue Thomiste* 96(1988): 440-459.

2179 Gaboriau, Florent. "Edith Stein Philosophie." *Revue Thomiste* 96(1988): 589-619.

2180 Gaboriau, Florent. "Sur le Concept de Révélation." *Revue Thomiste* 90(1990): 533-569.

2181 Garceau, Benoît. "Jugement et Vérité Chez Saint Thomas D'Aquin." *Tommaso Nel Suo Settimo Centenario VI: Atti del Congresso Internazionale: L'essere*. Napoli: Edizioni Domenicane Italiane, 1977. 189-195.

2182 Gauthier, A. "La Doctrine de la Conscience de Saint Thomas D'Aquin." *Revue Thomiste* 83(1983): 533-557.

2183 Gecse, Gustáv. "Les Enseignements de Saint Thomas D'Aquin sur la Justice." *Annales Universitatis Scientiarum Budapestinensis de Rolando Eötvös nominatae* 11(1977): 141-163.

2184 Gecse, Gustáv. "Les Enseignements de Saint Thomas D'Aquin sur le Mal et le Péché." *Annales Universitatis Scientiarum Budapestinensis de Rolando Eötvös nominatae* 12(1978): 153-165.

2185 Gecse, Gustáv. "Saint Thomas D'Aquin, Scolastique, Thomisme, I." *Annules Universitatis Scientiarum Budapestinensis de Rolando Eötvös nominatae* 13(1979): 165-185.

2186 Gecse, Gustáv. "Saint Thomas D'Aquin, Scolastique, Thomisme, II." *Annales Universitatis Scientiarum Budapestinensis de Rolando Eötvös nominatae* 14(1980): 109-136.

2187 Geffré, Claude. "Un Cas de Christianisation de L'hellénisme: La Sagesse Théologique de Thomas D'Aquin." *Archivio di Filosofia* 53(1985): 365-380.

2188 Geffré, Claude. "Thomas D'Aquin Ou la Dé christianisation de L'hellénisme." *L'être et Dieu*. Paris: Le Cerf, 1986. 23-42.

2189 Gils, P. -M. J. "Pour une Étude Du Ms: Pamplona." *Scriptorium* 32(1978): 221-230.

2190 Gils, P. -M. J. "L'édition Critique Des Questions Disputée *De Malo* de Saint Thomas D'Aquin." *Bulletin de Philosophie Ancienne et Médiévale* 22(1980): 81-85.

2191 Gils, P. -M. J. "*Intellectus Nude Aliquid Considerat.*" *Bulletin de Philosophie Ancienne et Médiévale* 23(1981): 91-92.

2192 Glorieux, Palémon. "Pro et Contra Thomam: Un Survol de Cinquante Années." *Sapientiae Procerum Amore*. 1977. 255-287.

2193 Gogacz, Mieczyslaw. "Proposition D'une Théorie Existentielle de la Personne Humaine." *Tommaso D'Aquino Nel Suo Settimo Centenario: Atti del Congresso Internazionale*. Napoli: Edizioni Domenicane Italiane, 1978. 236-244.

2194 Gogacz, Mieczyslaw. "Le Langage de Saint Thomas D'Aquin dans le *De Ente et Essentia.* " *Sprache und Erkenntnis Im Mittelalter II*. Eds. Jan P. Beckmann et al. Berlin: Walter de Gruyter, 1981. 761-768.

2195 Gogacz, Mieczyslaw. "Probléme Des Relations dans la Philosophie Médievale." *Journal Philosophique* 1(1985): 2101-2217.

2196 Gogacz, Mieczyslaw. "Qu'est-ce Que la Réalite?" *Journal Philosophique* 1(1985): 1-14.

2197 Guyot, Bertrand-Georges. "Dates et Lieux de Copie Des Manuscrits de Quelques Oeuvres de Saint Thomas." *Année Charniére—Mutations et Continuités: Colloques Internationaux Du Centre National de la Recherche Scientifique*. Paris: Éditions du Centre national de la rechereche scientifique, 1977. 633-643.

2198 Halbronn, Jacques. "L'itinéraire Astrologique de Trois Italiens Du XIII Siécle: Pietro D'Abano, Guido Bonatti, Thomas D'Aquin." *Actes Du Septiéme Congrés International de Philosophie Médiéval: L'homme et Son Univers Au Moyen Age II*. Ed. Christian Wenin. Philosophes Médiévaux 26-27. Louvain-la-Neuve: Éditions de l'Institut Supérieur de Philosophie, 1986. 668-674.

2199 Hamesse, Jacqueline, André Stainier, and Paul Tombeur. "Recherche de Méthodes Nouvelles Pour la Comparaison de Textes de Thomas et de Bonaventure." *Année Charniére—Mutations et Continuités: Colloques Internationaux Du Centre National de la Recherche Scientifique*. Paris: Éditions du Centre national de la rechereche scientifique, 1977. 589-623.

2200 Hana, Ghanem G. "Comment Saint Thomas et Averroés Ont-ils Lu la Définition de L'âme D'Aristote?" *Actas del V Congreso Internacional de Filosofia Medieval II*. Madrid: Nacional, 1979. 817-874.

2201 Hasumi, Toshimitsu. "Etude Comparative de la Théorie de la Connaissance Chez Saint Thomas D'Aquin, Kant, et de la Pensée Philosophique Du Zen." *Sprache und Erkenntnis Im Mittelalter II*. Eds. Jan P. Beckmann et al. Miscellanea Mediaevalia 13/2. Berlin: Walter de Gruyter, 1981. 1094-1098.

2202 Hissette, Roland. "Etat de L'*Index Thomisiticus*." *Bulletin de Philosophie Ancienne et Médiévale* 19(1977): 68.

2203 Hissette, Roland. "Albert le Grand et Thomas D'Aquin dans la Censure Parisienne Du 7 Mars 1277." *Studien Zur Mittelalterlichen Geistesgeschichte*. Ed. Albert Zimmermann. Miscellaenea Mediaevalia 15. Berlin: Walter de Gruyter, 1982. 226-246.

2204 Hissette, Roland. "Un Nouveau Début A L'édition Léonine Des Oeuvres de Saint Thomas D'Aquin." *Revue Philosophique de Louvain* 88(1990): 395-403.

*The first volume of the new ed. of the *Opera Omnia* of Thomas Aquinas, requested by Leo XIII, appeared 108 years ago. This first volume of the "Leonine Ed." contains the commentaries on the *Peri Hermeneias* and the *Posterior Analytics*. But a systematic listing of the whole tradition of textual evidence, which is now seen as a condition *sine qua non* of a critical ed., was not attempted; it was not then possible to classify the evidence scientifically, because it was not known that they were all dependent on a basic model or exemplar divided into *peciae* ("pieces": the consecutive folded *quarto* sheets from which the text was to be copied). Consequently, the handing on of the text has, in principle, to be studied *pecia* by *pecia*. As this prerequisite was not supplied, the two first volumes of the Leonine Ed. are not critical, and this has made necessary a complete overhauling of the work of the first Ed.s. Gratitude is due to Pére Gauthier for having done this. This note attempts to set out his method. It will be noticed that not only the texts of Thomas come within the compass of his work, but also the texts of Aristotle on which he commented.*

2205 Hoenen, J. F. M. "A Propos de Lectura I D. 39: Un Passage Dissimulé de Thomas D'Aquin Chez Duns Scot?" *Archives d'Histoire Doctrinale Littéraire du Moyen Âge* 52(1985): 231-236.

2206 Hosszu, Lajos. "L'expérience de Dieu de Saint Thomas D'Aquin." *Teologia* (Budapest) 4(1983): 207-211.

2207 Houde, Roland. "La Référence N'est Pas A *L'Index*." *Philosophiques* 6(1979): 341-346.

2208 Huant, Ernest. "Les Structures Intelligibles Du Réel dans la Science Actuelle et dans la Pensée de St. Thomas (Similitudes et Convergences)." *Tommaso D'Aquino Nel Suo Settimo Centenario IX: Atti del Congresso Internazionale: Il Cosmo e la Scienza.* Napoli: Edizioni Domenicane Italiane, 1978. 112-115.

2209 Hubert, Martin. "L'humour de Saint Thomas D'Aquin en Face de la Scolastique." *Année Charniére—Mutations et Continuités: Colloques Internationaux Du Centre National de la Recherche Scientifique*. Trans. Année charniére—Mutations et continuités: Colloques internationaux du Centre national de la recherche scientifique. Paris: Éditions du Centre national de la rechereche scientifique, 1977. 725-739.

2210 Hubert, Martin. "Eléments Provisoires de Linguistique Thomiste. Mots Outils et Ponctuation dans les Écrits de Saint Thomas." *Bulletin du Cange* 43(1981-1982): 57-63.

2211 Jacher, Wladyslaw. "Le Travail Humain: Son Objectif et Son Caractére Obligatoire Selon Saint Thomas D'Aquin." *Tommaso D'Aquino Nel Suo Settimo Centenario VIII: Atti del Congresso Internazionale: L'Uomo*. Napoli: Edizioni Domenicane Italiane, 1978. 120-127.

2212 Jacquin, Robert. "Deux Promoteurs Inattendus de la Philosophie de Saint Thomas D'Aquin." *Bulletin du Cercle Thomiste* 77-78(1977): 46-57.

2213 Jacquin, Robert. "L'oeuvre Philosophique de Flavien Hugonin." *Doctor Communis* 35(1982): 68-77.

2214 Jean-Paul II. "Discours de S. S. Jean-Paul II sur L'actualité de Saint Thomas." *Revue Thomiste* 80(1980): 5-12.

2215 Jordan, Mark D. "L Exégése de la Causalité Physique Chez Thomas D'Aquin." *Revue Thomiste* 82(1982): 550-574.

2216 Kalinowski, Georges. "Discours de Louange et Discours Métaphysique: Denys L'Aréopagite et Thomas D'Aquin." *Rivista di Filosofia Neo-Scolastica* 73(1981): 399-404.

*Jean-Luc Marion trouve dans *L'idole et la distance* que l'assimilation par Thomas d'Aquin de l'Etre à Dieu, d'une part, et son discours métaphysique sur Dieu, de l'autre, présentent un danger d'idolâtrie. L'auteur de l'article essaie de montrer qu'il n'en est rien.*

2217 Kalinowski, Georges, and Michel Villey. "La Mobilité Du Droit Naturel Chez Aristote et Thomas D'Aquin." *Archives de Philosophie du Droit* 29(1984): 187-199.

2218 Kalinowski, Georges. "Le Droit A la Vie Chez Thomas D'Aquin." *Archives de Philosophie du Droit* 30(1985): 315-330.

2219 Kalka, Richard. "Structure Métaphysique de la Relation Chez Thomas D'Aquin." *Journal Philosophique* 1(1985): 218-239.

2220 Kalka, Richard. "Une Introduction A la Problématique de la Présence dans les Écrits de Saint Thomas D'Aquin." *Journal Philosophique* 1(1985): 15-29.

2221 Kalka, Richard. "Définition de la Personne Chez Saint Thomas D'Aquin, I." *Journal Philosophique* 2(1986): 1-30.

2222 Kalka, Richard. "Définition de la Personne Chez Saint Thomas D'Aquin, II." *Journal Philosophique* 2(1986): 65-71.

2223 Kalka, Richard. "La Théorie de la Présence dans la Philosophie de Thomas D'Aquin (Un Aperçu Du Probléme)." *Journal Philosophique* 7(1986): 65-71.

2224 Kleber, Hermann. "La Théorie Thomiste Du Bonheur et Ses Rapports avec le *Roman de la Rose*." *Actes Du Colloque L' Idée de Bonheur Au Moyen Age.* Université de Picardie: Centre d'études médiévales: Danielle Buschinger, 1984. unknown.

2225 Klimski, Tadeusz. "La Définition de la Personne: Trois Étapes dans L'historie: Boéce, Thomas D'Aquin, Kant." *Journal Philosophique* 1(1985): 170-180.

2226 Kluxen, Wolfgang. "L'originalité de Saint Thomas D'Aquin et le Probléme D'un Thomisme Contemporain." *Tommaso D'Aquino Nel I Centenario Dell'Enciclica Aeterni Patris: Atti del Convegno Organizzato a Roma Dall Societá Internazionale Tommaso D'Aquino e Dalla Pontificia Universita San Tommaso D'Aquino.* Roma: Societá Internazionale Tommaso d'Aquino, 1979. 197-209.

2227 Koehler, T. "Le Vocabulaire, Misericordia, Misericiers, Misereri Chez Saint Thomas D'Aquin." *Divinitas* 24(1981): 34-42.

2228 Korn, Ernst R. "Thomas D'Aquin et la Libération de la Raison Métaphysique." *Tommaso Nel Suo Settimo Centenario VI: Atti del Congresso Internazionale: L'essere.* Napoli: Edizioni Domenicane Italiane, 1977. 206-218.

2229 Korolec, Jzerzy B. "Le Commentaire de Gilles D'Orléans A L'éthique A Nicomaque et le *Commentaire A L'éthique A Nicomaque* de Thomas D'Aquino (Le Probléme Du Libre Choix)." *Thomas von Aquin: Werk und Wirkung Im Licht Neuerer Forschungen*. Ed. Albert Zimmermann. Berlin/New York: Walter de Gruyter, 1988. 397-402.

2230 Kowalczyk, Stanislaw. "L'argument Eudémologique dans la Philosophie Thomistique de Dieu." *Divus Thomas* 81(1977): 109-140.

2231 Kowalczyk, Stanislaw. "L'argument Thomiste de Causalité Efficiente." *Divus Thomas* 81(1978): 109-140.

2232 Kowalczyk, Stanislaw. "La Sixiéme Voie de Maritain et la Philosophie Moderne de Dieu." *Jacques Maritain: Philosophe dans la Cité/ A Philosopher in the World.* Ed. Jean-Louis Allard. Philosophica 28. Ottawa: University of Ottawa Press, 1985. 73-83.

2233 Kozlowski, Joseph. "La Relation-une Lecture Évolutioniste: Saint Thomas D'Aquin et Teihard de Chardin." *Journal Philosophique* 2(1986): 72-89.

2234 Krapiec, Mieczyslaw A. "Traits Caractéristiques de la Philosophie de Saint Thomas." *Atti Del'VIII Congresso Tomistico Internazionale Vol. V: Problemi Metafisici. Studi Tomistici 14.* Città del Vaticano: Lib. Ed. Vaticana, 1982. 7-13.

2235 Kuc, Leszek. "Le Réel D'aprés Platon, Aristote et Thomas D'Aquin." *Diotima* 7(1979): 101-104.

2236 Kuc, Leszek. "La Connaissance de Son Propre Acte Intellectuel: Remarques sur Un Théme Anthropologique de Thomas D'Aquin." *Journal Philosophique* 1(1985): 241-253.

2237 Kuc, Leszek. "La Personne: Une Des Notions-clefs Du Moyen Age." *Journal Philosophique* 1(1985): 101-115.

2238 Kuc, Leszek. "Le Contenu Anthropologique Du Traité de la Trinité Divine de Thomas D'Aquin. A Propos Du Théme Des Relations: *Summa Theologie*, I, 28." *Journal Philosophique* 10-11(1986): 304-308.

2239 Kuksewicz, Zdzislaw. "Trois Lignes D'interprétation de la Théorie D'Aristote de L'ame: Albert le Grand, Siger de Brabant, Thomas D'Aquin." *Proceedings of the World Congress on Aristotle II.* Athens: Publication of the Ministry of Culture and Sciences, 1981. 125-129.

2240 La Croix, Benoit, and Albert M. Landry. "Quelques Thémes de la Religion Populaire Chez le Theologien Thomas D'Aquin." *La Culture Populaire Au Moyen-Age: Etudes Prentées Au IV Collogue de L'Institut D'Etudes Médiévales de L'Université de Montréal.* Ed. Pierre Boglioni. Montréal: Ed. Univers., 1979. 163-181. Also appears in *Proceedings of the Fifth Annual Symposium of the Ottawa-Carleton Medieval-Renaissance Club: Problems in the interpretation of Medieval and Renaissance Culture*, edited by Raymond St. Jacques and Lindsay Mann, 22-42.

2241 Labourdette, Michel. "Aux Origines Du Péché de L'homme, D'aprés Saint Thomas D'Aquin." *Revue Thomiste* 85(1985): 357-398.

*Le péché de l'homme a deux sortes d'origine:(1) *métaphysiques*: la défectibilité congénitale de la liberté, créée, qui provient de la potentialité. (2) *historiques* (en "historie sainte"): le péché *personnel* d'Adam infecte en lui la *nature* humaine, la met en État de péche (=privation de grâce); cette nature este transimise telle à tous ses descendents et infecte ainsi chaque personne. Celle-ci devra renaître à la grâce "de l'eau et de l'Esprit" (*Jean*, III, 5).*

2242 Labourdette, Michel. "Une Édition Française de la *Somme Théologique*." *Revue Thomiste* 85(1985): 302-305.

2243 Lacombe, Olivier. "Regards Thomistes sur la Pensée Hindoue." *Thomas Aquinas* (Annevoie) 7(1984): 8-14.

2244 Ladriére, Jean. "La Situation Actuelle de la Philosophie et la Pensée de Saint Thomas." *Tommaso D'Aquino Nel I Centenario Dell'Enciclica Aeterni Patris: Atti del Convegno Organizzato a Roma Dall Societá Internazionale Tommaso D'Aquino e Dalla Pontificia Universita San Tommaso D'Aquino.* Roma: Societá Internazionale Tommaso d'Aquino, 1979. 71-100.

2245 Lamy de la Chapelle, Marie. "Fils Jusque dans la Chair." *Doctor Communis* 33(1980): 130-168.

2246 Lavaud, Jean-Claude. "Le Statut Ontique de L'appréhension Simple (Conception) dans la *Somme de Théologie* de Thomas D'Aquin." *Journal Philosophique* 6(1986): 51-54.

2247 Lavelle, Louis. "L' existence des deux mondes." *Revue Philosophique de Louvain*, 81(1981): 5-35.

2248 Lebégue, Thomas. "La Critique de la Connaissance Intellectuelle de L'homme dans la Philosophie de Saint Thomas." *Atti Dell'VIII Congresso Tomistico Internazionale VII: L'uomo e Il Mondo Nella Luce Dell'Aquinate*. Studi Tomistici 16. Cittá del Vaticano: Pontificia Accademia di S. Tommaso e di Religione Cattolica, 1982. 51-61.

2249 Lechartier, Jean Jacques. "La Connaissance Selon Saint Thomas." *Bulletin du Cercle Thomiste* 83(1978): 28-33.

2250 Lechartier, Jean Jacques. "Saint Thomas et la Pédagogie." *Bulletin du Cercle Thomiste* 80-81(1978): 32-48.

2251 Lechartier, Jean Jacques. "La Connaissance Objective Du Bien Chez Saint Thomas D'Aquin." *Bulletin du Cercle Thomiste* 88-89(1980): 33-40.

2252 Lefévre, Charles. "Intersubjectivité et Promotion D'aprés Saint Thomas." *Tommaso D'Aquino Nel Suo Settimo Centenario: Atti del Congresso Internazionale*. Napoli: Edizioni Domenicane Italiane, 1978. 265-273.

2253 Léonard, André. "Dieu Toujours Plus Grand." *Thomas Aquinas* (Annevoie) 4(1983): 8-15.

2254 Leroy, Marie-Vincent. "La Troisiéme Voie de Saint Thomas et Ses Sources." *Recherches D'Islamologie*. Eds. Georges C. Anawati and Louis Gardet. Louvain: Éditions Peeters: Louvain-la-Neuve, Éditions de l'Institut Supérieur de Philosophie, 1977. 171-200.

2255 Leroy, Marie-Vincent. "Saint Thomas dans Son Oeuvre." *Revue Thomiste* 83(1983): 487-504.

2256 Leroy, Marie-Vincent. "Saint Thomas et le Thomisme." *Revue Thomiste* 83(1983): 668-678.

2257 Libera, Alain de. "L'instant Du Changement Selon Saint Thomas D'Aquin." *Métaphysique: Historie de la Philosophie*. Neuchâtel: Ed.s de la Baconniére, 1981. 99-109.

2258 Libera, Alain de. "Bulletin D'histoire de la Logique Médiévale." *Revue des Sciences Philosophiques et Théologiques* 71(1987): 590-634.

2259 Livi, Antonio. "Etienne Gilson: Il Tomismo Come Filosofia Cristiana." *Atti Dell'VIII Congresso Tomistico Internazionale VIII: San Tommaso Nella Storia del Pensiero*. Studi Tomistici 17. Cittá del Vaticano: Pontificia Accademia di San Tommaso e di Religione Cattolica, 1982. 285-300.

2260 Lobato, Abelardo. "Le Thomisme de Etienne Gilson." *Doctor Communis* 38(1985): 234-242.

2261 Louis, P., and B. Gillon. "Du Désir Naturel de Connaître Au Désir de Voir Dieu. Le Commentaire de Saint Thomas, sur Aristote, *Metaphysics* A, 1, 980a24." *Atti Del'VIII Congresso Tomistico Internazionale: Vol. IV: Prospettive Teologiche Moderne*. Studi Tomistici 13. Città del Vaticano, Pontificia Accademia di San Tommaso e di Religione Cattolica: Libreria Editrice Cattolica, 1981. 243-248.

2262 Lucien, Bernard. "Les Principes Fondamentaux de la Philosophie Politique Selon Saint Thomas D'Aquin." *Journal Philosophique* 15(1987): 207-223.

2263 Luyten, Norbert A. "Anthropologie Philosophique et Philosophie de la Nature." *Tommaso D'Aquino Nel Suo Settimo Centenario: Atti del Congresso Internazionale*. Napoli: Edizioni Domenicane Italiane, 1978. 9-19.

2264 Mansion, Suzanne. "L'anthropologie Latente Du *De Ente et Essentia*." *Tommaso D'Aquino Nel Suo Settimo Centenario: Atti del Congresso Internazionale*. Napoli: Edizioni Domenicane Italiane, 1978. 120-125, 483-533.

2265 Mansion, Suzanne. "L'intelligibilité Métaphysique D'aprés le Prooemium Du Commentaire de Saint Thomas A la *Métaphysique* D'Aristote." *Rivista di Filosofia Neo-Scolastica* 70(1978): 49-62.

*According to *Prooemium* metaphysics, the supreme science, has for its object what is most intelligible. The three criteria which help Aquinas define the *maxime intelligibilia* are certitude, universality, and separation from matter. Each of these, in turn, with the problems of interpretation they raise, are examined. Special attention is given to discussing how metaphysics can be defined both as the science of universal being and that of what is immaterial. This involves a difficulty because God, the supreme immaterial being, far from being enclosed in *ens commune*, is said to be its cause. A fresh solution to this much-debated problem is suggested.*

2266 Manteau-Bonamy, H. M. "La Liberté de L'homme Selon Thomas D'Aquin." *Archives d'Histoire Doctrinale Littéraire du Moyen Âge* 54(1978): 7-34.

2267 Mathonat, Bénédicte. "La Connaissance Scientifique Du Vivant et L'experience Interne." *L'anima Nell'antropologia Di San Tommaso D'Aquino IX: Atti del Congresso Societá Internazionale San Tommaso D'Aquino*. Ed. Abelardo Lobato. Milano: Editrice Massimo, 1987. 565-577.

2268 Mazierski, Stanislaw. "Temps et Éternité." *L'homme et Son Univers Au Moyen Age II*. Ed. Christian Wenin. Philosophes Médiévaux: Actes Du Septiéme Congrés International de Philosophie Médiéval 26-27. Louvain-la-Neuve: Éditions de l'Institut Supérieur de Philosophie, 1986. 876-881.

2269 McDermott, John Michel. "Un Inédit de Pierre Rousselot: Idéalisme et Thomisme." *Archives de Philosophie* 42(1979): 91-126.

*Only in consideration of the Primordial Adam hypothesis, presented in *Idealisme et Thomisme*, can one understand the apparent antinomies of Pierre Rousselot's doctoral thesis, "L'intellectualisme de Saint Thomas" and "Pour l'histoire du probléme de l'amour au Moyen Age." This sacramental vision provides the foundation for all the subsequent development of his thought.*

2270 McEvoy, James. "Philosophie Fondamentale." *Revue Philosophique de Louvain* 87(1989): 626-628.

2271 Milet, J. "Fondements Philosophiques de la Pensée de Vitoria: Rapports Entre Vitoria et Saint Thomas D'Aquin." *Le Supplément* (Paris) 160(1987): 100-102.

2272 Millet, Louis. "Analogie et Participation Chez Saint Thomas D'Aquin." *Les Études Philosophiques* 3-4(1989): 371-383.

2273 Mongillo, Antonio. "Le Conception Thomiste de L'histoire dans le Traité Des Lois, I II Q. 90-108." *Année Charniére—Mutations et Continuités: Colloques Internationaux Du Centre National de la Recherche Scientifique*. Paris: Éditions du Centre national de la rechereche scientifique, 1977. 873-880.

2274 Moreau, Pierre-François. "Loi Naturelle et Ordre Des Choses Chez Suarez." *Archives de Philosophie* 42(1979): 229-234.

The words "Natural Law" are to Saint Thomas and Suarez two profoundly different conceptions. To Saint Thomas, it means to root human nature in the characteristics of all reality and especially animal reality, while emphasizing what belongs only to Man. To Suarez, on the contrary, it means isolating Man in Nature as the only one belonging to a moral and juridical sphere.

2275 Motte, Antonin-René. "La Définition de la Vie Religieuse Selon Saint Thomas D'Aquin." *Revue Philosophie* 87(1987): 442-453.

2276 Moutsopoulos, É. "Thomisme et Aristotélisme A Byzance: Démétrius. Cydonés." *Jahrbuch der österreichischen Byzantinistik* (Wien) 32(1982): 307-310.

2277 Nader, Albert N. "Eléments de la Philosophie Musulmane Médiévale dans la Pensée de St. Thomas D'Aquin." *Thomas von Aquin. Werk und Wirkung Im Licht Neuerer Forschungen*. Ed. Albert Zimmermann. Berlin: Walter de Gruyter, 1988. 161-174.

2278 Nagakura, Hisako. "Le Probléme Du Langage dans la Théologie de L'image de Dieu Chez Saint Bonaventure et Saint Thomas." *Sprache und Erkenntnis Im Mittelalter II*. Eds. Jan P. Beckmann et al. Berlin: Walter de Gruyter, 1981. 952-960.

2279 Nau, Paul. "Pourquoi et Comment Suívre Saint Thomas." *Thomas Aquinas* 1(1983): 1-9.

2280 Nédoncelle, Maurice. "Unité de L'intellect et Pluralité Des Personnes." *Tommaso D'Aquino Nel Suo Settimo Centenario: Atti del Congresso Internazionale*. Napoli: Edizioni Domenicane Italiane, 1978. 317-332.

2281 Neyrand, Edith. "Auteurs Cités dans la *Somme Théologique*." *Somme Théologique I*. Paris: Cerf, 1984. 121-140.

2282 Nicolas, Hervé-M. "Maintenir la Place Privilégiée de Saint Thomas dans Un Enseignement Moderne de la Théologie." *Saint Thomas Aquinas in hodierna formatione sacerdotali: Seminarium* 29(1977): 878-897.

2283 Nicolas, Marie-Joseph. "Un Événement: Nouvelle Traduction Française de la *Somme Théologique*." *Thomas Aquinas* (Annevoie) 6(1984): 23-28.

2284 Nicolas, Marie-Joseph. "Vocabulaire de la *Somme Théologique*." *Somme Théeologique* I. Paris: Cerf, 1984. 91-120.

2285 Nicolas, Marie-Joseph. "Introduction a la *Somme Théologique*." *Somme Théeologique I*. Paris: Cerf, 1984. 13-66.

2286 Nicolas, Simonne. "La Conscience Humaine, I." *Thomas Aquinas* (Annevoie) 12(1985): 14-17.

2287 Nicolas, Simonne. "La Conscience Humaine, II." *Thomas Aquinas* (Annevoie) 13(1986): 1-7.

2288 Oliveira, Carlos-J. Pinto de "Image de Dieu et Dignité Huamine." *Freiburger Zeitschrift für Philosophie und Theologie* 27(1980): 401-436.

2289 Oliveira, C. -J. Pinto de. "Saint Thomas, le Concile et la Théologie Contemporaine." *Tommaso D'Aquino Nel I Centenario Dell'Enciclica Aeterni Patris: Atti del Convegno Organizzato a Roma Dall Societá Internazionale Tommaso D'Aquino e Dalla Pontificia Universita "San Tommaso D'Aquino."* Roma: Societá Internazionale Tommaso d'Aquino, 1979. 231-263.

2290 Oswald, Philippe. "La Philosophie Comparée Selon L'esprit de Saint Thomas D'Aquin." *Cahiers I.P.C. Faculté Libre de Philosophie Comparée* 23(1980): 69-75.

2291 Oswald, Philippe. "La Philosophie Comparée Selon L'esprit de Saint Thomas D'Aquin." *Atti Dell'VIII Congresso Tomistico Internazionale VIII: San Tommaso Nella Storia del Pensiero*. Studi Tomistici 17. Cittá del Vaticano: Pontificia Accademia di San Tommaso e di Religione Cattolica, 1982. 387-395.

2292 Patfoort, Albert. "Théorie de la Théologie Ou Réflexion sur le Corpus Des Ecritures? Le Vrai Sens, dans L'oeuvre de Saint Thomas, Des Prologues Du *Super Libros Sententiarum* et de la *Somme Théologique*." *Angelicum* 54(1977): 459-488.

2293 Patfoort, Albert. "La Finalité Apostolique de la *Somme Contre les Gentils*." *Angelicum* 59(1982): 3-22.

2294 Patfoort, Albert "*Sacra Doctrina*: Théologie et Unité de la I Pars." *Angelicum* 62(1985): 306-319.

2295 Patfoort, Albert. "*Cognitio Ista Est Quasi Experimentalis* (*I Sent.* , D. 14, Q. 2, A. 2, Ad 3m)." *Angelicum* 63(1986): 3-13.

2296 Pattin, Adrian. "La Relation Transcendantale et la Synthése Métaphysique Thomiste." *Tommaso Nel Suo Settimo Centenario VI: Atti del Congresso Internazionale: L'essere*. Napoli: Edizioni Domenicane Italiane, 1977. 303-310.

2297 Payen, Jean C. "Le Bonheur dans la Littérature Française Aux XIIe et XIIIe Siécles." *Romanistische Zeitschrift für Literaturgeschichte—Cahiers d'histoire des littératures Romanes* 4(1980): 1-18.

2298 Petuzzellis, Nicola. "Che Significa Vetera Novis Augere et Perficere." Cittá del Vaticano: Pontificia Accademia di San Tommaso e di Religione Cattolica, 1981. Vol. Atti dell'VIII Congresso Tomistico internazionale I. *L'enciclica Aeterni Patris Nell'arco Di Un Secolo*. Studi Tomistici 10. 472-490.

2299 Philippe, Marie-Dominique. "Analyse de L'étre Chez Saint Thomas." *Tommaso Nel Suo Settimo Centenario VI: Atti del Congresso Internazionale: L'essere*. Napoli: Edizioni Domenicane Italiane, 1977. 9-28.

2300 Philippe, Marie-Dominique. "La Lecture de la *Somme Théologique*." *Seminarium* (Città del Vaticano) 29(1977): 898-917.

2301 Philippe, Marie-Dominique. "La Démonstration de L'existence de Dieu dans les Premiéres Oeuvres de Saint Thomas." *Bulletin du Cercle Thomiste* 79(1977): 1-16.

2302 Philippe, Marie-Dominique. "Etude de la *Somme Théologique* (65 Leçon). Le Livre de Vie (Ia Q. 24)." *Bulletin du Cercle Thomiste* 77-78 (1977): 3-22.

2303 Philippe, Marie-Dominique. "Etude de la *Somme Théologique* (66 Leçon). Le Puissance de Dieu (I, Q. 25)." *Bulletin du Cercle Thomiste* 82(1978): 1-18.

2304 Philippe, Marie-Dominique. "La Puissance de Dieu Est-elle Infinie? (Ia, Q. 25, A. (2) [Etude de la *Somme Théologique* 67 Leçon]." *Bulletin du Cercle Thomiste* 84(1979): 3-15.

2305 Philippe, Marie-Dominique. "Dieu Est-il Tout-puissant? (Ia, Q. 25, A. (3) [Etude de la *Somme Théologique*, 68 Leçon, 69 Leçon)." *Bulletin du Cercle Thomiste* 85/86, 87(1979): 11-27, 1-17.

2306 Philippe, Marie-Dominique. "Y A-t-il Des Limites A la Toute-puissance de Dieu? (I, Q. 25, A. 4, 5 et 6)." *Bulletin du Cercle Thomiste* 88-89(1980): 7-24.

2307 Philippe, Marie-Dominique. "Y A-t-il Des Limites A la Toute-puissance de Dieu? (I, Q. 25, A. 4, 5 et 6)." *Bulletin du Cercle Thomiste* 90(1980): 1-22.

2308 Philippe, Marie-Dominique. "Etude de la *Somme Théologique* (73 Eme Leçon). La Création (I) De la Procession de Créatures A Partir de Dieu (Ia, Q. 44). Article 1: Dieu Est-il Cause Efficiente de Tous les Etres." *Cahiers de l'Ecole Saint Jean 1984-1985* 104-105(1984-85): 35-54.

2309 Philippe, Marie-Dominique. "Etude de la *Somme Théologique* (74 Eme Leçon). La Création (II) De la Procession de Créatures A Partir de Dieu (Ia, Q. 44)." *Cahiers de l'Ecole Saint Jean* 107(1985): 38-55.

2310 Philippe, Thomas. "Saint Thomas D'Aquin Au Service Des Pauvres." *Thomas Aquinas* 11(1985): 8-25.

2311 Pinckaers, Servais. "La Théologie Morale A la Période de la Grande Scolastique." *Nova et Vetera* 52(1977): 118-131.

2312 Pinckaers, Servais. "La Question Des Actes Intrinséquement Mauvais." *Revue Thomiste* 82(1982): 181-212.

Criticism of the "Proportionalism" of certain recent Catholic moralists, which is a system of moral evaluation based on the proportion between good and the bad effects of an act, taking into account the end pursued and all the attendant circumstances, rather than the object of the act. Thus there is the danger of utilitarianism and of relativism, and the difficulty of giving a theoretical foundation to the existence of intrinsically evil acts. Like post-Tridentine Catholic moral theology—which is the source of many of its categories—"proportionalism" lacks a scriptural content because of its concentration on obligations and on norms.

2313 Pinckaers, Servais. "La Béatitude dans L'éthique de Saint Thomas." *The Ethics of St. Thomas Aquinas*. Eds. L. Elders and K. Hedwig. Studi Tomistici 25. Città del Vaticano: Libreria Editrice Vaticana, 1984. 80-94.

2314 Pinckaers, Servais. "Liberté et Préceptes dans la Morale de Saint Thomas." *Lex et Libertas: Freedom and Law According to St. Thomas Aquinas*. Eds. L. J. Elders and K. Hedwig. Studi Tomistici 30. Città del Vaticano: Pontificia Accademia di San Tommaso e di Religione Cattolica, 1987. 15-24.

2315 Pinckaers, Servais. "Le Passions et la Morale." *Revue des Sciences Philosophiques et Théologiques* 74(1990): 379-391.

2316 Pines, Shlomo. "Maimonide et la Philosophie Latine." *Actas del V Congreso Internacional de Filosofia Medieval II*. Madrid: Nacional, 1979. 219-229.

2317 Plé, A. "La Morale Au Singulier." *Le Supplément* (Paris) 145(1983): 247-265.

2318 Quillet, Jeannine. "Note sur Démocrite Au Moyen Age: Hasard, Nécessité, Providence Chez Saint Thomas D'Aquin et Dante." *Revue Philosophie* 50(1984): 315-322.

2319 Quillet, Jeannine. "L'imagination et le Corps Selon Saint Thomas." *L'anima Nell'antropologia Di San Tommaso D'Aquino IX: Atti del Congresso Societá Internazionale San Tommaso D'Aquino.* Ed. Abelardo Lobato. Milano: Editrice Massimo, 1987. 383-389.

2320 Quillet, Jeannine. "L'art de la Politique Selon Saint Thomas." *Thomas von Aquin: Werk und Wirkung Im Licht Neuerer Forschungen.* Ed. Albert Zimmermann. Berlin/New York: Walter de Gruyter, 1988. 278-285.

2321 Renard, J. -P., Éd. "La *Lectura Super Matthaeum* V. 20-48de Thomas D'Aquin." *Recherches de Théologie Ancienne et Médiévale* 50(1983): 145-189. Ed. d'aprés le ms. Balc. University bibl. B. V. 12.

2322 Renaud, Michel. "Le Cercle Herméneutique Face A la Rationalité Du Discours Philosophique Chez Saint Thomas et Hegel." *Revue Philosophique de Louvain* 75(1977): 276-292.

*The philosophical discourse on God is taken as field of application for the question of rationality. How does the temporal distance which separates us from the philosophical productions of the past permit us to regain their thought? Three groups of problems are found on the path towards this recovery. Is the truth research-movement or stable correspondence? Are we not witnessing today the outmoding of the "primacy of representation" which characterizes the philosophical discourses of St. Thomas and Hegel (the concept of representation being taken in a non-Hegelian meaning)? Is not the problem of the horizon substituting itself for that of circularity? In a second section, theauthor aims, under the auspices of a specific interpretation of the hermeneutical circle, to resume the dialectical relationship between the *ratio theorica* and the elocutionary operativity of the discourse. He sketches succinctly the conclusions for a discourse on God, while emphasizing the rebounding influence of experienceon the discourse.*

2323 Rioux, Bertrand. "L'intuition de L'être Chez Maritain." *Jacques Maritain: The Man and His Metaphysics.* Ed. John F. X. Knasas. Mishawaka, IN: The American Maritain Association, 1988. 93-102.

2324 Rodriguez, Pedro. "Spontanéité et Caractére Légal de la Loi Nouvelle." *Lex et Libertas: Freedom and Law According to St. Thomas Aquinas.* Eds. L. J. Elders and K. Hedwig. Studi Tomistici 30. Città del Vaticano: Pontificia Accademia di San Tommaso e di Religione Cattolica, 1987. 254-264.

2325 Rosier, Iréne. "Signes et Sacrements: Thomas D'Aquin et la Grammaire Spéculative." *Revue des Sciences Philosophiques et Théologiques* 74(1990): 392-435.

2326 Rousseau, Félicien. "La Croissance Solidaire Des Droits de L'homme." *Laval Théologique et Philosophique* 39(1983): 349-360.

*Ce text fut rédigé à l'occasion d'un exposé fait dans le cadre des Conférences de la Faculté de théologie de l'Université Laval. Il constitue une présentation du livre intitulé: *La croissance solidaire des droits de l'homme*, publié le 15 décembre dernier chez Desclée et Bellarmin dans la collection *Recherches*," n. 29. Il met en relief l'ossature d'une recherche consacrée à retrouver le génie et l'étonnante actualité de la loi naturelle, telle que conçue par Thomas d'Aquin, et à renouer avec une partie de l'héritage moral de l'Occident qu'une théologie suffisante, hier comme aujourd'hui, n'a pas pleinement assimilée. Tout comme lors de cette présentation, le text est dépouillé, non de citations, mais de références, sauf quelques exceptions.*

2327 Roy, Réal. "Etre et Etres Chez Deux Philosophes Du XII-XIII Siécles: Zhu XI et Thomas D'Aquin." *Laval Théologique et Philosophique* 44(1988): 103-115.

*Presque contemporains, Zhu Xi, philosophe chinois de la dynastie Song, et Thomas d'Aquin ont chacun développé une synthése philosophique présentant d'étonnantes similarités lorsqu'elles sont comparées. Nous analysons, ici, l'ontologie telle que formulée par chaque auteur, en faisant bien ressortir les correspondances s'établissant entre *li* et existence, *qi* et essence, *Taijii* Dieu.*

2328 Samir, K. "Date de Composition de la *Somme Théologique* D'al-Mu' Taman B. Al-Assal." *Orientalia Christiana Periodica* 50(1984): 94-106.

2329 Samir, K. "Deux Citations D'al-Safi Ibn Al-Assal Au Ch. 46 de la *Somme Théologique* d' Al-Mu'taman." *Orientalia Christiana Periodica* 51(1985): 156-162.

2330 Scaltriti, Arturo. "Il Bicentenario Della Rivoluzione Francese: Vis-à-vis St. Thomas D'Aquin." *Aquinas* 30(1987): 487-511.

2331 Schwarz, Simon. "Source Théologique Des Actes Humains et Valeur Actuelle Des Actes." *Tommaso Nel Suo Settimo Centenario V: Atti del Congresso Internazionale: L'agire Morale*. Napoli: Edizioni Domenicane Italiane, 1977. 186-193.

2332 Scully, Edgar. "La Philosophie Politique de Saint Thomas D'Aquin: Economie Politique?" *Laval Théologique et Philosophique* 38(1982): 49-59.

Aquinas, in his rendering of the Aristotelian principle, "Man is by nature a political animal," sometimes uses the term "social" as an alternate or substitute for "political." In so doing, he does not identity the political with the social realm, though he grounds it in the social. Nor does he identify the social, in turn, with the economic, though he includes it within the social, which, for him, encompasses the total well-being of man.

2333 Serralda, Vincent. "La Philosophie Chrétienne de Alcuin et Saint Thomas D'Aquin." *Atti Dell'VIII Congresso Tomistico Internazionale VIII: San Tommaso Nella Storia del Pensiero*. Studi Tomistici 17. Cittá del Vaticano: Pontificia Accademia di S. Tommaso e di Religione Cattolica, 1982. 107-124.

2334 Serverat, Vincent. "Utopie et histoire. Les postulats théoriques de la praxis missionnaire." Raymond Lulle et le Pays d'Oc, E. Privat; Fanjeaux, Centre d'Etudes Historiques de Franjeaux, 1987, 191-229.

2335 Serverat, Vincent. "L'irrisio Fidei Chez Raymond Lulle et Saint Thomas D'Aquin." *Revue Thomiste* 90(1990): 436-448.

2336 Sigmond, Raymond. "Grandeur et Misére de L'homme: St. Thomas et les Sciences Humaines." *Tommaso D'Aquino Nel Suo Settimo Centenario: Atti del Congresso Internazionale*. Napoli: Edizioni Domenicane Italiane, 1978. 175-181.

2337 Silberstein, Jil. "C. -A. Cingria et G. K. Chesterton Face A Saint Thomas D'Aquin." *Thomas Aquinas* 10(1985): 26-32.

2338 Siwek, Paul. "Saint Thomas D'Aquin et L'évolutionnisme Biologique." *Tommaso D'Aquino Nel Suo Settimo Centenario IX: Atti del Congresso Internazionale: Il Cosmo e la Scienza*. Napoli: Edizioni Domenicane Italiane, 1978. 471-477.

2339 Sleiman, Jean. "Actualité Saint Thomas D'Aquin." *Bulletin du Cercle Philosophique* (Beyrouth) 10(1985): 45-47.

2340 Smagghue, Michel-Marie. "L'action de la Priére sur L'homme et sur Dieu." *Thomas Aquinas* 1(1983): 8-13.

2341 Spanneut, Michel. "Influences Stoïcennes sur la Pensée Morale de Saint Thomas D'Aquin." *The Ethics of St. Thomas Aquinas*. Eds. L. Elders and K. Hedwig. Studi Tomistici 25. Città del Vaticano: Libreria Editrice Vaticana, 1984. 50-79.

2342 Steel, Carlos. "*Omnis Corporis Potentia Est Finita*: L'interprétation d'un Principe Aristotélicienne: De Proclus A Saint Thomas." *Philosophie Im Mittelalter: Entwicklungslinien und Paradigmen*. Eds. Jan P. Beckmann et al. 65. Hamburg: Felix Meiner Verlag, 1987. 213-224.

2343 Steel, Carlos. "Ockham Versus Thomas D'Aquin: Le Sujet Des Vertus Morales." *Ockham and Ockhamists*. Eds. E. P. Bos and H. A. Krop. Artistarium, Supplementa IV. Nijmegen: Ingenium, 1987. 109-118.

2344 Steel, Carlos. "Guillaume de Moerbeke et Saint Thomas." *Guillume de Moerbeke I*. Eds. J. Brams and W. Vanhamel. *Ancient and Medieval Philosophy*. De Wulf-Mansion Centre 7. Leuven: University Press, 1989. 57-82.

2345 Steel, Carlos. "Guillaume de Moerbeke et Saint Thomas." *Guillaume de Moerbeke* II. *Ancient and Medieval Philosophy* 1/7. Leuven: Leuven University Press, 1989. 87-104.

2346 Swiezawski, Stefan. "Quelques Déformations de la Pensée de Saint Thomas dans la Tradition Thomiste." *Theory of Being to Understand Reality*. Eds. Stanislaw Kaminski, Marian Kurdzialek, and Zofa Józefa Zdybicka. Rozprawy Wydzialu Filozoficznego 34. Lublin: Towarzystwo Naukowe Katolickiego Uniwersytetu Lubelskiego, 1980. 269-284.

2347 Széll, Margit. "De la Vérité de la Connaissance et de la Vie (Au Point de Vue A Saint Thomas et Edith Stein)." *Tommaso Nel Suo Settimo Centenario VI: Atti del Congresso Internazionale: L'essere*. Napoli: Edizioni Domenicane Italiane, 1977. 568-572.

2348 Te Velde, Rudi. "Le Nominalisme dans la Doctrine Thomiste Des Noms Divins." *Werkgroep Thomas Van Aquino*. Amsterdam: Jaarboek, 1985. 39-70.

2349 Tiébey, Simon. "L'epistemologie Neothomiste en URSS." *Revue d'Histoire et de Philosophie Religieuses* 68(1988): 209-215.

2350 Tiébey, Simon. "La Perception Soviétique de la Philosophie Néo-thomiste." *Revue Thomiste* 89(1989): 91-96.

2351 Tirot, Paul. "Autour Du Débat sur L'analogie de Proportionnalité Propre Chez Saint Thomas D'Aquin." *Angelicum* 63(1986): 90-125.

2352 Toinet, Paul. "L'être, Demeure Commune Du Philosophe et Du Théologien." *Atti del Congresso Internazionale. Tommaso D'Aquino Nel Suo Settimo Centenario VI: L'essere*. Napoli: Edizioni Donemicane, 1977. 410-425.

2353 Torrell, Jean-Pierre. "Deux Remaniements Anonymes Des Collationes in Decem Praeceptis de Saint Thomas D'Aquin." *Mediaeval Studies* 40(1978): 1-29.

2354 Torrell, Jean-Pierre. "Frére Thomas D'Aquin Prédicateur." *Freiburger Zeitschrift für Philosophie und Theologie* 29(1982): 175-188.

2355 Torrell, Jean-Pierre. "La Pratique Pastorale D'un Théologien Du XIII Siécle: Thomas D'Aquin Prédicateur." *Revue Thomiste* 82(1982): 213-245.

2356 Torrell, Jean Pierre. "Quand Saint Thomas Meditait sur le Prophete Isaïe." *Revue Thomiste* 90(1990): 5-47.

2357 Trouillard, Jean. "La Connaissance Selon Saint Thomas." *Revue Philosophique de France et de l'étranger* 168(1978): 73-77.

*Cette bréve Étude est un commentaire critique du livre de Joseph Moreau, *De la connaissance selon Saint Thomas d'Aquin* (Paris: Beaucheshe, 1976): d'aprés J. Moreau, S. Thomas raeconcilierait l'idélisme Platonicien et le réalisme Aristotélicien. Tel à Été, en effet, le projet du Moyen Platonisme auquel se rattachent Prophyre et Saint Aqustin. Mais l'école néoplatonicienne de Plotin et Proclos s'oppose fermement à cette synthése. Proclos refuse d'identifier le Bien de Platon al'être, comme Plotin le placait au delà de la pensée de la pensée. La théologie négativeradicale ouvre la voie à une Autoconstitution peu Aristotélicienne de l'esprit dérive.*

2358 Turrini, Mauro. "Réginald de Piperno et le Texte Original de la *Tertia Pars* de Las *Somme de Théologie* de Saint Thomas D'Aquin." *Revue des Sciences Philosophiques et Théologiques* 73(1989): 233-246.

2359 Ushidà, Noriko. "Le Probléme de L'unité de la Forme Substantielle Chez Saint Thomas D'Aquin et Avicenne." *Actas del V Congreso Internacional de Filosofia Medieval II*. Madrid: Nacional, 1979. 1325-1329.

2360 Ushidà, Noriko. "Le Probléme de la Connaissance de Soi dans L'antiquite et dans le Moyen Age." *Siculorum Gymasium* 31(1979): 457-477.

2361 Van Banning, Joop. "Saint Thomas et L'Opus Imperfectum in Matthaeum." *Atti Dell'VIII Congresso Tomistico Internazionale VIII: San Tommaso Nella Storia del Pensiero*. Cittá del Vaticano: Pontificia Accademia di San Tommaso e di Religione Cattolica, 1982. 73-85.

2362 Van der Ploeg, J. P. M. "Le Traité de Saint Thomas de la Loi Ancienne." *Lex et Libertas: Freedom and Law According to St. Thomas Aquinas*. Eds. L. J. Elders and K. Hedwig. Studi Tomistici 30. Città del Vaticano: Pontificia Accademia di San Tommaso e di Religione Cattolica, 1986. 185-199.

2363 Van der Ven, J. J. M. "Permanence de la Philosophie Du Droit de Saint Thomas D'Aquin." *Atti Dell'VIII Congresso Tomistico Internazionale VI: Morale e Diritto Nella Prospettiva Tomistica*. Studi Tomistici 15. Cittá del Vaticano: Pontificia Accademia di San Tommaso e di Religione Cattolica, 1982. 150-161.

2364 Van Groenewoud, A. J. H. "Note sur la Position de la Raison dans la Théorie Thomiste Du Beau." *Revue Thomiste* 78(1978): 619-624.

*This article will prove that the (Latin) word *ratio*, in connection with the Thomistic aesthetics, means "proportion," not "reason." This appears from(1) *Summa theologica 1,5,4 ad 1*: "The sense enjoy well proportioned things, like things similar to themselves," after which: "for the sense is a *ratio*." (2) From related texts, whose meaning is almost equal to the mentioned, but ends with "the sense is a *proportio*." At the same time it appears what this proportion means. (a) In the organ: a specified proportion between the elements of which it is composed. (b) In the object: a specified proportion of qualities (colors, sound, tastes, etc.), which pleases the senses.*

2365 Van Riet, Georges. "La Liberté: Saint Thomas et Leibniz." *Tommaso Nel Suo Settimo Centenario V: Atti del Congresso Internazionale: L'agire Morale*. Napoli: Edizioni Domenicane Italiane, 1977. 368-372.

2366 Van Riet, Georges. "Le Titre L'Encyclique *Aeterni Patris*." *Revue Philosophique de Louvain* 80(1982): 35-63.

2367 Van Steenberghen, Fernand. "Corrections Au Text Du *De Unitate Intellectus* de Thomas D'Aquin." *Bulletin de Philosophie Médiévale* 19(1977): 65-67.

2368 Van Steenberghen, Fernand. "Le Mythe D'un Monde Eternel." *Revue Philosophique de Louvain* 76(1978): 157-179.

*In two previous studies, the author has shown that, if the argument of Saint Bonaventure based on the notion of *creation ex nihilo* is valueless in establishing the impossibility of an eternal world, his arguments founded on the impossibility of the *infinite in act* are irrefutable. In this new article he replies to the criticism put forward by an anonymous reviewer in the *Rassegna di Letteratura Tomistica* and by Professor A. Zimmermann. Bringing to light the variations of Saint Thomas on the notion of infinite in potentiality and on the impossibility of the infinite in act, he maintains that every infinite series cannot be realized and that, in consequence, the hypothesis of an eternal world, implying an infinite series of events accomplished, involves manifest contradictions. Only the extraordinary prestige of Aristotle can explain the fact that Saint Thomas defended the possibility of an eternal world, when he had excluded, with is customary lucidity, every infinite in act.*

2369 Van Steenberghen, Fernand. "Prolégoménes A la *Quarta Via*." *Rivista di Filosofia Neo-Scolastica* 70(1978): 99-112.

*The celebrated proof for the existence of God by the grades of perfection found in creatures, which is the *quarta via* in the series of five proofs given by Thomas Aquinas in his *Summa Theologiae*, is clearly inspired by neo-platonic principles. To determine the meaning of that very concise text, Van Steenberghen examines the two commentaries of neo-platonic writings given by Thomas: the *De Divinis Nominibus* of Pseudo-Dionysius Areopagita and the *Liber De Causis* (of an unknown author). This research leads him to fix very precisely the meaning of the *quarta via*. The value of the proof is another problem, which is not treated here.*

2370 Van Steenberghen, Fernand. "Connaissance Divine et Liberté Humaine." *Revue Théologique de Louvain* 2(1979): 46-68.

2371 Van Steenberghen, Fernand. "La Cinquiéme Voie Ex *Gubernatione Rerum*." *Quinque Sunt Viae*. Ed. Léon Elders. Studi Tomistici 9. Città del Vaticano, Pontificia Accademia di San Tommaso: Libreria Editrice Vaticana, 1980. 84-108.

2372 Van Steenberghen, Fernand. "La Philosophie Au XIII Siecle: Dialogue avec le P. Enrique Rivera de Ventosa." *Sapientiae Doctrina*. Ed. H. Bascour. 1980. 359-374.

2373 Van Steenberghen, Fernand. "Les Thomistes en Dialogue avec la Pensée Moderne." *Tommaso D'Aquino Nel I Centenario Dell'Enciclica Aeterni Patris*. Ed. Benedetto Amore. Roma: Societá Internazionale Tommaso d'Aquino, 1981. 137-158.

2374 Van Steenberghen, Fernand. "Esquisse D'une Anthropologie Philosophique de Thomas D'Aquin." *Wissen, Glaube, Politik*. Ed. von Otto König. Wien, Köln: Verlag Styria, 1981. 101-109.

2375 Van Steenberghen, Fernand. "Une Enquête sur L'existence de Dieu dans les Écrits de Saint Thomas." *Revue Philosophique de Louvain* 79(1981): 5-27.

*In these pages borrowed from the *Introduction* and especially from the *Doctrinal conclusions* of a work which has just appeared, the author sums up the investigation which he has made into the writings of St. Thomas. Certain demonstrations do not appear valid to him, but the contributions of St. Thomas to the solution of the problem of the existence of God is very important. One should use this contribution while taking into account the latest results of science and the view of the world which follows. It is accordingly necessary to bypass the letter of St. Thomas and to practice a Thomism broadly open to present-day scientific culture and philosophical criticism. Finally, only theism gives a satisfactory solution to the fundamental problem of the nature of the absolute.*

2376 Van Steenberghen, Fernand. "Une Enquête sur le Probléme de L'existence de Dieu dans les Écrits de Saint Thomas D'Aquin." *Académie Royale de Bulletin de la Classe des Lettres et des Sciences Morales et Politiques (Bruxelles)* 67(1981): 94-107.

2377 Van Steenberghen, Fernand. "Le Mythe D'un Monde Éternel: Note Complémentaire." *Revue Philosophique de Louvain* 80(1982): 486-499.

2378 Van Steenberghen, Fernand. "Les Derniéres Pages de Thomas D'Aquin sur le Probléme de L'existence de Dieu." *Vérité et Éthos*. Ed. Jaromir Danek. Québec: Les Presses de l'Université Laval, 1982. 93-99.

2379 Van Steenberghen, Fernand. "Thomas D'Aquin et Siger de Brabant en Quête D'arguments Pour le Monothéisme." *Graceful Reason: Essays in Ancient and Medieval Philosophy Presented to Joseph Owens on the Occasion of His Seventy-fifth Birthday and the Fiftieth Anniversary of His Ordination*. Ed. Lloyd P. Gerson. Papers in Mediaeval Studies 4. Toronto: Pontifical Institute of Mediaeval Studies, 1983. 381-400.

2380 Van Steenberghen, Fernand. "Note D'herméneutique: La Tournure Dialectique dans la Littérature de L'ecole." *Pascua Mediaevalia. Studia Voor Prof. Dr. J. M. De Smet.* Eds. R. Lievens et al. Mediaevalia Lovaniensia 10. Leuven: Universitaire Pers Leuven. 1983. 377-383.

2381 Van Steenberghen, Fernand. "Le Débat Du XIII Siécle sur le Passé de L'univers." *Revue Philosophique de Louvain* 83(1985): 231-238.

2382 Van Steenberghen, Fernand. "La Structure de la Philosophie Théorique Selon Saint Thomas D'Aquin." *Revue Philosophique de Louvain* 83(1985): 536-558.

*The division of speculative philosophy in three parts, resumed by Saint Thomas from the Aristotelian tradition, does not meet the present state of scientific knowledge, first of all because the Middle Ages ignored the distinction between philosophy and positive sciences. His *philosophia naturalis* is a complex knowledge, which partly belongs to positive sciences and partly to metaphysics, while the hypotheses concerning the heavenly spheres and the four elements are worthless. His *philosophia mathematica* coincides with the mathematics. Alone his *metaphysica* is a true philosophical knowledge, but general metaphysics must be prolonged in two special metaphysics: cosmology and (philosophical) anthropology. Besides metaphysics philosophy includes epistemology and the philosophy of sciences.*

2383 Van Steenberghen, Fernand. "Comment Etre Thomiste Aujourd'hui?" *Revue Philosophique de Louvain* 85(1987): 171-197.

The author discusses the history of the Thomistic revival revealing the existence of two divergent streams, which have been called "paleo-Thomism" and "neo-Thomism." An inquiry is desirable to determine the nature and the action of the two streams. To this inquiry the article offers the contribution of his personal experience. He first recalls the orientation of his own works, then he expounds the reaction of Thomists "of the strict observance." Some deny the very existence of paleo-Thomism. Many refuse every criticism of the famous "Five Ways" or of other proofs for the existence of God proposed by St. Thomas. Some refute every criticism of St. Thomas' positions in the problem of quantitative infinite or in the problem of eternal foreknowledge of our free acts. The conclusion of this inquiry is that the attitude of paleo-Thomists is disastrous for the future of Thomism.

2384 Van Steenberghen, Fernand. "La Conception de la Philosophie Au Moyen Age: Nouvel Examen Du Probléme." *Philosophie Im Mittelalter: Festschrift in Honor of Wolfgang Kluxen*. Eds. J. P. Beckmann et al. Hamburg: Felix Meiner Verlag, 1987. 187-199.

2385 Van Steenberghen, Fernand. "Philosophie et Christianisme: Epilogue D'un Débat Ancien." *Revue Philosophique de Louvain* 86(1988): 180-191.

2386 Van Steenberghen, Fernand. "Thomas D'Aquin." *Contemporary Philosophy: A New Survey II*. Ed. Guttorm Floistad. International Institute of Philosophy. Dordrecht: Kluwer Academie Publishers, 1990. 271-286.

2387 Vanneste, A. "Saint Thomas et le Probléme Du Surnaturel." *Ephemerides Theologicae Louvanienses* 64(1988): 348-370.

2388 Vanni Rovighi, Sofia. "La Vision Du Monde Chez Saint Thomas et Saint Bonaventure." *Année Charniére—Mutations et Continuités: Colloques Internationaux Du Centre National de la Recherche Scientifique*. Paris: Éditions du Centre national de la rechereche scientifique, 1977. 667-678.

2389 Vannier, Marie-Anne. "Sur le Probléme de la Création: Réflexion en Marge Des Textes de Saint Thomas." *Atti Del'VIII Congresso Tomistico Internazionale V: Problemi Metafisici*. Studi Tomistici 14. Città del Vaticano, Pontificia Accademia di San Tommaso e di Religione Cattolica: Libreria Editrice Cattolica, 1982. 435-451.

2390 Verbeke, Gérard. "L'univers Est-il L'oeuvre de Dieu? La Réponse de Thomas D'Aquin." *Quinque Sunt Viae*. Ed. Léon Elders. Studi Tomistici 9. Città del Vaticano, Pontificia Accademia di San Tommaso: Libreria Editrice Vaticana, 1980. 42-64.

2391 Verbeke, Gérard. "Saint Thomas et les Commentaires Grecs sur la *Physique* D'Aristotle." *La Philosophie de la Nature de Saint Thomas D'Aquin*. Ed. Léon Elders. Studi Tomistici 18. Cittá del Vaticano: Pontificia Accademia di San Tommaso, Libreria Editrice Vaticana, 1982. 134-154.

2392 Veres, Tomo. "Thomas D'Aquin Précurseur de Copernic?" *Tommaso D'Aquino Nel Suo Settimo Centenario IX: Atti del Congresso Internazionale: Il Cosmo e la Scienza*. Napoli: Edizioni Domenicane Italiane, 1978. 247-253.

2393 Villey, Michel. "Remarque sur la Notion de Droit Chez Suarez." *Archives de Philosophie du Droit* 42(1979): 219-227.

*When Suarez approaches the meaning of the word *jus*, he refers to Thomas Aquinas and to Roman Law; in fact, his use of references and quotations hides an embezzlement: the reduction of the old care *suum cuique tribuendi* to subjective right and to lex.*

2394 Villey, Michel. "Le Jugement Selon Saint Thomas et la Dialectique." *Archives de Philosophie du Droit* 28(1983): 303-313.

2395 Villey, Michel. "L'art Du Dialogue dans la *Somme Théologique*." *Archives de Philosophie du Droit* 29(1984): 55-71.

2396 Viola, Coloman. "Les Dimensions de la Vérité." *Journal Philosophique* 1(1985): 139-163.

2397 Viola, Coloman. "Table Générale et Index Analytique Des Oeuvres Complétes de Saint Thomas D'Aquin: Un Guide Pour L'édition Vivés." *Bulletin de Philosophie Médiévale* 29(1987): 178-192.

2398 Wéber, Édouard-Henri. "Dynamisme Du Bien et Statut Historique Du Destin Créé: Du Traité sur la Chute Du Diable Di Saint Anselme Aux Questions sur le Mal de Thomas D'Aquin." *Die Mächte Des Guten und Bösen*. Ed. Albert Zimmermann. Miscellanea Mediaevalia 11. Berlin: Walter de Gruyter, 1977. 154-205.

2399 Wéber, Édouard-Henri. "L'enchaînement Vertu-liberté." *Angelicum* 54(1977): 377-393.

2400 Wéber, Édouard-Henri. "Les Apports Postifs de la Noétique D'Ibn Rushd A Celle de Thomas D'Aquin." *Multiple Averroés*. Paris: Belles Lettres, 1978. 211-248.

2401 Wéber, Édouard-Henri. "La Négativité Méthodique comme Moment Critique de L'épistémologie et Du Langage Chez Albert le Grand et Thomas D'Aquin." *Sprache und Erkenntnis Im Mittelalter II*. Eds. Jan P. Beckmann et al. Miscellanea Mediaevalia 13/2. Berlin: Walter de Gruyter, 1981. 746-752.

2402 Wéber, Édouard-Henri. "*Commensuratio* de L'agir par L'objet D'activité et par le Sujet Agent Chez Albert le Grand, Thomas D'Aquin et Maître Eckhart." *Mensura, Mass, Zahl, Zahlensymbolik Im Mittelater*. Ed. Albert Zimmerman. Miscellanea Mediaevalia 16/1. Berlin: Walter de Gruyter, 1983. 43-64.

2403 Wéber, Édouard-Henri. "Resemblances et Disparités Concernant L'ame Intellective Entre la *Sententia* La *De Anima* et les Autres Oeuvres de Thomas D'Aquin." *Atti del Congresso Societá Internazionale San Tommaso D'Aquino Vol. IX: L'anima Nell'antropologia Di San Tommaso D'Aquino*. Ed. Abelardo Lobato. Milano: Editrice Massimo, 1987. 413-424.

2404 Wéber, Édouard-Henri. "L'élaboration de L'analogie Chez Thomas D'Aquin." *Les Études Philosophiques* 3-4(1989): 385-411.

2405 Weijers, Olga. "Contribution de L'histoire Des Thermes *Natura Naturans* et *Natura Naturata* Jusqu'à Spinoza." *Vivarium* 16(1978): 70-80.

2406 Wielockx, Robert. "Pour Un Portrait de Thomas D'Aquin Commentateur D'Aristote: La Contribution Des Manuscrits." *Scriptorium* 39(1985): 139-150.

2407 Wielockx, Robert. "Thomas D'Aquin, Commentateur Du *De Sensu*." *Scriptorium* 41(1987): 150-157.

2408 Wielockx, Robert. "Autour Du Procés de Thomas D'Aquin." *Thomas von Aquin: Werk und Wirkung Im Licht Neuerer Forschungen*. Ed. Albert Zimmermann. Berlin/New York: Walter de Gruyter, 1988. 413-438.

2409 Winance, Éleuthére. "Note de Logique sur la Démonstration Au Moyen Age." *Revue Thomiste* 78(1978): 32-53.

*The object of the "Note" is to analyse the Aristotelian model of a demonstration *propter quid* as it has been understood by an anonymous logician in a 13th century apocryphal work o

Thomas Aquinas. He shows that the middle term of a geometrical proof is the synthesis of the definition of the subject and the predicate. The *Note* is a tentative reduction of an ordinary inference to this complex pattern. What the Ancients called *a propositio per se secundo modo* was tentatively integrated with the *ratio* given for a statement of a modern textbook of geometry.*

2410 Winance, Éleuthére. "Métadiscours Du Discours sur Dieu." *Revue Thomiste* 74(1979): 546-574.

2411 Winance, Éleuthére. "Le Défi Du Positivisme Logique." *Revue Thomiste* 81(1981): 533-556.

2412 Winance, Éleuthére. "Réflexion sur la Logique de L'Aquinate: Son Intention, Son Objet, Son Horizon, Sa Nature." *Revue Thomiste* 87(1987): 391-434.

*Disciple of Aristotle, Thomas Aquinas describes the principles and the rules which control a living mind in search for truth. In this sense, logic is a philosophical science, reflexive and critical, dealing with an ideal objective order, *entia rationis*. The ultimate foundation is the intentionality of the intellect whose object is being, "allergic" to nonbeing. Then, logic guarantees the coherency of the mind, no longer knowledgeable of being and apprehensive of truth if it contradicts itself.*

2413 Winance, Éleuthére. "L'être et le Sensible: Edmund Husserl et Thomas D'Aquin." *Revue Thomiste* 89(1989): 357-404.

*The purpose of the article is to give a tentative answer to the question: Is Husserl's turn from the realism of the *Logical Investigations* to the idealism of the *Cartesian Meditations* logically predictable? An analysis of the concepts of being, sensible, categorical intuition suggest that his realism was enigmatic. Being was not, as in the Aristotelian tradition, the very constituent of the sensible. The comments of Thomas on Chapter 15 of the Posteriors Analytics II show us the intrinsic identity between the perceived and the understood, the sensible, and the universal (being). Therefore, idealism was already "virtual" in the 6th investigation. A descriptive account of the period between 1900 and 1907 (famous conferences: "The Idea of Phenomenology") tries to explain why; according to Lowit (French translator), the virtual became "actual" so slowly and unexpectedly.*

2414 Wohlman, Avital. "Amour Du Bien Propre et Amour de Soi dans la Doctrine Thomiste de L'amour." *Revue Thomiste* 81(1981): 204-234.

2415 Wohlman, Avital. "Lélaboration Des Éléments Aristotéliciens dans la Doctrine Thomiste de L'amour." *Revue Thomiste* 82(1982): 247-269.

In the order of friendship and love, one can observe a change in perspective parallel to that observed in the use of analogy. Thomas organizes a vertical order with reference to God, while the analogy of Aristotle is organized horizontally around substance. By this means, Aristotle's concept of friendship is applied to the order of charity to delineate the relationship between love of self, the root of all love, and the ultimate love of God, the loving creator.

2416 Wohlman, Avital. "De la Foi A la Foi par la Raison: Maïmonide et Thomas D'Aquin." *Revue des Sciences Philosophiques et Théologiques* 70(1986): 521-558.

2417 Wojciech, Felix, and B. Bednarski. "La Psychanalyse de L'agressivité A la Lumiére de la Psychosynthése de Saint Thomas D'Aquin." *Angelicum* 58(1981): 389-419.

2418 Zan, Ryszard. "La Relation Ame-corps Chez Thomas D'Aquin." *Journal Philosophique* 10-11(1986): 349-352.

2419 Zan, Ryszard. "La Personne et L'être." *Journal Philosophique* 13(1987): 117-125.

2420 Zdybicka, Zofia J. "Le Réalisme de la Connaissance et la Participation de L'etre." *Tommaso Nel Suo Settimo Centenario VI: Atti del Congresso Internazionale: L'essere*. Napoli: Edizioni Domenicane Italiane, 1977. 440-465.

2421 Ziemianski, Stanislaw. "La Finalité comme Anti-hasard Chez Aristote et St. Thomas D'Aquin." *Atti Del'VIII Congresso Tomistico Internazionale V: Problemi Metafisici*. Studi Tomistici 14. Città del Vaticano, Pontificia Accademia di San Tommaso e di Religione Cattolica: Libreria Editrice Cattolica, 1982. 351-358.

2422 Zimmermann, Albert. "Aristote et Averroés dans le Commentaire de Ferrandus de Hispania sur la Métaphysique D'Aristote." *Diotima* 8(1980): 159-163.

2423 Zum Brunn, Émilia. "La Métaphysique de L'*Exode* Selon Thomas D'Aquin." *Dieu et L'être: Exégesés D'Exode 3, 14 et de Coran 20, 11-24*. Ed. Centre d'études des religions du l. Etudes Augustiniennes. Paris: CNRS, 1978. 245-269.

C. GERMAN

2424 Aertsen, Johannes Adrianus. "Der Wissenschaftstheoretische Ort der Gottebeweise in der *Summa Theologiae* Des Thomas von Aquin." *Mediaeval Semantics and Metaphysics: Studies Dedicated to L. M. de Rijk, Ph. D., Professor of Ancient and Mediaeval Philosophy at the University of Leiden on the Occasion of His 60th Birthday*. Ed. E. P. Bos. Artistarium Supplementa 2. Nijmegen: Ingenium Publisher, 1985. 161-193.

2425 Aertsen, Johannes Adrianus. "Transzendental Versus Kategorial: Die Zwiespältigkeit von Thomas' Philosophie? Eine Kritische Studie." *Vivarium* 24(1986): 143-157.

2426 Aertsen, Johannes Adrianus. "Wendingen in Waarheid: Anselmus Van Canterbury, Thomas Van Aquino en Vico." *Tijdschrift voor Filosofie* 49(1987): 187-229. Also in German translation.

2427 Aertsen, Johannes Adrianus. "Die Lehre der Transzendentalien und die Metaphysik: Der Kommentar von Thomas von Aquin Zum IV: Buch der Metaphysica." *Freiburger Zeitschrift für Philosophie und Theologie* 35(1988): 293-316.

2428 Aertsen, Johannes Adrianus. "Die Transzendentalienlehre bei Thomas von Aquin in Ihren Historischen Hintergründen und Philosophischen Motiven." *Thomas von Aquin. Werk und Wirkung Im Licht Neuerer Forschungen*. Ed. Albert Zimmermann. Miscellanea Mediaevalia 19. Berlin/New York: Walter de Gruyter, 1988. 82-102.

2429 Albert, Karl. "Studien Zur Philosophie Des Thomas von Aquin." *Philosophischer Literaturanzeiger* 37(1984): 197-207.

2430 Albert, Karl. "Zu Thomas von Aquin: *Summa Theologiae* I, 4." *Freiburger Zeitschrift für Philosophie und Theologie* 31(1984): 207-209.

2431 Allgaier, Karl. "Engel und Intelligenzen: Zur Arabisch-Lateinischen Proklos-Rezeption." *Orientalische Kultur und Europäisches Mittelalter*. Eds. A. Zimmermann and I. Craemer-Ruegenberg. Berlin: Walter de Gruyter, 1985. 172-187.

2432 Anzenbacher, Arno. "Der Konflikt Zwischen Gesetz und Gewissen bei Thomas von Aquin." *Lex et Libertas: Freedom and Law According to St. Thomas Aquinas*. Eds. L. J. Elders and K. Hedwig. Studi Tomistici 30. Città del Vaticano: Pontificia Accademia di San Tommaso e di Religione Cattolica, 1987. 147-159.

2433 Anzenbacher, Arno. "Probleme der Thomas-Rezeption Im Aktuellen Kontext Praktischer Philosophie." *Jahrbuch F. Christliche Sozialwissenschaften*. Ed. A. Rauscher. Studi Tomistici 30. 1987. 59-89.

2434 Asveld, Paul. "Thomas und der Aristotelische Wissenschaftsbegriff." *Tommaso D'Aquino Nel Suo Settimo Centenario: Atti del Congresso Internazionale IX: Il Cosmo e la Scienza*. Napoli: Edizioni Domenicane Italiane, 1978. 92-98.

2435 Auer, Alfons. "Die Autonomie Des Sittlichen Nach Thomas von Aquin." *Christlich Glauben und Handeln: Fragen einer Fundamentalen Moraltheologie in der Diskussion*. Eds. Klaus Demmer and Bruno Schüller. Düsseldorf: Patmos, 1977. 31-54.

2436 Bauer, Johann. "Fält Gott Unter Einen Gattungsbegriff? Zu Thomas von Aquin, *Summa Theologicae* I Q. 3a. 5." *Salzburger Jahrbuch für Philosophie* 23-24(1978-1979): 89-98.

2437 Bäumer, Rolf, and Günter Helmes. "Tendenzen der Gegenwärtigen Glücksdiskussion: Ein Literaturbericht in Zwei Teilen." *Zeitschrift für Literaturwissenschaft und Linguistik* 13(1983): 99-127.

2438 Belmans, Théo G. "Hält Thomas von Aquin die Menschliche Natur Für Wandelbar?" *Münchener Theologische Zeitschrift* 30(1979): 208-217.

2439 Berg, Dieter. "Servitus Judaeorum. Zum Verhältnis Des Thomas von Aquin und Seines Ordens Zu Den Juden in Europa Im 13 Jahrhundert." *Thomas von Aquin: Werk und Wirkung Im Licht Neuerer Forschungen*. Ed. Albert Zimmermann. Berlin/New York: Walter de Gruyter, 1988. 439-458.

2440 Bernath, Klaus. "Einleitung." *Thomas von Aquin: Chronologie und Werkanalyse*. Ed. Klaus Bernath. Wege der Forschung 188. Darmstadt: Wissenschaftliche Buchgesellschaft, 1978. 1-11.

2441 Bernath, Klaus. "Bibliographie." *Thomas von Aquin II*. Ed. Klaus Bernath. Darmstadt: Wissenschaftliche Buchgesellschaft, 1981. 529-564.

2442 Bernath, Klaus. "Thomas von Aquin und die Erde." *Thomas von Aquin: Werk und Wirkung Im Licht Neuerer Forschungen*. Ed. Albert Zimmermann. Berlin/New York: Walter de Gruyter, 1988. 175-191.

2443 Berning, V. "Das Prinzip der Konnaturalität der Erkenntnis bei Thomas von Aquin." *Theologie und Glaube* (Paderborn) 72(1982): 291-310.

2444 Bertelloni, Carlos Francisco. "Die Thomasische Onto-theologische Auffassung der Politik in Ihrem Historischen Zusammenhang: Zur Entstehung Des Politischen Denkens Im Ausgehenden Mittelalter." *Freiburger Zeitschrift für Philosophie und Theologie* 35(1988): 331-352.

*First, the author makes a brief historical presentation of the situation of philosophy in the Faculty of Arts at Paris about 1240. Second, he analyzes the consequence of that situation for science and especially for ethics. Third, an attempt is made to demonstrate the existence in Paris of an interest for political themes before the Aristotelian *Politics* was known. These three points serve to show the context in which was born the political thought of later Middle Ages: Thomas Aquinas, Dante, and Marsilius. Finally, a reference is made regarding the onto-theological character of Thomas' political thought.*

2445 Bessner, Wolfgang. "Aspekte von Gemeinsamkeit in Den Lehren Ockhams und Des Hl. Thomas Gegenüber dem Averroismus." *Prima Philosophia* 1(1988): 218-255.

2446 Bien, Günther. "Die Philosophie und die Frage Nach dem Glück." *Die Frage Nach dem Glück*. Ed. Günther Bien. Problemata 74. Stuttgart, 1978. ix-xix.

2447 Bissels, Paul. "Die Seele Als Form und Einzelwesen bei Thomas von Aquin." *Franziskanische Studien* 61(1979): 1-7.

2448 Bochenski, Joseph M. "Die Fünf Wege." *Freiburger Zeitschrift für Philosophie und Theologie* 36(1989): 235-265.

*Mathematical-logical commentary to the proofs of existence God in Aquinas *Summa Theologiae*. Only the second proof is acceptable.*

2449 Böckle, Franz. "Moraltheologie und Exegese heute." *Ethik im Neuen Testament*. Ed. K. Kertelge. Freiburg: Verlag Herder, 197-210.

2450 Böckle, Franz. "Theonome Rationalitat Als Prinzip der Normbegründung bei Thomas von Aquin und Gabriel Vázquez." *Tommaso Nel Suo Settimo Centenario V: Atti del Congresso Internazionale: L'agire Morale*. Napoli: Edizioni Domenicane Italiane, 1977. 213-227.

2451 Borowsky, Wolfgang. "Die Wesentlichen Unterschiede Zwischen dem Menschen und dem Tier Nach Thomas von Aquin." *Tommaso D'Aquino Nel Suo Settimo Centenario: Atti del Congresso Internazionale VII: L'Uomo*. Napoli: Edizioni Domenicane Italiane, 1978. 211-218.

2452 Borzyszkowski, Marian. "Die Werke Des Hl. Thomas von Aquin in Den Bibliotheken in Pommerellen und Ermland." *Thomas von Aquin: Werk und Wirkung Im Licht Neuerer Forschungen*. Ed. Albert Zimmermann. Berlin/New York: Walter de Gruyter, 1988. 365-376.

2453 Browne, M. -D. "Die Echtheit Des Kommentars Des Hl. Thomas Zur Politik Des Aristoteles." 1920. *Thomas von Aquin: Chronologie und Werkanalyse*. Ed. Klaus Bernath. Wege der Forschung 188. Darmstadt: Wissenschaftliche Buchgesellschaft, 1978. 24-33.

2454 Bruch, Richard. "Das Wesen der Schweren Sünde Nach der Lehre Des Heiligen Thomas von Aquin." *Moralia Varia*. Ed. Richard Bruch. Düsseldorf: Patmos, 1981. 146-165.

2455 Bruch, Richard. "Intuition und Überlegung Beim Sittlichen Naturgesetz Nach Thomas von Aquin." *Theologie und Glaube* 67(1981): 29-54.

2456 Busa, Roberto. "Das Problem der Thomistischen Hermeneutik Nach der Veröffentlichung Des *Index Thomisticus*." *Thomas von Aquin: Werk und Wirkung Im Licht Neuerer Forschungen*. Ed. Albert Zimmermann. Berlin/New York: Walter de Gruyter, 1988. 359-364.

2457 Casula, Mario. "Die Beziehungen Wolff-Thomas-Carbo in der Metaphysica Latina: Zur Quellengeschichte der Thomas-Rezeption bei Christian Wolff." *Studia Leibnitiana* 11(1979): 98-123.

2458 Classen, Johannes. "Thomas von Aquin Als Philosophe und Lehrer." *Paedagicia Historica* 23(1983): 5-24.

2459 Comoth, Katharina. "Analogie und Reflexion bei G. W. F. Hegel und Thomas von Aquin." *Actualitas Omnium Actuum. Festschrift Für Heinrich Beck Zum 60. Geburtstag.* Ed. Erwin Schadel. Schriften Zur Triadik und Ontodynamik 3. Frankfurt: Peter Lang, 1989. 121-127.

2460 Courtés, P. -C. "Teilhabe und Kontingenz bei Thomas von Aquin." *Thomas von Aquin II.* Ed. Klaus Bernath. Darmstadt: Wissenschaftliche Buchgesellschaft, 1981. 266-313.

2461 Craemer-Ruegenberg, Ingrid. "Die Kritik Des Thomas von Aquin an der Origenistischen Seelenlehre." *Die Mächte Des Guten und Bösen.* Ed. Albert Zimmermann. Miscellanea Mediaevalia 11. Berlin: Walter de Gruyter, 1977. 235-252.

2462 De Mottoni, Faes Barbara. "Thomas von Aquin und die Sprache der Engel." *Thomas von Aquin. Werk und Wirkung Im Licht Neuerer Forschungen.* Ed. Albert Zimmermann. Berlin/New York: Walter de Gruyter, 1988. 140-155.

2463 Deku, Henry. "Formalisierungen." *Freiburger Zeitschrift für Philosophie und Theologie* 29(1982): 46-69.

2464 Donati, Silvia. "Egidius von Roms Kritik an Thomas von Aquins Lehre der Hylemorphen Zusammensetzung der Himmelskörper." *Thomas von Aquin: Werk und Wirkung Im Licht Neuerer Forschungen.* Ed. Albert Zimmermann. Studi Tomistici 19. Berlin/New York: Walter de Gruyter, 1988. 377-396.

2465 Dondaine, Antoine. "Die Sekretäre Des Hl. Thomas." 1963. *Thomas von Aquin: Chronologie und Werkanalyse.* Ed. Klaus Bernath. Wege der Forschung 188. Darmstadt: Wissenschaftliche Buchgesellschaft, 1978. 396-410.

2466 Donnell, R. A. "Individuation: Ein Beispiel Für die Entwicklung Im Denken Des Hl. Thomas von Aquin." *Thomas von Aquin II.* Ed. Klaus Bernath. Darmstadt: Wissenschaftliche Buchgesellschaft, 1981. 117-135.

2467 Echauri, Raúl. "Sein und Nichtsein bei Parmenides, Melissus, Platon und Thomas von Aquin." *Salzburger Jahrbuch für Philosophie* 26-27(1981-1982): 89-97.

2468 Elders, Léon J. "Die Person Im Bezug Zu Gott. Betrachtung Zur Grundlage Sittlicher Normen." *Die Person Im Anspruch Sittlicher Normen, St. Augustin.* 1980. 53-88.

2469 Elders, Léon J. "Zur Begründung der Fünf Wege." *Thomas von Aquin II.* Ed. Klaus Bernath. Darmstadt: Wissenschaftliche Buchgesellschaft, 1981. 136-162.

2470 Elders, Léon J. "Aufnahme und Erleüchtung in der Prophetischen Erkenntnis Nach Thomas von Aquin." *Veritati Catholicae: Festschrift Für Leo Scheffczykzum.* Eds. A. Ziegenaus, F. Courth, and Ph. Schäfer. Aschaffenburg: Pattloch, 1985. 628-648.

2471 Enders, Heinz W. "Die *Quinque Viae* Des Thomas Aquinas und das Argument Aus Anselm's *Proslogion*: Eine Bezeichnungstheoretische Analyse." *Wissenschaft und Weisheit* 40(1977): 158-188.

2472 Engelbert, Pius. "Eine Schule der Textkritik: Die Jüngsten Ed.en der Commissio Leonina." 1970. *Thomas von Aquin: Chronologie und Werkanalyse.* Ed. Klaus Bernath. Wege der Forschung 188. Darmstadt: Wissenschaftliche Buchgesellschaft, 1978. 438-452.

2473 Engelbert, Pius. "*De Veritate* und die Sekretäre Des Thomas von Aquin: Chronik einer ed." *Theologie und Philosophie* 55(1980): 78-100.

2474 Engelbert, Pius. "Zur Überlieferungsgeschichte der *Opuscula* Des Thomas von Aquin." *Studia Anselmiana* 85(1985): 289-301.

2475 Engelhardt (Bottrop-Münster), Paulus. "Menschwerdung Des Wortes und Menschliches Verlangen Nach Wahrheit: Ein Versuch, die Grundlegende Denk- und Glaubenserfahrung Des Thomas von Aquin Zu Erschliessen." *Thomas von Aquin: Werk und Wirkung Im Licht Neuerer Forschungen*. Ed. Albert Zimmermann. Berlin: Walter de Gruyter, 1988. 1-12.

2476 Ernst, Wilhelm. "Ursprung und Entwicklung der Menschenrechte in Geschichte und Gegenwart." *Gregorianum* 65(1984): 231-270.

2477 Fabro, Cornelio. "Zu einem Wesentlichen Thomismus." *Thomas von Aquin II*. Ed. Klaus Bernath. Darmstadt: Wissenschaftliche Buchgesellschaft, 1981. 221-238.

2478 Fabro, Cornelio. "Zu einem Vertieften Verständnis der Thomistischen Philosophie: Der Begriff der Partizipation." *Thomas von Aquin II*. Ed. Klaus Bernath. Darmstadt: Wissenschaftliche Buchgesellschaft, 1981. 386-432.

2479 Fabro, Cornelio. "Die Wiederaufnahme Des Thomistischen *Esse* und der Grund der Metaphysik." *Tijdschrift voor Filosofie* 43(1981): 90-116.

2480 Feder, Alfred. "Des Aquinaten Kommentar Zu Pseudo-Dionysius' *De Divinis Nominibus*: Ein Beitrag Zur Arbeitsmethode Des Hl. Thomas." 1926. *Thomas von Aquin: Chronologie und Werkanalyse*. Ed. Klaus Bernath. Wege der Forschung 188. Darmstadt: Wissenschaftliche Buchgesellschaft, 1978. 51-82.

2481 Fetz, Reto Luzius. "Personbegriff und Identitätstheorie." *Freiburger Zeitschrift für Philosophie und Theologie* 35(1988): 69-106.

2482 Fischer, Norbert. "Vernunftdeterminismus und Entscheidungsfreiheit: Die Doppelgesichtigkeit Des Intellektualismus-Problems in der Grundlegung der Philosophischen Ethik bei Thomas von Aquin." *Zeitshrift für Philosophische Forschung* 39(1985): 523-547.

Christian belief in God as an almighty creator and the resumption of Aristotle's philosophy are the reasons for Thomas Aquinas to reflect upon the responsibility of man for the decisions he takes. Thomas avoids the danger of an intellectual eudaemonistic determinism by showing that the responsibility for an evil decision becomes conceivable in man's inherent ambiguous faculty to deny his own finiteness and so to fall prey to haughtiness.

2483 Floss, Kare. "Thomas von Aquin und die Kategorie der Zeit." *Tommaso Nel Suo Settimo Centenario VI: Atti del Congresso Internazionale: L'essere*. Napoli: Edizioni Domenicane Italiane, 1977. 706-713.

2484 Fodor, Heinrich. "Die Gesellshaft Beim Hl. Thomas von Aquino (*Bonum Commune et De Regimine Principium*)." *Tommaso D'Aquino NelSuo Settimo Centenario VIII: Atti del Congresso Internazionale: L. Uomo*. Napoli: Edizioni Domenicane Italiane, 1978. 98-108.

2485 Fries, Albert. "Thomas von Aquin und Des Albertus Magnus *Quaestiones (Disputatae)* in Cod. Vat. Lat. 781." *Thomas von Aquin: Werk und Wirkung Im Licht Neuerer Forschungen*. Ed. Albert Zimmermann. Berlin/New York: Walter de Gruyter, 1988. 304-324.

2486 Fries, Albert. "Zur Problematik der *Summa Theologiae* Unter dem Namen Des Albertus Magnus." *Franziskanische Studien* 70(1988): 68-91.

2487 Fuchs, Josef. "Sittliche Wahrheit: Objektivismus und Subjektivismus." *Gregorianum* 63(1982): 631-646.

2488 Geenen, Godefridus. "Randglossen Zum Konzil von Chalkedon: Die Texte Des Vierten Konzils in Den Werken Des Hl. Thomas." *Thomas von Aquin: Chronologie und Werkanalyse*. Ed. Klaus Bernath. Wege der Forschung 188. Darmstadt: Wissenschaftliche Buchgesellschaft, 1978. 252-272.

2489 Geenen, Godefridus. "Thomas von Aquin und Seine Pseudepigraphischen Quellen." 1943. *Thomas von Aquin: Chronologie und Werkanalyse*. Ed. Klaus Bernath. Wege der Forschung 188. Darmstadt: Wissenschaftliche Buchgesellschaft, 1978. 209-223.

2490 Giacon, Carlo. "Der Hl. Thomas und das Sein Als Akt: Maritain, Gilson, Fabro." *Thomas von Aquin II*. Ed. Klaus Bernath. Darmstadt: Wissenschaftliche Buchgesellschaft, 1981. 482-512.

2491 Glorieux, Palémon. "De Regimine Judaeorum: Hypothesen und Klärungen." 1936. *Thomas von Aquin: Chronologie und Werkanalyse*. Ed. Klaus Bernath. Wege der Forschung 188. Darmstadt: Wissenschaftliche Buchgesellschaft, 1978. 132-143.

2492 Glorieux, Palémon. "Die *Quaestiones Disputatae* Des Hl. Thomas und Ihre Chronologische Aufeinanderfolge." *Thomas von Aquin*. Ed. Klaus Bernath. Wege der Forschung 188. Darmstadt: Wissenschaftliche Buchgesellschaft, 1978. 95-131.

2493 Gottzmann, Carola L. "Aspekte der Staatsauffassung Des Thomas von Aquin und die Nachhochhöfische Artusepik." *Thomas von Aquin: Werk und Wirkung Im Licht Neuerer Forschungen*. Ed. Albert Zimmermann. Berlin/New York: Walter de Gruyter, 1988. 286-303.

2494 Grabmann, Martin. "Die Persönlichen Beziehungen Des Hl. Thomas von Aquin." 1937. *Thomas von Aquin: Chronologie und Werkanalyse*. Ed. Klaus Bernath. Wege der Forschung 188. Darmstadt: Wissenschaftliche Buchgesellschaft, 1978. 144-166.

2495 Gumppenberg, Rudolf. "Zur Seinslehre in *De Ente et Essentia* Des Thomas von Aquin." *Thomas von Aquin II*. Ed. Klaus Bernath. Darmstadt: Wissenschaftliche Buchgesellschaft, 1981. 366-385.

2496 Gunthör, Anselm. "Natur Im Naturgesetz Nach Thomas von Aquin." *Lex et Libertas Freedom and Law According to St. Thomas Aquinas*. Ed. L. J. Elders and K. Hedwig. Studi Tomistici 30. Città del Vaticano: Pontificia Accademia di San Tommaso e di Religione Cattolica, 1987. 82-98.

2497 Hagemann, Ludwig B. "Missionstheoretische Ansätze bei Thomas von Aquin in Seiner Schrift *De Rationibus Fidei*." *Thomas von Aquin: Werk und Wirkung Im Licht Neuerer Forschungen*. Ed. Albert Zimmermann. Berlin/New York: Walter de Gruyter, 1988. 459-483.

2498 Heath, Thomas R. "Der Hl. Thomas und die Aristotelische Metaphysik: Einige Beobachtungen." 1955. *Thomas von Aquin: Chronologie und Werkanalyse*. Ed. Klaus Bernath. Wege der Forschung 188. Darmstadt: Wissenschaftliche Buchgesellschaft, 1978. 349-372.

2499 Hedwig, Klaus. "Analogie, Induktion, Experiment." *Sphaera Lucis: Studien Zur Intelligibilität Des Seienden Im Kontext der Mittelalterlichen Lichtspekulation.* Aschendorff: Münster Westfalem, 1980. 199-236.

2500 Hedwig, Klaus. "*Circa Particularia*: Kontingenz, Klugheit und Notwendigkeit Im Aufbau Des Ethischen Aktes bei Thomas von Aquin." *The Ethics of St. Thomas Aquinas.* Eds. L. Elders and K. Hedwig. Studi Tomistici 25. Città del Vaticano: Libreria Editrice Vaticana, 1984. 161-187.

2501 Hedwig, Klaus. "*Praecepta Negativa*: Die Axiomatik der Praktischen Vernunft und das Verbot." *Lex et Libertas: Freedom and Law According to St. Thomas Aquinas.* Eds. L. J. Elders and K. Hedwig. Studi Tomistici 30. Città del Vaticano: Pontificia Accademia di San Tommaso e di Religione Cattolica, 1987. 200-218.

2502 Hedwig, Klaus. "*Actus Indifferens*: Über die Theorie Des Undifferenzierten Handelns bei Thomas von Aquin und Duns Scotus." *Philosophisches Jahrbuch* 95(1988): 120-131.

2503 Hedwig, Klaus. "*Non Agere*: Über eine Verhältnisbestimmung von Freiheit und Bösem bei Thomas von Aquin." *Freiburger Zeitschrift für Philosophie und Theologie* 35(1988): 317-330.

2504 Heinzmann, Richard. "Die Theologie auf dem Weg Zur Wissenschaft. Zur Entwicklung der Theologischen Systematik in der Scholastik." 1974. *Thomas von Aquin: Chronologie und Werkanalyse.* Ed. Klaus Bernath. Wege der Forschung 188. Darmstadt: Wissenschaftliche Buchgesellschaft, 1978. 453-469.

2505 Heinzmann, Richard. "*Anima Unica Forma Corporis*: Thomas von Aquin Als Überwinder Des Platonisch-neoplatonischen Dualismus." *Philosophisches Jahrbuch* 93(1986): 236-259.

2506 Henle, Robert John. "Die Methodologie Des Hl. Thomas bei der Behandlung von Positiones Unter Besonderer Berücksichtigung der Positiones Platonicae." 1955. *Thomas von Aquin: Chronologie und Werkanalyse.* Ed. Klaus Bernath. Wege der Forschung 188. Darmstadt: Wissenschaftliche Buchgesellschaft, 1978. 291-312.

2507 Hoche, Hans-Ulrich. "Kausalgefüge, Irreale Bedingungssätze und das Problem der Definierbarkeit von Dispositionsprädikaten." *Zeitschrift für Allgemeine Wissenschaftstheorie* 8(1977): 257-291.

2508 Hödl, Ludwig. "Die Philosophische Gotteslehre Des Thomas von Aquin O. P. In der Diskussion der Schulen Um die Wende Des 13: Zum 14: Jahrhundert." *Rivista di Filosofia Neo-Scolastica* 70(1978): 113-134.

*Die Gottesnamen und die göttlichen Attribute (Eigenschaften) gründen nach Thomas von Aquin in der absoluten Fülle Gottes; ihre vielfältige Differenzierung geschieht nach Massgabe unseres menschlichen Erkennens. Heinrich von Gent machte die *rationes attributorum* in Gott aus, indem er das vollkommene Geist-Wesen Gottes in seiner Lebensfülle und (trinitarischen) Dynamik in acht nahm. In der Auseinandersetzung mit ihm legten die strengen Thomisten, u. a., Thomas von Sutton, die thomasische Position auf die Theorie der rein rationalen Unterscheidung der göttl. Attribute fest, obgleich Schüler des Thomas, u. a., Petrus von Tarentasie eine deutlich modifizierte Auslegung vertraten. Die Lehre von wesensimmanenten "rationes" griffen die Fransziskanertheologen Wilhelm von Ware, Duns Scotus, Robert Cowton, u. a., auf, indem sie sich (nicht ohne Widerspruch, z. B., des Peter von Baldeswell, Petrus von Sutton, u. a.) von der Tradition der mittleren Franziskanerschule lösten. Die Fülle der Wesensgründe hebt die Einfacheit nicht auf, die Formaldistinktion ist das Mittel ihrer Erkenntnis.*

2509 Hödl, Ludwig. "Das Intelligibile in der Scholastischen Erkenntnislehre Des 13 Jahrhunderts." *Freiburger Zeitschrift für Philosophie und Theologie* 30(1983): 345-372.

2510 Hödl, Ludwig. "Die Entdivinisierung Des Menschlichen Intellekts in der Mittelalterlichen Philosophie und Theologie." *Zusammenhänge, Einflüsse, Wirkungen.* 1988. 57-70.

2511 Hödl, Ludwig. "Philosophische Ethik und Moral-Theologie in der *Summa* Fr. Thomae." *Thomas von Aquin: Werk und Wirkung Im Licht Neuerer Forschungen.* Ed. Albert Zimmermann. Miscellanea Medievalia 19. Berlin/ New York: Walter de Gruyter, 1988. 23-42.

2512 Hödl, Ludwig. "Von der Theologischen Wissenschaft Zur Wissenschaftlichen Theologie bei Den Kölner Theologen Albert, Thomas und Duns Scotus." *Die Kölner Universität Im Mittelalter: Geistige Wurzeln und Soziale Wirkichkeit.* Ed. Albert Zimmermann. Miscellanea Medievalia 20. Berlin: Walter de Gruyter, 1989. 19-35.

2513 Hoffmann, A. "Ist der Hervorgang Des Wortes Beweisbar? Bemerkungen Zu *Summa Theologiae.* I 27,1 und I 32,1." *Münchener Theologische Zeitschrift* 34(1983): 214-223.

2514 Holz, Harald. "Hermeneutische Authenizität: Thomas von Aquin Als Streitfall?" *Archiv für Geschichte der Philosophie* 64(1982): 70-75.

2515 Honnefelder, Ludger. "*Conscientia Sive Ratio*: Thomas von Aquin und die Entwicklung Des Gewissensbegriffs." *Mittelalterliche Komponenten Des Europäischen Bewusstseins.* Berlin: Classical Folia Editions, 1983. 8-19.

2516 Hörmann, Karl. "Die Unveränderlichkeit Sittlicher Normen Im Anschluss an Thomas von Aquin." *Sittliche Normen: Zum Problem Ihrer Allgemeinen und Unwandelbaren Geltung.* Ed. W. Kierber. Düsseldorf: Patmos Verlag, 1982. 33-45.

2517 Hörmann, Karl. "Das Objekt Als Quelle der Sittlichkeit." *The Ethics of St. Thomas Aquinas.* Ed. L. Elders and K. Hedwig. Studi Tomistici 25. Città del Vaticano: Libreria Editrice Vaticana, 1984. 118-132.

2518 Horst, Ulrich. "Über die Frage einer Heilsökonomischen Theologie bei Thomas von Aquin: Ergebnisse und Probleme der Neueren Forschung." *Thomas von Aquin: Chronologie und Werkanalyse.* Ed. Klaus Bernath. Wege der Forschung 188. Darmstadt: Wissenschaftliche Buchgesellschaft, 1978. 373-395.

2519 Hoye, William J. "Die Unerkennbarkeit Gottes Als die Letzte Erkenntnis Nach Thomas von Aquin." *Thomas von Aquin. Werk und Wirkung Im Licht Neuerer Forschungen.* Ed. Albert Zimmermann. Berlin/New York: Walter de Gruyter, 1988. 117-139.

2520 Hoye, William J. "Sünden und Gottesliebe Nach Thomas von Aquin." *Die Mächte Des Guten und Bösen.* Ed. Albert Zimmermann. Miscellanea Mediaevalia 11. Berlin/New York: Walter de Gruyter, 1977. 206-234.

2521 Hufnagel, Alfonso. "Der Mensch Als Person Nach Thomas von Aquin." *Tommaso D'Aquino Nel Suo Settimo Centenario: Atti del Congresso Internazionale VII: L'Uomo.* Napoli: Edizioni Domenicane Italiane, 1978. 257-264.

2522 Hünemörder, Christian. "Thomas von Aquin und die Tiere." *Thomas von Aquin. Werk und Wirkung Im Licht Neuerer Forschungen.* Ed. Albert Zimmermann. Berlin/New York: Walter de Gruyter, 1988. 192-210.

2523 Imback, Ruedi. "Philosophisches Gespräch mit Thomas von Aquin: Zu einem Sammelband." *Freiburger Zeitschrift für Philosophie und Theologie* 25(1978): 217-223.

2524 Inciarte, Fernando. "Zur Rolle der Präedikation in der Theologie Des Thomas von Aquin: Am Beispiel der Trinitäetslehre." *Sprache und Erkenntnis Im Mittelalter*. Eds. Jan P. Beckmann et al. Miscellanea Mediaevalia 13. Berlin: Walter de Gruyter, 1981. 256-269.

2525 Inciarte, Fernando. "Kontingenz und Willensfreiheit: Bermerkungen Über Den Begriffder Menschenwürde." *Neue Hefte für Philosophie* 24/25(1985): 106-145.

2526 Jacobi, Klaus. "Thomas von Aquin Semantische Analyse Des Kontingenzbegriffs." *Tommaso Nel Suo Settimo Centenario VI: Atti del Congresso Internazionale: L'essere*. Napoli: Edizioni Domenicane, 1977. 624-637.

2527 Jacobi, Klaus. "Gut und Schlecht—Die Analyse Ihrer Entgegensetzung bei Aristoteles, bei Einigen Aristoteles—Kommentatoren und bei Thomas von Aquin." *Studien Zur Mittelalterlichen Geistesgeschichte und Ihre Quellen*. Ed. Albert Zimmermann. Miscellanea Mediaevalia 15. Berlin: Walter de Gruyter, 1982. 25-52.

2528 Jorissen, Hans. "Zur Struktur Des Traktates de Deo in der *Summa Theologiae* Des Thomas von Aquin." *Im Gespraech mit dem Dreieinen Gott*. Eds. M. Boehnke and H. Heinz. 1985. 231-257.

2529 Jung, Richard. "Sinnesphysiologische Bemerkungen Zu Thomas von Aquinos Maxime der Sinneserkenntnis." *Südhoffs Archiv* 64(1980): 371-384.

2530 Jüssen, Gabriel. "Thomistische Metaphysik und Analytische Philosophie." *Logik, Ethik, Theorie der Geistewissenschaften XI*. Ed. Wolfgang Patzig. Hamburg: Meiner, 1977. 399-404.

2531 Kaminski, Stanislaw. "Thomas von Aquin und Methodologische Typen von Ethik." *Tommaso Nel Suo Settimo Centenario V: Atti del Congresso Internazionale: L'agire Morale*. Napoli: Edizioni Domenicane Italiane, 1977. 488-498.

2532 Kaminski, Stanislaw. "Reduktive Erklärung in der Thomistischen Philosophie." *Atti Del'VIII Congresso Tomistico Internazionale V: Problemi Metafisici*. Studi Tomistici 14. Città del Vaticano, Pontificia Accademia di San Tommaso e di Religione Cattolica: Libreria Editrice Cattolica, 1982. 473-478.

2533 Kasper, Walter. "Das Wahrheitsverstaendnis der Theologie." *Wahrheit in Einheit und Vielheit*. Ed. E. Coreth. 1987. 170-193.

2534 Kleber, Hermann. "Literaturverzeichnis." *Glück Als Lebensziel: Untersuchungen Zur Philosophie Des Glücks bei Thomas von Aquin*. Beiträge Zur Geschichte der Philosophie und Theologie Des Mittelalters Neue Folge 31. Münster: Aschendorffsche Verlagsbuchhandlung Gmbh & Co., 1988. xii-xxvii.

2535 Klubertanz, George P. "Der Hl. Thomas und die Erkenntnis der Einzeldinge." *Thomas von Aquin II*. Ed. Klaus Bernath. Darmstadt: Wissenschaftliche Buchgesellschaft, 1981. 42-74.

2536 Kluxen, Wolfgang. "Glück und Glücksteilhabe: Zur Rezeption der Aristotelischen Glückslehre bei Thomas von Aquin." *Die Frage Nach dem Glück*. Ed. Günther Bien. Problemata 74. Stuttgart: Bad Canst, 1978. 77-91.

2537 Kluxen, Wolfgang. "Thomas von Aquin: Das Seiende und Seine Prinzipien." *Grundprobleme der Grossen Philosophen*. Ed. J. Speck. Göttingen, 1978. 210-216.

2538 Kluxen, Wolfgang. "Thomas von Aquin: Zum Gutsein Des Handelns." *Philosophisches Jahrbuch* 87(1980): 327-339.

2539 Kluxen, Wolfgang. "Seele und Unsterblichkeit bei Thomas von Aquin." *Seele*. Ed. Klaus Kremer. Leiden: Brill, 1984. 66-83.

2540 Kölmel, Wilhelm. "Geschichte und Geschichtlichkeit bei Thomas von Aquin." *Tommaso Nel Suo Settimo Centenario VI: Atti del Congresso Internazionale: L'essere*. Napoli: Edizioni Domenicane Italiane, 1977. 722-734.

2541 Korff, Wilhelm. "Der Rückgriff auf die Natur: Eine Rekonstruktion der Thomanischen Lehre Vom Natürlichen Gesetz." *Philosophisches Jahrbuch* 94(1987): 285-296.

2542 Korff, Wilhelm. "Thomas von Aquin und die Neuzeit." *Philosophie Im Mittelalter: Entwicklungslinien und Paradigmen*. Eds. Jan P. Beckmann et al. Hamburg: Felix Meiner Verlag, 1987. 387-408.

2543 Korff, Wilhelm. "Gnade Setzt Natur Voraus und Vollendet Sie: Thomas von Aquin und die Neuzeit." *Grundlagen und Probleme der Heutigen Morvaltheologie*. Ed. W. Ernst. 1989. 41-46.

2544 Kovach, Francis J. "Der Einfluss der Schrift Des Pseudo-Dionysius *De Divinis Nominibus* auf die Schönheitsphilosophie Des Thomas von Aquin." *Archiv für Geschichte der Philosophie* 63(1981): 150-166.

2545 Krämer, Hans. "Selbstverwirklichung." *Die Frage Nach dem Glück*. Ed. Günther Bien. Problemata 74. Stuttgart, 1978. 21-43.

2546 Küchenhoff, Günther. "Die Natur der Sache in der Lehre von Thomas Aquin." *Atti Di Congresso Internazionale. Tommaso D'Aquino Nel Suo Settimo Centenario VII: L'Uomo*. Eds. P. Alvigini et al. Napoli: Ed. Domenicane Italiane, 1978. 306-318.

2547 Küchenhoff, Günther. "Die Einwirkung von Lehren Des Hl. Thomas Durch die Enzyklik *Aeterni Patris* auf das Recht." *Atti Dell'VIII Congresso Tomistico Internazionale Vol. VI: Morale e Diritto Nella Prospettiva Tomistica*. Studi Tomistici 15. Napoli: Edizioni Domenicane Italiane, 1982. 207-212.

2548 Kühn, Ulrich. "Thomas von Aquin(1225-1274)." *Mittelalter II*. Ed. M. Greschat. 1983. 38-62. Also appears in *Klassiker der Theologie I*, Eds., H. Fries and G. Kretschmar, 212-225.

2549 Kühn, Ulrich. "*Nova Lex*: Die Eigenart der Christlichen Ethik Nach Thomas von Aquin." *Lex et Libertas: Freedom and Law According to St. Thomas Aquinas*. Ed. L. J. Elders and K. Hedwig. Studi Tomistici 30. Città del Vaticano: Pontificia Accademia di San Tommaso e di Religione Cattolica, 1987. 243-247.

2550 Kuksewicz, Zdzislaw. "Die Ägidianische Interpretation der Theorie der Seele bei Lambertus de Nonte." *Thomas von Aquin: Werk und Wirkung Im Licht Neuerer Forschungen*. Ed. Albert Zimmermann. Berlin/New York: Walter de Gruyter, 1988. 403-412.

2551 Kur, Mieczyslaw. "Auf der Suche Nach der Thomistischen Theorie Existentieller Urteile." *Przeglad Tomistyczny* 1(1980): 101-136, 136-137.

2552 Kurdzialek, Marian. "Über die Möglichkeit der Erdrotation in der Auffassung Thomas' von Aquin." *Tommaso D'Aquino Nel Suo Settimo Centenario IX: Atti del Congresso Internazionale: Il Cosmo e la Scienza*. Napoli: Ed. Domenicane Italiane, 1978. 229-234.

2553 Lakebrink, Bernhard. "Der Thomistische Seinbegriff und Seine Existentiale Umdeutung." *Tommaso Nel Suo Settimo Centenario VI: Atti del Congresso Internazionale: L'essere*. Napoli: Edizioni Domenicane Italiane, 1977. 219-238.

2554 Lakebrink, Bernhard. "Die Metaphysischen Voraussetzungen der Thomistischen Gottesbeweise und die Moderne Philosophie." *Quinque Sunt Viae*. Ed. Léon Elders. Studi Tomistici 9. Città del Vaticano, Pontificia Accademia di San Tommaso: Libreria Editrice Vaticana, 1980. 7-28.

2555 Landgraf, Artur. "Porretanisches Gut Beim Hl. Thomas von Aquin." 1939-1940. *Thomas von Aquin: Chronologie und Werkanalyse*. Ed. Klaus Bernath. Wege der Forschung 188. Darmstadt: Wissenschaftliche Buchgesellschaft, 1978. 196-208.

2556 Langlois, Jean. "Heidegger, Max Müller und der Thomismus." *Thomas von Aquin II*. Ed. Klaus Bernath. Darmstadt: Wissenschaftliche Buchgesellschaft, 1981. 91-116.

2557 Leijssen, L. "Martin Bucer und Thomas von Aquin." *Ephermerides Theologicae Lovanienses* 55(1979): 266-296.

2558 Leist, Fritz. "*Analogia Entis*." *Thomas von Aquin II*. Ed. Klaus Bernath. Darmstadt: Wissenschaftliche Buchgesellschaft, 1981. 75-90.

2559 Liebeschütz, Hans. "Mittelalter und Antike in Staatstheorie und Gesellschaftslehre Des Heilgen Thomas von Aquino." *Archiv für Kulturgeschichte* 61(1979): 35-68.

2560 Liske, Michael-Thomas. "Die Perspektive Des Sprechers und Ihre Logische Bedeutung: Ein Deutungsversuch Zu Thomas von Aquin *S. Th.* I, Q. 13, A. 10." *Theologie und Philosophie* 56(1981): 111-118.

2561 Liske, Michael-Thomas. "Die Sprachliche Richtigkeit bei Thomas von Aquin: Am Beispiel der Symmetrie Bzw. Asymmetrie von Relationen (Ehnlichkeit, *Relatio Realis-relatio Rationis*) Im Kontext der Trinitälslehre." *Freiburger Zeitschrift für Philosophie und Theologie* 32(1985): 373-390.

*Confronting the relations between the divine persons and the relation God—creature, the author discusses the symmetry of relations: Ordinary language terms (especially verbs) which refer to the symmetric relation of similarity connote asymmetric relations. *Relatio rationis* can consistently be understood as the converse of *relation realis*. A relation is real, if it presupposes in the subject an absolute reality which is sufficient to deduce the relational term from it.*

2562 Liske, Michael-Thomas. "Was Meint Thomas von Aquin mit Gott Weiss das Künftige Als Gegenwärtig?" *Theologie und Philosophie* 60(1985): 520-537.

2563 Lohr, Charles H. "Modelle Für die Überlieferung Theologischer Doktrin von Thomas von Aquin Bis Melchior Cano." *Studia Patristica XVI*. Ed. E. A. Livingstone. Texte und Untersuchuregen Zur Geschichte der Allchristlichen Literatur 129. Berlin: Akademie-Verlag, 1985. 148-167.

2564 Lotz, Johannés-Baptist. "Das Sein Nach Heidegger und Thomas von Aquin." *Tommaso Nel Suo Settimo Centenario VI: Atti del Congresso Internazionale: L'essere*. Napoli: Edizioni Domenicane Italiane, 1977. 35-49.

2565 Lotz, Johannés-Baptist. "Die Ontologische Differenz in Kant, Hegel, Heidegger und Thomas von Aquin." *Theologie und Philosophie* 53(1978): 1-26.

2566 Lotz, Johannés Baptist. "Mensch-Sein-Zeit-Gott: Zum Gespräch Zwischen Heidegger und Thomas von Aquin." *Theologie und Philosophie* 54(1979): 1-19.

2567 Lotz, Johannés Baptist. "Zur Thomas-Rezeption der Maréchal-Schule." *Thomas von Aquin II*. Ed. Klaus Bernath. Darmstadt: Wissenschaftliche Buchgesellschaft, 1981. 433-456.

2568 Luna, Concetta. "Die Ausgabe der Werke von Thomas von Aquin: Philologische Begriffe und Modelle der Übertragung." *Thomas von Aquin: Werk und Wirkung Im Licht Neuerer Forschungen*. Ed. Albert Zimmermann. Berlin/New York: Walter de Gruyter, 1988. 342-358.

2569 Luyten, Norbert A. "Der Erste Weg: *Ex Parte Motus*." *Quinque Sunt Viae*. Ed. Léon Elders. Studi Tomistici 9. Città del Vaticano, Pontificia Accademia di San Tommaso: Libreria Editrice Vaticana, 1980. 29-41.

2570 Luyten, Norbert A. "Der Begriff der *Materia Prima* Nach Thomas von Aquin." *La Philosophie de la Nature de Saint Thomas D'Aquin*. Ed. Léon Elders. Studi Tomistici 18. Cittá del Vaticano: Pontificia Accademia di San Tommaso, Libreria Editrice Vaticana, 1982. 28-44.

2571 Malik, Josef. "Gibt es Einen Eigenen Gottesbeweis, der Ausgeht Vom Streben Des Menschen Nach Erkenntnis und Glück?" *Quinque Sunt Viae*. Ed. Léon Elders. Studi Tomistici 9. Città del Vaticano, Pontificia Accademia di San Tommaso: Libreria Editrice Vaticana, 1980. 109-132.

2572 Malik, Josef. "Der Mensch Aus der Philosophischen Sicht Des Thomas von Aquin." *Theologie und Glaube* (Paderborn) 72(1982): 345-383.

2573 Mandonnet, Von Pierre. "Leben und Schriften Des Hl. Thomas in einem Kurzen Abriss." 1920. *Thomas von Aquin: Chronologie und Werkanalyse*. Ed. Klaus Bernath. Wege der Forschung 188. Darmstadt: Wissenschaftliche Buchgesellschaft, 1978. 11-23.

2574 Maritain, Jacques. "Der Humanismus Des Hl. Thomas von Aquin." 1941. *Thomas von Aquin II*. Ed. Klaus Bernath. Philosophisch Fragen: Wege der Forschung 538. Darmstadt: Wissenschaftliche Buchgesellschaft, 1981. 23-41.

2575 McDermott, John Michel. "Zwei Unendlichkeiten bei Thomas von Aquin: Gott und Materie." *Theologie und Philosophie* 61(1986): 176-203.

2576 McInerny, Ralph. "Thomas von Aquin: Kontemplation und Lehre." *Communio* 16(1987): 498-505.

2577 Meinhardt, H. "Einheitsmetaphysik-Seensmetaphysik." *Lexikon des Mittelalters* 1060(1985): 1739-1740.

2578 Merks, Karl-Wilhelm. "Anthropologische Perspektiven bei Thomas von Aquin." *Angelicum* 54(1977): 347-376.

2579 Meurers, Joseph. "Thomas und die Naturwissenschaft Heute." *Tommaso D'Aquino Nel Suo Settimo Centenario IX: Atti del Congresso Internazionale: Il Cosmo e la Scienza*. Napoli: Edizioni Domenicane Italiane, 1978. 41-59.

2580 Meyer, Gerbert. "Das Grundproblem der Bewegung bei Albert dem Grossen und Thomas von Aquin." *Albertus Magnus, Doctor Universalis: 1280-1980*. Ed. Gerbert Meyer and Albert Zimmermann. Walberberger Studien: Philosophische Reihe 6. Mainz: Mathias-Grünewald-Verlag, 1980. 249-277.

2581 Meyer, Gerbert. "Die Bewegungslehre Des Thomas von Aquin Im Kommentar Zum 3: Buch der Aristotelischen Physik." *La Philosophie de la Nature de Saint Thomas D'Aquin*. Ed. Léon Elders. Studi Tomistici 18. Cittá del Vaticano: Pontificia Accademia di San Tommaso, Libreria Editrice Vaticana, 1982. 45-65.

2582 Meyer, H. "Zur Empirischen Philosophie Arnold Gehlens." *Philosophia Naturalis* 23(1986): 399-423.

This article demonstrates that the "empirical" known philosophy of Arnold Gehlen really depends on traditional caused theories of European anthropology. Looking on Gehlen's theory of the special position of the human being, the origin of the human spirit, and institutions, this is demonstrated in detail. Gehlen's theory of the institutions for example seems to be based on the Roman Catholic theory of the sacraments.

2583 Mikat, Paul. "Gesetz und Staat Nach Thomas von Aquin Unter Besonderer Berücksichtigung der Lehre Vom Gesetz in der *Summa Theologiae.*" *Beiträge Zur Rechtsgeschichte*. Paderborn: Schöningh, 1979. 439-465.

2584 Motte, Antonin-René. "Abfassungszeit von *Contra Gentiles*." 1938. *Thomas von Aquin: Chronologie und Werkanalyse*. Ed. Klaus Bernath. Wege der Forschung 188. Darmstadt: Wissenschaftliche Buchgesellschaft, 1978. 167-172.

2585 Müller, Gerhard Ludwig. "Hebt das Sola-fide Prinzip die Moglichkeit einer Natürlichen Theologie? Eine Rückfrage bei Thomas von Aquin." *Catholica* 40(1986): 59-96.

2586 Müller, Ludger. "Das Schone Im Denken Des Thomas von Aquin." *Theologie und Philosophie* 57(1982): 413-424.

2587 Müller, Max. "Die Aktualität Des Thomas von Aquin." *Thomas von Aquin II*. Ed. Klaus Bernath. Darmstadt: Wissenschaftliche Buchgesellschaft, 1981. 513-527.

2588 Müller-Schmid, P. -P. "Kants Autonomie der Ethik und Rechtslehre und das Thomasische Naturrechtsdenken." *Jahrbuch für Christliche Sozialwissenschaften*(Münster) 27(1986): 35-60.

2589 Münk, H. J. "Ansätze Zu einer Neuen Sicht der Praktischen Philosophie Kants bei Katholischen Autoren der Gegenwart: Zugleich ein Beitrag Zum Vergleich der Naturrechtslehre bei Thomas von Aquin und Kant." *Jahrbuch für Christliche Sozialwissenschaften* (Münster) 26(1985): 97-122.

2590 Noelle-Neumann, Elisabeth. "Politik und Glück: Ein Versuch." *Freiheit und Sachzwang: Beiträge Zu Ehren Helmut Schelskys*. Ed. Horst Baier. Opladen, 1977. 208-262.

2591 Oberarzbacher, Franz Peter. "Die Urteilende Verstandestätigkeit und das Formelle Erkennen der Wahrheit bei Thomas von Aquin." *Tommaso Nel Suo Settimo Centenario VI: Atti del Congresso Internazionale: L'essere*. Napoli: Edizioni Domenicane Italiane, 1977. 290-295.

2592 Oeing-Hahnhoff, Ludger. "Mensch und Natur bei Thomas von Aquin." *Zeitschrift für Katholische Theologie* 101(1979): 300-315.

2593 Oeing-Hanhoff, Ludger. "Zur Rezeption und Kritik Des Averroistischen Hylemorphismus Durch Thomas von Aquin." *Actas del V Congreso Internacional de Filosofia Medieval II*. Madrid: Nacional, 1979. 1051-1057.

2594 Offermanns, Helga. "Philosophisch-theologische Gottesbeweise bei Platon, Aristoteles und Thomas von Aquin: Ein Beitrag Zur Fächerverbindung von Philosophie, Alten Sprachen und Religion." *Zeitschrift für Didaktik der Philosophie* 2(1980): 29-33.

2595 Owens, Joseph. "Metaphysische Trennung bei Thomas von Aquin." *Thomas von Aquin II*. Ed. Klaus Bernath. Darmstadt: Wissenschaftlich Buchgesellschaft, 1981. 339-365. Trans. Wenszel Peters of "Metaphysical separation in Aquinas," *Mediaeval Studies*, 34(1972): 287-306.

2596 Owens, Joseph. "Wissen und Realdistinktion bei Thomas von Aquin." *Thomas von Aquin II*. Ed. Klaus Bernath. Darmstadt: Wissenschaftliche Buchgesellschaft, 1981. 239-65. Trans. of "Quiddity and real distinction in St. Thomas Aquinas," *Mediaeval Studies*, 27(1965): 1-22.

2597 Pelster, Franz. "Zur Forschung Nach Den Echten Schriften Des Hl Thomas von Aquin." 1923. *Thomas von Aquin*. Ed. Klaus Bernath. Darmstadt: Wissenschaftliche Buchgesellschaft, 1978. 34-50.

2598 Pesch, Hermann Otto, "Introduction." *Thomas von Aquin. Grenze und Grobe mittelalterlicher Theologie Eine Einführung*. Mainz: Matthias-Grünewald, 1988. 452.

2599 Pesch, Hermann Otto. "Um Den Plan der *Summa Theologiae* Des Hl. Thomas von Aquin. Zu Max Secklers Neuem Deutungsversuch." 1965. *Thomas von Aquin: Chronologie und Werkanalyse*. Ed. Klaus Bernath. Wege der Forschung 188. Darmstadt: Wissenschaftliche Buchgesellschaft, 1978. 411-437.

2600 Pieper, Josef. "Der Philosophierende und die Sprache: Aphoristische Bemerkungen Eines Thomas-Lesers." *Philosophisches Jahrbuch* 93(1986): 226-235.

2601 Pöltner, Günther. "Die Stellung der Transzendentalen Seinsbestimmungen Im Gottesbeweis Des Thomas von Aquin." *Theologie und Glaube* (Paderborn) 7(1981): 17-34.

2602 Pöltner, Günther. "*Veritas Est Adaequatio Intellectus et Rei*: Der Gesprächsbeitrag Des Thomas von Aquin Zum Problem der Übereinstimmung." *Zeitschrift für Philosophische Forschung* 37(1983): 563-576.

2603 Pöltner, Günther. "Repräsentation und Partizipation: Zum Gedanken der Kreatürlichkeit Des Seienden bei Thomas von Aquin." *Theologie und Glaube* (Paderborn) 76(1986): 447-467.

2604 Ratzinger, Joseph. "Glaube, Philosophie und Theologie." *Zeitschrift für Katholische Theologie* 14(1985): 56-66.

2605 Reichwald, Ernst, and Elfi Reichwald. "Thomas von Aquino Über Di Gerechtigkeit und das Gerechte." *Wissenschaftliche Zeitschrift der Martin-Luther- Universität Halle-Wittenber. Gesellschafts-und sprachwissenschaftliche Reihe* 37(1988): 37-46.

2606 Reinhardt, H. "*Processio* und *Causa* bei Thomas von Aquin." *Forum Katholische Theologie* 5(1989): 44-50.

2607 Rieber, Arnulf. "Die Transzendentalienlehre Des Thomas von Aquin in Sprachphilosophischer Sicht." *Salzburger Jahrbuch für Philosophie* 23-24(1978-1979): 137-165.

2608 Rieber, Arnulf. "Der Ganzheitsbegriff bei Thomas von Aquin." *Z. f. Ganzheitsforschung* 28(1984): 99-131.

2609 Riedlinger, Helmut. "Zur Unterscheidung der Verstehensbereiche der Geschichtlichen und Geistlichen Schriftauslegung Anmerkungen Zu Thomas von Aquin *Summa Theologiae*, P. I, Q. 1 A. 10." *Veritati Catholicae* 1085(1985): 697-711.

2610 Riesenhuber, Klaus. "Partizipation Als Strukturprinzip der Namen Gottes bei Thomas von Aquin." *Sprache und Erkenntnis Im Mittelalter II*. Eds. Jan P. Beckmann et al. Miscellanea Mediaevalia 13/2. Berlin: Walter de Gruyter, 1981. 969-982.

2611 Roth, Gottfried. "Das Verhältnis von Angst und Freiheit Nach Thomas von Aquin." *The Ethics of St. Thomas Aquinas*. Eds. L. Elders and K. Hedwig. Studi Tomistici 25. Città del Vaticano: Libreria Editrice Vaticana, 1984. 216-225.

2612 Roth, Gottfried. "*Quod Anima Non Sit Complexio*: Zur Kritik Des Hl. Thomas von Aquin Am Seelenbegriff Galens." *Archiv für Religionpsychologie* 17(1985): 284-292.

2613 Runggaldier, Edmund. "*Sentencia Libri De Anima* und die Modernen Identitätstheorien." *L'anima Nell'antropologia Di San Tommaso D'Aquino IX: Atti del Congresso Societá Internazionale San Tommaso D'Aquino*. Ed. Abelardo Lobato. Milano: Editrice Massimo, 1987. 605-613.

2614 Salmann, Elmar. "Das Problem der Analysis *Fidei* bei A. Stolz und Pierre Rousselot." *Studia Anselmiana* 100(1988): 71-99.

2615 Saranyana, José Ignacio. "Thomas von Aquin: Signifikant, Signifikat und Grundwörter." *Sprache und Erkenntnis Im Mittelalter*. Eds. Jan P. Beckmann et al. Berlin: Walter de Gruyter, 1981. 424-433.

2616 Schäfer, Gerd. "Megalopsuhía und Magnanimitas bei Aristoteles und Thomas von Aquin. Zu Wesen und Wandlung Eines Antiken Wertbegriffes." *L'anima Nell'antropologia Di San Tommaso D'Aquino IX: Atti del Congresso Societá Internazionale San Tommaso D'Aquino*. Ed. Abelardo Lobato. Milano: Editrice Massimo, 1987. 18-25.

2617 Scheeben, Herbert. "Albert der Grosse und Thomas von Aquin in Köln." 1931. *Thomas von Aquin: Chronologie und Werkanalyse*. Ed. Klaus Bernath. Wege der Forschung 188. Darmstadt: Wissenschaftliche Buchgesellschaft, 1978. 87-94.

2618 Schenk, R. "*Perplexus Supposito Quodam*: Notizien Zu einem Vergessenen Schlüsselbegriff Thomanischer Gewissenlehre." *Recherches de Théologie Ancienne et Médiévale* 57(1990): 62-95.

2619 Scherer, Georg. "Die Unbergreiflichkeit Gottes und die Trinitaet bei Thomas von Aquin." *Im Gespräuch mit dem Dreieinigen Gott*. Eds. M. Boehnke and H. Heinz. Düsseldorf: Patmos, 1985. 258-275.

2620 Schönborn, C. "Die Autorität des Lehrers nach Thomas von Aquin." Ed. Fs. H. Chadwick. Berlin: Walter de Gruyter, 1988. 101-126.

2621 Schwarz, Balduin. "Die Irrtumslehre Des Heilger Thomas und der Transzendentale Idealismus." *Atti Dell'VIII Congresso Tomistico Internazionale V: Problemi Metafisici*. Città del Vaticano: Pontificia Accademia di San Tommaso e di Religione Cattolica, 1982. 452-463.

2622 Seibt, Ferdinand. "Thomas und die Utopisten: Planungsoptimismus und Universale Harmonie." *Die Mächte Des Guten und Bösen*. Ed. Albert Zimmermann. Miscellanea Mediaevalia 11. Berlin/New York: Walter de Gruyter, 1977. 252-270.

2623 Seidl, Horst. "Bemerkungen Zu Erkenntnis Als Massverhältnis bei Aristoteles und Thomas von Aquin." *Mensura: Mass, Zahl, Zahlensymbolik Im Mittelalter II*. Ed. von Albert Zimmermann. Miscellanea Mediaevalia 16/1. Berlin: Walter de Gruyter, 1983. 52-72.

2624 Seidl, Horst. "Natürliche Sittlichkeit und Metaphysische Voraussetzung in der Ethik Des Aristoteles und Thomas von Aquin." *The Ethics of St. Thomas Aquinas*. Eds. L. Elders and K. Hedwig. Studi Tomistici 25. Città del Vaticano: Libreria Editrice Vaticana, 1984. 95-117.

2625 Seidl, Horst. "Metaphysische Erörterungen Zu Boethius' Person-Definitiun und Ihrer Auslegung bei Thomas von Aquin." *Salzburger Jahrbuch für Philosophie* 30(1985): 7-27.

2626 Seidl, Horst. "Zur Geistseele Im Menschlichen Embryo Nach Aristoteles, Albert Dem Grossen und Thomas Von Aquin: Ein Diskussionsbeitrag." *Salzburger Jahrbuch für Philosophie* 31(1986): 37-63.

2627 Seidl, Horst. "Sittliche Freiheit und Naturgesetz bei Thomas von Aquin Angesichts Des Modernen Gegensatzes von Autonomie und Heteronomie." *Lex et Libertas: Freedom and Law According to St. Thomas Aquinas.* Eds. L. J. Elders and K. Hedwig. Studi Tomistici 30. Città del Vaticano: Pontificia Accademia di San Tommaso e di Religione Cattolica, 1987. 113-124.

2628 Seidl, Horst. "Zur Geistseele Im Menschlichen Embryo Nach Aristoteles, Albertus Magnus und Thomas von Aquin." *L'anima Nell'antropologia Di San Tommaso D'Aquino IX: Atti del Congresso Societá Internazionale San Tommaso D'Aquino.* Ed. Abelardo Lobato. Milano: Editrice Massimo, 1987. 123-157.

2629 Seidl, Horst. "Anmerkungen Zum Gottesbeweis Des Thomas von Aquin Aus dem Möglichen und Notwendigen." *Ontologie und Theologie. Beitr. Zum Problem D. Metaphysik bei Aristoteles U. Thomas von Aquin.* Ed. Matthias Bachmann-Lutz. Theologie 331. Frankfurt: Bern/Lang, 1988. 65-77.

2630 Seidl, Horst. "Über die Erkenntnis Erster, Allgemeiner Prinzipien Nach Thomas von Aquin." *Thomas von Aquin. Werk und Wirkung Im Licht Neuerer Forschungen.* Ed. Albert Zimmermann. Berlin: Walter de Gruyter, 1988. 103-116.

2631 Seidl, Horst. "Kommentar." *Über Seiendes und Wesenheit—De Ente et Essentia.* Ed. Horst Seidl. Philosophische Bibliothek 415. Hamburg: Meiner, 1988. 71-112.

2632 Senger, Hans Gerhard. "*Novitas Alicuius Entis*: Die Entstehung einer Neuen Philosophischen Frage Aus der Diskussion Um die Ewigkeit der Welt." *Studia Mediewistyczne* (Warszawa) 18(1977): 71-84.

2633 Senger, Hans Gerhard. "*Novitas Alicuis Entis* (Weltschöpfung und Erschaffung von Neuem in der Welt Nach Thomas von Aquin)." *Tommaso D'Aquino Nel Suo Settimo Centenario IX: Atti del Congresso Internazionale: Il Cosmo e la Scienza.* Napoli: Edizioni Domenicane Italiane, 1978. 455-470.

2634 Senger, Hans Gerhard. "Was Geht Lambert von Heerenberg die Seeligkeit Des Aristoteles An?" *Studien Zur Mittelalterlichen Geistesgeschichte und Ihre Quellen.* Ed. Albert Zimmermann. Berlin: Walter de Gruyter, 1982. 293-311.

2635 Sladeczek, Franz Maria. "Wann ist der Traktat Des Hl. Thomas *De Articulis Fidei et Ecclesiae Sacramentis* Entstanden?" 1927. *Thomas von Aquin: Chronologie und Werkanalyse.* Ed. Klaus Bernath. Wege der Forschung 188. Darmstadt: Wissenschaftliche Buchgesellschaft, 1978. 83-86.

2636 Sladeczek, Franz Maria. "Besagt der Satz der Identität Des Verschiedenen? Eine Ontologische Betrachtung Unter Bezugnahme auf Thomas von Aquin." *Salzburger Jahrbuch für Philosophie* 25(1980): 45-72.

2637 Spaemann, Robert. "Philosophie Als Lehre Vom Glücklichen Leben." *Die Frage Nach dem Glück.* Ed. B. Bien. Problemata 74. Stuttgart, 1978. 1-19.

2638 Speer, A. "Thomas von Aquin und Di Kunst: Eine Hermeneutische Anfrage Zur Mittelalterlichen Esthetik." *Archiv für Kulturgeschichte* 72(1990): 199-220.

2639 Stallmach, Josef. "Spontaneität Des Subjekts Im Aufbau Wissenschaftlicher Erkenntnis Nach der *Intellectus-Agens*-Lehre Thomas von Aquin." *Tommaso Nel Suo Settimo Centenario VI: Atti del Congresso Internazionale: L'essere*. Napoli: Edizioni Domenicane Italiane, 1977. 401-409.

2640 Steckner, Cornelius. "Der Städtegründende König Des Thomas von Aquin: Aristoteles und Vitruv, Politik und Städtebau Im Zeitalter der Kreuzzüge." *Aquinas* 29(1986): 233-253.

2641 Steel, Carlos. "De Metafysica Van Thomas Van Aquino." *Tijdschrift voor Filosofie* 45(1983): 459-74. In German translation.

2642 Stöhr, Johannes. "Theologie Als *Sacra Doctrina* bei Thomas von Aquin und in Neueren Auffassungen." *Veritati Catholicae*. Eds. A. Ziegenaus, F. Courth, and P. Schaefer. 1985. 672-696.

2643 Stöhr, Johannes. "Bewahrt das Sittengesetz Des Alten Bundes Seine Geltung Im Neuen Bund?" *Lex et Libertas: Freedom and Law According to St. Thomas Aquinas*. Eds. L. J. Elders and K. Hedwig. Studi Tomistici 30. Città del Vaticano: Pontificia Accademia di San Tommaso e di Religione Cattolica, 1986. 219-240.

2644 Stöhr, Johannes. "Die Theozentrik der Theologischen Wissenschaftslehre Des Hl. Thomas von Aquin und Ihre Diskussion bei Neuzeitlichen Kommentatoren." *Thomas von Aquin: Werk und Wirkung Im Licht Neuerer Forschungen*. Ed. Albert Zimmermann. Miscellanea Mediaevalia 19. Berlin/ New York: Walter de Gruyter, 1988. 484-498.

2645 Strohm, Hans. "Ps. Aristoteles *De Mundo* und Theilers Poseidonios." *Wiener Studien* (Wien) 100(1987): 69-84.

2646 Stroick, Clemens. "Die Ewigheit der Welt in Den Aristoteleskommentaren Des Thomas von Aquin." *Recherches de Théologie Ancienne et Médiévale* 51(1984): 43-68.

2647 Stürner, Wolfgang. "Die Gesellschaftsstruktur und Ihre Begründen bei Johannes von Salisbury, Thomas von Aquin und Marsilius von Padua." *Soziale Ordnungen Im Selbstverständnis Des Mittelalters I*. Miscellanea Mediaevalia 12. Berlin: Walter de Gruyter, 1979. 162-178.

2648 Stürner, Wolfgang. "Adam und Aristoteles Im Defensor Pacis Des Marsilius von Padua: Ein Vergleich mit Thomas von Aquin und Jean Quidort." *Medioevo* 6(1980): 379-396.

2649 Theis, Robert. "Struktur und Dialektik. Eine Strukturale Analyse von Thomas de Aquino *De Veritate* I, 4." *Filosofia Oggi* 5(1982): 227-245.

2650 Thum, Beda. "Ein Rückblick auf P. J. Gredts *Elementa Philosophiae Aristotelico-tomisticae*." *Studia Anselmiana* 97(1988): 245-255.

2651 Van Steenberghen, Fernand. "Lektüre und Studium Des Hl. Thomas: Überlegungen und Ratschläge." 1955. *Thomas von Aquin: Chronologie und Werkanalyse*. Ed. Klaus Bernath. Wege der Forschung 188. Darmstadt: Wissenschaftliche Buchgesellschaft, 1978. 273-290.

2652 Verbeke, Gérard. "Quellen und Chronologie Des Kommentars Zu *De Anima*." *Thomas von Aquin: Chronologie und Werkanalyse*. Ed. Klaus Bernath. Wege der Forschung 188. Darmstadt: Wissenschaftliche Buchgesellschaft, 1978. 224-251.

2653 Veres, Tomo. "Eine Fundamentale Ontologische Dichotomie Im Denken Des Thomas von Aquin." *Thomas von Aquin II*. Ed. Klaus Bernath. Darmstadt: Wissenschaftliche Buchgesellschaft, 1981. 314-338.

2654 Vergote, A. "Religie en Ethiek." *Tijdschrift voor Filosofie* 44(1982): 211-231. In German translation.

Criticism of the metaphysical concepts of law and finality leads to the distinction between the ontic and the ethical good, corresponding to two aspects: eudaemonism, obligation. These oppositions are corrected by a dialectic among the negativity of law (based on sanctity), human person, and psychic positivity. Religion does not form ethics but achieves its meaning.

2655 Von Gunten, François. "Gibt es eine Zweite Redaktion Des Sentenzenkommentars Des Hl. Thomas von Aquin?" 1956. *Thomas von Aquin: Chronologie und Werkanalyse*. Ed. Klaus Bernath. Wege der Forschung 188. Darmstadt: Wissenschaftliche Buchgesellschaft, 1978. 313-348.

2656 Wagner, Claus. "Alberts Naturphilosophie Im Licht der Neueren Forschung (1979-1983)." *Freiburger Zeitschrift für Philosophie und Theologie* 32(1985): 65-104.

2657 Walther, Helmut G. "Utopische Gesellschaftskritik oder Satirische Ironie? Jean de Meun und die Lehre Des Aquinaten Über die Entstehung Menschlicher Herrschaft." *Soziale Ordnungen Im Selbstverständnis Des Mittelalters I*. Miscellanea Mediaevalia 12. Berlin: W. de Gruyter, 1979. 84-105.

2658 Weidemann, Hermann. "Socrates Est/There is No Such Thing as Pegasus: Zur Logik Singulärer Existenzaussagen Nach Thomas von Aquin und Willard Van Orman Quine." *Philosophisches Jahrbuch* 86(1979): 42-59.

2659 Weidemann, Hermann. "Socrates Est: Zur Logik Singulärer Existenzaussagen Nach Thomas von Aquin." *Sprache und Erkenntnis Im Mittelalter II*. Eds. Jan P. Beckmann et al. Berlin: Walter de Gruyter, 1981. 753-758.

2660 Weidemann, Hermann. "Zum Problem der Begründung der Metaphysik bei Thomas von Aquin." *Ontologie und Theologie: Beitr. Zum Problem D. Metaphysik bei Aristoteles U. Thomas von Aquin*. Ed. Matthias Bachmann-Lutz. Theologie 331. Frankfurt: Bern/Lang, 1988. 37-63.

2661 Weier, W. "Seinsteilhabe und Sinnteilhabe Im Denken Des Hl. Thomas von Aquin." *Thomas von Aquin II*. Ed. Klaus Bernath. Darmstadt: Wissenschaftliche Buchgesellschaft, 1981. 192-220.

2662 Werner, Hans-Joachim. "Vom Umgang mit Den Geschöpfen: Welches ist die Ethische Einschätzung Des Tieres bei Thomas von Aquin?" *Thomas von Aquin. Werk und Wirkung Im Licht Neuerer Forschungen*. Ed. Albert Zimmermann. Berlin/New York: Walter de Gruyter, 1988. 211-232.

2663 Winkler, Friedrich. "*Deus-creatio-esse*: Der Denkansatz Des Thomas von Aquin." *Religion Wissenschaft Kultur* 25(1976-1977): 49-67.

2664 Wöerner, Markus H. "Der Sinn von Ewigkeit und Seine Deutung bei Thomas von Aquin." *Ontologie und Theologie. Beitr. Zum Problem D. Metaphysik bei Aristoteles U. Thomas von Aquin*. Ed. Matthias Bachmann-Lutz. Theologie 331. Frankfurt/New York: Bern/Lang, 1988. 79-101.

2665 Zan, Ryszard. "Gott ist die Umwelt Des Menschen: Über die Gotteserkenntnis Nach Thomas von Aquin." *Journal Philosophique* 1(1985): 293-300.

2666 Zimmer, C. "Logik der Thomasischen Gottesbeweise: Ein Beitrag Zur Aussagenlogik bei Thomas von Aquin." *Franziskanische Studien* 71(1989): 212-223.

2667 Zimmermann, Albert. "Zur Interpretation von Nous *Poetikos.*" *Proceedings of the World Congress on Aristotle II.* Berlin: Walter de Gruyter, 1981. 220-224.

2668 Zimmermann, Albert. "Bemerkungen Zu Thomas von Aquin, *Quaet. Disp. De Veritate* I." *Studien Zur Mittelalterlichen Geistesgeschichte und Ihre Quellen.* Ed. Albert Zimmermann. Miscellanea Mediaevalia 15. Berlin: Walter de Gruyter, 1982. 247-261.

2669 Zimmermann, Albert. "Zur Unterscheidung Des Sinnlichen Strebevermögens Gemäss Thomas von Aquin." *Aristotelisches Erbe Im Arabisch-Lateinischen Mittelalter.* Ed. Albert Zimmermann. Miscellanea Mediaevalia 18. Berlin: Walter de Gruyter, 1986. 43-52.

2670 Zimmermann, Albert. "Die Erkennbarkeit Des Natürlichen Gesetzes Gemäss Thomas Von Aquin." *Lex et Libertas: Freedom and Law According to St. Thomas Aquinas.* Eds. L. J. Elders and K. Hedwig. Studi Tomistici 30. Città del Vaticano: Pontificia Accademia di San Tommaso e di Religione Cattolica, 1987. 56-66.

2671 Zimmermann, Albert. "Gedanken Des Thomas von Aquin Über *Defectus Naturalis* und *Timor.*" *Thomas von Aquin. Werk und Wirkung Im Licht Neuerer Forschungen.* Ed. Albert Zimmermann. Miscellanea Mediaevalia 19. Berlin/New York: Walter de Gruyter, 1988. 43-52.

D. ITALIAN

2672 Abbà, Giuseppe. "La Funzione Dell'habitus Virtuoso Nell'atto Morale Secondo Lo *Scriptum Super Sententiis* Di San Tommaso D'Aquino." *Salesianum* 42(1980): 3-34.

2673 Abbà, Giuseppe. "La Nuova Concezione Dell'habitus Virtuoso Nella *Summa Theologiae* Di San Tommaso D'Aquino." *Salesianum* 43(1981): 71-118.

2674 Abbà, Giuseppe. "I Christian Moral Principles Di Germain Grisez e la *Secunda Pars* Della *Summa Theologiae.*" *Salesianum* 48(1986): 637-680.

2675 Agazzi, Evandro. "Il Messaggio Di Tommaso D'Aquino e la Razionalità Scientifica del Nostro Tempo." *Tommaso D'Aquino Nel Suo Settimo Centenario IX: Atti del Congresso Internazionale: Il Cosmo e la Scienza.* Napoli: Edizioni Domenicane Italiane, 1978. 60-67.

2676 Alberghi, Sante. "Moderne Risonanze del Principio Tomistico Di Analogia." *Tommaso Nel Suo Settimo Centenario VI: Atti del Congresso Internazionale: L'essere.* Napoli: Edizioni Domenicane Italiane, 1977. 75-80.

2677 Ales Bello, Angela. "Fenomenologia e Tomismo in Edith Stein." *Atti del Congresso Internazionale. Tommaso D'Aquino Nel Suo Settimo Centenario VI: L'essere.* Napoli: Edizioni Domenicane, 1977. 469-479.

2678 Alessi, Adriano. "La Struttura Metafisica Dell'esistente." *Aquinas* 32(1989): 353-380.

2679 Alfano, Giulio. "Il Tomismo Nel Pensiero Di Mariano F. Cordovani." *Sapienza* 41(1988): 71-91.

2680 Allegro, Giuseppe. "La Theologia Come Progetto Speculativo." *Giornale di Metafisica* 10(1988): 101-111.

2681 Alszeghy, Zoltan. "Teologia e Sistema." *Sapienza* 35(1982): 271-282.

2682 Alszeghy, Zoltan. "La Discussione Sul Peccato Originale." *Gregorianum* 67(1986): 133-139.

2683 Amato, Carmelo. "La Dottrina Tomistica del Bene." *Sacra doctrina* 22(1977): 117-147.

2684 Ambrosetti, Giovanni. "Natura, Persona e Diritto in San Tommaso D'Aquino." *Tommaso D'Aquino Nel Suo Settimo Centenario VIII: Atti del Congresso Internazionale: L'Uomo*. Napoli: Edizioni Domenicane Italiane, 1978. 247-263.

2685 Ambrosi, Annarosa. "Principio D'identità e Principio Di Non Contraddizione: Studio Su San Tommaso D'Aquino." *Verifiche* 10(1981): 205-234.

2686 Amerio, Romano. "Aporie Filosofiche e Uso Dell'indefinitó Quidam in Testi Tomistici." *Tommaso nel suo settimo centenario VI: Atti del Congresso internazionale: L'essere* Napoli: Edizioni Domenicane Italiane, 1977. 597-602.

2687 Andereggen, Ignacio E. M. "Differencias en la Comprensión Medioeval del *De Divinis Nominibus* de Dionisio Areopagita." *Sapientia* 44(1989): 197-210.

2688 Andrianopoli Cardullo, Mariacarla. "La Proposta Pedagogica Di San Tommaso." *Atti Dell'VIII Congresso Tomistico Internazionale VII: L'uomo e Il Mondo Nella Luce Dell'Aquinate*. Studi Tomistici 16. Napoli: Edizioni Domenicane Italiane, 1982. 233-242.

2689 Arata, Carlo. "La Metafisica Della Prima Persona (*Ego Sum Qui Sum*): Parte Prima." *Rivista di Filosofia Neo-Scolastica* 81(1989): 181-200.

2690 Arrighi, Gino. "Le Matematiche Nel Secolo Di Tommaso D'Aquino." *Tommaso D'Aquino Nel Suo Settimo Centenario IX: Atti del Congresso Internazional*. Napoli: Edizioni Domenicane Italiane, 1978. 87-91.

2691 Babolin, Sante. "La Cogitativa Di San Tommaso." *Tommaso D'Aquino Nel Suo Settimo Centenario IX: Atti del Congresso Internazionale*. Napoli: Edizioni Domenicane Italiane, 1978. 363-367.

2692 Baccari, Luciano. "Provvidenza: Una Proposta Di Intelligibilità del Mondo." *Aquinas* 32(1989): 411-433.

2693 Baldassarre, Walter. "La Collera Nella Concezione Di San Tommaso e Nella Psicologia Moderna. Il Doppio Aspetto Dell'aggressività Umana." *Euntes Docete* 39(1986): 409-428.

2694 Barbetta, Cecilia. "Un Trattato Inedito Di Scipione Maffei Sul Pensiero Di San Tommaso Intorno All'usura." *Studi storici veronesi Luigi Simeoni* 30-31(1980-1981): 166-204.

2695 Barbour, Hugo. "Eraclito e San Tommaso: Nota Su Una Scoperta." *Doctor Communis* 40(1987): 289-290.

2696 Barzaghi, Giuseppe. "Implicazioni del Pensiero Tomistico." *Sapienza* 39(1986): 5-121.

2697 Barzaghi, Giuseppe. "Analogia, Ordine e Il Fondamento Della Sintesi Tomista." *Sapienza* 40(1987): 65-97.

2698 Basso, Domingo M. "Un Pilar de la Moral Tomista: La Doctrina del Apetito Recto Natural." *Tommaso Nel Suo Settimo Centenario V: Atti del Congresso Internazionale: L'agire Morale*. Napoli: Edizioni Domenicane Italiane, 1977. 375-402.

2699 Basti, Gianfranco. "Una Riproposizione Operazionale Della Fisica Aristotelico-tomista Dell'intenzionalià." *L'anima Nell'antropologia Di San Tommaso D'Aquino IX: Atti del Congresso Societá Internazionale San Tommaso D'Aquino*. Ed. Abelardo Lobato. Milano: Editrice Massimo, 1987. 483-510.

2700 Bataillon, Louis Jacques. "Iacopo Da Varazze e Tommaso D'Aquino." *Sapienza* 32(1979): 22-29.

2701 Bazzi, Pio. "Il Principio Di Indeterminazione Di Heisenberg e la Dottrina Di San Tommaso Sul Determinismo in Natura." *Tommaso D'Aquino Nel Suo Settimo Centenario: Atti del Congresso Internazionale IX: Il Cosmo e la Scienza.* Napoli: Edizioni Domenicane Italiane, 1978. 269-275.

2702 Bednarski, Felice Adalberto. "La Cultura Alla Luce Della Teologia Di San Tommaso D'Aquino." *Atti del Congresso Internazionale VIII: Tommaso D'Aquino Nel Suo Settimo Centenario: L'Uomo.* Napoli: Ed. Domenicane Italiane, 1978. 383-392.

2703 Belic, Miljenko. "Hylemorphismi Locus Eiusque Momentum in Systemate Aristoteles et in Systemate Sancti Thomae." *Tommaso D'Aquino Nel Suo Settimo Centenario: Atti del Congresso Internazionale IX: Il Cosmo e la Scienza.* Napoli: Edizioni Domenicane Italiane, 1978. 276-282.

2704 Belic, Miljenko. "*Diversi Modi Analogiae Entis Quibus Tum Explicite Tum Implicite Utitur* San Tommaso." *Atti Del'VIII Congresso Tomistico Internazionale: Vol. V: Problemi Metafisici.* Studi Tomistici 14. Città del Vaticano, Pontificia Accademia di San Tommaso e di Religione Cattolica: Libreria Editrice Cattolica, 1982. 179-190.

2705 Berti, E. "Il Significato del Tomismo Nel Pensiero Contemporaneo." *Studium* (Roma) 77(1981): 59-66. Also appears in *Atti dell'VIII Congresso tomistico internazionale VIII: San Tommaso nella storia del pensiero.* Napoli: Edizioni Domenicane Italiane, 1982. 359-366.

2706 Bertola, Ermenegildo. "Tommaso D'Aquino Nella Storiografia Filosofica Medioevale Precedente Alla Enciclica *Aeterni Patris.*" *Atti Del'VIII Congresso Tomistico Internazionale II: L'enciclica Aeterni Patris 1981.* Studi Tomistici 11. Città del Vaticano, Pontificia Accademia di San Tommaso e di Religione Cattolica: Libreria Editrice Cattolica, 1981. 248-270.

2707 Bertuzzi, Giovanni. "L'estetica e L'arte in San Tommaso." *Sapienza* 39(1986): 106-117.

2708 Bertuzzi, Giovanni. "L'interpretazione Di Werner Jaeger Dell'Umanesimo e Della Teologia Di San Tommaso." *Sapienza* 41(1988): 299-311.

2709 Bessero Belti, Remo. "Rosmini Per San Tommaso." *Rivista Rosminiana di Filosofia e di Cultura* 75(1981): 189-201.

2710 Bessero Belti, Remo. "Rosmini Per Lo Studio Di San Tommaso." *Atti Del'VIII Congresso Tomistico Internazionale II: L'enciclica Aeterni Patris 1981.* Studi Tomistici 11. Città del Vaticano, Pontificia Accademia di San Tommaso e di Religione Cattolica: Libreria Editrice Cattolica, 1981. 271-281.

2711 Bianchi, Cirillo. "De Immortalitate Animae Huius Operationibus Deducta Apud Angelici Doctoris Doctrinam." *L'anima Nell'antropologia Di San Tommaso D'Aquino IX: Atti del Congresso Societá Internazionale San Tommaso D'Aquino.* Ed. Abelardo Lobato. Milano: Editrice Massimo, 1987. 201-205.

2712 Bianchi, Luca. "Guglielmo Di Baglione, Tommaso D'Aquino e la Condanna del 1270." *Rivista di Storia della Filosofia Medievale* 39(1984): 503-520.

2713 Bianco, Alberto. "La Nozione Di Creazione Nella Morale Di San Tommaso." *Atti Dell'VIII Congresso Tomistico Internazionale VI: Morale e Diritto Nella Prospettiva Tomistica*. Studi Tomistici 15. Cittá del Vaticano: Pontificia Accademia di San Tommaso e di Religione Cattolica, 1982. 39-44.

2714 Bianco, Alberto. "La Nozione Di Creazione Nella Morale Di San Tommaso." *Rivista Rosminiana di Filosofia e di Cultura* 76(1982): 158-163.

2715 Biffi, Inos. "Per Una Analisi Semantica Dei Lemmi *Theologia*, *Theologus*, *Theologicus*, *Theologico*, in San Tommaso: Un Saggio Metodologico Nell'uso Dell'*Index Thomisticus*." *Teologia* 3(1978): 148-163.

2716 Bini, Enrico. "Il Movimento Tomista a Prato." *Doctor Communis* 36(1983): 52-71.

2717 Bizzarri, Paolo. "De Gratia Della *Summa Theologiae* Di San Tommaso D'Aquino Secondo le Interpretazioni Di Alcuni Studiosi Recenti." *Doctor Communis* 30(1977): 339-377.

2718 Blandino, Giovanni. "Discussione Di Alcune Questioni Di Cosmologia Neo-tomista." *Aquinas* 33(1990): 29-38.

2719 Bof, Giampiero. "Sintomi Di Un'evoluzione Della Dottrina Circa L'anima in San Tommaso." *Lateranum* 46(1980): 379-413.

2720 Bogliolo, Don Luigi. "Sulla Fondazione Tomista Della Morale." *Tommaso Nel Suo Settimo Centenario V: Atti del Congresso Internazionale: L'agire Morale*. Napoli: Edizioni Domenicane Italiane, 1977. 107-121.

2721 Bogliolo, Don Luigi. "Problemas de la Analogía." *Sapientia* 35(1980): 359-372.

The scope of the article is to prove that analogy is not only a philosophical opinion but a real law of things. In fact, things speak to us. We must recognize that our daily and common intellectual experience offers to our mind neither an absolute multiplicity, nor an absolute unity. The world shows to us a great multiplicity of beings along a vertical and a horizontal line. To express this double multiplicity we need to use the principle of identity, the principle of participation, the principle of transcendency. Every other explanation of things would remain a pure illusion without the foundation of the principle of analogy. Naturally all this presupposes a real perfection making the existent existing, that is, to be, which is the perfection of all perfection, the root of every being.

2722 Bogliolo, Don Luigi. "Il Problema Dell'esistenza Di Dio Negli Scritti Di San Tommaso D'Aquino." *Doctor Communis* 35(1982): 185-204.

*It is a critical recension to the volume of Fernand Van Steenberghen's *Le probléme de l'existence de Dieu dans les Écrits de Saint Thomas d'Aquin*, Institut Supérieur de philosophie, Louvain-la-Neuve, 1980, page 375. According to Saint Thomas Aquinas, Van Steenberghen admits the validity of our reason to prove God's existence, but he reduces the five *viae* to the only proof from finite to infinite Being. The author of this article-recension, according to Van Steenberghen tries to demonstrate: it is true we by our reason can prove God's existence only through finite being, but finite being has many ontological properties and, therefore, it is possible to reach God's existence through many proofs.*

2723 Bogliolo, Don Luigi. "Fundamentación Ontológica de la Libertad Psicológica." *Sapientia* 39(1984): 249-256.

2724 Bogliolo, Don Luigi. "L'ottava Settimana Tomistica Argentina." *Doctor Communis* 37(1984): 292-314.

2725 Bogliolo, Don Luigi. "Dall'interiorità Agostiniana All'interiorità Tomista." *Augustinus et Thomas*. Città del Vaticano: *Rivista Doctor Communis*, Palazzo Canonici, 1986. 292-314. Omaggio dell'Accademia di San Tommaso d'Aquino a Sant'Agotino d'Ippona nel xvi centenario della conversione. *Doctor Communis*, 39(1986): n. (3).

2726 Bogliolo, Don Luigi. "La Chiave Risolutiva del Problema Dell'essere: La IV Via Di San Tommaso." *Doctor Communis* 41(1988): 3-17.

2727 Bonafede, Giulio. "L'attività Delle Cause Seconde in San Tommaso." *Atti Del'VIII Congresso Tomistico Internazionale V: Problemi Metafisici*. Studi Tomistici 14. Città del Vaticano, Pontificia Accademia di San Tommaso e di Religione Cattolica: Libreria Editrice Cattolica, 1982. 315-319.

2728 Bontadini, Gustavo. "La Concezione Classica Dell'essere e Il Contributo del Tomismo." *Tommaso Nel Suo Settimo Centenario VI: Atti del Congresso Internazionale: L'essere*. Napoli: Edizioni Domenicane Italiane, 1977. 29-34.

2729 Booth, Edward. "Conciliazioni Ontologiche Delle Tradizioni Platonica e Aristotelica in San Alberto e San Tommaso." *San Alberto Magno, L'uomo e Il Pensatore*. Ed. Studia Universitatis S. Thomas in Urbe. Ed. P Gieraths and D. Mathes. Milano: Studia Universitatis S. Thomas in Urbe, 1982. 59-81.

2730 Borzone Morera, Gabriella. "Il Concetto Di Persona Umana Nella Teoria Tomistica Dell'educazione." *Tommaso D'Aquino Nel Suo Settimo Centenario VIII: Atti del Congresso Internazionale: L'Uomo*. Napoli: Edizioni Domenicane Italiane, 1978. 400-425.

2731 Bourbon di Petrella, Fiammetta. "Il Tema Della Sopravvivenza Nel Pensiero Di Tommaso D'Aquino." *Tommaso D'Aquino Nel Suo Settimo Centenario: Atti del Congresso Internazionale VII: L'Uomo*. Napoli: Edizioni Domenicane Italiane, 1978. 442-449.

2732 Braakhuis, H. A. G. "Saint Thomas et L'astrologie." *Astrologia, Scienza, Filosofia e Società Nel Trecento Europeo*. Ed. Cattera di Storia della Filosofia Università di Parma. Parma: Università di Parma, 1990. Unavailable.

2733 Brena, Gian Luigi. "Interpretazione Antropologica Di San Tommaso." *Tommaso D'Aquino Nel Suo Settimo Centenario: Atti del Congresso Internazionale*. Napoli: Edizioni Domenicane Italiane, 1978. 83-100.

2734 Brunello, Bruno. "L'uomo in Tommaso D'Aquino e Nella Storia Contemporanea." *Tommaso D'Aquino Nel Suo Settimo Centenario: Atti del Congresso Internazionale VII: L'Uomo*. Napoli: Edizioni Domenicane Italiane, 1978. 228-235.

2735 Bucci, O. "Il Diritto Naturale Dalle Origini (Cristiane e Non Cristiane) a San Tommaso D'Aquino, a Proposito Di Una Recente Pubblicazione." *Apollinaris* 58(1985): 775-784.

2736 Busa, Roberto. "Introduzione Alla Bibliografia, Agli Indici e Lessici Tomistici." *Saint Thomas Aquinas in Hodierna Formation Sacerdotali. Seminarium*, 1977. 922-958.

2737 Busa, Roberto. "L'*Index Thomisticus*." *Studi Medievali* 21(1980): 411-421.

2738 Busa, Roberto. "Per San Tommaso *Ratio Seminalis* Significa Codice Genetico: Problemi e Metodi Di Lessicologia e Lessicografia Tomistiche." *Atti Dell'VIII Congresso Tomistico Internazionale: Morale e Diritto Nella Prospettiva Tomistica.* Studi Tomistici 15. Cittá del Vaticano: Pontificia Accademia di San Tommaso e di Religione Cattolica, 1982. 437-451.

2739 Busa, Roberto. "Voces *Realis-realiter* in S. Thomae Aquinate Cum Appendice de Voce *Res-rei.*" *Atti del III Colloquio Internazionale: Res.* Eds. M. Fattori and M. Bianchi. Lessico Intellettuale Europeo 26. Roma: Edizioni dell'Ateneo, 1982. 105-136.

2740 Busa, Roberto. "De Voce Spiritus in Operibus S. Thomae Aquinatis." *Spiritus IV.* Eds. M. Fattori and M. Bianchi. Lessico Intellettuale Europeo 32. Roma: Edizioni dell'Ateneo, 1984. 191-222.

2741 Busa, Roberto. "De Terminationum Latinarum Statisticis Mensuris Ex *Indice Tomistico.*" *Annales de la Faculté des Lettres et Sciences humaines de Nice* 52(1985): 147-161.

2742 Busa, Roberto. "Tommaso D'Aquino." *Grafia e Interpunzione del Latino Nel Medioevo.* Ed. A. Maieru. Roma: Lessico, 1987. 1-22.

2743 Caffarra, Carlo. "*Primum Quod Cadit in Apprehensione Practicae Rationis*(1, 2, Q. 94, A. (2). Variazioni Su Un Tema Tomista." *Euntes Docete* 39 (1986): 387-408.

2744 Campanini, Giorgio. "Potere e Proprietá Nella Riflessione Tomistica." *Tommaso D'Aquino Nel Suo Settimo Centenario VIII: Atti del Congresso Internazionale.* Napoli: Edizioni Domenicane Italiane, 1978. 50-63.

2745 Campodonico, Angelo. "Il Carattere Immediato Della Presenza Di Dio Nel Mondo Secondo Tommaso D'Aquino." *Rivista di Filosofia Neo-Scolastica* 76(1984): 245-268.

*This article is concerned with the immediateness of God's imminence in the world and in the human being. According to Aquinas, God's imminence permanently pervades the universe because He is both "Esse," i.e., the cause of created beings, and Spirit. The difference that exists in creatures between *esse* and *essentia* and the hierarchical participation (Proclus, Dyonisius) are also required. The author shows that God's immediate imminence is the basis of entities' value and complementarity.*

2746 Cantone, Carlo. "Partecipazione e Relazione." *Tommaso Nel Suo Settimo Centenario VI: Atti del Congresso Internazionale: L'essere.* Napoli: Edizioni Domenicane Italiane, 1977. 104-108.

2747 Caparello, Adriana. "Presenza Della Lingua Greca in Due Commentari Tomistici." *Doctor Communis* 30(1977): 250-269.

2748 Caparello, Adriana. "La Terminologia Greca Nel Commentario Al *De Caelo*: Tommaso D'Aquino e Lingua Greca." *Angelicum* 55(1978): 415-457.

2749 Caparello, Adriana. "Terminologia Greca Tomistica Nel *Commentarium Ad Meteorologica.*" *Sacra Doctrina* 23(1978): 243-287.

2750 Caparello, Adriana. "Note: Critiche-Discussioni." *Sapienza* 34(1981): 160-174.

2751 Caparello, Adriana. "Questioni Esegetiche e Problemi Di Confronto Nel I Libro Dell' Expositio Al *De Anima* Di Aristoteles: Temistio, Sigieri Di Brabante, Tommaso D'Aquino." *Sapienza* 34(1981): 160-174.

2752 Caparello, Adriana. "El I Libro de *De Anima* e la Reportatio: Piperno, Reginaldo Da." *Atti Dell'VIII Congresso Tomistico Internazionale VIII: San Tommaso Nella Storia del Pensiero*. Cittá del Vaticano: Pontificia Accademia di San Tommaso e di Religione Cattolica, 1982. 20-38.

2753 Capone, Domenico. "Prudenza e Veritá Di Coscienza in Situazione, Secondo San Tommaso." *Tommaso Nel Suo Settimo Centenario V: Atti del Congresso Internazionale: L'agire Morale*. Napoli: Edizioni Domenicane Italiane, 1977. 409-420.

2754 Cappello, Glori. "Umanesimo e Scolastica: Il Valla, Gli Umanisti e Tommaso D'Aquino." *Rivista di Filosofia Neo-Scolastica* 69(1977): 423-442.

2755 Cappelluti, Gerardo. "Ricerche Sulla Cultura Filosofica e Teologica Pre-post Tridentina Nel Sud Italia: La Provincia Domenicana Di San Tommaso D'Aquino in Puglia e Il Suo Studio Generale." *Memorie Domenicane* (Pistoia) 14(1983): 239-328.

2756 Cardoletti, Pietro. "Introduzione Allo Studio Di San Tommaso." *Saint Thomas Aquinas in Hodierna Formation Sacerdotali. Seminarium*, 1977. 959-969.

2757 Caspani, Andrea Mario. "Per Un'epistemologia Integrale: La Conoscenza Per Connaturalita in Jacques Maritain." *Doctor Communis* 35(1982): 39-67.

2758 Catan, John R. "Aristotele e San Tommaso Intorno All'*actus Essendi*." *Rivista di Filosofia Neo-Scolastica* 73(1981): 639-655.

*The essay shows a relationship between Thomas' conception of the *actus essendi* and the indications left by Aristotle in *De anima* 3. 5. Specifically the notion of "an act over and above form"; "form as a positive potency"; "the inconceivability of form as act of being." This established that the solving of the implicit aporia in Aristotle was a necessary practical condition for the full realization of the notion of the act of being elaborated by Thomas. Figures mentioned: Plato, Aristotle, Plotinus, Aquinas, J. Owens*

2759 Cattaneo, Vincenzo. "Alcune Osservaizioni Sulla Strutturazione e Sviluppo Logico Delle Cinque Vie Tomistiche." *Atti Del'VIII Congresso Tomistico Internazionale IV: Prospettive Teologiche Moderne*. Studi Tomistici 13. Città del Vaticano, Pontificia Accademia di San Tommaso e di Religione Cattolica: Libreria Editrice Cattolica, 1981. 36-41.

2760 Cavaciuti, Santino. "La Critica del Concetto Di Anima-sostanza Nel Primo Spiritualismo Ottocentesco." *L'anima Nell'antropologia Di San Tommaso D'Aquino IX: Atti del Congresso Societá Internazionale San Tommaso D'Aquino*. Ed. Abelardo Lobato. Milano: Editrice Massimo, 1987. 511-520.

2761 Cavalcoli, Giovanni. "La Resuurezione Della Sessualità Secondo San Tommaso." *Atti Dell'VIII Congresso Tomistico Internazionale VII: L'uomo e Il Mondo Nella Luce Dell'Aquinate*. Studi Tomistici 16. Cittá del Vaticano: Pontificia Accademia di San Tommaso e di Religione Cattolica, 1982. 207-219.

2762 Cavalcoli, Giovanni. "Sulla Differenza Tra L'anima Dell'uomo e Quella Della Donna." *L'anima Nell'antropologia Di San Tommaso D'Aquino IX: Atti del Congresso Societá Internazionale San Tommaso D'Aquino*. Ed. Abelardo Lobato. Milano: Editrice Massimo, 1987. 227-234.

2763 Cavallini, Stefano. "La Presenza Tomista Nell'opera Di Erich Przywara." *Atti Dell'VIII Congresso Tomistico Internazionale VIII: San Tommaso Nella Storia del Pensiero*. Studi Tomistici 17. Cittá del Vaticano: Pontificia Accademia di San Tommaso e di Religione Cattolica, 1982. 256-261.

2764 Cavallini, Stefano. "San Tommaso Nostro Contemporaneo: Un Saggio Sul Magistero del Prof. Luigi Bogliolo." *Doctor Communis* 39(1986): 213-215.

2765 Celli, Daniele. "Tommaso D'Aquino O Il Desierio Di Dio." *Il Nuovo Areopago* 2(1983): 94-112.

2766 Cenacchi, Giuseppe. "Il Primato Dell'intelletto in Tommaso D'Aquino." *Incontri Culturali* 10(1977): 169-176.

2767 Cenacchi, Giuseppe. "Liberare Il Lavoro Dall'alienzzione Secondo Il Pensiero Filosofico Di San Tommaso D'Aquino." *San Bonaventura e San Tommaso D'Aquino*. Ed. M. Cecchelli. 1978. 101-114.

2768 Cenacchi, Giuseppe. "Sulla Genesi Della Filosofia del Lavoro Nel Pensiero Di San Tommaso D'Aquino." *Tommaso D'Aquino Nel Suo Settimo Centenario VIII: Atti del Congresso Internazionale: L'Uomo*. Napoli: Edizioni Domenicane Italiane, 1978. 64-74.

2769 Cenacchi, Giuseppe. "Aspetti Esistenziali Dell'antropologia Di San Tommaso D'Aquino." *Atti Dell'VIII Congresso Tomistico Internazionale VII: L'uomo e Il Mondo Nella Luce Dell'Aquinate*. Studi Tomistici 16. Cittá del Vaticano: Pontificia Accademia di San Tommaso e di Religione Cattolica, 1982. 128-139.

2770 Cenacchi, Giuseppe. "Secolo XVI: Problema Dell'immortalità del *De Anima* Di Aristotele. Rilievi Critici Sulle Teorie Alessandriste, Tomiste e Della Scuola Di Pietro Pomponazzi." *L'anima Nell'antropologia Di San Tommaso D'Aquino IX: Atti del Congresso Societá Internazionale San Tommaso D'Aquino*. Ed. Abelardo Lobato. Milano: Editrice Massimo, 1987. 521-533.

2771 Centi, Tito S. "Ancora Sul Tomismo Di Santa Caterina Da Siena." Studi Tomistici 17. *Atti dell'VIII Congresso Tomistico Internazionale VIII: San Tommaso nella storia del pensiero*. Cittá del Vaticano: Pontificia Accademia di San Tommaso e di Religione Cattolica. 1982. 127-144.

2772 Centi, Tito S. "Riflessioni Sull'ascesa Tomistica a Dio." *Sacra Doctrina* 27(1982): 512-524.

2773 Chianese, Anna. "Imputabilitá, Responsabilità, Volontarietà in San Tommaso." *Tommaso Nel Suo Settimo Centenario V: Atti del Congresso Internazionale: L'agire Morale*. Napoli: Edizioni Domenicane Italiane, 1977. 421-425.

2774 Chiocchetta, Pietro. "Suggestioni Tomiste Sul Senso Della Storia." *Atti Dell'VIII Congresso Tomistico Internazionale VII: L'uomo e Il Mondo Nella Luce Dell'Aquinate*. Studi Tomistici 16. Cittá del Vaticano: Pontificia Accademia di San Tommaso e di Religione Cattolica, 1982. 245-257.

2775 Ciappi, Luigi. "L'omaggio a Paolo VI de la *Somma Teologica* Tradota e Commentata." *Doctor Communis* 31(1978): 248-252.

2776 Ciola, N. "La Ricerca Della Verità e L'attitudine Al Bene Come Apertura a Dio: Problematiche Contemporanne Ed Esposizione Della Dottrina Di San Tommaso." *Lateranum* 52(1986): 306-342.

2777 Clavell, Luis. "Il Primo Principio Della Conoscenza Intellectuale." *Atti Dell'VIII Congresso Tomistico Internazionale VII: L'uomo e Il Mondo Nella Luce Dell'Aquinate*. Studi Tomistici 16. Cittá del Vaticano: Pontificia Accademia di San Tommaso e di Religione Cattolica, 1982. 62-73.

2778 Clavell, Luis. "La Belleza en el Comentario Tomista Al *De Divinis Nominibus*." *Anuario Filosófico* 17(1984): 93-99.

2779 Clavell, Luis. "La Fondazione Della Liberta Nell'atto Di Essere Dell'anima." *L'anima Nell'antropologia Di San Tommaso D'Aquino IX: Atti del Congresso Societá Internazionale San Tommaso D'Aquino*. Ed. Abelardo Lobato. Milano: Editrice Massimo, 1987. 235-242.

2780 Colombu, Mario. "Il Fine Dell'educazione Secondo I Principi Di San Tommaso." *Tommaso D'Aquino Nel Suo Settimo Centenario VIII: Atti del Congresso Internazionale: L'Uomo*. Napoli: Edizioni Domenicane Italiane, 1978. 426-438.

2781 Colosio, Innocenzo. "La Vis Polemica Di San Tommaso Specialmente Nel *De Unitate Intellectus Contra Averroistas*." *Palestra del Clero* 62 (1983): 69-78.

2782 Composta, Dário. "Il Concetto Di Teologia in San Tommaso D'Aquino: Esame Di Una Recente Opera Di Michel Corbin." *Doctor Communis* 30(1977): 270-279.

2783 Composta, Dário. "Il Diritto Naturale Tomistico Nella Più Recente Ermeneutica." *Doctor Communis* 30(1977): 82-100.

2784 Composta, Dário. "Dimensioni Teologiche e Filosofiche del Diritto Nella Luce del Tomismo." *Doctor Communis* 31(1978): 170-173.

2785 Composta, Dário. "San Tommaso D'Aquino Oggi." *Doctor Communis* 31(1978): 237-247.

2786 Composta, Dário. "Ancora Sul Diritto Naturale: L'antropologia Classica Di Fronte Al Diritto Naturale, in Un Confronto Con le Recenti Filosofie Negatrici." *Euntes Docete* 32(1979): 117-138.

2787 Composta, Dário. "L'efficienza del Tomismo Oggi: A Proposito Di Un'opere del Cardinale Pietro Parente." *Doctor Communis* 33(1980): 91-96.

2788 Composta, Dário. "La Libertà Umana e le Sue Dimensioni." *Doctor Communis* 35(1982): 86-93.

This report on Professor Manno's miscellaneous volume on human freedom deals with various philosophical theories as propounded by Aquinas, Scotus, Marx, Scheler, Jaspers, and Soviet religious liberty. From such a historical survey on the problem, a double question might be offered to philosophical reflection: one, phenomenological; and the other one, metaphysical. As to this different treatment, a three-fold approach ought to be proposed: a clear terminology, a debate on existence and essence.

2789 Composta, Dário. "Il Fondamento Antropologico Della Morale e del Diritto Secondo San Tommaso." *Sapienza* 36(1983): 259-288.

*There are three foundations of Thomistic morals: biblical, because man is an image of God; ontological, because man is also body and soul and not an incarnate spirit; anthropological, because man knows not only the value of his actions, but also their general laws. The foundation of Thomistic law is the *res iusta* namely the objective social relationships binding man to others. These relationships are fixed and known through human needs, human speech, human inclinations.*

2790 Composta, Dário. "La Perenne Attualità Di San Tommaso D'Aquino." *Doctor Communis* 38(1985): 190-193.

2791 Composta, Dário. "Un Importante Traguardo Dell'Accademia Di San Tommaso D'Aquino." *Doctor Communis* 38(1985): 181-187.

2792 Composta, Dário. "Considerazioni Sull' "Intuizione Dell'essere:" Come Questione Fondamentale Della Metafisica." *Doctor Communis* 42(1989): 125-136.

2793 Conigliaro, Francesco. "L'uomo Imago Dei Fine Della Creazione: Antropologia Di Tommaso D'Aquino." *O Theologos* 5(1978): 5-100.

2794 Conticello, Carmelo Giuseppe. "San Tommaso Ed I Padri, La Catena Aurea Super Ioannem." *Archives d'Histoire Doctrinale et Littéraire du Moyen Age* 57(1990): 31-92.

2795 Cuciuffo, Michele. "*Ratio Essendi* e Funzione del Diritto Di Educare." *Tommaso D'Aquino Nel Suo Settimo Centenario: Atti del VIII Congresso Internazionale: L'Uomo*. Napoli: Edizioni Domenicane Italiane, 1978. 439-445.

2796 Cuciuffo, Michele. "Dalla Trascendenza Dell'essere la Laicità, Dalla Laictà Il Pluralismo." *Atti Del'VIII Congresso Tomistico Internazionale: Vol. V: Problemi Metafisici*. Studi Tomistici 14. Città del Vaticano, Pontificia Accademia di San Tommaso e di Religione Cattolica: Libreria Editrice Cattolica, 1982. 82-89.

2797 Cuciuffo, Michele. "I Due Poli Dell'anima Umana, Trascendenza e Immanenza." *L'anima Nell'antropologia Di San Tommaso D'Aquino IX: Atti del Congresso Societá Internazionale San Tommaso D'Aquino*. Ed. Abelardo Lobato. Milano: Editrice Massimo, 1987. 539-546.

2798 D'Amore, Benedetto. "Il Problema Dell'essere e del Dover Essere." *Tommaso Nel Suo Settimo Centenario VI: Atti del Congresso Internazionale: L'essere*. Napoli: Edizioni Domenicane Italiane, 1977. 138-154.

2799 D'Amore, Benedetto. "L'antropologia Filosofica." *Sapienza* 30(1977): 5-23.

2800 D'Amore, Benedetto. "La Filosofia Cristiana, Oggi (Presupposti Necessari Per Un'adequata Comprensione)." *Sapienza* 31(1978): 275-295.

2801 D'Ancona Costa, Cristina. "Aspetti del Rapporto Dell'Aquinate Con I Platonici Nel Commento Al *Liber de Causis*." *Atti Dell'VIII Congresso Tomistico Internazionale VIII: San Tommaso Nella Storia del Pensiero*. Studi Tomistici 17. Cittá del Vaticano: Pontificia Accademia di San Tommaso e di Religione Cattolica, 1982. 53-59.

2802 D'Ancona Costa, Cristina. "L'uso Della Sententia Dionysii Nel Commento Di San Tommaso e Egidio Romano Alle Proposizioni 3, 4, 6 del *Liber de Causis*." *Medioevo: Rivista di Storia della Filosofia Medievale* 8(1982): 1-42.

2803 D'Eredità, Pier Luigi. "Formalismo Kantiano e Formalità Tommasiana Nella Implicazione Dei Termini Dell'actio." *Giornale di Metafisica* 5(1983): 75-109.

2804 Dalledonne, Andrea. "L'autentico *Esse* Tomistico e L'equivoco Neoscolastico Sulla Esistenza Come Atto in Carlo Giacon." *Divus Thomas* 81(1978): 68-82.

2805 Dalledonne, Andrea. "La Metafisica Dell'essere e Il Primato Dottrinale del Tomismo Nel L'Enciclica *Aeterni Patris*." *Problemi Metafisici: Atti Dell'VIII Congresso Tomistico Internazional V*. Studi Tomistici 14. 1982. 14-23.

2806 Darms, Gion. "Il Problema Delle Norme Oggettive Dell'attività Morale Alla Luce Di San Tommaso." *Divinitas* (Roma) 21(1977): 191-214.

2807 De Finance, Joseph. "Il Pensiero Di San Tommaso: Valori Perenni e Nuovi Compiti." *Conmemoración* 1207(1979): 57-76.

2808 De Luca, Pietro. "I Principi Dello Stato Democratico Nella Concezione Politica Di San Tommaso." *Tommaso D'Aquino Nel Suo Settimo Centenario VIII: Atti del Congresso Internazionale.* Napoli: Edizioni Domenicane Italiane, 1978. 75-86.

2809 De Monticelli, Roberta, and Michele Di Francesco. "Lingua Degli Angli e Lingua Dei Bruti." *Teoria* 9(1989): 69-137.

2810 De Mottoni, Barbara Faes. "Enuntiatores Divini Silentii: Tommaso D'Aquino e Il Linguaggio Degli Angeli." *Medioevo* 12(1986): 197-228.

2811 De Scantimurgo, Joào. "Relazioni Di Politica e Morale Nella Filosofia Di San Tommaso." *Tommaso D'Aquino Nel Suo Settimo Centenario VIII: Atti del Congresso Internazionale: L'Uomo.* Napoli: Edizioni Domenicane Italiane, 1978. 87-93.

2812 De Stier, María Lillana Lukac. "Algunos Aspectos de la Doctrina Tomista del Entendimiento Posible." *Sapientia* 40(1985): 109-120.

2813 Degl'Innocenti, Umberto. "La Distinzione Reale Nel *De Ente et Essentia* Di San Tommaso." *Doctor Communis* 31(1978): 20-28.

2814 Del Cura, Alejandro. "Originalità Della Metafisica Di San Tommaso." *Aquinas* 31(1988): 7-23.

2815 Di Giannatale, Giovanni. "Considerazioni Sull'origine Dell'anima in Dante." *Sapienza* 30(1977): 450-454.

2816 Di Giannatale, Giovanni. "Dante Tra Aristotele e San Tommaso: L'argomento Logico-metafisico Dell Ordinatio Ad Unum Degli Enti." *Sapienza* 34(1981): 175-182.

2817 Di Giannatale, Giovanni. "La Posizione Di San Tommaso Sull'aborto (Note Sulla Concezione Genetica)." *Doctor Communis* 34(1981): 296-311.

2818 Di Giovanni, Alberto. "San Tommaso, Il Maggiore Degli Agostiniani." *Atti Dell'VIII Congresso Tomistico Internazionale VIII: San Tommaso Nella Storia del Pensiero.* Studi Tomistici 17. Cittá del Vaticano: Pontificia Accademia di San Tommaso e di Religione Cattolica, 1982. 86-106.

2819 Di Marino, Antonio. "La Fondazione Delle Norme Etiche Sessuali in San Tommaso D'Aquino." *Tommaso Nel Suo Settimo Centenario: Atti del Congresso Internazionale V: L'agire Morale.* Napoli: Edizioni Domenicane Italiane, 1977. 308-313.

2820 Di Russia, Dimitrij. "Giustizia Pratica in San Tommaso." *Atti Dell'VIII Congresso Tomistico Internazionale VI: Morale e Diritto Nella Prospettiva Tomistica.* Studi Tomistici 15. Cittá del Vaticano: Pontificia Accademia di San Tommaso e di Religione Cattolica, 1982. 318-328.

2821 Di Stefano, Tito. "Emergenza Dell'atto Di *Esse* Ed Emergenza Dell'atto Libero Nella Riflessione Radicale Di San Tommaso." *Tommaso D'Aquino Nel Suo Settimo Centenario: Atti del Congresso Internazionale VII: L'Uomo.* Napoli: Edizioni Domenicane Italiane, 1978. 392-399.

2822 Diodato, Roberto. "Tra *Esse* e Deissi: Note Per Una Conferma Linguistica Dell'ontologia Gilsoniana." *Revista di Filosofia Neo-Scolastica* 78(1986): 3-33.

2823 Dondaine, H. F. "Introduction." *Opera Omnia XXXXII: De Articulis Fidei.* By Sancti Thomae de Aquino. Rome: Ad Sanctae Sabinae, 1979. 211-241.

2824 Duro, Aldo. "*Index Thomisticus*: Un Monumento a San Tommaso." *Gregorianum* 60(1979): 156-171.

2825 Elders, Léon J. "Intellectto Pratico e Ricerca Di Dio." *Jacques Maritain Oggi: Atti del Convengno Internazionale Nel Centenario Della Nascita*. Milano, 1983. 456-462.

2826 Elders, Léon J. "L'edizione Critica del *Commento Al De Anima*." *Divus Thomas* 88(1985): 212-214.

2827 Esposito, Rosario F. "San Tommaso Nel Pensiero Di Don Orione." *Rivista di Ascetica e Mistica* 6(1981): 53-67.

2828 Estrada, Bernardo. "L'anima Nei Commenti Di San Tommaso D'Aquino Sul Nuovo Testamento." *L'anima Nell'antropologia Di San Tommaso D'Aquino IX: Atti del Congresso Societá Internazionale San Tommaso D'Aquino*. Ed. Abelardo Lobato. Milano: Editrice Massimo, 1987. 267-275.

2829 Fabriziani, Anna. "Tomismo e Filosofia Cristiana Nel Carteggio del Blondel Con Laberthonniére Dopo la Condanna del Pensiero Modernista." *Studia Patavina* 27(1980): 45-74.

2830 Fabro, Cornelio. "La Dialettica D'intelligenza e Volontà Nella Costituzione Dell'atto Libero." *Doctor Communis* 30(1977): 163-191.

2831 Fabro, Cornelio. "Rassegna Di Letteratura Tomistica." *Doctor Communis* 31(1978): 157-161.

2832 Fabro, Cornelio. "San Tommaso Davanti Al Pensiero Moderno." *Le Ragioni del Tomismo*. Ed. Carlos Cardona. Collan Sagitta, Problemi e Document, N. S. 29. Milano: Edizioni Ares, 1979. 50-95.

2833 Fabro, Cornelio. "Tomismo Essenziale e Crisi Dei Tomismi (Nel I Centenario Dell' Enciclica *Aeterni Patris*." *Renovatio* 15(1980): 81-102.

2834 Fabro, Cornelio. "Atto Esistenziale e Impegno Della Libertà." *Divus Thomas* 86(1983): 125-161.

2835 Fabro, Cornelio. "Il Trascendentale Moderno e Il Trascendentale Tomistico." *Angelicum* 60(1983): 534-558.

2836 Fabro, Cornelio. "Intorno Al Fondamento Dell'essere." *Graceful Reason: Essays in Ancient and Medieval Philosophy Presented to Joseph Owens, CSSR on the Occasion of His Seventy-fifth Birthday and the Fiftieth Anniversary of His Ordination*. Ed. Lloyd P. Gerson. Papers in Mediaeval Studies 4. Toronto: Pontifical Institute of Mediaeval Studies, 1983. 229-237.

2837 Fabro, Cornelio. "L'emergenza Dell'atto Di Essere in San Tommaso e la Rottura del Formalismo Scolastico." *Il Concetto Di Sapientia in San Bonaventura e San Tommaso*. Ed. Alessandro Muso. Biblioteca Dell'Enchiridion 1. Palermo: Officina di Studi Medievale, 1983. 35-54.

2838 Fabro, Cornelio. "Problematica del Tomismo Di Scuola." *Rivista di Filosofia Neo-Scolastica* 75(1983): 187-199.

2839 Fabro, Cornelio. "Atto Esistenziale e Inpegno Della Libertà." *Divius Thomas* 86(1983): 125-161.

2840 Fabro, Cornelio. "Partecipazione Agostiniana e Partecipazione Tomistica." ***Augustinus et Thomas***. Città del Vaticano: *Rivista Doctor Communis*, Palazzo Canonici, 1986. 282-291. Omaggio dell'Accademia di San Tommaso d'Aquino a Sant'Agotino d' Ippona nel xvi centenario della conversione, *Doctor Communis*, 39(1986): n. (3).

2841 Fabro, Cornelio. "Dall'anima Allo Spirito: L'enigma Dell'uomo e L'emergenzadell'atto." *Atti del Congresso Societá Internazionale San Tommaso D'Aquino IX: L'anima Nell'antropologia Di San Tommaso D'Aquino*. Ed. Abelardo Lobato. 1987. 457-467.

2842 Fabro, Cornelio. "La Teologia Come Scienza e Sapienza in San Tommaso." *Annales Theologici* 1(1987): 95-105.

2843 Fabro, Cornelio. "L'emergenza Dello *Esse* Tomistico Sull'atto Aristotelico: Breve Prologo. L'origine Trascendentale del Problema." *Angelicum* 66(1989): 149-177.

2844 Facchetti, Vittorio. "Il *De Magistro* Di Tommaso D'Aquino e L'odierna Problematica Pedagogica." *Tommaso D'Aquino Nel Suo Settimo Centenario VIII: Atti del Congresso Internazionale: L'Uomo*. Napoli: Edizioni Domenicane Italiane, 1978. 446-453.

2845 Fernández Sabaté, Aniceto. "Alcuni Principi Fondamentali Della Filosofia Di Tommaso D'Aquino." *Atti del Congresso Internazionale. Tommaso D'Aquino Nel Suo Settimo Centenario IX: Il Cosmo e la Scienza*. Napoli: Ed. Domenicane Italiane, 1978. 77-86.

2846 Ferrai, Valentino. "Il Compito Morale e la Sua Distribuzione (San Tommaso)." *Euntes Docete* 40(1987): 3-22.

2847 Ferrara, Vincenzo. "Premesse Tomistiche All'evoluzione del Diritto Penale." *Angelicum* 55(1978): 603-635.

2848 Ferrara, Vincenzo. "Attualità Della Dottrina Tomista Su Alcune Fondamentali Nozioni Di Diritto Penale." *Apollinaris* (Roma) 52(1979): 528-559.

2849 Ferrari, Mario Valentino. "L'ordine Morale e Il Conflitto Dei Doveri Nella Linea Di Tommaso D'Aquino." *Tommaso Nel Suo Settimo Centenario V: Atti del Congresso Internazionale: L'agire Morale*. Napoli: Edizioni Domenicane Italiane, 1977. 456-476.

2850 Ferrari, Mario Valentino. "Il Primo Principio Morale." *Angelicum* 57(1980): 45-53.

2851 Ferrari, Mario Valentino. "Una Feconda Formulazione del Principio Di Causalità Nella Linea Di Pensiero Di San Tommaso." *Atti Del'VIII Congresso Tomistico Internazionale: Vol. V: Problemi Metafisici*. Studi Tomistici 14. Città del Vaticano, Pontificia Accademia di San Tommaso e di Religione Cattolica: Libreria Editrice Cattolica, 1982. 320-328.

2852 Ferrari, Mario Valentino. "Il Compito Morale e la Sua Distribuzione (Rileggendo San Tommaso)." *Euntes Docete* (Roma) 40(1987): 3-22.

2853 Ferraro, Giuseppe. "La Pneumatologia Di San Tommaso D'Aquino Nel Suo Commento Al Quarto Vangelo: Aspetti Di Dottrina e Di Esegesi del Dottore Angelico." *Angelicum* 66(1989): 193-263.

2854 Fidelibus, F. "Realismo Critico e Critica Della Conoscenza in Jacques Maritain." *Sapienza* 37(1984): 3-28.

2855 Fioravanti, Luigi. "Il Dubbio Cartesiano e Il Realismo Tomistico." *Atti Dell'VIII Congresso Tomistico Internazionale VIII: San Tommaso Nella Storia del Pensiero*. Studi Tomistici 17. Cittá del Vaticano: Pontificia Accademia di San Tommaso e di Religione Cattolica, 1982. 173-180.

2856 Franchi, Alfredo. "*Sub Ratione* Ardui: Paura e Speranza Nella Filosofia." *Sapienza* 42(1989): 149-165.

2857 Frieri, Nicola Mario. "Le Teorie Gnoseologiche Sottese Alle Argomentazioni Sull'anima in Tommaso D'Aquino e in Immanuel Kant." *Atti del Congresso Societá Internazionale San Tommaso D'Aquino IX: L'anima Nell'antropologia Di San Tommaso D'Aquino*. 1987. 547-558.

2858 Galimberti, Andrea. "La Realtà Della Storia e San Tommaso." *Sapienza* 30(1977): 24-42.

2859 Galkowski, J. "Posizione Filosofica del Cardinale Karol Wojtyla." *Atti Dell'VIII Congresso Tomistico Internazionale VIII: San Tommaso Nella Storia del Pensiero*. Studi Tomistici 17. Cittá del Vaticano: Pontificia Accademia di San Tommaso e di Religione Cattolica, 1982. 308-322.

2860 Galli, Alberto. "La Legge Morale Naturale." *Sacra Doctrina* 31(1986): 126-158.

2861 Galli, Alberto. "La Legge Umana." *Sacra Doctrina* 31(1986): 582-619.

2862 Galli, Alberto. "Attualità del Realismo Tomista." *Atti Dell'VIII Congresso Tomistico Internazionale VIII: San Tommaso Nella Storia del Pensiero*. Studi Tomistici 17. Cittá del Vaticano: Pontificia Accademia di San Tommaso e di Religione Cattolica. 1982. 367-376.

2863 Galli, Dario. "La Filosofia Di San Tommaso Oggi." *Atti Dell'VIII Congresso Tomistico Internazionale VIII: San Tommaso Nella Storia del Pensiero*. Studi Tomistici 17. Cittá del Vaticano: Pontificia Accademia di San. Tommaso e di Religione Cattolica, 1982. 377-381.

2864 Galli, Giuseppe Mario. "Le Benemerenze Indirette Di San Tommaso D'Aquino Nella Nascita Della Scienza Moderna." *Atti Dell'VIII Congresso Tomistico Internazionale VII: L'uomo e Il Mondo Nella Luce Dell'Aquinate*. Studi Tomistici 16. Cittá del Vaticano: Pontificia Accademia di San Tommaso e di Religione Cattolica, 1982. 275-285.

2865 Garulli, Enrico. "La Differenza Ontologica e la Trascendentalità Dell'essere." *Atti del Congresso Internazionale. Tommaso D'Aquino Nel Suo Settimo Centenario VI: L'essere*. Napoli: Edizioni Domenicane, 1977. 196-205.

2866 Garzia, Raffaelle. "Il Valore Della Ragione in San Tommaso D'Aquino." *Atti Dell'VIII Congresso Tomistico Internazionale VII: L'uomo e Il Mondo Nella Luce Dell'Aquinate*. Studi Tomistici 16. Cittá del Vaticano: Pontificia Accademia di San Tommaso e di Religione Cattolica, 1982. 74-78.

2867 Gherardini, Brunero. "Un Tomista Per I Nostri Tempi L'Em. Mo Card. Pietro Parente." *Doctor Communis* 42(1989): 3-14.

2868 Ghio, Michelangelo. "Causa Emanativa e Causa Immanente: San Tommaso e G. Bruno." *Filosofia* 30(1979): 529-554.

*In the Introduction, the author emphasizes the relevance of the concept of expression in Leibniz and analyzes it briefly. The first chapter defines the *status quaestionis* by reviewing the critical writings on the question. Chapter Two gives a historical background of the concept from Plato to Niccolò da Cusa, showing later in Chapter Three the development, through platonic-Christian tradition, of two antithetical concepts (the emanative cause and the immanent cause, respectively, in St. Thomas and in G. Bruno) from the original ambiguity of the notion of expression in Plotinus. Chapter Four is a study of the doctrine of expression of the entire spectrum of Leibniz's speculative activity. The conclusion outlines "the re-discovery of the concept of expression" in European contemporary thought from Husserl and Heidegger to Gadmaer, Ricoeur, and Pareyson.*

2869 Ghisalberti, Alessandro. "La Concezione Della Natura Nel Commento Di Tommaso D'Aquino Alla Metafisica Di Aristotele." *Atti del Congresso Internazionale Vol IX: Il Cosmo e la Scienza Tommaso D'Aquino Nel Suo Settimo Centenario*. Napoli: Edizioni Domenicane Italiane, 1978. 222-228.

2870 Giacon, Carlo. "Il Contributo Originale Di San Tommaso All'ontologia Classica." *Tommaso Nel Suo Settimo Centenario VI: Atti del Congresso Internazionale: L'essere*. Napoli: Edizioni Domenicane Italiane, 1977. 61-71.

2871 Giacon, Carlo. "San Tommaso Filosofo, Continuatore Critico Di Aristotele." *Doctor Communis* 30(1977): 303-315.

2872 Giacon, Carlo. "Sussidi Lessicali e Bibliografici Per Lo Studio Di San Tommaso." *Seminarium* (Città del Vaticano) 29(1977): 918-993.

2873 Giacon, Carlo. "La Distinzione Tra L'essenza e L'esistenza E Logica in Avicenna Ed E Ontologica in San Tommaso." *Actas del V Congreso Internacional de Filosofia Medieval II*. Madrid: Nacional, 1979. 775-784.

2874 Giacon, Carlo. "Linguaggio e Scintilla Rationis in Aquinas." *Sprache und Erkenntnis Im Mittelater. Akten Des VI. Internationalen Kongresses Für Mittelalterliche Philosophie Des Société Internationale Pour L'Etude de la Philosophie Médiévale II*. Eds. Wolfgang Kluxen et al. Miscellanea Mediaevalia 13. Berlin: Walter de Gruyter, 1981. 1055-1065.

2875 Giacon, Carlo. "Postille Sulle Tesi del Tomismo Specifico." *Doctor Communis* 35(1982): 349-356.

2876 Giannini, Giorgio. "Ordine e Creazione." *Giornale di Metafisica* 32(1977): 129-131.

2877 Giannini, Giorgio. "Aspetti Dell'intenzionalità Corporea in San Tommaso." *Il Corpo, Perche? Saggi Sulla Struttura Corporea Della Persona*. Brescia: Morcelliana, 1979. 180-187.

2878 Giannini, Giorgio. "San Tommaso e Rosmini." *Rivista Rosminiana di Filosofia e di Cultura* 75(1981): 165-188.

2879 Gigante, Mario. "Validità e Attualità Delle Norme Morali in Tommaso D'Aquino e Maurizio Blondel." *Atti del Congresso Internazionale. Tommaso D'Aquino Nel Suo Settimo Centenario V: L'agire Morale*. Napoli: Edizioni Donemicane, 1977. 477-487.

2880 Gigante, Mario. "Thélsis e Boúlesis in San Tommaso." *Asprenas* (Napoli) 26(1979): 265-273.

2881 Gigante, Mario. "Egemonia Etica del Fine Ultimo in San Tommaso." *Asprenas* (Napoli) 27(1980): 313-330.

2882 Gigante, Mario. "*Actus Essendi* e Atto Libero Nel Pensiero Di San Tommaso." *Atti Del'VIII Congresso Tomistico Internazionale: Vol. V: Problemi Metafisici*. Studi Tomistici 14. Città del Vaticano: Lib. Ed. Vaticana, 1982. 249-282.

2883 Gillon, Ludovico Bertrando. "La Dottrina de Peccato Originale Lerie Oggi." *Sapienza* 35(1982): 345-357.

2884 Giordano, Agostino. "Il *De Magistro* Di San Tommaso e L'Ecclesiam Suam Di Paolo VI." *Incontri Culturali* 13(1980): 107-126.

2885 Giovanni Paolo II. "Il Metodo e la Dottrina Di San Tommaso in Dialogo Con la Cultura Contemporanea." *Doctor Communis* 33(1980): 259-270.

2886 Giovinazzo, Francesco. "Il Tomismo Dantesco Nella Critica del Novecento." *Asprenas* (Napoli) 28(1981): 445-456.

2887 Girotto, Bruno. "Il Problem Dell'essere Nel Pensiero Di Karl Rahner." *Filosofia* 30(1979): 555-584.

2888 Giustini, Pietro Alessandro. "San Tommaso e Il Pensiero Scientifico: Una Questione Sul Numbero." *Atti del Congresso Internazionale Vol. IX: Il Cosmo e la Scienza Tommaso D'Aquino Nel Suo Settimo Centenario*. Napoli: Edizioni Domenicane Italiane, 1978. 108-111.

2889 Giustiniani, Pasquale. "Tommaso D'Aquino Nel I Centenario Dell'enciclica *Aeterni Patris* Di Leone XIII." *Asprenas* (Napoli) 27(1980): 87-98.

2890 Grandinetti, Antonio. "L'attualità Della Pedagogia Metodologica Tomistica Nel *De Magistro*." *Tommaso D'Aquino Nel Suo Settimo Centenario VIII: Atti del Congresso Internazionale*. Napoli: Edizioni Domenicane Italiane, 1978. 464-466.

2891 Grasso, Giacomo. "La Liberazione Dell'intelligenza." *Annali Chieresi* 5(1985): 7-19.

2892 Grion, Alvaro. "Le Due Metafisiche in San Tommaso D'Aquino." *Atti del VII Congresso Internazionale Centro Internazionale Di Studi e Di Relazioni Culturali: Metafisica e Scienze Dell'uomo*. Ed. Benedetto D'Amore. 2. Roma: Borla, 1982. 421-444.

2893 Grygiel, Ludmilla. "La Santità Di Tommaso D'Aquino." *Divus Thomas* 88(1985): 89-99.

2894 Guzzo, Augusto. "San Tommaso e Bisanzio." *Filosofia* 28(1977): 137-138.

2895 Hölhuber, Ivo. "Il Tomismo Come Catalizzatore del Chardinismo." *Tommaso D'Aquino Nel Suo Settimo Centenario IX: Atti del Congresso Internazionale: Il Cosmo e la Scienza*. Napoli: Edizioni Domenicane Italiane, 1978. 389-396.

2896 Iammarrone, Luigi. "La Libertà in San Tommaso." *La Libertà*. Eds. F. Bellino and R. Belvederi. Napoli: Edizioni Dehoniane, 1980. 91-130.

2897 Iammarrone, Luigi. "Anima e Corpo Secondo San Bonaventura: Raffronti Con San Tommaso D'Aquino." *Doctor Seraphicus* (Bagnoregio, Viterbo) 31(1984): 5-29.

2898 Iammarrone, Luigi. "Il Problema Critico." *Aquinas* 27(1984): 373-404.

2899 Iammarrone, Luigi. "Il Fondamento Metafisico e Antropologico Dell'ascesa a Dio Nel Pensiero Di San Tommaso." *Aquinas* 31(1988): 171-184.

2900 Incardona, Nunzio. "Determinazione Della Cognitio e Cognitio Sapientiae." *Il Concetto Di Sapientia in San Bonaventura e San Tommaso*. Ed. Alessandro Muso. Biblioteca Dell'Enchiridion 1. Palermo: Officina di Studi Medievale, 1983. 55-68.

2901 Inciarte, Fernando. "La Verità in San Tommaso e Nella Filosofia Attuale." *Studi Cattolici* 21(1977): 3-10.

2902 Iona, Giorgio. "La Neuropsichiatria Oggi e la Concezione Tomistica Dell'uomo." *Atti del Congresso Internazionale. Tommaso D'Aquino Nel Suo Settimo Centenario VII: L'Uomo*. Napoli: Ed. Domenicane Italiane, 1978. 101-106.

2903 Izquierdo Labeaga, José A. "La Teologia del Verbo en la *Summa Contra Gentiles*." *Scripta Theologica*, Pamplona 14(1982): 551-580.

2904 Joannes Paulus II (Pope). "Tommaso D'Aquino, Maestro e Guida." *Angelicum* 57(1980): 121-132.

2905 Jossa, Franco. "Attualità Di San Tommaso Nel Problema del Rapporto Tra Scienza e Fede." *Tommaso D'Aquino Nel Suo Settimo Centenario IX: Atti del Congresso Internazionale: Il Cosmo e la Scienza*. Napoli: Edizioni Domenicane Italiane, 1978. 123-139.

2906 Kaczynski, Edward. "*Lex Nova* in San Tommaso: Le Tendenze Spiritualistiche e Legalistiche Nella Téologia Morale." Studi Tomistici 15. *Atti dell'VIII Congresso Tomistico internazionale VI: Morale e diritto nella prospettiva tomistica*(1982): 22-33.

2907 Kalinowski, Georges. "Il Diritto Alla Vita in Tommaso D'Aquino." *Rivista de Filosofia* 74(1983): 43-61.

2908 Klakowicz, Beatrix E. "San Tommaso e la Sua Acculturazione Della Filosofia Greca." *Atti Dell'VIII Congresso Tomistico Internazionale VIII: San Tommaso Nella Storia del Pensiero*. Studi Tomistici 17. Cittá del Vaticano: Pontificia Accademia di San Tommaso e di Religione Cattolica, 1982. 7-19.

2909 La Scala, Francesco. "Il Pensiero Di San Tommaso D'Aquino Sull'anima." *L'anima Nell'antropologia Di San Tommaso D'Aquino IX: Atti del Congresso Societá Internazionale San Tommaso D'Aquino*. Ed. Abelardo Lobato. Milano: Editrice Massimo, 1987. 277-281.

2910 La Via, Vincenzo. "Necessità O Amore? Introduzione Al Concetto Della Filosofia Come Via a Dio *Ad Mentem* Divi Thomae." *Tommaso Nel Suo Settimo Centenario VI: Atti del Congresso Internazionale: L'essere*. Napoli: Edizioni Domenicane Italiane, 1977. 252-261.

2911 La Via, Vincenzo. "Filosofia e Idea Di Dio." *Teoresi* 35(1980): 3-10.

2912 Lamacchia, Ada. "Tommaso D'Aquino e Kant: Strutturazione Dei Fantasmi e Schematismo Trascendentale." *Tommaso Nel Suo Settimo Centenario VI: Atti del Congresso Internazionale: L'essere*. Napoli: Edizioni Domenicane Italiane, 1977. 239-251.

2913 Lambertino, Antonio. "Eudemonologia Tomista e Critica Kantiana All'eudemonismo." *Tommaso Nel Suo Settimo Centenario V: Atti del Congresso Internazionale: L'agire Morale*. Napoli: Edizioni Domenicane Italiane, 1977. 261-269.

2914 Lambertino, Antonio. "Pensiero Ed Essere in San Tommaso D'Aquino: In Margine a Un Rilievo Di Heidegger." *Sapíenza Antica: Studi in Onore Di Domenico Pesce*. Ed. V. E. Alfieri. Collana Della Facoltà Di Magistero: Università Degli Studi Di Parma 1. Milano: Franco Angeli, 1985. 348-357.

2915 Laurenti, Renato. "Spunti Per Un Confronto Tra la Concezione Dell'ira in Aristotele e in Tommaso." *Atti Dell'VIII Congresso Tomistico Internazionale VI: Morale e Diritto Nella Prospettiva Tomistica*. Studi Tomistici 15. Cittá del Vaticano: Pontificia Accademia di San Tommaso e di Religione Cattolica, 1982. 73-87.

2916 Liuzzi, Tiziana. "L'*esse* in Quanto Similitudine Di Dio Nel Commento Di Tommaso D'Aquino Al *De Divinis Nominibus* Di Dionigi Areopagita." *Vetera Novis Augere*. Roma: La Goliardica, 1982. 19-34.

2917 Liverziani, Filippo. "Esperienzialità Delle Cinque Vie? Nota Su Aspetti del Tomismo Di Giorgio Giannini." *Aquinas* 22(1979): 414-427.

2918 Livi, Don Antonio. "Il Ritorno Allo Studio Di San Tommaso Prima e Dopo L'*Aeterni Patris*." *Scripta Theologica*, Pamplona 11(1979): 599-616.

2919 Livi, Don Antonio. "Etienne Gilson: Metafisica e Metodologia Dell'esperienza Storica." *Filosofia Oggi* 7(1984): 547-556.

2920 Livi, Don Antonio. "Bibliografia Gilsoniana." *Doctor Communis* 38(1985): 381-390.

2921 Livi, Don Antonio. "Il Contributo Di Etienne Gilson Alla Migliore Conoscenza Di San Tommaso Nel Novecento." *Doctor Communis* 43(1990): 3-15.

2922 Lobato, Abelardo. "Vigencia de la Filosofia Cristiana y del Tomismo." *Angelicum* 57(1980): 257-279.

2923 Lobato, Abelardo. "Le Tre Dimensioni Dell'uomo." *Sapienza* 34(1981): 87-149.

It tries to integrate in a true synthesis the three constituent dimensions of man: individual, social and historical. Classical thought is analyzed first. The other two receive more emphasis in modern conscience. Attempting to understand man from every one of them has had little success. It is necessary to answer the question from the very being of man. The contribution of human sciences must be an open road for a metaphysical anthropology. The author receives inspiration from St. Thomas Aquinas in this comprehensive essay which is published in its first half here.

2924 Lobato, Abelardo. "Anima Quasi Horizon et Confinium." *L'anima Nell'antropologia Di San Tommaso D'Aquino IX: Atti del Congresso Societá Internazionale San Tommaso D'Aquino*. Ed. Abelardo Lobato. Milano: Editrice Massimo, 1987. 53-80.

2925 Lobato, Abelardo. "L'attualità Di San Tommaso Nel Pensiero e Nell'insegnamento del Santo Padre Giovanni Paolo II." *Doctor Communis* 40(1987): 3-28.

2926 Lobato, Abelardo. "Ziglara, Filosofo Tomista." *Angelicum* 65(1988): 240-270.

2927 Lotz, Johannés Baptist. "Il Valore Religioso Nella Filosofia Dell'essere Di Martin Heidegger." *Sapienza* 31(1978): 257-264.

In Heideggers' Philosophieren finden sich religiöse Züge. Der Mensch ist vom Sein als dem Grund des Seienden in Anspruch genommen. Das Sein teilt sich ihm in Huld und Gunst mit; darauf antwortet das Denken als Danken samt der Fragen als der Frömmigkeit des Denkens. Doch ist das Sein nicht Gott; vielmehr ist es zeitlich und auf den Menschen angewiesen; letztlich stammt es aus dem Ereignis. Zugleich kann man die Frage nach Gott einzig innerhalb des Seins stellen; gefragt wird, ob sich Gott nahe oder entziehe. An die Anwort rührt das Ringen um das Es, das uns das Sein gibt. Doch verbirgt sich der Gott der Religion dem heutigen Menschen, weshalb es gilt, Über ihn zu schweigen.

2928 Lotz, Johannés Baptist. "Mi Pensamiento Filsófico." *Revista de Filosofia* (Mexico) 11(1978): 45-72.

Der Aufsatz gibt einen Einblick in mein Denken, indem er zunächst von, meinem Lebsensweg und meinem Ansatz mitmeinen. Haupt-Themen umschreibt. Einflüsse habe ich vor allem von Thomas von Aquin, verdeutlicht durch Maréchal, von Kant, Hegel und Heidegger empfangen. Mein Ausgangspunkt ist die Rückführung des menschlichen Wirkens durch die transzendentale Methode auf sein ermöglichenden Gründe. So komme ich zur Metaphysik des Seins als Fülle, die sich in einer personalen Anthropologie und Gottleslehre auswirkt und auch der Meditation eine philosophische Basis liefert. Den Hintergrund von allem bildet die transzendentale Erfahrung.

2929 Lotz, Johannés Baptist. "Uomo-essere-tempo-Dio: Sul Dialogo Tra Heidegger e Tommaso D'Aquino." *Rassengna di Teologia* (Roma) 19(1978): 292-306.

2930 Lotz, Johannés Baptist. "*Magis Anima Continet Corpus.. quam e Converso* (*STh* I, Q. 76, A. (3)." *L'anima Nell'antropologia Di San Tommaso D'Aquino IX: Atti del Congresso Societá Internazionale San Tommaso D'Aquino*. Ed. Abelardo Lobato. Milano: Editrice Massimo, 1987. 293-302.

2931 Lozzi, Carlo. "Incunaboli Delle Opere Di San Tommaso D'Aquino Non Posseduti Dalle Biblioteche Italiane." *Doctor Communis* 31(1978): 253-258.

2932 Lozzi, Carlo. "Gli Incunaboli Delle Opere Scientifiche Di San Tommaso." *Atti Dell'VIII Congresso Tomistico Internazionale VII: L'uomo e Il Mondo Nella Luce Dell'Aquinate*. Studi Tomistici 16. Cittá del Vaticano: Pontificia Accademia di San Tommaso e di Religione Cattolica, 1982. 342-346.

2933 Lucchetta, Francesca. "Sulla Critica Tomistica Alla Noetica Di Averroé." *Rivista di Filosofia Neo-Scolastica* 73(1981): 596-602.

2934 Luna, Concetta. "Essenza Divina e Relazioni Trinitarie Nella Critica Di Egidio Romano a Tommaso D'Aquino." *Medioevo* 14(1988): 3-69.

2935 Lunetta, Loredano. "La Pluralità Delle Forme Nel Correctorium Fratris Thomae Di Guglielmo de La Mare." *Studi Medievali* 28(1987): 729-749.

2936 Lupi, Carlo. "Il Problema Della Creazione in San Tommaso. I." *Filosofia Oggi* 3(1980): 30-65.

2937 Lupi, Carlo. "Il Problema Della Creazione in San Tommaso. II." *Filosofia Oggi* 3(1980): 305-333.

2938 Luppi, Sergio. "Società Bene Comune e Limiti del Potere Nella Filosofia Politica Di San Tommaso D'Aquino." *Atti Dell'VIII Congresso Tomistico Internazionale VI: Morale e Diritto Nella Prospettiva Tomistica*. Studi Tomistici 15. Cittá del Vaticano: Pontificia Accademia di San Tommaso e di Religione Cattolica, 1982. 253-269.

2939 Malatesta, Michele. "La Problematica Tomistica Delle Relazioni Alla Luce Della Logica Matematica e Dei Moderni Indirizzi Di Pensiero." *Tommaso D'Aquino Nel Suo Settimo Centenario IX: Atti del Congresso Internazionale: Il Cosmo e la Scienza.* Napoli: Edizioni Domenicane Italiane, 1978. 140-167.

2940 Mamiani, Maurizio. "La Definizione Formale Della Veritá e la Genesi Delle Nozioni Trascendentali Nell Quaestio I *De Veritate* Di Tommaso D'Aquino." *Tommaso Nel Suo Settimo Centenario VI: Atti del Congresso Internazionale: L'essere*. Napoli: Edizioni Domenicane Italiane, 1977. 262-266.

2941 Marabelli, Costante. "Note Preliminari Allo Studio del Commento Di San Tommaso D'Aquino Ai Secondi Analitici Di Aristotele." *Divus Thomas* 88(1985): 77-88.

2942 Marchesi, Angelo. "Trascendentalitá Dell'essere e Sua Compossibilità Con la Dottrina Dell'*Analogia Entis*." *Metafore Dell' Invisibile: Ricerche Sull'analogia*. Brescia: Morcelliana, 1984. 128-136.

2943 Marongiu Pico, Tiziana. "Il Concetto Di Tirannide in San Tommaso e in Egidio Colonna Romano." *Tommaso D'Aquino Nel Suo Settimo Centenario VIII: Atti del Congresso Internazionale*. Napoli: Edizioni Domenicane Italiane, 1978. 150-159.

2944 Mauro, Letterio. "Le Passioni Nell'antropologia Di San Tommaso." *Tommaso Nel Suo Settimo Centenario V: Atti del Congresso Internazionale: L'agire Morale*. Napoli: Edizioni Domenicane Italiane, 1977. 337-343.

2945 Mauro, Letterio. "Il Problema del Fato in Boezio e Tommaso D'Aquino." *Atti Congresso Internazionale Di Studi Boeziani*. Ed. Luca Obertello. Roma: Editrice Herder, 1981. 355-365.

2946 Mazzarella, Pasquale. "Creazione Partecipazione e Tempo Secondo San Tommaso D'Aquino." *Studia Patavina* 29(1982): 308-335.

2947 Mazzarella, Pasquale. "Aristotelismo, Platonismo, Neoplatonismo Nel Pensiero Di Tommaso D'Aquino." *Programmi Di Ricerca Relativi Alla Genesi, Fenomenologia e Storia Delle Categorie Costitutive Dell'idea Di Europa*. Ed. Maria Adelaide Raschini. Studi Critici 2. 1985. 133-154.

2948 McNicholl, Ambrogio. "La Conoscenza Umana Oggi e Il Pensiero Tomista." *Sapienza* 34(1981): 37-86.

2949 Melloni, Alberto. "Christianitas Negli Scritti Di Tommaso D'Aquino." *Cristianesimo nella storia* 6(1985): 45-69.

2950 Mininni, G. "Il Pensiero Linguistico in Tommaso D'Aquino." *Linguistica Medievale: Anselmo D'Aosta, Abelardo, Tommaso D'Aquino, Pietro Ispano, Gentile Da Cingoli, Occam*. Ed. Francesco Corvino. Bari: Ed. Adriatica, 1983. 55-122.

2951 Miyakawa, T. "La Conoscenza Divina del Futuro Libro: Il Pensiero Di San Tommaso Condiviso Da M. J. Scheeben." *Divinitas* 32(1988): 113-122.

2952 Molinaro, Aniceto. "Introduzione: Il Debito Critico Verso Jacques Maritain." *Aquinas* 25(1982): 393-395.

2953 Mondin, Battista. "La Dottrina Tomistica Della Conoscenza Nel Commento Alle Sentenze." *Doctor Communis* 30(1977): 206-218.

2954 Mondin, Battista. "Che Cosa Farebbe San Tommaso Di Fronte a Marx?" *Sapienza* 31(1978): 469-475.

Is it possible to do with Marx what St. Thomas has done with Aristotle? This is the problem faced in this paper. Helder Camara and the theologians of liberation believe that it is feasible and have applied Marxist analysis of society and Marxist political theory to the interpretation of the Gospel and to the construction of a new Christian theology. But their results are unacceptable: the means and the end of the Church (which are both essentially supernatural) are no longer safeguarded. Theology needs a metaphysical interpretation of reality such as that of Plato or Aristotle. Because Marxist philosophy excludes metaphysics, it cannot be employed for the interpretation of the Word of God. Therefore, it is impossible to do with Marx what St. Thomas has done with Aristotle.

2955 Mondin, Battista. "*Esse, Actus Essendi* e *Essentia* Secondo San Tommaso." *Doctor Communis* 22(1979): 86-95.

2956 Mondin, Battista. "La Filosofia Cristiana de San Tommaso." *Incontri Culturali* 13(1980): 139-145.

2957 Mondin, Battista. "Le Ragioni del Tomismo." *Divinitas* (Roma) 24(1980): 221-224.

2958 Mondin, Battista. "La Filosofia Cristiana Di San Tommaso D'Aquino: Linee Fondmentali e Attualità." *Atti Dell'VIII Congresso Tomistico Internazionale I: L'enciclica Aeterni Patris Nell'arco Di Un Secolo*. Studi Tomistici 10. Cittá del Vaticano: Pontificia Accademia di San Tommaso e di Religione Cattolica, 1981. 218-237.

2959 Mondin, Battista. "Perenne Validità Delle Cinque Vie." *Quinque Sunt Viae: Actes Du Symposium sur les Cinq Voies de la Somme Théologique 1981*. Ed. Léon Elders. Studi Tomistici 9. Città del Vaticano, Pontificia Accademia di San Tommaso: Libreria Editrice Vaticana, 1981. 94-97.

2960 Mondin, Battista. "Il Ruolo Della Filosofia in Teologia Secondo San Tommaso e Secondo le Nuove Teologie." *Sapienza* 35(1982): 283-326.

*This long essay is divided into three main sections. The first deals with Aquinas' use of philosophy in theology and shows how his philosophy of being contributed to the development of some of his theological doctrines. The second analyzes how *de facto* the relationship between philosophy and theology has functioned in contemporary theology. The third presents a critical analysis of how the relationship has been formally conceived by contemporary thinkers, through the study of such theories as harmony, dialectical opposition, polarity, correlation, form-content, subalternation, etc.*

2961 Mondin, Battista. "Perenne Validità Delle Cinque Vie." *Doctor Communis* 35(1982): 94-101.

2962 Mondin, Battista. "Le Cinque Vie Di Fronte Alla Fisica Recente." *Doctor Communis* 37(1984): 216-235.

2963 Mondin, Battista. "I Valori Fondamentali: Definizione e Classificazione Dei Valori." Ragione e Tempo 7. Roma: Edizione Dino, 1985. 210.

2964 Mondin, Battista. "Aristotele e Tommaso D'Aquino Sulla Libertà." *Energeia: Etudes Aristotéliciennes Offertes A Mgr Antonio Jannone*. Ed. Evanghélos A. Moutsopoulos. Recherches 1. Paris: J. Vrin, 1986. 303-312.

2965 Mondin, Battista. "Dio e la Filosofia Di Etienne Gilson." *Doctor Communis* 39(1986): 79-81.

2966 Mondin, Battista. "Fecondità Antropologica Della Concezione Tomistica Dell'essere: Brevi Annotazioni in Margine Alla Q. D. *De Anima*." *Atti del Congresso Societá Internazionale San Tommaso D'Aquino IX: L'anima Nell'antropologia Di San Tommaso D'Aquino*. 1987. 343-353.

2967 Mondin, Battista. "La Persona e le Sue Proprietà Essenziali." *Sapienza* 41(1988): 361-387.

2968 Mondin, Battista. "Per Una Metafiscia Dei Valori." *Aquinas* 31(1988): 69-82.

Against traditional Thomistic philosophy which tends to identify value with the transcendental of goodness, this article tries to prove that value cannot be identified with goodness or with any other of the transcendentals. Value is a transcendental of its own, distinct from being, unity, truth, goodness, and beauty. It is one of the fundamental aspects of being; it has its objective side in the dignity of being and its subjective side in estimation (which is a special operation which may include intuition, feeling, and sometimes also reasoning).

2969 Mongillo, Dalmazio. "Ispirarsi Ancora a San Tommaso D'Aquino in Teologia Morale?" *Tommaso D'Aquino Nel I Centenario Dell'Enciclica Aeterni Patris: Atti del Convegno Organizzato a Roma Dall Societá Internazionale Tommaso D'Aquino e Dalla Pontificia Universita "San Tommaso D'Aquino."* Roma: Societá Internazionale Tommaso d'Aquino, 1979. 179-196.

2970 Morandi, Emmanuele. "Ermeneutica e Tomismo." *Doctor Communis* 43(1990): 103-125.

2971 Moretti, Roberto. "Natura e Compito Della Teologia Nel Pensiero Di San Tommaso e Nel Recent Insegnamento del Magistero." *Doctor Communis* 34(1977): 11-40.

2972 Müller, Paola. "Nominare L'essenza Divina: La Distinzione XXII Dell'Ordinatio Di Ockham." *Rivista di Filosofia Neo-Scolastica* 8(1989): 224-254.

2973 Mura, Gaspare. "Ermeneutica, Gnoseologia e Metafisica: Attualità del Commento Di San Tommaso Al *Perihermeneias* Di Aristotele." *Virtualità e Attualità Della Filosofia Cristiana*. Ed. B. Mondin. 1988. 181-209.

2974 Muraro, G. "Povertà e Perfezione: La Funzione Liberatrice Della Povertà Religiosa Secondo San Tommaso." *Sapienza* 34(1981): 257-309.

2975 Muraro, Marcolino. "Come Possiamo Conoscere Dio." *Sacra Doctrina* 28(1983): 154-172.

2976 Muraro, Marcolino. "I Fondamenti del Pluralismo in Filosofia." *Annali Chieresi* 5(1985): 45-57.

2977 Muratore, S. "Uno Instrumento Di Recera L'*Index Thomisticus*." *Rassegna di Teologia* 22(1981): 314-322.

2978 Narciso, Enrico. "Autoritarismo e Dissenso Nel Pensiero Di San Tommaso D'Aquino." *Atti del Congresso Internazionale. Tommaso D'Aquino Nel Suo Settimo Centenario VII: L'Uomo*. Napoli: Edizioni Domenicane, 1978. 160-169.

2979 Nave, Alberto. "Punti Di Convergenza Tra Filosofia Aristotelico-tomistica e Filosofia Crociana." Studi Tomistici 17. *Atti dell'VIII Congresso tomistico internazionale VIII: San Tommaso nella storia del pensiero*. Cittá del Vaticano: Pontificia Accademia di S. Tommaso e di Religione Cattolica, 1982. 209-219.

2980 Negroni, Bruno. "Essenza Ed Esistenza Nell'omonimo Opusculo Di Tommaso D'Aquino." *Tommaso Nel Suo Settimo Centenario VI: Atti del Congresso Internazionale: L'essere*. Napoli: Edizioni Domenicane Italiane, 1977. 283-289.

2981 Neva, Mario. "Concordanza Tra Agostino e Tommaso Nella Problematica Della Conoscenza Secondo Mons. Amato Masnova." *Atti Dell'VIII Congresso Tomistico Internazionale VIII: San Tommaso Nella Storia del Pensiero*. Studi Tomistici 17. Cittá del Vaticano: Pontificia Accademia di San Tommaso e di Religione Cattolica, 1982. 249-255.

2982 Nicoletti, Enrico. "L'analogia in San Tommaso." *Origini e Sviluppi Dell'analogia: Da Parmenide a San Tommaso*. Ed. Giuseppe Casetta. Settimane Filosofiche Di Vallombrosa 1. Roma: Edizioni Vallombrosa, 1987. 116-175.

2983 Nicolosi, Salvatore. "Politica e Morale Secondo Tommaso D'Aquino." *Tommaso D'Aquino Nel Suo Settimo Centenario VIII: Atti del Congresso Internazionale: L'Uomo*. Napoli: Edizioni Domenicane Italiane, 1978. 170-184.

2984 Nicolosi, Salvatore. "Casistica e Probabilismo Nella Crisi Della Coscienza Morale Europea." *Aquinas* 31(1988): 279-309.

2985 Noonan, John T. "*Maxima Amicitia.*" *Tommaso Nel Suo Settimo Centenario V: Atti del Congresso Internazionale: L'agire Morale*. Napoli: Edizioni Domenicane Italiane, 1977. 344-351.

2986 O'Farrell, F. "Il Contributo Dell'analitica Trascendentale Di Kant Alla Filosofia Cristiana." *Aquinas* 31(1988): 97-109.

The purpose of the article is to show that the Transcendental Analytic contains the development of elements not elaborated in St. Thomas' theory of human cognition as regards sensation and our intellect's dependence on it. It reviews the Aristotelian and Thomistic texts on sensation before exposing the Kantian theory of sensation and its completing the Thomistic one. It then shows how by reason of this theory of sensation the object of our direct cognition is the phenomenon. Finally it treats principles of Thomism containing germinally the distinction of man's phenomenal and noumenal knowing: whatever is received is received in the mode of the receiver; operation follows being; man's mode of being is spirit that is also form of the body.

2987 Obertello, Luca. "Conoscenza Divina e Creazione: Alle Origini Della Problematica Scolastica." *Archivio di Filosofia* 53(1985): 351-363.

2988 Ocàriz, Fernando. "Il Pensiero Di San Tommaso." *Le Ragioni del Tomismo*. Ed. Carlos Cardona. Collan Sagitta, Problemi e Document, N. S. 29. Milano: Edizioni Ares, 1979. 96-160.

2989 Orlando, Pasquale. "L'esperienza Intellettiva Tomista: Intellectus-ratio, I: Semantica Dei Termini Nell'Antichità Greco-latina." *Doctor Communis* 30(1977): 316-338.

2990 Orlando, Pasquale. "L'esperienza Intellettiva Tomista: *Intellectus-ratio*, II: Semantica Dei Termini Nell'Antichità Greco-latina." *Doctor Communis* 30(1978): 187-204.

2991 Orlando, Pasquale. "L'argomento Delle Verità Eterne in San Tommaso D'Aquino." *Una Hostia*. Ed. Saturnino Muratore. Napoli: d'Auria, 1984. 517-544.

2992 Orlando, Pasquale. "San Tommaso Anticipatore Della Esigenza Della Filosofia D'oggi." *Cinquant'anni Di Magistero Teologico, Scritti in Onore Di Mons. Antonio Piolanti Nel 50 del Suo Sacerdozio*. Studi Tomistici 26. Città del Vaticano: Libreria Editrice Vaticana, 1985. 197-214.

2993 Orlando, Pasquale. "L'immutabilita di Dio. Il pensiero di San Tommaso di fronte ad Hegel e a Kierkegaard." *Doctor Communis*. 40(1987): 278-284.

2994 Ottonello, Pier Paolo. "Rosmini, Tommaso, Il Tomismo." *Rivista Rosminiana di Filosofia e di Cultura* 80(1986): 367-389.

2995 Pangallo, Mario. "La Trascendenza Dell'essere in San Tommaso: Sintesi e Superamento Di Platonismo e Aristotelismo." *Doctor Communis* 50(1987): 187-197.

2996 Pangallo, Mario. "Per Una Fondazione Metafisica Della Dottrina Dell'animazione Immediata: *Actus Essendi* Tomistico e Spiritualità Dell'anima." *L'anima Nell'antropologia Di San Tommaso D'Aquino IX: Atti del Congresso Societá Internazionale San Tommaso D'Aquino*. Ed. Abelardo Lobato. Milano: Editrice Massimo, 1987. 355-361.

2997 Pangallo, Mario. "Essere e Infinito: Lévinas e San Tommaso." *Doctor Communis* 41(1988): 189-193.

2998 Pangallo, Mario. "Causalità e Libertà: La Questione del Fondamento Metafisco Dell Libertà Creata Nel Pensiero Di Cornelio Fabro Interprete Di San Tommaso." *Doctor Communis* 43(1990): 203-233.

2999 Paoli, Germano. "Tommaso D'Aquino e Il Diritto Internazionale." *Tommaso D'Aquino Nel Suo Settimo Centenario VIII: Atti del Congresso Internazionale.* Napoli: Edizioni Domenicane Italiane, 1978. 328-340.

3000 Paolinelli, Marco. "Sapienza e Filosofia in San Tommaso D'Aquino." *Rivista di Filosofia Neo-Scolastica* 79(1987): 196-216.

3001 Paolo II, Giovanni. "Allocuzione Finale del San Padre." *Tommaso d'Aquino nel I Centenario dell'Enciclica Aeterni Patris: Atti del convegno organizzato a Roma dall Societá internazionale Tommaso d'Aquino e dalla Pontificia Universita San Tommaso d'Aquino.* Roma: Societá Internazionale Tommaso d'Aquino: 271-281. 1979.

3002 Paolo II, Giovanni. "Apertura e Universalismo Della Filosofia Di San Tommaso." *Sapienza* 32(1979): 385-395.

3003 Paolo II, Giovanni. "Il Metodo e la Dottrina Di San Tommaso in Dialogo Con la Cultura Contemporanea." *Doctor Communis* 33(1980): 259-270.

3004 Paolo II, Giovanni. "Perenne Validità del Pensiero Di San Tommaso." *Doctor Communis* 33(1980): 3-11.

3005 Paolo II, Giovanni. "Sapere Teologico e Scienza Tecnologica." *Doctor Communis* 34(1981): 243-246.

3006 Paolo II, Giovanni. "La Dottrina Dell'Aquinate Chiarisce Il Vero Bene Dell'uomo Redento Da Cristo." *Doctor Communis* 39(1986): 107-112.

3007 Paolo VI. "Lumen Ecclesiae: Lettera Al P. Vincenzo de Cousnongle, Maestro General Dell'Ordine Domenicano. Nel VII Centenario Della Morte Di San Tommaso D'Aquino." *Tommaso D'Aquino Nel Suo Settimo Centenario IX: Atti del Congresso Internazionale: Il Cosmo e la Scienza.* Napoli: Edizioni Domenicane Italiane, 1978. 499-533.

3008 Parente, Pietro. "Tre Geni in Azione Tra Cielo e Terra Per Richiamare Gli Uomini a Dio: San Tommaso- Dante- San Caterina." *Palestra del Clero* 58(1979): 1359-1373.

3009 Paschetto, Eugenia. "La Natura del Moto in Base Al *De Motu Cordis* Di San Tommaso." *Thomas von Aquin: Werk und Wirkung Im Licht Neuerer Forschungen.* Ed. Albert Zimmermann. Berlin/New York: Walter de Gruyter, 1988. 247-260.

3010 Pasquale Magni, Ulderico D. "Protologia Ed Escatologia Da Principium Individuationis Alla Immortalità Della Persona Umana in San Tommaso e Nella Epistemologia Moderna." *Atti Dell'VIII Congresso Tomistico Internazionale VII: L'uomo e Il Mondo Nella Luce Dell'Aquinate.* Studi Tomistici 16. Cittá del Vaticano: Pontificia Accademia di San Tommaso e di Religione Cattolica, 1982. 315-324.

3011 Patfoort, Albert. "La Concezione Della Teologia Secondo San Tommaso." *Sapienza* 35(1982): 259-270.

3012 Patfoort, Albert. "La Finalité Apostolique de la *Somme Contre les Gentils.*" *Angelicum* 59(1982): 3-22.

3013 Pedrini, Arnaldo. "L'ispirazione a San Tommaso in San Francesco Di Sales." *Atti Dell'VIII Congresso Tomistico Internazionale VIII: San Tommaso Nella Storia del Pensiero.* Studi Tomistici 17. Cittá del Vaticano: Pontificia Accademia di San Tommaso e di Religione Cattolica, 1982. 145-166.

3014 Pegoraro, Olindo. "La Verità in San Tommaso e Martin Heidegger." *Tommaso Nel Suo Settimo Centenario VI: Atti del Congresso Internazionale: L'essere*. Napoli: Edizioni Domenicane Italiane, 1977. 311-319.

3015 Pellegrino, Piero. "Il Concetto Di Promulgatio Nella *Summa Theologiae* Di San Tommaso D'Aquino: Dal Diritto Romano Al Decreto Di Graziano." *Ius Canonicum* 19(1979): 265-313.

3016 Pellerey, Roberto. "Tommaso D'Aquino: Semiotica Naturale e Processo Gnoseologico." *Semiotica Medievale* 95(1984): 39-62.

3017 Penzo, Giorgio. "La Differenza Ontologica e Il Problema Di Dio in Heidegger, in San Tommaso D'Aquino e in Gogarten." *Euntes Docete: Commentaria Urbaniana* (Roma) 35(1982): 125-137.

3018 Penzo, Giorgio. "La Differenza Ontologica e Il Problema Di Dio in Heidegger e in San Tommaso." *Atti Del'VIII Congresso Tomistico Internazionale V: Problemi Metafisici*. Studi Tomistici 14. Città del Vaticano, Pontificia Accademia di San Tommaso e di Religione Cattolica: Libreria Editrice Cattolica, 1982. 70-81.

3019 Percivale, Franco. "Rosmini, San Tommaso e L'*Aeterni Patris*." *Rivista Rosminiana di Filosofia e di Cultura* 75(1981): 121-164.

3020 Peretti, Gaetano. "Spazio e Tempo Nel Pensiero Di Tommaso D'Aquino e Nell'attuale Gnoseologia." *Tommaso D'Aquino Nel Suo Settimo Centenario IX: Atti del Congresso Internazionale: Il Cosmo e la Scienza*. Napoli: Edizioni Domenicane Italiane, 1978. 415-421.

3021 Perini, Giuseppe. "Contínuitá Ed Evoluzione Delle Disposizioni Della Chiesa Sul Ruolo Della Dottrina Di San Tommaso Nelle Scuole Cattoliche." *Seminarium* (Cittá del Vaticano) 29(1977): 604-673.

3022 Perini, Giuseppe. "Pagine Recenti Di Letteratura Tomista." *Divus Thomas* 80(1977): 398-422.

3023 Perini, Giuseppe. "Pagine Recenti Di Letteratura Tomista (Continua)." *Divus Thomas* á81(1978): 141-168.

3024 Perini, Giuseppe. "Dall' *Aeterni Patris* Al Concilio Vaticano II. Le Direttive del Magistero Sulla Dottrina Di San Tommaso." *Scripta Theologica*, Pamplona 11(1979): 619-656.

3025 Perini, Giuseppe. "La Chiesa Ha Fatta Sua Propria la Dottrina Di San Tommaso." *Divus Thomas* 83(1980): 217-224.

3026 Perini, Giuseppe. "Thomae Doctrinam Ecclesia Suam Fecit." *Atti Dell'VIII Congresso Tomistico Internazionale I: L'enciclica Aeterni Patris Nell'arco Di Un Secolo*. Studi Tomistici 10. Cittá del Vaticano: Pontificia Accademia di San Tommaso e di Religione Cattolica, 1981. 89-121.

3027 Petruzzellis, Nicola "Ritorni Immaginari." *Doctor Communis* 39(1986): 113-128.

3028 Pirola, Giuseppe. "Eterogeneità Tra Teologia Cristiana e Metafisica in Tommaso D'Aquino." *Il Senso Della Filosofia Cristiana, Oggi: Atti del XXXII Convegno del Centro Di Studi Filosofici Tra Professori Universitari*. Brescia: Morcelliana, 1978. 156-167.

3029 Piscione, Enrico. "Bernardo Di Chiaravalle e Tommaso D'Aquino Di Fronte Al Problema Dell'amore: Due Posizioni Antitetiche O Complementari?" *Sapienza* 36(1983): 405-414.

3030 Pizzorni, Reginaldo M. "Diritto Naturale e Diritti Naturali Secondo San Tommaso D'Aquino." *Apollinaris* (Roma) 50(1977): 47-94.

3031 Pizzorni, Reginaldo M. "Persona Umana e Diritto Naturale." *Atti del Congresso Internazionale. Tommaso D'Aquino Nel Suo Settimo Centenario VII: L'Uomo*. Napoli: Edizioni Domenicane, 1978. 341-351.

3032 Pizzorni, Reginaldo M. "I Diritti Dell'uomo Di Fronte Allo Stato Secondo San Tommaso D'Aquino." *Lo Stato e I Cittadini*. Ed.Giacomo Ambrogio Manno. Problemi Di Attualità 5. Napoli: Edizioni Dehonaiane, 1982. 117-154.

3033 Pizzorni, Reginaldo M. "In Che Senso si Può Dire Che Ogni Uomo E Legge a Se Stesso (*S. Theol.* , I-II, Q. 90, A. 3, Ad(1)." *Angelicum* 6(1984): 602-626.

3034 Pizzorni, Reginaldo M. "La Conoscenza Della Legge O Diritto Natural Per Connaturalitatem O Per Inclinationem." *Apollinaris* (Roma) 58(1985): 47-67.

3035 Pizzorni, Reginaldo M. "La Pace Nel Pensiero Di San Tommaso D'Aquino." *Per la Filosofia* 4(1987): 62-72.

3036 Pizzorni, Reginaldo M. "La Pace Frutto Della Giustizia e Della Carità Secondo San Agostino e San Tommaso D'Aquino." *La Pace: Sfida All'Università Cattolica. Atti del Simposio Fra le Università Ecclesiastiche e Gli Istituti Di Studi Superiori Di Roma*. Ed. Federazione Internazional Università Cattoliche. Roma: Herder, 1988. 561-572.

3037 Pizzutti, Giuseppe Mario. "Le Strutture Speculative del Problema Morale in Karl Barth e Nell'esistenzialismo Jaspersiano Nella Prospetiva Della Metafisica Di San Tommaso D'Aquino." *Atti del Congresso Internazionale Tommaso Nel Suo Settimo Centenario VI: L'essere*. Napoli: Edizioni Domenicane Italiane, 1977. 338-359.

3038 Pizzutti, Giuseppe Mario. "Convergenze Tomistiche Nell'opera Di Soren Kierkegaard." *Atti Dell'VIII Congresso Tomistico Internazionale VIII: San Tommaso Nella Storia del Pensiero*. Studi Tomistici 17. Cittá del Vaticano: Pontificia Accademia di San Tommaso e di Religione Cattolica, 1982. 191-208.

3039 Poli, Cristoforo Oddone. "San Tommaso D'Aquino e L'economia Moderna." *Tommaso D'Aquino Nel Suo Settimo Centenario VIII: Atti del Congresso Internazionale*. Napoli: Edizioni Domenicane Italiane, 1978. 201-213.

3040 Pollini, Pierluigi. "Bartolomé de Las Casas E. J. Ginés Sepúlveda Di Fronte Alla Questione Della Libertá Degli Indios." *Rivista Filosofia di Neo-Scolastica* 74(1982): 343-354.

3041 Pompei, Alfonso. "Le Virtu Cardinali Di San Tommaso D'Aquino: Note Sulle Fonti Dottrinali." *Parola e Spirito II*. Ed. C. Marcheselli. 1982. 1051-1070.

3042 Poppi, Antonino. "Lo Studio Di Aristotele Nella Scuola Di Padova." *Scienza e Cultura* (Padova) 2(1980): 137-159.

3043 Poppi, Antonino. "Eredità Clássica e Innovazione Cristiana Nel Concetto Dei Sapientia in San Bonaventura e Tommaso D'Aquino." *Il Concetto Di "Sapientia" in San Bonaventura e San Tommaso*. Ed. Alessandro Muso. Biblioteca Dell'Enchiridion 1. Palermo: Officina di Studi Medievale, 1983. 13-33.

3044 Portalupi, Enzo. "Gregorio Magno Nelle *Quaestiones Disputatae de Veritate* Di Tommaso D'Aquino." *Rivista di Filosofia Neo-Scolastica* 77(1985): 556-598.

3045 Portalupi, Enzo. "Gregorio Magno Nelle *Index Thomisticus*." *Bulletin de Philosophie Médiévale* 31(1989): 103-146.

3046 Portalupi, Enzo. "Gregorio Magno Nelle *Index Thomisticus*: Corrigendum." *Bulletin de Philosophie Médiévale* 32(1990): 136-137.

3047 Possenti, Vittorio. "L'intuizione Astrattiva e I Primi Principi Speculativi Nel Tomismo." *Atti Dell'Viii Congresso Tomistico Internazionale V: Problemi Metafisici*. Studi Tomistici 14. Editrice Vaticana: Città del Vaticano, 1982. 93-146.

3048 Prestipino, Vincenzo. "Adaequatio e Razionalitá: Aspetti Della Gnoseologia Di San Tommaso e Di Hegel." *Giornale di Metafisica* 32(1977): 205-216.
*L'articolo vuol dimostrare la comune esigenza, nella filosofia di S. Tommaso e di Hegel, della razionalità del reale e della conseguente gnoseologia intesa come adeguazione di realtà e di pensiero. Ne sorge una sorta di integrazione di istanze idealistiche e realistiche nei termini della loro validità. El il problema della verità posto nel rapporto fra soggetto e oggetto, del dualismo superato nella teoria della *adequazione*. Su tale problema nella dottrina di S. Tommaso e di Hegel si possono cogliere affinità rispondenti alla loro comune postulazione de diritti della ragione e della sua determinante presa sulla natura razionale dell'oggetto in una correlazione che coglie la verità oggettiva, ontologicamente fondata sull'Essere.*

3049 Puglisi, Flippo. "Il Compito Dell'artista Nell'estetica Di Tommaso D'Aquino." *Tommaso D'Aquino Nel Suo Settimo Centenario VIII: Atti del Congresso Internazionale: L'Uomo*. Napoli: Edizioni Domenicane Italiane, 1978. 517-520.

3050 Pulvirenti, Rosalia Azzaro. "La Rinascità del Tomismo Nella Sicilia Occidentale." *Doctor Communis* 35(1982): 212-244.

3051 Quarello, Eraldo. "Tommaso D'Aquino Situazionista in *IV Sent.*, D. 33, Q. L, A. 2?" *Tommaso Nel Suo Settimo Centenario V: Atti del Congresso Internazionale: L'agire Morale*. Napoli: Edizioni Domenicane Italiane, 1977. 178-185.

3052 Quinto, Riccardo. "Latino Patristico e Latino Scolastico: Dalla Comprensione Della Lingua All'interpretazione del Pensiero." *Rivista Filosofia Neo-Scolastica* 80(1988): 115-123.

3053 Quirito, Riccardo. "*Timor* e *Timiditas*: Note Di Lessicografia Tomista." *Rivista di Filosofia Neo-Scolastica* 77(1985): 387-410.

3054 Raschini, Maria Adelaide. "La Soluzione Tommasiana Della Questione Degli Universali Nella Critica Di Giovanni Gentile." *Il Pensiero Giovanni Gentile II*. Firenze: Instituto della Enciclopedia Italiana, 1977. 741-745.

3055 Regina, Umberto. "Tommaso D'Aquino e Heidegger: Le Ragioni Di Un Raffronto." *Tommaso Nel Suo Settimo Centenario VI: Atti del Congresso Internazionale: L'essere*. Napoli: Edizioni Domenicane Italiane, 1977. 365-373.

3056 Riccati, Carlo. "L'immagine Di Platone in Tommaso D'Aquino." *Filosofia* 35(1984): 85-116.

3057 Rigobello, Armando. "Orizzonte Fenomenologico e Problema Metafisico in San Tommaso." *Sapienza* 34(1981): 19-36.

3058 Rindone, Elio. "L'antropologia Tomista E Unitaria O Dualistica?" *Aquinas* 31(1988): 477-499.

3059 Riondato, Ezio. "Il Metodo Della Filosofia Morale in Tommaso D'Aquino." *Tommaso Nel Suo Settimo Centenario V: Atti del Congresso Internazionale: L'agire Morale*. Napoli: Edizioni Domenicane Italiane, 1977. 516-520.

3060 Rizzacasa, Aurelio. "Il Pensiero Di Tommaso D'Aquino Interpretato Quale Paradigma Per Una Filosofia Della Religione Elaborata in Un Dialogo Con la Scienza." *Tommaso D'Aquino Nel Suo Settimo Centenario IX: Atti del Congresso Internazionale: Il Cosmo e la Scienza*. Napoli: Edizioni Domenicane Italiane, 1978. 168-172.

3061 Rizzello, Raffaele. "L'educazione Intellettuale in Tommaso D'Aquino: Ruolo del Docente e del Discente." *Annali Chieresi* 1101(1985): 85-103.

3062 Rizzello, Raffaele. "Il Rapporta Educativo Nel Pensiero Di Tommaso D'Aquino." *Annali Chieresi* 2(1986): 105-128.

3063 Roccaro, Giuseppe. "Il Concetto Di Sapienza in San Bonaventura e San Tommaso." *Schede Medievali* 2(1982): 203-209.

3064 Rolandetti, Vittorio. "Tomismo e Modernità: L'uomo Alla Luce Dell'essere Ovvero Come si Fa Filosofia Secondo Luigi Bogliolo." *Problemi Metafisici: Atti Dell'VIII Congresso Tomistico Internazional V*. Studi Tomistici 14. Napoli: Edizioni Domenicane Italiane, 1982. 341-355.

3065 Rolandetti, Vittorio. "Profonde Virtualita e Nuove Prospettive del Tomismo Nel Pensiero del Prof. Luigi Bogliolo." *Virtualita e Attualita Della Filosofia Cristiana*. Ed. B. Mondin. 1988. 77-113.

3066 Rossi, Amedeo. "Immediatezza Della Conoscenza Sensitiva e Intellettiva, Scetticismo, Relativismo e Agnosticismo." *Tommaso Nel Suo Settimo Centenario VI: Atti del Congresso Internazionale: L'essere*. Napoli: Edizioni Domenicane Italiane, 1977. 388-400.

3067 Roth, Gottfried. "Amentia Ex Aegritudinibus Cerebralibus: Psychopathologia in Doctrina Sancti Thomae et Psychiatria Biologica Contemporanea." *L'anima Nell'antropologia Di San Tommaso D'Aquino IX: Atti del Congresso Societá Internazionale San Tommaso D'Aquino*. Ed. Abelardo Lobato. Milano: Editrice Massimo, 1987. 597-604.

3068 Roverselli, Carla. "Linee Di Antropologia Nel Contra Impugnantes Di Tommaso D'Aquino." *Sapienza* 41(1988): 429-445.

3069 Ruffinengo, Pier Paolo. "Astrazione, Separazione, Fondazione Della Metafisica." *Annali Chieresi* 2(1986): 25-63.

3070 Russo, Giuseppe. "L'accademia Filosofica e Teologica Di San Tommaso D'Aquino in Modena." *Atti Del'VIII Congresso Tomistico Internazionale III: L'enciclica Aeterni Patris 1981*. Studi Tomistici 12. Città del Vaticano, Pontificia Accademia di San Tommaso e di Religione Cattolica: Libreria Editrice Cattolica, 1981. 148-156.

3071 Saavedra, Alejandro. "Perspectiva Tomista Para Una Meta-antropologia." *Doctor Communis* 43(1990): 126-134.

3072 Sacchi, Mario Enrique. "El Rescate Neotomista del Acto de Ser." *Problemi Metafisici: Atti Dell'VIII Congresso Tomistico Internazional V*. Studi Tomistici 14. 1982. 24-30.

3073 Sales, Giovanni. "L'attualità Scientifica Di San. Tommaso." *Tommaso D'Aquino Nel Suo Settimo Centenario IX: Atti del Congresso Internazionale: Il Cosmo e la Scienza*. Napoli: Edizioni Domenicane Italiane, 1978. 173-176.

3074 Salmona, Bruno. "Intelligere e Ratiocinari in San Tommaso." *Tommaso D'Aquino Nel Suo Settimo Centenario: Atti del Congresso Internazionale VII: L'Uomo*. Napoli: Edizioni Domenicane Italiane, 1978. 418-424.

3075 Sanchez Sorondo, Marcelo. "L'idea Dell'evoluzione (*Entwicklung*) Storica Della Libertà Come Stimolo Per la Filosofia Cristiana." *Aquinas* 31(1988): 45-59.

3076 Santoro, Liberato. "Alcune Riflessioni Sul Commentario Di San Tommaso Al *De Anima* Di Aristotele." *L'anima Nell'antropologia Di San Tommaso D'Aquino IX: Atti del Congresso Societá Internazionale San Tommaso D'Aquino*. Ed. Abelardo Lobato. Milano: Editrice Massimo, 1987. 115-121.

3077 Sava, Giuseppe. "Vincenzo Lilla Nella Filosofia Italiana Dell'Ottocento." *Il Protagora* 6(1986): 153-172.

3078 Savagnone, Giuseppe. "La Conoscibilità del Mondo Della Natura Secondo San Tommaso." *Aquinas* 21(1978): 63-93.

3079 Savagnone, Giuseppe. "L'amicizia Nel Pensiero Di San Tommaso D'Aquino." *Sapienza* 34(1981): 431-441.

3080 Schurr, Adolf. "La Concezione Della Libertà Nel *De Veritate* Di San Tommaso D'Aquino (Una Interpretazione Filosofico-trascendentale Per Una Teologia Fondamentale)." *Tommaso D'Aquino Nel Suo Settimo Centenario: Atti del Congresso Internazionale VII: L'Uomo*. Napoli: Edizioni Domenicane Italiane, 1978. 425-435.

3081 Scilironi, Carlo. "Tommaso D'Aquino e la Critica Della Religione. Un Confronto Con Barth e Bonhoeffer." *Asprenas* (Napoli) 27(1980): 331-354.

3082 Selvaggi, Filippo. "San Tommaso e la Mentalitá Scientifica Moderna." *Saint Thomas Aquinas in Hodierna Formatione Sacerdotali. Seminarium* 29(1977): 855-877.

3083 Sequeri, Pier Angelo. "Analogia." *Nuovo Dizionario Di Teologia*. Eds. Giuseppe Barbaglio and Severino Dianich. Roma: Ed. Paoline, 1977. 341-351.

3084 Spiazzi, Raimondo. "La Dottrina Sociale Di San Tommaso Ed I Principi Fondamentali Dell'umanesimo Cristiano." *Saint Thomas Aquinas in hodierna formatione sacerdotali: Seminarium* (Città del Vaticano) 29(1977): 812-854.

3085 Spiazzi, Raimondo. "La Scelta Di San Tommaso Da Parte Della Chiesa." *Doctor Communis* 34(1981): 3-10.

3086 Spiazzi, Raimondo. "La Lettera *Lumen Ecclesiae* Di Paolo VI Sul Tomismo a Dieci Anni Dalla Sua Promulagazione." *Doctor Communis* 38(1985): 3-22.

3087 Spiazzi, Raimondo. "Conoscenza Con Amore in San Agostino e in San Tommaso." *Augustinus et Thomas*. Città del Vaticano: Rivista Doctor Communis, Palazzo Canonici, 1986. 315-328. Omaggio dell'Accademia di San Tommaso d'Aquino a Sant'Agotino d'Ippona nel xvi centenario della conversione (*Doctor Communis*, 39(1986): n. (3).

3088 Spiazzi, Raimondo. "Laicitá Dello Stato e Motivazioni Religiose Della Politica Secondo San Tommaso D'Aquino, Appendice: Il Passaggio Dal Laicismo Al Totalitarismo Nell'ordinamento Politico Secondo Luigi Sturzo." *Doctor Communis* 40(1987): 227-248.

3089 Spiazzi, Raimondo. "Armonia del Pensiero Dell'Aquinate e Dello Scheeben Sul Cristianesimo Come Perfezionamento Dei Valiori Umani." *Divinitas* 32(1988): 175-190.

3090 Stagnitta, Antonino. "Il Posto Della Logica in Tommaso D'Aquino." *Angelicum* 56(1979): 42-61.

3091 Stagnitta, Antonino. "Precisazioni Su Essere e Autocoscienza Assoluta in Tommaso D'Aquino." *Sapienza* 32(1979): 72-88.

Viene precisato come Tommaso riinterpreta Aristotele nella ricerca sul tema dell'essere e del divenire. Inevitabilmente é condotto ad una certa "secolarizzazione" della tematica teologica. Lo sforzo di superare le aporie metafisiche aristoteliche derivanti dal concetto di materia e divenire eterni (il problema della creazione non é meno importante di quello del divenire come concetto della cultura umana): non consente però a Tommaso di sciogliere definitivamente ogni difficoltà. Nello schema della giustificazione del divenire si riscontra una "petitio principii." Il "senso dell'essere" coincide con l'assoluto autopercepirsi dell'indivenibile: autocoscienza assoluta, e medesimamente coll'autocoscienza intramondana.

3092 Stagnitta, Antonino. "L'idealismo Logico Di Tommaso D'Aquino." *Angelicum* 58(1981): 323-338.

3093 Stagnitta, Antonino. "Tommaso D'Aquino e L'intuizione Dei Concetti Moderni Di Frustrazione Ed Aggressivtà." *Atti Dell'VIII Congresso Tomistico Internazionale VII: L'uomo e Il Mondo Nella Luce Dell'Aquinate*. Studi Tomistici 16. Cittá del Vaticano: Pontificia Accademia di San Tommaso e di Religione Cattolica, 1982. 166-194.

3094 Stagnitta, Antonino. "La Ragione Pratica: Gli Habitus Etici Come Costitutive Psicometafisico Dell'agire in Tommaso D'Aquino." *Atti Del'VII Congresso Tomistico Internazionale: Metafisica e Scienze Dell'uomo*. Roma: Borla, 1982. 350-371.

3095 Stagnitta, Antonino. "Una Parafrasi Storicistico—trascendentale. Per Un Ripensamento Filosofico Della Terza Prova Tomasiana Di Dio (*Summa Theologiae*. I, Q. 2, A. (3)." *Angelicum* 61(1984): 543-579.

3096 Stagnitta, Antonino. "Tommaso D'Aquino e I Precorrimenti Da Sistema: La Psicologia. Le Passioni Dell'uomo Come Tendenze Istintive Ed Affettive (Pulsioni)." *Angelicum* 62(1985): 531-564.

3097 Stickler, Alfonso. "San Tommaso e L'*Index Thomisticus*." *Doctor Communis* 3(1978): 162-164.

3098 Széll, Margit. "Sándor Horváth O. P. Ed Il Concetto Dell'anima." *L'anima Nell'antropologia Di San Tommaso D'Aquino IX: Atti del Congresso Societá Internazionale San Tommaso D'Aquino*. Ed. Abelardo Lobato. Milano: Editrice Massimo, 1987.

3099 Terzi, Carlo. "Il Maestro in San Tommaso." *Tommaso D'Aquino Nel Suo Settimo Centenario VIII: Atti del Congresso Internazionale: L'Uomo*. Napoli: Edizioni Domenicane Italiane, 1978. 467-473.

3100 Todescan, Franco. "Presupposti Antropologici Della Filosofia Morale e Giuridica Di San Tommaso." *Tommaso D'Aquino Nel Suo Settimo Centenario VIII: Atti del Congresso Internazionale*. Napoli: Edizioni Domenicane Italiane, 1978. 367-372.

3101 Tognolo, Antonio. "Il Problema Della Struttura Metafisica Dell'uomo in Avicenna e Tommaso D'Aquino." *Actas del V Congreso Internacional de Filosofia Medieval II*. Madrid: Nacional, 1979. 1283-1289.

3102 Tognolo, Antonio. "L'analogia Dell'entre in Tommaso D'Aquino." *Metafore Dell'invisibile: Ricerche Sull'analogia*. Brescia: Morcelliana, 1984. 97-119.

3103 Toso, Mario. "Etienne Gilson e la Filosofia Realista Di San Tommaso." *Salesianum* 44(1982): 641-667.

3104 Toso, Mario. "Etienne Gilson e Il Realismo Tomista, I." *Salesianum* 45(1983): 553-573.

3105 Toso, Mario. "Etienne Gilson e Il Realismo Tomista, II." *Salesianum* 45(1983): 845-880.

3106 Trapé, Agostino. "Centenario Della Conversione Di Sant'Agostino: Da Ippona Ad Aquino." *Augustinus et Thomas*. Città del Vaticano: *Rivista Doctor Communis*, Palazzo Canonici, 1986. 267-281.

3107 Trifogli, Cecilia. "Il Luogo Dell'ultima Stera Nei Commenti Tardo-antichi e Medievali a *Physica* IV, 5." *Giornale Critico della Filosofia Italiana* 68(1989): 144-160.

3108 Truini, Fabrizio. "Attualità Delle Riflessioni Di San Tommaso Sulla Pace." *Tommaso D'Aquino Nel Suo Settimo Centenario VIII: Atti del Congresso Internazionale: L'Uomo*. Napoli: Edizioni Domenicane Italiane, 1978. 214-243.

3109 Tyn, Tomás M. "Lo Studio Della Teologia Sotto la Guida Di San Tommaso." *Sapienza* 39(1986): 5-37.

*The foundation of Thomism consists in epistemological realism. Human intellect can rise up from sensible data to universal essences and to the Act of Being. The object of *sacra doctrina* is the Essence of God identical with the *actus purus essendi*. There is no theology without a metaphysical basis. The object of the holy science determines its theocentrical nature and an *ordo disciplinae* given by the essential structure of a rational reflection about God, which cannot undergo temporal changes.*

3110 Tyn, Tomás M. "L'interpretazione del Rapporto Tra Dio e Il Mondo Secondo San Tommaso D'Aquino." *Per la Filosofia* 4(1987): 51-73.

3111 Umberto, Eco. "*Latratus Canis*." *Tijdschrift voor Filosofie* 47(1985): 3-14.

3112 Uscatescu, Georges. "L'antropologia e I Suoi Problemi in San Tommaso D'Aquino: Dalla Physis Aristotelica Alla Metafisica Dei Valori." *Giornale di Metafisica* 32(1977): 197-204.

3113 Uscatescu, Georges. "L'antropologia e I Suoi Problemi in Tommaso D'Aquino (Dalla Physis Aristotelica Alla Metafisica Dei Valori)." *Tommaso D'Aquino Nel Suo Settimo Centenario: Atti del Congresso Internazionale VII: L'Uomo*. Napoli: Edizioni Domenicane Italiane, 1978. 192-199.

3114 Uscatescu, Georges. "L'antropologia e I Suoi Problemi in San Tommaso D'Aquino (Dalla Physis Aristotelica Alla Metafisica Dei Valori)." *Energeia. Etudes Aristotéliciennes Offertes A Mgr Antonio Jannone*. Ed. Evanghélos A. Moutsopoulos. Centre International D'études Platoniciennes et Aristotéliciennes. Publications. Séerie "Recherches" 1. Paris: J. Vrin, 1986. 313-321.

3115 Ushida, Noriko. "Le Probléme de L'unité de la Forme Substantielle Chez Saint Thomas D'Aquin et Avicenne." *Actas del V Congreso Internacional de Filosofia Medieval II*. Madrid: Nacional, 1979. 1325-1330.

3116 Vagaggini, Aldo. "La Svolta Trascendentale Alla Luce del Concetto Di Essere Di San Tommaso Di Aquino." *Atti Del'VIII Congresso Tomistico Internazionale V: Problemi Metafisici. Studi Tomistici* 14. Città del Vaticano, Pontificia Accademia di San Tommaso e di Religione Cattolica: Libreria Editrice Cattolica, 1982. 48-54.

3117 Van Steenberghen, Fernand. "La Eleccio de Un Maestro." *Revista de Filosofia* 23(1990): 230-242.

3118 Vanni Rovighi, Sofia. "C'é Un'etica Filosofica in San Tommaso D'Aquino?" *Tommaso Nel Suo Settimo Centenario V: Atti del Congresso Internazionale: L'agire Morale.* Napoli: Edizioni Domenicane Italiane, 1977. 194-210.

3119 Vanni Rovighi, Sofia. "C'é Un Ética Filosofica in San Tommaso D'Aquino?" *Studi Di Filosofia Medioevale II: Secoli XIII e XIV.* Ed. Sofia Vanni Rovighi. Scienze Filosofiche 20. Milano: Vita e Pensiero, 1978. 129-148.

3120 Vanni Rovighi, Sofia. "*Contemplata Aliis Tradere.*" *Studi Di Filosofia Medioevale II: Secoli XIII e XIV.* Ed. Sofia Vanni Rovighi. Scienze Filosofiche 20. Milano: Vita e Pensiero, 1978. 203-206.

3121 Vanni Rovighi, Sofia. "Il Fondamento Dell'etica Di San Tommaso." *Studi Di Filosofia Medioevale II: Secoli XIII e XIV.* Ed. Sofia Vanni Rovighi. Scienze Filosofiche 20. Milano: Vita e Pensiero, 1978. 118-128.

3122 Vanni Rovighi, Sofia. "Il Secolo XIII: Bonaventura Da Bagnoregio e Tommaso D'Aquino." *Studi Di Filosofia Medioevale II: Secoli XIII e XIV.* Ed. Sofia Vanni Rovighi. Scienze Filosofiche 20. Milano: Vita e Pensiero, 1978. 53-71.

3123 Vanni Rovighi, Sofia. "L'antropologia Filosofica Di San Tommaso." *Studi Di Filosofia Medioevale II: Secoli XIII e XIV.* Ed. Sofia Vanni Rovighi. Scienze Filosofiche 20. Milano: Vita e Pensiero, 1978. 107-117.

3124 Vanni Rovighi, Sofia. "L'unità del Sapere Secondo Tommaso D'Aquino." *Studi Di Filosofia Medioevale II: Secoli XIII e XIV.* Ed. Sofia Vanni Rovighi. Scienze Filosofiche 20. Milano: Vita e Pensiero, 1978. 72-87.

3125 Vanni Rovighi, Sofia. "Le Novità Di Tommaso D'Aquino." *Studi Di Filosofia Medioevale II: Secoli XIII e XIV.* Ed. Sofia Vanni Rovighi. Scienze Filosofiche 20. Milano: Vita e Pensiero, 1978. 189-202.

3126 Vanni Rovighi, Sofia. "Legge e Coscienza in San Tommaso." *Studi Di Filosofia Medioevale II: Secoli XIII e XIV.* Ed. Sofia Vanni Rovighi. Scienze Filosofiche 20. Milano: Vita e Pensiero, 1978. 149-160.

3127 Vanni Rovighi, Sofia. "Natura e Moralità Nell'etica Di San Tommaso D'Aquino." *Studi Di Filosofia Medioevale II: Secoli XIII e XIV.* Ed. Sofia Vanni Rovighi. Scienze Filosofiche 20. Milano: Vita e Pensiero, 1978. 174-188.

3128 Vanni Rovighi, Sofia. "Perenne Validità Delle Cinque Vie Di San Tommaso." *Studi Di Filosofia Medioevale II: Secoli XIII e XIV.* Ed. Sofia Vanni Rovighi. Scienze Filosofiche 20. Milano: Vita e Pensiero, 1978. 88-106.

3129 Vanni Rovighi, Sofia. "Prego Con San Tommaso." *Studi Di Filosofia Medioevale II: Secoli XIII e XIV.* Ed. Sofia Vanni Rovighi. Scienze Filosofiche 20. Milano: Vita e Pensiero, 1978. 299-302.

3130 Vanni Rovighi, Sofia. "Studi Tomistici Dal 1945." *Studi Di Filosofia Medioevale II: Secoli XIII e XIV*. Ed. Sofia Vanni Rovighi. Scienze Filosofiche 20. Milano: Vita e Pensiero, 1978. 207-221.

3131 Vanni Rovighi, Sofia. "San Tommaso D'Aquino e Averroé." *L'averroismo in Italia*. Convegno Internazionale. Accademia Nazionale Dei Lincei: Atti Dei Convegni Lincei 40. Roma: Accademia Nazionale dei Lincei, 1979. 221-236.

3132 Vanni Rovighi, Sofia. "Un Esemplare Ricercatore Della Verità—San Tommaso Nel Discorso del Papa Per Il Centenario Dell'*Aeterni Patris*." *Vita e Pensiero* 63(1980): 58-60.

3133 Vanni Rovighi, Sofia. "La Fondazione Metafisica Dell'etica in San Tommaso." Ed. and Trans. *Atti dell'VIII Congresso Tomistico Internazionale I: L'enciclica Aeterni Patris nell'arco di un secolo*. Studi Tomistici 10. Cittá del Vaticano: Pontificia Accademia di San Tommaso e di Religione Cattolica, 1981. 307-313.

3134 Vanni Rovighi, Sofia. "San Tomaaso D'Aquino." *Storia Delle Idee Politiche, Economiche e Sociali II*. Torino: Laet, 1983. 367-463.

3135 Vansteenkiste, Clems M. J. "Il Metodo Di San Tommaso." *Le Ragioni del Tomismo*. Ed. Carlos Cardona. Collan Sagitta, Problemi e Document, N. S. 29. Milano: Edizioni Ares, 1979. 161-196.

3136 Ventimiglia, Giovanni. "La Relazione Trascendentale Nella Neoscolastica." *Rivista di Filosofia Neo-Scolastica* 81(1989): 416-465.

3137 Viganò, Mario. "Il Mondo Di San Tommaso e Il Mondo del Secolo XX." *Atti del Congresso Internazionale IX: Il Cosmo e la Scienza: Tommaso D'Aquino Nel Suo Settimo Centenario*. Napoli: Ed. Domenicane Italiane, 1978. 254-262.

3138 Viglino, Ugo. "Autoriflessione Tomistica Come Riflessione Trascendentale." *Tommaso Nel Suo Settimo Centenario VI: Atti del Congresso Internazionale: L'essere*. Napoli: Edizioni Domenicane Italiane, 1977. 435-439.

3139 Viola, Francesco. "L'autorità Come Principio." *Aquinas* 25(1982): 331-348.

3140 Viola, Francesco. "Per Una Filosofia Dell'autorità Secondo San Tommaso D'Aquino." *Atti Dell'VIII Congresso Tomistico Internazionale VI: Morale e Diritto Nella Prospettiva Tomistica*. Studi Tomistici 15. Cittá del Vaticano: Pontificia Accademia di San Tommaso e di Religione Cattolica, 1982. 270-283.

3141 Vrana, Karel. "La Genesi Della Conoscenza Umana." *Geist und Erkenntnis*. Ed. K. Macha. 1985. 215-228.

3142 Wave, A. "Punti Di Convergenza Tra Filosofia Aristotelico-tomistica e Filosofia Crociana." *Atti Dell'VIII Congresso Tomistico Internazionale VIII: San Tommaso Nella Storia del Pensiero*. Studi Tomistici 17. Cittá del Vaticano: Pontificia Accademia di San Tommaso e di Religione Cattolica, 1982. 209-219.

3143 Weinberg, Julius R. "La filosofia di Tommaso d'Aquino." *Introduzione Alla Filosofia Medievale*. Bologna: Mulino, 1985. 189-219.

3144 Wilder, Alfred. "Un Confronto Fra L'etica Tomista e L'etica Kantiana." *Antonianum* 64(1989): 84-97.

3145 Wojtyla, Karol (John Paul II). "La Dottrina Dell'Aquinate Chiarisce Il Vero Bene Dell'uomo Redento Da Cristo." *Doctor Communis* 39(1986): 107-112.

3146 Zoffoli, Enrico. "Origine Nelle Idee e Astrazione Dell'intelletto Agente in San Tommaso D'Aquino." *Atti Dell'VIII Congresso Tomistico Internazionale VII: L'uomo e Il Mondo Nella Luce Dell'Aquinate*. Studi Tomistici 16. Cittá del Vaticano: Pontificia Accademia di San Tommaso e di Religione Cattolica, 1982. 7-50.

E. SPANISH

3147 Aguer, Héctor. "La Verdad del Alma. Una Lectura de la Cuestión 10 *De Veritate*." *Teologia* 21(1984): 101-115.

3148 Aguilar, Arnulfo. "Estructura y Función de la Metafisica Según Santo Tomás de Aquino." *Libro Anual* (Mexico) 8(1980): 305-339.

3149 Alberto Sacheri, Carlos. "Interacción de la Inteligencia y de la Voluntad en el Orden Prudencial." *Philosophica* 1(1978): 129-144.

3150 Alcocer, Antonio Pérez. "El Acto Moral Según Santo Tomás y Las Distintas Corrientes en Etica." *Revista de Filosofia* (México) 10(1977): 223-232.

El objeto del articulo es demonstrar que los grandes sistemas de Ética que muestra la historia de filosofía—los sistemas de Aristóteles, Epicuro, Kant, Scheler y Nietzsche—no son otra cosa que las distintas posiciones que sé obtienen identificando el soberano bien con los distintos elementos que constituyen el acto moralmente bueno, según lo concibe Santo Tomás de Aquino.

3151 Alcocer, Antonio Pérez. "Acerca de la Analogie de Ser." *Revista de Filosofia* (México) 11(1978): 379-387.

(1)La analogia de atribución propia no existe pues la ilamada asi es una analogía residual que queda cuando se niega la distinción real entre la esencia y la existencia. (2) Esa analogia residual es la única posible en la ontologia del Padre Suárez.

3152 Alcorta, J. I. "Vacilaciones Tomistas Sobre el Ser *Primum Cognitum*." *Folia Humanistica* 19(1981): 187-195.

3153 Almedia, Enrique. "Tomás de Aquino y la Antropología Actual." *Tommaso D'Aquino Nel Suo Settimo Centenario: Atti del Congresso Internazionale VII: L'Uomo*. Napoli: Edizioni Domenicane Italiane, 1978. 65-72.

3154 Alonso, Luz García. "La Abstracción en el Pensamiento Tomista. I." *Logos* (Mexico) 12(1983): 39-48.

3155 Alonso, Luz García. "La Abstracción en el Pensamiento Tomista. II." *Logos* (Mexico) 13(1984): 103-115.

3156 Alonso, Luz García. "La Ética y los Derechos Humanos en la Filosofia Clásica." *Logos* (Mexico) 18(1990): 33-46.

3157 Alonso González, Andrés. "Las Vías del Tomismo: Comparación Critica Con el Evolucionismo de Bergson y Whitehead." *Studium* 27(1987): 313-358.

3158 Alvarez, Margarita Mauri. "La Prudencia en la Actividad Práctica." *Sapientia* 42(1987): 233-238.

3159 Alvarez Gómez, Mariano. "Sobre la Verdad en Tomás de Aquino y Hegel: Estudio Comparativo." *Tommaso Nel Suo Settimo Centenario VI: Atti del Congresso Internazionale: L'essere*. Napoli: Edizioni Domenicane Italiane, 1977. 81-103.

3160 Alvira, Rafael. "Casus et Fortuna en Sto. Tomás de Aquino." *Anuario Filosófico* 10(1977): 27-69.

3161 Alvira, Tomás. "Significado Metafisico del Acto y la Potencia en la Filosofia del Ser." *Anuario Filosófico* 12(1979): 9-46.

3162 Andrade, Ciro Schmidt. "La Sabiduría en Santo Tomás: Ascensión a la Intimidad Con Dios Por la Participación de la Verdad y el Amor." *Sapientia* 39(1984): 119-132.

3163 Aquino, M. F. de. "Analogia e Dialética: A Propósito de Tomás de Aquino e de Hegel, I." *Sintese* 13(1985): 41-55.

3164 Aquino, M. F. de. "Analogia e Dialética: A Propósito de Tomás de Aquino e de Hegel, II." *Sintese* 13(1985): 55-57.

3165 Archideo, Lila Blanca. "La Actualidad de la Cogitativa Tomista." *Atti Dell'VIII Congresso Tomistico Internazionale VII: L'uomo e Il Mondo Nella Luce Dell'Aquinate*. Studi Tomistici 16. Cittá del Vaticano: Pontificia Accademia di San Tommaso e di Religione Cattolica, 1982. 79-88.

3166 Arias-Muñoz, José Adolfo. "Una Teoria del Lenguaje en San Agustin y Santo Tomás." *Tommaso Nel Suo Settimo Centenario VI: Atti del Congresso Internazionale: L'essere*. Napoli: Edizioni Domenicane Italiane, 1977. 607-617.

3167 Arregui, Jorge Vicente. "El Carácter Práctico del Conocimento Moral Según Sto. Tomás." *Anuario Filosófico* 13(1980): 101-128.

3168 Arruda Campos, Fernando. "El Tomismo en el Diálogo Con el Pensamiento Contemporáneo." *Revista de Filosofia University Iberoamericana* (México) 18(1985): 493-507.

3169 Aubert, Jean-Marie. "La Objetividad de la Moral Cristiana y la Filosofia del Ser." *Etica y Teologia*. Eds. P. De Sousa Alves and T. Lopez. 1980. 145-160.

3170 Avezac de Castera, Bernard d'. "La Maître Saint Thomas." *Cahiers I. P. C. Faculté libre de Philosophie Comparée* 24(1981): 61-67.

3171 Ballesteros, Juan Carlos Pablo. "La Desigualdad Humana Según Santo Tomás." *Mikael* 6(1978): 63-73.

3172 Balmaceda, Federico. "La Doble Causalidad Ejemplar Divina en Santo Tomás de Aquino." *Philosophica* (Valparaiso) 9-10(1986-1987): 155-166.

3173 Barbosa, Tito Montenegro. "A Relaçào Na Concepçào Tomista Da Matéria-primeira." *Veritas* 28(1983): 276-286.

3174 Barone, Gulia. "Universidad y Escuelas de Las Ordenes Mendicantes en Paris a Mediados del Siglo XIII." *Il Concetto Di Sapientia in San Bonaventura e San Tommaso*. Ed. Alessandro Musco. Biblioteca Dell'Enchiridion 1. Palermo, 1983. 1-11.

3175 Barrientos Garcia, José. "El Estatuto y Juramento(1627) de Enseñar y Leer a San Agustin y Santo Tomás en la Universidad de Salamanca: Un Simple Proyecto?" *Cuadernos Salmantinos de Filosofia* 12(1985): 103-124.

3176 Barrio Maestre, José Maria. "La Disputa Averroismo-tomismo en el Op. *De Unitate Intellectus Contra Averroisitas*, de Tomás de Aquino." *Anales del Semminario Hist. Filosophia* 6(1986-1987): 88-89, 131-141.

3177 Barrio Maestre, José Maria. "Contribución Al Esclarecimiento de la Noción Aristotélica de Substancia." *Pensamiento* 45(1989): 223-226.

The author analyzes the basic elements of the Aristotelian doctrine about "substance" and remarks about some frequent errors in the positivism, particularly in its global judgments about the so-called substantialism. He revises the historical-theoretical keys on the darkening of the original Aristotelian notion, especially in rationalism and empiricism, from which the positivism takes its prejudices about Aristotle. To detach the originality of the Aristotelian notion of substance, the author refers to some essential points in the doctrine of Thomas Aquinas about the human soul and to the importance that the Aristotelian concept of substance has in the Thomist demonstration of its immortality.

3178 Basave, Augustin. "La Doctrina Metafisica de la Participación en Santo Tomás de Aquino." *Giornale di Metafisica* 30(1979): 257-266.

3179 Basso, Domingo M. "La Naturaleza de la Voluntad." *Estudios Teológicos y Filosóficos* (Buenos Aires) 8(1977): 7-16.

3180 Benito Alzaga, José Ramón. "El Pensamiento de Santo Tomás Sobre Las Relaciones Entre el Maestro y el Alumino." *Tommaso D'Aquino Nel Suo Settimo Centenario VIII: Atti del Congresso Internazionale: L'Uomo*. Napoli: Edizioni Domenicane Italiane, 1978. 393-399.

3181 Benito y Durán, Angel. "El Ocio Perfectivo del Hombre Según Santo Tomás de Aquino." *Tommaso D'Aquino Nel Suo Settimo Centenario VIII: Atti del Congresso Internazionale*. Napoli: Edizioni Domenicane Italiane, 1978. 20-43.

3182 Bertelloni, Carlos Francisco. "La Pregunta Por le Ser en Heidegger y Santo Tomás de Aquino." *Realisimo pluridimensional* 13-14(1983): 131-140.

3183 Bertelloni, Carlos Francisco. "De la Politíca Como Ontoteologia a la Politíca Como Teología (De Tomás de Aquino a Guillermo de Ockham)." *Revista de Filosofia* (Argentina) 2(1987): 119-134.

This paper deals with the antecedents of the medieval political thought on the basis of the M S Ripoll 109. The evolution of this thought from Aquinas to Ockham is also briefly analyzed.

3184 Beuchot, Mauricio. "El Problema de los Universales en Tomás de Aquino." *Revista de Filosofia* (México) 11(1978): 389-420.

3185 Beuchot, Mauricio. "Estructura y Función de la Metafisica Según Aristoteles, San Alberto Magno y Santo Tomás de Aquino. Y Estructura y Función de la Metafisica en la Filosofia Analitica." *Libro Anual* (Mexico) 8(1980): 181-303.

3186 Beuchot, Mauricio. "La Substancia en el Tomismo y en la Filosofia Analitica." *Revista de Filosofia* 8(1980): 293-319.

3187 Beuchot, Mauricio. "La Metafisica de Las Causas en Aristóteles y Santo Tomás." *Logos* (Mexico) 9(1981): 9-28.

3188 Beuchot, Mauricio. "Necesidad y Contingencia en Aristóteles, Tomás Aquino y Saúl Kripke." *Revista de Filosofia* (México) 15(1982): 211-230.

3189 Beuchot, Mauricio. "La Metafisica y el Ente en la Filosofia Analitica y en el Tomismo." *Revista de Filosofia* 16(1983): 367-391.

3190 Beuchot, Mauricio. "La Filosofia y Las Ciencias en la Filosofia Analitica y en el Tomisimo." *Logos* 11(1983): 13-34.

3191 Beuchot, Mauricio. "La Distincion Entre Esencia y Existencia en la Alta Edad Media: Mario Victorino, Severino Doecio, Gilberto Porretano y Hugo de San Victor." *Revista de Filosofia* (México) 18(1985): 203-218.

3192 Beuchot, Mauricio. "Acerca de la Argumentación Filosófico-metafísica." *Critica* 18(1986): 57-66.

3193 Beuchot, Mauricio. "La Distincion Entre Esencia y Existencia en los escolasticos anteriores a Tomás de Aquino." *Revista de Filosofia* (México) 19(1986): 71-87.

3194 Beuchot, Mauricio. "Nombres Propios, Sujetos y Predicados en la Semántica Escolastica y en la Actual." *Filosofia Oggi* 9(1986): 105-123.

3195 Beuchot, Mauricio. "La Esencia y la Existencia en Tomás de Aquino." *Revista de Filosofia* (Mexico) 22(1989): 149-165.

3196 Beuchot, Mauricio. "La Persona Humana y Su Proyección a Lo Social, Según Santo Tomás." *Logos* (Mexico) 17(1989): 55-65.

3197 Beuchot, Mauricio. "Los Factores Originales de la Sociedad en Tomás de Aquino." *Logos* (Mexico) 18(1990): 33-39.

3198 Bianchi, Cirillo. "Umanesimo Tomista." *Tommaso D'Aquino Nel Suo Settimo Centenario: Atti del Congresso Internazionale*. Napoli: Edizioni Domenicane Italiane, 1978. 375-378.

3199 Blanco, Guillermo P. "El Estudio del Aima." *Sapientia* 33(1978): 249-266.

3200 Blanco Cendon, Fernando. "Filosofia del Numero en Santo Tomás." *Studium* 24(1984): 463-487.

3201 Blandino, Giovanni. "Discussione Sulla Causalità, I." *Aquinas* 23(1980): 93-113.

*G. Blandino thinks that the three Thomistic principles: *Nemo dat quod non habet* (Nobody gives what he has not): *Nihil reducitur de potentia in actum nisi per aliquod ens actu*, *Quidquid movetur, ab alio movetur* are not right, because they, especially the first one, imply the interpretation of causality as pure "communication." Blandino admits that the causality is for us very mysterious, but he maintains that it cannot be reduced to "a communication of something which one already had," because it is essentially "the production of something which before did not exist and which, therefore, one had not." On the contrary, P. Pellecchia maintains the validity of those three principles.*

3202 Blandino, Giovanni. "Discussione Sulla Causalità, II." *Aquinas* 25(1982): 515-552.

*The article is a discussion between C. Manzia and G. Blandino about the two principles: *Nemo dat quod non habet* and *quidquid movetur ab alio movetur*.*

3203 Blandino, Giovanni. "Discussione Sul Problema Critico." *Aquinas* 28(1985): 519-533.

3204 Blázques, Niceto. "Los Tratados Sobre la Ley Antiqu y Nueva en la *Summa Theologiae*." *Scripta Theologica*, Pamplona 15(1983): 421-467.

3205 Blázquez, Niceto. "Tomás de Aquino Cien Años Depués de la *Aeterni Patris* de Leó XIII." *Studium* 20(1980): 101-113.

3206 Blázquez, Niceto. "Refléxión Analógica y Comprensión Humana Según Santo Tomás." *Atti Del'VIII Congresso Tomistico Internazionale: Vol. V: Problemi Metafisici.* Studi Tomistici 14. Città del Vaticano, Pontificia Accademia di San Tommaso e di Religione Cattolica: Libreria Editrice Cattolica, 1982. 191-200.

3207 Blázquez, Niceto. "La Pena de Muerta: Lectura Crítica del Pensamiento de Santo Tomás." *Moralia: Revista de Ciencias Morales* (Madrid) 7(1985): 107-128.

3208 Blázquez, Niceto. "El Valor de Las Cinco Vias de Santo Tomás." *Studium* 26(1986): 77-103.

3209 Boff, Clodovis. "Santo Tomás de Aquino e a Teologia Da Libertaçao." *Revista Eclesiastica Brasileira* 41(1981): 426-442.

3210 Boff, Clodovis. "Santo Tomás de Aquino y la Teologia de la Liberación: Carta a Un Joven Te." *Theologica Xaveriana* 32(1982): 65-79.

3211 Bolzán, J. E. "Hilemorfismo y Corporalidad." *Sapientia* 40(1985): 25-32.

*Se desecha el hilemorfismo de Aristóteles y especialmente la *materia prima*, recurriéndose a la mixis o "combinación entre substanicas" (*Gen. Corr.* 1, 10) para explicar la corporalidad del hombre; el alma aparece aquí como la causa radical estructurante de un cuerpo preexistente sólo como posibilidad de ser en las diversas substancias cósmicas capaces de ser asimiladas por la actividad megemónica del alma.*

3212 Bolzán, J. E. "Ente Natural, Artefacto y Natural-facto." *Revista de Filosofia* (México) 20(1987): 262-269.

3213 Bonnín Aguiló, Francisco. "Santo Tomás de Aquino y la Felicidad Imperfecta." *Estudios Filosóficos* 27(1978): 111-125.

3214 Bordón, Nelibe Judith. "Aproximaciones a la Concepción de Sto. Tomás de Aquino Sobre el Conocimiento de la Esencia de Dios." *Anuario de Filosofia* (Tucumán) 1(1982): 39-46.

3215 Bourke, Vernon J. "El Principio de la Sindéresis: Fuentes y Función en la Ética de Tomás de Aquino." *Sapientia* (Buenos Aires) 35(1980): 615-626.

3216 Brasa Díez, Mariano. "La Historicidad del Hombre Según Sto. Tomás." *Tommaso D'Aquino Nel Suo Settimo Centenario: Atti del Congresso Internazionale: L'Uomo*. Napoli: Edizioni Domenicane Italiane, 1978. 219-222.

3217 Brasa Díez, Mariano. "La Filosofia en el Mundo de Tomás de Aquino." *Studium* 19(1979): 87-109.

3218 Brasa Díez, Mariano. "El Lenguaje Sobre Dios en Tomás de Aquino." *Studium* 21(1981): 487-502.

3219 Brasa Díez, Mariano. "Conocimiento Analógico y Negativo de Dios en Tomás de Aquino." *Studium* 27(1987): 127-141.

3220 Briancesco, E. "La Exploración del Mal Moral en el Ultimo Tomás de Aquino: Introducción a la Lectura de la Q. D. *De Malo*." *Teologia* 23(1986): 5-36.

3221 Buela, Alberto Eduardo. "El Método Empirico-reflexivo." *Sapientia* 40(1985): 67-72.

3222 Caldera, Rafael-Tomas. "*Primo Cadit Ens*." *Anuario Filosófico* 22(1989): 57-94.

3223 Calderón Bouchet, Rubén. "El Sistema del Mundo de Acuerdo Con Santo Tomás." *Philosophica* (Valparaiso) 7(1984): 117-129.

3224 Campos, Fernando Arruda. "El Tomismo en el Mundo Contemporáneo." *Revista de Filosofia* 14(1981): 9-25.

3225 Campos, Fernando Arruda. "El Tomisimo en el Dialogo Con el Pensamiento Contemporaneo." *Revista de Filosofia* (México) 19(1986): 3-16.

3226 Canals, Vidal. "La Actitud Filosófica de Santo Tomás Como Orientación Para Un Búsqueda de Sintesis en el Pensamiento Contemporaneo." *Tommaso D'Aquino Nel I Centenario Dell'Enciclica Aeterni Patris.* Ed. Benedetto Amore. Roma: Societá Internazionale Tommaso d'Aquino, 1981. 211-229.

3227 Caponnetto, Mario. "La Voluntad de Sentido en la Antropología Psiquiátrica de Frankl: Examen Critico de la Categoria Frankeleana de la Voluntad de Sentido a la Luz de la Filosofia de Tomás de Aquino." *Philosophica* (Valparaiso) 8(1985): 113-124.

3228 Cappelletti, Angel J. "El Aristotelismo Político de Tomás de Aquino." *Revista de Filosofia de la Universidad de Costa Rica* 25(1987): 201-205.

*Usually it is said that Aquinas had "Christianized" Aristotle. Many doctrines of Aristotelian metaphysics are, however, not compatible with Christian *Weltanschauung*. But in political philosophy Thomas follows Aristotle's teaching closer than in other fields, in open contradictions sometimes with Augustine and the Greek fathers.*

3229 Cappelletti, Angel J. "La Analogia del Ser Como Fundamento de la Metafisica Tomista." *Revista Venezolana Filosofia* 24(1988): 7-14.

3230 Cardona, Carlos. "El Acto de Ser y la Acción Creatural." *Scripta Theologica*, Pamplona 10(1978): 1081-1096.

3231 Cardona, Carlos. "La Ordenación de la Criatura a Dios Como Fundamento de la Moral." *Scripta Theologica*, Pamplona 11(1979): 801-822.

3232 Cardozo Biritos, Dennis. "Unificación de Las Ciencias y Unidad del Saber." *Philosophica* (Valparaiso) 7(1984): 191-200.

3233 Carubini, Oscar Alfredo. "La Animación Según Santo Tomás y la Actual Biologia." *Filosofar Cristiano* (Argentina) 8-9(1984-1985): 99-105.

3234 Carvalho, Ubirajara Calmon. "O Argumento Ontológico Em Kant e a 1. a Via Da Demonstraçào de Deus En Santo Tomás." *Revista Brasileira de Filosofia* 35(1986): 22-42.

3235 Casado, F. "El Apriorismo del Conocimiento en Santo Tomás de Aquino." *Estudio Agustiniana* (Valladolid) 12(1977): 493-509.

3236 Casaubón, Juan A. "Apéndice: Sobre Intencionalidad." *Sapientia* 34(1979): 47-54.

*In this article I try to show that, in the study of human intentional cognition, two ways may be followed:(1) a cosmological-psychological-metaphysical way (P. Hayen) and (2) a gnosiological-reflexive way. In this second way we begin by showing that human intelligence is specified pre-conscientiously and that this specification factor must exercise also a stimulation function. Then, we show that this *specifying-stimulating-factor* must have its origin in the material being, which shows itself as penetrated by supra-material influences. Then, I discuss Husserl's "constitution" theory.*

3237 Casaubón, Juan A. "Los Tres Estados de la Esencia Según Santo Tomás de Aquino." *Sapientia* 45(1990): 87-94.

3238 Casaubón, Tomás A. "En Torno Al Concepto de Dignidad." *Sapientia* 41(1986): 306-309.

3239 Castro de Cabanillas, Rosa Ana. "Santo Tomás y el Derecho de Gentes." *Filosofar Cristiano* (Argentina) 5-6(1981-1982): 411-422.

3240 Caturelli, Alberto. "La Antropología y Sus Problemas en Santo Tomás de Aquino." *Tommaso D'Aquino Nel Suo Settimo Centenario: Atti del Congresso Internazionale VII: L'Uomo*. Napoli: Edizioni Domenicane Italiane, 1978. 20-36.

3241 Caturelli, Alberto. "Significado del Pensamiento de Michele F. Sciacca Para el Hombre de Hoy." *Sapientia* 41(1986): 265-280.

3242 Caturelli, Alberto. "La Estudiosidad y la Vida Espiritual." *Sapientia* 42(1987): 167-176.

3243 Caturelli, Alberto. "Premisas Metafísicas de la Bioética." *Sapientia* 44(1989): 35-46.

3244 Cayetano, Tomás. "Comentarío del Cardenal Cayetano: I, Q. 4, A. 1. Cuestion Cuarta: Sobre la Perfección de Dios." *Ethos* 9(1981): 285-318. Trans. Gustavo D. Corbi.

3245 Celada, Gregorio. "Introduction." *Suma de Teologia*. By Tomás de Aquino. Trans. Provincias Dominicanas. Ed. Provincias Dominicanas. BAC Maior 31. Madrid: Editorial Catolica, 1988. i-xxxviii.

3246 Cercós Soto, José Luis. "Substancia y Sustantividad: Tomás de Aquino y X. Zubiri." *Anuario Filosófico* 23(1990): 9-27.

3247 Cerezo-De Diego, Prometeo. "El Problema de la 'Infidelidad' en Fray Alonso de la Veracruz." *Revista de Filosofia* (México) 17(1984): 291-310.

*The problem of the "infidelity" of the American Indians is studied by Fr. Alosno de la Veracruz in his treatise *De dominio infidelium et iusto bello*. Starting from the known classification of unbelievers by Cardinal Caietanus, he works out a complete new classification of unbelievers, and he concludes that no power, neither spiritual (the Roman Pontiff) nor political (the Emperor) may justly wage war against unbelievers to deprive them of their rights because of their unbelief.*

3248 Chacón, Alfonso C. "El Tratado Sobre la Gracia en la *Summa Contra Gentiles*." *Scripta Theologica* 16(1984): 113-146.

3249 Chacón, Alfonso C. "Sobre la Autoria de la *Summa Theologiae* del Card. Pedro de Capua (+1214)." *Hispania Christiana*. Eds. J. I. Saranyana and E. Tejero. Colección Historia de la Iglesia 14. Pampelune: EUNSa, 1988. 379-387.

3250 Chalmeta, Gabriel. "Fenomenología de la Sensación." *Sapientia* 40(1985): 33-48.

3251 Chalmeta, Gabriel. "Materialidad e Inmaterialidad del Alma Sensitiva en la Abstracción Sensible." *L'anima Nell'antropologia Di San Tommaso D'Aquino IX: Atti del Congresso Societá Internazionale San Tommaso D'Aquino*. Ed. Abelardo Lobato. Milano: Editrice Massimo, 1987. 219-226.

3252 Chico Sánchez, Gabriel. "La Quaestio Como Método Filosófico en Tomás de Aquino." *Analogia* 1(1987): 3-44.

3253 Ciliberto, Vicente O. "El Ser en Santo Tomás y en la Fenomenologia." *Sapientia* 32(1977): 93-110.

3254 Cipriani, Juan Luis. "Estudio de la Virtud de la Prudencia en Las Obras de Santo Tomás." *Rev. Teol.* (Limense) 17(1983): 69-96.

3255 Clavell, Luis. "El Estudio de Santo Tomás en el Magisterio de Juan Pablo II." *Sapientia* 35(1980): 589-600.

3256 Colomer, Eusebio. "La Critica Marxista de la Idea de Creación y Santo Tomás de Aquino." *Atti Del'VIII Congresso Tomistico Internazionale IV: Prospettive Teologiche Moderne*. Studi Tomistici 13. Città del Vaticano, Pontificia Accademia di San Tommaso e di Religione Cattolica: Libreria Editrice Cattolica, 1981. 60-72.

3257 Colon Rosado, Anibal. "Filosofia de la Substancia: Aristóteles y Santo Tomás de Aquino." *Dialogos* 18(1983): 95-116.

3258 Composta, Dário. "Ley Eterna y Ley Natural." *Revista Filosofia* (México) 12(1979): 187-214.

*The purpose of this paper is to show historical exegetical and metaphysical meaning of the two-sided normative system, usually called *lex aeterna lex naturalis*. Exegetically it derives from pantheistic stoic conception of cosmic order, but corrected by Christian theology. Historically, this conception underwent three steps: pagan period, Christian period (until the XVIII century), and modern refusal period. Metaphysically, the conception still is vital in those cultural centers in which not reason (Kant), not *Obiektives Geist* or History (Hegel, Marx), but intelligence discovers part of universal order.*

3259 Corbi, Gustavo Daniel. "La Manuductio del Erro en la Vida de la Inteligencia." *Philosophica* (Valparaiso) 7(1984): 157-177.

3260 Corcuera, Francisco Ugarte. "Estudio Sobre la Esencia, I." *Sapientia* 36(1981): 171-194.

3261 Corcuera, Francisco Ugarte. "Estudio Sobre la Esencia, II." *Sapientia* 36(1981): 255-262.

3262 Cordero Pando, Jesús. "Instancias Parentales y Heteronomia de la Conciencia." *Atti del Congresso Internazionale Tommaso D'Aquino Nel Suo Settimo Centenario V: L'agire Morale*. Napoli: Edizioni Donemicane, 1977. 228-238.

3263 Corti, Enrique Camilo. "Las Pruebas Tomistas de la Existencia de Dios: Rasgos Comunes." *Logos* (México) 9(1981): 29-54.

3264 Corti de Pérez, Myriam. "Del Ser y de la Esencia del Hombre Según Santo Tomás." *Filosofar Cristiano* (Argentina) 8-9(1984-1985): 33-39.

3265 Corvino, Francesco. "Observaciones Sobre el Concepto de Sapientia en San Buenaventura." *Il Concetto Di Sapientia in San Bonaventura e San Tommaso*. Ed. Alessandro Musco. Biblioteca Dell'Enchiridion 1. Palermo: 1983. 71-90.

3266 Crosby, John F., and Caprile De Leaniz. "Son Ser y Bien Realmente Convertibles? Una Investigación Fenomenológica." *Diálogo Filosófico* 6(1990): 170-194.

*Se establecen en este trabajo las diferencios entre la concepción tomista del *esse* y la concepción fenomenológica, especialmente apoyada en la filosofía de Von Hildebrand, de valor. El valor aparece con un carácter absoluto, mientras que el *bonum*—idéntico con el *esse*—tiene un cierto carácter relativo—aunque no relativista—, por ser el mismo ser en cuanto apetecido. Se muesta con profusión de argumentos que el valor no es reducible al ser, concebido por la filosofía tomistra, pero que tampoco se debe entender la relación entre ser y valor en un sentido dualista radical. El valor no es una carcterística constitutiva del ser sustancial, pero sí uno caracteristica "consecuencial" del mismo, por lo que no puede concebirse al margen del ser mismo.*

3267 Cselényi, István Gábor. "Le Cinque Vie Ed Il Dialogo Odierno: Dialogo Sull'origine Dello Sviluppo." *Atti Del'VIII Congresso Tomistico Internazionale IV: Prospettive Teologiche Moderne*. Studi Tomistici 13. Città del Vaticano, Pontificia Accademia di San Tommaso e di Religione Cattolica: Libreria Editrice Cattolica, 1981. 42-46.

3268 Cunningham, Francis A. "La Compositio in Re de Santo Tomás." *Pensamiento* 33(1977): 123-154.

3269 Curiel, José Luis. "La Persona Humana en la Filosofia del Derecho de Sto. Tomás." *Tommaso D'Aquino Nel Suo Settimo Centenario VIII: Atti del Congresso Internazionale: L'Uomo.* Napoli: Edizioni Domenicane Italiane, 1978. 282-285.

3270 Darós, William R. "La Interpretación Rosminiana del Intelecto Agente Tomista." *Pensamiento* 34(1978): 47-72.

*This article presented the agreement between the light of agent intellect in Saint Thomas' philosophy and the ideal being in Rosmini's philosophy. Moreover, the necessity of putting the idea of being as an innate one is discussed. The suppositions of this philosophy are then manifested. For the traditional philosophy and for Rosmini it is evident that if we think, we think the being (*esse*) and by the being. But in this article we reach the conclusion that this way of thinking about thought is only a way of making a philosophy with metaphysical and empirically unproven suppositions.*

3271 Darós, William R. "Nota Sobre el Concepto de Ente en Tomás de Aquino (Dios: Ser O Ente?)." *Sapientia* 33(1978): 285-296.

*Thomistic philosophers don't want to call God *ens*. According to them, God is the *esse subsistens*: He is not an *ens*. In this article, on the contrary, it is shown that St. Thomas thinks God is also an *ens* by essence and the other things are thought as *ens* by participation. The article tries then to indicate the difference between *ens* and *esse* according to Saint Thomas' mind. As Heidegger said, God is not *esse*: He is the *esse subsistens*, but He is also—in opposition to Heidegger—*ens* by essence.*

3272 Darós, William R. "Verdad y Relativismo Según el Pensamiento de Tomás de Aquino." *Sapientia* 34(1979): 231-254.

Truth is the concept of a relation between the idea in the mind and the thing to which the idea refers. It is essential to truth to be a relation, but it is a relation of analogy. Truth is absolutely a relation, but this relation is conditioned by the mind and by the thing that can change. Truth differs, changes if things change or if our ideas change our mind. The identity of truth depends on the identity of thing and of mind.

3273 Darós, William R. "Lo A-priori en la Teoria Tomista del Conocimiento Según J. Marechal." *Pensamiento* 36(1980): 401-423.

La teoria tomista del conocimiento se basa en un elemento a-priori y metafísico: la ratio essendi de nuestros pensamiento como luz inteligible innata de la inteligencia humana. Se trata de un elemento formal metafísico que interviene en todo conocimiento, como condición det todo pensar. Este elemento no puede ser ni aceptado ni rechazado por los argumentos basados en meros datos empíricos. Sin embargo esta teoría no carece de sentido.

3274 Darós, William R. "Diversidad de la Verdad y Relativismo en el Pensamiento de Tomás de Aquino." *Atti Del'VIII Congresso Tomistico Internazionale: Vol. V: Problemi Metafisici*. Studi Tomistici 14. Città del Vaticano, Pontificia Accademia di San Tommaso e di Religione Cattolica: Libreria Editrice Cattolica, 1982. 222-245.

3275 Darós, William R. "Educación y Función Docente en el Pensamiento de Tomás de Aquino." *Sapientia* 38(1983): 45-66.

3276 Darós, William R. "La Espiritualidad de la Persona Humana en el Pensamiento de Ph Lersch: Observaciones Desde Una Perpectiva Tomista." *Sapientia* 38(1983): 187-202.

3277 Darós, William R. "Qué es la Filosofía, en Pensamiento de John Dewey." *Sapientia* 38(1983): 121-138.

3278 Darós, William R. "La Analogía en el Concepto de Ciencia Aristotélico-tomista." *Sapientia* 39(1984): 19-36.

3279 Darós, William R. "Ciencia O Actividad Política en la Docencia? Perspectiva Tomista Sobre la Relativa Dependencia y Autonomia del Proceso Didactico." *Sapientia* 40(1985): 197-216.

3280 Darós, William R. "La Educación del Alma en el Hombre." *Atti del Congresso Societá Internazionale San Tommaso D'Aquino IX: L'anima Nell'antropologia Di San Tommaso D'Aquino*. 1987. 559-563.

3281 De Diez, Maria Raquel Fischer. "El Orden Al Bien y la Libertad Humana: Una Lectura de la Cuestión *Disputada De Libero Arbitrio*." *Patristica et Mediaevalia* 7(1986): 65-82.

3282 De Estrada, Jose M. "Libertad y Temporalidad." *Sapientia* 41(1986): 67-70.

3283 De Finance, Joseph. "Las Dos Formas del Obrar y Su Raíz Metafísica." *Sapientia* 34(1979): 9-36.

The scope of the article is to show how immanent and transitive actions—classically distinguished since Aristotle—express two aspects of being, viz. intrinsic perfection and "generosity" ("self-communicativity"). The main forms of immanence and transitivity are considered on the various levels of being. A higher degree of immanence expresses a higher degree of ontological unity and gives a new expression to being's communicativity. In the pure immanence of the Absolute, being's generosity is creation. According to the non-philosophical doctrine of the Trinity, this generosity expresses itself in the very core of the immanence.

3284 De Finance, Joseph. "Metafisica y Concepto del Mundo: A Proposito del Problema Filosofico de la Evolución de Una Perspectiva Tomista." *Sapentia* 35(1980): 637-654.

3285 De Gandolfi Donadio Maggi, María Celestina. "Libertad-necesidad en la Quaestio Disputata *De Malo*, VI." *Sapientia* 39(1984): 257-266.

3286 De Gandolfi Donadio Maggi, Maria Celestina. "Juicios Morales y Verdad." *Sapientia* 40(1985): 97-108.

3287 De Gandolfi Donadio Maggi, Maria Celestina. "Contemplación y Praxis: II-II *Suma Teológica*, Qq. 179-182." *Doctor Communis* 41(1988): 34-46.

3288 De Gandolfi Donadio Maggi, Maria Celestina. "Etica y Metafisica." *Doctor Communis* 42(1988): 155-166.

3289 De la Cierva, Santiago. "Las Potencias Sensibles y el Alma Separada." *L'anima Nell'antropologia Di San Tommaso D'Aquino IX: Atti del Congresso Societá Internazionale San Tommaso D'Aquino.* Ed. Abelardo Lobato. Milano: Editrice Massimo, 1987. 243-251.

3290 De La Puente Miguel, Maria Candelas. "La Visión Tomista de la Belleza Como Resultado del Amor y de la Belleza Divinos." *Revista Agustiniana* 25(1984): 107-160.

3291 De Stier, María Lillana Lukac. "Compatibilidad Entre la Presciencia Divina y la Libertad de los Actos Humanos: Refutación a Las Objectiones de Anthony Kenny." *Sapientia* 39(1984): 267-276.

*This author intends to refute Anthony Kenny's objections to Thomas Aquinas' arguments proving the compatibility between God's foreknowledge and the freedom of human actions, which the former exposes in his paper *Divine foreknowledge and human freedom*, published in *Aquinas: A Collection of Critical Essays*. The main critique consists in an erroneous interpretation of Aquinas' divine knowledge and his fundamental notion of future as *presentialiter* known. Besides, methodologically, Kenny omits not only other very important Aquinas' texts but even the *corpus* of the article he analyzes.*

3292 De Stier, Maria Lillana Lukac. "Naturaleza y Ética en Hobbes y Tomás de Aquino." *Sapientia* 43(1988): 123-138.

3293 De Stier, María Lillana Lukac. "Qué Conocemos de Dios? Hobbes Versus Tomas." *Logos* (Mexico) 18(1990): 59-71.

3294 De Vries, Josef. "Lo Inevitable de la Percepción del Ser a la Luz de la Critica de la Razón Pura de Kant." *Revista de Filosofia* (Mexico) 12(1979): 7-20.

3295 Del Cura, Alejandro. "Verdad y Ser en Santo Tomás de Aquino." *Tommaso Nel Suo Settimo Centenario VI: Atti del Congresso Internazionale: L'essere*. Napoli: Edizioni Domenicane Italiane, 1977. 155-173.

3296 Del Cura, Alejandro. "De Nuevo Las Cinco Vías." *Estudios Filosóficos* 30(1981): 519-531.

3297 Delgado, V. Munoz. "La Lógica en Las Condenaciones de 1277." *Cuadernos Salmantinos de Filosofia* 4(1977): 36-39.

3298 Derisi, Octavio Nicolás. "El Maestro Según Santo Tomás." *Sapientia* 32(1977): 321-324.

*En la *Cuestion XI: Acerca del Maestro* de las *Cuestiones Disputadas*, Santo Tomás trata de resolver la esencia de la acción docente y del Maestro que la imparte. Frente a dos concepciones antagónicas, Santo Tomás toma la via media: la vida del conocimiento y de la voluntad procedente del interior, pero son a su vez determinadas por los objetos formales externos. La educación es llevada a cabo por el propio educando mediante el desarrollo armónico de su naturaleza en orden a su fin trascendente divino. El educador solamente lo ayuda: encauza y corrige ese desarrollo. El Maestro, ya en posesión de la ciencia, la presenta al discipulo para que Él mismo la pueda adquirir por su propio esfuerzo. Al final, Santo Tomás hace ver que la acción educadora pertenece, en parte, a la vida contemplativa, poroque cultiva las ciencias; pero en si misma pertence a la vida activa, como tramisión de la misma.*

3299 Derisi, Octavio Nicolás. "El Sentido de la Nada en la Filosofia Moderna Contemporánea y en la Filosofia de Santo Tomás." *Filosofar Cristiano* (Córdoba, Argentina) 1(1977): 25-37.

3300 Derisi, Octavio Nicolás. "Nuevos Aportes a la Metafisica Tomista." *Anuario del Centro de Estudios Humanisticos* (México) 19(1978): 27-45.

3301 Derisi, Octavio Nicolás. "El Significado de la Enciclica *Aeterni Patris* de Leon XIII, A los Cien Anos de Su Publicacion." *Sapientia* 34(1979): 303-308.

3302 Derisi, Octavio Nicolás. "Actualidad de la Doctrina Tomista del Conocimiento." *Scripta Theologica*, Pamplona 11(1980): 773-800.

3303 Derisi, Octavio Nicolás. "El Fundamento de la Metafisica Tomista: El *Esse* e *Intelligere Divino*, Fundamento y Causa de Todo Ser y Entender Participados." *Sapientia* 35(1980): 9-26.

*El Racionalismo panteista Hegel y el empirismo sensista Hume reducen el conocimiento a un inmanentismo. El realismo intelectualista de Santo Tomás restaura la auténtica realidad del conocimiento: la aprehensión de un ser trascendente en la inmanencia del acto. Desde ese ser la inteligencia llegal al *Esse subsistente*, en cuyo Acto puro se identifica el Entender con el Ser. El ser inmediatamente dado es participado, finito y contingente, porque su esencia no es la existencia. Ambas son por participación inmediata el *Esse divino*: la esencia por causalidad ejemejemplar necesaria del *Esse* y *Verbo divino*; la existencia por causa eficiente libre de la Voluntad divina. El *Esse divino* es el fundamento metafísico inmediato de todo el ser tanto en su esencia como en su existencia.*

3304 Derisi, Octavio Nicolás. "La Contribución Fundamental de Santo Tomás de Aquino a la Filosofia. La Ubicación de la Inteligencia en Su Objeto Formal: El Ser Trascendente." *La Filosofia del Cristiano, Hoy. Vetera Novis Augere et Perficere*. Cordoba: General de Public. UNC, 1980. 39-56.

3305 Derisi, Octavio Nicolás. "Ser y Duración." *Sapientia* 36(1981): 15-42.

*La duración es la permanencia en el ser; y, como Éste, se expresa con un concepto análogo que comprende(1) La *eternidad*; permanencia en el Acto Puro Imparticipado de Ser, sin principio ni fin, y todo a la vez—sin cambio—; (2) La *eviternidad*: duración de los seres participados espirituales cuya esencia no es su ser ni su actividad y, por eso, poseen cambio de actos; (3) El *tiempo* duración del ser corpóreo, cuya esencia no es el ser, y cuyo acto esencial está limitado también por la materia y, por eso, es corruptible y continuamente cambiante.*

3306 Derisi, Octavio Nicolás. "Ser, Entender y Acto." *Atti Dell'VIII Congresso Tomistico Internazionale I: L'enciclica Aeterni Patris Nell'arco Di Un Secolo*. Studi Tomistici 10. Cittá del Vaticano: Pontificia Accademia di San Tommaso e di Religione Cattolica, 1981. 291-306.

3307 Derisi, Octavio Nicolás. "Del Ente Participado Al Ser Imparticipado." *Filosofar Cristiano* 5-6(1981): 19-33.

3308 Derisi, Octavio Nicolás. "La Participación del Ser." *Sapientia* 37(1982): 5-10, 83-86, 243-248.

3309 Derisi, Octavio Nicolás. "Del Ente Participado Al Ser Imparticipado." *Doctor Communis* 35(1982): 26-38.

El ente es lo que es o puede ser, está compuesto de esencia y el acto de ser. El Ser participado es el que nos rodea y se nos manifiesta como finito y contingente, caracteres que implican la distinción y composición real de esencia y acto de ser. La esencia es participada por vía ejemplar de la Esencia divina y del Verbo de Dios que, al contemplar su Esencia, ve y constituye todas las esencias. La participación del Ser es por causalidad eficiente de la Voluntad divina libre: por Creación, Conservación y Premoción y Concurso. Por eso, el ser participado, por su esencia y acto de ser, implican necesariamente el Acto puro de ser, el Ser imparticipado.

3310 Derisi, Octavio Nicolás. "Del Ente Participado Al Ser Imparticipado." *Sapientia* 39(1984): 169-180.

3311 Derisi, Octavio Nicolás. "El Ser y los Entes." *Sapientia* 39(1984): 91-100.

Todo ente finito consta de esencia y acto de ser, ambos participados del Ser divino. La esencia es por particpación de la Esencia y del Entendimiento divino de un modo comunica por creación conservación libre del Acto puro de ser, quient lo comunica por creación conservación, concurso y premoción. "Todo el ser es por Dios" (Santo Tomás). Por consiguiente, tanto la esencia como el acto de ser participados implican necesariamente la existencia del Ser imparticipado, ya que sin. El no se concibe esencia alguna posible ni el acto de ser que les da actualidad.

3312 Derisi, Octavio Nicolás. "Aspectos Fundamentales del Conocimiento Humano." *Sapientia* 39(1984): 5-8, 83-90, 163-168, 243-248.

3313 Derisi, Octavio Nicolás. "Carácter Racional de la Libertad." *Sapientia* 40(1985): 9-12.

La libertad de la voluntad se funda en el juicio de indiferencia de la inteligencia frente a un determinado bien. La decisión libre es la conjundión de un acto de la voluntad como fuerza o causa eficiente y de un acto de inteligencia como causa formal: la elección es un acto de la voluntad informada por un juicio práctico de la inteligencia. El útimo fin el hombre, que es Dios o el Bien infinito está siempre presente en cualquier acto libre, ya que el bien apetecido por Éste, es por participación de aquél.

3314 Derisi, Octavio Nicolás. "La Partecipación de la Esencia." *Cinquant'anni Di Magistero Teologico, Scritti in Onore Di Mons. Antonio Piolanti Nel 50 del Suo Sacerdozio.* Studi Tomistici 26. Città del Vaticano: Libreria Editrice Vaticana, 1985. 173-184.

3315 Derisi, Octavio Nicolás. "La Verdad." *Sapientia* 40(1985): 5-8, 83-88, 163-170, 243-248.

3316 Derisi, Octavio Nicolás. "La Filosofia Frente a la Fisica Moderna." *Sapientia* 40(1985): 171-184.

3317 Derisi, Octavio Nicolás. "El Acto Constitutivo del Conocimiento y de la Cognoscibilidad O Verdad." *Sapientia* 42(1987): 97-104.

3318 Derisi, Octavio Nicolás. "Ser y Entender en Hegel y Santo Tomás." *Doctor Communis* 40(1987): 269-277.

3319 Derisi, Octavio Nicolás. "Significación Fundamental de la Abstractio en Santo Tomás de Aquino." *Atti del Congresso Societá Internazionale San Tommaso D'Aquino IX: L'anima Nell'antropologia Di San Tommaso D'Aquino*. Napoli: Edizioni Domenicane Italiane, 1987. 253-265.

3320 Derisi, Octavio Nicolás. "La Realidad del Concepto de la Trascendentalidad y Predicamentalidad. I." *Sapientia* 43(1988): 237-242.

3321 Derisi, Octavio Nicolás. "La Realidad del Concepto de la Trascendentalidad y Predicamentalidad. II." *Sapientia* 43(1988): 317-330.

3322 Derisi, Octavio Nicolás. "La Semana Tomista." *Sapientia* 43(1988): 383-386.

3323 Derisi, Octavio Nicolás. "Un Acontecimento Acera del Tema del Alma en la Antropología de Santo Tomás de Aquino." *Sapientia* 43(1988): 382-383.

3324 Derisi, Octavio Nicolás. "La XIII Semana Tomista en Argentina." *Doctor Communis* 42(1989): 68-71.

3325 Derisi, Octavio Nicolás. "Naturaleza del Conocimiento Humano: El Significado de la Abstracción en Santo Tomás. III." *Sapientia* 44(1989): 163-170.

Compuesto de cuerpo y alma espiritual, el hombre se vale de dos conocimientos, intimamente unidos: el sensitivo, que es un intuición o aprehensión inmediata de la realidad, sin intermediarios. Este conocimiento no aprehende el ser o la realidad y el yo como tal. El entendimiento inteligible, a través de la abstracción del conocimiento sensitivo, aprehende el ser o esencia de las cosas y sabe que las cosas son y que Él es. El trabajo denuncia los errores tanto del sensismo antiguo y moderno, como del espiritualismo exagerado racionalismo, que escinde estos dos conocimientos y por caminos diversos conducen al inmanentismo. Sólo por la abstracción es posible la unión de estos dos conocimientos, que permiten la aprehensión de la realidad como tal.

3326 Domenech, M. M. "La *Suma Teológica* y Sus Contrastes Con la Ciencia." *Cristiandad* 36(1980): 143-147.

3327 Echauri, Raúl. "Sobre Una Nueva Confrontación de Heidegger Con Santo Tomás." *Sapientia* 42(1987): 371-380.

3328 Elders, Léon J. "La Naturaleza de la Metafisica Según San Alberto Magno y Santo Tomás de Aquino." *Scripta Theologica*, Pamplona 12(1980): 547-651.

3329 Elders, Léon J. "Las Ciencias de la Naturaleza y la Existencia de Dios." *Dios y el Hombre*. Ed. VI Simposio Internacional de Teologia. Pamplona: Universidad de Navarra, 1985. 47-65. German Trans. in *Salzburger Jahrbuch für Philosophie* 30(1985): 73-86.

3330 Escandón, Carlos. "Derecho de Propiedad en el Contexto de la *Summa Theologica* de Tomás de Aquino." *Medellin* 4(1978): 212-231.

3331 Escandón, Carlos. "Freud y Skinner Frente a la Moral." *Revista de Filosofia* 14(1981): 91-117.

The purpose of this conference is to analyze Freud's and Skinner's main affirmations related to human conduct, in view of Aquinas' moral postulates. The conclusion of the analysis is a judgment of the foregoing psychological affirmation by differentiating subjective and objective conscience, substantial and accidental axiological reality.

3332 Ewbank, Michael Berton. "Observaciones Sobre Tomás de Aquino y el Derecho Natural." *Pensamiento* 35(1979): 59-73.

*This presentation gives an overview of Aquinas' moral theory. Recognition is given to Aquinas' cautious inductions based on reflective observation upon evidence given in experience concerning men's tendencies. His demonstrative procedure is noted, as well as his acknowledgment of the limitations akin to ethical speculation. A proper grasp of Aquinas' notion of *recta ratio*, which must be understood in terms of his metaphysics and theory of cognition, is central to his ethical thinking. A true understanding of how Aquinas portrays *recta ratio* will permit one to more fully comprehend his teaching concerning natural law.*

3333 Fabro, Cornelio. "El *Actus Essendi* en Santo Tomás y la Ruptura del Formalismo Escoástico." *Il Concetto Di Sapientia in San Bonaventura e San Tommaso*. Ed. Alessandro Musco. Biblioteca Dell'Enchiridion 1. Palermo: 1983. 37-54.

3334 Fabro, Cornelio. "Libertad y Persona en Santo Tomás." *Gladius* 2(1986): 5-32.

3335 Falgueras Salinas, Ignacio. "Consideraciones Filosóficas en Torno a la Distinción Real *Esse-essentia*." *Revista de Filosofia* (Madrid) 8(1985): 223-252.

3336 Fernández, I. P. "La Doctrina de Santo Tomás en la Mente y en la Acción del Padre Las Casas." *Studium* 27(1987): 297-312.

3337 Fernández, M. "La Naturaleza del Alma Según Santo Tomás." *Studium* 27(1987): 63-75.

3338 Fernández Sabaté, Aniceto. "Del Hombre a la Persona." *Tommaso D'Aquino Nel Suo Settimo Centenario: Atti del Congresso Internazionale*. Napoli: Edizioni Domenicane Italiane, 1978. 245-256.

3339 Ferreira, Graciela Beatriz. "Dignidad Humana e Indignación." *NAO* 5(1984): 55-70.

3340 Ferrer, Urbano. "En Torno Al Concepto de Recta Razón." *Anuario Filosófico* 19(1986): 181-193.

3341 Ferrer Rodríguez, Pilar. "La Inmaterialidad de Las Sustancias Espirituales." *Excerpta e Dissertationibus in Sacra Theologia* 15(1988): 153-220.

3342 Ferrer Santos, Urbano. "La Intencionalidad de la Voluntad, Según Santo Tomás." *Studium* 17(1977): 529-539.

3343 Filippi, Silvana. "El Hombre, Sujeto de la Educación, en la Perspectiva de Tomás de Aquino." *Sapientia* 44(1989): 11-34.

3344 Filippi, Silvana. "Heidegger y la Noción Tomista de Verdad." *Anuario Filosófico* 22(1989): 135-158.

*This work tries to show notable coincidences that—without forgetting the differences—can be observed between the conception of truth by Heidegger and Thomas Aquinas. Supporting that thesis, three aspects from both philosophers are comparatively examined: the notion, the ordinary place, and the scope of truth. The author considers then the Heideggerian conception of truth presented in *Sein und Zeit*, and at the same time the author tries to determine the accurate sense of the Thomist doctrine of truth as *adaequatio intellectus et rei*, frequently misinterpreted because of the transformation that it suffered during modern age.*

3345 Forment, Eudaldo. "El *Esse* en Santo Tomás." *Espiritu* 32(1983): 59-70.

3346 Forment, Eudaldo. "Problemática de la Analogia." *Espiritu* 33(1984): 147-158.

3347 Forment, Eudaldo. "El Ser en Domingo Báez, Por Eudaldo Forment Giralt." *Espiritu* 34(1985): 25-48.

3348 Forment, Eudaldo. "El Concepto Tradicional de Verdad en Santo Tomás." *Espiritu* 35(1986): 111-125.

3349 Forment, Eudaldo. "La Interpretación de Santo Tomás en García Movente." *Espiritu* 35(1986): 13-34.

3350 Forment, Eudaldo. "En Torno Al Tomismo y la Modernidad." *Anuario Filosófico* 19(1986): 133-141.

3351 Forment, Eudaldo. "La Interpretación de Santo Tomás en Garcia Morente." *Espiritu* 35(1986): 13-34.

3352 Forment, Eudaldo. "El Personalismo de Santo Tomás." *Sapientia* 45(1990): 277-294.

3353 Formentin, Justo. "La Educación del Hombre en Función de la Angelologia de Tomás de Aquino." *Tommaso D'Aquino Nel Suo Settimo Centenario VIII: Atti del Congresso Internazionale: L'Uomo*. Napoli: Edizioni Domenicane Italiane, 1978. 454-463.

3354 Fuster, Sebastian. "Presencia del Dios Trinitario en el Hombre Creyente Según el Pensamiento de Tomás de Aquino." *Escritos del Vedat* 13(1983): 49-55.

3355 Galíndez de Caturelli, Celia I. "La Metafisica Realista de la Educación de Santo Tomás y Las Exigencias de la Pedagogia Contèmporánea." *Filosofar Cristiano* (Argentina) 7(1983): 313-315.

3356 Gamarra, Daniel O. "Tiempo e Inmanencia." *Sapientia* 42(1987): 213-232.

3357 Garcia, Javier. "Santo Tomás de Aquino e a Teologia Da Libertaçao." *Communio* 4(1985): 109-130.

3358 Garcia, Javier. "Santo Tomás de Aquino y la Teologia de la Liberación." *Medellin* 8(1982): 518-534.

3359 Garcia de Haro, Ramón. "La Libertad Creada, Manifestación de la Omnipotencia Divina." *Atti Dell'VIII Congresso Tomistico Internazionale IV: Morale e Diritto Nella Prospettiva Tomistica*. Studi Tomistici 15. Cittá del Vaticano: Pontificia Accademia di San Tommaso e di Religione Cattolica, 1982. 45-72.

3360 García Marqués, Alfonso. "La Individuación de Las Substancias Materiales en Averroes y Santo Tomás." *Sapientia* 35(1980): 601-613.

3361 García Marqués, Alfonso, and Marcelino Otero. "A Proposito de la Cronologia del *De Substantiis Separatis* de Tomás de Aquino." *Anuario Filosófico* 16(1983): 109-122.

3362 Garcia Vieyra, Alberto. "Fiat Lux: El Ambito de Visibilidad de Las Creaturas Intelectuales." *Philosophica* (Valparaiso) 1(1978): 35-51.

3363 Gilbert, Paul. "El Acto der Ser: Un Don." *Revista de Filosofia* (México) 23(1990): 28-52.

3364 Gils, P. -M. J. "Busa's *Index Thomisticus* en 100 Jaar Thomas-uitgave Anno 1980." *Tijdschrift voor Filosofie* 42(1980): 122-126.

3365 Gilson, Étienne Henry. "La Filosofia Cristiana a la Luz de la *Aeterni Patris*." 1967. *Razon y Teologia*. Ed. P. Rodriguez. 1979. 253-273.

3366 Gironella, Juan Roig. "Cómo Debe Ser Hoy Dia la Investigación y la Enseñanza de la Filosofia Siguiendo Las Directrices de Santo Tomás, Según la Constante Recomendación y Ordenación de la Iglesia?" *Espiritu* 26(1977): 40-47.

3367 Gironella, Juan Roig. "La Metafisica de Santo Tomás y la Transcendencia del Pensamiento, Planteada Por la Fenomenologia." *Tommaso Nel Suo Settimo Centenario VI: Atti del Congresso Internazionale: L'essere*. Napoli: Edizioni Domenicane Italiane, 1977. 546-560.

3368 Gironella, Juan Roig. "La Analogía del Ser y la Originalidad de la Intención Profunda del Aquinatense." *Espiritu* 30(1981): 57-69.

*Aristóteles ve que debe admitirse una determinación o *necesidad* (Acto) para rechazar el relativismo. Pero los griegos eran *finitistas* (porque concebían el *in-finito* como *no-determinado* o *no-acabado*);entonces el Acto Pure Aristotélico es finito. Así no fundamenta la verdad o inteligibilidad del ámbito del Ser; por tanto no puede *conocer* el cosmos cambiante (pues El cambiaría); por tanto no puede *pre-ver*, ni *pro-veer*—En cambio Tomás de Aquino fundamenta hasta el paso del *no-ser* a *ser* en un Acto absolutamente Acto; entonces admite que todo procederá de El hasta en cuanto a *ser* creación); fundamentará *toda* la intelgibilidad del orizonte illmitado del Ser; y por *pre-ver*, por tanto *pro-veer*, amar y ser amado.*

3369 Gironella, Juan Roig. "La Analogia del Ser y la Originalidad de la Intención Profunda del Aquinatense." *Atti Del'VIII Congresso Tomistico Internazionale: Vol. V: Problemi Metafisici*. Studi Tomistici 14. Città del Vaticano, Pontificia Accademia di San Tommaso e di Religione Cattolica: Libreria Editrice Cattolica, 1982. 166-178.

3370 González, Angel Luis. "Notas Sobre Creación y Cuarta Via." *Atti Del'VIII Congresso Tomistico Internazionale IV: Prospettive Teologiche Moderne*. Studi Tomistici 13. Napoli: Edizioni Domenicane Italiane, 1981. 47-59.

3371 González, Orestes J. "Tomás de Aquino: La Aprehensión del Acto der Ser." *Anuario Filosófico* 22(1989): 147-159.

3372 González Alió, J. Lez. "El Entender Como Perfección: La Operación Inmanente." *Sapientia* 40(1985): 249-290.

3373 González Alió, J. Lez. "El Entender Como Posesión: La Función Gnoseológica del Verbo Mental. I." *Sapientia* 43(1988): 243-268.

3374 González Alió, J. Lez. "El Entender Como Posesión: La Función Gnoseológica del Verbo Mental. II." *Sapientia* 43(1988): 331-368.

3375 González Alió, J. Lez. "El Reflejo de la Unidad de Dios Uno y Trino en la Unidad de la Iglesia." *Dios y Hombre*. Ed. A. Aranda. 1986. 377-398.

3376 González Alvarez, Angel. "Tomás de Aquino y Las Tres Esferas del Espíritu." *Sapientia* 33(1978): 87-98.

3377 Gracia, Diego. "Persona y Comunidad: De Boecio a Tomás de Aquino." *Cuadadernos Salmantinos de Filosofia* 11(1984): 63-106.

3378 Granados, Tomás Melendo. "La Mediación del Error en la Génesis del Saber Practico." *Pensamiento* 42(1986): 385-412.

3379 Granados, Tomás Melendo. "El Carácter Trascendental del Alma Humana en Relación a la Belleza." *L'anima Nell'antropologia Di San Tommaso D'Aquino IX: Atti del Congresso Societá Internazionale San Tommaso D'Aquino*. Ed. Abelardo Lobato. Milano: Editrice Massimo, 1987. 325-342.

3380 Guerra Campos, José. "El Saber Teológico Según Santo Tomás." *Cuenca* 6(1977): 73-121.

3381 Hankey, Wayne J. "San Agustín, San Anselmo y Santo Tomás." *Augustinus* 26(1981): 83-94.

*This is a Spanish translation of an article previously published in *Dionysius*, 31(1979) showing that Anselm and Thomas both transform the use of Augustine's psychological image of the Trinity. They do this by proceeding from the image to the Persons rather than in Augustine's opposite order.*

3382 Hernández, Héctor H. "Acerca de la Verdad Politica." *Philosophica* (Valparaiso) 7(1984): 179-190.

3383 Hernández, Héctor H. "Obligación Ético-juridica, Naturaleza y Recta Razón (Una Cuestión en I-II, 94, (2)." *Ethos* 12-13(1984-1985): 161-180.

3384 Hernández, Héctor H. "Libertad Política: Liberalismo y Tomismo." *Sapientia* 40(1985): 13-24.

3385 Hoelhuber, Ivo. "Tomás de Aquino, Filósofo: Inculpado de Fideismo Absoluto." *Espiritu* 26(1977): 49-61.

3386 Incardona, Nunzio. "La Cognitio y la Sapientia." *Il Concetto Di Sapientia in San Bonaventura e San Tommaso.* Ed. Alessandro Musco. Palermo: Biblioteca Dell'Enchiridion 1, 1983. 57-68.

3387 Inciarte, Fernando. "Sobre la Etica de la Responsabilidad y Contra el Consecuencialismo Teologico-moral." *Etica y Teologia.* Eds. Alves De Sousa and T. Lopez. Pamplona: Universidad de Navanra, 1980. 399-417.

3388 Inciarte, Fernando. "La Importancia de la Unión Predicado-sujeto en la Doctrina Trinitaria de Tomás de Aquino." *Scripta Theologica* 12(1980): 871-884.

3389 Izquierdo Labeaga, José A. "Homo Analogicus." *Gregorianum* 69(1988): 505-545.

3390 Jáñez Barrio, Tarcisio. "La Muerte Como Paso Al Limite: Aporias y Exigencias." *Tommaso D'Aquino Nel Suo Settimo Centenario: Atti del Congresso Internazionale VII: L'Uomo.* Napoli: Edizioni Domenicane Italiane, 1978. 457-466.

3391 Juan Pablo II. "El Valor Perenne del Pensamiento Filosófico Teológico de Santo Tomás de Aquino." *Filosofar Cristiano* (Argentina) 4(1980): 3-17.

3392 Juan Pablo II. "Santo Tomás de Aquino, *Doctor Communis* Ecclesiae y Doctor Humanitatis." *Sapientia* 36(1981): 5-14.

3393 Kaufmann, Arthur. "Entre Iusnaturalismo y Positivismo Hacia la Hermenéutica Juridica." *An Cated Suarez* 17(1977): 351-362.

3394 La Croce, Ernesto. "La Analogia de Las Causas en Aristóteles y Santo Tomás." *Philosophica* (Valparaiso) 5(1982): 127-140.

3395 Ladusans, Stanislavs. "Uma Investigaçap Filosofológica Comemorativa Do Centenário Da Encíclica *Aeterni Patris* de Leo XIII." *Humanitas* (Mexico) 21(1980): 89-108.

3396 Laje, E. J. "El Derecho de Propiedad en Puebla: Una Constante Doctrinal en el Magisterio de la Iglesia." *Stromata* 36(1980): 3-23.

3397 Landaburu Saguillo, Gonzalo. "Los Signos de la Divinidad de la Revelación Según Santo Tomás." *Sacra Theologia* 10(1986): 259-315.

3398 Lazcano, Pedro E. B. "Poder y Persona en la Sociedad Humana." *Sapientia* 39(1984): 101-106.

3399 Lefevre, Charles. "Intersubjectivité et Promotion D'aprés Santo Tomás." Napoli: Edizioni Domenicane Italiane, 1978. 265-273.

3400 León XIII. "Sobre la Restauración de la Filosofia Cristiana Conforme Al Pensamiento de Santo Tomás de Aquino." *Filosofar Cristiano* (Argentina) 3(1979): 1-28.

3401 Lértora Mendoza, Celina Ana. "La Unidad Especifica Humana y la Inferiordad Psicofisica de la Mujer Según Santo Tomás." *L'anima Nell'antropologia Di San Tommaso D'Aquino IX: Atti del Congresso Societá Internazionale San Tommaso D'Aquino.* Ed. Abelardo Lobato. Milano: Editrice Massimo, 1987. 283-291.

3402 Lértora Mendoza, Celina Ana. "La Teoria de la Ciencia Según Santo Tomás y en la Actualidad." *Conferenciss Cifina 1976 I*. Buenos Aires: Pontificia Universidad Catolica Argentena, 1977. 33-61.

3403 Lira Pérez, Osvaldo. "Caracter Analógico del Conocer." *Philosophica* 1(1978): 65-101.

3404 Llamera, Marceliano. "El Concepto de Moral Teologica y Sus Caracteres Teocéntrico y Antropológico Según Santo Tomás." *Atti del Congresso Internazionale. Tommaso D'Aquino Nel Suo Settimo Centenario V: L'agire Morale*. Napoli: Edizioni Donemicane, 1977. 50-104.

3405 Lobato, Abelardo. "El Principio Libertad: El Dinamismo Originario de la Voluntad en la Cuestión VI *De Malo* de Santo Tomás de Aquino." *Doctor Communis* 30(1977): 33-88.

3406 Lobato, Abelardo. "El Humanismo de la Ley Según Santo Tomás de Aquino." *Verbo* 151-152(1977): 79-88.

3407 Lobato, Abelardo. "La Persona en el Pensamiento de Santo Tomás de Aquino." *Tommaso D'Aquino Nel Suo Settimo Centenario: Atti del Congresso Internazionale VII: L'Uomo*. Napoli: Edizioni Domenicane Italiane, 1978. 274-293.

3408 Lobato, Abelardo. "Tomismo y Antitomismo a Lo Largo de Cien Años." *Tommaso D'Aquino Nel I Centenario Dell'Enciclica Aeterni Patris*. Ed. Benedetto Amore. Roma: Soc. Internaz. Tommaso d'Aquino, 1981. 101-136.

3409 Lobato, Abelardo. "Densidad Ontologica del Individuo Humano." *Parola e Spirito II*. Ed. C. Marcheselli. 1982. 1383-1410.

3410 Lobato, Abelardo. "La Filosofia de Santo Tomás y Su Estructura Dialógica." *Angelicum* 61(1984): 63-95.

3411 Lobato, Abelardo. "La Cogitativa en la Antropologia de Santo Tomás de Aquino." *Journal Philosophique* 1(1985): 117-138.

3412 Lobato, Abelardo. "Verdad y Libertad: San Agustin y Santo Tomás, Exégetas de Juan 8, 32." *Augustinus et Thomas*. Città del Vaticano: *Rivista Doctor Communis*, Palazzo Canonici, 1986. 329-338.

3413 Lobato, Abelardo. "Maimonides, Averroes y Tomás de Aquino: Diálogo de Tres Culturas." *Communio* 20(1986): 33-64.

3414 Lobato, Abelardo. "El Maestro en Teología en el Proyecto de Santo Tomás." *Sapientia* 42(1987): 177-198.

3415 Lobato, Abelardo. "Santo Tomás, Magister in *Sacra Theologia*: El Principium Du Su Magisterio." *Communio* 21(1988): 49-70.

3416 Lobato, Abelardo. "El Lenguaje y la Palabra en Tomás de Aquino." *Revista de Filosofia* (México) 22(1989): 132-148.

3417 Lobo-Gomez, Alfonso. "Derecho Natural: Un Análisis Contemporáneo de Sus Fundamentos." *Revista Latinoamericana de Filosofia* 12(1986): 143-160.

In this paper it is argued that the foundations of Natural Law according to Aquinas consist of an analytical principle that defines the basic practical predicate ("good") and of a set of principles that state which are the basic human goods. Principles of the latter sort are held to be empirical generalizations for the common run of people. For specialists, i.e., for philosophers of the appropriate persuasion, they would be analytical propositions which are nevertheless known to be true a posteriori. An outcome of this thesis is that Natural Law is not founded upon human nature and is thus immune to the positivist objection that it commits the naturalistic fallacy.

3418 López, Antonio Marlasca. "La Eternidad del Mundo: Un Capítulo de Filosofía Medieval." *Revista de Filosofia* (Costa Rica) 23(1985): 169-182.

We present here the old discussion of the eternal and temporal character of the world, beginning with St. Augustine. Our exposition centers on the antagonical positions of Bonaventure and Aquinas. The former affirms that the beginning of the world can be rationally demonstrated. The latter holds exactly the opposite. In the final selection a critique is made of the theses of dialectical materialism, as well as of the "popular" interpretations of modern astrophysics concerning the eternity or non-eternity of the world. The author ends with an agnostic viewpoint: so far, it has not been demonstrated either the absolute beginning or the eternity of the world.

3419 López, Jesús Garcia. "El Concepto de Filosofía Cristiana." *Sapientia* 42(1987): 199-212.

3420 Lopez Gonzales, Luis. "Santo Tomás de Aquino: Vida y Significado. Breve Resena." *Philosophica* (Valparaiso) 1(1977): 9-20.

3421 Lotz, Johannés Baptist. "A Diferença Ontológica Em Kant, Hegel, Heidegger e Tomás de Aquino. I." *Revista Portuguesa de Filosofia* 33(1977): 21-36.

Die ontologische Differenz unterscheidet nach Heidegger vom Seienden (Mensch und Dinge) das Sein als dessen Grund. Bei Kant kommt das Wissen nur zum Erscheinenden statt zum Seienden, weil die Vernunft das Sein nicht erreicht, sondern auf den regulativen Gebrauch der Ideen eingeschränkt ist. Bei Hegel tritt das Seiende als Moment der dialektischen Bewegung auf, in der das Absolute oder das Sein seine Vermittlung oder Entfaltung findet, Doch wird wegen der Dialektik die Differenz verkürzt, weshalb weder das Sein ganz Sein noch das Seiende ganz Seiendes ist. Heidegger und Thomas von Aquin werden in einem folgenden Heft behandelt.

3422 Lotz, Johannés Baptist. "A Diferença Ontológica Em Kant, Hegel, Heidegger e Tomás de Aquino. II." *Revista Portuguesa de Filosofia* 33(1977): 270-284.

Die ontologische Differns hebt das Sein vom Seienden ab. Wie Kant und Hegel dazu stehen, zeigt ein früherer Artikel. Wach ihrer geschichtlichen Auslegung bei Heidegger schickt sich das Sein vor allem dem Menschen epochal zu;jede Mitteilung eröffnet eine Epóche der Geschicte, wobei sich das Sein zugleich entzieht (Epoché). Das eine Überepochale Sein läss sich nicht fassen. Thomas von Aquin nimmt die ontologische Differenz als Partizipation. Gott als die unendliche Füle des subsistierenden Seins teilt durch Erschaffen aus dem Nichts jedem Seienden seine endlichen Anteil des Seins mit. Der Mensch allein kann das Sein vom Seienden unterscheiden und so Gott erreichen.

3423 Lotz, Johannés Baptist. "El Problema de Dios en la Filosofía del Ser de Martin Heidegger." *Revista de Filosofia* (México) 19(1986): 225-241.

3424 Luceros, Ignacio Toribio. "Las Dos Dimensiones Esenciales de la Verdad Forma." *Sapientia* 41(1986): 47-54.

3425 Machado, Geraldo Pinheiro. "Jacques Maritain, Filósofo Da Inteligência." *Revista Portuguesa de Filosofia* 41(1985): 60-68.

3426 Magnasco, Benito Raffo. "Ciencia Política y Teología." *Sapientia* 35(1980): 239-250.

3427 Manzanedo, Marcos F. "El Hombre Como Microcosmos O Mundo Menor [Santo Tomás]." *Arbor* 99(1978): 18-24.

3428 Manzanedo, Marcos F. "La Inteligencia y Las Manos Según Santo Tomás." *Tommaso D'Aquino Nel Suo Settimo Centenario: Atti del Congresso Internazionale VI: L'Uomo*. Napoli: Edizioni Domenicane Italiane, 1978. 400-417.

3429 Manzanedo, Marcos F. "El Hombre Como Microcosmos Seqún Santo Tomás." *Angelicum* 56(1979): 62-92.

3430 Manzanedo, Marco F. "Los Seis Ultimos Predicamentos Según la Doctrina Aristotélico-tomista, I-II." *Studium* 19(1979): 199-227.

3431 Manzanedo, Marcos F. "La Naturalezza de Las Pasiones O Emociones." *Studium* 23(1983): 47-69.

3432 Manzanedo, Marcos F. "La Clasificación de Las Pasiones O Emociones." *Studium* 23(1983): 357-378.

3433 Manzanedo, Marcos F. "El Amor y Sus Causas." *Studium* 25(1985): 41-69.

3434 Manzanedo, Marcos F. "La Antropologia Filosofica en el Commentario Tomista Al *Libro de Job*." *Angelicum* 62(1985): 419-471.

3435 Manzanedo, Marcos F. "Propiedades y Efectos del Amor." *Studium* 25(1985): 423-443.

3436 Manzanedo, Marcos F. "El Odio Según Santo Tomás." *Studium* 26(1986): 3-32.

3437 Manzanedo, Marcos F. "La Naturaleza del Alma Según Santo Tomás." *Studium* 27(1987): 63-76.

3438 Manzanedo, Marcos F. "La Naturaleza del Alma Según Santo Tomás." *L'anima Nell'antropologia Di San Tommaso D'Aquino IX: Atti del Congresso Societá Internazionale San Tommaso D'Aquino*. Ed. Abelardo Lobato. Milano: Editrice Massimo, 1987. 303-312.

3439 Manzanedo, Marcos F. "El Deseo y la Aversión Según Santo Tomás." *Studium* 27(1987): 189-234.

3440 Manzanedo, Marcos F. "La Delectación y Sus Causas." *Studium* 28(1988): 265-295.

3441 Manzanedo, Marcos F. "Efectos y Propiedades de la Delectación." *Studium* 29(1989): 107-139.

3442 Marcos Rodriguez, Florencio. "Un Autógrafo de Santo Tomás en Salamanca." *Revista Española de Teologia* (Madrid) 38(1978): 169-172.

3443 Marimón Batlló, Ricardo. "El Conocimiento Humano en Santo Tomás de Aquino." *Sapientia* 32(1977): 25-50.

Human knowledge in Thomas Aquinas is the result of the "assimilation" of the intellect to the thing known. This similitude guarantees the true cognition of human intellect. But the "mode" of thing in the outward world is different from the "mode" of the thing in our intellect. The difference, however, is also caught by the intellect in its act of judgment, which attains indirectly the existence itself of the thing known by its "turning over the phantasm." This article points out the correspondence of the three-dimensional operation of human intellect—concept, judgment, and reasoning—with the three metaphysical dimensions of the common being—essence, existence, and operation.

3444 Marimón Batlló, Ricardo. "El Concepto del Ser, Primer Principio del Entendimento en Santo Tomás de Aquino." *Estudios Filosóficos* 27(1978): 127-135.

3445 Marimón Batlló, Ricardo. "Ontología, Gnoseología y Teología, Tres Estadios de la Metafisica." *Sapientia* 33(1978): 187-200.

For the Divine Understanding its unique and perfect being is enough to constitute the object of its Metaphysics. For human understanding the sensible beings which are our proper object of knowledge are not enough. In a first step we focus on the ontological panorama of their "being in common," which is limited and claims for the non-limited First Being (God). As Aristotle said, the"theological" step will be the last one in human metaphysics. But to reach this theological term we must become conscious of the special mode of being known in human intellect, according to Aquinas' doctrine. This is the second step in human Metaphysics, namely the "gnoseological" one. Thus, Ontology, Gnoseology, and Theology are three steps of human Metaphysics.

3446 Marimón Batlló, Ricardo. "Orden Natural y Orden Sobrenatural en Santo Tomás de Aquino (Un Reajuste del Llamado Humanisimo Integral Cristiano." *Sapientia* 33(1978): 17-38.

This article describes, according to St. Thomas Aquinas, the "natural order" in human nature, which is ordinated to natural perfection through its natural potentialities and virtues. Second, it describes the "supernatural order" to which man has been elevated by the participation of divine grace. This ordains man to divine vision in Heaven through the activity of "infused virtues," gifts of the Spirit and theological virtues. Finally the author states, according to St. Thomas, the relations between both "orders" making a readjustment of Maritain's "integral humanism," by ascribing to human nature an instrumental role related to the supernatural, and ascribing to this a perfective function which "integrates" the whole human nature itself.

3447 Marimón Batlló, Ricardo. "El Concepto de Ser, Primer Principio del Entendimiento Para Santo Tomás de Aquino." *Actas del V Congreso Internacional de Filosofia Medieval II*. Madrid: Nacional, 1979. 943-950.

3448 Marimón Batlló, Ricardo. "Lenguaje y Metafisica en Santo Tomás de Aquino: Dos Anlogias, Ontológica y Teológico-metafisica, *S. Th.* I, Q. 13." *Estudios Filosóficos* 28(1979): 315-328.

3449 Marimón Batlló, Ricardo. "El Alma Humana O Ente Intelectual en Potencia Según Tomás de Aquino." *Sapientia* 36(1981): 273-282.

This article is a study of rational psychology. Thomas Aquinas with Aristotle and Avicenna consider the human soul as a spiritual substance, "separated" from matter, and at the same time a "form" of a physical body. The spiritual nature of this soul is as a "pure potentiality," specified by the universal world of beings known and loved from the sensible world in which it lives now. This study opens a way too for a metaphysical consideration of the human soul.

3450 Marimón Batlló, Ricardo. "Los Fundamentos de la Ética en Tomás de Aquino." *Atti Dell'VIII Congresso Tomistico Internazionale VI: Morale e Diritto Nella Prospettiva Tomistica*. Studi Tomistici 15. Cittá del Vaticano: Pontificia Accademia di San Tommaso e di Religione Cattolica, 1982. 7-71.

3451 Marimón Batlló, Ricardo. "El Fundamento de la Filosofía del Arte y de la Cultura en Tomás de Aquino." *Sapientia* 38(1983): 275-286.

*The author reports a research on the ground of Philosophy of Art and Culture in Thomas Aquinas and Aristotle. For both, Art is one of the four philosophical sciences.

Its object is the beautiful produced by anyone. For both philosophers, beautiful is compounded by proportion, perfection, and clarity, three elements which are in logical sequence with modality, specificity, and ordination, the three components of good. In these metaphysical structures are grounded all the rules of Art, under the First Art of the Supreme Being.*

3452 Marimón Batlló, Ricardo. "El Alma Humana Ente Intelectual en Potencia Según Tomás de Aquino?" *L'anima Nell'antropologia Di San Tommaso D'Aquino IX: Atti del Congresso Societá Internazionale San Tommaso D'Aquino*. Ed. Abelardo Lobato. Milano: Editrice Massimo, 1987. 313-324.

3453 Marlasca Lopez, Antonio. "El Supuesto Derecho Natural a la Propiedad Privada." *Revista de Filosofia de la Universidad de Costa Rica* 17(1979): 123-137.

3454 Marlasca Lopez, Antonio. "La Eternidad del Mundo: Un Capitulo de Filosofia Medieval." *Revista de Filosofia de la University de Costa Rica* 23(1985): 169-182.

3455 Marques, Alfonso Garcia. "Averroes, Una Fuente Tomista de la Noción Metafísica de Dios." *Sapientia* 37(1982): 87-106.

3456 Mas Herrera, Oscar E. "Transmisibilidad O Intransmisibilidad del Pensamiento: Estudio de la Cuestión XI (*De Magistro*) de Las Cuestiones *De Veritate* de Santo Tomás de Aquino." *Revista de Filosofia de la Universidad de Costa Rica* 16(1978): 41-58.

3457 Massini Correas, Carlos Ignacio. "La Analitica de la Ley Según Santo Tomás." *Ethos* 9(1981): 93-102.

3458 Massini Correas, Carlos Ignacio. "La Categorización Metafísica del Derecho Seqún Santo Tomás." *Sapientia* 37(1982): 11-20.

*The purpose of the work is to establish in which of the categories of Thomists' thinking one must include *ius* in an objective sense. Points of view that consider it to be categorized as *relatio* are refuted. On the basis of the analyzes of Thomistic texts, we can say that *ius* belongs to the *actio* category as regard external behavior. In its internal dimension *ius* belongs to the *qualitas* category.*

3459 Massini Correas, Carlos Ignacio. "Reflexiones Sobre Un Texto de Santo Tomás Acerca de la Verdad Práctica." *Philosophica* (Valparaiso) 7(1984): 147-156.

3460 Massini Correas, Carlos Ignacio. "La Cuestión del Paso Indebido de Las Proposiciones Especulativas a Las Prácticas y la Respuesta de Tomás de Aquino." *Sapientia* 41(1986): 249-264.

3461 Massini Correas, Carlos Ignacio. "Santo Tomás y el Desafío de la Ethica Analitica Contemporánea." *Anuario Filosófico* 23(1990): 161-172.

3462 Mateo Seco, Lucas Francisco. "El Concepto de Verdad en Santo Tomás de Aquino y en la Teologia de la Liberación." *Scripta Theologica*, Pamplona 9(1977): 1043-1062.

3463 Mateo Seco, Lucas Francisco. "La Muerte Como Mal en el Pensmiento de Santo Tomás de Aquino." *Tommaso D'Aquino Nel Suo Settimo Centenario: Atti del Congresso Internazionale VII: L'Uomo*. Napoli: Edizioni Domenicane Italiane, 1978. 467-480.

3464 Mateo Seco, Lucas Francisco. "Santo Tomás Ante la Muerte (Un Punto Crucial de la Antropologia Tomista)." *Atti Dell'VIII Congresso Tomistico Internazionale VII: L'uomo e Il Mondo Nella Luce Dell'Aquinate*. Studi Tomistici 16. Cittá del Vaticano: Pontificia Accademia di San Tommaso e di Religione Cattolica, 1982. 195-206.

3465 Matilla Martínez, M. "Escolástica Medieval y Escolástica Renacentista: Comparación Suárez-Santo Tomás." *Durius Boletin Castellano de Estudios Clásicos* (Valladolid) 5(1977): 162-172.

3466 McCarthy, B. "El Modo del Conocimiento Profético y Escrituristico Según Santo Tomas de Aquino." *Scripta Theologica* 9(1977): 425-484.

3467 McInerny, Ralph. "Santo Tomás de Aquino: La Razonabilidad de la Fe." *La Filosofia del Cristiano, Hoy, Vetera Novis Augere et Perficere: Congreso Mundial de Filosofia Cristiana*. Cordoba: Dir. General de Public. UNC, 1980. 251-263.

3468 McInerny, Ralph. "Acerca del Reconocimiento de la Ley Natural." *El hombre* 1066(1985): 135-140.

3469 McInerny, Ralph. "La Materia Prima es Conocida Por Analogía." *Revista de Filosofia* (Argentina) 2(1987): 99-105.

3470 Melendo, Tomás. "Oposición y Contradicción en Aristóteles y Tomás de Aquino." *Anuario Filosófico* 14(1981): 63-100.

3471 Melendo, Tomás. "La Naturaleza de la Verdad Práctica." *Studium* 26(1986): 51-76.

3472 Méndez, Julio Raúl. "Participacion y actitud contemplativa." *Sapientia* 34(1979): 124-128.

3473 Méndez, Julio Raúl. "El Principium Essendi del Hombre y Su Conocimiento." *Sapientia* 37(1982): 191-200.

*The author attempts to establish the entitative structure of man; to do this he seeks first to establish the experience which permits this analysis. In Saint Thomas' analysis of the act of self-consciousness (*In Librum De Causis Expositio, XV*), the entitative principle of man appears as a being-in-and-unto-oneself which opens itself onto a being-unto-other-than-oneself. All of the properties of man derive from this entitative structure.*

3474 Méndez, Julio Raúl. "Las Tesis de Cornelio Fabro." *Sapientia* 39(1984): 181-192.

*The 54 Thomistic hermeneutical theses of Fabro seem as a whole to be critically founded. The notions of *esse ut actus*, metaphysical participation, and the integrative function of the cognitive faculty are recovered authentically from St. Thomas. The primacy of the will in the concrete decision of the ultimate end, however, represents an original contribution beyond what St. Thomas says explicitly. It seems, nonetheless, a legitimate development consistent with his thought.*

3475 Méndez, Julio Raúl. "El Aporte del *Liber de Causis* en la Noción Tomista del Alma." *L'anima Nell'antropologia Di San Tommaso D'Aquino IX: Atti del Congresso Societá Internazionale San Tommaso D'Aquino*. Ed. Abelardo Lobato. Milano: Editrice Massimo, 1987. 95-113.

3476 Méndez, Julio Raúl. "El Principio del Amor." *Stromata* 43(1987): 387-391.

*This paper deals with the determination of the metaphysical principle of love in Saint Thomas. The notion of love is enunciated as *habitudo ad perfectum*. Love is an originating fact, a transcendental. The principle of love is the unity of *esse* itself, which as *perfectum* is its own *perfectivum* and therefore its own *bonum*. The first love in every being is to itself and consequently to those found in the line of its metaphysical continuity.*

3477 Méndez, Julio Raúl. "Emergencia y Sentido del Hombre en la Reflexión Ética de la *Suma Contra Gentiles*." *Sapientia* 43(1988): 51-58.

3478 Miceli, Vincent P. "Santo Tomás, la Justicia y el Marxismo." *La Filosofia del Cristiano, Hoy, Vetera Novis Augere et Perficere*. Cordoba: Dir General de Public. UNC, 1982. 598-607.

3479 Miralles, Antonio. "La Perspectiva Sapiencial de la Téologia del Mérito en Santo Tomás de Aquino." *Atti del VIII Congresso Tomistico Internazional IV: Prospettive Teologiche Moderne*. Studi Tomistici 13. Città del Vaticano: Libreria Editrice Vaticana, 1981. 293-303.

3480 Miralles, Antonio. "El Gobierno Divino en la Teologia del Mérito de Santo Tomás de Aquino." *Teresianum* 35(1984): 73-97.

3481 Mirete Navarro, José L. "La Idea de Pacto en Santo Tomás de Aquino." *Caudernos de Real. Sociales* 16-17(1980): 97-102.

3482 Monckeberg Balmaceda, Federico. "La Doble Causalidad Ejemplar Divina en Santo Tomás de Aquino." *Philosophica* 9-10(1986-1987): 155-166.

3483 Mondin, Battista. "Las Cinco Vias de Frente a la Fisica Reciente." *NAO* 5(1984): 9-28.

3484 Montané, Pedro Ribes. "Conoció Santo Tomás la Explicatio Symboli de Ramón Marti?" *Espiritu* 26(1977): 93-97.

3485 Muñoz Alonso, Adolfo. "El Hombre en el Pensamiento de Agustin y Tomás de Aquino." *Tommaso D'Aquino Nel Suo Settimo Centenario: Atti del Congresso Internazionale*. Napoli: Edizioni Domenicane Italiane, 1978. 304-316.

3486 Navarro Cordón, Juan Manuel. "Ser y Trascendentalidad: Un Estudio en Tomás de Aquino." *Anales del Seminario de Metafisica* 19(1984): 11-62.

3487 Nogueira, Joao Carlos. "O Valor Obrigatório Da Consciência Moral Na Ética Tomista e a Análise Rosminiana Da Consciência Errônea." *Reflexao* 7(1982): 31-49.

3488 Obradors, Pedro Javier Moya. "El Ser en Santo Tomás de Aquino, Según Etienne Gilson." *Anuario Filosófico* 4(1986): 175-185.

3489 Obradors, Pedro Javier Moya. "Etienne Gilson Ante Las Falsas Interpretaciones del Pensamiento de Santo Tomás de Aquino." *Sapientia* 44(1988): 185-196.

3490 Ocariz, Fernando. "Dignidad Personal, Trascendencia e Historicidad del Hombre." *Dios y el Hombre: VI Simposio Internatcional de Teologia*. Pamplona: Universidad de Navarra, 1985. 175-195.

3491 Ochoa, Hugo Renato. "La Libertad Según Santo Tomás de Aquino." *Philosophica* (Valparaiso) 7(1984): 93-107.

3492 Ollero, Andrés. "Hermeneutica Juridica y Ontologia en Tomás de Aquino." *Tommaso D'Aquino Nel Suo Settimo Centenario VIII: Atti del Congresso Internazionale: L'Uomo*. Napoli: Edizioni Domenicane Italiane, 1978. 319-327.

3493 Ortiz Bustos, Belisario Miguel. "De la Naturaleza Social del Hombre a la Luz de la Doctrina Tomista." *Filosofar Cristiano* (Argentina) 8-9(1984-1985): 151-162.

3494 Ossandón Valdés, Juan Carlos. "El *A Priori* en Santo Tomás de Aquino." *Philosophica* (Valparaiso) 1(1978): 103-127.

3495 Ossandón Valdés, Juan Carlos. "Décima Semana de Estudios Tomistas: Por Qué Tomistas?" *Philosophica* (Valparaiso) 7(1984): 131-145.

3496 Ossandón Valdés, Juan Carlos. "En Torno a los Primeros Principios de la Razón." *Philosophica* (Valparaiso) 11(1988): 123-139.

3497 Osuna, P. "Una Nueva Edición de la *Suma* de Santo Tomás de Aquino." *La Ciencia Tomista* 115(1988): 331-336.

3498 Owens, Joseph. "Los Tres Conceptos de Existencia en Maritain." *Revista de filosofia* (México) 14(1979): 399-414. Trans. of "Maritain's Three Concepts of Existence," by Joseph Owens, *The New Scholasticism*, 49(1975): 295-309.

The author examines Maritain's "first concept of existence," acquired by ordinary abstraction from sensible things; his "second," conceptualizing the existence already intuited in judgment; and his "third," attained by the metaphysician in the third degree of abstraction. This is shown to be in accord with Maritains's own epistemology, though in locating metaphysics in an abstraction independent of what is grasped through judgment it differs significantly from the philosophy of Aquinas.

3499 Oyaneder Jara, Patricio. "Notas Acerca del Bien Común en Santo Tomás de Aquino." *Philosophica* (Valparaiso) 5(1982): 141-148.

3500 Palma Villarreal, Laura. "Fundamento Teórico de la Fe Práctica en la Divina Providencia, en el Pensamiento de Santo Tomás de Aquino." *Philosophica* 1(1978): 53-63.

3501 Palma Villarreal, Laura. "Contemplación y Vida Contemplativa en Santo Tomás de Aquino." *Philosophica* 2-3(1979-1980): 73-86.

3502 Paradinas, Jesús Luis. "Visión del Mundo y Religión." *Tommaso D'Aquino Nel Suo Settimo Centenario IX: Atti del Congresso Internazionale: Il Cosmo e la Scienza.* Napoli: Edizioni Domenicane Italiane, 1978. 235-239.

3503 Pegueroles, Juan. "Lineas Fundamentales de la Filosofia de San Agustin." *Pensamiento* 35(1979): 75-84.

3504 Pegueroles, Juan. "Moral de la Ley y Moral del Bien: Kant y Santo Tomás." *Espiritu* 33(1984): 17-26.

Se exponen primero las objeciones de Kant: el fundamento de la moral no es Dios, no es el ser, no es el bien. Después, la teoría moral de Santo Tomás: la naturaleza y el bein, la naturaleza y la ley, el bein y el valor. Tercero, se responde a las objeciones de Kant. Finalment, se nota la afinidad moral entre Ockham, Kant y Nietzsche.

3505 Pegueroles, Juan. "Fragmentos de Filosofía." *Espiritu* 34(1985): 145-155.

*Contiene los siguientes temas: Crítica agustinana a dos textos de Santo Tomás, La libertad agustiniana en S. Tomás, La *dispensatio temporalis* en San Agustín. La ley la verdad y el bien en Kant, Historia de un error (Nietzsche): Si hay Dios no hay hombre? La impotencia del Dios de Ockham, Valor absoluto y libertad. Dios fin del hombre en Platón y en Aristóteles, Ulises o Abrahán? (Levinas)*

3506 Pegueroles, Juan. "Fragmentos de Filosofía." *Espiritu* 34(1985): 77-94.

3507 Pérez Delgado, Estebán. "La Prudencia Cristiana Virtud del Hombre Señor de Sus Actos." *Tommaso Nel Suo Settimo Centenario V: Atti del Congresso Internazionale: L'agire Morale.* Napoli: Edizioni Domenicane Italiane, 1977. 270-280.

3508 Pérez Fernández, Isacio. "La Metafisica Nasce Con Santo Tomás de Aquino." *Tommaso Nel Suo Settimo Centenario VI: Atti del Congresso Internazionale: L'essere*. Napoli: Edizioni Domenicane Italiane, 1977. 328-337.

3509 Pérez Ruiz, Francisco. "Protágoras, Reexaminado." *Pensamiento* 33(1977): 61-75.

Partiendo del conocido principio de Protágoras y teniendo en cuenta algunas cosas importantes que nos dicen Platón, Aristóteles y Santo Tomás examinamos el problema del papel de la subjetividad en la constitución de la obligación moral. La solución se busca en aceptar lo subjetivo y lo objetivo, no como dos cosas meramente yuxtapuetas sino como dos aspectos de la realidad humana esencialmente relacionados entre sí. La exigencia de objetividad se manifiesta dentro de la propia subjetividad y la fidelidad a las exigencias de la subjetividad incluye necesariamente una ordenación esencial al reconocimiento objetivo de la realidad.

3510 Pérez-Estevez, Antonio. "Razón y Femineidad en el Pensamiento Cristiano Medieval." *Revista de Filosofia* (Venezuela) 10(1986): 127-153.

This is the second part of "Reason and Feminity." Masculine values (reason, power, formality, activity, repression, being) are not only human attributes, they become the attributes of the Christian God. On the contrary for Christian tradition (Paul, Holy Fathers, Augustine, Anselm, Thomas Aquinas), woman and her values (matter, body, nature, life, individuality, pleasure) become diabolic attributes. Sin, guilt, and condemnation enter into the Western culture linked to woman, instrument of Satan. Union with a woman implies in some way union with the devil. Man will be saved and will go to Heaven because of reason and repression, but he will to Hell because of irrationality and body pleasure.

3511 Peroni, José L. Martínez. "*Esse et Bonum*: Reflexiones Metafísicas en Torno Al Beien Común." *Sapientia* 38(1983): 249-274.

3512 Petit Sullá, José Maria. "El Concepto de Movilidad Requerido Para Una Fundamentación de la Filosofia de la Naturaleza." *Atti Dell'VIII Congresso Tomistico Internazionale VII: L'uomo e Il Mondo Nella Luce Dell'Aquinate*. Studi Tomistici 16. Cittá del Vaticano: Pontificia Accademia di San Tommaso e di Religione Cattolica, 1982. 308-314.

3513 Pieper, Josef. "La Actualidad de Santo Tomás de Aquino." *Folia Humanistica* 16(1978): 571-581.

3514 Pieper, Josef. "Creaturidad: Observaciones Sobre los Elementos de Un Concepto Fundamental." *Philosophica* 2-3(1979-1980): 35-54.

3515 Pieper, Josef. "El Filosofar y el Lenguaje." *Anuario Filosófico* 21(1988): 73-83.

3516 Ponferrada, Gustavo Eloy. "Fundamentos Ontológicos de la Ética Tomista." *Atti del Congresso Internazionale: L'agire Morale V: Tommaso Nel Suo Settimo Centenario*. Napoli: Edizioni Domenicane Italiane, 1977. 171-177.

3517 Ponferrada, Gustavo Eloy. "Nota Sobre los Grados de Abstracción." *Sapientia* 33(1978): 267-284.

3518 Ponferrada, Gustavo Eloy. "Los Primeros Principios." *Sapientia* 34(1979): 171-206.

3519 Ponferrada, Gustavo Eloy. "Las Causas en Aristóteles y Santo Tomás II." *Philosophica* (Valparaiso) 6(1983): 121-128.

3520 Ponferrada, Gustavo Eloy. "Las Causas en Aristóteles y Santo Tomás I." *Sapientia* 38(1983): 9-36.

3521 Ponferrada, Gustavo Eloy. "El Tema de la Verdad en Santo Tomás: Sus Fuentes." *Sapientia* 41(1986): 11-36.

3522 Ponferrada, Gustavo Eloy. "Las Potencias del Alma en el Acto de la Libertad." *Atti del Congresso Societá Internazionale San Tommaso D'Aquino IX: L'anima Nell'antropologia Di San Tommaso D'Aquino*. 1987. 363-381.

3523 Ponferrada, Gustavo Eloy. "El Tema de la Libertad en Santo Tomás: Fuentes y Desarrollo." *Sapientia* 43(1988): 7-50.

3524 Ponferrada, Gustavo Eloy. "Tomás de Aquino, la Metafisica y los Tomistas." *Philosophica* (Valparaiso) 11(1988): 89-101.

3525 Poppi, Antonino. "Herencia Clásica e Innovación Cristiana en el Concepto de Sapientia en Santo Tomás y San Buenaventura." *Il Concetto Di Sapientia in San Bonaventura e San Tommaso*. Ed. Alessandro Musco. Biblioteca Dell'Enchiridion 1. Palermo: 1983. 15-33.

3526 Pozo, C. "Perfil Teológico de Santo Tomás." *Burgense* 23(1982): 343-349.

3527 Quiles, Ismael. "La Noción de Causa Segun la Filosofìa de la India y Santo Tomás de Aquino." *Oriente-Occidente* (Buenos Aires) 2(1981): 65-74.

3528 Rego, Francisco. "La Inmortalidad del Alma en Santo Tomás." *El hombre* 8-9(1984-1985): 121-132.

3529 Rego, Francisco. "En Torno a Tre Concepciones de la Verdad Formal." *Sapientia* 41(1986): 37-46.

3530 Riccati, Carlo. "La Imagen de Platón en Tomás de Aquino, I-II." *Revista de Filosofia* (México) 19(1986): 481-500.

3531 Riccati, Carlo. "La Imagen de Platón en Tomás de Aquino, II-II." *Revista de Filosofia (México)* 20(1987): 6-27.

3532 Rigobello, Armando. "Possibilità Di Una Seconda Lettura Dei Testi Tomisti Sulla Persona." *Tommaso D'Aquino Nel Suo Settimo Centenario*. Napoli: Edizioni Domenicane Italiane, 1978. 333-339.

3533 Ritacco de Gayoso, Graciela L. "La Verdad y la Medida de la Verdad." *NAO* 5(1984): 16-32.

3534 Ritacco de Gayoso, Graciela L. "Eternidad Divina y Libertad Humana." *NAO* 6(1985): 7-23.

3535 Rivera Cruchaga, Jorge Eduardo. "El Conocimiento Por Connaturalidad en Santo Tomás de Aquino." *Philosophica* (Valparaiso) 2-3(1979-1980): 87-99.

3536 Rivera De Ventosa, Enrique. "Significación de Juan de Santo Tomás en la Historia del Pensamiento." *Revista Portuguesa de Filosofia* 38(1982): 581-592.

3537 Robles Sierra, Adolfo. "Nuevo Fragmento Autógrafo de Sto Tomás de Aquino." *Escritos del Vedat* (Torrente) 7(1977): 381-388.

3538 Robles Sierra, Adolfo. "Fragmento Autógrafo del IV de Las Sentencias de Sto Tomás." *Escritos del Vedat* (Torrente, Valencia) 10(1980): 565-581.

3539 Rodriguez, Javier. "La Libertad en el Pensamiento." *Sapientia* 34(1979): 135-142.

3540 Rodriguez, Victorino. "Dios, Espiritu Simple." *Philosophica* 2-3(1979-1980): 19-33.

3541 Rodriguez, Victorino. "Grandes Rasgos de la Antropologia Tomista." *Atti del Congresso Internazionale. Tommaso D'Aquino Nel Suo Settimo Centenario VII: L'Uomo.* Napoli: Ed. Domenicane Italiane, 1978. 144-174.

3542 Rodriguez Arias Bustamante, Lino. "Santo Tomás y el Derecho Natural." *Atti Dell'VIII Congresso Tomistico Internazionale: Morale e Diritto Nella Prospettiva Tomistica.* Studi Tomistici 15. Cittá del Vaticano: Pontificia Accademia di San Tommaso e di Religione Cattolica, 1982. 142-149.

3543 Rodriguez Bachiller, Angelo. "Los Fundamentos de la Teologia de Santo Tomás." *Incontri Culturali* 10(1977): 541-543.

3544 Rodriguez Luño, Angel. "La Virtud Moral Como Hábito Electivo Según Santo Tomás de Aquino." *Persona y Derecho* 10(1983): 209-234.

3545 Rodríguez Pascural, Francisco. "Interpretación Antropológica del Pensamiento: Reflexiones Sobre Escoto y Santo Tomás." *Home et Mundus: Acta Quinti Congressus Scotistici Internationalis.* Ed. Camille Bérubé. Studi Scholastico-Scotistica 8. Romae: Societas Internationalis Scotistica, 1984. 181-185.

3546 Rosado, Anibal Colón. "Filosofía de la Substancia: Aristóteles y Santo Tomás de Aquino." *Dialogos* 18(1983): 95-116.

*The purpose of the essay is to investigate the use of the term *substance* in Aristotle and St. Thomas. The latter analyzed the ontology of the former and developed its virtualities, but introduced theological categories which gave a radical transformation to the philosophy of substance. Some factors complicate and illuminate the question: ambiguity of the original term and its translations, the Thomistic metaphysics of "existence," the Catholic dogma, and the Neoplatonic influence.*

3547 Rotella, Oscar Sabino. "Santo Tomás y Wittgenstein." *Tommaso Nel Suo Settimo Centenario VI: Atti del Congresso Internazionale: L'essere.* Napoli: Edizioni Domenicane Italiane, 1977. 665-676.

3548 Ruiz, Francisco Perez. "A Propósito de Etica y Política en Aristóteles." *Pensamiento* 33(1977): 317-323.

Con motivo de una nota de Capelletti examinamos algunos aspectos de la teoria sobre el estado en Platon, Aristóteles, S. Agustin y Sto. Tomás. Como consecuencia creemos que no hay razón para interpretar el pensamiento de Aristóteles como totalitario en sentido moderno y menos aún para decir que toda concepción del estado termina identificándolo con la clase gobernante y poniéndolo todo al servicio del bien de esa clase. En Platón, en Sto. Tomás y en S. Agustín encontramos un modo de concebir totalmente distinto. Tampoco encontramos fundamento para oponer en este punto el pensamiento de S. Agustin al de Sto. Tomás.

3549 Ruiz de Santiago, Jaime. "Conciencia Erronea y Reflexión Moral." *Tommaso Nel Suo Settimo Centenario V: Atti del Congresso Internazionale: L'agire Morale.* Napoli: Edizioni Domenicane Italiane, 1977. 521-526.

3550 Ruiz Rodríguez, Virgilio. "Virtud y Justo Medio." *Revista de Filosofia* (México) 20(1987): 374-382.

3551 Sacchi, Mario Enrique. "La Continuidad Metafisica del Ser en Santo Tomás de Aquino." *Estudios Teológicos y Filosóficos* (Buenos Aires) 8(1977): 47-80.

3552 Sacchi, Mario Enrique. "La Terapéutica del Dolor y la Tristeza Según Santo Tomás." *Psychologica* (Buenos Aires) 2(1979): 85-104.

3553 Sacchi, Mario Enrique. "Pedagogía y Filosofía." *Sapientia* 36(1981): 209-224.

3554 Sacchi, Mario Enrique. "*Utrum Deus Cognoscat Alia a Se*: La Teoría de Aristóteles Sobre el Conocimiento Divino del Mundo y la Exégesis de Santo Tomás de Aquino." *Divinitas* (Roma) 26(1982): 123-161.

3555 Sáinz, J. J., and J. Solabre, Trans. "San Agustin, San Anselmo y Santo Tomás. La Imagen Psicológica de la Trinidad en *De Trinitate*, *Monologion* y *Summa Theologiae*." *Augustinus* 26(1981): 83-94.

3556 Salvans Camps, Francesco. "El Tiempo y Su Testimonio." *Tommaso D'Aquino Nel Suo Settimo Centenario IX: Atti del Congresso Internazionale: Il Cosmo e la Scienza*. Napoli: Edizioni Domenicane Italiane, 1978. 437-444.

3557 Sanabria, José Rubén. "Ser, Persona, Dios." *Revista de Filosofia* (México) 12(1978): 399-436.

El artículo pretende insistir en la vinculación necesaria y profunda entre ser, persona y Dios. Hoy en algunas partes la Filosofía se concreta al estudio del lenguaje y olvida lo más fundamental. Nadie puede negar que el ser es lo primero y que la persona es la convergencia de los trascendentales del ser: es la suprema exigencia del ser. Cuando el hombre busca al ser, busca a Dios. El hombre es una tendencia al Absoluto. Es urgente volver al ser, a la persona y a Dios pues el hombre se precipita en el vacio.

3558 Sanabria, José Rubén. "Trascendentalidad de la Belleza en la Filosofia de Santo Tomás." *Tommaso D'Aquino Nel Suo Settimo Centenario VIII: Atti del Congresso Internazionale: L'Uomo*. Napoli: Edizioni Domenicane Italiane, 1978. 521-529.

3559 Sanabria, José Rubén. "Realismo y Conocimiento en Santo Tomás." *Atti Del'VIII Congresso Tomistico Internazionale V: Problemi Metafisici*. Studi Tomistici 14. Città del Vaticano, Pontificia Accademia di San Tommaso e di Religione Cattolica: Libreria Editrice Cattolica, 1982. 211-221.

3560 Sanabria, José Rubén. "Metafisica Todavia. I." *Revista de Filosofia* (México) 21(1988): 334-360.

3561 Sanabria, José Rubén. "Metafisica Todavia. II." *Revista de Filosofia* (México) 22(1988): 6-31.

Hace tiempo se viene negando todo valor a la metafísica. Se le niega desde diferentes posturas filosóficas y aun científicas. Pero para ver si son válidas las razones de la negación, es necesario saber primero qué es la metafísica. El autor hace un breve recorrido por la historia de la metafísica para que quede en claro qué han entendido los filósofos por esa venerable disciplina filosófica y poder llegar a la conclusíon si está viva o ya murió la metafisica.

3562 Sánchez Alvarez-Castellanos, Juan José. "La Inteligencia Sentiente y la Cogitativa: Zubiri y Santo Tomás." *Anuario Filosófico* 3(1985): 159-169.

3563 Sánchez, Marcelino. "Murió Envenenado Santo Tomás de Aquino?" *Studium* 18(1978): 3-37.

3564 Sanchis, Antonio. "De la Autonomia Personal a la Liberación." *Atti del Congresso Internazionale Tommaso Nel Suo Settimo Centenario V: L'agire Morale*. Napoli: Edizioni Domenicane Italiane, 1977.

3565 Sanguineti, Juan José. "La Unidad y Multiplicidad del Universo." *Anuario Filosófico* 12(1979): 135-170.

3566 Sanguineti, Juan José. "Libertad de Dios y Orden del Mundo." *Atti Del'VIII Congresso Tomistico Internazionale: Vol. IV: Prospettive Teologiche Moderne.* Studi Tomistici 13. Città del Vaticano, Pontificia Accademia di San Tommaso e di Religione Cattolica: Libreria Editrice Cattolica, 1981. 73-83.

3567 Sanguineti, Juan Jóse. "La Filosofia del Progreso en Kant y Tomás de Aquino." *Anuario Filosófico* 18(1985): 199-210.

3568 Sanguineti, Juan José. "La Naturaleza Como Principio de Racionalidad." *Sapientia* 41(1986): 55-66.

3569 Sanguineti, Juan José. "La Vida Corpórea en Tomás de Aquino." *Atti del Congresso Societá Internazionale San Tommaso D'Aquino IX: L'anima Nell'antropologia Di San Tommaso D'Aquino.* Napoli: Edizione Domenicane Italiane, 1987. 391-400.

3570 Santos Ferrer, Urbano. "La Intencionalidad de la Voluntad, Según Santo Tomás." *Studium* 17(1977): 529-539.

3571 Saranyana, José Ignacio. "La Escatologia del Mundo Según Santo Tomás de Aquino." *Atti del Congresso Internazionale (Teoria e Prassi) I.* Napoli: Edizioni Domenicane Italiane, 1977. 507-512.

3572 Saranyana, José Ignacio. "Sobre el Fin de los Días." *Anuario Filosófico* 10(1977): 219-241.

3573 Saranyana, José Ignacio. "Sobre la Inmaterialidad de Las Sustancias Espirituales (Santo Tomás Versus Avicebrón)." *Rivista di Filosofia Neo-Scolastica* 70(1978): 63-97.

*The Spanish Jewish philosopher Ibn-Gabirol, better known as Avicebrón(1020-1058), wrote a treatise entitled *Fons vitae*, which was discovered by Munk(1857) and edited by Baeumker(1895). It is of enormous importance for the history of mediaeval philosophy because it was the principle inspirer of "universal hylomorphism," systematized in the 13th century by Saint Bonaventure and Duns Scotus. Saint Thomas took Avicebrón as his opposite number in his discussion of the perfect or positive immateriality of the angels and of the human soul. Discussing with Ibn-Gabirol, the Angelic Doctor was able to crystallize his great discovery of the *actus essendi*, declaring that not all potency is necessarily prime matter. He also showed that his way of philosophizing was incompatible with the metaphysics of Bonaventure and of Duns Scotus.*

3574 Saranyana, José Ignacio. "Tomás de Aquino: Significante, Significado y Palabras Fundamentales." *Anuario Filosófico* 11(1978): 197-207.

3575 Saranyana, José Ignacio. "La Crisis de la Edad del Espíritu Santo (Santo Tomás Versus Joaquín de Fiore)." *Soziale Ordnungen Im Selbstverständnis Des Mittelalters I.* Ed. Albert Zimmermann. Miscellanea Mediaevalia 12. Berlin: Walter de Gruyter, 1979. 106-121.

3576 Saranyana, José Ignacio. "Tomás de Aquino: Significante, Significado y Palabras Fundamentales." *Studium* 19(1979): 111-119.

3577 Saranyana, José Ignacio. "Tomás de Aquino: Significante, Significado y Palabras Fundamentales." *Scripta Theologica* 11(1979): 187-195.

3578 Saranyana, José Ignacio. "Nota Sobre Las Discrepancias Entre Santo Tomás y San Buenaventura en Tres Manuscritos Bajomedievales." *Bulletin de Philosophie Médiévale* 24(1982): 91-92.

3579 Saranyana, José Ignacio. "Sobre el In Boethii *De Trinitate* de Tomás de Aquino." *Thomas von Aquin. Werk und Wirkung Im Licht Neuerer Forschungen*. Ed. Albert Zimmermann. Miscellanea Mediaevalia. Veröffentlichungen Des Thomas Instituts der Universitat Zu Köln 19. Berlin: Walter de Gruyter, 1988. 71-81.

3580 Sardina-Páramo, Juan Antonio. "Derecho, Razón Práctica e Ideología en la Obra de Michel Villey." *An Cated Suarez* 17(1977): 183-200.

Michel Villey entiende que el derecho, por ser el arte de hacer justicia, pertenece a la razón práctica. La ciencia del derecho, y particularmente la filosofía del derecho, sin embargo, son únicamente legitimas como ciencias prácticas pero en el plano de la razón especulativa. La incidencia de la ideologia de cualquier signo en la indagación de lo justo tiene únicamente una función pertubadora, limitando la observación de la realidad, del ser, que es la única fuente de investigación válida.

3581 Sarmiento, Augusto. "El Binomio Medios-fin en Santo Tomás y en la Teologia de la Liberación." *Incontri Culturali* 10(1977): 639-646.

3582 Seeber, Federico Mihura. "Presupuestos Necesarios Para Una Recta Formulación del Concepto de Ciencia Práctica." *Sapientia* 42(1987): 105-124.

3583 Segura, Carmen. "La Dimensión Reflexiva de la Verdad en Tomás de Aquino." *Anuario Filosófico* 15(1982): 271-279.

3584 Segura, Carmen. "Verdad, Juicio y Reflexión Según Tomás de Aquino." *Anuario Filosófico* 21(1988): 159-169.

3585 Silva, Emilio. "Francisco Zumel, Excelente Interprete y Acerrimo Defensor de Sto. Tomás." *Sapientia* 35(1980): 541-558.

3586 Skarica Zuñiga, Mirko. "Verdad y Lenguaje Según Austin y Tomás de Aquino Paralelos y Discrepancias." *Philosophica* (Valparaiso) 6(1983): 47-71.

3587 Skarica Zuñiga, Mirko. "*Peri Hermeneias*, Algunas Divergencias Entre los Commentarios de Boecio y Tomás de Aquino." *Philosophica* (Valparaiso) 2-3(1979-1980): 143-150.

3588 Skarica Zuñiga, Mirko. "La Disputatio en Tomás de Aquino, Su Validez Para la Scientia." *Philosophica* (Valparaiso) 1(1978): 155-171.

3589 Soaje Ramos, Guido. "Esbozo de Una Respuesta Tomista Al Problema del Valor." *Ethos* 8(1980): 69-106.

3590 Soaje Ramos, Guido. "Ensayo de Una Interpretación de la Doctrina Moral Tomista en Términos de Participación." *Ethos* 10-11(1982-1983): 271-294.

3591 Soaje Ramos, Guido. "Santo Tomás y el Ilamado Principio de Finalidad." *Philosophica* (Valparaiso) 6(1983): 137-150.

3592 Soaje Ramos, Guido. "Sobre el Llamado Principio de Finalidad en la Obra de Tomás de Aquino: Nota Sobre Una Recensión Critica." *Philosophica* (Valparaiso) 8(1985): 247-250.

3593 Soaje Ramos, Guido. "Algunas Notas Sobre el Concepto de Praxis en Santo Tomás de Aquino." *Philosophica* (Valparaiso) 11(1988): 103-111.

3594 Sola, Francisco Bartina De P., and Juan Sebastián Roig Gironella. "Que Importancia Se Ha de Señalar Hoy a Tomás de Aquino en la Investigación y en la Enseñanza?" *Espiritu* 26(1977): 29-47.

3595 Soria, Fernando. "Santo Tomás de Aquino y la Informática: El *Index Thomisticus*." *Estudios Filosóficos* 29(1980): 357-363.

3596 Sorondo, Marcelo Sánchez. "La Querella Antropológica del Siglo XIII." *Sapientia* 35(1980): 325-358.

3597 Soto Cercós, José. "Notas Sobre el Triple Estado de la Esencia en Tomás de Aquino." *Studium* 29(1989): 329-336.

3598 Soto Cercós, José. "La Determinación de la Esencia en: X. Zubiri y Tomás de Aquino." *Sapientia* 45(1990): 95-104.

3599 Souza, Francisco de Paula. "A Inovaçao Existencialista Da Filosofia de Santo Tomás." *Reflexao* 4(1979): 74-88.

3600 Stein, Edith. "La Fenomenología de Husserl y la Filosofía de Santo Tomás de Aquino." *Diálogo Filosófico* 62(1990): 148-169.

La autora ensaya en este artículo una confrontación entre la filosofía de Sto. Tomás y la fenomenología de Edmundo Husserl. Ambos coinciden en considerar la filosofía como ciencia estricta que trata de obtener una imagen del mundo lo más universal y fundamentada posible. En esta tarea para Santo Tomás, la fe tiene un papel fundamentador (Filosofía teocéntrica): mientras que para Husserl el punto de partida es la conciencia pura transcendental (filosofía egocéntrica). Mientras que la fenomenología trata de establecerse como ciencia de escencias para una conciencia trascendental, para Tomás a las investigaciones de esencias deben añadirse los hechos de la experiencia natural y los que aporta la fe. Finalmente, el análisis de la cuestión de la "intuición" revela nuevas coincidencias y divergencias metodológicas entre los dos autores.

3601 Stella, P. T. "Erronea et Horrenda-pulchra et Solemnis-antropologie in Concorrenza Nel Com. in I-II *De Anima* Di Pietro Tomás." *Aquinas* 21(1978): 400-438.

**Com. in I-II De anima*, anonymous in Codes; Vaticano, Biblioteca Apostolica, lat. 869)ff. 51 vb-101rb) and 3092 (ff. 45vb-53ra, 71Ar-72rb, 95vb-97rb, 107rb-vb, 64va-67rb, 70v-71Ar, 101ra-107vb) belongs to the Franciscan Peter Thomas. In the question *Utrum diffinitio de anima posita a Philosopho sit talis ut sit sensus anima est actus corporis id est dans esse corporeum ipsi corpori, ita quod in animato non sit alia forma qua animatum habet esse et alia qua habet esse corporeum*, the anthropologies of Thomas Aquinas, John Pecham, Giles from Rome, Henry of Ghent, John Duns Scotus, and Thomas Wylton are contrasted.*

3602 Tábet, M. Angel. "La Perspectiva Sobrenatural de la Hermeneutica Biblica de Santo Tomás." *Scripta Theologica* 18(1986): 175-196.

3603 Tato, I. Garcià. "Ortodoxia Luterana y Escolástica Mediéval: Juan Jorge Dorsch y Su Interpretación de Tomás de Aquino." *Diálogo Euménico* 22(1987): 5-26.

3604 Tobio Fernández, Jesús. "Honor y Fama en Santo Tomás." *Tommaso Nel Suo Settimo Centenario V: Atti del Congresso Internazionale: L'agire Morale*. Napoli: Edizioni Domenicane Italiane, 1977.

3605 Tovar G., Leonardo. "Santo Tomás de Aquino en la Bibliografia Filosófica Colombiana del Siglo XX." *Análisis* 23(1987): 111-130.

3606 Turiel, Quintin. "El Deseo Natural de Ver a Dios." *Atti Del'VIII Congresso Tomistico Internazionale IV: Prospettive Teologiche Moderne*. Studi Tomistici 13. Città del Vaticano, Pontificia Accademia di San Tommaso e di Religione Cattolica: Libreria Editrice Cattolica, 1981. 249-262.

3607 Turiel, Quintín. "Es la Resurrección Una Verdad Accesible a la Razón? Posición de Sto. Tomás Al Respecto." *L'anima Nell'antropologia Di San Tommaso D'Aquino IX: Atti del Congresso Societá Internazionale San Tommaso D'Aquino*. Ed. Abelardo Lobato. Milano: Editrice Massimo, 1987. 401-412.

3608 Turiel Sandin, Bienvenido. "Lo Primario en el Habito."*Studium* 17(1977) 540-549.

3609 Turiel Sandin, Bienvenido. "Una Doctrina Viva: La de Santo Tomás." *Studium* 17(1977): 365-373.

3610 Urdánoz, Teófilo. "Función de la Razón en la Etica." *Sapientia* 33(1978): 99-132.

Después de breve prolegómeno sobre el origen de las nociones fundamentales de razón teórica y práctica, de teoria y praxis, en el pensamiento griego, el autor expone los cuatro grandes sistemas principales sobre el modo de entender la función de la razón en la estructuración de la Ética. El primero es el de Tomás de Aquino, heredero de Aristóteles, en quien la razón práctica obtiene una función universal en la construcci ón de la Ética como principio constitutivo de la moralidad en cuanto norma del bein y del mal de las acciones, en la formación de la ley moral y de las leyes, de la conciencia y de la última norma de la prudencia. Esta razón práctica se funda no obstante en la teoria, en el orden objetivo de los bienes. El segundo sistema estudiado es el de Kant, que introduce un cambio profundo en el sentido de la razón práctica como principio moral, independizándola del orden teórico y convirtiéndola en autolegisladora, de donde deriva su desarrollo de una moral convirtiéndola en autolegisladora, de donde deriva su desarrollo de una moral autónoma y subjetivista. El tercer sistema estdudiado es el de la razón vital de Ortega y Gasset, principio de una moral vitalista, cuya norma consiste en servir a la vida.

3611 Urdánoz, Teófilo. "La Filosofia Analitica Actual y Su Terapia Mediante la Filosofia Cristiana y Tomista." *Sapientia* 34(1979): 207-230.

3612 Urdánoz, Teófilo. "La Teología Moral Desde la Encícliva *Aeterni Patris*." *Sapientia* 35(1980): 405-434.

3613 Vallet de Goytisolo, Juan. "Santo Tomás de Aquino y la Lógica de Lo Razonable y de la Razón Vital e Histórica." *Anuario Filosófico* 19(1976-1977): 17-28.

3614 Vallet de Goytisolo, Juan. "Propiedad y Iusticia, a la Luz de Santo Tomás de Aquino." *Verbo* 188(1980): 1065-1122.

3615 Van Steenberghen, Fernand. "Introducción a la Antropología de Santo Tomás de Aquino." *Revista de Filosofia* (México) 10(1977): 233-250.

3616 Van Steenberghen, Fernand. "La Estructura de la Filosofía Teórica Según Santo Tomás." *Diálgo Filosófico* 3(1987): 289-301.

3617 Vanni Rovighi, Sofia. "Se Puede Hablar de Límites del Racionalismo Ético en la Teoria de Sto. Tomás Sobre el Conocimiento Moral?" *Studi Di Filosofia Medioevale II: Secoli XIII e XIV*. Ed. Sofia Vanni Rovighi. Scienze Filosofiche 20. Milano: Vita e Pensiero, 1978. 161-173.

3618 Vázquez, Rodolfo. "La Religion Según Santo Tomás de Aquino." *Revista de Filosofia* (México) 16(1983): 245-283.

3619 Vicente Burgoa, Lorenzo de G. "*Omne Agens Agit Propter Finem*: El Principio de Finalidad en Santo Tomás de Aquino." *Burgense: Collectanea Scientifica* (Bargos) 21(1980): 505-531.

3620 Vicente-Burgoa, Lorenzo. "Los Problemas de la *Quinta Via* Para Demonstrar la Existencia de Dios." *Divus Thomas* 84(1981): 3-37.

3621 Vicente Guida, Lorenzo. "*Omne Agens Agit Propter Finem*: El Principio de Finalidad en Santo Tomás de Aquino." *Atti Del'VIII Congresso Tomistico Internazionale V: Problemi Metafisici*. Studi Tomistici 14. Città del Vaticano, Pontificia Accademia di San Tommaso e di Religione Cattolica: Libreria Editrice Cattolica, 1982. 329-341.

3622 Vicente Rodrigo, José. "El Verdadero Objeto de la Metafisica Según Santo Tomás." *Tommaso Nel Suo Settimo Centenario VI: Atti del Congresso Internazionale: L'essere*. Napoli: Edizioni Domenicane Italiane, 1977. 426-434.

3623 Vidal, Francisco Canals. "La Actitud Filosófica de Santo Tomás Como Orientación Para Una Búsqueda de Sintesis en el Pensamiento Contemporáneo." *Tommaso d'Aquino nel I Centenario dell'Enciclica Aeterni Patris: Atti del convegno organizzato a Roma dall Societá internazionale Tommaso d'Aquino e dalla Pontificia Universita "San Tommaso d'Aquino."* Roma: Societá Internazionale Tommaso d'Aquino, 1979. 211-229.

3624 Vidal, Francisco Canals. "Actual Inteligibilidad y Posesión Originaria de Toda Ciencia." *L'anima Nell'antropologia Di San Tommaso D'Aquino IX: Atti del Congresso Societá Internazionale San Tommaso D'Aquino*. Ed. Abelardo Lobato. Milano: Editrice Massimo, 1987. 207-218.

3625 Vigil Lagarde, C. "El Mundo y la Felicidad." *Tommaso Nel Suo Settimo Centenario V: Atti del Congresso Internazionale: L'agire Morale*. Napoli: Edizioni Domenicane Italiane, 1977. 551-556.

3626 Vigo, Rudolfo Luis. "Versión Subjetivista y Realista de los Llamados Derechos Subjetivos dc la Personalidad O Esenciales del Hombre." *Sapientia* 35(1980): 47-62.

3627 Villoro Toranzo, Miguel. "Una Explicación Moderna del Concepto Tomista del Derecho." *Tommaso D'Aquino Nel Suo Settimo Centenario VIII: Atti del Congresso Internazionale*. Napoli: Edizioni Domenicane Italiane, 1978. 373-380.

3628 Von Rintelen, Fritz-Joachim. "O Bonum e O Summum Bonum No Pensamento de Tomás de Aquino." *Revista Portuguesa de Filosofia* 33(1977): 182-195.

3629 Webster, Richard T. "Che Cosa *Significa Anima Enim Est in Corpore Ut Continens et Non Ut Contenta* (*S. T.* Ia 52,1)?" *L'anima Nell'antropologia Di San Tommaso D'Aquino IX: Atti del Congresso Societá Internazionale San Tommaso D'Aquino*. Ed. Abelardo Lobato. Milano: Editrice Massimo, 1987. 425-430.

3630 Widow, Juan Antonio. "La Democracia en Santo Tomás." *Philosophica* (Valparaiso) 1(1978): 203-217.

3631 Widow, Juan Antonio. "Las Virtudes Morales en la Vida Intelectual. La Sabiduraia Como Fin de la Vida Práctica, Según Tomás de Aquino." *Philosophica* (Valparaiso) 8(1985): 9-31.

3632 Widow, José Antonio. "El Verbo Interior, Según Tomás de Aquino." *Philosophica* (Valparaiso) 9-10(1986-1987): 167-176.

3633 Widow, Juan Antonio. "Saber Metafisico y Experiencia." *Philosophica* (Valparaiso) 11(1988): 141-155.

3634 Wilhelmsen, Frederick D. "Las Presuposiciones de la Demonstración de la Existencia de Dios en *De Ente et Essentia*, C. 4." *Revista de Filosofia* (México) 20(1987): 212-229.

3635 Yarza, Ignacio. "Anotaciones en Torno Al Vivir." *Revista de Filosofia* (México) 20(1987): 159-165.

3636 Zalba, Marcelino. "*Nihil Prohibet Unius Actus Esse Duos Effectus* (*Summa Theologica* 2-2, Q. 64, A. 7): Numquid Applicari Potest Principium in Abortu Therapeutico?" *Tommaso Nel Suo Settimo Centenario V: Atti del Congresso Internazionale: L'agire Morale*. Napoli: Edizioni Domenicane Italiane, 1977. 557-568.

3637 Zarco Neri, Miguel Angel. "De la Naturaleza del Conocimiento en el Pensamiento de Santo Tomás de Aquino." *Tommaso D'Aquino Nel Suo Settimo Centenario: Atti del Congresso Internazionale*. Napoli: Edizioni Domenicane Italiane, 1978. 436-441.

3638 Zimmermann, Albert. "En Torno a la Doctrina de Tomás de Aquino Sobre el Ius Naturale." *Anuario Filosófico* 11(1978): 169-184.

F. POLISH

3639 Aduszkiewicz, Adam. "Piekno I Milosc W Mysli Filozoficznej Sw. Tomasza Z Akwinu [Le Beau et L'amour dans la Pensée Philosophique de Saint Thomas D'Aquin]." *Studia Philosophiae Christianae* 21(1985): 9-22.

*En se référant aux textes Saint Thomas l'auteur de l'article a l'intention de présenter trois théses. Premiérement, il faut considérer le beau en tant que notion transcendentale révélant la conveyance (*convenientia*) spécifique entre l'âme et l'être. Deuxiemement, il faut examiner à quoi consiste cette conveyance. Troisiément le beau de l'être se révéle au croisement de l'action de volonté, amour et connaissance. Des remarques de St. Thomas concernant l'art complétent ces Études. Or, l'oevre d'art est avant tout une manifestation de la conception du beau présentée ci-dessus, c'est le fondement de sa signification.*

3640 Bakies, B. "Dieu comme Objet de la Métaphysique." *Studia Philosophiae Christiane* 15(1979): 7-32.

3641 Bartel, Tomasz. "Psychologia Filozoficzna." *Przeglad Tomist* 2(1986): 33-49.

3642 Bartnik, Czeslaw. "Znaczenie Tomizmu Na Tle Kryzysu Umyslowego W Europie XII I XIII Wieku." *Roczniki Teologiczno-Kanoniczne* 31(1984): 59-70.

3643 Bartnik, Czeslaw. "Z Badan Nad Oryginalnoscia Tomizmu." *Roczniki Teologiczno-Kanoniczne* 32(1985): 207-220.

3644 Bednarski, Feliks Wojciech. "Le Principe Constitutif Des Valeurs Morales dans L'ethique de Saint Thomas D'Aquin." *Studia Philosophiae Christiane* 25(1989): 59-78.

L'auteur s'efforce de prouver que saint Thomas d'Aquin a bien exposé la question du principe constitutif de la valeur morale, c'est-à-dire, de la bonte reelle du comportement humanin; tandis que le mal est plutôt une privation de la valeur, laquelle n'est pas un idéal hors d'atteindre mais une realite accessible. La nature humaine integrale et ordoné, est le fondement de la valeur morale et non son principe constitutif. Par contre la conformité du comportement humain à la nature de l'homme en accord avec les exigences de la raison bien orientée a la vraie fin deniére de la vie humaine—voila vraiment le principe constitutif de bonté morale, parce que la rationalité est la distinction spécifique de la nature humaine, mais la conduite humaine n'est raisonnable que dans la concordance avec la finalité de la vie humaine, et en conséquence quand les moyens sont ordonnés à la fin et les fins secondaires subordonnées à la vraie fin deniére de l'homme.

3645 Belch, Stanislav. "Aquinas' *Summa Theologica* in Polish Trans." Studi Tomistici 17. *Atti dell'VIII Congresso tomistico internazionale VIII: San Tommaso nella storia del pensiero*. Cittá del Vaticano: Pontificia Accademia di San Tommaso e di Religione Cattolica, 1982. 169-172.

3646 Dec, Ignacy. "Le Probléme Du Point de Départ de la Théorie de L'homme de Saint Thomas D'Aquin et de Gabriel Marcel." *Roczniki Filozoficzne* 30(1982): 189-217.

3647 Dec, Ignacy. "Teoria Bytu W Ujeciu Sw. Tomasza Z Akwinu I Gabriela Marcela [La Théorie de L'être D'aprés Saint Thomas D'Aquin et Gabriel Marcel]." *Studia Philosophiae Christianae* 18(1982): 41-62.

3648 Dec, Ignacy. "La Conception de la Philosophie de Saint Thomas D'Aquin et de Gabriel Marcel." *Studia Philosophiae Christianae* 19(1983): 25-58.

L'article traite de la conception de la philosophie de saint Thomas d'Aquin et de Gabriel Marcel. Il se compose de trois parties. La premiére présente genése, objet, but et méthodes de la philosophie thomiste. On constate ici que la philosophie de saint Thomas prendre sa source de l'étonnement. Elle a pour l'objet tout ce qui existe. Le but de la philosophie selon saint Thomas est d'expliquer toute la réalité par les causes définitives. Dans cette philosophie le rôle principal est joué par l'induction heuristique. La deuxiéme partie traite des mêmes problémes chez G. Marcel. D'apres lui la philosophie prendre sa source de l'inquiétude intérieure. Au centre de considerations marcelliennes se trouve l'homme concret. Dans la méthode de cette philosophie le rôle principal joue l'expérience intérieure et la seconde reflexion. La troisiéme partie de l'article est une comparison de ces deux conceptions. En conclusion finale on constate que ces deux conceptions de la philosophie sont complémentaires.

3649 Dec, Ignacy. "Remarques sur le Langage Philosophique de Saint Thomas D'Aquin et de Gabriel Marcel." *Collectanea Theologica* (Warszawa) 54(1984): 59-64.

3650 Domanski, Julusz. "Sw. Tomasz, Erazma Rotterdamu I Humanizum Biblijny [St. Thomas, Erasmus of Rotterdam and Biblical Humanism]." *Studia Z Dziejów Mysli Swietego Tomasza Z Akwinu [Studies on the History of St. Thomas Aquinas' Thought]*. Ed. Stefan Swiezwaski and Jana Czerkawskiego. Towarzystwo Naukowe Kul, Zródla I Monografie 105. Lublin: Towarzystwo Naukowe Katolickiego Uniwersytetu Lubelskiego, 1978. 91-96.

3651 Gawronski, Alfred. "Existential Thomism in the Face of New Philosophical and Grammatical Studies." *Studia Philosophiae Christiane* 23(1987): 25-43.

*This is a brief account of the last volume of a series of studies analyzing the verb "to be" and/or synonyms in a number of languages. This volume—*The Verb "Be" in Ancient Greek* by Charles H. Kahn—presents an analysis of the syntax and semantics of the verb "be" (*einai*) in the language in which it acquired its central role for the logic and metaphysics of the West: ancient Greek. Kahn attempts to assess the linguistic and philosophical impact of all the contributions. His conclusions are of great importance for the development of modern ontology and metaphysics. The description of the various uses of the verb, illustrated in detail and supplemented by a systematic discussion of the theoretical problems raised by the concepts of subject, predicate, copula, and existence, is of particular interest for the development (if such a development is necessary) of "Existential Thomism."*

3652 Gogacz, Mieczyslaw. "Tomizm W Polskeich Srodowiskach Uniwersyteckich XX Wieku." *Studia Z Dziejów Mysli Swietego Tomasza Z Akwinu*. Eds. Stefana Swiezawkiego and Jana Czerkawskiego. Lublin: Tow. Nauk. KUL, 1978. 335-350.

3653 Gogacz, Mieczyslaw. "Philosophical Identification of the Dignity of Person." *Studia Philosophiae Christiane* 25(1989): 181-207.

The literature of the subject shows that dignity is identified with the person, or with one of its properties, or with relation, which is bandaged by person with surrounded beings. Therefore, dignity appears like a freely pointed element, which distinguishes person. It is not a separate being structure. That state of the problem induces us to undertake strictly philosophical research, which lies in establishing internal and examined object.

3654 Gogacz, Mieczyslaw. "Conscience, Contemplation, Wisdom." *Studia Philosophiae Christiane* 25(1989): 65-71.

Conscience is man's interior tendency to make good and avoid evil. Conscience is, because of intellectual reception of principles of being, a tendency of will to being as shown by intellect to will as good. Contemplation is giving evidence with the help of intellect and will that personal relations are persisting. Wisdom is an intellectual capacity of connecting the effects with the causes. By the same it is the grasp of the dependence between good and truth. It is recognition whether the being is giving us the good while being opened. When the being is causing good, our intellect advises will to tie the relations upon this being. This relation shelters us, because good shelters us always.

3655 Gombocz, Wolfgang L. "The Philosophy of Language in Scholasticism." *Filozofska Instrazivanja* 30(1989): 1011-1029.

3656 Greniuk, F. "Le Néo-Thomisme en Théologie Morale Au XX." *Roczniki Teologicznokanoniczne* 28(1981): 67-84.

3657 Herbstrith, Waltraud. *Edith Stein I Toma Akvinski. Obnovljeni Zivot* 35(1980): 52-58.

3658 Korolec, Jerzy B. "Itinerarium S. Thomae Jana Sartoris." *Studia Z Dziejów Mysli Swietego Tomasza Z Akwinu [Studies on the History of St. Thomas Aquinas' Thought]*. Ed. Stefan Swiezwaski and Jana Czerkawskiego. Towarzystwo Naukowe Kul, Zródla I Monografie 105. Lublin: Towarzystwo Naukowe Katolickiego Uniwersytetu Lubelskiego, 1978. 185-193.

3659 Kowalczyk, Stanislaw. "L'argument Thomiste de Causalité Efficiente." *Studia Philosophiae Christiane* 13(1977): 47-93.

3660 Kowalczyk, Stanislaw. "Argument Eudajmologiczny W Tomistycznej Filozofii Boga." *Studia Philosophiae Christianae* 13(1977): 47-93.

3661 Kowalczyk, Stanislaw. "Swietego Tomasz Z Akwinu Z Perspektywy Wspolczesnej." *Chrzescijanin w Swiecie* 4(1980): 37-55.

3662 Krapiec, Mieczyslaw A. "O Tomaszowe Rozumienie Bytu Jako Bytu (La Podstawie Wybraych, Charakterystyczych Tekstów) [About St. Thomas' Idea of Existence as Existence]." *Studia Z Dziejów Mysli Swietego Tomasza Z Akwinu [Studies on the History of St. Thomas Aquinas' Thought]*. Ed. Stefan Swiezwaski and Jana Czerkawskiego. Towarzystwo Naukowe Kul, Zródla I Monografie 105. Lublin: Tow. Nauk. KUL, 1978. 11-28.

3663 Krapiec, Mieczyslaw A. "Dusza Ludzka-Wspolczesne I Tomaszewe Podejscie." *Zeszyty Naukowe* 28(1985): 45-57.

3664 Kuc, Leszek. "Z Badán Nad Projeciem *Theoria* W Szkole Tomistycznej XV Wieku [The Notion of *Theoria* in the Thomist School in the 15th Century]." *Studia Z Dziejów Mysli Swietego Tomasza Z Akwinu [Studies on the History of St. Thomas Aquinas' Thought]*. Eds. Stefan Swiezwaski and Jana Czerkawskiego. Towarzystwo Naukowe Kul, Zródla I Monografie 105. Lublin, 1978. 47-90.

3665 Kur, Miroslaw. "*Iudicium Per Inclinationem* Chez Saint Thomas D'Aquin." *Przeglad Tomistyczny* 4(1988): 19-32.

3666 Markowski, Mieczyslaw. "Tomizm W Logice, Teorii Poznania, Filozofii Przyrody I Psychologii W Polsce W Latach 1400-1525 [Thomism in the Logic, Theory of Knowledge, Philosophy of Nature and Psychology in Poland in the Year 1400-1525]." *Studia Z Dziejów Mysli Swietego Tomasza Z Akwinu [Studies on the History of St. Thomas Aquinas' Thought]*. Ed. Stefan Swiezwaski and Jana Czerkawskiego. Towarzystwo Naukowe Kul, Zródla I Monografie 105. Lublin: Towarzystwo Naukowe Katolickiego Uniwersytetu Lubelskiego, 1978. 195-261.

3667 Mercep, Vladimir. "Rozlozi Tomizma." *Obnovljeni Zivot* 36(1981): 545-54.

3668 Mirewicz, Jerzy. "Wsplolna Troska Tomza Z Akwinu I Horacjusza." *Trzy Minuty Filozofii*. London: Ojcowie Jezuici, 1978. 36-38.

3669 Morawiec, Edmund. "La Critique de la Metaphysique Classique Au Moyen-Age et Aux Temps Modernes." *Studia Philosophiae Christiane* 18(1982): 123-160.

The aim of this paper is to show the base and direction in the critique of metaphysics understood as the most general theory of reality. The author has shown, using historical data, that the basis of that critique is a trend to make metaphysics a scientific science. This tendency was carried out in different ways in each epoch. It resulted in the loss of the true field of metaphysics and denial of its necessity.

3670 Morawiec, Edmund. "A Props de la Métaphysique Du Thomisme Traditionaliste." *Analecta Cracov* 14(1982): 21-38.

3671 Morawiec, Edmund. "About a Road to Discover the Authentic Philosophical Thinking of Thomas Aquinas." *Studia Philosophiae Christiane* 22(1986): 109-131.

The author of this paper makes an attempt to produce reasons which are at the origin, in his view, of the mistaken understanding of the philosophical thought of Thomas Aquinas by Thomists most close to him or those more distant in time. He is trying to make it by showing the development of the Thomism and circumstances under which it has grown since its origin. Particular attention is given to the period from the middle of the thirteenth to the fifteenth century. He maintains that this period has finally shaped the understanding of Thomas Aquinas' philosophy, which has finally established itself until the twentieth century without any essential change.

3672 Morawiec, Edmund. "Appréciation de L'oeuvre Théologicao-philosophie de Thomas D'Aquin Au Tournant Des XIIIe-XIVe Ss." *Studia Philosophiae Christiane* 25(1989): 73-87.

Des le début, l'oeuvre théologico-philosophique de Thomas d'Aquin a recontre une appréciation qui s'est manifestée par la critique et par l'acceptation. Ce qui est devenu l'objet de l'appréciation c'est, contenue dans l'oeuvre la doctrine chrétienne vue du point de vue de sa position face à la philosophie d'Aristote. L'article se propose de reproduire les positions directes prises face à la doctrine de Thomas d'Aquin par les théologiens et les philosophes chrétiens et non chrétiens qui lui sont les plus proches quant au temps. Les plus proches, car le sujet de l'article embrase la période de la seconde moitié du XIIIe s. et la premiére du XIVe s.

3673 Nieznanski, Edward. "A Formalization of Thomistic Foundations of a Proof for the Existence of a Necessary First Being." *Studia Philosophiae Christianae* 15(1979): 163-180.

3674 Pawlak, Dzislaw. "Sens Negatywnych Okreslen Boga U Sw. Tomasza Z Akwinu." *Archiv f. Liturgiewissenschaft* 102(1984): 465-473.

3675 Radvan, Eduard. "K Otázce Pojetí Cloveka V Tomismu a Neotomismu [On the Question of the Conception of Man in Thomism and Neothomism]." *Studia minora facultatis philosophicae Universitatis Brunenis—series B (philosophica)* 30(1983): 53-60.

3676 Reding, Marcel. "Toma Akvinski I Karl Marx." *Obnovljeni Zivot* 32(1977): 445-453.

3677 Rut Wosiek, Barbara. "Sw. Tomasz W. Srodowiskach Mlodziezy Akademickiej I Mlodej Inteligencij Polskiej Okresum Miedywojennego." *Studia Z Dziejów Mysli Swietego Tomasza Z Akwinu.* Eds. Stefana Swiezawkiego and Jana Czerkawskiego. Lublin: Tow. Nauk. KUL, 1978. 351-366.

3678 Salij, Jacek. "Sw. Tomasza Z Akwinu *De Rationibus Fidei*." *Studia Theologica Varsaviensia* 18(1980): 219-250.

3679 Salij, Jacek. "Bóg Jako Dobro Powszechne W Ujeciu Sw. Tomasza Z Akwinu [Dieu comme Bien Universel Selon Saint Thomas D'Aquin]." *Collectanea Theologica* 51(1981): 53-61.

3680 Salij, Jacek. "Madrosc I Giupota W Refleksji Sw. Tomasza Z Akwinu [Wisdom and Folly in the Thought of St. Thomas Aquinas]." *Collectanea Theologica* 52(1982): 21-28.

3681 Senko, Wladyslaw. "Kilka Uwag Na Temat Historii Tomaszowego Projecia Istnienia We Wczesnej Szkole Tomistycznej." *Przeglad Tomistyczny* 3(1987): 21-27.

3682 Senko, Wladyslaw. "Quelques Remarques Concernant L'histoire de la Notion D'existence Selon St. Thomas D'Aquin dans L'école Thomiste Primitive." *Przeglad Tomistyczny* 3(1987): 21-27.

3683 Slaga, Sz W. "Essai de Preciser la Notion de L'essence de la Vie Chez St. Thomas." *Studia Philosophiae Christiane* 15(1979): 9-26.

3684 Slipko, Tadeusz. "The Interpretation of Dynamic Character of Natural Law According to St. Thomas Aquinas." *Roczniki Filozoficzne* 25(1977): 148-157.

3685 Sparty, Andrzej. "La Doctrine de Jean Philopon dans *De Intellectu* et Son Application Chez Thomas D'Aquin." *Acta Mediaevalia (Lublin)* 3(1978): 167-230.

3686 Swiezawski, Stefan. "Note sur les Conceptiones Universales Chez Saint Thomas D'Aquin." *Studia Z Teorii Poznania I Filozofii Wartosci.* Ed. Wladyslaw Strozewski. Wroclaw-Warszawa: Ossolineum, 1978. 81-90.

3687 Swiezawski, Stefan. "Apercu sur L'ouvage: Histoire de la Pensée de Saint Thomas." *Studia Z Dziejów Mysli Swietego Tomasza Z Akwinu [Studies on the History of St. Thomas Aquinas' Thought].* Eds. Stefan Swiezwaski and Jana Czerkawskiego. Towarzystwo Naukowe Kul, Zródla I Monografie 105. Lublin: Towarzystwo Naukowe Katolickiego Uniwersytetu Lubelskiego, 1978. 379-391.

3688 Swiezawski, Stefan. "Aperçu sur L'ouvrage: Histoire de la Pensée de Saint Thomas: Recherches Polonaises." *Studia Z Dziejów Mysli Swietego Tomasza Z Akwinu.* Eds. Stefana Swiezawkiego and Jana Czerkawskiego. Lublin: Towarzystwo Naukowe Katolickiego Uniwersytetu Lubelskiego, 1978. 379-391.

3689 Veres, Tomo. "Beogradski Dijalog O Tomi Akvinskom." *Obnovljeni Zivot* 37(1982): 157-162.

3690 Wistuba, Halina. "Teoria Doskonalosci Bytu Tomasza Z Akwinu W Relacji Do Kultury." *Poznanskie Studia Teologiczne* 6(1986): 423-430.

3691 Wlodek, Zofia. "Tomasza Suttona Filozoficna Interpretacja Po Wstawania Bytów Materialnych [Thomas Sutton's Interpretation of the Origins of Material Existences]." *Studia Z Dziejów Mysli Swietego Tomasza Z Akwinu [Studies on the History of St. Thomas Aquinas' Thought].* Eds. Stefan Swiezwaski and Jana Czerkawskiego. Towarzystwo Naukowe Kul, Zródla I Monografie 105. Lublin: Towarzystwo Naukowe Katolickiego Uniwersytetu Lubelskiego, 1978. 31-45.

3692 Woznicki, Andrew. "A la Recherche Du Sens de L'existence Humaine." *Zeszyty Naukowe Kat. University Lubelskiego* 21(1978): 25-33.

3693 Wronski, Stanislaw. "Osoba Ludzka Na Tle Ogólnego Pojecia Osoby I Nauki O Czlowieku U Sw. Tomasza Z Akwinu [Notions of the Person with Particular Reference to the Anthropology of Aquinas]." *Studia Mediewistyczne* 22(1983): 113-140.

3694 Ziemianski, Stanislaw. "Essai D'une Réinterprétation de la Troisiéme Voie de Saint Thomas D'Aquin." *Studia Philosophiae Christianae* 13(1977): 145-161.

G. MISCELLANEOUS

3695 Anawati, Georges C. "Psychologie Avicennienne et Psychologie de Saint Thomas: Estude Comparée." *Acta Antiqua Academiae Scientiarum Hungaricae* (Budapest) 29(1981): 1-4, 13-32.

3696 Baning, Benedict. "Een Foutje Bij Thomas Van Aquino? De Analogie in Onze Kennis Van God Volgens *Summa Theologiae* I, 13, 5 C." *Werkgroep Thomas Van Aquino.* Amsterdam: Jaarboek, 1985. 9-22.

3697 Borges, Anselmo. "A Imortalidade Na *Summa Theologica.*" *Humanistica e Teologia* (Porto) 6(1985): 151-197.

3698 Braakhuis, H. A. G. "Heymeric Van de Velde (A. Campo): Denker OP Een Kruispunt Van Wegen: De Logische Kwesties Uit Zijn." *Algemeen Nederlands Tijdschrift voor Wijsbegeerte Assen* 75(1983): 13-24.

*The logical questions of Heymeric's *Problemata inter Albertum Magnum et Sanctum Thomam* (ca 1496) (ed. Cologne, 1496, ff 5-14v) are discussed. It is argued—this also in view of the fact that Heymeric starts the treatise with a defense of the realist view on universals that he borrowed from Johannes *De Nova Domo*—that for Heymeric the Thomist view is to be combated as such.*

3699 Campos, Fernando Arruda. "Posiçao Do Tomismo, Na Histôria Do Pensamento Filosófico." *Revista Brasileira de Filosofia* 35(1986): 304-317.

3700 Cavalho, Ubirajara Calmon. "O Argumento Ontológico Em Kant e a L. Via Da Demonstraçap de Deus Em Santo Tomás." *Revista Brasileira de Filosofia* 35(1986): 22-42.

3701 De Grijs, Ferdinand. "Filosoof Over Theoloog: Het Thomasboek Van Delfaauw." *Bijdragen* 43(1982): 199-204.

3702 De Grijs, Ferdinand. "Het Schriftgebruik in De Regno Van Thomas Van Aquino." *Jaarboek* 1102(1985): 34-72.

3703 Delfgaauw, B. "Thomisme en Neo-thomisme." *Algemeen Nederlands Tijdschrift Wijsbegeerte* 73(1981): 229-240.

3704 Delfgaauw, B. "Kan Hedendaagse Filosofie Nog Inspiratie Vinden Bij Thomas Van Aquino?" *Annalen van het Thymgenootschap* (Baarn) 72(1984): 10-27.

3705 Dengerink, J. D. "Structuur en Persoon." *Philosophia Reformata* 51(1986): 29-44.

3706 Dufeil, Michel-Marie. "Oriens Apud Tomam." *Images et signes de l'Orient dans l'Occident médiéval* 11(1982): 163-176.

3707 Fujimoto, Y. "*Visio Dei* in St. Thomas' *De Veritate*." *Studies in Medieval Thought* 20(1978): 88-102.

3708 Iizuka, T. "A Consideration of Thomas' Theory of Capacity for Activity." *Studies in Medieval Thought* 22(1980): 83-92.

3709 Iizuka, T. "Thomas Aquinas' Theory of Creation." *Studies in Medieval Thought* 28(1986): 119-128.

3710 Imamichi, Tomonobu. "Genjitsu to Keisha [Pronum et Realitas]." *Chusei Shiso Kenkyu* 29(1987): 1-20.

3711 Inagaki, Bernard Ryôsuke. "Metaphysics and *Habitus* in Thomas Aquinas." *Studies in Medieval Thought* 20(1978): 181.

3712 Jacobi, Klaus. "Kontingente Naturgeschehnisse." *Studia Mediewistyczne (Warszawa)* 18(1977): 3-70.

3713 Kaneko, R. "Thomas on Abstraction." *Studies in Medieval Thought* 22(1980): 93-102.

3714 Kawazoe, S. "Self-cognition of the Human Intellect in Thomas Aquinas." *Studies in Medieval Thought* 24(1982): 132-140.

3715 Klima, Gyula. "Thomas Aquinas on the Meaning of the Words." *Magyar Filozof Szemle* 3-4(1984): 298-312.

*The article is an attempt at reconstructing, at least partially, Aquinas' theory of meaning. Because Aquinas' theory of meaning rests upon his theory of abstraction, in recent time, however, abstractionist theories have, since the time of Berkeley, been under severe attack, first it is pointed out that, in spite of the apparent similarities, Aquinas is not an abstractionist in a Lockean sense, by showing how Berkeley's criticism, cogent against Locke, is incogent against Aquinas. On the basis of this argument three main elements are distinguished: a term *significatio*, its *significatum*, and its *suppositum*.*

3716 Klima, Gyula. "Thomas Aquinas on the Principles of Nature." *Studies in Medieval Thought* 27(1987) 41-80.

*The general aim of the study is to present a conceptual apparatus which, as the author claims, despite Kuhn's incommensurability thesis, is able to mediate between different paradigms. In particular, it is shown how this mediation is achieved by applying this apparatus to Thomas Aquinas' *De principiis naturae* and *De mixtione elementorum*.*

3717 Kosugi, M. "*Esse* and *Essentia* in St. Thomas Aquinas." *Studies in Medieval Thought* 21(1979): 155-163.

3718 Kreling, G. P. "Het Intellectualisme Van de H. Thomas Van Aquino." *Het Goddelijk Geheim*. Amsterdam: Dordrecht, 1979. 166-179.

3719 Kumachi, Y. "On the Cognitional Structure of Human Intellect in Thomas Aquinas." *Studies in Medieval Thought* 25(1983): 135-145.

3720 Maltha, A. H. "Over de Menselijke Ziel." *Articuli* 4(1978): 67-116.

3721 Matsuda, Teiji. "On the Division and Methods of the Sciences in Thomas Aquinas." *Jimbunronshu* 33(1983): 27-52.

3722 Miyauchi, Hisamitsu. "On Good in Thomas Aquinas." *Studies in Medieval Thought* 21(1978): 1-18.

3723 Miyauchi, Hisamitsu. "The Doctrine of *Analogia Entis* in Thomas of Aquin." *Studies in Medieval Thought* 24(1982): 47-68.

3724 Mizuta, Hidemi. "*Quarta Via* and *De Ente*." *Studies in Medieval Thought* 25(1983): 81-105.

3725 Nagakura, Hisako. "The Theory of Creation in Thomas Aquinas." *Studies in Medieval Thought* 21(1979): 119-136.

3726 Nagakura, Hisako. "Reality and Language in Saint Thomas Aquinas: From Analysis of Language to the Apperception of *Esse*." *Studies in Medieval Thought* 32(1990): 225.

3727 Nyiri, Tamas. "The Destiny of Being from Thomas Aquinas to Heidegger." *Magyar Filozof Szemle* 3-4(1984): 313-328.

In diesen Thesen wird der Versuch unternommen, die Metaphysik des Thomas v. Aquin unter das Licht eines zentralen Gedanken von Martin Heidegger, nämlich deiniger der Seinsvergessenheit in der abendländischen Philosophie zu stellen. E. Gilson, J. B. Lotz, C. Fabro und andere Neothomisten nehmen Thomas v. Aquin in Schutz; sie geben zwar zu dass die Anklage—wen es eine ist—der Seinsvergessenheit im allgemeinen auf die Abendländische Philosophie zutrifft, aber nicht auf Thomas.

3728 Papadis, Dimitrios. "Die Einheit und die Vielheit der Seele Nach Aristoteles, Alexander von Aphrodisias und Thomas von Aquin." *Philosophia* (Athens) 15-16(1985-1986): 298-315.

3729 Pattin, Adriaana. "De Deugd Van Voorizichtigheid Naar Het Manuale Repertorium Libri Ethicorum Aristoteles Van Johannes Van Hasselt." *Tijdschrift voor Filosofie* 41(1979): 503-513.

3730 Persson, Pererik. "Thomas Av Aquino: Hans Betydelse for Aktuell Debatt Om Den Kristina Gudstrons Innebord." *Vardag Och Eviheit*. Ed. B. Hanson. Amsterdam: Dordrecht, 1981. 211-218.

3731 Ravensloot, V. Ch. "De Thomistisch-realistische Verhouding Van Zijn en Kennen. Enkele Overwegingen An de Hand Van *De Veritate*." *Ariculi* 6(1980): 46-59.

3732 Riesenhuber, Klaus. "Platonism in Thomas Aquinas." *Studies in Medieval Thought* 19(1977): 148-156.

3733 Riesenhuber, Klaus. "Participation as a Structuring Principle in Thomas Aquinas' Teaching on Divine Names." *Studies in Medieval Thought* 20(1978): 240-242.

3734 Riesenhuber, Klaus. "Knowledge of the Good According to Thomas Aquinas." *Studies in Medieval Thought* 21(1981): 19-40, 240-242.

3735 Sakai, K. "A Consideration of Thomas' Theory of Sensation: *S. T.* I. 17. 2. 3." *Studies in Medieval Thought* 21(1979): 164-176.

3736 Swiezawski, Stefan. "On Some Distortions of Thomas Aquinas' Ideas in Thomist Tradition." *Dialectics and Humanism* 11(1984): 599-612.

3737 Takahashi, Wataru. "Self-knowledge According to Augustine and Thomas Aquinas." *Studies in Medieval Thought (Kyoto)* 19(1977): 1-17.

3738 Tanaka, C. "On the Unity of Intellects—Averroes' Opinion and Thomas' Refutation." *Studies in Medieval Thought* 21(1979): 106-118.

3739 Tani, Ryuichíro. "An Aspect of the Human Act and Good in St. Thomas Aquinas." *Studies in Medieval Thought* 20(1978): 182.

3740 Te Velde, E. A. "Een Theologie Van de Goddelijke Namen? Deel I: Structuur en Structuurbeginselen Inde Godsleer Van de Summa Theologiae (Qq. 2-26)." *Werkgroep Thomas Van Aquino*. Amsterdam: Jaarboek, 1987. 8-31.

3741 Te Velde, Rudi. "Het Metafysische Karakter Van Thomas' Waarheidsbegrip." *Stoicheia* 1(1986): 24-48.

3742 Tsuzaki, S. "Metaphysics of *Verbum Interius* According to St. Thomas Aquinas." *Studies in Medieval Thought* 21(1979): 137-154.

3743 Van de Wiele, J. "Is de Waarheid Alleen in Het Verstand?" *Wijsgerig Perspectief op Maatschappij en Wetenschap* 19(1978-1979): 102-104.

3744 Van den Eijnden, J. G. J. "Onderzoek Draaiboek Voor Een Onderzoeksprogramma Betreffende de Invloed Van Thomas Van Aquino Op de Theologie." *Werkgroep Thomas Van Aquino* 2. Utrecht: Transitorium, 1985. 78-80.

3745 Van Tongeren, Paul. "The Virtues of the Proprietor (Aristotle and Thomas Aquinas on Truth, Wealth and Poverty)." *Magyar Filozóf Szemle* 2-3(1989): 273-286.

3746 Van Veldhuijsen, Peter. "Heeft God de Wereld Eerder Kunnen Maken Dan Hij Daadwerkelijk Gedaan Heeft? Albertus Magnus, Thomas Van Aquino en Een Vergeten Kwestie Over de Oorsprong Van de Wereld." *Werkgroep Thomas Van Aquino*. Amsterdam: Jaarboek, 1985. 71-91.

3747 Van Veldhuijsen, Peter. "Hendrik Van Gent (Vóór 1240-1293) Contra Thomas Van Aquino(1224/25-1274): Over de Mogelijkheid Van Een Eeuwig Geschapen Wereld." *Stoicheia* 2(1987): 3-26.

3748 Veres, Tomo. "Toma Akvinski I Dante Alighieri." Warsaw: Lublin University, 1982. 427-443.

3749 Vos, Arvin. "Thomas Van Aquino, de Gelovige Denker." *Emmaus* 10(1979): 281-290.

3750 Vos, Arvin. "Thomas' en Duns Scotus' Theorie Van de Goddelijke Alwetendheid." *Werkgroep Thomas Van Aquino*. Amsterdam: Jaarboek, 1982. 40-68.

3751 Vos, Arvin. "Thomas en Duns Scotus Over de Goddelije Wil." *Werkgroep Thomas Van Aquino*. Utrecht: Transitorium II, 1982. 7-30.

3752 Waragai, T. "On the Type Difference Between Singular Existential Sentences and Predication in St. Thomas." *Studies in Medieval Thought* 22(1980): 103-114.

3753 Watabe, Kikuo. "The Intellectual Cognition of Man According to St. Thomas Aquinas." *Studies in Medieval Thought* 27(1985): 77-100.

3754 Watabe, M. "On the Problem of Truth in Thomas Aquinas." *Studies in Medieval Thought* 22(1980): 115-125.

3755 Wohlman, Avital. "From Faith to Faith Through Reason: Maimonides and Aquinas." *Iyyum* 35(1986): 212-239.

The comparison of the relations between reason and faith, according to Thomas Aquinas and Maimonides, who start off from a common adherence to their respective religious traditions, shows a fundamental dissymmetry. The comparison proceeds in three sections:(1) criticism of natural knowledge leading to the doctrine of negative attributes versus analogy; (2) the analogy of light as unifying the two orders of nature and grace; (3) the limitations of natural reason and the revelation of natural truth. The comparison leads to a conclusion as to the importance of analogy as a conceptual tool which enabled the use Thomas made of Jewish thought in constructing his own Christian world.

3756 Yagi, Y. "A Study of Comparison: Thomistic and Scotistic Thoughts on Practical Cognition." *Studies in Medieval Thought* 24(1982): 151-162.

3757 Yamada, Akira. "On the Meaning of *Aliquid* in Aquinas, Especially in the Demonstration of God's Existence." *Studies in Medieval Thought* 23(1981): 218.

3758 Yamada, Akira. "Tomasu Akuinasu Ni Okeru Kobutsu No Mondai [On the Problem of Individuation in St. Thomas Aquinas]." *Chusei Shiso Kenkyu* 28(1986): 1-26.

I. CONGRESSES, SPECIAL COLLECTIONS, UNPUBLISHED PAPERS, AND DISSERTATIONS

3759 *Atti del Congresso Internazionale Tommaso Nel Suo Settimo Centenario V: L'agire Morale 1977.* Napoli: Edizioni Domenicane Italiane, 1977. 571.

3760 *Atti del Congresso Internazionale Tommaso D'Aquino Nel Suo Settimo Centenario VI: L'essere 1977.* Napoli: Edizioni Domenicane Italiane, 1977. 750.

3761 *Atti del Congresso Internazionale VII-VIII: L'uomo. Tommaso D'Aquino Nel Suo Settimo Centenario.* Napoli: Edizioni Domenicane Italiane, 1978. 483-533.

*Wilder, A., *Angelicum*, 60(1983): 652-653.*

3762 *Atti del XXXII Convengno del Centro Di Studi Filosofici 1978: Il Senso Della Filosofia Cristiana Oggi*: Brescia: Morcelliana, 1978.

3763 *Atti del Convengno Di Studi Promosso Dalla Collegiata Di San Biagio Nel VII Centenario Della Morte 1978: San Bonaventura e San Tommaso D'Aquino.* Ed. Marco Ceechelli. Biblioteca Cente se 2. Roma: G. Baruffaldi, 1978. 263.

3764 *Atti del Congresso Internazionale IX: Cosmo e la Scienza: Tommaso D'Aquino Nel Suo Settimo Centenario.* Napoli: Edizioni Domenicane Italiane, 1978. 523.

3765 *Atti del Convegno Organizzato a Roma Dall Societá Internazionale Tommaso D'Aquino e Dalla Pontificia Universita San Tommaso D'Aquino: Tommaso D'Aquino Nel I Centenario Dell'Enciclica Aeterni Patris.* Ed. Benedetto D'Amore. Roma: Societá Internazionale Tommaso d'Aquino, 1979. 319.

3766 *Actas del V Congreso internacional medieval I-II.* 1979. Madrid: Nacional, 1979. 1409.

3767 *Atti del VIII Congresso Tomistico in L'Enciclica Aeterni Patris I 1981.* Studi Tomistici 10. Città del Vaticano, Pontificia Accademia di San Tommaso e di eligione Cattolica: Libreria Editrice Cattolica, 1981. 512.

*O'Brien, Thomas, *The Thomist*, 48(1984): 473-475.*

3768 *Atti Del'VIII Congresso Tomistico Internazionale: L'enciclica Aeterni Patris II: Significato e Preparazione 1981.* Studi Tomistici 11. Città del Vaticano, Pontificia Accademia di San Tommaso e di Religione Cattolica: Libreria Editrice Cattolica, 1981. 484.

*Orlando, Pasquale, *Doctor Communis*, 35(1982): 374-378.*

3769 *Atti del'VIII Congresso Tomistico Internazionale: L'enciclica Aeterni Patris III: Suoi riflessi nel tempo 1981.* Studi Tomistici 12. Città del Vaticano, Pontificia Accademia di San Tommaso e di Religione Cattolica: Libreria Editrice Cattolica, 1981. 493.

3770 *Atti Del'VIII Congresso Tomistico Internazionale: Prospettive Teologiche Moderne IV.* Studi Tomistici 13. Città del Vaticano, Pontificia Accademia di San Tommaso e di Religione Cattolica: Libreria Editrice Cattolica, 1981. 457.

3771 *Atti Dell'VIII Congresso Tomistico Internazionale I: L' Enciclica Aeterni Patris Nell'arco Di Un Secolo.* Studi Tomistici 10. Cittá del Vaticano: Pontificia Accademia di San Tommaso e di Religione Cattolica, 1981. 512.

3772 *Atti Congresso Internazionale Di Studi Boeziani 1981.* Ed. Luca Obertello. Roma: Editrice Herder, 1981.

3773 *Atti del Convegno Organizzato a Roma Dalla Società Internazional Tommaso D'Aquino e Dalla Pontificia Università San Tommaso D'Aquino 1981*: Tommaso D'Aquino Nel I Centenario Dell'Enciclica *Aeterni Patris*: Università San Tommaso D'Aquino 1981. Ed. Benedetto Amore. Roma: Societá Internazionale Tommaso d'Aquino, 1981. 319.

3774 *Atti del III Colloquio Internazionale del Lessico Intellettuale Europeo: Res.* Eds. M. Fattori and M. Bianchi. Lessico Intellettuale Europeo 26. Roma: Edizioni dell'Ateneo, 1982. xiii-594.

3775 *Atti del VII Congresso Internazionale Centro Internazionale Di Studi e Di Relazioni Culturali: Metafisica e Scienze Dell'uomo.* Ed. Benedetto D'Amore. 2. Roma: Borla, 1982.

*Anon., *Rassegna di Letteratura Tomistica*, 18(1985): 400-402.*

3776 *Atti Dell'VIII Congresso Tomistico Internazionale: Morale e Diritto Nella Prospettiva Tomistica VI.* Studi Tomistici 15. Cité del Vatican: Pontificia Accademia di San Tommaso e di Religione Cattolica, 1982. 342.

3777 *Atti Dell'VIII Congresso Tomistico Internazionale: L'uomo e Il Mondo Nella Luce Dell'Aquinate VII. Studi Tomistici* 16. Citté del Vatican: Pontificia Accademia di San Tommaso e di Religione Cattolica, 1982. 350.

3778 *Atti Dell'VIII Congresso Tomistico Internazionale: San Tommaso Nella Storia del Pensiero VIII.* Studi Tomistici 17. Cittá del Vaticano: Pontificia Accademia di San Tommaso e di Religione Cattolica, 1982. 419.

3779 *Atti Dell'VIII Congresso Tomistico Internazionale: L'uomo e Il Mondo Nella Luce Dell'Aquinate VII. Studi Tomistici* 16. Citté del Vatican: Pontificia Accademia di San Tommaso e di Religione Cattolica, 1982. 350.

3780 *Atti Dell'VIII Congresso Tomistico Internazionale V: Problemi Metafisici.* Studi Tomistici 14. Città del Vaticano: Pontificia Accademia di San Tommaso e di Religione Cattolica, 1982. 485.

3781 *Atti del Convengno Internazionale Di Studio Promosso Dall'Università Cattolica Nel Centenario Della Nascita: J. Maritain Oggi.* Ed. Vittorio Possenti. Milano: Vita e Pensiero, 1983. 582.

*Cardoletti, P., *La Civiltà Cattolica*, 135(1984): 96-97.*
*Castellano, D., *Filosofia Oggi*, 9(1986): 161-166.*
*Gioia, G., *Giornale di Metafisica*, 8(1986): 387-389.*
*Pizzorni, R. M., *Angelicum*, 61(1984): 535-536.*
*Pizzorni, R. M., *Aquinas*, 27(1984): 227-228.*

3782 *Atti del Congresso Societá Internazionale San Tommaso D'Aquino Vol. IX: L'anima Nell'antropologia Di San Tommaso D'Aquino 1987.* Ed. Abelardo Lobato. Studia Universitatis S. Thomae in Urbe 28. Milano: Editrice Massimo, 1987. 645.

II. SPECIAL COLLECTIONS

A. ENGLISH

3783 *A Straight Path: Studies in Medieval Philosophy and Culture: Essays in Honor of Arthur Hyman.* Eds. Jeremiah Hackett et al. Washington, DC: The Catholic University of America Press, 1988. xiv-310.

3784 *Albertus Magnus and the Sciences: Commemorative Essays 1980.* Ed. James A. Weisheipl. Studies and Texts 49. Toronto: Pontifical Institute of Mediaeval Studies, 1980. xiv-658.

*Carroll, William E., *The Thomist*, 44(1980): 647-651.*
*Daly, P. H., *Scriptorium*, 39(1985): 114-115.*
*Federici, Vescovini G., *RCSF*, 38(1983): 225-228.*
*Hedwig, K., *Philosophischer Literaturanzeiger*, 36(1983): 284-286.*
*Lindberg, D. C., *Isis*, 72(1981): 137-138.*
*McEvoy, J., *Bulletin de Théologie Ancienne et Médiévale*, 470-474.*
*Steel, C., *Tijdschrift voor Filosofie*, 45(1983): 486-487.*
*Sturlese, L., *Annali della Scuola Normale Superiore di Pisa (Lettere e Filosofia)*, 11(1981): 1427-1431.*
*Zamora, G., *Collectanea Franciscana*, 53(1983): 143-144.*

3785 *Approaches to Nature in the Middle Ages: Papers of the Tenth Annual Conference of the Center for Medieval & Early Renaissance Studies 1982.* Ed. Lawrence D. Roberts. Medieval & Renaissance Texts & Studies 16. Binghamton, NY: Center for Medieval & Renaissance Studies, 1982. 220.

3786 Kenny, Anthony John Patrick. *Aquinas: A Collection of Critical Essays.* Ed. Patrick John Anthony Kenny. Modern Studies in Philosophy. Notre Dame, IN: University of Notre Dame Press, 1977. 389.

3787 *Being and Knowing: Studies in Thomas Aquinas and Later Medieval Philosophers.* Ed. Armand Augustine Maurer. Papers in Mediaeval Studies 10. Toronto: Pontifical Institute of Mediaeval Studies, 1990. 496.

3788 *Being and Predication: Thomistic Interpretations 1986.* Ed. Ralph McInerny. Studies in Philosophy and the History of Philosophy 16. Washington, DC: The Catholic University of America Press, 1986. xii-323.

3789 *Calgary: Aquinas Studies.* Ed. Anthony Parel. Toronto: Pontifical Institute of Mediaeval Studies, 1978. viii-174. Papers originally presented at the Aquinas Septicentennial conference, held at the University of Calgary in October 1974.

3790 *Celebrating the Medieval Heritage: A Colloquy on the Thought of Aquinas and Bonaventure 1978.* Ed. David Tracy. Chicago: University of Chicago Press, 1978. ix-239.

3791 *Collected Works of Bernard Longergan I-V.* Eds. Frederick Crowe et al. Toronto: University of Toronto, 1980-1988.

3792 *Divine and Human Action.* Ed. Thomas V. Morris. Ithaca, NY: Cornell University Press, 1988.

3793 *Divine Omniscience and Omnipotence in Medieval Philosophy: Islamic, Jewish, and Christian Perspectives.* Ed. Tamar Rudavsky. Dordrecht: D. Reidel Publishing Company, 1985.

*Decorte, J., *Tijdschrift voor Filosofie*, 50(1988): 148-149.*
*Kent, Bonnie, *The Review of Metaphysics*, 39(1986): 783-784.*
*Mulligan, R. W., *The Modern Schoolman*, 64(1987): 207-209.*
*Redpath, Peter A., *The Thomist*, 51(1987): 716-718.*
*Stubbens, N. A., *Idealistic Studies*, 18(1988): 185-186.*

3794 *From Cloister to Classroom: Monastic and Scholastic Approaches to Truth 1986.* Ed. E. R. Elder. Cistercian Studies 90. Kalamazoo, MI: Cistercian Publications, 1986. vi-275.

3795 *Graceful Reason: Essays in Ancient and Medieval Philosophy Presented to Joseph Owens, CSSR on the Occasion of His Seventy-fifth Birthday and the Fiftieth Anniversary of His Ordination.* Ed. Lloyd P. Gerson. Papers in Mediaeval Studies 4 58. Toronto: Pontifical Institute of Mediaeval Studies, 1983.

*Bianchi, L, *Rivista di Storia della Filosofia*, 41(1986): 405-406.*
*Burrell, D., *The New Scholasticism*, 62(1988): 239-241.*
*Freudenthal, G., *Iris*, 77(1986): 183-184.*
*Madigan, A., *Ancient Philosophy*, 5(1985): 136-140.*
*Peña, Lorenzo, *Philosophia* (Israel) 19(1989): 73-79.*

3796 *Infinity and Continuity in Ancient and Medieval Thought.* Ed. Norman Kretzmann. London: Cornell University Press, 1982. 367.

*Benardete, J. A., *Nous*, 18(1984): 367-373.*
*Inwood, B., *International Studies in Philosophy*, 16(1984): 88-90.*
*Lolli, Gabriele, *Scientia*, 119(1984): 20-21.*
*Longeway, John, *The Philosophical Review*, 94(1985): 263-265.*
*Minonzio, F., *Estudios Lulianos*, 6(1985): 221-228.*
*Sweeney, Leo, *Journal of the History of Philosophy*, 21(1983): 399-400.*

3797 *Lex et Libertas: Freedom and Law According to St. Thomas Aquinas. Proceedings of the Fourth Symposium on St. Thomas Aquinas' Philosophy 1987*. Eds. L. J. Elders and K. Hedwig. Studi Tomistici 30. Città del Vaticano: Libreria Editrice Vaticana, 1987.

*Composta, Dario, *Doctor Communis*, 50(1988): 96-97.*

3798 *Metaphysical Themes in Thomas Aquinas 1984*. Ed. John F. Wippel. Studies in Philosophy and the History of Philosophy 10. Washington, DC: The Catholic University of America Press, 1984. xi-293.

*Anon., *Rassegna di Letteratura Tomistica* 20(1987): 162-164.*
*Inagaki, Y., *Studies in Medieval Thought*, 27(1985): 206-210.*
*Wilder, A., *Angelicum*, 63(1986): 150-152.*

3799 *Nature and Motion in the Middle Ages*. Ed. William E. Carroll. Studies in Philosophy and the History of Philosophy 11. Washington, DC: The Catholic University of America Press, 1985. 292. Selected Bibliography of the works of Weisheipl, James A., 283-285.

3800 *One Hundred Years of Thomism*. Ed. Victor B. Brezik. Houston, TX: Center for Thomistic Studies, University of St. Thomas, 1981. 210.

3801 *Philosophy and the God of Abraham: Essays in Memory of James A. Weisheipl, OP*. Ed. James Long. Toronto: Pontifical Institute of Mediaeval Studies, In press. 296.

3802 *Rationality and Religious Belief*. Ed. C. F. Delaney. Notre Dame, IN: University of Notre Dame Press, 1979. 176.

*Ferreira, M. J., *The Thomist*, 46(1982): 328-334.*
*Kennedy, L. A., *The New Scholasticism*, 56(1982): 258-260.*
*Young, Robert, *Religious Studies*, 17(1981): 128.*

3803 *Rationality, Religious Belief, and Moral Commitment 1986*. Eds. Robert Audi and William J. Wainwright. Ithaca, NY: Cornell University Press, 1986. 341.

*Austin, William H., *Nôus*, 23(1989): 383-386.*

3804 *St. Thomas Aquinas on the Existence of God: Collected Papers of Joseph Owens, C. Ss. R.* Ed. John R. Catan. Albany, NY: State University of New York Press, 1980. 291.

3805 *Studies in Medieval Philosophy*. Ed. John F. Wippel. Studies in Philosophy and the History of Philosophy 17. Washington, DC: The Catholic University of America Press, 1987. viii-302.

3806 *The Cambridge History of Later Medieval Philosophy: From the Rediscovery of Aristotle to the Disintegration of Scholasticism 1100-1600*. Eds. Norman Kretzmann, Anthony Kenny, and Jan Pinborg. New York: Cambridge University Press, 1988. xiv-1035.

3807 *The Cambridge History of Mediaeval Political Thought (350-1450) 1988*. Ed. J. H. Burns. Cambridge: Cambridge University Press, 1988.

*Genet, Jean-Phillippe, *History of Political Thought*, 10(Summer 1989): 359-362.*

3808 *The Eternity of the World in the Thought of Thomas Aquinas and His Contemporaries*. Ed. J. B. M. Wissink. Studien und Texte Zur Geistesgeschichte Des Mittelalters 27. Leiden: E. J. Brill, 1990. viii-100.

3809 *The Ethics of St. Thomas Aquinas: Proceedings of the Third Symposium on St. Thomas Aquinas' Philosophy*. Eds. L. Elders and K. Hedwig. Studi Tomistici 25. Città del Vaticano: Libreria Editrice Vaticana, 1984. 259.

3810 *The Georgetown Symposium on Ethics 1984*. Ed. Rocco Porreco. Lanham, MD: University Press of America, 1984.

3811 *The Medieval Tradition of Natural Law*. Ed. H. J. Johnson. Studies in Medieval Culutre 22. Kalamazoo, MI: Medieval Institute Publications, 1987. 211.

3812 *Theory of Being to Understand Reality*. Eds. Stanislaw Kaminski, Marian Kurdzialek, and Zofia Zdybicka. Lublin: Towarzystwo Naukowe Katolickiego Uniwersytetu Lubelskiego, 1980. 322.

3813 *Thomas Aquinas*. 15/16(1986): 1-21. Listing of primary sources translated into French.

3814 *Thomistic Bibliography, 1940-1978*. Terry L. Miethe and Vernon J. Bourke, comps. Westport, CT: Greenwood Press, 1980. xxii-318.

3815 *Thomistic Papers I*. Ed. Victor S. Brezik. Notre Dame, IN: University of Notre Dame Press, 1985. 156.

3816 *Thomistic Papers II*. Eds. A. Kennedy and C. Marler. Houston, TX: Center for Thomistic Studies, University of St. Thomas, 1986. 163.

*Baldner, S., *Canadian Philosophical Reviews*, 6(1986): 492-493.*

3817 *Thomistic Papers III*. Ed. A. Kennedy. Houston, TX: Center for Thomistic Studies, University of St. Thomas, 1987. 140.

3818 *Thomistic Papers IV*. Ed. Leonard A. Kennedy. Houston, TX: University of St. Thomas, Center for Thomistic Studies, 1988. 207.

3819 *Thomistic Papers V*. Ed. Thomas A. Russman. Houston, TX: Center for Thomistic Studies, University of Saint Thomas, 1990.

B. MISCELLANEOUS

3820 *Année Charniére—Mutations et Continuités: Colloques Internationaux Du Centre National de la Recherche Scientifique 1977*. Ed. Michel Mollat. Colloques Internationaux Du CNRS 558. Paris: Éditions du CNRS, 1977. 1009.

3821 *Annali Chieresi*. Ed. Intituto di filosofia San Tommaso d'Aquino. Chieri, 1985. 127.

3822 *Archives D'histoire Doctrinale et Littéraire Du Moyen-âge 1985*. Eds. Marie-Thérése D'Alverny and Marie-Dominique Chenu. Paris: Vrin, 1985. 284.

3823 *Associacion Catolica Interamericana. De Filosofia: Realismo Pluridimensional*. Córdoba, 1983. 449. Especially Caturelli, Celia Galíndes de, "La metafíisica realista de la educación de Santo Tomás" and Poradowski, Miguel, "El Tomismo en las Encíclicas Sociales."

3824 *Attualità Filosofica Di San Tommaso 1980*. Ed. Sacra Doctrina. Napoli: Edizioni Domenicane Italiane, 1980. 160.

3825 *Augustinus et Thomas: Numero Speciale Di Doctor Communis. Omaggio Dell'Accademia Di San Tommaso D'Aquino a Sant'Agostino D'Ippona Nel XVI Centenario Della Conversione (Doctor Communis*, 39(1986): N. 3, 235-457. Città del Vaticano: *Rivista Doctor Communis*, Palazzo Canonici, 1986. 282-291.

3826 *Autour de Saint Thomas D'Aquin: Recueil D'études sur Sa Pensée Philosophique et Théologique II: L'agir Moral Approches Théologiques 1987*. Ed. Léon Elders. Paris: FAC-éditions, 1987. 229.

3827 *Cinquant'anni Di Magistero Teologico, Scritti in Onore Di Mons. Antonio Piolanti Nel 50 del Suo Sacerdozio 1985*. Studi Tomistici 26. Città del Vaticano: Libreria Editrice Vaticana, 1985. 261.

3828 *De Gelovige Thomas: Beschouwingen Over de Hymne Sacris Sollemniis Van Thomas Van Aquino 1986*. Eds. A. Bastiaensen et al. *Annalen Van Het Thymgenoots* 74. 2. Baarn: Amboboeken, 1986. 126.

3829 *Die Frage Nach dem Glück 1978*. Ed. Günther Bien. Problemata 74. Stuttgart-Bad Cannstatt: Frommann-Holzboog, 1978.

3830 *Die Mächte Des Guten und Bösen 1977*. Ed. Albert Zimmermann. Miscellanea Mediaevalia 11. Berlin: Walter de Gruyter, 1977. viii-548.

3831 *Die Philosophie Des Thomas von Aquin 1977*. Philosophische Bibliothek 100. Hamburg: Meiner, 1977. xviii-224.

3832 *Die Philosophie Im 14. und 15. Jahrhundert: In Memoriam Kostanty Michalski(1879-1947)*. Ed. Olaf Pluta. Bochumer Studien Zur Philosophie 10. Amsterdam: Verlag B. R. Grüner, 1988. lx-639.

3833 *Doctrine de la Révélation Divine de Saint Thomas D'Aquin: La Actes Du Symposium sur la Pensée de Saint Thomas D'Aquin*. Ed. L. Elders. *Studi Tomistici* 37(1990). Roma: Pontificia Accademia di San Tommaso. 278.

3834 *Energeia: Etudes Aristotélicienne Offertes A Mgr. Antonio Jannone*. Ed. Evanghélos A. Moutsopoulos. Recherches 1. Paris: J. Vrin, 1986. 412.

3835 *Ethique, Religion et Foi 1985*. Le Point Théologique 43. Paris: Beauchesne, 1985. 270. Especially M. Corbin, "L'homme passe l'homme: Essai sur l'éthique théologique chez Saint Thomas Aquinas."

3836 *Etienne Gilson et Nous: La Philosophie et Son Histoire*. Eds. M. -Th. D'Alvery and P. Aubenque. Bibliothéque D'histoire de la Philosophie. Paris: J. Vrin, 1980. 160.

3837 *Fe, Razón y Teologia. En el I Centenario de la Enciclica Aeterni Patris*. Ed. Pedro Rodriguez. Pampelune: Ediciones Universidad de Navarra, 1979. 488.

*Van Steenberghen, Fernand, *Revue Philosophique de Louvain*, 79(1981): 591.*

3838 *Foi et Raison A Partir de Saint Thomas: Préalables A la Question D'une Rationalité Pour les Psychanalystes 1983*. Psychanalytique 6. Paris: Le Discours, 1983. 64. Especially R. P. M. Capitte, "La structure du psychisme humain d'apres Thomas d'Aquin."

3839 *Grundprobleme der Grossen Philosophen: Philosophie Des Altertums und Des Mittelalters: Slkrates, Platon, Aristoteles, Augustinus, Thomas von Aquin, Nikolaus von Kues 1983*. Ed. Josef Speck. Göttingen: Vandenhoeck und Ruprecht, 1983. 261.

3840 *Il Concetto Di Sapientia in San Bonaventura e San Tommaso*. Ed. Alessandro Musco. Biblioteca Dell'Enchiridion 1. Palermo: 1983. x-95.

*Ruello, F., *Recherches de Science Religieuse*, 74(1986): 280-281.*

3841 *Il Risveglio Della Coscienza Nella Civiltà Medievale 1981*. Ed. Marie-Dominique Chenu. Trans. Inos Biffi. Biblioteca Di Cultura Medievale 57. Milan: Ed.ial Jaca Book, 1981. 116. Especially James Weisheipl, "Tommaso d'Aquino: La vita, il pensiero, le opere: Cultura Medievale." Conversazioni con M. D. Chenu, F. Van Steenberghen, R. Bultot, J. Harnesse, P. Tombeur, R. Busa, J. G. Bougerol, S. Varini-Rovighi, M. T. Beonio-Brocchieri Fumagalli, M. Dal Pra, A. Ghisalberti, e altri.

3842 *Implicazione del Pensiero Tomistico*. Napoli: Editrice Domenicana Italiana, 1986. 128.

3843 *Index Thomisticus, Sancti Thomae Aquinatis Operum Omnium Indices et Concordantiae in Quibus Verborum Omnium et Singulorum Formae et Lemmata Cum Suis Frequentiis et Contextibus Variis Modis Referuntur Quaeque.. electronico IBM Automato Usus*. Sectio prima: Vol. I-X: Indices. Sectio secunda: Concordantiae operum thomisticorum. Concordantia prima. Vol I-XXIII. Sectio secunda: Concordantiae operum thomisticorum. Concordantia altera. Vol. I-VIII. Sectio tertia: Concordantiae operum aliorum auctorum. Concordantia prima. Vol. I-VI. Sectio tertia: Concordantiae operum aliorum auctorum. Concordantia altera. Vol. I-II. Ed. Roberto Busa. 49. Stuttgart-Bad Cannstatt: Frommann-Holzboog, 1974-1980. 21840.

*Blanchette, Oliva, *International Philosophical Quarterly*, 17(1977): 101-103.*
*Burton, D. M., *Speculum*, 59(1984): 891-894.*

3844 *L'homme et Son Univers Au Moyen Age: Actes Du Septiéme Congrés International de Philosophie Médievale I-II 1986*. Ed. Christian Wenin. Philosophes Médiévaux 26-27. Louvain-la-Neuve: Éditions de l'Institut Supérieur de Philosophie, 1986. xiv-480, xiii-961.

*Luch-Baixauli, M. *Scripta Theologica*, Pamplona: 19(1987): 475-477.*
*Van Steenberghen, F. *Bulletin de Théologie Ancienne et Médiévale*, 14(1987): 234-235.*

3845 *L'Uomo, 1 Tomo. Congress, Tommaso D'Aquino Nel Suo Settimo Centenario 1978*. Ed. Norbert A. Luyten. Naples: Edizioni Domenicane Italiane, 1978. 483.

3846 *La Fondazione Della Morale e del Diritto Naturale Nella Concezione Tomistica*. Ed. Società Internazionale Tommaso d'Aquino. Napoli: San Domenico Maggiore, 1983. 257-384.

3847 *La Metafisica e le Sue Forme Dialettiche: Sciacca Da Tommaso D'Aquino a Platone*. Genova: Tilgher, 1985. 171-403.

3848 *La Philosophie de la Nature de Saint Thomas D'Aquin: Actes Du Symposium sur la Pensée de Saint Thomas Tenu A Rolduc*. Ed. Léon Elders. Studi Tomistici 18. Rome: Libreria Editrice Vaticana, 1982. 178.

*Van Steenberghen, F., *Revue Philosophique de Louvain*, 83(1985): 289-292.*

3849 *La Scolastique: Certitude et Recherche: En Hommage A Louis Marie Régis 1980*. Ed. Ernest Joós. Montréal: Les Éditions Bellarmin, 1980.

3850 *Las Razones del Tomismo 1980*. Baranain: Universidad de Navarra, 1980. 144.

3851 *Le Ragioni del Tomismo: Dopo Il Centenario Dell'enciclica Aeterni Patris*. Ed. Cardona Carolos. Collana Sagitta: Problemi e Documenti 29. Milano: Edizioni Ares, 1979. 238.

*Colonnello, P., *Sapienza*, 33(1980): 235-237.*
*Leroy, M. -V., *Revue Thomiste*, 83(1983): 675-677.*
*Musco, A., *Schede Medievali*, 1(1981): 88-89.*

3852 *Les Machines Du Sens: Fragments D'une Sémiologie Médievale. Textes de Hugues de Saint-Victor, Thomas D'Aquin et Nicolas de Lyre 1987.* Ed. and Trans. Yves Delégue. Archives Du Commentaire. Paris: Éd. des Cendres, 1987. 118.

3853 *Lex et Virtus: Studi Sull'evoluzione Della Dottrina Morale Di San Tommaso D'Aquino.* Ed. G. Abbà. Biblioteca Di Scienze Religiose 56. Rome: Libreria Ateneo Salesiano, 1983.

3854 *Lexikon Des Mittelalters 1986.* 9. München-Zürich: Artemis, 1986.

3855 *Linguistica Medievale: Anselmo D'Aosta, Abelardo, Tommaso D'Aquino, Pietro Ispano, Gentile Da Cingoli, Occam.* Ed. Francesco Corvino. Bari: Ed. Adriatica, 1983. 315.

3856 *Mensura. Mass, Zahl, Zahlensymbolik Im Mittelalter.* Ed. Gudrun Vuillemin-Diem. Miscellanea Mediaevalia 16. 1-2. Berlin: Walter de Gruyter, 1983-1984. x-260, viii-494.

3857 *Metafisica Iijecia Jednosci: Platon, Tomasz Z Akwinu, Giovanni Pico Della Mirandola, Aristoteles 1985.* 2. Warszawa: Akad Teol Katol, 1985.219/237.

3858 *Nel Centenario Dell'Enciclica Aeterni Patris (Doctor Communis, 3(1980) 1980.* Città del Vaticano: Palazzo Canonici, 1980. 259-390.

3859 Maritain, Jacques. *Oeuvres II:(1940-1963) 1979.* Paris: Desclée De Brouwer, 1979. 926.

3860 Maritain, Jacques, and Räissa Maritain. *Oeuvres Complétes. I.(1906-1920) 1986.* Fribourg: Ed. Universitaires, 1986. xxviii-1178.

3861 *Ontologie und Theologie: Beiträge Zum Problem der Metaphysik bei Aristoteles und Thomas von Aquin 1988.* Ed. Matthias Lutz-Bachmann. Europäische Hochschulschriften, Reihe 23, Theologie, 331. Frankfurt/New York: Bern/Lang, 1988. 109.

3862 *Orientalische Kultur und Europäisches Mittelalter.* Eds. Albert Zimmermann and Ingrid Craemer-Ruegenberg. Miscellanea Mediaevalia 17. Berlin: Walter de Gruyter, 1985. ix-440.

3863 *Origini e Sviluppi Dell'analogia: Da Parmenide a San Tommaso.* Eds. E. Berti and Giuseppe Casetta. Settimane Filosofiche Di Vallombrosa 1. Roma: Edizioni Vallombrosa, 1987. 178.

*Fontana, S., *Bollettino Filsofico*, 22(1988): 131-133.*

3864 *Over God Spreken. Een Tekst Van Thomas Van Aquino Uit de Summa Theologiae* (I, Q. 13) 1988. Ed. H. W. M. Rikhof. Sleutelteksten in Godsdienst en Theologie 6. Delft: Meinema, 1988. 159.

3865 *Philosophes Médiévaux 1986.* Ed. R. Imbach. Paris: Union Génerale d'Editores, 1986. 408.

*Fornet-Betancourt, R., *Concord*, 7(1985): 362-364.*

3866 *Philosophie Im Mittelalter: Festschrift in Honor of Wolfgang Kluxen.* Eds. J. P. Beckmann et al. Hamburg: Felix Meiner Verlag, 1987.

*Van Steenberghen, Fernand, *Revue Philosophique de Louvain*, 87(1989): 348-349.*

3867 *Polska Bibliografia Nauk Koscielnych Za Lata 1972-1973.* Warszawa: Akad. Teol. Katol, 1979. 516.

3868 *Quinque Sunt Viae: Actes Du Symposium sur les Cinq Voies de la Somme Théologique 1980*. Ed. Léon Elders. Studi Tomistici 9. Rome, Pontificia Accademia di San Tommaso-Città del Vaticano: Libreria Editrice Vaticana, 1980. 150.

*Hedwig, K., *Philosophischer Literaturanzeiger*, 35(1982): 156-159.*
*Leroy, M. -V., *Revue Thomiste*, 83(1983): 125-127.*

3869 *Rassegna Di Letteratura Tomistica: Thomistic Bulletin, Boletin Tomista, Thomistische Literaturschau Vol. XIIII: Letteratura Dell'anno 1978*. Nuova Serie del Bulletin Thomiste. Napoli: Editrice Domenicana Italiana, 1981. 485.

3870 *Rassegna Di Letteratura Tomistica: Thomistic Bulletin, Boletin Tomista, Thomistische Literaturschau Vol. XV: Letteratura Dell'anno 1979*. Napoli: Editrice Domenicana Italiana, 1982. 493.

3871 *Rassegna Di Letteratura Tomistica: Thomistic Bulletin, Boletin Tomista, Thomistische Literaturschau Vol. XIIII: Letteratura Dell'anno 1978*. Nuova Serie del Bulletin Thomiste. Napoli: Editrice Domenicana Italiana, 1983. 511.

3872 *Rassegna Di Letteratura Tomistica: Thomistic Bulletin, Boletin Tomista, Thomistische Literaturschau Vol. XVII: Letteratura Dell'anno 1981*. Nuova Serie del Bulletin Thomiste 29. Napoli: Editrice Domenicana Italiana, 1984. 509.

3873 *Rassegna Di Letteratura Tomistica: Thomistic Bulletin, Boletin Tomista, Thomistische Literaturschau Vol. XVIII: Letteratura Dell'anno 1982*. Nuova Serie del Bulletin Thomiste 30. Napoli: Editrice Domenicana Italiana, 1985. 375.

3874 *Rassegna Di Letteratura Tomistica: Thomistic Bulletin, Boletin Tomista, Thomistische Literaturschau Vol. XIX: Letteratura Dell'anno 1983*. Nuova Serie del Bulletin Thomiste. Napoli: Editrice Domenicana Italiana, 1986.

3875 *Rassegna Di Letteratura Tomistica: Thomistic Bulletin, Boletin Tomista, Thomistische Literaturschau Vol. XX: Letteratura Dell'anno 1984*. Nuova Serie del Bulletin Thomiste. Napoli: Editrice Domenicana Italiana, 1987. 438.

3876 *Rassegna Di Letteratura Tomistica: Thomistic Bulletin, Boletin Tomista, Thomistische Literaturschau Vol. XXI: Letteratura Dell'anno 1985*. Nuova Serie del Bulletin Thomiste. Napoli: Editrice Domenicana Italiana, 1988. 463.

3877 *Rassegna Di Letteratura Tomistica: Thomistic Bulletin, Boletin Tomista, Thomistische Literaturschau Vol. XXIII: Letteratura Dell'anno 1987*. Nuova Serie del Bulletin Thomiste. Napoli: Editrice Domenicana Italiana, 1990.

3878 *Rassegna Di Letteratura Tomistica: Thomistic Bulletin, Boletin Tomista, Thomistische Literaturschau Vol. XXII: Letteratura Dell'anno 1986*. Nuova Serie del Bulletin Thomiste. Napoli: Editrice Domenicana Italiana, 1989. 438.

3879 *Saggi e Ricerche Sul Pensiero Tomistico*. Napoli: Sapienza, 1981. 253.

3880 *Saint-Thomas D'Aquin Pour le Septiéme Centenaire de Sa Mort: Essai D'actualisation de Sa Philosophie*. Eds. Stanislaw Kaminski, Marian Kurdzialek, and Zofia Zdybicka. Lublin: Towarzystwo Naukowe Katolickiego Uniwersytetu Lubelskiego, 1978. 351.

3881 *San Tomás de Aquino, Suma de Teologia*. Ed. D. Byrne. Biblioteca de Autores Cristianos 31. Madrid: La Editorial Católica, 1988. xxxviii-992.

3882 *Schönheit: Eine Untersuchung Zum Ursprung Des Denkens bei Thomas von Aquin 1978*. Ed. Günther Pöltner. Wien, Freiburg: Herder, 1978. 214.

3883 *Sein und Geist. Systemat. Unters. Über Grundproblem U. Aufbau Mittelalteri.* Ed. Max Müller. Ontologie 2. Freiburg: Alber, 1981. viii-245.

3884 *Sein-Wahrheit-Wort: Thomas von Aquin und die Lehre von der Wahrheit der Dinge 1984.* Ed. Rudolf B. Schmitz. Philosophie 1. Münster, 1984. xxix-657.

3885 *Soziale Ordnungen Im Selbstverständnis Des Mittelalters I-II.* Ed. Albert Zimmermann. Miscellanea Mediaevalia 12/1 und 12/2. Berlin: Walter de Gruyter, 1979-1980. vi-335, viii-337-619.

3886 *Sprache und Erkenntnis Im Mittelalter: Akten Des VI. Internationalen Kongresses Für Mittelalterliche Philosophie der Sociéte Internationale Pour L'étude de la Philosophie Médiévale 1981.* Eds. Jan P. Beckmann et al. Miscellanea Medievalia 13. 1-2. Berlin: Walter de Gruyter, 1981. xxiv-547-1113.

3887 *Studi Di Filosofia Medioevale 2: Secoli XIII e XIV: Collected Essays of Sofia Vanni Rovighi 1978.* Ed. Sofia Vanni Rovighi. 1978.

3888 *Studia Z Dziejów Mysli Swietego Tomasza Z Akwinu [Studies on the History of St. Thomas Aquinas' Thought].* Eds. Stefan Swiezwaski and Jana Czerkawskiego. Towarzystwo Naukowe Kul, Zródla I Monografie 105. Lublin: Tow. Nauk. KUL, 1978. 403.

3889 *Studien Zur Mittelalterlichen Geistesgeschichte Und Ihren Quellen 1982.* Ed. Albert Zimmermann. Miscellanea Mediaevalia 15. Berlin: Walter de Gruyter, 1982. 318.

3890 *Studien Zur Mittelalterlichen Geistesgeschichte und Ihren Quellen.* Ed. Albert Zimmermann. Miscellanea Mediaevalia 15. Berlin: Walter de Gruyter, 1982. viii-318.

3891 *Thematische Geschriften: Thomas Aquinas, J. H. Newman 1982.* Eds. J. H. Walgrave, G. de Schrijver, and J. Kelly. Bibliotheca Ephemeridum Theologicarum Lovaniensium 57. Leuven: Uitgeverij Peeters, 1982. xliii-425.

3892 Schütz, Ludwing. Stuttgart: Frommann-Holzboog, 1983. x-889.

3893 *Thomas von Aquin: Werk und Wirkung Im Licht Neuerer Forschungen.* Ed. Albert Zimmermann. Miscellanea Mediaevalia 19. Berlin: Walter de Gruyter, 1988. xi-507.

3894 *Thomas von Aquin. Bd I: Chronologie und Werkanalyse.* Ed. Klaus Bernath. Wege der Forschung 188. Darmstadt, Wissenschaftliche Buchgesellschaft: Abt. Verl., 1978. x-491.

3895 *Thomas von Aquin II: Philosophische Fragen.* Ed. Klaus Bernath. Wege der Forschung 538. Darmstadt: Wissenschaftliche Buchgesellschaft, 1981. Abt. Verl. Viii-572.

3896 *Vérité et Éthos: Recueil Commémoratif Dédié A Alphonse-Marie Parent 1982.* Ed. Jaromir Danek. Québec: Les Presses de l'Université Laval, 1982.

3897 *Virtualità e Attualità Della Filosofia Cristiana.* Ed. Battista Mondin. Pontificia Universitas Urbaniana 32. Roma: Pontificia Universita Urbaniana, 1988. 506.

*Giannini, G., *Doctor Communis*, 42(1989): 78-80.*

*Perazzoli, B., *Rivista Rosminiana di Filosofia e di Cultura*, 83(1989): 250-257.*

*Pizzorni, R. -M., *Angelicum*, 65(1988): 485.*

3898 *War and Peace I-III.* By Aquinas and others. Ed. Faculty members of Lynchburg College. Classical Selections on Great Issues 1. Washington, DC: University Press of America, 1982. 635.

3899 *Werkgroep Thomas Van Aquino*. Transitorium 2. Amsterdam: Jaarboek, 1981. 142.

3900 *Werkgroep Thomas Van Aquino*. Amsterdam: Jaarboek, 1982. 134.

3901 *Werkgroep Thomas Van Aquino*. Amsterdam: Jaarboek, 1985. 144.

3902 *Wissen, Glaube, Politik: Festschrift Für Paul Asveld 1981*. Ed. Winfried Gruber, Jean Ladriére, and Norbert Leser. Verlag, Styria, 1981.

III. UNPUBLISHED PAPERS

3903 Artus, Walter. "Aquinas and Llull on Truths Believed and Demonstratively Known." Fifteenth International Conference on Patristic Mediaeval and Renaissance Studies. Villanova University, Villanova, PA: September 21-23, 1990.

3904 Bazán, Bernardo Carlos. "The Turning Point of Thomas' Anthropology: Questions Disputate *De Anima*." American Philosophical Association, Eastern Division: December 1989.

3905 Bazán, Bernardo Carlos. "Thirteenth Century Controversies: Concerning the Intellect: Siger of Brabant and Thomas Aquinas." American Philosophical Association, Pacific. San Francisco: 1980.

3906 Berquist, Duane. "Aquinas and the First Errors About the Modes of Procedure." Ninth International Conference on Patristic Mediaeval and Renaissance Studies. Villanova University, Villanova, PA: September 21-23, 1984.

3907 Boyle, William John. "Process Philosophy: A Thomistic Evaluation." ACPA Round Table of Philosophy. New York: April 16, 1988.

3908 Braine, Stephen. "Analogy in the Thirteenth and Fourteenth Centuries." Society for Medieval and Renaissance Philosophy. American Philosophical Association Division Meeting. Boston: December 1990.

3909 Brock, Stephen Louis. "What is a First Practical Principle? St. Thomas' Doctrine of the Habit of First Moral Principles—Background and Meaning." Ninth International Conference on Patristic Mediaeval and Renaissance Studies. Villanova University, Villanova, PA: September 21-23, 1984.

3910 Brock, Stephen Louis. "The Setting of the Account of Natural Law in *Summa Theologiae*." Thirteenth International Conference on Patristic Mediaeval and Renaissance Studies. Villanova University, Villanova, PA: September 23-25, 1988.

3911 Bronson, Larry L. "My Heart is Harden'd: Marlowe's Dr. Faustus and the Thomistic Concept of *Acedia*." Fifth Mid-Atlantic States Conference: Patristic Mediaeval and Renaissance Studies. Villanova University, Villanova, PA: October 3-5, 1980.

3912 Brown, Montague. "Aquinas on the Resurrection of the Body." Thirteenth International Conference on Patristic Mediaeval and Renaissance Studies. Villanova University, Villanova, PA: September 23-25, 1988.

3913 Brown, Stephen F. "Analogy in the Thirteenth and Fourteenth Centuries." Society for Medieval and Renaissance Philosophy. American Philosophical Association, Eastern Division. Boston: December 1990.

3914 Caputo, John D. "Heidegger and Thomas Aquinas: A Confrontation." American Philosophical Association, Eastern Division 53. New York: 1979.

3915 Carl, Maria Theresa. "Law and Virtue in St. Thomas' Ethics." Fourteenth International Conference on Patristic Mediaeval and Renaissance Studies. Villanova University, Villanova, PA: September 15-17, 1989.

3916 Cizewski, Wanda. "The Concept of Eternal Law in Thomas Aquinas and Richard Hooker." Thirteenth International Conference on Patristic Mediaeval and Renaissance Studies. Villanova University, Villanova, PA: September 23-25, 1988.

3917 Clarke, W. Norris. "Thomas Aquinas on *Romans* 1:20 and the Possibility of a Natural Theology." Society of Christian Philosophers. American Philosophical Association, Eastern Division. Washington, DC: March 1988, 1989.

3918 Corrigan, Kevin. "Light and Metaphor in Plotinus (Robert Grosseteste) and St. Thomas Aquinas." Thirteenth International Conference on Patristic Mediaeval and Renaissance Studies. Villanova University, Villanova, PA: September 23-25, 1988.

3919 Dennehy, Raymond. "The Changing and the Unchanging in St. Thomas' Natural Law Doctrine." Eighth International Conference on Patristic Mediaeval and Renaissance Studies. Villanova University, Villanova, PA: September 21-23, 1983.

3920 Donnelly, Dorothy F. "The Impact of Thomas Aquinas' Thought on the Reappearance of Utopian Speculation in the Renaissance." Fifth Mid-Atlantic States Conference: Patristic Mediaeval and Renaissance Studies. Villanova University, Villanova, PA: October 3-5, 1980.

3921 Donnelly, Dorothy F. "The Idea of Membership in Augustine and Aquinas." Twelfth International Conference on Patristic Mediaeval and Renaissance Studies. Villanova University, Villanova, PA: October 16-18, 1986.

3922 Drost, Mark P. "Intentionality in Aquinas' Theory of the Emotions." American Philosophical Association, Eastern Division: December 28, 1989.

3923 Drost, Mark P. "Intentionality in Aquinas' Theory of the Emotions." ACPA Round Table of Philosophy. New York: March 10, 1990.

3924 Etzwiler, James P. "The Natural in Aquinas' Natural Law." Eighth International Conference on Patristic Mediaeval and Renaissance Studies. Villanova University, Villanova, PA: September 21-23, 1983.

3925 Fashbaugh, Jack. "Form and Two Related Concepts in the Thomist and Bonaventurian Models of Creation." Fifth Mid-Atlantic States Conference: Patristic Mediaeval and Renaissance Studies. Villanova University, Villanova, PA: October 3-5, 1980.

3926 Fay, Thomas A. "Thomas Aquinas on the Justification of Revolution." Fifteenth International Conference on Patristic Mediaeval and Renaissance Studies. Villanova University, Villanova, PA: September 21-23, 1990.

3927 Ford, Lewis S. "Process and Thomist Views Concerning Divine Perfection." American Philosophical Association Meeting, Eastern Division. Washington, DC: 1985.

3928 Frost, William P. "The Catholic Imagination of Thomas Aquinas." Sixth International Conference on Patristic Mediaeval and Renaissance Studies. Villanova University, Villanova, PA: September 25-27, 1981.

3929 Gulley, Anthony D. "*De Magistro* of Saint Thomas Aquinas." Twelfth International Conference on Patristic Mediaeval and Renaissance Studies. Villanova University, Villanova, PA: October 16-18, 1986.

3930 Hall, Pamela. "Aristotelian Practical Wisdom and Thomistic Natural Law." American Philosophical Association, Eastern Division. December 1989.

3931 Hanagan, John J. "*Via Efficacissima*: St. Thomas' Most Powerful Way to God." Fourteenth International Conference on Patristic Mediaeval and Renaissance Studies. Villanova University, Villanova, PA: September 15-17, 1989.

3932 Hankey, Wayne J. "Theology as System and as Science: Proclus and Thomas Aquinas." Sixth International Conference on Patristic Mediaeval and Renaissance Studies. Villanova University, Villanova, PA: September 25-27, 1981.

3933 Herrera, Robert A. "Maimonides and St. Thomas on the Tetragrammaton: The Exodus of Philosophy?" Fifth Mid-Atlantic States Conference: Patristic Mediaeval and Renaissance Studies. Villanova University, Villanova, PA: October 3-5, 1980.

3934 Ingardia, Richard. "Thomas Aquinas' Discussion of *Scientia Media*." Seventh International Conference on Patristic Mediaeval and Renaissance Studies. Villanova University, Villanova, PA: September 24-26, 1982.

3935 Ingardia, Richard. "Aquinas' Doctrine of Common Nature and the Morality of the Moral Act Itself." Eighth International Conference on Patristic Mediaeval and Renaissance Studies. Villanova University, Villanova, PA: September 21-23, 1983.

3936 Keenan, James F. "Charity or Prudence, Goodness or Rightness." International St. Thomas Society. American Philosophical Association, Eastern Division. Washington, DC: December 1989.

3937 Knasas, John F. X. "*Ad Mentem Thomae* Does Natural Philosophy Prove God?" Twelfth International Conference on Patristic Mediaeval and Renaissance Studies. Villanova University, Villanova, PA: October 16-18, 1986.

3938 Knasas, John F. X. "Transcendental Thomism and the Thomistic Texts." Thirteenth International Conference on Patristic Mediaeval and Renaissance Studies. Villanova University, Villanova, PA: September 23-25, 1988.

3939 Knasas, John F. X. "Does Gilson Theologize Thomistic Metaphysics?" Fourteenth International Conference on Patristic Mediaeval and Renaissance Studies. Villanova University, Villanova, PA: September 15-17, 1989.

3940 Kondoleon, Theodore J. "Augustine and Aquinas on Divine Foreknowledge and Free Will." Twelfth International Conference on Patristic Mediaeval and Renaissance Studies. Villanova University, Villanova, PA: October 16-18, 1986.

3941 Kondoleon, Theodore J. "A Critical Approach of the IVth Way in Light of Some Recent Criticism." Fourteenth International Conference on Patristic Mediaeval and Renaissance Studies. Villanova University, Villanova, PA: September 15-17, 1989.

3942 Koterski, Joseph W. "Ulrich of Strasbourg and Thomas Aquinas: A Comparison of Their Treatises *De Bono*." Thirteenth International Conference on Patristic Mediaeval and Renaissance Studies. Villanova University, Villanova, PA: September 23-25, 1988.

3943 Lauder, Robert. "Phenomenology, Thomism, Personalism and the Meaning of a World Community." ACPA Round Table of Philosophy. New York: November 3, 1990.

3944 Leftow, Brian. "Aquinas on Anselm." Ninth International Conference on Patristic Mediaeval and Renaissance Studies. Villanova University, Villanova, PA: September 21-23, 1984.

3945 Leftow, Brian. "Anselm and Aquinas on Impeccability." American Philosophical Association Meeting, Central Division. Chicago, April 28, 1985.

3946 Lewis, John H. "Secularization of Natural Law." Thirteenth International Conference on Patristic Mediaeval and Renaissance Studies. Villanova University, Villanova, PA: September 23-25, 1988.

3947 Lewis, John Underwood. "Epistemological in Aquinas' Treatment of the Relation Between the Old Law and the Natural Law." Eighth International Conference on Patristic Mediaeval and Renaissance Studies. Villanova University, Villanova, PA: September 21-23, 1983.

3948 Lewis, John Underwood. "John Finnis on Some Alleged Inadequacies in Aquinas' Theory of Natural Law." Ninth International Conference on Patristic Mediaeval and Renaissance Studies. Villanova University, Villanova, PA: September 21-23, 1984.

3949 Lewis, John Underwood. "On the Secularization of Natural Law Theory." Thirteenth International Conference on Patristic Mediaeval and Renaissance Studies. Villanova University, Villanova, PA: September 23-25, 1988.

3950 Lisska, Anthony. "Aquinas on the Role of Emotion in Moral Judgment and Activity." Society for Medieval and Renaissance Philosophy. American Philosophical Association Meeting, Central Division. Chicago: April 28, 1985.

3951 Lisska, Anthony. "God, Aquinas and Natural Law." American Philosophical Association Meeting, Central Division. St. Louis: May 3, 1986.

3952 MacDonald, Scott. "The Role of Ultimate Ends in Practical Reasoning: Aquinas' Aristotelian Moral Psychology and Anscombe's Fallacy." American Philosophical Association Meeting, Central Division. Chicago: April 28, 1985.

3953 MacDonald, Scott. "Demons, Doxastic, Voluntarism, and Aquinas' Account of Faith." Colloquium, Medieval Philosophy. American Philosophical Association, Eastern Division 87: December 29, 1990.

3954 Martin, James T. H. "Aquinas' *Intellectus Agens* and Aristotle's *Nous Poietikos*." ACPA Round Table of Philosophy: April 13, 1990.

3955 McCool, Gerald A. "The Tradition of St. Thomas: Its Problems and Promise." Lecture. ACPA Round Table of Philosophy. New York: April 4, 1987.

3956 McCord, Adams, and John Wippel. "Truth in Aquinas and Ockham." American Philosophical Association, Eastern Division. Washington, DC: March 1989.

3957 McGrade, S. Stephen. "Aquinas, Oresme, and Richard Hooker as Political Aristotelians." Thirteenth International Conference on Patristic Mediaeval and Renaissance Studies. Villanova University, Villanova, PA: September 23-25, 1988.

3958 Mournion, William. "Aquinas on Revolution." ACPA Round Table of Philosophy. New York: November 7, 1989.

3959 Nota, John. "The Importance and Relevance of Knowledge by Connaturality." International St. Thomas Society. American Philosophical Association, Eastern Division: December 1990.

3960 O'Neil, Patrick. "A Re-examination of the Augustinian and Thomistic Approaches to the Role of Obedience to Just Authority in the Natural Law Tradition." Fifth Mid-Atlantic States Conference: Patristic Mediaeval and Renaissance Studies. Villanova University, Villanova, PA: October 3-5, 1980.

3961 Owens, Joseph. "Thomistic Distinctions Between Essence and Existence." International Thomas Aquinas Society. American Philosophical Association Meeting, Eastern Division. Washington, DC: December 28, 1985.

3962 Ramos, Alice. "Activity and Finality in St. Thomas Aquinas." ACPA Round Table of Philosophy. New York: November 7, 1989.

3963 Ramos, Alice. "Aquinas on the Divine Ideas and the Truth of Creation." Fifteenth International Conference on Patristic Mediaeval and Renaissance Studies. Villanova University, Villanova, PA: September 21-23, 1990.

3964 Ramos, Alice. "The Divine Ideas and the Intelligibility of Creation: A Way Toward Universal Signification in Aquinas." ACPA Round Table of Philosophy. New York: November 3, 1990.

3965 Redpath, Peter. "The Moral Teaching of Aquinas and Bonaventure." Fifth Mid-Atlantic States Conference: Patristic Mediaeval and Renaissance Studies. Villanova University, Villanova, PA: October 3-5, 1980.

3966 Redpath, Peter. "How Did the Principle of Double Effect Get Lost in St. Thomas?" Eighth International Conference on Patristic Mediaeval and Renaissance Studies. Villanova University, Villanova, PA: September 21-23, 1983.

3967 Reilly, James P. "Some Reflections on the Foundations of St. Thomas' Theory of Natural Law." Ninth International Conference on Patristic Mediaeval and Renaissance Studies. Villanova University, Villanova, PA: September 21-23, 1984.

3968 Reilly, James P. "Eternal Law, the Ground of Natural Law." Thirteenth International Conference on Patristic Mediaeval and Renaissance Studies. Villanova University, Villanova, PA: September 23-25, 1988.

3969 Reilly, James P. "The Articulation of the Precepts of the Natural Law." Thirteenth International Conference on Patristic Mediaeval and Renaissance Studies. Villanova University, Villanova, PA: September 23-25, 1988.

3970 Riedl, John O. "Thomas Aquinas' Commentary on the Fourth Proposition of the *Book of Causes* Appraised as a Measure of His Mature Understanding of Platonist Philosophy." Sixth International Conference on Patristic Mediaeval and Renaissance Studies. Villanova University, Villanova, PA: September 25-27, 1981.

3971 Ross, James F. "Aquinas on Belief and Knowledge." American Philosophical Association, Eastern Division, New York: December 28, 1984.

3972 Schindler, David. "St. Thomas & Whitehead: A Dialogue on Existence and the Unity of the Universe." American Philosophical Association, Eastern Division. Washington, DC: 1981.

3973 Schultz, Janice Lee. "Aquinas on Predication and Moral Principles." Twelfth International Conference on Patristic Mediaeval and Renaissance Studies. Villanova University, Villanova, PA: October 16-18, 1986.

3974 Schultz, Janice Lee. "Goodness, Intention, and Willing Freely in Aquinas." Thirteenth International Conference on Patristic Mediaeval and Renaissance Studies. Villanova University, Villanova, PA: September 23-25, 1988.

3975 Schultz, Janice Lee. "On Aquinas on Boethius: *De Hebdomadibus*." Fourteenth International Conference on Patristic Mediaeval and Renaissance Studies. Villanova University, Villanova, PA: September 15-17, 1989.

3976 Scully, Robert A. "Aquinas' State: A Household Writ Large?" Fifth Mid-Atlantic States Conference: Patristic Mediaeval and Renaissance Studies. Villanova University, Villanova, PA: October 3-5, 1980.

3977 Sommers, Mary C. "Pseudo-Dionysius and Aquinas' Polemic of Perfection." International Society for Neoplatonic Studies. American Philosophical Association Meeting, Central Division. Chicago: April 27, 1985.

3978 Spitzer, Robert. "Toward a Thomistic Metaphysics of Time." International St. Thomas Society. American Philosophical Association Eastern Division Meeting: December 1989.

3979 Spoerl, Joseph. "Practical Truth in Aquinas." Fourteenth International Conference on Patristic Mediaeval and Renaissance Studies. Villanova University, Villanova, PA: September 15-17, 1989.

3980 Staley, Kevin Michael. "Natural Law and the Community of Being." Ninth International Conference on Patristic Mediaeval and Renaissance Studies. Villanova University, Villanova, PA: September 21-23, 1984.

3981 Staley, Kevin Michael. "Parts and Whole; Another Look/Universals in Aquinas." Fourteenth International Conference on Patristic Mediaeval and Renaissance Studies. Villanova University, Villanova, PA: September 15-17, 1989.

3982 Strasser, Michael W. "On the Virtue of Religion in Aquinas." Fifteenth International Conference on Patristic Mediaeval and Renaissance Studies. Villanova University, Villanova, PA: September 21-23, 1990.

3983 Sweeney, Eileen Carroll. "*Resolutio* and the Dialectical Structure of Reasoning in Aquinas." Fourteenth International Conference on Patristic Mediaeval and Renaissance Studies. Villanova University, Villanova, PA: September 15-17, 1989.

3984 Sweeney, Leo. "Thomas Aquinas, Immanuel Kant, Edmund Husserl: Christian Philosophers?" Fourteenth International Conference on Patristic Mediaeval and Renaissance Studies. Villanova University, Villanova, PA: September 15-17, 1989.

3985 Synan, Edward A. "Chaos and Order in Thomism." General address. Fourteenth International Conference on Patristic Mediaeval and Renaissance Studies. Villanova University, Villanova, PA: September 15, 1989.

3986 Wawrykow, Joseph. "On Merit: Thomas Aquinas and the *Divina Ordinatio*." Thirteenth International Conference on Patristic Mediaeval and Renaissance Studies. Villanova University, Villanova, PA: September 23-25, 1988.

3987 Weithman, Paul Jude. "Thomas Aquinas on Private Property and Acts of Injustice." Society of Christian Philosophers. American Philosophical Association: Pacific Division. March 1989.

3988 Westra, Laura. "The Soul's Noetic Ascent to the One in Plotinus and to God in Aquinas: A Comparison." American Philosophical Association, Eastern Division. Washington, DC: 1981.

3989 Wippel, John F. "Unreal Possibles in Thirteenth Century Ontology." American Philosophical Association, Eastern Division. Boston: 1980.

3990 Woznicki, Andrew Nicholas. "Being and Becoming According to St. Thomas and William of Ockham." Twelfth International Conference on Patristic Mediaeval and Renaissance Studies. Villanova University, Villanova, PA: October 16-18, 1986.

3991 Woznicki, Andrew Nicholas. "Realistic Foundations of Existentialist Metaphysics of Being." American Philosophical Association Meeting, Pacific Division. Oakland, CA: March 22, 1989.

IV. DISSERTATIONS

A. ENGLISH

3992 Adams, Donald E. I. "Love and Morality in Socrates, Plato, Aristotle and Aquinas." Diss. Cornell University. Ann Arbor, MI: UMI, 1989.

3993 Andrews, Robert R. "Peter of Auvergne's Commentary on Aristotle's *Categories*: Ed., Trans., and Analysis." Diss. Cornell University. *DAI* 49(1988) Ann Harbor, MI: UMI: 02A. 8804534.

3994 Anslow, Thomas Chenowith. "*Intellectus* as the Proper Mode of Metaphysics According to St. Thomas Aquinas." Diss. University of Toronto. *DAI* 45(1983) Ann Harbor, MI: UMI: 02A. 0553863 (not available).

3995 Armenti, Joseph. "Elements of Divine Power in the Old Testament: A Philosophical and Comparative Study." Diss. Dropsie College. 1982.

3996 Baasten, Matthew Jacob. "Pride in the *Moralia* of Gregory the Great." Diss. University of Notre Dame. *DAI* 44(1984) Ann Arbor, MI: UMI: 11A. 8403961.

3997 Bagnall, J. J. "Aquinas' Theory of the Rational Soul in the *Summa Contra Gentiles*." Diss. University of London. 1983.

3998 Bagus, L. "Religious Language According to Ian Thomas Ramsey in the Light of St. Thomas." Diss. Pontifical University Greg. 1986.

3999 Baldner, Steven Earl. "Four Hitherto Unedited Questiones on Creation Attributed to St. Bonaventure." Diss. University of Toronto. *DAI* 43(1982) Ann Arbor, MI: UMI: 12A. 0551386 (not available).

4000 Barad, Judith A. "Consent: The Means to an Active Faith According to St. Thomas Aquinas." Diss. Northwestern University. *DAI* 45(1984): 07A. Ann Arbor, MI: UMI. 8423203.

4001 Bartlett, Dennis Alan. "The Evolution of the Philosophical and Theological Elements of the Jesuit *Ratio Studiorum*: An Historical Study." Diss. University of San Francisco. *DAI* 46(1984) Ann Arbor, MI: UMI: 03A. 8509196.

4002 Blythe, James Morgan. "Ideal Government and the Mixed Constitution." Diss. Cornell University. *DAI* 48(1987) Ann Arbor, MI: UMI: 05A. 8715587.

4003 Bonjean, Sr. Ronald Dean. "Fundamental Option in Theology of Karl Rahner and Its Relationship to Moral Development." Diss. Marquette University. Ann Arbor, MI: 1983.

4004 Boyle, William John. "Weakness of Will and Self-control According to St. Thomas Aquinas." Diss. University of Toronto. *DAI* 44(1982) Ann Arbor, MI: UMI: 03A. 0551890 (not available).

4005 Brett, Stephen Francis. "The Justification of Slavery: A Comparative Study of the Use of Concepts of *Jus* and *Dominium* by Thomas Aquinas, Francisco de Vitoria and Domingo de Soto in Relationship to Slavery." Diss. The Catholic University of America. *DAI* 48(1987) Ann Arbor, MI: UMI: 03A. 8712919.

4006 Brock, Stephen Louis. "The Legal Character of Natural Law According to St. Thomas Aquinas." Diss. University of Toronto. *DAI* 50(1988) Ann Arbor, MI: UMI: 01A. 0564912 (not available).

4007 Brockette, Ann Harrington. "The Mass as Metaphor: A Study of the Aesthetic Nature of the Eucharistic Liturgy." Diss. The University of Texas at Dallas. *DAI* 46(1985) Ann Arbor, MI: UMI: 11A. 529722.

4008 Broderick, David Gregory. "Objectivity: Thomas Aquinas and Karl Popper." Diss. Boston College. *DAI* 44(1984) Ann Arbor, MI: UMI: 11A. 8405171.

4009 Brown, Montague. "Permanent Creation: A Study in the Thought of St. Thomas Aquinas." Diss. Boston College. *DAI* 46(1986) Ann Arbor, MI: UMI: 12A. 8604109.

4010 Brush, Jack Edmund. "Language and Verification in Thomas Aquinas: A Contribution to Fundamental Theology." Diss. Zürich University 1984.

4011 Butterworth, Edward Joseph. "The Doctrine of the Trinity in Saint Thomas Aquinas and Saint Bonaventure." Diss. Fordham University. *DAI* 46(1985) Ann Arbor, MI: UMI: 08A. 8521405.

4012 Canale, Fernando Luis. "Toward a Criticism of Theological Reason: Time and Timelessness as Primordial Presuppositions." Diss. Andrews University. *DAI* 44(1983): 04A. AAC8318612.

4013 Carl, Maria Theresa. "The First Principles of Natural Law Ethics: A Study of the Moral Theories of Aristotle and Saint Thomas Aquinas." Diss. Marquette University. *DAI* 50(1989) Ann Arbor, MI: UMI: 12A. 9014051.

4014 Carley, Moira Teresa. "Bernard J. F. Lonergan, S. J.: On Teaching." Diss. Harvard University. *DAI* 50(1989) Ann Arbor, MI: UMI: 11A. 9009834.

4015 Casey, C. J. "The Enigma of Revealed Discourse: A Study of Development in Aquinas's Application of the Phrase *per Revelationem Divinam* to Theological Discourse, and the Relevance of This to Recent Discussions of the Problem of Reference in Theology." Diss. Oxford University. *Indexes to Theses* 31(1981).

4016 Cashore, Joseph Michael. "The Proof of God's Existence in the Work of Joseph Marechal." Diss. McMaster University (Canada). *DAI* 41(1980) Ann Arbor, MI: UMI: 09A. 0534514.

4017 Celano, Anthony John. "Aristotle's Concept of Happiness in the 13th Century." Diss. University of Toronto. *DAI* 44(1980) Ann Arbor, MI: UMI: 02A. 0551397 (not available).

4018 Christou, Jacovas. "The Influence of Aspects of the Common Law on the Political Thought of Richard Hooker." Diss. Council for National Academic Awards (United Kingdom). *DAI* 50(1988) Ann Arbor, MI: UMI: 08A. 86620.

4019 Cullinan, E. G. "Contemplation as the Basis of the Christian Life in St. Thomas' treatise on the New Law." Diss. Academia Alphonsiana. 1986.

4020 Davis, Richard A. "Hegel's Concept of Property." Diss. Marquette University. *DAI* 47(1985) Ann Arbor, MI: UMI: 01A. 8604951.

4021 Dillon, Thomas Edward. "The Real Distinction Between Essence and Existence in the Thought of St. Thomas Aquinas." Diss. University of Notre Dame. *DA* 37(1977) Ann Arbor, MI: UMI: 03A. 7719521.

4022 Dobbs-Weinstein, Idit. "The Concept of Providence in the Thought of Moses Maimonides and St. Thomas Aquinas." Diss. University of Toronto. *DAI* 48(1987) Ann Arbor, MI: UMI: 12A. 0562190 (not available).

4023 Donart, Arthur Charles. "Some Implications of the Philosophy of St. Thomas Aquinas for the Teaching of English in Secondary Schools." Diss. University of Illinois at Urbana—Champaign. *DAI* 39(1978) Ann Arbor, MI: UMI: 12A. 7913433.

4024 Downey, Michael. "An Investigation of the Concept of Person in the Spirituality of *L'Arche* as Developed in the Writings of Jean Vanier." Diss. The Catholic University of America. *DAI* 43(1982) Ann Arbor, MI: UMI: 07A. 8226676.

4025 Duffey, Michael Kerrigan. "A Study of the Principle of Double Effect, Its Evaluation in Contemporary Philosophical Ethics and Catholic Moral Theology, and Especially Its Role in the Thought of Richard McCormick." Diss. University of Notre Dame. *DAI* 41(1981) Ann Arbor, MI: UMI: 11A. 8109103.

4026 Duncan, S. E. "Natural Law and the Diversity of Morals." Diss. Aberdeen University. *Index of Theses* 35(1984): 524.

4027 Dunne, Thomas Aquinas. "Lonergan on Social Progress and Community: A Developmental Study." Diss. Institute of Christian Thought, University of St. Michael's College (Canada). *DAI* 43(1975) Ann Arbor, MI: UMI: 04A. 8219863.

4028 Edwards, Steven Anthony. "The Inward Turn: Justice and Responsibility in Religious Ethics of Thomas Aquinas." Diss. Stanford University. *DAI* 42(1981) Ann Arbor, MI: UMI: 05A. 8124057.

4029 Engram, Ann Toms. "Renaissance Humanism and the Decline of the Medieval Contemplative Ideal: An Intellectual History of the *Via Contemplativa/vita Activa* Debate." Diss. The Florida State University. *DAI* 46(1984) Ann Arbor, MI: UMI: 01A. 8505294.

4030 Ess, Charles Melvin. "Analogy in the Critical Works: Kant's Transcendental Philosophy as Analytical Thought." Diss. The Pennsylvania State University. 1983.

4031 Farrell, J. "St. Thomas Aquinas' Treatment of the Gifts of the Holy Spirit in the *Summa Theologiae*." Diss. Edinburgh University. *Index to Theses* 35. 3(1985): 1067-1068.

4032 Farthing, John Lee. "Images of St. Thomas Aquinas in the Academic Theology of Gabriel Biel." Diss. Duke University. *DAI* 40(1978) Ann Arbor, MI: UMI: 01A. 7915577.

4033 Ferrara, Dennis Michael. "*Imago Dei*: Knowledge, Love, and Bodiliness in the *Summa Theologiae* of St. Thomas Aquinas— A Study in Development and Ambiguity." Diss. The Catholic University of America. *DAI* 49(1988) Ann Arbor, MI: UMI: 11A. 8903205.

4034 Figurski, Leszek Stanley. "Final Cause and Its Relations to Intelligence in St. Thomas Aquinas." Diss. Fordham University. *DA* 38(1977) Ann Arbor, MI: UMI. 7714892.

4035 Finan, William Joseph. "Shame and Grace in the Context of Questions of Privacy." Diss. Yale University. *DAI* 41(1980) Ann Arbor, MI: UMI: 06A. 8026989.

4036 Flint, Thomas Patrick. "Divine Freedom." Diss. University of Notre Dame. *DAI* 41(1980) Ann Arbor, MI: UMI: 03A. 8020959.

4037 Fortuna, Joseph John. "Two Approaches to the Role of Language in Sacramental Efficacy Compared: Thomas Aquinas in the *Summa Theologiae* and Louis-Marie Chauvet." Diss. The Catholic University of America. *DAI* 50(1989) Ann Arbor, MI: UMI: 04A. 8913818.

4038 Foster, David Ruel. "A Study and Critique of Thomas Aquinas' Arguments for the Immateriality of the Intellect." Diss. The Catholic University of America. *DAI* 49(1988) Ann Arbor, MI: UMI: 11A. 8905341.

4039 Froelich, Gregory Lawrence. "Thomas Aquinas on Friendship and Political Common Good." Diss. University of Notre Dame. *DAI* 49(1988) Ann Arbor, MI: UMI: 08A. 8821045.

4040 Gallagher, David Michael. "Thomas Aquinas on the Causes of Human Choice." Diss. The Catholic University of America. *DAI* 50(1989) Ann Arbor, MI: UMI: 04A. 8912974.

4041 Geraghty, Richard Patrick. "The Object of Moral Philosophy According to St. Thomas Aquinas." Diss. University of Toronto. *DAI* 42(1980) Ann Arbor, MI: UMI: 01A. 0535207 (not available).

4042 Girodat, Clair Raymond. "The Development of Man as a Person According to the Philosophy of St. Thomas Aquinas." Diss. University of Toronto. *DAI* 39(1978) Ann Arbor, MI: UMI: 3A (Not Available).

4043 Griffin, James J. "*Caritas* and *Ren*: A Comparative Study of Thomas Aquinas and Zhu Xi in the Contexts of Their Traditions." Diss. Edinburgh University (United Kingdom). *DAI* 50(1989) Ann Arbor, MI: UMI: 02A. 85025.

4044 Guagliaro, Vincent Anthony. "The Future of an Origin: Being and God in the Philosophy of Martin Heidegger." Diss. Graduate Theological Union. 1981.

4045 Haladus, Jerome Joachim. "The Negative Judgement of Separation According to Saint Thomas Aquinas' *Commentary on the De Trinitate* of Boethius." Diss. P. U. S. Thomae. Roma, 1979.

4046 Hall, Pamela. "Natural Law, *Phronesis* and *Prudentia*: Is Aquinas' Natural Law Theory Compatible with His Aristotelianism." Diss. Vanderbilt University. 1988.

4047 Hankey, Wayne J. "The Structure of the First Forty-five Questions of the *Summa Theologiae* of St. Thomas Aquinas." Diss. Oxford University. *Index to Theses* 32-33. 115(1981): 4.

4048 Harak, G. Simon. "The Role of the Passions in the Formation of Character." Diss. University of Notre Dame. *DAI* 47(1986) Ann Arbor, MI: UMI: 05A. 8616932.

4049 Hartmann, Jr., Herbert Edward. "St. Thomas and Prudence." Diss. University of Toronto. *DA* 40. 12(1980): 6310A.

4050 Hayden, Mary R. "Love and the First Principles of St. Thomas' Natural Law." Diss. University of St. Thomas. *DA* 50(1988): 7. 2. 8924435.

4051 Healy, Paul Joseph. "Philosophical Truth and Its Relation to Empirical Science." Diss. Pennsylvania State University. 1984.

4052 Henninger, Mark Gerald. "Some Late Medieval Theories of the Category of Relation." Diss. University of California, Los Angeles. *DAI* 45(1984) Ann Arbor, MI: UMI: 06A. 8420188.

4053 Hibbs, Thomas Stewart. "The Pedagogy of Law and Virtue in the *Summa Theologia*." Diss. University of Notre Dame. *DAI* 48(1987) Ann Arbor, MI: UMI: 03A. 8712944.

4054 Houser, Rollen Edward. "Thomas Aquinas on Transcendental Unity: Scholastic and Aristotelian Predecessors." Diss. University of Toronto. *DAI* 42(1981) Ann Arbor, MI: UMI: 10A. 0536803.

4055 Hughes, Christopher Mark. "On a Complex Theory of a Simple God: Limitative and Ampliative Properties in Aquinas' Theology." Diss. University of Pittsburgh. 1983.

4056 Hunter, A. Richard. "Analogy and Beauty: Thomistic Reflections on the Transcendentals." Diss. Bryn Mawr College. *DA* 39(1978).

4057 Ihejiofor, T. "Freedom and the Natural Inclination of the Will According to Saint Thomas Aquinas." Diss. Katholieke Universiteit Leuven. *DA* 51(1990): 2.

4058 Incandela, Joseph Michael. "Aquinas' Lost Legacy: God's Practical Knowledge and Situated Human Freedom." Diss. Princeton University. *DAI* 47(1986) Ann Arbor, MI: UMI: 09A. 8629434.

4059 Jarnevic, Donald Peter. "Faith and Knowledge: An Examination of Aquinas Theory of Theology." Diss. The University of Pittsburgh. 1987.

4060 Jordan, Mark D. "Creation and Intelligibility in Thomas Aquinas: A Reading of the *Contra Gentiles*." Diss. The University of Texas at Austin. 1977.

4061 Kaiser, Kenneth John. "A Critique of Harry V. Jaffa's Study: Thomism and Aristotelianism." Diss. Claremont Graduate School. *DAI* 47(1986) Ann Arbor, MI: UMI: 02A. 8607829.

4062 Kay, Judith Webb. "Human Nature and the Natural Law Tradition." Diss. Graduate Theological Union. *DAI* 49(1988) Ann Arbor, MI: UMI: 07A. 8816910.

4063 Keenan, James F. "Being Good and Doing the Right in Saint Thomas' *Summa Theologia*." Diss. Pontificia Universitas Gregoriana (Vatican). *DAI* 50(1988) Ann Arbor, MI: UMI: 02C (not available).

4064 Kennedy, Robert George. "Thomas Aquinas and the Literal Sense of Sacred Scripture." Diss. University of Notre Dame. *DAI* 46(1985) Ann Arbor, MI: UMI: 05A. 8515220.

4065 Kent, Bonnie Dorrick. "Aristotle and the Franciscans: Gerald Odonis' Commentary on the *Nichomachean Ethics*." Diss. Columbia University. *DAI* 45(1984) Ann Arbor, MI: UMI: 10A. 8429900.

4066 Kim, Chung Gun. "Thomistic Parallels in the Epistemology of Coleridge." Diss. University of Missouri, Columbia. 1983.

4067 Kolbeck, Kevin Dean. "The *Prima Via*: Natural Philosophy's Approach to God." Diss. University of Notre Dame. *DAI* 50(1989) Ann Arbor, MI: UMI: 7. 8923638.

4068 Kries, Douglas Lee. "Friar Thomas and the Politics of Sinai: An Inquiry Concerning the Status of the Mosaic Law in the Christian Theology of Thomas Aquinas." Diss. Boston College. *DAI* 49(1988) Ann Arbor, MI: UMI: 11A. 8904014.

4069 Kuss, Karen Marie. "Obedience as a Virtue: A Thomistic Consideration." Diss. The University of Notre Dame. 1990-1991.

4070 Laird, Walter Roy. "The *Scientiae Mediae* in Medieval Commentaries on Aristotle's *Posterior Analytics*." Diss. University of Toronto. *DAI* 45(1983) Ann Arbor, MI: UMI: 01A. 8328243.

4071 Landen, Laura L. "Thomas Aquinas and the Dynamism of Natural Substances." Diss. The Catholic University of America. *DAI* 46(1985) Ann Arbor, MI: UMI: 02A. 8507813.

4072 Langan, John Patrick. "Desire, Beatitude and the Basis of Morality in Thomas Aquinas." Diss. University of Michigan. *DAI* 40(1979) Ann Arbor, MI: UMI: 05A. 25181.

4073 Langston, Douglas Charles. "When Willing Becomes Knowing: The Voluntarist Analysis of God Omniscience." Diss. University of California, Irvine. 1982.

4074 Laumakis, Stephen J. "The *Sensus Communis* and the Unity of Perception According to Saint Thomas Aquinas." Diss. The University of Notre Dame. 1990-1991.

4075 Lee, William Patrick. "The Natural Law and the Decalogue in St. Thomas Aquinas and Blessed John Duns Scotus." Diss. Marquette University. *DAI* 41(1980) Ann Arbor, MI: UMI: 09A. 8104807.

4076 Lehrberger, James Joseph. "Incarnate Intellect: Man's Soul-body Union According to the *Pars Prima* of St. Thomas Aquinas' *Summa Theologiae*, Questions Seventy-five and Seventy-six." Diss. The University of Dallas. *DAI* 44(1983) Ann Arbor, MI: UMI: 02A. 8315048.

4077 Ling, Daniel Hok-Pin. "Virtue and Obligation in Thomas Aquinas and Immanuel Kant." Diss. Drew University. *DAI* 42(1981) Ann Arbor, MI: UMI: 03A. 8119748.

4078 Little, Joyce A. "*Esse*/essence and Grace: A Theological Inquiry Into Thomist Methodology." Diss. Marquette University. *DAI* 45(1984) Ann Arbor, MI: UMI: 07A. 8422823.

4079 Macierowski, Edward Michael. "The Thomistic Critique of Avicennian Emanationism from the Viewpoint of the Divine Simplicity, with Special Reference to the *Summa Contra Gentiles*." Diss. University of Toronto. *DA* 40(1979): 6312A.

4080 Malloy, Michael Patrick. "Civil Authority in Medieval Philosophy: Selected Commentaries of Aquinas and Bonaventure." Diss. Georgetown University. 1983.

4081 Maloney, Anne Mercedes. "Gabriel Marcel's Critique of the Thomist Proofs for God's Existence." Diss. Marquette University. *DAI* 49(1988) Ann Arbor, MI: UMI: 12A. 8904274.

4082 Manding, Benito O. "An Analysis of the *Quinque Viae*: A Descriptive Analysis of Aquinas' Proofs of God's Existence in the Context of Current Interpretations." Diss. Syracuse University. 1977.

4083 Martin, Christopher F. J. "A Distinction Between Different Notions of Existence in the Writings of St. Thomas Aquinas and Its Use to Distinguish Logic from Metaphysics." Diss. Oxford University. 1984.

4084 Martz, John Robert. "The Implications for Religious Language in the Thought of Herman Dooyeweerd as Contrasted with Thomas Aquinas and Paul Tillich." Diss. Drew University. *DAI*: 07A. Ann Arbor, MI: UMI, 1988. 8817636.

4085 Massobrio, Simona Emilia. "Aristotelian Matter as Understood by St. Thomas Aquinas and John Duns Scotus." Diss. McGill University. 1990-1991.

4086 McCartney, James Joseph. "The Relationship Between Wojtyla's Personalism and the Contemporary Debate Over the Ontological Status of Human Embryological Life." Diss. Georgetown University. *DAI* 42(1981) Ann Arbor, MI: UMI: 04A. 8122472.

4087 McCleary, Rachel M. "Toward a Contemporary Approach to Conscience: A Study of Judgment and Guilt in the Thought of Thomas Aquinas and Sigmund Freud." Diss. The University of Chicago. *DAI* ADD(1986) Ann Arbor, MI: UMI: X1986. 03752202 (not available).

4088 McClements, C. "The Distinction *Intellectus-ratio* in the Philosophy of Thomas Aquinas: A Historical and Critical Study." Diss. Katholieke Universiteit Leuven. 1990.

4089 McGovern, Mark. "Aquinas and Scotus on Certitude." Diss. Saint Louis University. *DAI* 43(1982) Ann Arbor, MI: UMI: 05A. 8223702.

4090 McGowan, Richard J. "The Imperfections of Woman in St. Thomas' Doctrine of Woman." Diss. Marquette University. 1985.

4091 McLean, Michael Frank. "An Exposition and Defense of St. Thomas Aquinas' Account of the Rational Justification of Religious Belief." Diss. University of Notre Dame. *DAI* 42(1981) Ann Arbor, MI: UMI: 07A. 8129283.

4092 Merriell, Donald Franklin. "The Image of the Trinity in Man According to St. Thomas Aquinas." Diss. University of Toronto. *DAI* 45(1984) Ann Arbor, MI: UMI: 09A. 0555141.

4093 Miller, Hal. "Beyond Tragedy: Reinhold Niebuhr's Idea of Divine Providence." Diss. Boston College. *DAI* 45(1984) Ann Arbor, MI: UMI: 04A. 8416009.

4094 Mills, James Carleton. "Emerging Finite Aspects in the Concept of God." Diss. The Florida State University. *DAI* 09A(1985) Ann Arbor, MI: UMI. 8524615.

4095 Mohamad, I. G. "God's Knowledge and the Concept of Predestination in the Thought of Averroes and St. Thomas Aquinas." Diss. St. Andrews. 1985.

4096 Morrice, D. S. "A Comparative Study of the Positions of St. Thomas Aquinas, John Locke and David Hume Relating to the Problem of Natural Law." Diss. University of Aberdeen. *Index to Theses* 29. 2(1978): 182.

4097 Moskop, John Charles. "Divine Omniscience and Human Freedom in Thomas Aquinas and Charles Hartshorne." Diss. The University of Texas at Austin. *DAI* 40(1979) Ann Arbor, MI: UMI: 07A. 28330.

4098 Nelson, Daniel Mark. "The Priority of Prudence: Virtue and Natural Law in Thomas Aquinas and the Implications for Modern Ethics." Diss. Princeton University. *DAI* 47(1986) Ann Arbor, MI: UMI: 064A. 8621730.

4099 Nelson, Joseph Edward. "Knight's Tale: A Vision of a Secular Ideal of Chivalry." Diss. University of Kansas. *DAI* 41(1979) Ann Arbor, MI: UMI: 01A. 14432.

4100 Netzer, Judith Hannah. "Freedom as a Metaphysical Endowment: A Study in Thomas Aquinas." Diss. Boston University. *DAI* 47(1987) Ann Arbor, MI: UMI: 11A. 8704809.

4101 Nobuhara, Tokiyuki. "God and Analogy: In Search of a New Possibility of Natural Theology." Diss. Claremont Graduate School. *DAI* 42(1981) Ann Arbor, MI: UMI: 07A. 8129369.

4102 O'Connor, Bernadette. "Martin Heidegger, Saint Thomas Aquinas, and the Forgottenness of Being." Diss. Duquesne University. *DAI* 43(1983) Ann Arbor, MI: UMI: 01A.

4103 O'Neil, William Richard. "The Hermeneutical Foundations of Ethical Theory." Diss. Yale University. *DAI* 50(1988) Ann Arbor, MI: UMI: 11A. 9009024.

4104 O'Rourke, Francis A. "Being and the Good. A Study in the Metaphysics of Pseudo-Dionysius and Aquinas." Diss. Katholieke Universiteit Leuven. 1986.

4105 Peña, Braulio. "The Relation of the Concept of Nature on the Ethical Criterion of Human Behavior." Diss. U. S. Tomás. Manila: U. S. T. Press, 1979. vii-172.

4106 Pentz, Rebecca. "A Defense of the Formal Adequacy of St. Thomas Aquinas' Analysis of Omnipotence." Diss. University of California, Irvine. *DAI* 40(1979) Ann Arbor, MI: UMI: 03A. 19307.

4107 Petersen, Thomas R. "The Albertus Magnus Lyceum: A Thomistic Approach to Science Education." Diss. University of Illinois. Urbana, IL: 1977.

4108 Poissant, Leeward J. "An Analysis and Evaluation of Bernard Lonergan's Proposed Method for Verification in Metaphysics." Diss. University of Toronto. 1978.

4109 Porter, Mildred Jean. "The Concept of Rational Agency in the Thought of Aristotle and Thomas Aquinas." Diss. Yale University. *DAI* 46(1984) Ann Arbor, MI: UMI: 03A. 8509765.

4110 Rafferty, K. A. "Concepts of Mind and Will in Aquinas." Diss. Newcastle upon Tyne. *Index to Theses* 37. 2(1987): 418-19.

4111 Rebard, Theodore Paul. "Germain Grisez's Natural Law Theory: A Thomistic Critique." Diss. Boston College. *DAI* 50(1989) Ann Arbor, MI: UMI: 07A. 8922254.

4112 Reeve, P. J. "The Metaphysical and Noetic Foundations of the Return to God in Thomas Aquinas." Diss. University of Toronto. 1990.

4113 Reichberg, Gregory Martin. "Moral Choice in the Pursuit of Knowledge: The Ethics of Knowing According to Thomas Aquinas." Diss. Emory University. 1990-1991.

4114 Renick, Timothy Mark. "Political Obligation and the Common Good: A Study in Philosophical and Theological Ethics." Diss. Princeton University. *DAI* 47(1986) Ann Arbor, MI: UMI: 10A. 8701916.

4115 Reynolds, Robert Blair. "Towards a Process Pneumatology." Diss. The University of Pittsburgh. 1983.

4116 Rioux, Jean. "Aristotle, Aquinas, and the Foundations of Arithmetic." Diss. University of St. Thomas Center for Thomistic Studies. 1990.

4117 Rocca, Gregory Philip. "Analogy as Judgment and Faith in God's Incomprehensibility: A Study in the Theological Epistemology of Thomas Aquinas." Diss. The Catholic University of America. *DAI* 50(1989) Ann Arbor, MI: UMI: 05A. 8917038.

4118 Rogers, Katherine Anne. "St. Anselm of Canterbury on Divine and Human Ideas." Diss. University of Notre Dame. 1982.

4119 Rousseau, Mary F. "Toward a Thomistic Philosophy of Death: The Natural Cognition of the Separated Soul." Diss. Marquette University. 1977.

4120 Sajama, Seppo Eino. "Idea, Judgment and Will: Essays on the Theory of Judgment." Diss. Turun Yliopisto. 1983.

4121 Schultz, Janice Lee. "Thomas Aquinas and R. M. Hare: The Good and Moral Principles." Diss. State University of New York, Buffalo. *DAI* 39(1978) Ann Arbor, MI: UMI: 09A. 7905319.

4122 Sinnott-Armstrong, Walter Preston. "Moral Dilemmas." Diss. Yale University. 1982.

4123 Snyder, Steven Craig. "Albert the Great's Analysis of Time in Its Historical and Doctrinal Setting." Diss. University of Toronto. *DAI* 46(1984) Ann Arbor, MI: UMI: 05A.

4124 Sparrow, Mary Frances. "The *Praeambula Fidei* According to St. Thomas Aquinas." Diss. University of Notre Dame. *DAI* 50(1989) Ann Arbor, MI: UMI: 07A. 8923430.

4125 Spencer, Stephen Robert. "Reformed Scholasticism in Medieval Perspective: Thomas Aquinas and Francois Turrettini on the Incarnation." Diss. Michigan State University. *DAI* 50(1988) Ann Arbor, MI: UMI: 03A. 8912643.

4126 Staley, Kevin Michael. "Happiness: A Study of Man's Natural Perfection in the Philosophy of Thomas Aquinas." Diss. University of Toronto. *DAI* 48(1986) Ann Arbor, MI: UMI: 11A. 0562072 (not available).

4127 Steenkamp, Lourens Johannes Stephanus. "Aristotle's Concept of God." Diss. University of Pretoria (South Africa). *DAI* 48(1987) Ann Arbor, MI: UMI: 11A. 0561959. Afrikaans text.

4128 Steinbuch, Thomas Anthony. "Leibniz: Unity, Thought, and Being." Diss. University of Massachusetts. *DAI* 42(1981) Ann Arbor, MI: UMI: 03A. 8118045.

4129 Stewart, Melville Yorke. "The Greater-good Defense." Diss. University of Minnesota. 1983.

4130 Stypinsk, Andrzej-Bobola. "Aquinas on the Communicability of Creation: The *Scriptum* and the *Liber de Causis*." Diss. University of Toronto. *DAI* 45(1983) Ann Arbor, MI: UMI: 2A. 0553960 (not available).

4131 Sweeney, Eileen Carroll. "Aquinas' Notion of Science: Its Twelfth-century Roots and Aristotelian Transformation." Diss. The University of Texas at Austin. *DAI* 48(1986) Ann Arbor, MI: UMI: 03A. 8706111.

4132 Taylor, Michael Allyn. "Human Generation in the Thought of Thomas Aquinas: A Case Study on the Role of Biological Fact in Theological Science." Diss. The Catholic University of America. *DAI* 42(1982) Ann Arbor, MI: UMI: 11A. 8208772.

4133 Tekippe, Terry Joseph. "An Investigation of the Balance Between Conceptual and Primordial Knowing in Major Figures of the Western Philosophical Tradition." Diss. Tulane University. 1980.

4134 Thompson, Edward Collins. "From Theory of Truth to Theory of Methodology and Back Again." Diss. The University of Texas at Austin. 1983.

4135 Tolimieri, Jane. "Medieval Concepts of Time and Their Influence on Structure and Meaning in the Works of the Gawain-Poet." Diss. The University of Connecticut. *DAI* 49(1988): 12A. AAC8905986.

4136 Utrecht, Daniel Stuart. "*Esse* in the *Summa Contra Gentiles* of Saint Thomas Aquinas." Diss. University of Toronto. *DAI* 44(1983) Ann Arbor, MI: UMI: 03A. 0552057.

4137 Vinson, Jr., William Edward. "The Kingdom of God According to Thomas Aquinas: A Study of the Relationship Between Thomas' Philosophy and Theology Reflected in His Doctrine of Church and State." Diss. Southwestern Baptist Theological Seminary. *DAI* 49(1987) Ann Arbor, MI: UMI: 05A. 8806943.

4138 Wadell, Paul. "An Interpretation of Aquinas' *Treatise on the Passions*, *The Virtues*, and *The Gifts from the Perspective of Charity as Friendship with God*." Diss. University of Notre Dame. 1985.

4139 Wagner, John V. "A Study of What Can and Cannot Be Determined About *Separatio* as It is Discussed in the Works of St. Thomas Aquinas." Diss. The Catholic University of America. *DAI* 40(1979) Ann Arbor, MI: UMI: 05A.

4140 Wehrle, Walter Ernest. "The Old Academic Dichotomy in Aristotle: Essence and Accident; Existence; Form and Universal." Diss. The Florida State University. *DAI* 49(1988) Ann Arbor, MI: UMI: 12A. 8906243.

4141 Weithman, Paul Jude. "Justice, Charity and Property: The Centrality of Sin to the Political Thought of Thomas Aquinas." Diss. Harvard University. *DAI* 50(1988) Ann Arbor, MI: UMI: 02A. C8909021.

4142 Westra, Laura. "Truth and Existence in Thomas Aquinas." Diss. University of Toronto. *DAI* 44(1983) Ann Arbor, MI: UMI: 09A. 0553172 (not available).

4143 Whitcomb, Philip Wright. "Existence and Essence in Scholastic Metaphysics." Diss. University of Kansas. *DAI* 42(1981) Ann Arbor, MI: UMI: 10A. 8202127.

4144 White, Kevin. "Two Studies Related St. Thomas Aquinas' Commentary on Aristotle's *De Sensu et Sensato*, Together with an Ed. of Peter of Auvergne's *Quaestiones Super Parva Naturalia*." Diss. University of Ottawa (Canada). ADD C1977 Ann Arbor, MI: UMI. 1986. 0377568.

4145 Winiewicz, David Casimer. "Self-knowledge and Self-presence in Aquinas: An Investigation Into the Meaning and Significance of Man's Presence in the World." Diss. University of Toronto. 1980.

4146 Zanoni, Mary Louise. "Divine Order and Human Freedom in Chaucer's Poetry and Philosophical Tradition." Diss. Cornell University. 1982.

4147 Zeno, Carl. "The Meaning of Real According to Bernard Lonergan." Diss. Marquette University. 1977.

B. MISCELLANEOUS

4148 Baier, Karl. "Die Einwände Des Aristoteles Gegen die Ideenlehre Platons. Unter Berücks: D. Metaphysik-Kommentars von Thomas von Aquin." Diss. Universitat Salzburg. Wien: VWGö, 1981. v-187.

4149 Balmaceda, Federico. "Ejemplaridad y Causalidad: Estudio de Las Ideas Divinas en Tomás de Aquino." Diss. University de Navarra. 1980.

4150 Banares Parera, Leticia. "Revelacion y Lumen Propheticum en Santo Tomas de Aquino." Diss. Universidad de Navarra, Spain. *DAI* 49(1986) Ann Arbor, MI: UMI: 02C (not available).

4151 Belmans, Theo G. "La Spécification de L'agir Humanin par Son Objet Chez Saint Thomas D'Aquin." Diss. P. U. Gregroiana. Città del Vaticano, 1979.

4152 Bujo, Bénézet. "Begründung Des Sittlichen: Zur Frage Des Eudämonismus bei Thomas von Aquin." Diss. Würzburg. *RHE* 74(1983).

4153 Casella, Pietro. "La Pace in San Tommaso (*Summa Theologica*: II-II, Q. 29). Interiorizzazione e Attualità Di Un Concetto." Diss. P. U. Lateranense. Piacenza, 1978.

4154 Coggi, R. "Il Problema Teologico del Libro Di Giobbe Secondo L'intrerpretazione Di San Tommaso." Diss. Roma, 1981.

4155 Domínguez, T. Alvira. "Naturaleza y Libertad en Santo Tomás de Aquino." Diss. University de Navarra. 1980.

4156 Escobar Valencia, Juan Jóse. "El Justo Precio Según Santo Tomás." Diss. P. U. S. Thomae. Roma, 1986.

4157 Fleischmann-Kessler, Eva. "Funktion und Bedeutung der Himmelskörper in der *Summa Theologica* Des Thomas von Aquin." Diss. University Zürich. 1983. vi-198.

4158 Follo, F. "Il Vocabolario Della Storia in San Tommaso D'Aquino. Saggio Di Ermeneutica Lessicologica." Diss. Pontificia Universitas Gregoriana. 1980.

4159 García Marqués, Alfonso. "Presencia de Averroes en la Génesis de la Metafísica de Santo Tomás." Diss. University de Navarra. 1980.

4160 Granados, Tomás Melendo. "Metafísica de los Opuestos Según Santo Tomás." Diss. University de Navarra. 1980.

4161 Hermes, Mechtild. "Die Gotteslehre Des Thomas von Aquin Im Siegel Frühreformatorischer Kritik (Von Luther Bis Zum Ende der Altlutherischen Orthodoxie)." Diss. Münster (Westfalen) Universität. *HO* 7(1977).

4162 Krajski, S. "Les Problémes Métaphysiques dans le *De Ente et Essentia* de Saint Thomas D'Aquin." Diss. Académie de Théeologie Catholique. Varsovie, 1982.

4163 Krasevac, Edward L. "Revelation and Experience: An Analysis of the Theology of George Tyrrell, Karl Rahner, Edward Schillebeeckx, and Thomas Aquinas." Diss. Graduate Theological Union. *DAI* 47(1986) Ann Arbor, MI: UMI: 08A. 8628715.

4164 Leijseen, Lambert. "Martin Bucer et Thomas Van Aquino: De Involed Van Thomas Op Het Denkpatroon Vpt Bucer in de Commentaar of de Romeinenbrief(1536)." Diss. Katholieke Universiteit Leuven. 1978-1979.

4165 Lopez Lopez, R. "Análisis Filosófica de la Experiencia Mistica Según Santo Tomás de Aquino." Diss. Angelicum. Roma, 1988.

4166 Luño, A. Rodrígues. "La Virtud Moral Como Hábito Electivo Según Santo Tomás de Aquino." Diss. University de Navarra. 1980.

4167 Mahillo Monte, Antonio Javier. "El Sufrimiento Humano Según Santo Tomás de Aquino." Diss. Universidad de Navarra (Spain). *DAI* 51(1989) Ann Arbor, MI: UMI: 02C (not available).

4168 Mariano Gonzalez, Jose Maria Arsenio. "El Numero y la Singularidad en Frege y Tomás de Aquino." Diss. Universidad de Navarra (Spain). *DAI* 51(1988) Ann Arbor, MI: UMI: 02C (not available).

4169 Masota, F. Altarejos. "El Ser en Las Proposiciones Según Santo Tomás de Aquino." Diss. University de Navarra. 1980.

4170 Meli, Antonio. "*Beatitudo Imperfecta*: Considerazioni Su Un Tema Della *Summa Theologiae* Di San Tommaso D'Aquino." Diss. U. P. Salesiana. Roma, 1986.

4171 Mendes de Almedia, Luciano Pedro. "A Imperfeiçao Intelectiva Do Espirito Humano. Introduçao A Teoria Tomista Do Conhecimiento Do Outro." Diss. P. U. Gregoriana. Sao Paulo, 1980.

4172 Mendez, Julio Raul. "El Amor Fundamento Di la Participación Metafisica: Hermenutica de la *Summa Contra Gentiles*." Diss. Pontifical University Lateranense. Roma: Pontifical University Lateranense, 1985. viii-431.

4173 Moreno Narvaez, Fabio. "Demostrabilidad Racional de la Creación Según Santo Tomás de Aquino." Diss. P. U. S. Thomae. Bogotá: Ed. Nueva América, 1983. 144.

4174 Müeller, Klaus. "Theorie und Praxis der Analogie in der *Summa Theologiae* Des Thomas von Aquin: Der Streit Um das Rechte Vorturteil Un die Analyse einer Aufschlussreichen Diskrepanz." Diss. Pontificia Università Gregoriana. *DA* 45(1983).

4175 Prokopowicz, M. "L'ordo Naturae D'aprés la *Summa Theologiae* de Saint Thomas D'Aquin." Diss. Académie de Théeologie Catholique. Varsovie, 1982.

4176 Restrepo Escobar, Jaime. "El *Compendium Theologiae* de Santo Tomás de Aquino." Diss. Universidad de Navarra. 1979.

4177 Ri, B. -H. V. "La Connaissance par Connaturalité et Son Rôle dans la Vie Chrétienne Selon Saint Thomas D'Aquin." Diss. Paris: Institut Catholique, 1982.

4178 Rodriguez Pascual, Francisco. "Sociedad y Persona: Un Estudio Sobre el Hombre Desde Presupuestos Tomistas." Diss. P. U. S. Thomae. Salamanca, 1979. 153.

4179 Sanguineti, Juan José. "La Estructura del Cosmos Según Sto. Tomás." Diss. University de Navarra. 1980.

4180 Tanghetti, Franco. "La Questione Sociale Nel Pensiero Di San Tommaso e Il Suo Influsso Nelle Encicliche Sociali." Diss. P. U. Lateranensis. Roma: Pontifical University Lateranense, 1977.

4181 Tran Duc Anh, J. "Morale Bouddhique et Morale Chrétienne en Dialogue: Les Concepts Fondamentaux de la Morale Bouddhique Selon le Traité de L'Abhidharmakosa de Vasubandu Confrontes avec la Doctrine de Saint Thomas D'Aquin dans la Ia-IIae de la *Somme Théologique*." Diss. Freiburg-im-Breisgau, 1983.

4182 Van Veldhuijsen, Peter L. "Thomas Van Aquino en de Eeuwigheid Van de Wereld." Diss. VU Amsterdam. 1983.

4183 Velasco, Góñez J. O. "La Virtud de la Fortaleza: Estudio en Santo Tomás de Aquino y en Algunos de Sus Comentarios." Diss. University de Navarra. 1980.

4184 Verhulst, J. "L' *esse intentionale* Chez Saint Thomas D'Aquin: L'être de la Vertu Instrumentale et Du Concept." Diss. Université libre de Bruxelles. 67. 1978-1979.

V. OTHERS

4185 Adams, Don. "Aquinas on Aristotle on Happiness." *Mediaeval Philosophy and Theology* 1 (In press): 98-118.

4186 Aertsen, Johannes Adrianus. "Beauty in the Middle Ages: A Forgotten Transcendental." *Mediaeval Philosophy and Theology* 1 (In press): 68-97.

4187 Anderegggen, Ignacio E. M. "El Conocimiento de Dios en la Exposición de Tomás de Aquino Sobre el *De Divinis Nominibus* de Dionisio Areopagita." *Sapientia* 45(1990): 269-276.

4188 Ashworth, E. J. "Signification and Modes of Signifying in Thirteenth Century Logic: A Preface to Aquinas on Analogy." *Mediaeval Philosophy and Theology* 1 (In press): 39-67.

4189 Blandino, Giovanni. *Discussioni Sul Neo-Tomismo: Per Il Progresso Della Filosofia Cristiana*. Vatican City: Pontifical U. Lateranense, 1990.

4190 Blandino, Giovanni. *Le Existentia de Deo e le Immortalitate del Anima: Lineas de Philosophia del Esser*. Vatican City: Pontifical U. Lateranense, 1990.

4191 Coreth, Emerich et al., eds. *Christilich Philosophie Im Katholischen Denken Des 19 und 20. Jarhunderts*. Vol. 2. Graz: Styria, 1988. Especially Armand Maurer's article on Étienne Gilson, 519-645.

4192 Coulter, Gregory. "Aquinas on the Identity of Mind and Substantial Form." *The American Catholic Philosophical Association Proceedings* 64(1990): 161-179.

4193 Dales, Richard C. "Early Latin Discussions of the Eternity of the World in the Thirteenth Century." *Traditio* 43(1987): 171-197.

4194 Dales, Richard C. "Time and Eternity in the Thirteenth Century." *Journal of the History of Ideas* 49(1988): 27-45.

4195 Ellos, William J. *Ethical Practice in Clinical Medicine*. New York: Routledge, 1990.

In this study, basic yet controversial issues such as death and dying, truth-telling, confidentiality, and physician-patient relationships are treated in great depth—issues whose principles and complexities it is vital for the practicing medical ethicist to grasp. It first presents the theoretical sources of virtue ethics and then works through a number of medical ethics cases using the materials from the sources. In addition, it is the first book to address directly practical clinical problems from an historical perspective by using classic texts.

4196 Gallagher, David. "Aquinas on Moral Action: Interior and Exterior Acts." *The American Catholic Philosophical Association Proceedings* 64(1990): 118-129.

4197 Gallagher, Kenneth T. *The Philosophy of Knowledge*. New York: Fordham University Press, 1982. 307.

4198 Gy, Pierre-Marie. "The Original Text of the *Tertia Pars* of St. Thomas Aquinas *Summa Theologica* in the *Apparatus Criticus* of the Leonine ed." *Revue des Sciences Philosophiques et Théologiques* 65(1981): 608-616.

*The manuscripts from Naples, the variants of which are given in the *Apparatus Criticus* of the Leonine Ed., contain the original text of the *Tertia Pars*. These variants contribute to the understanding of the final state of St. Thomas' Eucharistic theology.*

4199 Hayden, Mary R. "Natural Inclinations and Moral Absolutes: A Mediated Correspondence for Aquinas." *The American Catholic Philosophical Association Proceedings* 64(1990): 130-115.

4200 Klubertanz, George P. *St. Thomas Aquinas on Analogy: A Textual Analysis and Systematic Synthesis*. Chicago: Books on Demand, 1978.

4201 Knasas, John F. X. "The Fundamental Nature of Aquinas' *Secunda Operatio Intellectus*." *The American Catholic Philosophical Association Proceedings* 64(1990): 190-202.

4202 Langan, John. "Egoism and Morality in the Theological Teleology of Thomas Aquinas." *Journal of Philosophical Research* 15 (In press): 411-426.

4203 Laumakis, Stephen. "The *Sensus Communis* and the Unity of Perception According to Saint Thomas Aquinas." Diss. University of Notre Dame. 1990-1991.

4204 MacDonald, Scott, ed. *Being and Goodness: The Concept of the Good in Metaphysics and Philosophical Theology*. Ithaca, NY: Cornell University Press, In press. 328.

4205 Malusa, Luciano. *Neotomismo e Intransigentismo Cattolico Ai Tempi del Sillabo*. Vol. 2. Milano: IPL, 1989.

*Bizzotto, Mario, *Filosofia*, 41(1990): 436-443.*

4206 Massini Correas, Carlos Ignacio. "Santo Tomás y el Desafio de la Ética Analitica Contemporánea." *Anuario Filosófico* 23(1990): 161-172.

4207 Massobrio, Simona Emilia. "Aristotelian Matter as Understood by St. Thomas Aquinas." Diss. McGill University. 1990-1991.

4208 Mavrodes, George I. "How Does God Know the Things He Knows." *Divine and Human Action*. Ed. Thomas V. Morris. Ithaca, NY: Cornell University Press, 1988. 345-361.

4209 McCool, Gerald A. "Is Thomas' Way of Philosophizing Still Viable Today?" *The American Catholic Philosophical Association Proceedings* 64(1990): 1-13.

4210 Mora, George. "Thomas Aquinas and Modern Psychology: A Reassessment." *Psychoanalytic Review* 64(1977): 495-530.

4211 Narciso, Enrico. "Autoritarismo e Dissenso Nel Pensiero Di San Tommaso D'Aquino." *Tommaso D'Aquino Nel Suo Settimo Centenario VIII: Atti del Congresso Internazionale*. Napoli: Edizioni Domenicane Italiane, 1978. 160-169.

4212 Phillippe, Marie-Dominique. "L'âme Humaine Selon Saint Thomas." *L'anima Nell'antropologia Di San Tommaso D'Aquino IX: Atti del Congresso Societá Internazionale San Tommaso D'Aquino*. Ed. Abelardo Lobato. Milano: Editrice Massimo, 1987. 169-180.

4213 Pope, Stephen J. "Aquinas on Almsgiving, Justice and Charity: An Interpretation and Reassessment." *The Heythrop Journal* 32 (In press): 167-191.

The author attempts to correct the current view of charity as opposed by justice by examining the treatment of this subject in the writings of Aquinas. He argues that the Thomistic notions of charity and almsgiving are much richer and more complex than what one finds in modern uses of the same terms, that the harmony between justice and charity is superior to the opposition between these terms, that charity in Thomas' view is more stringent than charity in classical liberalism and that these must not be confused or identified, and that at the same time charity in Thomas' view may be "ordered," i.e., intelligently and wisely submitted to the priorities established by practical wisdom. Finally, he argues that the strength of Thomas' views lies in the balance of universalism with an incorporation of the moral centrality of natural priorities.

4214 *Rassegna Di Letteratura Tomistica: Thomistic Bulletin, Boletin Tomista, Thomistische Literaturschau Vol. XIII: Letteratura Dell'anno 1977*. Nuova Serie del Bulletin Thomiste 13. Napoli: Editrice Domenicana Italiana, 1980. 507.

4215 Simon, Yves R. *An Introduction to Metaphysics of Knowledge*. Trans. Vukan Kuic, and Richard J. Thompson. 1934. New York: Fordham University Press, 1990. 180.

4216 Steel, Carlos. "Thomas Aquinas and the Renewal of Philosophy: Some Reflections on the Thomism of Mercier." In Dutch. *Tijdschrift voor Filosofie* 53 (In press): 44-89.

*The article is a critical examination of the particular form of Thomism developed by Désiré Mercier, the first president of the Louvain Institute of Philosophy. Mercier bases his philosophical option for Thomism on his judgment that it is better than any other philosophy offers a metaphysical synthesis within which the investigations of the modern sciences can be integrated, while at the same time being in concordance with the Christian view on man and world. At the end of the paper it is argued that no intrinsic philosophical argument can be given for a normative preference for Thomas. The demand to philosophize *ad mentem Thomae* only makes sense when the relation of reason to faith is considered.*

4217 Thomas Aquinas. *An Aquinas Reader: Selections from the Writings of Thomas Aquinas*. Ed. Mary T. Clark. 1972. New York: Fordham University Press, 1988. 597.

4218 Thomas Aquinas. *Treatise on Happiness*. Questions 1-21, *Summa Theologiae* I-II. Trans. John A. Oesterle. 1964. Notre Dame, IN: University of Notre Dame Press, 1983. xvi-208.

4219 Thomas Aquinas. *Treatise on Virtues*. Trans. John A. Oesterle. 1966. Notre Dame, IN: University of Notre Dame Press, 1983.

*Zedler, B. H., *The Modern Schoolman*, 64(1986-1987): 147-148.*

4220 Tomás de Aquino. "Del Magestro II." *Revista di Filosofia (México)* 10(1977): 121-144. Trans. Maurico Beuchot.

4221 Uyl, Douglas J. *The Virtue of Prudence*. Studies in Moral Philosophy. New York: Peter Lang, 1990. Especially Chapter 3: "Aquinas," 85-106.

4222 Vernier, Jean-Marie. "Physique Aristotélicienne et Métaphysique Thomiste." *Revue Thomiste* 9 (In press): 5-33.

4223 Weinreb, Lloyd L. *Natural Law and Justice*. Cambridge: Harvard University Press, 1987. 320.

4224 Werne, Stanley J. "Natural Law: A Way to Meaning in the World of Law." *The American Catholic Philosophical Association Proceedings* 64(1990): 231-239.

AUTHOR INDEX

English Authors

A

B

C

D

E

F

G

H

I

J

K

L

M

N

O

P

Q

R

S

T

U

V

W

Y

Z

Non-English Authors

A

B

C

D

E

F

G

H

I

J

K

L

M

N

O

P

S

T

U

V

W

Y

Z

NAMES WITHIN TITLES

A

B

C

D

E

F

G

H

I

M

N

O

P

Q

R

S

T

U

V

W

Z

BOOK REVIEWS

A

Abbà, G. *Salesianum* 432 579
Abelson, R. *Canadian Philosophical Reviews* 312
Ackrill, J. L. *Classical Review* 188
Aertsen, Jan A. *Speculum* 268 614 *Vivarium* 574
Aeschliman, M. D. *The Thomist* 259
Alarcón, E. *Anuario Filosófico* 651
Albert, K. *Philosophischer Literaturanzeiger* 60 65 68 574 594
Allion, J-M. *Revue Thomiste* 152
Alvira, T. *Anuario Filosófico* 423
Amato, S. *Rivista Internazionale di Filosofia del Diritto* 725
Anderson, Robert D., *The Thomist* 23
Anon., *Rassegna di Letteratura Tomistica* 34 39 40 49 52 60 62 63 64 81 86 88 91 96 98 100 101 102 108 109 114 120 169 174 175 177 190 203 213 228 247 279 329 330 337 345 368 423 429 443 458 510 527 528 540 566 584 592 594 602 605 636 643 644 669 670 671 675 680 696 700 701 704 705 714 716 717 725 735 736 743 745 749 762 769 772 776 803 838 843 852 860 869 871 875 3775 3798
Antoniotti, Louise-Marie *Revue Thomiste* 174 659 744
Appel, Fredrick *Philosophy and the Social Sciences* 313
Arregui, J. V. *Anales de Filosofia* 819
Ashley, Benedict *The Modern Schoolman* 234
Austin, William H. *Nôus* 3803

B

Baertschi, Bernard *Revue de Théologie et de Philosophie* 248
Baldner, Steven *The New Scholasticism* 424 *Canadian Philosophical Reviews* 276 3816
Bandera, A. *Ciencia Tomista* 109
Barbiero, Daniel *Critical Texts* 220
Barbotin, E. *Revue d'Histoire et de Philosophie Religieuses* 247
Barcala, A. *Revista Espanola de Teologia* 484
Barham, P. *HHS* 313
Barry, Brian *Ethics* 313
Barry, Robert *The Thomist* 228
Bascour, H. *Bulletin de Théologie Ancienne et Médiévale* 527
Bataillon, Louis-Jacques *Laval Théologique et Philosophique* 497
Bazán, Bernardo Carlo *The Review of Metaphysics* 14 *Dialogue* 100 528 529 *Speculum* 248
Benardete, J. A. *Nous* 3796
Berna, Francis *Speculum* 18
Bertoncini, L. *Divus Thomas* 329
Bérubé, C. *Collectanea Franciscana* 166 527 528
Beuchot, *Mauricio Revista de Filosofia* 720 *Nôus* 294
Bertoncini, L. *Divus Thomas* 329
Bharati, *Agehananda Philosophischer Literaturanzeiger* 628
Bianchi, L. *Rivista di Storia della Filosofia* 429 3795

C

Carlen, C. *The Thomist* 7 274
Caroti, S. *Memorie Dom* 636
Carpino, Joseph L. *Interpretation* 427
Carroll, William E. *The Thomist* 3784
Catania, Francis. *The Modern Schoolman* 14
Cartechini, Sisto *Doctor Communis* 80 166 658 742
Carter, Curtis *The Modern Schoolman* 344
Casey, J. *Philosophical Quarterly* 312
Castellano, D. *Filosofia Oggi* 3781
Catan, John R. *Nous* 177
Catania, Francis J. *The Modern Schoolman* 14 177
Catechini, P. Sisto *Doctor Communis* 738
Cauvel, Jane *Teaching Philosophy* 312
Cavadi, Augusto *Sapienza* 664 733
Cennacchi, Giuseppe *Doctor Communis* 734
Centore, F. F. *Dialogue* 357
Cesareo, Rosa *Filosofia* 648
Cessario, Romanus *Theological Studies* 24 *The Thomist* 26 368
Charlton, W. *The British Journal of Aesthetics* 344
Cheetham, Mark A. *Canadian Philosophical Review* 219
Cheneval, Francis *Freiburger Zeitschrift für Philosophie und Theologie* 71 577
Chisholm, R. M. *Religious Studies* 432
Clarke, P. A. *Mind* 369
Clarke, W. Norris *Canadian Philosophical Reviews* 174 *International Philosophical Quarterly* 24 *New Blackfriars* 210
Clavell, L. *Anuario Filosófico* 852
Cohen, Ted *Journal of Philosophy* 344
Colish, Marcia L. *History of European Ideas* 249
Collins, James *The Modern Schoolman* 278
Collins, Peter *South African Journal of Philosophy* 312
Collinson, Diané *British Journal of Aesthetics* 219
Colonnello, P. *Sapienza* 247 3851
Composta, Dario *Divus Thomas* 753 754 755 *Doctor Communis* 36 223 224 329 346 520 646 696 710 724 727 742 745 753 754 755 759 760 768 769 858 3797
Connolly, William E. *Political Theory* 312
Contat, Alain *Doctor Communis* 479 562 670
Copleston, Frederick C. *Classical Review* 294 *The Heythrop Journal* 259
Corvez, M. *Revue Thomiste* 778 779
Courtney, W. I. *Speculum* 294
Cronin, J. *Revue Philosophique de Louvain* 182
Crosson, Frederick J. *Canadian Philosophical Reviews* 259
Cruz, J. *Anuario Filosófico* 821
Culiani, Joan P. *The Journal of Religion* 220
C. V. *Angelicum* 66
Cvek, P. P. *Canadian Philosophical Reviews* 267
Czapiewski, W. *Salzburger Jahrbuch für Philosohie* 605

D

E

F

G

H

Henle, Robert J. and Linu J. Thro *The Modern Schoolman* 266
Hill, W. J. *Theological Studies* 247 *The Thomist* 178
Hiorth, F. *Philosophia* 282
Hissette, R. *Archiv für Geschichte der Philosophie* 562 *Bulletin de Théologie Ancienne et Médiévale* 95 100 101 102 294 574 605 *Revue Philosophique de Louvain* 295 527 627
Hittinger, John P. *The Modern Schoolman* 229 *The New Scholasticism* 312 *The Review of Metaphysics* 259 329
Hittinger, R. *The Review of Metaphysics* 329
Holtz, L. *Revue des Études Latines* 100
Honner, John *The Heythrop Journal* 218
Hornsby, Jennifer *Inquiry* 217
Horowitz, M. *Nouvelle Revue Théologique* 539
Hossefeld, P. *Zeitschrift für Religions und Geistesgeschichte* 294
Hudson, Deal W. *International Philosophical Quarterly* 326
Huerga, A. *Angelicum* 109 *Revista Espanola de Teologica* 861
Hundersmarck, Lawrence F. *Vera Lex* 267
Husain, Martha *International Studies in Philosophy* 188

I

Iammarrone, L. *Miscellanea Francescana* 717
Igartua, J. M. *Pensamiento* 527 636
Iglesias, Teresa *Philosophical Studies* (Ireland) 313
Imbach, Ruedi *Freiburger Zeitschrift für Philosophie und Theologie* 467 *Revue de Théologie et de Philosophie* 36 65 68 465 539
Inagaki, Y. *Studies on Medieval Thought* 3798
Inciarte, F. *Philosophisches Jahrbuch* 423
Ingardia, Richard *The New Scholasticism* 218 *The Thomist* 161
Innis, Robert E. *The Thomist* 177
Inwood, B. *International Studies in Philosophy* 3796
Isaac, Jeffrey C. *Political Theory* 313

J

Johnson, Mark *Personalist Forum* 312
Jolivet, J. *Revue Philosophique de la France et de l'étranger* 36 101 102 247 528 537 642
Jordan, Mark D. *Rassengna di Letteratura Tomistica* 159 195 218 *Revue Philosophique de la France Speculum* 234 *The Journal of Religion* 318 *The Review of Metaphysics* 177 *The Thomist* 770 860
Jori, A. *Bollettino Filosofico* 758

K

Kachi, Y. *Archives Internationales d'Histoire des Sciences* 188
Kaczynski, E. *Angelicum* 49 275
Kafel, S. *Collectanea Franciscana* 714
Kalinowski, G. *Archives de Philosophie du Droit* 228 *Ethos* 228

L

Lindberg, Carter *Church History* 225 *Isis* 3784
Lindblad, Ulrika *Frieburger Zeitschrift für Philosophie und Theologie* 60 548 *Revue Théologique de Louvain* 14
Lippens, Elisabeth *Tijdschrift voor Filosofie* 617 871 872
Lisska, Anthony J. *Teaching Philosophy* 20
Livi, Antonio *Doctor Communis* 744 *La Ciencia Tomista* 744 *Rivista di Filosofia Neo-Scholastica* 482
Lluch-Baixauli, M. *Scripta Theologica* 710
Lobato, Abelardo *Angelicum* 574 744 *Doctor Communis* 737
Lolli, Gabriele *Scientia* 3796
Long, E. T. *Review of Metaphysics* 432
Longeway, John *The Philosophical Review* 3796
Lopéz, Clemente Garciá *Revista Espanola de Teologia* 806
Lorenzon, A. *Revista de Filosofia* 110 *Presenca Filosófica* 110 *Ciências Humanas* 110
Loth, H. -J. *Zeitschrift für Religions-und Geistesgeschichte* 247
Luch-Baixauli, M. *Scripta Theologica* (Pamplona) 3844
Lunetta, L. *Studi Medievali* 683

M

MacDonald, S. *Archiv für Geschichte der Philosophie* 318
MacIntyre, A. *Teaching Philosophy* 329
Macierowski, E. M. *The Thomist* 318
Macken, R. *Franziskanische Studien* 428 527
Madigan, Arthur *Ancient Philosophy* 234 3795
Madigan, Patrick *Revue Philosophique de Louvain* 325
Maer, A. *Rivista Rosminiana di Filosofia Cultura* 101
Maglione, G. *Asprenas* 732
Magraner, Rulián J. 854
Mahoney, E. P. *Journal of the History of Philosophy* 415
Maidan, Michael *History of European Ideas* 312 *Revista Latinoamericana de Filosofia* 312
Malatesta, Michele *Sapienza* 677
Mangiagalli, M. *Rivista di Filosofia Neo-Scolastica* 166 646
Mann William, E. *Faith and Philosophy* 231
Manno, A. G. *Sapienza* 721
Marmiroli, E. *Theologie und Phiosophie* 605
Manselli, R. *Revue d'Histoire Ecclésiastique* 861
Mansion, Suzanne *Revue Philosophique de Louvain* 354
Manzanedo, M. F. *Angelicum* 735
Manzano, I. *Antonianum* 573
Marabotto de Grau, M. I. *Antropos* 432
Marlet, Mich. *Philosophia Reformata* 540
Marmiroli, E. *Theologie und Philosophie* 605
Marsh, J. L. *International Philosophical Quarterly* 182
Martinez-G., L. *Pensamiento* 428
Mascall, E. L. *Religious Studies* 177
Massini, C. I. *Filosofar Cristiano* (Córdoba Argentina) 536 *Sapienza* 228
Masterson, Patrick *Review of Metaphysics* 166

N

O

O'Brien, Thomas C. *The Thomist* 171 172 187 188 355 417 751 3767
Ogiermann, H. *Theologie und Philosophie* 218 280
O'Leary, Joseph Stephen *The Thomist* 182
Ols, D. *Angelicum* 243
Olson, Jeannine *Church History* 264
Oppenheimer, H. *The Journal of the Theological Studies* 202
Orlando, Pasquale *Doctor Communis* 710 782 3768
Osuna, A. *La Ciencia Tomista* 122 799
Owens, Joseph *Dialogue* 279 *International Journal for Philosophy of Religion* 178 *The Review of Metaphysics* 446 574 *The Thomist* 563
Ozaeta, J. M. *Ciudad de Dios* 675

P

Paggi, C. *Aquinas* 670
Palmer, Humphrey *Philosophical Books* 278
Panaccio, C. *The Philosophical Review* 294
Pangallo, Mario *Doctor Communis* 92 174 331 449 477 711
Pappin, Joseph *The Heythrop Journal* 166 *The Thomist* 432
Parain-Vial, J. *Les Études Philosophiques* 537
Pasqua, Hervé *Revue Philosophique de Louvain* 486 487 488 495 834
Pattin, A. *Tijdschrift voor Filosofie* 574
Paulson, S. L. *Philosophical Books* 228
Paván-S., C. *Episteme NS* 785 *Revista Venezolana de Filosofia* 446
Peccorini, F. L. *Speculum* 177
Pegueroles, J. *Espiritu* 432
Penna, James V. *Canadian Philosophical Reviews* 357
Peña, Lorenzo *Philosophia* (Israel) 3795
Perazzoli, B. *Rivista Rosminiana di Filosofia e di Cultura* 3897
Perego, A. *Divus Thomas* 166 190 848
Perini, G. *Divus Thomas* 100 102 108 109 856
Perreiah, Alan *Teaching Philosophy* 318
Petino, Cosimo *Divinitas* 732 *Doctor Communis* 48 673 677 705 720
Petino, C. *Divinitas* 733
Phillips, D. Z. *Mind* 312
Pinckaers, Servais-Th. *Freiburger Zeitschrift für Philosophie und Philosophie und Theologie* 552 *Revue Thomiste* 312 617
Pizzorni, R. M. *Angelicum* 700 736 758 3781 3897 *Aquinas* 3781 *Divus Thomas* 645
Pleydell-Pearce, A. G. *The Journal of the British Society for Phenomenology* 182
Pollard, D. E. B. *Philosophical Studies* 228
Pöltner, G. *Salzburger Jahrbuch für Philosophie* 60 548
Ponton, L. *Laval Théologique et Philosophique* 40
Post, Stephen G. *Medical Humanities Review* 313
Poutet, Y. *Divus Thomas* 513
Prakash, M. S. and Weinstein, M. *Études* 312
Prozesky, Martin H. *Philosophical Papers* 177

Q

R

S

Scheffler, Samuel *Philosophical Review* 312
Schenk, Richard *The Thomist* 643
Scherer, Donald *International Journal of Applied Philosophy* 312
Scherer, Georg *Zeitschrift für Philosophische Forschung* 605
Schreier, Josep *Philosophischer Literaturanzeiger* 75
Schmitz, R. M. *Doctor Communis* 563
Schneider, M. *Wissenschaft und Weisheit* 247
Schreier, Josep *Philosophischer Literaturanzeiger* 75
Schuller, Peter M. *Teaching Philosophy* 313
Schuster, J. *Theologie und Philosophie* 617
Scott, James H. *Philosophical Topics* 344
Seddon, F. *Studies in Soviet Thought* 161
Sell, Alan P. *Philosophical Studies* 417
Senner, W. *Bulletin de Théologie Ancienne et Médiévale* 594
Sessa, D. *Sapienza* 90 778 779
Shute, Sara *Journal of the History of Philosophy* 306
Sia, Santiago *Modern Theology* 202
Sieben, H. J. *Theologie und Philosophie* 40
Silagi, G. *Daem* 2126
Silva, C. Ferreira *Salesianum* 643
Sirat, C. *Revue des Études Juives* 294
Skarica, Zuñiga, M. *Philosophica Valparaiso* 137
Skousgaard, S. *International Journal for Philosophy of Religion* 432
Smith, Raymond *The Thomist* 163
Snider, Eric W *Metaphilosophy* 313
Snyder, S. C. *Speculum* 102
Sokolowski, Robert *Faith and Philosophy* 178
Solignac, A. *Aporia* 101 579
Soria, F. *Estudios Filosóficos* 843
Soskice, O. *The Heythrop Journal* 263
Spade, P. V. *Dialogue* 188 355
Spiazzi, R. *Divinitas* 746
Spitz, J. -F. *Critique* 312
Spitzer, Robert *The Modern Schoolman* 177
Stack, George J. *The Review of Metaphysics* 268 *The Modern Schoolman* 161
Steel, C. *Bulletin de Théologie Ancienne et Médiévale* 52 *Tijdschrift voor Filosofie* 312 875 3784
Stefani, M. *Filosofia Oggi* 704
Stella, P. T. *Aquinas* 174 700 *Salesianum* 294
Stephenson, Günther *Philosophischer Literaturanzeiger* 581
Stern, J. *The Journal of Philosophy* 379
Stohrer, Walter J. *The Modern Schoolman* 432
Stout, J. *The Journal of Religion* 313
Stramare, Tarcisio *Doctor Communis* 792
Stubbens, N. A. *Idealistic Studies* 3793
Stump, E. *International Studies in Philosophy* 355 *Speculum* 247 *The Philosophical Review* 177 *The Thomist* 209
Sturlese, L. *Annali della Scuola Normale Superiore di Pisa* (Lettere e Filosofia) 3784

Vitale, V. *Rivista Internazionale di filosofia del Ditto* 228 841
Volpi, F *Veritas* 548
Volta, S. *Journal Philosophique* 772

W

Wagner, Claus *Freiburger Zeitschrift für Philosophie und Theologie* 428
Walgrave, J. H. *Ephemerides Theologicae Lovanienses* 60 *Tijdschrift voor Filosofie* 177
Walhout, D. *International Studies in Philosophy* 166
Wallace, R. Jay *History and Theory* 312 313
Wallach, J. R. *Telos* 312
Walton, A. S. *Bulletin of the Hegel Society of Great Britain* 312
Warnock, M. *The Journal of the Theological Studies* 229
Wawrykow, Joseph *The Thomist* 225
Wéber, E. *Les Études* 446
Weber, Stephen L. *Philosophical Books* 200
Weiler, G. Grazer *Philosophische Studien* 229
Weisheipl, James A. *The Review of Metaphysics* 428 429
Weithman, P. J. *Review of Metaphysics* 19
Wells, N. J. *The Journal of the History of Philosophy* 428
Wenin, Christian *Revue Philosophique de Louvain* 96 182 337 528 529 534 749 863
Westphal, M. *International Journal for Philosophy of Religion* 366
Weston, Anthony *Free Inquiry* 312
Widow, J. A. *Philosophica Valparaiso* 458
Wielockx, R. *Bulletin de Théologie Ancienne et Médiévale* 91 642 *Ephemerides Theologicae Lovanienses* 528 *Louvain Studies* 213 *Revue Philosophique de Louvain* 574 *Scriptorium* 101 102 627
Wierenga, E. *Philosophy and Phenomenological Research* 379
Wilcox, W. H. *The Philosophical Review* 228
Wilder, A. *Angelicum* 166 213 322 429 691 719 3761 3798
Wiles, M. *The Journal of the Theological Studies* 278
Wilhelmsen, Frederick D. *Faith and Philosophy* 360
Wilkinson, Winston A. *The Modern Schoolman* 182
Williams, Bruce A. *The Thomist* 247
Wippel, John F. *Journal of the History of Philosophy* 12
Wong, David *Philosophical Books* 313
Wood, F. *International Journal for Philosophy of Religion* 196
Wood, Robert E. *Review of Metaphysics* 219 220
Woods, Richard *The Thomist* 18
Wucherer-Huldenfeld, A. K. *Philosophisches Jahrbuch* 605
Wuppertal, Rainer B. *Philosophischer Literaturanzeiger* 67
Wykstra, S. *Faith and Philosophy* 366

Y

Yarnold, E. J. *The Journal of the Theological Studies* 423
Young, Robert *Religious Studies* 278 3802

Z

LATIN WORDS AND PHRASES

A

C

D

E

H

I

L

N

O

P

Q

R

S

T

U

V

LATIN BOOKS

L

M

P

Q

R

S

GENERAL INDEX

ENGLISH

A. KEYWORDS

B

C

E

F

G

H

I

J

K

M

N

O

R

S

T

U

V

W

Z

FOREIGN

A

B

C

D

E

G

H

M

N

O

P

Q

R

T

U

V